# The Literature of PROPAGANDA

VOLUME 1

# The Literature of PROPAGANDA

## APPROACHES

**THOMAS RIGGS,** *editor*

**ST. JAMES PRESS**
*A part of Gale, Cengage Learning*

GALE
CENGAGE Learning·

Detroit • New York • San Francisco • New Haven, Conn • Waterville, Maine • London

GALE
CENGAGE Learning·

**The Literature of Propaganda**

Thomas Riggs, Editor

Michelle Lee, Project Editor

Artwork and photographs for *The Literature of Propaganda* covers were reproduced with the following kind permission.

*Volume 1*

For foreground "We Can Do It!" World War II poster, c. 1942. © MPVHistory/Alamy.

For background photograph of women working in Douglas aircraft assembly plant during WWII. © Bettmann/CORBIS.

*Volume 2*

For foreground illustration of a page from a Nazi schoolbook, c. 1935. © INTERFOTO/Alamy.

For background photograph of soldiers at a Nazi Party rally in Nuremberg, Germany, 1936. © Bettmann/CORBIS.

*Volume 3*

For foreground poster featuring Cuban communist heroes including Fidel Castro and Che Guevara. Cuba, 1969 (colour litho), Martinez, Raul (1927–95)/ Private Collection/Peter Newark American Pictures/The Bridgeman Art Library/Used with permission by Xin Dong Cheng/Beijing, China/Xin Dong Cheng Space for Contemporary Art.

For background photograph of Cuban rebel soldiers posing with guns in Havana, Cuba, 1959. © Lester Cole/CORBIS.

WITHDRAWN
UTSA Libraries

© 2013 Gale, Cengage Learning

ALL RIGHTS RESERVED. No part of this work covered by the copyright herein may be reproduced, transmitted, stored, or used in any form or by any means graphic, electronic, or mechanical, including but not limited to photocopying, recording, scanning, digitizing, taping, Web distribution, information networks, or information storage and retrieval systems, except as permitted under Section 107 or 108 of the 1976 United States Copyright Act, without the prior written permission of the publisher.

For product information and technology assistance, contact us at **Gale Customer Support, 1-800-877-4253.** For permission to use material from this text or product, submit all requests online at **www.cengage.com/permissions.** Further permissions questions can be emailed to **permissionrequest@cengage.com**

While every effort has been made to ensure the reliability of the information presented in this publication, Gale, a part of Cengage Learning, does not guarantee the accuracy of the data contained herein. Gale accepts no payment for listing; and inclusion in the publication of any organization, agency, institution, publication, service, or individual does not imply endorsement of the editors or publisher. Errors brought to the attention of the publisher and verified to the satisfaction of the publisher will be corrected in future editions.

**LIBRARY OF CONGRESS CATALOGING-IN-PUBLICATION DATA**

The literature of propaganda / Thomas Riggs, editor.
    volumes cm
  Summary: Contains 300 entries that explore literary works that deal with propaganda. The set includes a wide variety of genres and has an international scope. It explores the works of authors shaped by a variety of political, social, and economic movements, and places each work in its historical context. Each entry includes an overview of the work, historical context, primary themes and style, and critical discussion -- Provided by publisher.
  Includes bibliographical references and index.
  ISBN 978-1-55862-858-8 (set) -- ISBN 978-1-55862-859-5 (vol. 1) -- ISBN 978-1-55862-860-1 (vol. 2) -- ISBN 978-1-55862-861-8 (vol. 3) -- ISBN 978-1-5586-2878-6 (e-book) -- ISBN 1-5586-2878-9 (e-book)
  1. Literature in propaganda. 2. Persuasion (Psychology) in literature.
3. Persuasion (Rhetoric) in literature. 4. Authors--Political and social views.
I. Riggs, Thomas, 1963- editor.
  PN51.L5744 2013
  809'.93358--dc23
                                                              2013001494

*Gale*
27500 Drake Rd.
Farmington Hills, MI, 48331-3535

ISBN-13: 978-1-55862-858-8 (set)      ISBN-10: 1-55862-858-4 (set)
ISBN-13: 978-1-55862-859-5 (vol. 1)    ISBN-10: 1-55862-859-2 (vol. 1)
ISBN-13: 978-1-55862-860-1 (vol. 2)    ISBN-10: 1-55862-860-6 (vol. 2)
ISBN-13: 978-1-55862-861-8 (vol. 3)    ISBN-10: 1-55862-861-4 (vol. 3)

This title will also be available as an e-book.
ISBN-13: 978-1-55862-878-6 ISBN-10: 1-55862-878-9
Contact your Gale, a part of Cengage Learning, sales representative for ordering information.

Printed in the United States of America
1 2 3 4 5 6 7 17 16 15 14 13

**Library**
**University of Texas**
**at San Antonio**

# ADVISORY BOARD

## CHAIR

**Russ Castronovo**
Dorothy Draheim Professor of English and American Studies, University of Wisconsin-Madison. Author of *Beautiful Democracy: Aesthetics and Anarchy in a Global Era* (2007); *Necro Citizenship: Death, Eroticism, and the Public Sphere in the Nineteenth-Century United States* (2001); and *Fathering the Nation: American Genealogies of Slavery and Freedom* (1995). Coeditor, with Jonathan Auerbach, of *The Oxford Handbook of Propaganda Studies* (forthcoming).

## ADVISORS

**Laura R. Braunstein**
Librarian, English Language and Literature, Dartmouth College, Hanover, New Hampshire.

**Maria Teresa Micaela Prendergast**
Associate Professor of English, College of Wooster, Wooster, Ohio. Author of *Railing, Reviling and Invective in Early Modern Literary Culture, 1588–1617* (2012); and *Renaissance Fantasies: The Gendering of Aesthetics in Early Modern Fiction* (2000). Coauthor, with Thomas Prendergast, of "The Invention of Propaganda: A Translation and Critical Commentary of *Inscrutabili Divinae*," in *The Oxford Handbook of Propaganda Studies*, edited by Jonathan Auerbach and Russ Castronovo (forthcoming).

**Thomas Prendergast**
Associate Professor of English and Department Chair, College of Wooster, Wooster, Ohio. Author of *Chaucer's Dead Body: From Corpse to Corpus* (2004). Coauthor, with Maria Teresa Micaela Prendergast, of "The Invention of Propaganda: a Translation and Critical Commentary of *Inscrutabili Divinae*," in *The Oxford Handbook of Propaganda Studies*, edited by Jonathan Auerbach and Russ Castronovo (forthcoming). Coeditor, with Barbara Kline, of *Rewriting Chaucer: Culture, Authority and the Idea of the Authentic Text, 1400–1602* (1999).

ADVISORY BOARD

**Harilaos Stecopoulos**
Associate Professor of English, University of Iowa, Iowa City. Author of
*Reconstructing the World: Southern Fictions and U.S. Imperialisms, 1898–1976*
(2008). Coeditor, with Michael Uebel, of *Race and the Subject of Masculinities*
(1997).

**Matthew Stratton**
Assistant Professor of English, University of California, Davis. Author of *The
Politics of Irony in American Modernism* (forthcoming) and articles on topics
ranging from propaganda to capital punishment in literature and popular culture.

**Mark Wollaeger**
Professor of English, Vanderbilt University, Nashville, Tennessee. Author of
*Modernism, Media, and Propaganda: British Narrative from 1900 to 1945* (2006);
and *Joseph Conrad and the Fictions of Skepticism* (1990). Editor of *The Oxford
Handbook of Global Modernisms* (2012); and *James Joyce's A Portrait of the Artist as a
Young Man: A Casebook* (2003). Coeditor, with Victor Luftig and Robert Spoo, of
*Joyce and the Subject of History* (1996).

# EDITORIAL AND PRODUCTION STAFF

**ASSOCIATE PUBLISHER**
Marc Cormier

**PRODUCT MANAGER**
Philip J. Virta

**PROJECT EDITOR**
Michelle Lee

**EDITORIAL SUPPORT**
Matthew Derda

**EDITORIAL ASSISTANCE**
Sara Constantakis, Andrea Henderson,
Lisa Kumar, Rebecca Parks, and Marie Toft

**ART DIRECTOR**
Kristine Julien

**COMPOSITION AND IMAGING**
Evi Seoud, John Watkins

**MANUFACTURING**
Wendy Blurton

**RIGHTS ACQUISITION AND MANAGEMENT**
Kimberly Potvin, Robyn V. Young

**TECHNICAL SUPPORT**
Luann Brennan, Mike Weaver

EDITORIAL AND
PRODUCTION STAFF

# TABLE OF CONTENTS

# INTRODUCTION

If in the beginning was the Word, propaganda soon followed. The relationship between discourse and persuasion is intimate and almost always troubling. Our modern notion of propaganda is suffused by pejorative connotations involving falsification and manipulation. The term is often used to discount opponents' views or to invalidate a contrasting perspective. This book encourages an understanding that is at once neutral and explanatory, one that seeks to define propaganda as neither good nor bad and instead promotes a definition that is more pragmatic: Propaganda is publicly disseminated information intended to influence others in belief, action, or both. A reconsideration of the subject in this light can produce corresponding changes in our understandings of literature.

The proper use of rhetoric—oral and written communication or persuasion—was a hotly debated issue in ancient Greece, as any of Plato's interlocutors or Aristotle's students knew. Across the centuries the debate has only intensified. The word "propaganda" first appeared in modern languages as part of Pope Gregory XV's establishment of the Sacra Congregatio de Propaganda Fide (Sacred Congregation for Propagating the Faith) in 1622. The mission of this body was to spread what the Catholic Church considered to be the one true faith during the crisis of the Counter Reformation. The next notable use of the term is associated with the cataclysmic upheavals of the French Revolution. From the perspective of alarmists in England, the revolutionaries in Paris had organized various institutions of propaganda to spread their radical creed across Europe.

Our negative understanding of propaganda emerged during World War I, when the Allies waged an information war accusing Germany of spreading atrocity stories and distorting events; Germany similarly denounced the Allies. Wartime governments also directed biased media persuasion at their own populations in order to mobilize support for the war. Some sixty years earlier, when Harriet Beecher Stowe penned the best-selling novel of the nineteenth century, *Uncle Tom's Cabin* (1852), she did not see herself as peddling false or deceptive information; her aim was to educate readers about the fundamental humanity of the so-called "merchandise" that was legally sold in the antebellum United States. Jumping forward a century and a half, in 2010 Julian Assange uploaded "The WikiLeaks Manifesto" in an equally daring endeavor: to challenge the monopoly on information held by corporations and governments. The German cultural critic Siegfried Kracauer asks in his 1960 book *Theory of Film,* "Is not truth the best propaganda weapon?"[1] Like many of the authors discussed in the following pages, Pope Gregory, Stowe, and Assange would have agreed, approving the spread and circulation of information as both enlightening and persuasive.

From ancient Greek times to the present, propaganda has served many different masters, has appeared across many media, from engraving to film, and has been variously condemned and appreciated. Written propaganda can be sorted according to three overlapping functions. It can be literature that (1) attempts to persuade, manipulate, or even deceive; (2) depicts the use of propaganda and its impact upon people and the society that they inhabit; (3) theorizes about propaganda, examining its techniques and psychological mechanisms, its media, and its modes of dissemination and circulation.

Rarely does a work of literature satisfy only one of these conditions. More often, it bleeds across categories. In a radio address in spring 1941, George Orwell took stock of World War I, the Russian Revolution, and the advance of Hitler and Nazi Germany across Europe. In conclusion, he contended that "propaganda in some form or other lurks in every book."[2] From this perspective, all texts are susceptible to propaganda. Authors often inveigh against propaganda while employing it themselves. Consider Upton Sinclair's muckraking novel of the meatpacking industry, *The Jungle* (1906), which exposes the emptiness of capitalist propaganda by delivering impassioned sermons about the Christian virtues of socialism. Try to determine whether Langston Hughes's six-line poem "Johannesburg Mines" (1928) is an example of or a critique of propaganda. Observe the ways in which Edward Bernays's seemingly definitive book *Propaganda* (1928), while explaining modern techniques of advertising and mass persuasion, becomes a public relations pitch for ad men and other spin artists. These examples support Orwell's conclusion that "literature has been swamped by propaganda."[3]

The ubiquity of propaganda is neither cause for despair nor a reason to give up on literature. In fact, Orwell construed its prevalence as an urgent reminder that "every work of art has a meaning and purpose—a political, social and religious purpose."[4] The surest sign that art is intended to engage the world in these ways is that it seeks to affect our beliefs, attitudes, and actions. Writers labor over manuscripts in the hopes of intervening in the course of human events, whether through straightforward confrontation, by means of gripping or gentle narrative, or in a more elliptical fashion that employs irony, satire, and other tactics. And writing does engage: readers pore over books, debating meanings and wresting interpretations to support their individual view of the work and its applications to life. Looking at literature through the lens of propaganda reminds us that it is not produced simply for its own sake but rather to change history and how people understand it.

An overview of the table of contents for this book reveals that authors have combined imagination, outrage, accusation, and wit with any number of goals: abolishing slavery; reforming slum conditions; creating scapegoats and targeting internal enemies; rallying support for war; fomenting revolution; and many more. Unquestionably, utopian optimism and commitment, cynicism and hatred have been poured into such efforts. What remains debatable, however, is the effectiveness of these appeals. Can a discrete set of social events ever be tied to a specific work of literature? This incalculability generates further questions about propaganda's possibilities of success. Does it risk galvanizing opponents even as it seeks to encourage the most ardent supporters? When it focuses on a specific social ill—for example, squalid tenements and unsafe factory conditions in the early twentieth century—does it miss the need for more thoroughgoing, systemic reform? Why do its utopian dimensions so often seem destined for failure? The huge range of literature examined in these volumes—from the rhetoric of the classical world to the digital spread of information in the twenty-first century—provides readers with plenty of material to ponder in regard to these questions. It also generates new lines of debate and inquiry.

*The Literature of Propaganda*'s three-part structure affords multiple lenses through which to assess plays, novels, poems, exposés, manifestoes, short stories, biographies, memoirs, and essays that circulate as or comment on propaganda and mass persuasion. Divided into Approaches (volume 1), Groups (volume 2), and Effects (volume 3), this work seeks to account for the diversity and richness, the optimism, and the terror that have resulted from efforts to create change through textual means.

Because the definitions and connotations of the term "propaganda" have shifted over time, the first volume, Approaches, registers varied understandings and uses of the concept. It sets out theories of persuasion formulated in ancient Greece, the World War I era, the postcolonial world, and postmodern society. With this foundation in place, the volume then identifies different types of propaganda, including appeals and exhortations, exposés, education and indoctrination, histories, and political declarations. The "Formal Innovations" chapter explores texts that respond to political crises and social exigencies—for example, Theodore Dwight Weld's cut-and-paste method in *American Slavery As It Is* (1839) and Art Spiegelman's illustrated panels in his graphic novel *The Complete Maus* (1991). The selections in this first volume invite readers to consider literature as variously surveying, commenting on, deploring, and utilizing propaganda. Only a fraction of the works represent "pure" propaganda (if such a category could be defined). Instead, such texts as W. E. B. Du Bois's "Criteria of Negro Art" (1926) and Theodor W. Adorno's "Freudian Theory and the Pattern of Fascist Propaganda" (1951) embody earnest attempts to unlock the mechanisms that have given misrepresentation, paranoia, and fear such a hold over modern life.

Volume 2, Groups, studies texts produced by parties and factions, dissidents and rebels, various social classes, and cultural critics. These works suggest that, whereas in its most negative incarnations, propaganda becomes weaponized speech, with its own targets and triggers, literature carries liberating potential as well. The chapter "Social Classes" explores writing that, among other things, advocates for the economically oppressed. Works ranging from Rebecca Harding Davis's "Life in the Iron Mills" (1861) to the "Preamble to the Constitution of the IWW" (1905) have been crafted to rally public opinion in support of human rights. Literature has also been used to promote group cohesion in the form of nationalism. The chapter titled "Nations" features a discussion of one of the most infamous pieces of propaganda in history, Adolf Hitler's *Mein Kampf* (1925). Invidious language that appeals to feelings of superiority or fear is often associated with xenophobic nationalism, but those seeking to redress a problem or call attention to a social movement may also draw on emotion in propagating a message. While this potential may often go unrealized, it is hard to overestimate the poignant force of such a piece (included in the chapter "Dissidents and Rebels") as Rodolfo Walsh's "Open Letter from a Writer to the Military Junta," written the day before his death at the hands of government soldiers. Including such works as Aristophanes's *Lysistrata* (411 BCE), this volume offers readers a literature that allows human actors to comment upon and intervene in political and social affairs.

Because the impact of such interventions can be difficult to gauge, the final volume, Effects, considers literary works that have been tied to legislative reform, religious conversion, changes in economic policy, and other aspects of historical significance. The chapter "Myths and Martyrs" explores the ways in which real-world results often ensue from mythic representations, such as those that render a figure such as George Washington larger than life or depict Joan of Arc as a martyr. Embellishment can play an instrumental role in making national heroes of ordinary men and women. As the chapter "Distortions and Delusions" reveals, people can eagerly gobble up these fictive portraits; we consume fanciful versions of history as readily as the characters in Aldous Huxley's *Brave New World* (1932) consume drugs to adjust to a deluded view of reality. The chapters "Dystopias and Utopias," "Legislation and Reform," "Predictions and Prescriptions," and "Suppression and Scapegoating" round out the volume. Analyzing perspectives on such reactionary texts as Ayn Rand's *Atlas Shrugged* (1957) and William Luther Pierce's *Turner Diaries* (1978) alongside those on progressive documents such as Elizabeth Cady Stanton's "Declaration of Sentiments" (1848) and Charlotte Perkins Gilman's *Herland* (1915), the chapters span the political spectrum. The settings evoked by this literature are just as diverse, ranging from the jail cell of American Indian activist Leonard Peltier evoked in his *Prison Writings: My Life Is My Sun Dance* (1999) to the repressive landscapes of Margaret Atwood's *The Handmaid's Tale* (1985) and Suzanne Collins's *The Hunger Games* (2008). The fact that Collins's novel depicting teenage gladiatorial combat, like many of the works discussed in these pages, also achieved blockbuster status as a Hollywood film evidences the popularity of the literature of propaganda and its capacity to inspire and generate other creative media projects.

Many believe that the value of literature rests on its enduring artistic merit (determined by assessing style, tone, and other formal features) rather than on its political and social impacts. By implicitly fusing it with propaganda, these volumes confirm literature not only as a zone of aesthetic contemplation but also as an impetus for action, so that our ideas about the social and political force of words are reinvigorated. The 300 individual essays that comprise *The Literature of Propaganda* add nuance and complexity to the concept of mass persuasion—through literature—that leads to action. The essays do not coalesce into a single viewpoint; there is no unity to be found among the revolutionary writings of Edmund Burke, Bertolt Brecht, and Ho Chi Minh—and the same might be said of any cohort of authors represented in the pages that follow. This diversity makes the collection, above all else, an arena for debate and continued investigation.

**Russ Castronovo,**
**Advisory Board Chair**

---

[1] Siegfried Kracauer. *Theory of Film: The Redemption of Physical Reality* (New York: Oxford University Press, 1960) 161.

[2] Orwell, George. "The Frontiers of Art and Propaganda." BBC Overseas Service. 30 Apr. 1941.

[3] Orwell 30 Apr. 1941.

[4] Orwell 30 Apr. 1941.

# EDITOR'S NOTE

*T*he *Literature of Propaganda,* a three-volume reference guide, provides critical introductions to 300 texts from around the world. Some of these texts function as propaganda, while others discuss propaganda or use propaganda as a theme or setting. For this guide the term propaganda is defined as information spread publicly in order to influence others in belief, action, or both, regardless of whether the intent is seen as honorable or evil-minded.

An early text covered in this guide is the *History of the Kings of Britain,* written by English bishop Geoffrey of Monmouth around 1136. Purportedly a complete history of the British monarchy, it includes inaccuracies, heroic legends presented as truth, and supernatural content. The book helped popularize King Arthur as a national hero and create a British historical and cultural identity. A much different example of propaganda discussed in the guide is the "Battle Hymn of the Republic," a pro-Union poem published during the Civil War by American abolitionist Julia Ward Howe and set to the popular tune of "John Brown's Body." A well-known propaganda text from India is *Hind Swaraj,* written in 1909 by Mohandas Gandhi, who urged his country to reject materialist Western culture in favor a homegrown, spiritually based movement and to use satyagraha, or nonviolent resistance, against British authority. Among more recent propaganda works covered in the guide is *The Coming Insurrection,* written in 2007 by the Invisible Committee, an anonymous French group, which called for an end to capitalism.

The structure and content of *The Literature of Propaganda* was planned with the help of the project's advisory board, chaired by Russ Castronovo, Dorothy Draheim Professor of English and American Studies, University of Wisconsin-Madison. His introduction to this guide provides an overview of the literature of propaganda.

## ORGANIZATION

All entries share a common structure, providing consistent coverage of the works and a simple way of comparing basic elements of one text with another. Each entry has six parts: overview, historical and literary context, themes and style, critical discussion, sources, and further reading. Entries also have either an excerpt from the original text or a sidebar discussing a related topic, such as the life of the author.

*The Literature of Propaganda* is divided into three volumes, each with 100 entries. Volume 1, Approaches, has seven sections—appeals and exhortations, education and indoctrination, exposés, formal innovations, histories, political action, and theories. The works covered in this volume are examples of how propaganda is used. *The Feminine Mystique,* for example, an exposé published in 1963 by American feminist Betty Friedan, exposes and critiques the social pressure on women to become mothers and housewives. Volume 2, Groups, has five sections—cultural critics, dissidents and rebels, nations, parties and factions, and social classes. These entries provide examples of how propaganda works for or against groups of people. Volume 3, Effects, has six sections—distortions and delusions, dystopias and utopias, legislation and reform, myths and martyrs, predictions and prescriptions, and suppression and scapegoating. The texts covered in this volume illustrate common results of propaganda.

Among the criteria for selecting entry topics were the importance of the work in university curricula, the genre, the region and country of the author and text, and the time period. Entries can be looked up in the author and title indexes, as well as in the subject index.

**ACKNOWLEDGMENTS**

Many people contributed time, effort, and ideas to *The Literature of Propaganda*. At Gale, Philip Virta, manager of new products, developed the original plan for the book, and Michelle Lee, senior editor, served as the in-house manager for the project. *The Literature of Propaganda* owes its existence to their ideas and involvement.

We would like to express our appreciation to the advisors, who, in addition to creating the organization of *The Literature of Propaganda* and choosing the entry topics, identified other scholars to work on the project and answered many questions, both big and small. We would also like to thank the contributors for their accessible essays, often on difficult topics, as well as the scholars who reviewed the text for accuracy and coverage.

I am grateful to Erin Brown, senior project editor, especially for her work with the advisors and on the entry list; Greta Gard, project editor, who managed the writers; Mary Beth Curran, associate editor, who oversaw the editing process; David Hayes, associate editor, whose many contributions included organizing the workflow; and Hannah Soukup, assistant editor, who identified and corresponded with the academic reviewers. Other important assistance came from Mariko Fujinaka, managing editor; Anne Healey, senior editor; and Janet Moredock and Lee Esbenshade, associate editors. The line editors were Heather Campbell, Cheryl Collins, Tony Craine, Holli Fort, Laura Gabler, Harrabeth Haidusek, Ellen Henderson, Joan Hibler, Constance Israel, Jane Kupersmith, Dehlia McCobb, Kathy Peacock, Donna Polydoros, Natalie Ruppert, Mary Russell, Lisa Trow, Will Wagner, and Whitney Ward.

**Thomas Riggs**

# CONTRIBUTORS

**DAVID AITCHISON**

*Aitchison is a PhD candidate in literary studies and a university instructor.*

**GREG BACH**

*Bach holds an MA in classics and is a freelance writer.*

**CRAIG BARNES**

*Barnes holds an MFA in creative writing and has been a university instructor and a freelance writer.*

**MARIE BECKER**

*Becker holds an MA in humanities.*

**KAREN BENDER**

*Bender holds an MFA in creative writing and an MPhil in Anglo-Irish literature. She has taught high school English.*

**KATHERINE BISHOP**

*Bishop is a PhD student in English literature and has been a university instructor.*

**ALLISON BLECKER**

*Blecker is a PhD candidate in Near Eastern languages.*

**ELIZABETH BOEHEIM**

*Boeheim holds an MA in English literature and has been a university instructor.*

**WESLEY BORUCKI**

*Borucki holds a PhD in American history and is a university professor.*

**GERALD CARPENTER**

*Carpenter holds an MA in U.S. intellectual history and a PhD in early modern French history. He is a freelance writer.*

**ADAM CARSON**

*Carson is a PhD student in history and a university instructor.*

**MARK CASELLO**

*Casello is a PhD candidate in American literature and a university professor.*

**CURT CLONINGER**

*Cloninger holds an MFA in studio arts and is a university professor.*

**KEVIN COONEY**

*Cooney holds a PhD in English literature and is a university professor.*

**ALEX COVALCIUC**

*Covalciuc is a PhD candidate in English literature. He has been a university instructor and a freelance writer.*

**GIANO CROMLEY**

*Cromley holds an MFA in creative writing and is a university instructor.*

**COLBY CUPPERNULL**

*Cuppernull holds an MA in writing and has been a university instructor and a freelance writer.*

**ANNA DEEM**

*Deem holds an MA in education and is a freelance writer.*

**CHAD DUNDAS**

*Dundas holds an MFA in creative writing and has been a university instructor and a freelance writer.*

**RICHARD ESBENSHADE**

*Esbenshade holds a PhD in history and has been a university professor and a freelance writer.*

**TAYLOR EVANS**

*Evans is a PhD student in English literature and has been a university instructor.*

**DAISY GARD**

*Gard is a freelance writer with a background in English literature.*

**GRETA GARD**

*Gard is a PhD candidate in English literature and has been a university instructor and a freelance writer.*

**SARAH GARDAM**

*Gardam is a PhD candidate in English literature and has been a university instructor.*

**CLINT GARNER**

*Garner holds an MFA in creative writing and is a freelance writer.*

**TINA GIANOULIS**

*Gianoulis is a freelance writer with a background in English literature.*

**CYNTHIA GILES**

*Giles holds an MA in English literature and a PhD in interdisciplinary humanities. She has been a university instructor and a freelance writer.*

**QUAN MANH HA**

*Ha holds a PhD in American literature and is a university professor.*

**HARRABETH HAIDUSEK**

*Haidusek holds an MA in English literature and is a university instructor.*

**GREG HALABY**

*Halaby is a PhD candidate in Arabic and Islamic studies and a teaching fellow.*

**RODNEY HARRIS**

Harris is pursuing a PhD in history and has been a university instructor.

**MICHAEL HARTWELL**

Hartwell holds an MFA in creative writing. He has been a university instructor and a freelance writer.

**RON HORTON**

Horton holds an MFA in creative writing and has been a high school English instructor and a freelance writer.

**FRANKLYN HYDE**

Hyde holds a PhD in English literature and is a university instructor.

**LAURA JOHNSON**

Johnson holds a PhD in English literature and is a university professor.

**EMILY JONES**

Jones holds an MFA in creative writing and has been a university instructor.

**ALICIA KENT**

Kent holds a PhD in English literature and is a university professor.

**ROBERT KIBLER**

Kibler holds a PhD in English literature and is a university professor.

**DENNIS KLEIN**

Klein holds a PhD in history and is a university professor.

**LISA KROGER**

Kroger holds a PhD in English literature and has been a university instructor.

**HANA LAYSON**

Layson holds a PhD in English literature and has been a university instructor and a freelance writer.

**GREGORY LUTHER**

Luther holds an MFA in creative writing and has been a university instructor and freelance writer.

**THEODORE MCDERMOTT**

McDermott holds an MFA in creative writing and has been a university instructor and a freelance writer.

**MAGGIE MAGNO**

Magno has an MA in education. She has been a high school English teacher and a freelance writer.

**PHILLIP MAHONEY**

Mahoney is a PhD candidate in English literature and has been a university instructor.

**ABIGAIL MANN**

Mann holds a PhD in English literature and is a university professor.

**RACHEL MINDELL**

Mindell holds an MFA in creative writing and has been a freelance writer.

**JIM MLADENOVIC**

Mladenovic holds an MS in clinical psychology and is pursuing an MA in library science.

**KATHRYN MOLINARO**

Molinaro holds an MA in English literature and has been a university instructor and a freelance writer.

**CAITIE MOORE**

Moore holds an MFA in creative writing and has been a university instructor.

**JANET MOREDOCK**

Moredock is an editor and has been a university instructor and a freelance writer.

**ROBIN MORRIS**

Morris holds a PhD in English literature and has been a university instructor.

**AARON MOULTON**

Moulton holds an MA in Latin American studies. He is a PhD candidate in history and a university instructor.

**JANET MULLANE**

Mullane is a freelance writer and has been a high school English teacher.

**ELLIOTT NIBLOCK**

Niblock holds an MTS in the philosophy of religion.

**ELIZABETH ORVIS**

Orvis is a freelance writer with a background in English literature.

**JAMES OVERHOLTZER**

Overholtzer holds an MA in English literature and has been a university instructor.

**MARC OXOBY**

Oxoby holds a PhD in English literature and has been a university instructor.

**MEGAN PEABODY**

Peabody is a PhD candidate in English literature and a university instructor.

**EVELYN REYNOLDS**

Reynolds is pursuing an MA in English literature and an MFA in creative writing and has been a freelance writer.

**CHRIS ROUTLEDGE**

Routledge holds a PhD in English literature and is a university lecturer and a freelance writer.

**REBECCA RUSTIN**

Rustin holds an MA in English literature and is a freelance writer.

**CATHERINE E. SAUNDERS**

Saunders holds a PhD in English literature and is a university professor.

**CARINA SAXON**

Saxon is a PhD candidate in English literature and has been a university instructor and a freelance editor.

**JACOB SCHMITT**

Schmitt holds an MA in English literature and has been a freelance writer.

**GINA SHERRIFF**

Sherriff holds a PhD in Spanish and is a university professor.

**KIRKLEY SILVERMAN**

Silverman is pursuing her PhD in English literature and has been a university instructor.

**NANCY SIMPSON-YOUNGER**

Simpson-Younger is a PhD candidate in literary studies and a university instructor.

**CLAIRE SKINNER**

Skinner holds an MFA in creative writing and is a university instructor.

**ROGER SMITH**

Smith holds an MA in media ecology and has been a university instructor and a freelance writer.

**HANNAH SOUKUP**

Soukup holds an MFA in creative writing.

**NICHOLAS SNEAD**

Snead is a PhD candidate in French language and literature and has been a university instructor.

**SCOTT STABLER**

Stabler holds a PhD in history and is a university professor.

**SARAH STOECKL**

*Stoeckl holds a PhD in English literature and is a university instructor and a freelance writer.*

**SARA TAYLOR**

*Taylor holds an MA in theater history, theory, and literature and is pursuing her PhD in the same field.*

**PAMELA TOLER**

*Toler has a PhD in history and is a freelance writer and former university instructor.*

**ELIZABETH VITANZA**

*Vitanza holds a PhD in French and Francophone studies and has been a university and a high school instructor.*

**JOHN WALTERS**

*Walters is pursuing a PhD in English literature and has been a university instructor.*

**KATRINA WHITE**

*White is a PhD candidate in Spanish language and literature and a university instructor.*

# ACADEMIC REVIEWERS

**RAJA ADAL**

*Assistant Professor of History, University of Cincinnati, Ohio.*

**KHALED AL-MASRI**

*Assistant Professor of Arabic, Swarthmore College, Pennsylvania.*

**JOHN ALVIS**

*Professor of English and Director, American Studies Program, University of Dallas, Irving, Texas.*

**ARLENE AVAKIAN**

*Emeritus Professor and former Department Chair of Women, Gender, Sexuality Studies, University of Massachusetts-Amherst.*

**ROBERT BANNISTER**

*Professor Emeritus of History, Swarthmore College, Pennsylvania.*

**IAN BARNARD**

*Associate Professor of English, California State University-Northridge.*

**CONSTANTIN BEHLER**

*Associate Professor of German Studies, University of Washington, Bothell.*

**STEPHEN BEHRENDT**

*George Holmes Distinguished Professor of English, University of Nebraska, Lincoln.*

**WILLIAM BELDING**

*Professorial Lecturer, School of International Service, American University, Washington, D.C.*

**DORON BEN-ATAR**

*Professor of History, Fordham University, New York.*

**JILL BERGMAN**

*Professor of English and Chair, Department of English, University of Montana, Missoula, Montana.*

**STEPHEN BLACKWELL**

*Professor of Russian, University of Tennessee, Knoxville.*

**FLORENCE BOOS**

*Professor of English, University of Iowa, Iowa City.*

**MOULAY-ALI BOUÂNANI**

*Professor of Africana Studies, Binghamton University, Vestal, New York.*

**MICHAEL BREEN**

*Associate Professor of History and Humanities, Reed College, Portland, Oregon.*

**PAUL BRIANS**

*Professor Emeritus of English, Washington State University, Pullman.*

**STEPHEN BRONNER**

*Distinguished Professor of Political Science, Rutgers University, New Brunswick, New Jersey.*

**JAMES BROWN**

*Assistant Professor of English, University of Wisconsin-Madison.*

**ALISON BRUEY**

*Assistant Professor of History, University of North Florida, Jacksonville.*

**PETER BUTTON**

*Assistant Professor of East Asian Studies, New York University.*

**VERA CAMDEN**

*Professor of English, Kent State University, Ohio; Clinical Assistant Professor of Psychiatry, Case Western Reserve University, Cleveland, Ohio; Clinical Professor of Social Work, Rutgers University, New Brunswick, New Jersey.*

**RUSS CASTRONOVO**

*Dorothy Draheim Professor of English and American Studies, University of Wisconsin Madison.*

**SARAH E. CHINN**

*Associate Professor of English, Hunter College, New York.*

**ANN CIASULLO**

*Assistant Professor of English and Women's and Gender Studies, Gonzaga University, Spokane, Washington.*

**PAULA CIZMAR**

*Adjunct Assistant Professor of Playwriting, University of Southern California, Los Angeles.*

**NATHAN CLARKE**

*Assistant Professor of History, Minnesota State University-Moorhead.*

**WILLIAM CLEMENTE**

*Professor of Literature, Peru State College, Nebraska.*

**MARC CONNER**

*Jo M. and James Ballengee Professor of English, Washington and Lee University, Lexington, Virginia.*

**JANE CRAWFORD**

*Faculty, History and Political Science Department, Mount St. Mary's College, Los Angeles, California.*

LAWRENCE J. CUSHNIE

*PhD candidate in Political Science,
University of Washington, Seattle.*

JOHN T. DALTON

*Assistant Professor of Economics, Wake Forest
University, Winston-Salem, North Carolina.*

ALISTAIR DAVIES

*Senior Lecturer in English, University of
Sussex, Brighton, United Kingdom.*

KIRK DENTON

*Professor of East Asian Languages and
Literatures, Ohio State University, Columbus.*

MUSTAFAH DHADA

*Professor of African, Middle Eastern,
and World History, California State
University-Bakersfield.*

GABRIELE DILLMANN

*Associate Professor of German, Denison
University, Granville, Ohio.*

JANE DOWSON

*Reader in Twentieth-Century Literature, De
Montfort University, Leicester, United
Kingdom.*

JEANNE DUBINO

*Professor of English and Global Studies,
Global Studies Faculty Member,
Appalachian State University, Boone,
North Carolina.*

JILLIAN DUQUAINE-WATSON

*Senior Lecturer I, School of Interdisciplinary
Studies, University of Texas-Dallas.*

ELIZABETH DUQUETTE

*Associate Professor of English, Gettysburg
College, Pennsylvania.*

MICHAEL J. DUVALL

*Associate Professor of English, College of
Charleston, South Carolina.*

TAYLOR EASUM

*Assistant Professor of Global Histories,
Faculty Fellow of Draper Program,
New York University.*

SIÂN ECHARD

*Professor of English, University of British
Columbia, Vancouver.*

JAMES ENGLISH

*John Welsh Centennial Professor of English,
Director of the Penn Humanities Forum,
University of Pennsylvania, Philadelphia.*

MICHAEL FALETRA

*Associate Professor of English and Humanities,
Reed College, Portland, Oregon.*

DANINE FARQUHARSON

*Associate Professor of English, Memorial
University of Newfoundland, St. John's.*

CHARLES FORD

*Professor of History and Chair, History
Department, Norfolk State University,
Virginia.*

LUANNE FRANK

*Associate Professor of English, University of
Texas-Arlington.*

JOANNE E. GATES

*Professor of English, Jacksonville State
University, Alabama.*

JAMES GIGANTINO

*Assistant Professor of History, University of
Arkansas, Fayetteville.*

ROBERT W. GLOVER

*CLAS Honors Preceptor of Political Science,
University of Maine, Orono.*

SHARON GORMAN

*Walton Professor of Music, University of the
Ozarks, Clarksville, Arkansas.*

QUAN MANH HA

*Assistant Professor of American Literature
and Ethnic Studies, University of
Montana, Missoula.*

RAFEY HABIB

*Professor of English, Rutgers University, New
Brunswick, New Jersey.*

ANDREW HALEY

*Associate Professor of American Cultural
History, University of Southern
Mississippi, Hattiesburg.*

EIRIK LANG HARRIS

*Assistant Professor of Philosophy, City
University of Hong Kong, Kowloon.*

BRUCE HARVEY

*Associate Professor of English, Associate Director
of SEAS, and Director of Liberal Studies,
Florida International University, Miami.*

ROBERT HEGEL

*Professor of Chinese and Comparative
Literature, Washington University,
St. Louis, Missouri.*

MARGUERITE HELMERS

*Professor of English, University of Wisconsin-
Oshkosh.*

RICHARD HIGGINS

*Lecturer of English, Franklin College, Indiana.*

WALTER HÖLBLING

*Professor of American Studies, Karl-
Franzens-Universität, Graz, Austria.*

PIPPA HOLLOWAY

*Professor of History and Program Director,
Graduate Studies, Middle Tennessee State
University, Murfreesboro.*

TED HUMPHREY

*President's Professor, Barrett Professor,
Lincoln Professor of Ethics and Latin
American Intellectual History, and
Professor of Philosophy at the School of
Historical, Philosophical and Religious
Studies, Arizona State University, Tempe.*

FRANKLYN HYDE

*Adjunct Professor of English, University of
Manitoba, Winnipeg.*

WILLIAM IRWIN

*Professor of Philosophy, Kings College,
Wilkes-Barre, Pennsylvania.*

STEVEN JACOBS

*Associate Professor of Religious Studies
and Aaron Aronov Endowed Chair in
Judaic Studies, University of Alabama,
Tuscaloosa.*

JAKE JAKAITIS

*Associate Professor of English and Director,
Undergraduate Studies in English,
Indiana State University, Terre Haute.*

JENNIFER JAY

*Professor of History and Chinese, University
of Alberta, Edmonton.*

KELLY JEONG

*Assistant Professor of Comparative Literature
and of Korean Studies, University of
California, Riverside.*

JAMES JONES

*Professor of History, West Chester University,
Pennsylvania.*

ISAAC KAMOLA

*American Council for Learned Societies
(ACLS) New Faculty Fellow, Department
of Political Science, Johns Hopkins
University, Baltimore, Maryland.*

**AHMED KANNA**

Assistant Professor of Anthropology, University of the Pacific, Stockton, California.

**WARD KEELER**

Associate Professor of Anthropology, University of Texas-Austin.

**STEVEN G. KELLMAN**

Professor of Comparative Literature, University of Texas-San Antonio.

**DAVID KENLEY**

Associate Professor of History, Elizabethtown College, Pennsylvania.

**ALICIA A. KENT**

Associate Professor of English, University of Michigan-Flint.

**ROBERT KIBLER**

Professor of English Literature and Humanities, as well as Coordinator, English Program, Minot State University, North Dakota.

**RICHARD KING**

Professor of Chinese Studies, University of Victoria, British Columbia.

**HIROSHI KITAMURA**

Associate Professor of History, College of William and Mary, Williamsburg, Virginia.

**CHRISTOPHER KNIGHT**

Professor of English, University of Montana, Missoula.

**KRISTIN KOPTIUCH**

Associate Professor of Anthropology, Arizona State University at the West campus, Phoenix.

**JOSÉ LANTERS**

Professor of English, University of Wisconsin-Milwaukee.

**MURRAY LEAF**

Professor of Anthropology and Political Economy, University of Texas-Dallas.

**MARY LEDERER**

Independent Scholar of African Literature, Botswana.

**MICHAEL LEVY**

Professor of English, University of Wisconsin-Stout, Menomonie.

**HUA LI**

Assistant Professor of Chinese, Coordinator of Chinese, Montana State University, Bozeman.

**GRANT LILFORD**

Lecturer in English, University of Zululand, South Africa.

**RUTH LOOPER**

Professor of English, Dean of the Division of Humanities, Young Harris College, Georgia.

**DAVID MCCANN**

Korea Foundation Professor of Korean Literature, Harvard University-Korea Institute, Cambridge, Massachusetts.

**DEREK MAUS**

Associate Professor of English and Communication, State University of New York-Potsdam.

**RICHARD J. MOLL**

Associate Professor of English Literature, University of Western Ontario, London, Canada.

**JOHN MORILLO**

Associate Professor of English Literature, North Carolina State University, Raleigh.

**MICHAEL MUNGER**

Professor of Political Science, Economics, and Public Policy, as well as Director, PPE Program, Duke University, Durham, North Carolina.

**BRIAN MURDOCH**

Professor Emeritus of Languages, Cultures, and Religions, University of Stirling, Scotland, United Kingdom.

**SARA MURPHY**

Clinical Assistant Professor, New York University-Gallatin.

**EVAN MWANGI**

Associate Professor of English, Northwestern University, Evanston, Illinois.

**MICHAEL NIMAN**

Professor of Journalism and Media Studies, SUNY Buffalo State, New York.

**STACEY OLSTER**

Professor of English, Stony Brook University, New York.

**FEMI OSOFISAN**

Professor of Drama, University of Ibadan, Nigeria.

**ANDREW PARKER**

Professor of French and Comparative Literature, Rutgers University, New Brunswick, New Jersey.

**MICHEL PHARAND**

Director, Disraeli Project, Queen's University, Kingston, Ontario.

**ADAM PIETTE**

Professor of English Literature, University of Sheffield, United Kingdom.

**ELIZABETH PIKE**

Undergraduate Advisor and Instructor, Department of Geography, University of Colorado-Boulder.

**MARIA POLSKI**

Associate Professor of English and Communications, East-West University, Chicago, Illinois.

**JANET POWERS**

Professor Emerita of Interdisciplinary Studies and Women, Gender, and Sexuality Studies, Gettysburg College, Pennsylvania.

**H. L. T. QUAN**

Assistant Professor of Justice and Social Inquiry, Arizona State University, Tempe.

**PATRICK QUINN**

Professor of English Literature, Chapman University, Orange, California.

**KENNETH REEDS**

Assistant Professor of Spanish, Salem State University, Massachusetts.

**PATRICIO RIZZO-VAST**

Instructor of Spanish and Portuguese, Northeastern Illinois University, Chicago.

**PHILLIP ROTHWELL**

Professor of Portuguese, Rutgers University, New Brunswick, New Jersey.

**ELI RUBIN**

Associate Professor of History, Western Michigan University, Kalamazoo.

**ELIZABETH RUSS**

Associate Professor of Spanish, Southern Methodist University, Dallas, Texas.

**BURTON ST. JOHN III**

*Associate Professor of Communication, Old Dominion University, Norfolk, Virginia.*

**BRETT SCHMOLL**

*Lecturer of History, California State University-Bakersfield.*

**ROBERT SCHUHMANN**

*Associate Professor of Political Science and Head, Criminal Justice Department, University of Wyoming, Laramie.*

**DANIEL SCHWARTZ**

*Assistant Professor of History, George Washington University, Washington, D.C.*

**BEDE SCOTT**

*Assistant Professor of World Literature, Nanyang Technological University, Singapore.*

**KEN SEIGNEURIE**

*Associate Professor of Literature and Director, World Literature Program, Simon Fraser University, Surrey, British Columbia.*

**HORACIO SIERRA**

*Assistant Professor of English, Bowie State University, Maryland.*

**MICHAEL SIZER**

*Assistant Professor of History and Intellectual History, Maryland Institute College of Art, Baltimore.*

**MAREK STEEDMAN**

*Associate Professor of Political Science and Director, American Studies, University of Southern Mississippi, Hattiesburg.*

**ALAN STEWART**

*Professor of English and Comparative Literature, Columbia University, New York.*

**NANCY STOCKDALE**

*Associate Professor of History, University of North Texas, Denton.*

**GARY TAYLOR**

*Distinguished Research Professor, Florida State University, Tallahassee. General Editor of the Oxford editions of Shakespeare's Complete Works and Middleton's Collected Works.*

**LARRY THORNTON**

*Professor of History, Hanover College, Indiana.*

**JOHN TONE**

*Professor of History, Technology, and Society, as well as Associate Dean, Ivan Allen College of Liberal Art, Georgia Institute of Technology, Atlanta.*

**THOMAS UNDERWOOD**

*Senior Lecturer (Master Level), College of Arts and Sciences Writing Program, Boston University, Massachusetts.*

**RUJIE WANG**

*Associate Professor of Chinese and Chair, Chinese Department, College of Wooster, Ohio.*

**ANNETTE WANNAMAKER**

*Associate Professor of Children's Literature and Coordinator of the Children's Literature Program, Eastern Michigan University, Ypsilanti. North American Editor-in-Chief of* Children's Literature in Education: An International Quarterly.

**ALLYNA WARD**

*Assistant Professor of English, Booth University College, Winnipeg, Manitoba.*

**JEFF WEINTRAUB**

*Lecturer, Philosophy, Politics and Economics Program, University of Pennsylvania, Philadelphia.*

**JOLEE WEST**

*Director of Academic Computing and Digital Library Projects, Wesleyan University, Middletown, Connecticut.*

**CRAIG WHITE**

*Professor of Literature, University of Houston-Clear Lake, Texas.*

**KENNETH WILBURN**

*Assistant Professor of History, East Carolina University, Greenville, North Carolina.*

**PHILIP WILLIAMS**

*Visiting Professor of Chinese, Montana State University, Bozeman, and Professor Emeritus of Chinese, Arizona State University, Tempe.*

**DONALD WOLFF**

*Professor of English, Eastern Oregon University, La Grande.*

**SIMONA WRIGHT**

*Professor of Italian, College of New Jersey, Ewing.*

**RALPH YOUNG**

*Professor of History, Temple University, Philadelphia, Pennsylvania.*

**YU ZHANSUI**

*Assistant Professor of Chinese, Nazareth College, Rochester, New York.*

**PETER ZINOMAN**

*Professor of History, University of California-Berkeley.*

# APPEALS AND EXHORTATIONS

# "An Address to the Slaves of the United States"

*Henry Highland Garnet*

## OVERVIEW

Henry Highland Garnet's "An Address to the Slaves of the United States," delivered in 1843 and published in 1848, is often referred to as his "call to rebellion." In it Garnet melds high emotion with powerful rhetoric to bid southern (male) slaves to free themselves at whatever cost necessary. He asks slaves to acknowledge the strong ties among African Americans and to recall the countless horrors implicit in a history of servitude. Furthermore, the address proposes that those who "submit" as slaves are just as guilty of sin as those who promote the institution and that the time had arrived for slaves to act as men, to loosen their own chains. Garnet's speech served as an important, if radical, part of the abolition movement in the antebellum United States.

Born a slave in Maryland in 1815, Garnet escaped with his family to the North at the age of eight. He received an excellent education and went on to become a Presbyterian minister. Due to an early interest in opportunities for freed slaves abroad, he traveled to Cuba several times, but upon one return, in 1829, Garnet found that slave hunters had looted his family home—an experience that forever marked him. The perceived violent and dangerous revolutionary character of his 1843 address caused a commotion among abolitionists, many of whom initially rejected his ideas, only to later adopt them as slavery continued in spite of considerable efforts to the contrary. Although perhaps less frequently regarded than other abolitionist figures, Garnet is recognized as an early supporter of the African American-led freedom movement.

## HISTORICAL AND LITERARY CONTEXT

The 1840s were marked by the continued growth of abolitionism, combined with divisiveness among its ranks and the memory of recent slave-led rebellions that ended violently. Several significant events occurred the year before Garnet's speech. The decision in *Prigg v. Pennsylvania* upheld the fugitive slave law of 1793 but allowed states the option to prevent their own courts from hearing and prosecuting these cases, which interfered greatly with the fugitive retrieval process and greatly angered the South. In that same year, U.S. Congressman Joshua Giddings was removed from the House of Representatives for his antislavery position. There was a growing rift between white and black abolitionists regarding the most effective opposition to slavery and whether it should be political, religious, or militant. Further, a reliance on science to validate racism based upon biological distinctions was fully entrenched—a stance Garnet wholeheartedly rejected. He did, however, embrace "complexionally distinct" organization, believing that the black community needed to combat slavery as its own united front.

Garnet delivered his address at the National Convention of Colored Citizens in Buffalo, New York, to a relatively small audience of mixed race, age, and ideology, opening with only forty men, women, and children on August 15. Buffalo, which had a small population of abolitionists, had become a staging ground for confrontation between abolitionist groups and was selected for the convention with this aim. Despite these factors and the smallness of the Buffalo hall in which the meeting was held, Garnet spoke with charismatic strength. A white correspondent from the *Buffalo Commercial Advertiser* wrote, "I have heard some of the first men of our land speak, but they never held their audience under such complete control as Garnet." The address would remain unpublished, however, until 1848.

"An Address to the Slaves of the United States" was clearly influenced by several sources, including David Walker's *Appeal to the Coloured Citizens of the World,* which Garnet had printed alongside his own address. In the *Appeal,* Walker recalls his experience as the free son of a slave mother, relating in four "articles" the cruelties of slavery and the immediate need for violent revolt. Two speeches that preceded Garnet's and whose orators purported to address slaves as their audience were those of Gerrit Smith in 1842 and William Lloyd Garrison in 1843. Smith was a personal friend of Garnet's, and his speech was the first to acknowledge the importance of addressing slaves directly, to bid them to seek escape even if the result proved brutal. Garrison was opposed to Smith's ideology and instead reminded slaves of their friends in the North and that they must be patient, waiting for God to harshly punish their sinning masters.

*Key Facts*

**Time Period:**
Mid-19th Century

**Genre:**
Speech

**Events:**
Growth of abolitionism before the Civil War

**Nationality:**
American

## PRIMARY SOURCE

### EXCERPT FROM "AN ADDRESS TO THE SLAVES OF THE UNITED STATES"

In a few years the colonists grew strong, and severed themselves from the British Government. Their independence was declared, and they took their station among the sovereign powers of the earth. The declaration was a glorious document. Sages admired it, and the patriotic of every nation reverenced the God like sentiments which it contained. When the power of Government returned to their hands, did they emancipate the slaves? No; they rather added new links to our chains. Were they ignorant of the principles of Liberty? Certainly they were not. The sentiments of their revolutionary orators fell in burning eloquence upon their hearts, and with one voice they cried, Liberty or Death. Oh what a sentence was that! It ran from soul to soul like electric fire, and nerved the arm of thousands to fight in the holy cause of Freedom. Among the diversity of opinions that are entertained in regard to physical resistance, there are but a few found to gainsay that stern declaration. We are among those who do not. Slavery! How much misery is comprehended in that single word. What mind is there that does not shrink from its direful effects? Unless the image of God be obliterated from the soul, all men cherish the love of Liberty. The nice discerning political economist does not regard the sacred right more than the untutored African who roams in the wilds of Congo. Nor has the one more right to the full enjoyment of his freedom than the other. In every man's mind the good seeds of liberty are planted, and he who brings his fellow down so low, as to make him contented with a condition of slavery, commits the highest crime against God and man. Brethren, your oppressors aim to do this. They endeavor to make you as much like brutes as possible. When they have blinded the eyes of your mind when they have embittered the sweet waters of life then, and not till then, has American slavery done its perfect work.

Garnet's address, although initially regarded with considerable aversion for its rebellious content, contributed to his already substantial notoriety. He was indeed admired by agitators such as John Brown of the Harper's Ferry raid, who helped print and circulate his speech. However, as the war drew closer, more abolitionists aligned with the need for urgency, and Frederick Douglass, with whom Garnet had been at odds, worked with him to recruit soldiers for the Union Army. In 1865 President Abraham Lincoln invited Garnet to be the first African American to deliver a sermon in the House of Representatives. Today, "An Address to the Slaves of the United States" is regarded as an essential expression of abolitionist fervor that sought to build a black community to combat the institution of slavery.

### THEMES AND STYLE

Central to "An Address to the Slaves of the United States" is the necessity for a fiercely committed and unified move toward emancipation. Garnet opened the speech by establishing the close relationship among his designated audience—slaves. "Many of you," he said, "are bound to us, not only by the ties of a common humanity, but we are connected by the more tender relations of parents, wives, husbands, children, brothers, and sisters, and friends. As such we most affectionately address you." At the address's apex, Garnet insisted with powerful repetition, "let your motto be RESISTANCE! RESISTANCE! RESISTANCE! No oppressed people have ever secured their liberty without resistance." He encouraged slaves to approach their masters and "inform them that all you desire is FREEDOM, and that nothing else will suffice … and forever cease to toil," for if they "commence the work of death, they, and not you, will be responsible for the consequences." Thus, violence is portrayed as a possibility, if necessary, but not an ultimate desired outcome.

Portrait of Henry Highland Garnet. SCHOMBURG CENTER, NYPL/ART RESOURCE, NY.

TO SUCH DEGREDATION IT IS SINFUL IN THE EXTREME FOR YOU TO MAKE VOLUNTARY SUBMISSION. The divine commandments you are in duty bound to reverence and obey. If you do not obey them, you will surely meet with the displeasure of the Almighty. He requires you to love him supremely, and your neighbor as yourself—to keep the Sabbath day holy—to search the Scriptures—and bring up your children with respect for his laws, and to worship no other God but him. But slavery sets all these at nought, and hurls defiance in the face of Jehovah. The forlorn condition in which you are placed, does not destroy your moral obligation to God. You are not certain of heaven, because you suffer yourselves to remain in a state of slavery, where you cannot obey the commandments of the Sovereign of the universe. If the ignorance of slavery is a passport to heaven, then it is a blessing, and no curse, and you should rather desire its perpetuity than its abolition. God will not receive slavery, nor ignorance, nor any other state of mind, for love and obedience to him. Your condition does not absolve you from your moral obligation. The diabolical injustice by which your liberties are cloven down, NEITHER GOD, NOR ANGELS, OR JUST MEN, COMMAND YOU TO SUFFER FOR A SINGLE MOMENT. THEREFORE IT IS YOUR SOLEMN AND IMPERATIVE DUTY TO USE EVERY MEANS, BOTH MORAL, INTELLECTUAL, AND PHYSICAL THAT PROMISES SUCCESS. If a band of heathen men should attempt to enslave a race of Christians, and to place their children under the influence of some false religion, surely Heaven would frown upon the men who would not resist such aggression, even to death. If, on the other hand, a band of Christians should attempt to enslave a race of heathen men, and to entail slavery upon them, and to keep them in heathenism in the midst of Christianity, the God of heaven would smile upon every effort which the injured might make to disenthral themselves.

SOURCE: *A Memorial Discourse,* pp. 44–51. J. M. Wilson, 1865.

Bringing a unique perspective to his era's acceptance of slavery as sin, Garnet relies upon both religious and political rhetoric to bolster his claims. Instead of solely reprimanding slaveholders for their sins, he critiques the slaves themselves, stating: "TO SUCH DEGREDATION IT IS SINFUL IN THE EXTREME FOR YOU TO MAKE VOLUNTARY SUBMISSION" for "NEITHER GOD, NOR ANGELS, OR JUST MEN COMMAND YOU TO SUFFER FOR A SINGLE MOMENT." Garnet also invokes the American Revolution and the cultural need to respect anyone willing to sacrifice life for liberty. He tells detailed stories of four slave rebels—Denmark Vescy, Nat Turner, Joseph Cinque, and Madison Washington—who risked their lives for freedom, their own and that of others. He asserts, "RATHER DIE FREEMEN THAN LIVE TO BE SLAVES. Remember that you are THREE MILLIONS."

Passion, drama, shaming, and sarcasm mark the language of the address. "Your brethren of the North, East, and West," he remarks, "have been accustomed to meet together in National Conventions and sympathize with each other and weep over your unhappy condition." Here, and elsewhere, he indicates how little abolitionists have accomplished by addressing slavery at such a distance and convening only with each other. Several large sections of the address are printed entirely in capitals, and exclamation marks run throughout. Although he directs the address to slaves generally, he is clearly speaking to male members of this group, as women are portrayed as belonging to their slave men. Garnet questions the masculinity of his addressees in harsh tones and warns them to remember their ancestors. He chides, "You act as though your daughters were born to pamper the lusts of your masters and overseers.... You tamely submit while your lords tear your wives from your embraces.... In the name of God we ask, are you men? Where is the blood of your fathers?"

**CRITICAL DISCUSSION**

The address received immediate reaction from Frederick Douglass and other Garrisonians at the convention who felt it advocated excessive force that would have dangerous consequences for free blacks, both in the North and South. A highly emotional debate ensued, often provoking tears in the audience. Garnet defended his position while Douglass begged that abolitionists promote "the moral means just a little longer." Members voted on whether to include Garnet's address in their conference publications; the result was nineteen to eighteen in favor of censure. After the conference, Garnet was widely criticized, including by Maria Weston Chapman, the editor of the *Liberator,* who claimed he should have sought the advice of other abolitionists before proposing violence. He responded, "I can think on the subject of human rights without 'counsel' from the men of the West or the women of the East."

Through his address, Garnet helped create the foundation for what has come to be known politically as black nationalism. Though Walker's *Appeal* is widely considered to be the seminal work in this regard, Garnet seemingly followed suit. He bid slaves create their own solution unique to their situation (one of slavery based exclusively on race), to empower themselves through direct action rather than by waiting for the biracial abolitionist movement to do it for them. As Eddie S. Claude Jr. observes in *Exodus!* (2000), Garnet "exposed the ambivalence at the heart of the convention's efforts (its simultaneous rejection of American racism and its embrace of American identity) and forced a choice." Criticism in recent years has examined Garnet's shifting perspectives, including his rejection of violence in a Boston speech from 1842 and his dismissal in "An Address to the Slaves of the United States" of the Exodus movement, which favored relocating freed slaves to Africa—a movement he would support at other times.

According to Stanley Harrold in *The Rise of Aggressive Abolitionism* (2004), until the 1960s few if any of the addresses to slaves received appropriate attention within American literature. However, "An Address to the Slaves of the United States" first gained recognition around this time as an early example of black militancy. Current scholarship looks critically at this designation, questioning whether Garnet truly advocated violence as strongly as it has been argued. Garnet's relationship with the major abolitionists of the time, especially Garrison and Douglass, has also been further explored with a greater emphasis on their commonalities. Still, according to scholar Harry Reed, as quoted in *Exodus!* Garnet believed slavery and slaveholding to be sins: his notion of "the slave as an agent in his own liberation" makes Garnet unique.

## BIBLIOGRAPHY

### Sources

Claude, Eddie S., Jr. *Exodus!* Chicago: U of Chicago P, 2000. Print.

Harrold, Stanley. *The Rise of Aggressive Abolitionism: Addresses to the Slaves.* Lexington: UP of Kentucky, 2004. Print.

Schor, Joel. "The Rivalry between Frederick Douglass and Henry Highland Garnet." *Journal of Negro History* 64.1 (1979): 30–38. *JSTOR.* Web. 28 Oct. 2012.

Stuckey, Sterling. *The Ideological Origins of Black Nationalism.* Boston: Beacon, 1972. Print.

### Further Reading

Adeleke, Tunde. "Violence as an Option for Free Blacks in Nineteenth-Century America." *Canadian Review of American Studies* 351 (2005): 87–107. *Literature Resource Center.* Web. 30 Oct. 2012.

Davis, Hugh. *We Will Be Satisfied with Nothing Less: The African American Struggle for Equal Rights in the North during Reconstruction.* Ithaca: Cornell UP, 2011. Print.

Faulkner, Carol. "The Root of the Evil: Free Produce and Radical Antislavery, 1820–1860." *Journal of the Early Republic* 27.3 (2007): 377–405. *Literature Resource Center.* Web. 1 Nov. 2012.

Hutchinson, Earl Ofari. *Let Your Motto Be Resistance; the Life and Thought of Henry Highland Garnet.* Boston: Beacon, 1972. Print.

Marable, Manning, and Leith Mullings. *Let Nobody Turn Us Around: Voices of Resistance, Reform, and Renewal: An African American Anthology.* Lanham: Rowman & Littlefield, 2009. Print.

Miller, Floyd J. "African Dreams Deferred." *The Search for a Black Nationality: Black Emigration and Colonization 1787–1863.* Champaign: U of Illinois P, 1975. 250–63. *Literature Resource Center.* Web. 1 Nov. 2012.

Newman, Richard S. *The Transformation of American Abolitionism: Fighting Slavery in the Early Republic.* Chapel Hill: U of North Carolina P, 2002. Print.

Quarles, Benjamin. *Black Abolitionists.* New York: Oxford UP, 1969. Print.

### Media Adaptation

*Emancipation Day Celebration: Songs of Freedom and Words of Black Emancipation.* Prod. Howard Dodson and Roberta Yancy. Dir. James Briggs. Perf. Alvin Durant, Howard Dodson, and Ossie Davis. New York: Schomburg Media Productions, 1998. VHS.

*Rachel Mindell*

# AN ALMOND FOR A PARRAT

*Thomas Nashe*

## OVERVIEW

*An Almond for a Parrat* (c. 1590), a tract signed by Cuthbert Curry-knave but attributed to Thomas Nashe (sometimes spelled "Nash"), is an entry in the pamphlet war known as the Marprelate controversy, in which Episcopal Anglican bishops, who wielded significant control over affairs of state, were subjected to scrutiny and ridicule in a series of seven tracts signed by a militant Presbyterian who called himself Martin Marprelate. The bishops took the tracts as a serious threat to their authority and therefore may have employed Thomas Nashe, a gifted, Cambridge-educated rhetorician and clergyman's son, to write several pamphlets, including *An Almond for a Parrat*, in defense of the Episcopalian system. In the work Nashe accuses Martin of a power grab and questions the Puritan stance on women's role in the church.

The end of the Marprelate controversy (if not the debate over church governance) came about after the legal prosecution of those involved and the publication of longer, more serious works by the Anglican bishops. Both Martin and Nashe have been accused of flyting—virtuosic verbal sparring without much in the way of substantive argument. Nevertheless, the Marprelate tracts take up specific points of theology, demanding changes to the Anglican Book of Common Prayer, denouncing the inclusion of Apocrypha in officially sanctioned editions of the Bible, and criticizing Anglican translations of contentious portions of scripture. The Puritan John Penry, the man whom Nashe identifies as Martin, probably helped write the Marprelate tracts; he wrote other anti-Episcopal works under his own name. Penry was later convicted of publishing seditious and scandalous works and was executed in 1593. However, Nashe also served time in prison as a result of his later writing. Today *An Almond for a Parrat* is viewed as the product of a grimly repressive political climate.

## HISTORICAL AND LITERARY CONTEXT

In 1588, with the defeat of the Spanish Armada—which had attempted on behalf of the King of Spain and the Holy Roman Emperor to overpower England and force it back into the Catholic fold—the first Marprelate texts were unleashed on a British public that may have been wary of theological discourse. The English queen was eager to squelch internal dissent wherever possible, and the bishops in charge of the inchoate post-Reformation church were easily incensed by any opposition or critique of their methods. A 1586 ordinance decreed that all published matter required a license from either the archbishop of Canterbury or the bishop of London. Thus, the Marprelate tracts were printed on an illegal press and circulated via clandestine methods, and the participants in the printing and distribution were sought out and prosecuted. The government held that Martin was not merely concerned with church governance and liturgy but also was attempting to undermine the government, thereby committing treason.

By the time *An Almond for a Parrat* was published, British public opinion regarding religion was in a transitional period. Various published screeds, tracts, missives, and pamphlets competed with theatrical representations of a culturally enervated society and vivid sermons including those issued from Paul's Cross, which functioned as the monarch's unofficial mouthpiece. Authorities such as the powerful archbishop of Canterbury and leader of the Church of England, John Whitgift, surveyed literature and theater with intense scrutiny, looking for signs of sedition. Nashe is known to have been a guest in Whitgift's summer retreat at Croydon 1592; nevertheless, the next year Nashe was imprisoned.

Pamphlets responding to the Marprelate tracts included officially sanctioned responses and independently produced texts. Famous writers such as John Lyly and Robert Greene, along with Nashe, are thought to have been employed by the government to write their pamphlets; however, their use of the scurrilous Martinist style eventually led authorities to rethink the strategy. Lyly's *Pappe with a Hatchet* (c. 1589) struggles to maintain an appropriate tone; the writer of the fashionable and influential work *Euphues, The Anatomy of Wit: Very Pleasant for all Gentlemen to Read* (1578), Lyly had hoped to secure a position as court dramatist. However, in *Martin's Month's Minde* (c. 1589), the authors—who likely included Anthony Munday—claimed Lyly's work to be anti-Martinist theater in that "everie stage Plaier made a jest of [Martin]."

Nashe's engagement with Martinism is believed to have helped shape his later writing style. Since in 1590 he was still trying to establish a career for himself, *An Almond for a Parrat* was useful in garnering

**Key Facts**

**Time Period:**
Late 16th Century

**Genre:**
Tract

**Events:**
Reformation; rise of Martinism

**Nationality:**
English

# JOHN PENRY: THE MAN WHO COULD NOT STOP CONVERTING

John Penry—whom Thomas Nashe accused of writing the Martin Marprelate tracts—converted to several different religions over the course of his lifetime, which scarcely spanned thirty years. Born in Wales in 1562 or 1563, he matriculated at Cambridge in 1580 and was likely a Catholic. Nashe writes of Penry's childhood Catholicism in *An Almond for a Parrat*: "I tell you I. a P. in those daies would haue run a false gallop ouer his beades with anie man in England, and helpt the Priest for a shift to saie Masse at high midnight; which, if need were, I doubt not but he would do at this houre."

While at Cambridge, inspired by Thomas Cartwright, Penry switched to Presbyterianism. However, after attempting to convert the Welsh church to Presbyterianism, an energetically undertaken campaign during which Penry referred to the bishops of Wales as "excrements of romish vomits," he was drawn to Robert Browne's Congregationalism. Separatism would be Penry's last church, and under its banner he advocated that a person should be allowed to pray to whatever form of God he or she wanted to without being accused of treason. Because of accusations of treason, however, he was executed in 1593.

attention within the literary community. Greene, a popular romance writer, had already permitted Nashe to write the preface to *Menaphon* (1589), and Whitgift was briefly pleased with Nashe's work. In *Pierce Peniless: His Supplication to the Devill* (1592), a short comic prose work that sold well, Nashe mocks a range of London types, including the writer seeking patronage (*Pierce* is a play on *purse*). At the time of his passing around 1601, Nashe had earned the respect of such writers as Ben Jonson, who wrote in his elegy for Nashe that the writer's death begot "a general dearthe of witt throughout this land."

## THEMES AND STYLE

Central to *An Almond for a Parrat*—which R. B. McKerrow in *The Works of Thomas Nashe* (1905) interprets as meaning "an answer for a fool"—is the denunciation of the Marprelate author as an enemy of the state. The official condemnation of Martin was already known to the public, largely via the Paul's Cross sermons preached by Richard Bancroft, the bishop of London, who would go on to succeed Whitgift as archbishop of Canterbury. Nashe uses Martin's outlaw status to gibe at repressive publishing laws: "wee can cracke halfe a score blades in a backe-lane though a Constable come not to part us." However, he quickly doubles back, accusing Martin of seeking power under the guise of piety: "Malicious hipocryt … that thou shouldst filch thy selfe, as a new disease, into our gouernement…. Wert thou the last instrument of Sathans enuy, that,

as the abortive childe of a Chaos of heresies, thou sholdst adorne thy false dealing with the induments of discipline?"

Nashe's unique combination of literary, scholarly, and polemical elements is woven throughout the text. For example, the opening epistle mentions French social and religious satirist François Rabelais and his patron, Margaret of Navarre—"for that she was a maintainer of mirth in her life"—whose brother and grandson were kings of France. This noting of a politically powerful woman confronts Puritan Presbyterianism's aim to reduce the role of women in the church. Moreover, Nashe tells of a Presbyterian priest who, refusing Anglican funeral rites, "tombled his wife naked into the earth at high noone" and another who, deciding that veils were unchristian, shamed a veiled woman who came to his church: "she is a straunger, and we haue nothing to do with her; I take her to be Dinah the harlot, that sat by the way side, for she hath a vayle over her face." In Elizabeth I's London, when countries including France had laws forbidding female monarchs, it was politic to defend women.

*An Almond for a Parrat* uses Martin's style against him, dipping into the Marprelate tracts for ammunition. In *Hay Any Work for Cooper* (1589), Martin mocks Whitgift for failing to reply to works by the Presbyterian Thomas Cartwright: "Thomas hath now these many years let him alone and said nothing unto him for not answering his books." Nashe retorts: "Ile ribroste my brother Martin a litle, for objecting to my Lord Archbishop the not answering of his books." In *The Epitome* (1588), Martin writes: "the Church of Christ be a thing so prescribed by the Lord in the New Testament, as it is not lawful for any man to alter the same." Nashe answers: "One thing I am perswaded, that he neither respects the propagation of the Gospel, nor the prosperity of the Church, but only the benefite that may fall to him and his boulsterers." Unimpressed by Martin's use of classical logic, Nashe vows to "cutte off the traynes of your tedious syllogisms, that nowe haue no lesse than seuen or eight Termini waiting on them."

## CRITICAL DISCUSSION

Given the equally scurrilous nature of the pamphlets written in response to Martin, initial reactions were mixed—although Nashe's reputation enjoyed a boost of notoriety. An early complaint regarding the Marprelate controversy and Nashe's share in it came from Richard Harvey, brother to Nashe's longtime rival Gabriel Harvey. Richard Harvey's *Theologicall Discourse of the Lamb of God* (1590) "comprises a general attack on both sides of the pamphlet war, seasoned with violent abuse of Thomas Nashe," writes Sydney Anglo in *Machiavelli—The First Century: Studies in Enthusiasm, Hostility, and Irrelevance* (2005). In response to Harvey, Greene composed *Quip for an Upstart Courtier* (1592), to which Nashe probably contributed. Gabriel Harvey's subsequent *Four Letters and Certain Sonnets* (1592) refers to Nashe as "the prattling Parrat with his ignorant discourses" and an "elvish gnat." Over the course of the next few years, Nashe and the Harveys—mainly Gabriel—continued their feud in print. However, in 1599 Whitgift and Bancroft declared all works by the Harveys and Nashe illegal.

*An Almond for a Parrat* may have helped Nashe cut his teeth as a satirist, but the social and religious issues it raised came to haunt him. He was sent to prison for a passage in *Christ's Tears over Jerusalem* (1593), in which he compares the sinful population of Christ's Jerusalem with the people of London: "London, thou art the seeded garden of sinne, the sea that sucks in all the scumy channels of the realm." The words were edited in the 1594 version of the tract, as Charles Nicholl notes in the *Oxford Dictionary of National Biography* (2008), because Nashe, for all his wit and levity, had "a vein of troubled religiosity in him." Nashe's time in prison, his fight with the Harveys, and the reasons behind his departure from Cambridge—which are hinted at in another, smaller pamphlet skirmish between Nashe and Richard Lichfield—continue to interest literary scholars. Of similar scholarly interest are Nashe's possible interactions with playwrights Thomas Kyd and Christopher Marlowe, who were both arrested in 1593, and William Shakespeare.

Although Nashe's authorship of *An Almond for a Parrat* was debated for some time, there has been no dispute since Donald McGinn affirmed Nashe as the author in 1944, taking cues from McKerrow's and Nashe's texts. Scholars have examined several avenues of criticism of the document. For example, in his 1969 essay in *PMLA*, David C. McPherson explores Italian eroticism as both Nashe's inspiration and a source of his strength as a writer. Meanwhile, Stephen S. Hilliard, in *The Singularity of Thomas Nashe* (1986), examines Nashe's strained relationship with Whitgift in light of his participation in the Marprelate controversy and an anti-Presbyterian play Nashe wrote: "Neither the play nor the more corrosive Marprelate pamphlets won Nashe the support he needed."

**BIBLIOGRAPHY**

*Sources*

Anglo, Sydney. *Machiavelli—The First Century: Studies in Enthusiasm, Hostility, and Irrelevance.* Oxford: Oxford UP, 2005. *Google Books.* Web. 3 Sept. 2012.

Hilliard, Stephen S. *The Singularity of Thomas Nashe.* Lincoln: U of Nebraska P, 1986. Print.

McGinn, Donald J. "Nashe's Share in the Marprelate Controversy." *PMLA* 59 (1944): 952–84. *JSTOR.* Web. 3 Sept. 2012.

McKerrow, R. B., ed. *The Works of Thomas Nashe.* Oxford: Oxford UP, 1905. Print.

McPherson, David C. "Aretino and the Harvey-Nashe Quarrel." *PMLA* 84.6 (1969): 1551–58. *JSTOR.* Web. 3 Sept. 2012.

Thomas Nashe

*From a very scarce Pamphlet entitled The Trimming of Thomas Nashe Gentleman, by the high-tituled patron Don Richardo de Medico campo, Barber Chirurgion to Trinitie Colledge in Cambridge. Faber quas fecit compedes ipse gestat. London Printed for Philip Scarlet 1597. Published by T. Rodd, 9, Gt. Newport Street, Long Acre.*

Nicholl, Charles. "Thomas Nashe." *Oxford Dictionary of National Biography.* Oxford UP, 2008. Web. 3 Sept. 2012.

*Further Reading*

Andersen, Jennifer L. "Anti-Puritanism, Anti-Popery, and Gallows Rhetoric in Thomas Nashe's *The Unfortunate Traveller.*" *Sixteenth Century Journal* 35.1 (2004): 43–63. *JSTOR.* Web. 3 Sept. 2012.

Black, Joseph L. *The Martin Marprelate Tracts: A Modernized and Annotated Edition.* Cambridge: Cambridge UP, 2008. Print.

Hibbard, G. R. *Thomas Nashe: A Critical Introduction.* London: Routledge and Kegan Paul, 1962. Print.

McLuhan, Marshall. *The Classical Trivium: The Place of Thomas Nashe in the Learning of His Time.* Ed. W. Terrence Gordon. Corte Madera: Gingko, 2005. Print.

Nashe, Thomas. *The Unfortunate Traveller and Other Works.* Ed. J. B. Steane. Harmondsworth: Penguin, 1985. Print.

Nicholl, Charles. *A Cup of News: The Life of Thomas Nashe.* London: Routledge and Kegan Paul, 1984. Print.

Ward, Allyna E. "The 'Hyperbolical Blasphemies' of Nashe and Marlowe in Late Tudor England." *Marlowe Studies* 2 (2012): 125–42. Print.

*Rebecca Rustin*

English writer Thomas Nashe, to whom *An Almond for a Parrat* has been attributed. The c. 1590 work defends the Anglican Church in the Marprelate Controversy. © MARY EVANS PICTURE LIBRARY/ALAMY.

# CRUSADE SERMONS

*James of Vitry*

✣ *Key Facts*

**Time Period:**
Mid-13th Century

**Genre:**
Sermon

**Events:**
The Crusades

**Nationality:**
French

## OVERVIEW

James of Vitry, also known as Jacques de Vitry, wrote his *sermones vulgares* between 1225 and 1240 CE—the first comprehensive collection of so-called *ad status* sermons, written as examples of sermons for delivery to specific groups rather than to general congregations. The collection includes two lectures intended as models for preaching to "those who are or will become crusaders." An active proponent of the Crusades, James did not intend for the sermons to be spoken verbatim; rather they were intended to provide inexperienced preachers with a formula for writing their own perorations. Like other Crusade sermons, those included in James de Vitry's *sermones vulgares* were explicitly intended as propaganda, making use of the only mass medium available—the pulpit.

By the time James of Vitry wrote his well-received sermons, the concept of crusading had spread to target both non-Catholic Christian heretics in Europe and Muslim countries outside the Holy Lands. James himself had preached on behalf of one of the early crusades against heretics. Despite setbacks in the Holy Lands in the 1180s, when Turkish leader Saladin recaptured Jerusalem, the crusading movement remained vigorous. Over the course of the thirteenth century, crusaders fought against the Mongols, the non-Christian peoples of the Baltic region, and heretics in southern France, Italy, Germany, and the Balkans, as well as against Muslims in Spain, North Africa, and the Holy Lands. Today these sermons offer new insights into the religious history of the era.

## HISTORICAL AND LITERARY CONTEXT

The First Crusade began in 1095 following a sermon Pope Urban II delivered to a group of clergy and noblemen in a field outside the French town of Clermont. Urban called on Christian knights to stop warring among themselves and fight for control of the Holy Lands from the Turks. Following Urban II's exhortation, sermons became a critical element of the Crusades. Papal legates and bishops preached sermons that recruited crusaders and raised money for new campaigns. Clergy traveling with crusade armies preached to men prior to battle as a way of raising their spirits, while in Europe, pastors asked their parishioners for prayers in support of the crusaders.

James wrote his collection of model sermons during a revival of the art of preaching that was centered on the newly formed University of Paris. As a young man, he studied theology at the university, where he came under the influence of moral theologian Peter the Chanter and teachings about practical ethics. Many in Peter's circle, including James, became famous preachers and prolific writers of preaching texts. Around 1210 James left Paris and was ordained as a priest. After a brief period working as a parish priest, he settled in the town of Oignies, where he became a canon at St. Nicholas priory. In 1213 Pope Innocent III commissioned him to preach about the crusade in Lotharingia (modern Lorraine) and France against the Albigensian heresy; James subsequently preached for crusades to the Holy Lands. His success as a preacher led to his promotion within the church: in 1216 he was elected bishop of the crusader kingdom of Acre, where he participated in the Fifth Crusade against Egypt. He returned to Europe in 1225 and was made the cardinal bishop of Tusculum in 1229. After his return, he took to heart a phrase common to preaching manuals—*experiencia docet* (experience teaches)—and composed most of his model sermons.

Crusade preaching benefited from innovations pioneered by the pastoral reform movement that began in Paris in the late twelfth century. The central idea was that the clergy should make theological doctrine understandable to the laity, allowing even uneducated people to make that doctrine the basis of their daily lives. This idea was part of a larger trend that included the development of the Dominican and Franciscan preaching orders, as well as heretical movements such as the Waldensians. However, many clergy members did not have enough education or training to teach others. As a result, learned clergy at the University of Paris and elsewhere produced *pastoralia*, a body of instructional materials. With the aid of a new system of rapid copying, *pastoralia* spread across Europe. Since sermons were the primary medium by which pastors educated their flocks, the most useful of these instructional materials were collections of model sermons. Most were tied to the liturgical year; a few, like James of Vitry's *sermones vulgares*, were *ad status* collections, composed for delivery to specific groups in society.

James himself described the impact that a well-preached crusade sermon could have on a crowd, explaining that many people who had "decided in their heart not to be signed" took the cross after a successful sermon. Although it is doubtful that James's model sermons were ever preached as written, Crusade historian Norman Housely argues in a 2000 review for *English Historical Review,* "[I]n these texts we surely come close to the crusading message which was communicated to the faithful."

## THEMES AND STYLE

James of Vitry's two crusade sermons were written as invitations to "take the cross." The first is clearly designed with a crusade to the Holy Lands in mind, with sections titled "About the destruction and desolation of the Holy Land" and "Against those who put off being signed and are slow in coming to the aid of the Holy Land." James suggests in the protheme, or introductory section, that the material can be used to preach to "those who do not care about the Holy Land." The second sermon does not refer to a particular crusade and may well have been written in response to an emphasis on support for the Crusades from those left at home, since James addresses—in addition to enlistment—the value of attending sermons, making confession, and financing a crusader.

In his first crusade sermon, James urges men to action by describing the degradations suffered by Jerusalem and its Christian residents at the hands of the Turks. Jerusalem, the site of Christ's Passion, is portrayed as "a nest of serpents and the feeding ground of sparrows." Stating that Christians have a moral obligation to go on crusade, James offers his listeners prototypes for their action from the Old Testament, including Eli, Matthias, the Maccabees, and Samson. In his second crusade sermon, he focuses on the image of the cross and the value of the papal indulgence earned by crusaders. In this sermon, he uses extended metaphors to develop his themes. The cross is described as the key to God's treasure, a ship that carries men to salvation, the shepherd's rod, and Jacob's ladder to heaven. Linking the cross to the crusade, he suggests that the crusade is an imitation of Christ's self-sacrifice. In fact, he completes his construction of the crusade as an imitation of Christ's death on the cross by extending the benefits of the indulgence—which frees crusaders from "venial and mortal sins and from every penance enjoined upon them"—to members of the crusaders' families. James essentially suggests that the crusader dies for his family's sins.

Stylistically, the two sermons reveal their origins as instructional texts. Organized roughly in the form of a finished sermon, they are divided into three parts: the protheme, in which James discusses the purpose of the sermon; a main section, in which he develops an exposition of an initial Bible passage; and a final section listing possible subthemes. The model sermons include more material than a preacher needs for one

# THE CRUSADER KINGDOMS

Jerusalem fell to the armies of the First Crusade on July 15, 1099. Many of the crusaders considered that they had fulfilled their vows and returned home; others saw the newly conquered lands as an opportunity. A substantial number of the knights who joined the First Crusade were younger sons of European aristocrats with no prospect of inheriting land. Settling in the Kingdom of Jerusalem and the associated states of Edessa, Antioch, and Tripoli offered them the chance of wealth and status that they could not find at home.

For almost one hundred years the crusader kingdoms were European outposts in the Holy Lands, known collectively as *Outremer,* the lands over the seas. They fought among themselves and with their Greek Orthodox coreligionists as often as they fought with their Muslim neighbors. The need to protect themselves from Muslim attack inspired new crusades. Although politically divided and in constant turmoil, Outremer controlled the Holy Lands until 1187, when Islamic forces under the leadership of Saladin reconquered Jerusalem. By 1189 the crusader kingdoms had been reduced to a few outposts in Antioch and Tripoli. Finally, in 1291, Muslim forces drove Europeans out of the last crusader stronghold, Acre.

sermon and comprise a collection of themes, arguments, biblical authorities, brief illustrative stories known as *exempla,* and comparisons from which a preacher could select to develop his sermon.

## CRITICAL DISCUSSION

James was renowned as a preacher in his own time. Carolyn Muessig in *The Faces of Women in the Sermons of Jacques de Vitry* (1999) reports that a contemporary of James, Dominican Thomas of Cantimpré, was "so impressed by this preacher that he claimed that simply the mention of Jacques de Vitry's name would bring him great joy." Edward Tracy Brett in *Humbert of Romans: His Life and View of Thirteenth-Century Society* (1984) quotes another thirteenth-century preacher, Humbert of Romans, as saying that when James de Vitry preached in France, he "moved all of that nation to such a degree that no one either before or after has proved his equal."

James's model sermons had a profound influence on later collections of sermons, particularly those of Gilbert of Tournai (ca. 1200–1284), who borrowed from them on a grand scale. According to medievalist Penny J. Cole in *The Preaching of the Crusades to the Holy Land, 1095–1270* (1991), it is "a sign of the stature of Jacques de Vitry that so many of his writings have survived," including a hagiography of the holy woman Marie de Oignies, two histories, collections of *exempla,* and four collections of model sermons. At least fourteen manuscripts of the *sermones vulgares* still exist, suggesting that the collection must have

No full-length study of James's life and writings is available in English, and few of his sermons have been published in critical editions, but aspects of his work are the subject of a growing number of monographs. He is generally considered one of the most important popular preachers of the thirteenth century. Housely sums up his accomplishment, saying James of Vitry "weaves rich and varied patterns of imagery around the central symbol of the Passion and those who wore it to follow Christ."

### BIBLIOGRAPHY

*Sources*

Brett, Edward Tracy. *Humbert of Romans: His Life and View of Thirteenth-Century Society.* Toronto: Pontifical Institute of Medieval Studies, 1984. Print.

Cole, Penny J. *The Preaching of the Crusades to the Holy Land, 1095–1270.* Cambridge: Medieval Academy of America, 1991. Print.

Housely, Norman. Rev. of *Crusade Propaganda and Ideology: Model Sermons for the Preaching of the Cross,* ed. by Christoph T. Maier. *English Historical Review* 115.463 (2000): 939–40. *JSTOR.* Web. 15 Oct. 2012.

James of Vitry. "Sermo I" and "Sermo II." *Crusade Propaganda and Ideology: Model Sermons for the Preaching of the Cross.* Ed. Christoph T. Maier. Cambridge: Cambridge UP, 2000. 83–128. Print.

Muessig, Carolyn. *The Faces of Women in the Sermons of Jacques de Vitry.* Toronto: Peregrina, 1999. Print.

*Further Reading*

Andrea, Alfred J. "Walter, Archdeacon of London, and the 'Historia Occidentalis' of Jacques de Vitry." *Church History* 50.12 (1981): 146–51. *JSTOR,* Web. 15 Oct. 2012.

D'Avray, D. L. *The Preaching of the Friars: Sermons Diffused from Paris Before 1300.* Oxford: Clarendon, 1985. Print.

de Joinville, Jean. *Chronicles of the Crusades.* New York: Penguin, 2009. Print.

Ferrulo, S. C. "Preaching to the Clergy and Laity in Early Thirteenth-Century France: Jacques de Vitry's Sermones ad status." *Proceedings of the Annual Meeting of the Western Society for French History* 12 (1984): 12–43. Print.

Holt, Andrew, and James Muldoon, eds. *Competing Voices from the Crusades.* Westport: Greenwood, 2008. Print.

LeGoff, Jacques. "Social Realities and Ideological Codes in the Early Thirteenth Century: An Exemplum by James of Vitry." *The Medieval Imagination.* Trans. Arthur Goldhammer. Chicago: U of Chicago P, 1988. Print.

Maier, Christoph T. *Preaching the Crusades: Mendicant Friars and the Cross in the Thirteenth Century.* Cambridge: Cambridge UP, 1994. Print.

Riley-Smith, Jonathan. *The Crusades: A History.* New Haven: Yale UP, 2005. Print.

———. *What Were the Crusades?* 3rd ed. New York: Palgrave Macmillan, 2002. Print.

*Pamela Toler*

PETER THE HERMIT PREACHING THE FIRST CRUSADE

Peter the Hermit preaching the First Crusade before Pope Urban II in 1095. Hand-colored woodcut of a nineteenth-century illustration. © NORTH WIND PICTURE ARCHIVES/ALAMY.

been fairly well known. His historical writings have long been used as sources for the religious history of twelfth- and thirteenth-century Europe. His *Historia Occidentalis,* in particular, is one of the primary sources for the preaching revival, the careers of Peter the Chanter and his circle, and the development of the Dominican and Franciscan preaching orders.

Despite the widespread use of his historical writings, James's crusade sermons, like the genre as a whole, received limited scholarly attention for many years. Although Valmar Cramer published a full-length study of crusade preaching in 1939, the subject did not receive significant study until 1991, when Cole published *The Preaching of the Crusades.* Since then, a small body of scholarly work has appeared on the subject. For the most part, these works focus on the placement of crusade sermons in the context of the pastoral reform movement, theology, and rhetoric.

# THE EPISTLE, THE EPITOME, AND HAY ANY WORK FOR COOPER

*Martin Marprelate*

## OVERVIEW

*The Epistle, The Epitome,* and *Hay Any Work for Cooper* were the first, second, and fourth installments in a series of seven pamphlets (published between October 1588 and September 1589) that came to be known as the Martin Marprelate tracts. The pamphlets were composed by the pseudonymous Martin Marprelate, who wrote on behalf of—though not necessarily with the support of—Presbyterians, who opposed the Episcopalian Church of England under Elizabeth I. Written with a trenchant flair for language and a gossipy viciousness that came to be known as the Martinate style, the tracts enumerate a range of behaviors, both historically documented and otherwise, that painted certain clergymen as greedy, poorly educated, violent, cuckolded, extortionate, and otherwise lacking in priestly dignity, when they were not being downright "popish" (acting like Catholics). The text engaged directly with, among others, the militantly anti-Presbyterian archbishop of Canterbury, John Whitgift; Thomas Cooper, bishop of Winchester; John Aylmer, bishop of London; the dean of Salisbury, John Bridges, whose 1,400-page work denouncing the Presbyterian movement Marprelate frequently held up to ridicule; and the twice-converted Andrew Perne, dean of Ely. The true identity of Martin Marprelate remains unconfirmed. Two likely contributors were John Penry, an impassioned Welsh Presbyterian who (also) wrote under his own name and who was imprisoned and executed in May 1593 by English authorities for his efforts, and Job Throckmorton, a country gentleman whose extensive social connections may have been what saved him from suspicious authorities.

The search for the author responsible for the tracts commenced almost immediately after the first, *The Epistle,* came out in October 1588, printed in secret on an illegal press. Marprelate was seen as a direct threat to the ruling authorities the pamphlets attacked. In addition to mocking the bishops' antics and elaborate garb, the text describes how Presbyterians—the term "puritan" was used interchangeably—wanted the Church to be run, drawing inspiration from adherents of the Geneva school of the Protestant Reformation, led until 1564 by John Calvin.

## HISTORICAL AND LITERARY CONTEXT

After the end of the Marian reign in 1559, when the Reformation was imposed on the Church of England, people were encouraged to think of their former Catholicism as a foreign and superstitious religion. Martin Luther's exegesis had identified Rome as the devil's province. Some puritans called for the removal of maypoles and a halt to various popular festivals beloved by the people. The term "antichrist" was used on all sides to describe the others. John Udall, an early assistant to the Marprelate project who authored the pro-Presbyterian *A Demonstration of the Trueth of That Discipline* (1588), was first deprived of his parish and then executed. Catholics were also being targeted, and public executions were commonplace.

A war in print between the Presbyterian theologian Thomas Cartwright and Whitgift (who took over Cartwright's Cambridge fellowship after Cartwright was pushed out) had taken place in the 1570s after two of Cartwright's followers, John Field and Thomas Wilcox, published *An Admonition to the Parliament* (1572). Whitgift responded with accusations of treason in *Answere to a Certain Libel Intituled, 'An Admonition'* (1572). Cartwright then published *Replye* in 1573 before fleeing to Europe to escape warrants for his arrest. On the continent, Reformation politics were also divisive and frequently violent—French Protestants were killed by the thousands in the St. Bartholomew's Day massacre of 1572.

The Marprelate pamphlets revived one of the many contentious issues of Whitgift's fight with Cartwright, calling a debated translation of verse 28 of Psalm 105 in the Book of Common Prayer an example of the bishops' "palpable corruptions by subscribing unto things mere contrary to the word" (*The Epistle*). In the Presbyterian's preferred version, the line that refers to God's interventions in Egypt should read, according to Marprelate, "And they were not disobedient unto his word," while the Book of Common Prayer presents the line as "And they were not obedient unto his word"—"which is a plain corruption of the text," *The Epistle* states. As archbishop of Canterbury, Whitgift had required in 1584 that all clergy subscribe to certain articles of belief, including an affirmation of the Book of Common Prayer

Key Facts

**Time Period:**
Late 16th Century

**Genre:**
Pamphlet

**Events:**
Protestant Reformation

**Nationality:**
English

# MURDER PAMPHLETS

In the sixteenth and seventeenth centuries, "murder pamphlets" described violent crime in graphic detail, and as the pamphlets achieved popularity, they often featured gory woodcut illustrations. Buyers considering a Marprelate tract or one of the responses to it may have been tempted, for example, by the murder pamphlet *Sundrye Strange and Inhumaine Murthers, Lately Committed* (1591). It contained a woodcut featuring an ax-wielding man in a field strewn with dead people. A black-clad humanoid figure with claws for hands and feet lurks to one side—the devil figure typical of such illustrations—while a dog sniffs at one of the corpses.

Murder pamphlets could sometimes be used for propagandistic purposes, as demonstrated following the murders committed by Enoch ap Evan, a Puritan, of his mother and brother in 1633. *A Mirror for Murderers Wherein Is Briefly Set Forth the Life and Death of Enoch ap Evan* (1633) describes the captured murderer as one who "knew not where he was," who behaved "like a distracted bedlam and disquieted the whole jail with his tumultuous uproar." *A True Relation of a Barbarous and Most Cruel Murder Committed by One Enoch ap Evan* (1633), however, has ap Evan lucidly repenting in prison and writing a verse confession that implores "non-conformists" to "take heed in pulpits how you rail and bawl,/ Draw not poor laymen quite beyond true sense,/ Which caused me to do this foul offence."

as being in perfect agreement with scripture. Presbyterians disapproved of many parts of the Book of Common Prayer, such as the inclusion of Apocrypha and ceremonial guidelines such as "churching of women, the cross in baptism, the ring in marriage" (*The Epistle*). (Churching was a blessing for women who had recently given birth.)

After Marprelate's seventh tract, the *Protestatyon* (September 1589), authorities closed in on the secret press used to print it. Publisher Robert Waldegrave was forced to flee to Europe, though he would eventually continue his career in Scotland. "Martinist" style was appropriated in a number of pamphlets responding to Marprelate's, some of them commissioned by the bishops themselves. During the English Civil Wars of the seventeenth century, the Marprelate tracts were reissued, along with new ones written in a similar vein, such as those by "Margery Mar-prelate" (1640–41). Also reprinted at that time were refutations of the pamphlets and of Presbyterianism in general, such as Richard Bancroft's *Dangerous Positions and Proceedings* (1593).

## THEMES AND STYLE

Apart from laying out basic tenets of Presbyterianism, the Marprelate pamphlets use shock tactics and humor to draw in a lay audience perceived as apathetic.

*Hay Any Work* defends the use of gossip and jokes in the text as a means of attracting readers: "I saw the cause of Christ's government, and of the bishops' antichristian dealing, to be hidden. The most part of men could not be gotten to read anything in defense of the one and against the other." Many Presbyterian clergymen had been excommunicated without due process and deprived of work. Echoing clergyman Anthony Gilby's "Hundred Pointes of Poperie, Yet Remayning, Which Deforme the Englishe Reformation," *The Epistle*'s "Conditions of Peace to Be Inviolably Kept Forever" sets out a list of "things as all the world will think you unworthy to live, if you grant them not," including an exhortation to the bishops "that never hereafter they profane excommunication as they have done, by excommunicating alone in their chambers, and that for trifles."

Scriptural exegesis, syllogisms, animadversion, and various forms of classical rhetoric are also deployed in the pamphlets. The Marprelate writer uses rumor and anecdote to further leaven the theology; reference is made more than once to the lewd "Libel of Oxford" (c. 1564), circulated in manuscript, which suggested that Bishop Cooper's wife and Dr. John Day of Magdalen College, later a vicar general in Wells, were lovers. *Hay Any Work* mocks Cooper's *An Admonition to the People of England* (1589): "The style and the phrase is very like her husband's, who was wont to write unto Doctor Day of Wells." "Hay any work for cooper" was a common cry heard in the street from itinerant coopers (barrel-makers) soliciting work ("have ye any"). The Marprelate tract of that title claims that "church government by archbishops and bishops is an unlawful church government"—in other words, that Cooper ought to be unemployed. Bishop Aylmer was reprimanded for selling trees for profit from his episcopal estate. *The Epitome* quotes from a work Aylmer wrote before he was transferred to the powerful London diocese: "'Come off you bishops, away with your superfluities, yield up your thousands, be content with your hundredths.... Let your portion be priestlike, and not princelike.'" The hypocrisy does not go unnoticed by Marprelate: "And may not all the former speeches be fitly applied unto him? Is, without doubt."

Overall, the Marprelate writer evinces a passionate engagement with the society in which he lives. The pamphlets combine folksy sayings—"Ye but it is an old said saw, enough is as good as a feast" (*Hay Any Work*)—with preacherly wrath against the bishops—"But you three, like furious and senseless brute beasts, dread no peril, look no farther than your feet, spare none, but with tooth and nail cry out" (*The Epitome*)—and entertaining anecdotes such as the one about the bishop who came to dinner in full regalia—"The dog flies at the bishop and took off his corner cap (he thought belike it had been a cheesecake)" (*The Epistle*). All serve to erode the image of bishops as all powerful and beyond reproach.

## CRITICAL DISCUSSION

Most of the initial reactions to the Marprelate tracts were centered on the suspicion that it was political power their authors were after, not theological exactitude. In a 1588 letter to Archbishop Whitgift, Lord Treasurer Burghley called *The Epistle* "a Seditious book against ye Ecclesiastical Government of ye Church by Bishops" and demanded that the author be found and captured at once. Cooper's *Admonition* fretted that the Marprelate author "wil proue himselfe to bee, not onely *Mar-prelate*, but *Mar-prince, Mar-state, Mar-lawe, Mar-magistrate*," terms *Hay Any Work* turns back against Cooper. In *An Advertisement Touching the Controversies of the Church of England* (c. 1590), philosopher and statesman Francis Bacon quotes the apostle Paul: "'While there is amongst you zeal and contention, are ye not carnal?'" (1 Corinthians 3:3). Bacon recommended the tracts "be censured, by all that have understanding and conscience."

By May 1593, with Penry executed and Waldegrave in exile, the Marprelate controversy had subsided. Whitgift's chaplain and successor, Richard Bancroft, published *Survay of the Pretended Holy Discipline* (1593), which engages with Presbyterian theological contentions; his Marprelate-like *Dangerous Positions and Proceedings* (1593) chronicles the details of the other side's activities. Richard Hooker's *Lawes of Ecclesiastical Politie* (1593) equates Presbyterianism with treason. Regardless of such setbacks, "Puritanism was more than a movement: it was already an institution, a church within the Church, with its own standards of nascent traditions, and even its own discipline and spiritual government," writes Patrick Collinson in *The Elizabethan Puritan Movement* (1967), adding that Presbyterian disapproval of Marprelate's tactics was widespread: "He made fun of a solemn matter and defiled the cause with unprecedented scurrility."

In his 1879 scholarly collection of documents related to the controversy, Edward Arber observes that "hitherto the Martinists have been largely vilified, their works considered blasphemous, and their purposes treasonable. There is neither blasphemy nor treason to be found in their writings." Tessa Watt's *Cheap Print and Popular Piety, 1550–1640* (1991) notes that puritanism was perceived as overly strict by "playwrights and pamphleteers who made 'precise' religion (along with 'godly ballads') the butt of mockery, and a threat to 'good fellowship.'" In *The Anti-Christ's Lewd Hat* (2002), Peter Lake comments on revisionist accounts of the "clash between the culture of 'the godly' (a.k.a. the puritans)—sober, pious, word- and sermon-centred—and, on the other hand, a residual popular culture, centred on the alehouse and the village green."

## BIBLIOGRAPHY

*Sources*

Arber, Edward, ed. "An Introductory Sketch to the Martin Marprelate Controversy, 1588–1590." *The English Scholar's Library of Old and Modern Works*. No. 8. Westminster: Constable, 1879. *Google Books*. Web. 23 Oct. 2012.

Bacon, Francis. *The Works of Francis Bacon, Baron of Verulam, Viscount of St. Alban, and Lord High Chancellor of England*. Vol. 2. London: Rivington, 1819. *Google Books*. Web. 24 Oct. 2012.

Black, Joseph L., ed. *The Martin Marprelate Tracts*. Cambridge: Cambridge UP, 2008. Print.

Collinson, Patrick. *The Elizabethan Puritan Movement*. Berkeley: U of California P, 1967. Print.

Lake, Peter, and Michael C. Questier. *The Anti-Christ's Lewd Hat*. New Haven: Yale UP, 2002. Print.

*Puritan Discipline Tracts. Re-printed from the Black Letter Edition*. Introduction and notes by John Petheram. 2nd ed. London: Petheram, 1843. Print.

A sixteenth-century English lord mayor and bishop depicted in an 1882 illustration. Sixteenth-century tracts such as *The Epistle*, *The Epitome*, and *Hay Any Work for Cooper* attacked English religious figures. © IVY CLOSE IMAGES/ALAMY.

Watt, Tessa. *Cheap Print and Popular Piety, 1550–1640*. Cambridge: Cambridge UP, 1991. Print.

*Further Reading*

Anselment, Raymond A. "Rhetoric and the Dramatic Satire of Martin Marprelate." *Studies in English Literature, 1500–1900,* 10.1 (1970). *JSTOR*. Web. 14 Sept. 2012.

Coolidge, John S. *The Pauline Renaissance in England: Puritanism and the Bible.* Oxford: Clarendon, 1970. Print.

Egan, James. "Nathaniel Ward and the Marprelate Tradition." *Early American Literature* 15.1 (1980). *JSTOR*. Web. 12 Sept. 2012.

Lander, Jesse M. *Inventing Polemic: Religion, Print, and Literary Culture in Early Modern England.* Cambridge: Cambridge UP, 2006. Print.

McGinn, Donald. "The Real Martin Marprelate." *PMLA* 58.1 (1943). *JSTOR*. Web. 14 Sept. 2012.

Poole, Kristen. "Saints Alive! Falstaff, Martin Marprelate, and the Staging of Puritanism." *Shakespeare Quarterly* 46.1 (1995). *JSTOR*. Web. 14 Sept. 2012.

Walsham, Alexandra. *Providence in Early Modern England.* Cambridge: Cambridge UP, 1999. Print.

*Rebecca Rustin*

# GRAVESIDE ORATION FOR JEREMIAH O'DONOVAN ROSSA

*Padraig Pearse*

## OVERVIEW

At the funeral of legendary Irish nationalist Jeremiah O'Donovan Rossa on August 1, 1915, poet, educator, and prominent nationalist Padraig Pearse delivered a graveside oration venerating Rossa and encouraging escalation in campaigns for Irish independence. Pearse had been recruited by the very secretive Irish Republican Brotherhood (IRB) in 1913 because of his contributions to the nationalist movement, particularly his aid in the formation of the Irish Volunteers (a nationalist militia) earlier that year. In the course of the speech Pearse aligns IRB values and aims with those of earlier nationalist movements—particularly those led by Theobald Wolfe Tone, John Mitchel, and Rossa himself—and asks all active republican organizations to unite in a concentrated push for sovereignty. Including the IRB and the Fenian Volunteers (another nationalist militia), attendance was reported to have been in the hundreds of thousands, effectively turning Rossa's funeral into a republican rally.

Though Pearse had delivered several such orations since being recruited by the IRB, many considered the tribute to Rossa his finest. The speech was immediately embraced by Pearse's nationalist cohort, and he quickly rose in the ranks of the IRB. He eventually was appointed the first president of the provisional government of the Republic of Ireland during the Easter Rising of 1916. The closing remark of the speech, "Ireland unfree shall never be at peace," became the battle cry for nearly all nationalist militance thereafter. If Tone was the "father of Irish republicanism," Pearse had become the father of Irish independence. Today the oration is seen not only as the most influential speech of the Irish nationalist movement but as one of the greatest speeches of the twentieth century.

## HISTORICAL AND LITERARY CONTEXT

Ireland had been a separate nation under British rule for nearly two hundred years when the Acts of Union (1800) joined the Kingdom of Great Britain and the Kingdom of Ireland to form the United Kingdom of Great Britain and Ireland. Irish opposition to the union appeared early and took many forms. Because nationalists had not heeded Tone's message of unity, however, dozens of organizations emerged, including the Home Rule League, the Land League, Sinn Fein, the Ulster Volunteer Force, and the Irish Republican Brotherhood. The organizations campaigned independently and sometimes even against one another, rendering all of them ineffectual. Then, in 1914, several of Ireland's nationalist members of Parliament (MPs) became outraged when their one small victory—the Third Home Rule Bill—was used as leverage to retain British conscription rights over Irish soldiers going into World War I, and they returned to Ireland determined to mount a substantial military opposition.

These MPs, who belonged to various nationalist organizations, understood that the time for unity had come. They searched for a figurehead, a voice through which to mount their campaign. Pearse had made a name for himself with the Irish Volunteers from their inception, and he had been the Irish Republican Brotherhood's go-to orator since being recruited to their ranks in 1913. He was known for his rousing speeches at the gravesides of national heroes, and when republican legend Rossa died in the summer of 1915, the MPs and the republican leaders they were working with saw before them a unique opportunity. The funeral service was widely promoted, and Pearse delivered his call for a united front against British rule to hundreds of thousands of nationalist sympathizers.

The speech draws heavily on the panegyric tradition, particularly as originally employed by the ancient Greeks to honor great public figures in death. The *Olympiacus* of Gorgias and the *Olympiacus* of Lysias are the most prominent examples, displaying the ornate language and lavish praise characteristic of the early panegyric. By contrast, English language adaptations of the form had been written mostly in honor of living public figures to mark a momentous occasion, as in the numerous compositions honoring Charles II's ascendancy to the British throne in 1660. All variations included passages promoting the emulation of the subject's deeds.

Although Pearse's oration more closely resembles those of the Greeks, the attention paid by English panegyrics to national pride factors heavily in his composition as well. Rather than touting Rossa's contributions as the products of an exceptional individual, Pearse portrays Rossa as an ordinary man made

#### ✢ *Key Facts*

**Time Period:**
Early 20th Century

**Genre:**
Speech

**Events:**
Irish nationalist movement

**Nationality:**
Irish

# ON HALLOWED GROUNDS

Padraig Pearse's graveside oration was delivered at Jeremiah O'Donovan Rossa's funeral service on the grounds of the Glasnevin Cemetery, which housed the remains of nearly all of Ireland's nationalist heroes. Along with Rossa, Michael Collins, Maud Gonne McBride, Daniel O'Connell, Charles Stewart Parnell, and Éamon de Valera were all buried at Glasnevin. After Pearse was tried and executed following the rising, Sir John Maxwell, commander of British forces in Ireland, suggested to the prime minister that his body not be returned to Ireland for burial, as his grave was sure to attract crowds of unruly nationalist sympathizers.

The ploy was in vain, however, as people instead began gathering at Rossa's grave to pay their respects and on occasion reenact Pearse's famous speech. In commemoration of their support and Pearse's contributions to Irish independence, the Glasnevin Cemetery and Museum hosted a month-long event in August 2012. An actor dressed as Pearse in his Volunteer uniform delivered the speech in full every day at 2:30 in the afternoon, the same time Rossa's funeral began on August 1, 1915.

exceptional by his allegiance to a noble cause. In so doing, the speech enjoined all able-bodied Irish citizens to emulate Rossa by dedicating their lives to Irish independence.

## THEMES AND STYLE

The presiding themes of Pearse's graveside oration are the presentation of a united Irish front against Britain and the promotion of escalated armed resistance as a means to national sovereignty. Pearse makes sure to align himself with his predecessors' visions of Irish independence, assuring all in attendance that "we know only one definition of freedom: it is Tone's definition, it is Mitchel's definition, it is Rossa's definition." In pursuit of that vision, he insists that "we of the Irish Volunteers, and you others who are associated with us in to-day's task and duty, are bound together and must stand together henceforth in brotherly union." Feeling condescended to and patronized by the British government, who think they have subdued Irish resistance by "purchas[ing] half of us and intimidat[ing] the other half," Pearse encourages a move to armed resistance, defiantly declaring that "Ireland unfree shall never be at peace."

The speech's greatest rhetorical strength lies in its insistence on laying aside internal political and religious differences in the interest of presenting a united front. Pearse eschews discussion of Catholic or Protestant allegiance or allegiance to any one organization, insisting instead that "here we avow ourselves, as [Rossa] avowed himself in the dock, Irishmen of one allegiance only," "re-baptised in the Fenian faith"

only. He further enjoins his fellow Irishmen to forego affiliating themselves with any one faction, lest they "blaspheme the cause … by giving it any other name and definition than" Tone's, Mitchel's, and Rossa's—indeed any other than Ireland's.

The sole emotional tenor of the speech is defiance. Pearse saw in Rossa "all that was olden and beautiful and Gaelic in Ireland, the holiness and simplicity of patriotism," and he refused to let his countrymen wait patiently for fair treatment any longer. "They think that they have pacified Ireland," he put forth to the crowd, "they think that they have foreseen everything, think that they have provided against everything" Ireland could possibly muster. In response to their self-assuredness he could only exclaim, "the fools, the fools, the fools!"

## CRITICAL DISCUSSION

Pearse's oration was as thoroughly praised within Irish republican circles as it was ignored outside them. Only republican periodicals covered the speech, and their sentiments generally fell closely in line with those that appeared on a souvenir produced within days of the speech. It contained text positing that "cold, lifeless print cannot convey even an idea of the depth and intensity of feeling in which [Pearse's] words were couched." In response to public murmurs that the oration was nothing more than an orchestrated, rehearsed publicity stunt, the text of the souvenir further offered that "it was the soul of a patriot breathing" life into the movement for his nation's freedom.

The speech accomplished the republican mission, as thousands joined and thousands more rededicated themselves to the nationalist cause. The Volunteers and IRB gained enough support and momentum to stage an uprising—albeit an unsuccessful one—some eight months later during Easter week 1916. Pearse himself read aloud the constitution of the provisional government of the Republic of Ireland as the opening act of the rebellion and was shortly thereafter named the first provisional president of Ireland. In the decades that followed, the rebellion overshadowed the oration that had ensured its inception.

Contemporary scholarship places the speech in much the same context. F. X. Martin sees it not as starting the rising, or even starting preparations for the rising, but as presaging the perseverance that embodied both the rising and the push for independence that followed. Pearse's words, Martin argues, "clearly expressed … the greatest danger of the rising, the declaration that the insurgents acting in the names of Tone, Emmet, Davis, Mitchel and O'Donovan Rossa represented the political aspirations of an oppressed Irish people" no longer content with incremental placation. Also frequently noted—by Martin and many others—is the significance of a poet's giving voice to a movement so concerned with the retention of cultural and artistic heritage.

In 2012 members of Sinn Fein pose in period costumes to commemorate the 1916 Easter Uprising in Ireland. © STEPHEN BARNES/NI POLITICS/ ALAMY.

**BIBLIOGRAPHY**

*Sources*

MacArthur, Brian. *The Penguin Book of Twentieth-Century Speeches.* New York: Penguin, 1994. Print.

Martin, F. X. "1916: Myth, Fact, and Mystery." *Studia Hibernica* 7 (1967): 7–126. *JSTOR.* Web. 23 Aug. 2012.

———. *Leaders and Men of the Easter Rising: Dublin 1916.* Ithaca: Cornell UP, 1967. Print.

Townshend, Charles. *Easter 1916: The Irish Rebellion.* Chicago: Ivan R. Dee, 2006. Print.

*Further Reading*

Dangerfield, George. *The Damnable Question: A Study in Anglo-Irish Relations.* Boston: Little, 1976. Print.

O'Donnell, Ruan. *The Impact of the 1916 Rising: Among the Nations.* Dublin: Irish Academic, 2008. Print.

O'Donovan, Rossa J. *My Years in English Jails.* Tralee: Anvil, 1967. Print.

O'Donovan, Rossa J., and Seán Ó. Lúing. *Rossa's Recollections, 1838 to 1898: Memoirs of an Irish Revolutionary.* Guilford: Lyon's, 2004. Print.

Pearse, Padraic, Joseph Campbell, and Patrick Browne. *Collected Works of Padraic H. Pearse.* New York: Stokes, 1917. Print.

Regan, Stephen. *Irish Writing: An Anthology of Irish Literature in English 1789–1939.* Oxford: Oxford UP, 2004. Print.

*Clint Garner*

# "HOPE SPEECH"

*Harvey Milk*

✛ *Key Facts*

**Time Period:**
Late 20th Century

**Genre:**
Speech

**Events:**
Rise of the gay rights
movement; growth and
success of anti-gay
rights efforts

**Nationality:**
American

## OVERVIEW

Harvey Milk's "Hope Speech," delivered in the summer of 1978, describes the gay community in America as being discriminated against just as much as any other minority group and proposes that the first step toward ending that discrimination is for citizens and political leaders to come out of the closet. Milk argues that all communities, marginalized or not, ought to be judged not by their "criminals and myths" but by their leaders. He adds that in order to have such leaders, members of the gay community need to stop hiding their identities. He had delivered a condensed version of the speech during his campaign to become a member of the San Francisco Board of Supervisors in 1977. But the extended version, which he delivered as the nation's first self-identified gay public official in 1978 at San Francisco's Gay Freedom Day Parade, is the version for which Milk became famous.

Neither speech received much attention outside of San Francisco. Having been unsuccessful in three previous campaigns for public office, Milk was largely dismissed even within San Francisco—the one notable exception being the Castro district, a primarily gay neighborhood at the time. It was not until Milk and Mayor George Moscone were assassinated by former Supervisor Dan White inside City Hall in November 1978 that he gained national recognition. If, as some suggested at the time, the gay community had yet to find a martyr—as the African American civil rights movement had in Abraham Lincoln and Martin Luther King Jr.—Milk would soon fill that role. Since his death, Milk's messages of pride and equality under law have bolstered the continued efforts of gay rights activists, and his "Hope Speech" is seen as a fundamental text in their rhetorical strategies.

## HISTORICAL AND LITERARY CONTEXT

Although the counterculture movement of the 1960s had supplied much needed momentum to the gay rights movement, the 1970s saw just as many setbacks as advances in the cause. Activist Jim Foster, cofounder of the Society for Individual Rights, had become the first openly gay man to speak at a national political convention, delivering an address at the 1972 Democratic National Convention, where he was joined by lesbian activist Madeline Davis. Their appearance at the convention was possible in large part because progress made by grassroots gay rights activism had rendered "gay" issues socially acceptable subjects for public discussion. Meanwhile, prominent popular figures were waging successful anti-gay rights campaigns around the country. Most notable among them was singer and former Miss Oklahoma Anita Bryant's 1977 campaign in Dade County, Florida, which ended in the repeal of a local ordinance prohibiting discrimination on the basis of sexuality. Later that same year, Dade County also passed a law revoking adoption rights for gay couples.

Milk began delivering a rough version of his now famous speech shortly thereafter, during the early stages of his 1977 campaign for the board of supervisors. These early versions were marked by an emphasis on legal equality for gay individuals, an element prompted by the Dade County decisions and others like them. Milk insisted that the only way to bring about legal equality was for openly gay individuals to have a say in the enactment and enforcement of the law—namely, via the election of openly gay officials. It was in part the strength and conviction of this message that enabled him to become the first openly gay man in the nation to be elected to public office.

The speech follows a long American tradition of oratorical responses to legal inequality. Patrick Henry's address to the Virginia House of Burgesses in 1775, which calls for immediate action against the unjust policies enacted in the colonies by the British Empire, marks perhaps the first notable instance. From it Milk inherited the sense of urgency that imbues much of what became known as the "Hope Speech." Informing that urgency also are King's speeches insisting that the "right moment" not be waited for, but rather that equality be demanded immediately and unconditionally.

By the beginning of his campaign in 1977, Milk felt the time for timidity and patience had passed for the gay community. What separated his early speeches from King's, though, was a sense of hope. It was a close friend and colleague who urged Milk to include not only a message about hope but to use the word itself repeatedly. Versions of the speech that incorporated these suggestions became increasingly popular, and it was the longest of these, the version delivered on June 25, 1978, at the San Francisco Gay Freedom Day parade (now known as the Gay Pride parade), that made famous his closing refrain: "You have to give them hope ... and you and you and you, have to give the people hope." The refrain became a rallying cry for progressive politicians campaigning for all manner of individual rights. It was later echoed in the speeches, slogans, and posters for the successful 2008 presidential campaign of Barack Obama, who occasionally cited Milk in his speeches and posthumously awarded him the Presidential Medal of Freedom in 2009.

## THEMES AND STYLE

The central theme of the "Hope Speech" is the insistence on equal rights and protection under the law for the gay community and the need for that equality to be ensured by the election of openly gay public officials. "The black community made up its mind to that a long time ago," he argues, "that the myths against blacks can only be dispelled by electing black leaders" so the community can be judged by them and not by its criminal members. He argues that the same needs to be true of the gay community and that "the first gay people we elect must be strong ... they must be—for the good of all of us—independent, unbought." Only then, Milk argues, will real change be possible.

The speech draws most of its rhetorical power from Milk's ability to align the struggles of the gay community with those of other minority communities. He maintains that the loss of hope is equally devastating to all individuals, "be they gay, be they seniors, be they blacks looking for an almost-impossible job, be they Latins trying to explain their problems and aspirations in a tongue that's foreign to them." Building on this sense of shared hopes, Milk then posits that "if you help elect to the central committee and other offices, more gay people, that gives a green light to all who feel disenfranchised," because, in a predominantly anti-gay political climate, "if a gay person makes it, the doors are open to everyone."

The emotional tenor of the speech is wide-ranging. Milk opens with a political joke, announcing, "My name is Harvey Milk—and I want to recruit you!" Milk is playing here on statements made by California conservatives to the effect that the gay community was "recruiting" vulnerable youths to their ranks. He then moves into more pragmatic passages, addressing the perceived "move to the right" in the American political climate and discussing the importance of "open[ing] the walls of dialogue." It is only toward the end of the speech that Milk begins making impassioned pleas, invoking the plight of young gay people coming out in "the Altoona, Pennsylvanias and the Richmond, Minnesotas" and their need for signs of hope.

## CRITICAL DISCUSSION

None of Milk's speeches attracted much media attention outside San Francisco until after his assassination. Even then, papers such as the *Washington Post* frequently focused more on Mayor Moscone's life and death than Milk's. One significant exception was Larry

## MOBILIZING COMMUNITIES

Though Milk's election in 1977 was perhaps the most noteworthy, he was not the only supervisor sworn in that year who represented a new demographic. Also elected in 1977 were Carol Ruth Silver, Gordon Lau, and Ella Hill Hutch, San Francisco's first single mother, Chinese American, and African American female, respectively, to be elected to public office. Milk, with the help of Lau and Hutch, formed close working relationships between the gay community and both the Chinese American and African American communities and was able to mobilize large numbers of voters in his campaigns for and against legislative initiatives.

The biggest of Milk's legislative contributions was the defeat of Proposition 6 (known as the Briggs Initiative), which would have made firing teachers on the basis of sexuality not only acceptable but mandatory. The initiative worried Milk particularly because of its timing, as State Senator John Briggs had introduced it following a 1977 trip to Miami, where the national spotlight was on the successful repeal of a law providing protection against discrimination on the basis of sexuality. Milk toured California, debating Briggs at every stop and promising that he could mobilize the gay community—a promise that carried weight in San Francisco, where 25 percent of the voting public was gay—as well as other minority communities to vote down the initiative.

Kramer, who wrote in the *New York Times,* "I am not a crying man, but I had tears in my eyes, as well as shivers of pride" while attending the marches and candlelight vigils in which San Franciscans mourned their loss. Reflecting on the state of gay rights activism in his home state of New York, Kramer lamented the fact that while San Francisco "homosexuals mobilized an entire state to defeat" anti-gay legislation, "New York City's one million homosexuals cannot mobilize a city." "Harvey Milk," Kramer said in closing, "we have no one like you here."

Though he was virtually unheard of outside the Bay Area prior to his death, Milk's efforts forged the mold for a new direction in civil rights activism. By becoming the first openly gay elected official, and by attending to all public concerns in that capacity, not just those of the gay community, Milk provided a much-needed model for minority public officials. Journalist Randy Shilts hinted that, in some ways, the movement and its leaders struggled for years to live up to Milk's standard, remarking in his best-selling biography *The Mayor of Castro Street* (1982) that what remained in Milk's wake were "the dream and its lengthening shadow."

Contemporary scholarship tends to place Milk, and his "Hope Speech," in the contexts of rhetoric and identity studies. John Loughery, in his book *The Other Side of Silence* (1998), applauds Milk for his

Harvey Milk campaigning in 1976. Later elected to the San Francisco Board of Supervisors, Milk was one of the first openly gay politicians in the United States. His ardent support of gay rights is reflected in a 1978 speech about hope. © ROBERT CLAY/ALAMY.

contributions to awareness not just of gay rights but of civil rights in general. Loughery finds special merit in the composure with which Milk handled continued discrimination, never allowing his words to "[reach] the level of irrational or destructive anger" for which other activists had been dismissed as reactionaries. Charles Morris addresses both topics in his book *Queering Public Address* (2007), examining the complexity of Milk's rhetoric—by which, Morris offers, "he constructed a queer world in which the possibilities of freedom, identification, and inclusion" were foregrounded, providing a new model and "meaning for community."

## BIBLIOGRAPHY

### Sources

Kramer, Larry. "Gay 'Power' here." *New York Times* 13 Dec. 1978: A27. *ProQuest Historical Newspapers: The New York Times (1851–2008)*. Web. 13 Aug. 2012.

Loughery, John. *The Other Side of Silence: Men's Lives and Gay Identities: A Twentieth Century History.* New York: Holt, 1998. Print.

Milk, Harvey. "The Hope Speech" (1978). *Great Speeches on Gay Rights*. Ed. James Daley. Mineola: Dover, 2010. 65–70. Print.

Morris, Charles E. *Queering Public Address: Sexualities in American Historical Discourse.* Columbia: U of South Carolina P, 2007. Print.

Shilts, Randy. *The Mayor of Castro Street: The Life & Times of Harvey Milk.* New York: St. Martin's, 2008. Print.

### Further Reading

Bull, Chris. *Come Out Fighting: A Century of Essential Writing on Gay and Lesbian Liberation.* New York: Thunder's Mouth/Nation Books, 2001. Print.

Crewdson, John M. "Harvey Milk, Led Coast Homosexual-Rights Fight." *New York Times* 28 Nov. 1978: B12. *ProQuest Historical Newspapers: The New York Times (1851–2008)*. Web. 13 Aug. 2012.

Foss, Karen A. "Harvey Milk: 'you have to give them hope.'" *Journal of the West* 27.2 (1988): 75+. Print.

Robinson, Paul. "Gays in The Streets." *New Republic* 180.23 (1979): 9–10. *Academic Search Complete*. Web. 13 Aug. 2012.

Stewart-Winter, Timothy. "The Castro: Origins of the Age of Milk." *Gay & Lesbian Review Worldwide* 16.1 (2009): 12+. *Academic OneFile*. Web. 13 Aug. 2012.

Weigle, Kristin. "Harvey Milk Day: Chapter 626 Gives a Controversial Figure's Birthday Special Significance for California Public Schools." *McGeorge Law Review* 41.3 (2010): 558–567. *Academic Search Complete*. Web. 13 Aug. 2012.

### Media Adaptation

*Milk.* Dir. Gus Van Sant. Perf. Sean Penn, Josh Brolin, and Emile Hirsch. Focus Features, 2008. Film.

*Clint Garner*

# "IN FLANDERS FIELDS"

*John McCrae*

## OVERVIEW

Written on the battlefield, John McCrae's lyric poem "In Flanders Fields" (1915) is both a mournful elegy for fallen soldiers and a fervent call to arms. Rhythmic and rich in evocative imagery, the poem is told from the perspective of a soldier killed in combat in World War I. McCrae, a Canadian soldier and physician, captures the charged and conflicting emotions felt by troops and citizens alike: woe and despair mingling with hope and grim perseverance. "In Flanders Fields" encourages readers to remember and memorialize war victims by supporting the military effort. Although not necessarily intended as propaganda, the poem was widely used by the Canadian, British, and American governments to enlist soldiers, sell war bonds, and bolster national morale during World War I.

"In Flanders Fields" was published anonymously in the widely read journal *Punch* and quickly became popular internationally. Purportedly written in response to a friend's death in the Second Battle of Ypres, the poem is thought to be the most commonly read war poem of the era, when it was reprinted in Allied newspapers, used in war posters, and even set to music. The poem is still evoked and quoted on Remembrance Day in Canada and similar memorial days in the United Kingdom and the United States. The poppy, mentioned in the poem as "blow[ing]" over the graves of fallen soldiers, remains a widespread symbol of commemoration for the military dead. Although many contemporary scholars view it as both anachronistic and propagandist, "In Flanders Fields" has had a major influence on war poetry and military culture, particularly in Canada—where part of its prose appears on the ten-dollar bill—and also in the United Kingdom and United States.

## HISTORICAL AND LITERARY CONTEXT

Like most of the countries that entered the fighting in World War I, Canada felt confident that the conflict would be quickly and easily won. Yet a stalemate on the Western Front dashed any hopes for a speedy resolution. New weapons, including poison gas and the long-range rifle, made warfare increasingly grim and deadly. A soldier's life in the trenches was terrifying and physically uncomfortable, marked by stretches of intense action that were interspersed with periods of boredom. "No man's land"—a battered, lifeless zone riddled with mortar shells and barbed wire—separated each side's complex system of trenches, which snaked from northern Belgium into France.

After its publication on December 6, 1915, "In Flanders Fields" was widely circulated as the war, which many thought would be finished by Christmas in 1914, dragged on. Allied governments ramped up the production of propaganda—from posters to pamphlets to popular songs—encouraging men to enlist and everyone else to support the troops and war effort. Although not explicitly propagandist, McCrae's poem did indeed reinforce the pro-war message. In fact, an excerpt from it appeared on a poster that was used to sell Canadian war bonds (securities for funding military action). The poster depicts a soldier solemnly standing over a gravesite blooming with bright red poppies. Above the soldier's head, McCrae's words hover: "If ye break faith—we shall not sleep."

World War I inspired a rich and diverse canon of poetry, from Rupert Brooke's affirmative vision of war in "The Soldier" to Siegfried Sassoon's and Wilfred Owen's darker, more complicated portrayals. As with "In Flanders Fields," "The Soldier" was used to encourage military recruitment. Both "In Flanders Fields" and "The Soldier" exhort readers to serve their country by joining the bravehearted war effort. In addition, both poems skim over the appalling aspects of warfare, instead focusing on abstract ideals such as honor, duty, and love of country. While "In Flanders Fields" acknowledges the death and destruction brought about by war, it minimizes these horrors.

"In Flanders Fields" is Canada's best-known poem from World War I. Throughout the conflict, pro-war poetry, song, and artwork served as daily reminders to citizens to continue helping in the war effort, and "In Flanders Fields" inspired imitation poems that were sent to newspapers across Canada and England. The poem was also translated into many languages. McCrae, reportedly gratified by the poem's widespread popularity, quipped: "It needs only Chinese now." After many promotions within the military, McCrae died of cerebral meningitis in 1918 in France. *In Flanders Fields: and Other Poems* was published soon thereafter, solidifying the poem's ongoing influence as a tribute to those who have died in war.

❖ *Key Facts*

**Time Period:**
Early 20th Century

**Genre:**
Poetry

**Events:**
World War I

**Nationality:**
Canadian

# MCCRAE'S POPPIES

Combat in World War I wreaked havoc on the French and Belgian countryside. Poppies, which thrive in disturbed soils, soon began to bloom in battlefields and impromptu graveyards. Poppies, hardy flowers, lie dormant for years until something comes along—a farmer's tractor, a war—and agitates the soil. McCrae was deeply touched and inspired by the profusion of vivid flowers growing near his station in Ypres, Belgium. According to legend, "In Flanders Fields" was composed in a few minutes, between McCrae's taxing duties as a frontline physician.

Because of the poem's worldwide popularity, the poppy and war trauma became connected. Yet before McCrae ever saw Flanders' poppies, the flowers were already associated with sleep and oblivion. The poem's final lines—"We shall not sleep, though poppies grow"— infer that even the sleep-inducing power of poppies will not be able to placate the dead if the living do not take up the fight. Inspired by McCrae's poem, the Young Men's Christian Association (YMCA) began to sell red poppies in 1918 to raise funds for those in need, especially veterans. Poppies remain vivid reminders of fallen soldiers, particularly on memorial days (sometimes called "Poppy Days") when mourners often wear the red flower tucked in their lapels.

## THEMES AND STYLE

Purposefully heartrending, "In Flanders Fields" makes an appeal to its readers to honor fallen soldiers by redoubling their support of the war. At first glance, "In Flanders Fields" can be mistaken solely as a mournful memorialization of men killed in battle. In actuality, the poem goes much further, suggesting that if readers "break faith with us who die" or fail to carry on the fight, the dead will never be able to fully rest or, by inference, forgive the living. Veiled behind calm descriptions of a graveyard scene is a powerfully aggressive and unsettling message that is meant to motivate civilian men and women to take up the fight themselves: "To you from failing hands we throw / The torch; be yours to hold it high." The implication is clear: if citizens do not catch "the torch," the Allied world will tumble into darkness.

Addressing the reader directly, McCrae further underscores the gravity of the poem's message through his choices of setting, speaker, and form. "In Flanders Fields" is told from the point of view of a recently killed soldier lying in his grave watching the "poppies blow" and "larks, still bravely singing, fly[ing]" above him. This perspective increases the forcefulness of the poem's ultimate goal to bolster and sustain support for the war in any way possible. "In Flanders Field" is a rondeau, a French form created in the thirteenth century and generally chosen for melancholy subjects. Fifteen lines long, a rondeau requires a strict meter and rhyme, as well as a specific phrase to be repeated three times, in this case the poem's title, "In Flanders Fields."

The repetition of this location creates a claustrophobic sensation of inescapability, as if all roads lead back to the World War I battlegrounds.

Stark, poignant imagery and candid language create a rousing poem targeting an audience just beginning to feel disillusioned with war. McCrae explores the speedy interval between bodily, passionate life and irrevocable death: "We are the Dead. Short days ago / We lived, felt dawn, saw sunset glow." Such a moving and intense topic does much to spark emotional reactions in the reader. The poem is filled with straightforward and affecting avowals and declarations—such as, "[We] loved and were loved" and "Take up our quarrel with the foe"—creating for the reader a sense of intimacy with the speaker. William Wordsworth described poetry as the "spontaneous overflow of powerful feelings." This axiom rings true in "In Flanders Fields," a poem that both expresses and elicits "powerful feelings," all for the purpose of furthering military support.

## CRITICAL DISCUSSION

Following World War I, "In Flanders Fields" received favorable responses in literary journals and reviews. Some critics, however, contended that poetry (including McCrae's popular rondeau) that is produced in the turmoil of war loses its timeliness and emotional efficacy in the calm days of armistice. In particular, war prose written between 1914 and 1915, termed the "days of idealism" by poet Robert Graves, began to appear increasingly anachronistic, because of its almost pitiful optimism. Nevertheless, Harriet Monroe noted in a 1919 issue of *Poetry* that while war poetry rarely "lift[s] the emotion of the moment into song," "In Flanders Fields" moves beyond the confines of ordinary war writing and is enduring art.

"In Flanders Fields" is, by far, McCrae's most popular poem, still memorized by school children and recited on memorial days. Among the lasting influences of the poem is the widespread use of the poppy as a symbol of war remembrance, particularly for World War I. The power of "In Flanders Fields" springs from its ability to discuss war, death, and sacrifice in a manner that ordinary citizens can empathize with and understand. Canadian poet Bruce Meyer wrote that "In Flanders Fields" is "couched in poetic language that made the experience of war accessible to the general reader," who shared with others the knowledge of death and sacrifice. However, this very accessibility, coupled with the poem's propagandist turn, discouraged many later critics from treating the poem as anything more than a war artifact.

"In Flanders Fields" receives little scholarly attention today, although it is part and parcel of Canadian culture. Canadian poet Nancy Holmes wrote in 2012 that the work is "lavishly honored yet studiously ignored." What attention the poem does receive is sporadic and diverse, ranging from praise of its expressive intensity to derision of its rather obvious militaristic

A painting (c. 1919) of a World War I soldier's grave in a field of poppies.
© MARY EVANS PICTURE LIBRARY/ALAMY.

leanings. Paul Fussell, author of *The Great War and Modern Memory,* argues that its "recruiting-poster rhetoric" ruins an otherwise satisfactory, if occasionally hackneyed, poem. Fussell contends that McCrae's poem amounts to a "propaganda argument" against "negotiated peace," going so far as to call it "vicious." On the other hand, Holmes argues that "In Flanders Fields" has received harsher criticism than is warranted and calls the poem "a rather assured little word machine." Holmes praises the poem's formal inventiveness and metrical intricacy, as well as its uncanny imagery and effective use of the supernatural. Regardless of the stance they take, most critics agree that "In Flanders Fields" is, in the words of Holmes, a moving "war monument" of a specific era.

## BIBLIOGRAPHY

### Sources

Fussell, Paul. "Arcadian Recourses." *The Great War and Modern Memory.* New York: Oxford University Press, 1975. 231–69. Detroit: Gale Research, 1984. *Literature Resource Center.* Web. 11 June 2012.

Hemmings, Robert. "Of Trauma and Flora: Memory and Commemoration in Four Poems of the World Wars." *University of Toronto Quarterly* 77.2 (2008): 738–56. *Project MUSE.* Web. 11 Jun. 2012

Holmes, Nancy. "'In Flanders Fields'—Canada's Official Poem: Breaking Faith." *Studies in Canadian Literature / Études en Littérature Canadienne, North America,* 30 Jan. 2005. Web. 11 June 2012.

Meyer, Bruce. "Critical Essay on 'In Flanders Fields.'" *Poetry for Students.* Vol. 5. Detroit: Gale Group, 1999. *Literature Resource Center.* Web. 11 June 2012.

Monroe, Harriet. "Other Poets of the War." *Poetry.* Vol. 14, No. 4 (July 1919). 220–25. Web. 11 June 2012.

### Further Reading

Cassar, George H. *Hell in Flanders Fields: Canadians at the Second Battle of Ypres.* Toronto: Dundurn Press, 2010. Print.

Fussell, Paul. *The Great War and Modern Memory.* New York: Oxford University Press, 1975. Print.

Harmon, H. E. "Two Famous Poems of the World War." *South Atlantic Quarterly* 19.1 (Jan. 1920): 9–17. Detroit: Gale Research, 1984. *Literature Resource Center.* Web. 11 June 2012.

*In Flanders Fields: And Other Poems of the First World War.* Ed. Brian Busby. London: Arcturus, 2005. Print.

Kelly, David. "Critical Essay on 'In Flanders Fields.'" *Poetry for Students.* Vol. 5. Detroit: Gale Group, 1999. *Literature Resource Center.* Web. 11 June 2012.

McCrae, John. *In Flanders Fields and Other Poems, by Lieut.-Col. John McCrae, M.D., with an Essay in Character, by Sir Andrew Macphail.* New York: G. P. Putnam, 1919. Print.

Neilson, S. "John McCrae on Death." *Canadian Medical Association. Journal* 181.10 (2009): 717–19. Web. 11 June 2012.

### Media Adaptation

McCrae, John. *John McCrae's War: In Flanders Field.* Dir. Robert Duncan. Produced by Jonathan Desbarats, Barbara Shearer, and Selwyn Jacob. [Montreal, Quebec]: National Film Board of Canada, © 1998. VHS.

*Claire Skinner*

# "IRON CURTAIN" SPEECH

*Winston Churchill*

✣ *Key Facts*

**Time Period:**
Mid-20th Century

**Genre:**
Speech

**Events:**
Aftermath of World
War II; beginning of
Cold War

**Nationality:**
English

## OVERVIEW

On March 5, 1946, the former British prime minister Winston Churchill delivered an address, now referred to as the "Iron Curtain" speech, in which he discussed post-World War II international relations and issued a warning about the intentions of the Soviet Union regarding Europe, argued against an approach of appeasement, and urged stronger ties between the United Kingdom and the United States. Churchill, whose title for the speech was Sinews of Peace, had been asked by U.S. president Harry S. Truman to speak at Westminster College, a small school in Fulton, Missouri—Truman's home state. The oratorical skills of Churchill were already legendary, and on the occasion of his first major postwar speech the world listened attentively. His call for heightened concern about the Soviet Union quickly crystallized competing political positions and raised public awareness of the topic.

Churchill's speech was delivered less than one year after World War II had ended in Europe. The Soviet Union had delayed withdrawing its troops from certain occupied territories in Eastern Europe and Iran, raising concerns that the Soviets did not intend to honor agreements made at the end of the war. In addition, Great Britain was facing severe financial stress, the close wartime alliance between Britain and the United States had become increasingly distant, and many war-weary people were hoping that the newly formed United Nations would bring about a period of peace. Churchill, whose Conservative Party had lost in the general election to the Labour Party in Britain shortly after the war's end, wanted to maintain his presence on the world stage by making a bold statement at Fulton—and he succeeded not only in attracting attention but also in affecting the course of history. Although the United States government initially distanced itself from Churchill's remarks and the Soviet Union immediately attacked the speech, it proved to be a defining element in the rapidly emerging Cold War.

## HISTORICAL AND LITERARY CONTEXT

During the massive conflict in Europe that began in 1939 and officially ended in May of 1945, Britain sustained tremendous losses in combat in Europe and suffered through frequent bombing attacks at home. Prime Minister Churchill not only rallied the British with memorable speeches but also promoted a strategic relationship with the United States, which entered the war in 1942. The communist-controlled Soviet Union signed a nonaggression pact with Germany in 1939 but joined the Allies after becoming a target of German aggression in 1941. Because the contributions of the Soviet Union were crucial to the war effort, Churchill and U.S. president Franklin Roosevelt tried to maintain cooperation with Soviet premier Joseph Stalin, despite concerns that the Soviet Union would try to secure territorial gains in Eastern Europe after the war.

By the time Churchill spoke in Fulton, questions about Soviet intentions had increased, based on such indicators as the Soviet Union's failure to allow free elections in Poland, their resistance to withdrawal from Iran, and their lack of cooperation with the other Allies in the postwar management of Germany. Early in 1946 George Kennan, deputy chief of the U.S. mission in Moscow, further raised apprehensions with a very long telegram to Secretary of State James Byrnes, detailing the danger he saw in Soviet attitudes toward the West. At the same time, Great Britain was struggling to recover from the extensive damage caused by German bombing and from the tremendous financial cost of the war. The United States, on the other hand, was returning to prosperity, but an increasingly isolationist and cost-conscious Congress was reluctant to approve the massive loan needed by Britain. Against the background of this complex situation, Churchill undertook to sound a warning about the Soviet Union, and at the same time, to issue a call for reinvigoration of the Anglo-American alliance.

The Fulton speech was a continuation of concerns expressed throughout Churchill's long, dynamic career, which included serving in the British army, as a member of Parliament since 1900, and in various government cabinet posts. In eloquent, impassioned speeches before the House of Commons in 1938, he had protested Prime Minister Neville Chamberlain's policy of appeasing the Germans, and of course his warnings proved to be prophetic. Churchill had also foreseen the importance of educating Americans about the magnitude of the looming disaster in Europe. In a radio address to the United States less than a year before the war began, Churchill called for a "swift gathering of forces" and appealed to the "English-speaking peoples" for a "resolute and sober acceptance of their duty."

As Churchill's first major postwar speech, the Fulton address attracted worldwide attention, sparking both immediate criticism and ongoing debate. Churchill's use of the phrase "iron curtain"—initially criticized as harsh and inflammatory—established a new shorthand for discussing postwar Europe. This vigorous reaction fit Churchill's own agenda perfectly, and the speech served as something of a platform for his revitalized public role. A few months later he expanded on his core themes in another seminal address at the University of Zurich, this time focusing on the need for a unified Europe. He continued in his role as an outspoken citizen of the world until his Conservative Party regained power in the general election of 1951, when he returned to the prime minister's office. The aging Churchill resigned in 1955, but his "Sinews of Peace" speech lived on in the policies of Conservative prime minister Margaret Thatcher, who served from 1979 to 1990 and collaborated with U.S. president Ronald Reagan to hasten the end of Soviet dominance in Eastern Europe.

**THEMES AND STYLE**

Although the Fulton speech is remembered mainly for calling attention to the Soviet threat, John W. Young explains in *Winston Churchill's Last Campaign* (1996) that it was actually a more complex and nuanced presentation, asserting "the need for Anglo-American partnership, the necessity for Western rearmament, and the eventual hope of an East-West settlement." In fact, according to John P. Rossi's article "Winston Churchill's Iron Curtain Speech" (1986), the "main thrust" of the speech was not the Iron Curtain section but rather the "call for a revival of the Anglo-American cooperation that had prevailed during the war." Rossi also points out the often overlooked importance of Churchill's "argument that the atomic monopoly of the West not be shared either with the UN or with the Soviet Union." This contention, along with other elements of the speech, can be seen as provocative rather than persuasive, intended mainly to increase public awareness of the issues.

In constructing the speech, according to Lynn Boyd Hinds and Theodore Otto Windt Jr. in *The Cold War as Rhetoric* (1991), Churchill drew on "the dominant rhetoric of World War II ... to give a new sense of understanding and mission in the postwar world." He enhanced his own authority by subtly reminding the audience of his prophetic warnings about Nazi Germany, and he engaged their sympathy by evoking those "sacred values of the American people" that had been protected by Allied cooperation during the war. At the same time, Churchill picked up the "subordinate rhetoric of anticommunism" that had remained latent during the war, when messaging had necessarily

## ROOSEVELT ADDRESSES THE NATION

Like his wartime ally Winston Churchill in England, U.S. President Franklin Delano Roosevelt was a skilled communicator, but the two men had very different styles. While Churchill is most remembered for his inspiring wartime oratory, Roosevelt is best known for a series of thirty-one radio addresses delivered between 1933 and 1944. These "Fireside Chats" were designed in part to create a sense of national unity, encouraging Americans across the country to gather around their radios and listen together as the president discussed crucial current events. The talks were also intended to create public support for Roosevelt's policies.

Roosevelt presented the first address at the height of a financial crisis that had closed the nation's banks. The president calmly reassured his listeners, explaining not only the problem at hand but the approach that would lead to recovery. This speech, which used plain language and simple concepts to ensure that average Americans could understand the president's message, set a precedent for those to follow. Roosevelt made complicated topics accessible by means of anecdotes, examples, and real-life stories.

The Fireside Chats were broadcast on the national radio networks, often on Sunday evenings. Facing the difficulties of the Great Depression and then World War II, many Americans took comfort in hearing FDR's steady voice calling them "friends" and inviting them to write to him or to their representatives. Millions did write, influencing legislation and supporting the president's agenda.

As a legacy of the Fireside Chats, most U.S. presidents after Roosevelt delivered regular radio addresses. The importance of these communications has steadily declined, however, as cultural conditions have changed.

stressed the importance of the Soviet Union's contribution to the war effort. In his Fulton speech Churchill skillfully cast a new situation in terms of an old one, linking Stalin's designs on Eastern Europe with the horrors that Hitler had unleashed.

Notwithstanding Churchill's sophisticated use of rhetorical strategy, the Fulton speech has been remembered primarily for a single image: that of the Iron Curtain. The phrase was not original to Churchill, who gleaned it from sources that dated all the way back to 1914, when the queen of Belgium used it in describing how the German invasion had divided her country. Churchill himself had used the phrase on several occasions prior to Fulton—and in fact, according to David Reynolds's book *From World War to Cold War* (2006), he played with variations such as "iron veil" or "iron screen" in preparing for the speech. The image of iron, of course, denoted an impenetrable material, hard and opaque. "Curtain" proved the most powerful choice of metaphors, as Hinds and Windt suggest, in part because it "also connoted mystery,"

Winston Churchill, who delivered the "Iron Curtain" speech on March 5, 1946, AT WESTMINSTER COLLEGE IN FULTON, MISSOURI. © BETTMANN/CORBIS.

as in a "theatrical convention" that divides the audience from events taking place on stage. Throughout the speech, they suggest, Churchill's use of language "supplied basic elements for a vocabulary that would be picked up and widely spread by opinion leaders, so that these linguistic elements eventually became the way to perceive and to talk about disputes between the Soviet Union and the West."

## CRITICAL DISCUSSION

Churchill's Fulton speech was immediately attacked, not only in the Soviet newspapers *Pravda* and *Izvestia* but also by American liberals (including Eleanor Roosevelt) who believed that Churchill was proposing a special alliance between Britain and America that would cripple the newly formed United Nations. In Britain Churchill's commentary was aggressively criticized by members of the Labour Party, and in the United States President Truman and his chief of staff, Admiral William Leahy, distanced themselves from the speech—despite the fact that, as was later revealed, both had approved the text in advance. Rossi explains that "even many individuals who accepted Churchill's pessimistic diagnosis of the international scene were disconcerted by the implications of his charges" and that "for days the American press was filled with hostile comments about Churchill's views." Churchill, however, was far from dismayed. According to Rossi, "he thought that the American public, and the American political leadership and press in particular, were naive in their perception of Soviet intentions in the world." Therefore, he had concluded, they must be shocked into a more realistic view.

Churchill's success in this respect was even greater than he might have hoped—his "Iron Curtain" speech became a foundation document for the ensuing political conflict that became known as the Cold War. Churchill had brought together several concepts that were known to many analysts and politicians but that had not previously been connected and delivered

with such skill to such a broad audience. Ultimately, however, the Americans—who were Churchill's true target in the speech—took the anti-Soviet message seriously but rejected the claim that a renewed alliance of English-speaking peoples was necessary for the defense of Western civilization's most cherished values. The kind of aligned response Churchill envisioned might arguably have prevented or at least shortened the Cold War. In retrospect, however, such an alliance may have been nearly impossible, given the chaotic postwar conditions and the two countries' differences in political, military, and social interests.

During the later twentieth century, as correspondence and other materials became available, scholars continued to refine and expand their understanding of Churchill's Fulton strategy. In 1996 many of them gathered at Westminster College to discuss the speech and its ramifications—and to hear an address by Margaret Thatcher, who spoke prophetically of new threats that might be set in motion by the Soviet Union's relatively recent collapse. Proceedings of the event are gathered in James W. Muller's 1999 volume *Churchill's "Iron Curtain" Speech Fifty Years Later*. Now recognized as a milestone in modern history and a classic example of persuasive rhetoric, Churchill's Fulton speech is regarded by contemporary scholars as one element in a larger study of Cold War origins and early anti-Soviet propaganda.

## BIBLIOGRAPHY

### Sources

Hinds, Lynn Boyd, and Theodore Otto Windt Jr. *The Cold War as Rhetoric: The Beginnings, 1945–1950*. New York: Praeger, 1991. Print.

Muller, James W., ed. *Churchill's "Iron Curtain" Speech Fifty Years Later*. Columbia: U of Missouri P, 1999. Print.

Reynolds, David. *From World War to Cold War: Churchill, Roosevelt, and the International History of the 1940s*. New York: Oxford UP, 2006. Print.

Rossi, John P. "Winston Churchill's Iron Curtain Speech: Forty Years After." *Modern Age* 30.2 (1986): 113–19. Print.

Young, John W. *Winston Churchill's Last Campaign: Britain and the Cold War, 1951–1955*. Oxford: Clarendon, 1996. Print.

### Further Reading

Boyle, Peter G., et al. *The Origins of the Cold War, 1945–1950*. London: InterUniversity Film, 1999. Print.

Brewer, Susan A. *To Win the Peace: British Propaganda in the United States during World War II*. Ithaca: Cornell UP, 1997. Print.

Churchill, Winston S. *Never Give In! The Best of Winston Churchill's Speeches*. New York: Hyperion, 2003. Print.

Churchill, Winston, and Martin Gilbert. *Churchill: The Power of Words: His Remarkable Life Recounted through His Writings and Speeches*. Boston: Da Capo, 2012. Print.

Harbutt, Fraser J. *The Iron Curtain: Churchill, America, and the Origins of the Cold War.* New York: Oxford UP, 1986. Print.

Humes, James C. *Eisenhower and Churchill: The Partnership That Saved the World.* New York: Three Rivers, 2004. Print.

Schwartz, Lowell. *Political Warfare against the Kremlin: US and British Propaganda Policy at the Beginning of the Cold War.* Basingstoke: Palgrave, 2009. Print.

Wevill, Richard. *Britain and America after World War II: Bilateral Relations and the Beginnings of the Cold War.* London: Tauris, 2012. Print.

White, Philip. *Our Supreme Task: How Winston Churchill's Iron Curtain Speech Defined the Cold War Alliance.* New York: PublicAffairs, 2012. Print.

*Cynthia Giles*

# "LIBERTY OR DEATH"

*Jean-Jacques Dessalines, Louis Félix Boisrond-Tonnerre*

✛ **Key Facts**

**Time Period:**
Early 19th Century

**Genre:**
Speech

**Events:**
French colonization of
Haiti; Haitian Revolution

**Nationality:**
Haitian

## OVERVIEW

Issued January 1, 1804, "Liberty or Death," Jean-Jacques Dessalines and Louis Félix Boisrond-Tonnerre's three-part declaration of independence, seeks to unite the people of the former French colony of Saint-Domingue under the independent nation of "Hayti." With bold and colorful rhetoric, the proclamation urges Haitians to remember their suffering under the French, their struggles against slavery, and their sacrifices for liberty. The text lambasts the French "barbarians" and the various factions who, vying for power, created even more victims and conflict among the recently designated "indigenous" or "native" of Haiti. By focusing on the past atrocities perpetrated by French masters and soldiers, the proclamation endeavors to create a common bond among divided and diverse peoples in an attempt to form a single Haitian body politic.

At the heart of the proclamation are the dual symbols of the French "barbarians" and the "native" Haitians. For more than a decade during the Haitian Revolution, persons of African descent struggled against French colonialism, foreign powers, and internal divisions; however, there was no single identity that incorporated all of these diverse peoples. Because of the island's heterogeneous population of Africans and mixed-race peoples, emerging leaders and factions throughout the Haitian Revolution sought political stability, often through literary metaphors and cultural symbols. The proclamation's symbols illustrate similar efforts by Dessalines and his officers to access the history of the region and to locate common social causes and symbols. Despite the drafting of Haiti's 1804 declaration of independence and 1805 constitution, however, the country would continue to face invasions, wars, violence, and divisions throughout the nineteenth century. Thus, the proclamation represents the ongoing challenges of division and nation building that have plagued the newly independent Haitian people in their long pursuit of self-determination.

## HISTORICAL AND LITERARY CONTEXT

After a massive, well-coordinated slave revolt on August 22, 1791, sparked the Haitian Revolution, the peoples of French Saint-Domingue faced uncertainty over their futures. Slaves demanded abolition while free blacks and mulattoes sought to obtain citizenship (whites had long denied freedpersons of African descent equal rights and privileges). Nevertheless, former masters and many whites held onto their monopoly over the region's resources and power. Additionally, French commissioners, the British army, and the Spanish government at Santo Domingo on Saint-Domingue's eastern border invaded or offered alliances to some of the revolution's factions, further exacerbating the region's instability. Although slavery was officially, and unofficially, abolished multiple times beginning in 1793, some of these factions and foreign invaders had sought to return the newly freed to slavery or similar forms of forced labor. For example, when the island's forces under liberator Toussaint Louverture made peace with the French in 1802, the French betrayed Louverture and attempted to reimpose slavery.

At the end of 1803, the revolution's future remained contested. French commanders had initiated a horrific counterinsurgency campaign with mass murders, the drowning of prisoners of war, and discussions of killing all black men on the island. In November Dessalines defeated the last French troops that had been deployed by Napoleon to retake the region, but the revolution's figurehead, Louverture, had passed away in a French prison. Dessalines and his officers thus hoped to bring together the island's divided peoples and factions in a declaration of independence. On the eve of the new year, Dessalines rejected the first proposed document. Officer Louis Félix Boisrond-Tonnerre agreed to create a new draft, allegedly declaring, "In order to draw up our act of independence, we need the skin of a white to serve as a parchment, his skull as an inkwell, his blood for ink, and a bayonet for a pen." These authors decided to design a document that would inspire former slaves and free blacks and mulattoes to remember their abuse under the French colonial system.

The authors of founding documents and declarations in the Atlantic world faced similar challenges throughout the late eighteenth and early nineteenth centuries as they debated their colonial history and cultural origins. Leaders in the United States and Latin America endeavored to move beyond colonialism, to unite their diverse peoples, and to forge nations. The architects of the 1776 U.S. Declaration of Independence, the model for the first draft of Haiti's declaration of independence, acknowledged a British heritage, though it refused to address slaves and indigenous peoples. In contrast, the American Indian noble Túpac Amaru II's rebellion in 1780 and 1781 against Spanish colonialism in the Andes incorporated symbols that fused the region's indigenous heritage with Spanish Catholicism.

After the Haitian Revolution, other movements in the Atlantic world followed the cultural pattern put forward in "Liberty or Death." Propagandistic literature was dominated by reminders of peoples' common exploitation under racial and colonial systems. From Mexico to Colombia to Peru, from Simón Bolívar to Cuban patriots in the late 1800s such as Antonio Maceo, Latin American declarations incorporated support for indigenous, African, and mixed-race nationalisms and derisions against colonial exploitation. One of the most important examples was Father Miguel Hidalgo's 1810 "Grito de Dolores" in colonial Mexico, which reminds indigenous and mixed-race peoples of their suffering under the Spanish empire. The revolutionary nature and cultural icons of all such declarations became ingrained in national histories, although the legacy of the racial violence of the Haitian Revolution is still disputed.

**THEMES AND STYLE**

Drawing on the violence and suffering of the Haitian Revolution, Dessalines and Boisrond-Tonnerre's "Liberty or Death" presents unity, independence, and a single Haitian body or family as the antitheses to slavery, the French, and death. To galvanize a people divided by more than a decade of war and invasion, the authors stress that "independence or death" is the standard that must unite Haitians. They bind slavery with French influences found throughout Haiti, even mocking those who believe freedom and independence are possible if the French remain on the island. The authors call for a single body of "native citizens, men, women, girls, and children" to find "on all parts of this island" their "spouses," "husbands," "brothers," and "sisters." Rather than noting social or historical differences among the population, the authors direct the citizens toward "avenging" their "children" and their "fathers," claiming a shared enmity against the French.

Dessalines and Boisrond-Tonnerre convey their message by using metaphors to portray the French as predators of liberty and the Haitian family, the most precious symbols of the Haitian Revolution that the authors claim to defend. The French are "tigers still dripping with their blood" from Haitian "victims" or "vultures" who prey upon Haitians' "suckling infants." After demonstrating how the shared Haitian body has been ravaged by the French, the authors describe their military victories in order to tap into a common enmity and to claim authority as political leaders. The authors allege that the soldiers and generals "spilled their

## AN ORIGINAL COPY: LOST AND RECOVERED

During the years following the Haitian Revolution, the fledgling Haitian government printed numerous copies of its declaration of independence for widespread distribution. The declaration's text was printed throughout the Atlantic world, from France and Britain to the United States and Latin America, in order to obtain global recognition of Haitian independence. In the midst of this publicity campaign, the Haitian government did not preserve any of the original printed copies with the signatures of Dessalines and his officers. As the government became engaged in nation building and defense projects, the overwhelming majority of the copies were either lost or destroyed.

Haitian historians spent decades in a search of the originals. For many, the search reflected the nation's ongoing pursuit of independence. Fleeing slave owners continued to claim Haiti's peoples as slaves, and foreign powers' invasions represented an international disregard for Haitians' sacrifices and liberation. As the nation repeatedly fought for self-determination, its historians hoped to obtain an original declaration to display as evidence of Haiti's independence and to stand with similar documents from other nations. It was only in early 2010 that such a printed copy was finally discovered in the British National Archives in London.

blood," swearing "to forever renounce France" and "to die rather than to live under its domination." Dessalines portrays himself as the epitome of valor: he has "sacrificed everything" for Haiti, including his "family" and "children." Now, as "despots and tyrants curse" him, he takes on a role as "sentinel who would watch over the idol" of liberty for which Haiti would "sacrifice." To bind together his authority and Haitian liberty, he concludes by asking Haitians to "vow ... to live free and independent" and "to prefer death to anything that will try to place you back in chains."

A powerful and emotional appeal against slavery and for constant vigilance underlies the whole of "Liberty or Death." Castigations against a "barbarous people," a "nation of executioners," and an "inhuman government" represent the visceral hated against the French that is woven throughout the text. Because Haitians had only been recently liberated from slavery, the repetition of the key terms of "slavery" and "enslaved" stoke intense emotion in readers. Parallelism keeps the pace steady and passionate. The phrases "to ourselves, to posterity, to the entire universe" and "that they are not our brothers, that they never will be" build energy throughout the text, and the repetition and parallelism of the phrase "let us" in the middle of the document ensures that the authors' message does not lose its emotional appeal.

A bicyclist passes a monument to Jean-Jacques Dessalines in the Champ de Mars plaza in Port-au-Prince, Haiti, 2008. © AURORA PHOTOS/ALAMY.

## CRITICAL DISCUSSION

The assessment of the declaration's legacy poses great challenges. Soon after it was drafted, Dessalines proclaimed himself emperor, causing observers to ponder the precise definitions of liberty put forward in the declaration. The declaration's promises for "vengeance" and the elimination of the French were quickly realized in early 1804 when Dessalines spearheaded a series of trials that resulted in the deaths of whites found guilty of participating in or supporting earlier massacres against blacks during the Haitian Revolution. While Dessalines defended sentencing the white criminals to death, opponents claimed Haiti had degenerated into the very barbarity "Liberty or Death" condemned. Similarly, although the proclamation speaks of allowing "neighbors to breathe in peace," Dessalines attempted an invasion of Santo Domingo in 1805, and domestic attempts to revive Haiti's sugar economy through forced labor also threw evaluations of the document's significance into question.

The call for constant vigilance against slavery presents the most important and lasting legacy of "Liberty or Death." Despite the discrepancies between the document's ideas and Dessalines's legacy, Dessalines and his proclamation join Louverture and the French "Rights of Man" as inspirations for slave revolts throughout the Atlantic. For example, the leader of the 1812 Aponte Rebellion in Cuba displayed pictures of Dessalines, and black soldiers in 1805 Brazil wore images of the Haitian leader. However, the document and the Haitian Revolution's impact on abolition varied throughout the Atlantic world. Some abolitionists used the events in Haiti to encourage antislavery projects; nevertheless Caribbean states increased imports of slaves and passed laws protecting slavery, which further entrenched the institution in the Atlantic world.

Throughout the scholarly literature on the Haitian Revolution, "Liberty or Death" often signals the end of the Revolution. Laurent Dubois's *Avengers of the New World* (2004) places the proclamation and Dessalines as the final figures in the revolution. Scholars of Haiti and Atlantic slavery, such as David Geggus, stress how various movements in the Americas echoed "Liberty or Death" in resurrecting indigenous symbols to contest European colonialism. More generally, however, the declaration is overshadowed by similar Atlantic national documents, such as the U.S. Declaration of Independence, the French "Rights of Man," and Latin American proclamations, in part because the connection between "Liberty or Death" and Dessalines hinders more nuanced studies. Essentially, Dessalines has been the subject of far less scholarship than figures such as Louverture, Napoleon, or George Washington.

### BIBLIOGRAPHY

*Sources*

Dessalines, Jean-Jacques, and Louis Félix Boisrond-Tonnerre. "The Haitian Declaration of Independence, January 1, 1804." *Slave Revolution in the Caribbean, 1789–1804*. Ed. Laurent Dubois and John D. Garrigus. Boston: Bedford / St. Martin's, 2006. Print.

Dubois, Laurent. *Avengers of the New World: The Story of the Haitian Revolution.* Cambridge: Harvard UP, 2004. Print.

Fick, Carolyn E. *Making Haiti: The Saint Domingue Revolution from Below.* Knoxville: U of Tennessee P, 1990. Print.

Geggus, David Patrick. *Haitian Revolutionary Studies.* Bloomington: Indiana UP, 2002. Print.

Klooster, Wim. *Revolutions in the Atlantic World: A Comparative History.* New York: New York UP, 2009. Print.

Popkin, Jeremy D. *You Are All Free: The Haitian Revolution and the Abolition of Slavery.* New York: Cambridge UP, 2010. Print.

*Further Reading*

Clavin, Matthew J. *Toussaint Louverture and the American Civil War: The Promise and Peril of a Second Haitian Revolution.* Philadelphia: U of Pennsylvania P, 2010. Print.

Davis, David Brion. *Inhuman Bondage: The Rise and Fall of Slavery in the New World.* New York: Oxford UP, 2006. Print.

Garrigus, John D. *Before Haiti: Race and Citizenship in French Saint-Domingue.* New York: Palgrave Macmillan, 2006. Print.

Gaspar, David Barry, and Darlene Clark Hine, eds. *More Than Chattel: Black Women and Slavery in the Americas.* Bloomington: Indiana UP, 1996. Print.

Geggus, David P., ed. *The Impact of the Haitian Revolution in the Atlantic World.* Columbia: U of South Carolina P, 2001. Print.

Geggus, David P., and Norman Fiering, eds. *The World of the Haitian Revolution.* Bloomington: Indiana UP, 2009. Print.

Ghachem, Malick W. *The Old Regime and the Haitian Revolution.* New York: Cambridge UP, 2012. Print.

Klein, Herbert S., and Ben Vinson. *African Slavery in Latin America and the Caribbean.* 2nd ed. New York: Oxford UP, 2007. Print.

*Aaron Moulton*

# A Manifesto of the Lord Protector to the Commonwealth of England, Scotland, Ireland, &c.

*Published by Consent and Advice of His Council, Wherein Is Shewn the Reasonableness of the Cause of This Republic against the Depredations of the Spaniards*

*Oliver Cromwell*

✥ *Key Facts*

**Time Period:**
Mid-17th Century

**Genre:**
Manifesto

**Events:**
Anglo-Spanish War

**Nationality:**
English

## OVERVIEW

Attributed to the English lord protector Oliver Cromwell and translated into Latin by poet John Milton for dissemination to the European international community, *A Manifesto of the Lord Protector to the Commonwealth of England, Scotland, Ireland, &c. Published by Consent and Advice of His Council, Wherein Is Shewn the Reasonableness of the Cause of This Republic against the Depredations of the Spaniards* (1655) officially declares war on Spain and argues that the English cause is religiously, politically, and economically just. The proclamation retroactively justifies hostilities in the Anglo-Spanish War (1654–60), which had already begun with an attack that Cromwell ordered on Spanish holdings in the West Indies. Addressed to both the English and the greater European public, Milton's Latin translation has survived as the most widely available copy of the proclamation—although scholarly debate continues as to how much of the composition was Cromwell's, Milton's, or a third party's.

Because the Anglo-Spanish War was widely known to be in progress at the time *A Manifesto of the Lord Protector* was issued, the persuasive impact of Cromwell's proclamation was minimal. Derided by the European community as the explanations of an embarrassed protector, the proclamation was not well received by the English public, which remained largely unsupportive of the war. The proclamation also infuriated the Spanish government under King Philip IV, who ordered the seizure of numerous English ships and goods in Spanish ports. Only the French responded positively to *A Manifesto of the Lord Protector,* largely because France was already at war with Spain. Despite failing to achieve the intended propagandistic effect of justifying the English cause, the text marks an important turn in English foreign policy toward imperial ambition and the pursuit of international power status.

## HISTORICAL AND LITERARY CONTEXT

The proclamation responds to generations of antagonism between the English and Spanish dating to the sixteenth century. The conflict stemmed from religious discord between Catholic Spain and Protestant England, competing trading interests, and colonial ambitions in the Americas. By the mid-seventeenth century, the Spanish Empire, a once-dominant power in Europe, was waning, and English imperial ambitions were on the rise. England had a contentious history with both Spain and France, though anti-Spanish sentiment was especially strong in England dating back to the failed Spanish Armada invasion of 1588. English privateers frequently raided Spanish and French ships, and both nations had reason to seek an English alliance in order to tip the balance of power on the continent. However, France was in a better military and financial position to propel English interests in Europe, and Cromwell's correspondence indicates he was aware of this fact in his negotiations with both nations.

By 1654 England's lord protector had decided to go to war with Spain and had launched an English fleet to attack the Spanish West Indies, a plan he referred to as Western Design. Some members of Cromwell's council of state opposed the policy, chiefly Major-General John Lambert, but Cromwell persisted with Western Design even as he continued to negotiate with the Spanish and the French over a proposed alliance. In fact, the Spanish ambassador to England, Don Alonso Cardenas, was led to believe that England might still side with Spain up to the eve of the attack on the West Indies. When news reached Cromwell that English forces had failed to seize their primary objective, Santo Domingo, and had retreated to Spanish Town in Jamaica, he ordered the commanders of the campaign, William Penn and Robert Venables, imprisoned in the Tower of London. He retreated into depressed seclusion and emerged days later to find the English government in disarray; in response he ordered the issuance of *A Manifesto of the Lord Protector.*

*A Manifesto of the Lord Protector* continues in a tradition of political and religious proclamations issued at the behest of Cromwell to the English people and to Europe at large. Many of these documents were composed with Milton's input. Chief among them is Milton's defense of the English people, *Defensio pro Populo Anglicano* (1651), another propagandistic work that defended the legitimacy of Cromwell's government. *A Manifesto of the Lord Protector* was also influenced by Bartolomé de Las Casas's *A Short Account of the Destruction of the Indies* (1552), which vividly details a variety of Spanish atrocities committed against the native population of the Americas. The proclamation also draws on numerous possibly apocryphal accounts of Spanish injustices committed against English sailors.

After *A Manifesto of the Lord Protector* was issued, its themes were echoed in other works of anti-Spanish propaganda. It encouraged John Phillips, Milton's nephew, to publish an English translation of Las Casas's *Short Account* titled *The Tears of the Indians* (1656). Its themes are also indirectly echoed in Milton's later and better known poetic works *Paradise Lost* (1667) and *Paradise Regained* (1671), in which the Devil is at one point represented in the figure of a conquistador engaged in colonial enterprise. The proclamation also influenced the writing of William Davenant's Puritan opera *The Cruelty of the Spaniards in Peru* in 1658. Today *A Manifesto of the Lord Protector* remains one of Cromwell's lesser-known proclamations and one of Milton's lesser-known prose works.

## THEMES AND STYLE

The central themes of *A Manifesto of the Lord Protector* are the villainy of Spain toward the English and native peoples and the righteousness of the English cause. The proclamation asserts that the English attack on the West Indies is "exceeding just and reasonable, every one will easily see" because the Spanish are "continually murdering, and sometimes even in cold blood butchering, any of our countrymen in America they think fit." The work also emphasizes the economic and religious benefits of an Anglo-Spanish War for England, claiming that the English fleet should be put to "profitable" enterprise and that the conquest of the West Indies will enlarge "the bounds of Christ's Kingdom" and end the "bloody Spanish inquisition." These themes are augmented by an exhaustive recounting of past Spanish transgressions against the English dating to the sixteenth century, which points to the general conclusion that the Spanish are an arrogant and immoral people deserving of military punishment.

The proclamation achieves its rhetorical effect through religious and political appeals to English nationalist sentiment, specifically neo-Elizabethan anti-Catholicism and the ostensibly republican ideals of the English Civil War and Cromwell's Protectorate government. The argument is designed to persuade through a list of historical appeals. Each instance of

## OLIVER CROMWELL AS GOD'S AGENT

Famous for referring to himself as an instrument of divine agency, English lord protector Oliver Cromwell might very well have believed that Western Design was God's will. His belief would have been grounded in his numerous previous military successes, often against long odds. He did not personally see to the preparations or execution of Western Design—unlike previous military campaigns—and was astonished upon learning of the English defeat at Santo Domingo. After imprisoning the generals who had failed in the campaign, he is said to have retreated to his room for a period of spiritual questioning that lasted several days. Presumably, he received some kind of reassurance—at least enough to reemerge and issue *A Manifesto of the Lord Protector.*

Spanish insult is held out as an example of the need for English military action. Some of the instances are examples of broad national disagreement, such as the failed Spanish Armada invasion and the Spanish violation of free trade treaties in 1542. Others are anecdotal and specific, such as the murder of the English crew of the *Mary* by Spaniards in 1605 and the account of an English captain "stript of his clothes, and fastened to a tree" by Spaniards and "exposed naked to be bit by the flies and vermin."

The language of *A Manifesto of the Lord Protector* is strident, emphatic, and relatively hyperbolic in its account of Spanish deprivations. The shrill emotional tenor of the writing is intended to persuade an English audience to support the war while also convincing other European nations that such a war is justified. Some scholars have argued that the numerous religious appeals are intended to downplay the underlying economic incentive for the English attack. Nevertheless, the language of the proclamation is righteous and aggrieved, even if the aggravation is more rhetorical than realistic.

## CRITICAL DISCUSSION

There is little evidence that *A Manifesto of the Lord Protector* was successful in convincing the English people or the European community that Cromwell's Western Design was justified. Not surprisingly, the Spanish rejected the proclamation as ludicrous. Scholars acknowledge that had the Spanish advanced the same reasoning to support an attack on English holdings in North America, Cromwell would have also rejected their claims. In addition, the work was largely overshadowed by the fact that the war had already commenced months earlier. As a piece of propaganda, *A Manifesto of the Lord Protector* enjoyed a second life in a 1738 republication in support of the English cause in the War of Jenkins' Ear (Jenkins, an English merchant captain, supposedly had returned to England holding

OLIVER CROMWELL. PROT.

Oliver Cromwell, Lord Protector of England, in a 1650 painting by Robert Walker. NATIONAL ARMY MUSEUM/THE ART ARCHIVE AT ART RESOURCE, NY.

Protectorate; at the same time they note the irony that the Anglo-Spanish War ultimately forced him to recall Parliament. Contemporary scholarship has continued to focus on the intersection of Cromwell's and Milton's views as expressed in the proclamation, in particular the paradoxes that seemingly result from this collaboration.

Recent scholarship has focused on the relationship between *A Manifesto of the Lord Protector* and Milton's later poetical works. In the 2003 book *Reforming Empire: Protestant Colonialism and Conscience in British Literature* (2003), Christopher Hodgkins emphasizes the use of the "dark figure" of the Spaniard in Milton's *Paradise* poems. Scholars have also explored how the proclamation relates to Milton's views on the European treatment of Native Americans. Robert Fallon argues in an essay in *Milton and the Imperial Vision* (1999) that it is "unlikely that a document used to justify conquering the West Indies was anti-imperial" and that Milton's references to Native Americans "have the flavor of an advocate seeking the moral high ground in controversy rather than one truly incensed over atrocities." Fallon also asserts that anti-imperialism was not Cromwell's focus—in fact, it was just the opposite.

## BIBLIOGRAPHY

### Sources

Abbot, Wilbur Cortez. *The Writings and Speeches of Oliver Cromwell.* Vol. III. Cambridge: Harvard UP, 1945. Print.

Armitage, David. "The Cromwellian Protectorate and the Languages of Empire." *Historical Journal* 35.3 (1992): 531–55. Print.

Battick, John F. "Cromwell's Diplomatic Blunder: The Relationship between the Western Design of 1654–1655 and the French Alliance of 1657." *Albion* 5.4 (1973): 279–98. Print.

Fallon, Robert Thomas. "Cromwell, Milton, and the Western Design." *Milton and the Imperial Vision.* Ed. Balachandra Rajan and Elizabeth Sauer. Pittsburg: Duquesne UP, 1999. 133–54. Print.

Hodgkins, Christopher. *Reforming Empire: Protestant Colonialism and Conscience in British Literature.* Columbia: U of Missouri P, 2003. Print.

### Further Reading

Carlyle, Thomas. *Oliver Cromwell's Letters and Speeches with Elucidations.* Vol. 4. New York: Scribner's, 1900. Print.

Fraser, Antonia. *Cromwell: The Lord Protector.* New York: Knopf, 1974. Print.

Howell, Roger, Jr. *Cromwell.* Boston: Little, Brown, 1977. Print.

Hughes, Merritt Y. *Ten Perspectives on Milton.* New Haven: Yale UP, 1965. Print.

Paul, Robert S. *The Lord Protector: Religion and Politics in the Life of Oliver Cromwell.* London: Lutterworth, 1955. Print.

Purkiss, Diane. *The English Civil Wars: Papists, Gentlewomen, Soldiers, and Witchfinders in the Birth of Modern Britain.* New York: Basic Books, 2006. Print.

his shriveled ear after it was cut off by a member of the Spanish coast guard). With English public opinion already in favor of the war, Cromwell's original proclamation met with a more receptive audience.

This 1738 republication, drawn from Milton's original Latin translation of *A Manifesto of the Lord Protector,* has served as the primary copy of Cromwell's proclamation and has provoked scholarly debate regarding Milton's reputation as a supporter of republican government and as an anti-imperialist. There is also debate as to whether the composition was entirely Milton's or if he simply signed his name to the translation. Regarding Cromwell's scholarship, scholars have pointed to the text as an example of the lord protector's increasingly authoritative position as ruler of the English

*Craig Barnes*

# "THE NEGRO'S COMPLAINT"

*William Cowper*

## OVERVIEW

William Cowper's poem "The Negro's Complaint" (1788) is a powerful appeal for the abolition of the slave trade in the British Empire. Written in a simple meter characteristic of English hymns of the day, the poem juxtaposes the cruelties of slavery with the specious luxuries it provides merchants and consumers. The poem's speaker, an unnamed African slave, deflates European claims of cultural superiority, arguing that those who practice chattel slavery are themselves brutes and beasts. The slave also derides the hypocrisy of those who claim to be Christians while systematically mistreating their fellow human beings. In seven compact stanzas, "The Negro's Complaint" contests all the typical rationalizations of slavery before concluding that it is the masters, not the slaves, whose humanity is truly in question; the masters, too, are themselves slaves, bonded to wealth and luxury.

Late-eighteenth-century Britain had seen a sharp increase in abolitionist sentiment, fomented by a coalition of Quakers, Evangelical Protestants, and Unitarians, all of whom firmly opposed slavery on religious grounds. A landmark 1772 court case had failed to find support in English or Welsh law for slavery, but the ruling stopped short of an explicit prohibition and remained mute on the subject of the slave trade per se. By the time "The Negro's Complaint" was printed, tracts describing the horrors of slavery were in frequent circulation, and public opinion was inflamed against the entrenched interests of slave traders. In his long poem *The Task* (1785), Cowper had already voiced the opinion that English law and custom were inimical to slavery, and he published several new poems in 1788 supporting the abolitionist cause. Widely reprinted, "The Negro's Complaint" served as the literary emblem of a prolonged campaign that contributed to the outlawing of the slave trade in 1807 and, a quarter-century later, the total abolition of slavery in Britain.

## HISTORICAL AND LITERARY CONTEXT

The abolitionist movement had already undergone a century of maturation when Cowper wrote "The Negro's Complaint." The Society of Friends had nonviolently agitated against slavery since at least 1688, when a group of Pennsylvania Quakers published the "Germantown Petition against Slavery." The English branch of the movement gained immediate momentum in the wake of "Somersett's Case" (1772), which established that slavery was not supported by positive law in England or Wales and formally ended the practice of slaveholding in those nations. However, the Somersett ruling did little to mitigate the infamous triangular trade, which brought English industrial products to Africa, slaves to America, and the products of slaveholding plantations, such as sugar, tobacco, and rum, to England. The events following the 1781 *Zong* massacre (see sidebar) further demonstrated that the "slavery question" was still open on a legal level, but they also revealed a mounting public disgust with the treatment of slaves as property rather than as persons.

By the publication of "The Negro's Complaint," Cowper had established an association between the dictates of his evangelical Christian faith and the cause of abolition. In the 1760s, he befriended clergyman John Newton, a former slave trader with whom he cowrote the *Olney Hymns* (1779). Cowper was also an attentive reader of contemporary developments in the English slavery debates: his monumental blank-verse poem *The Task* (1785) closely echoes the arguments of Somersett's advocates in its claim that "Slaves cannot breathe in England; if their lungs / Receive our air, that moment are they free […]." The Society for Effecting the Abolition of the Slave Trade was formed in 1787, and Cowper, while not a charter member, contributed several poems to its campaigns. "The Negro's Complaint" would prove to be the most enduring and memorable of these works.

By the late 1780s, antislavery sentiment had penetrated virtually every literary genre and artistic medium. Many of these works urged the public to take the initiative via boycotts of slavery-based industries. Pottery manufacturer Josiah Wedgwood helped to popularize the abolitionist cause with the production of the now-famous "Am I Not a Man and a Brother" medallion, which depicts the Society's seal and gave abolitionism a clear visual identity. "The Negro's Complaint" shares many characteristics with the Wedgwood medallion, including its emphasis on common humanity over superficial differences of appearance.

Cowper's poetry is often seen as an inciting force in the Romantic movement, whose products defined English poetry in the early nineteenth century. William Wordsworth and Samuel Taylor Coleridge displayed a

### ❖ *Key Facts*

**Time Period:**
Late 18th Century

**Genre:**
Poetry

**Events:**
Abolitionist agitation; Zong massacre

**Nationality:**
English

# THE *ZONG* MASSACRE

"The Negro's Complaint," like much abolitionist literature of its time, addressed an audience for which personal slavery was uncommon. However, the economic role of slavery in the colonies impeded the passage of abolition laws. The aftermath of the 1781 massacre aboard the slave ship *Zong* codified slaves' legal status, even as it galvanized the public in favor of abolition.

Bound for Jamaica in November 1781, the *Zong* began to suffer massive casualties from malnutrition and rampant disease. Captain Luke Collingwood and his crew proceeded to throw overboard 130 of the remaining slaves, who were legally considered property and, therefore, were insured. Upon the *Zong*'s return, the ship's owners sought compensation for the jettisoned human cargo, but their insurers contested the claim.

The court ruled in favor of the owners, but the very terms of the *Zong* case were odious to pro-abolition onlookers, who considered the crew guilty not of insurance fraud but of murder. Noted abolitionist Granville Sharp attempted to intervene in the case to this effect, but John Lee, solicitor general for England and Wales, infamously responded that "the case is the same as if wood had been thrown overboard." Despite Sharp's efforts and those of former slave Olaudah Equiano, no criminal prosecution was ever mounted.

familiarity with Cowper's poetry as a whole, but the specific import of "The Negro's Complaint" remains difficult to discern. The subgenre of "complaint," written in the persona of a tragically suffering character, certainly found renewed emphasis in Wordsworth's and Coleridge's *Lyrical Ballads* (1798). However, Cowper's less overtly political poetry, including *The Task* and his translations of Homer, capture the Romantic imagination more fully and influenced the movement's depictions of nature and its emphasis on spontaneous, "un-artificial" verse.

## THEMES AND STYLE

The argument of "The Negro's Complaint" is summarized in the speaker's closing injunction: "Prove that you have human feelings, / Ere you proudly question ours!" The speaker maintains that English people who support slavery, whether directly (by participating in the trade) or indirectly (by a cowardly refusal to forgo the goods it produces), forfeit any claims of moral and cultural superiority over, and even equality with, the slaves they despise. By illustrating the insensitivity of both the slave traders and the consumers, Cowper appeals to those most likely to be swayed in favor of the abolitionist cause.

Cowper's poem adopts the perspective of an African slave, wrenched from a rather vaguely defined "Afric" homeland and tortured into submission by English captors. Declaring that "minds are never to

be sold," the speaker takes aim at a culture insulated from the direct experience of slavery, contrasting the plenty of England's "jovial boards" with the "knotted scourges, / Matches," and "blood-extorting screws" used to extract labor from unwilling subjects. This principle of contrast applies throughout, occasioned by what might be termed a knowing ignorance of English law and the principles of the Christian religion. The speaker, claiming a kind of incredulity at the tenets of Christianity, mocks those who interpose themselves, rather than God, as masters: "Has He bid you buy and sell us, / Speaking from his throne, the sky?" Finally, the speaker asserts that the European traders, who act as tyrants over their fellow men and women, are more contemptible than the literal slaves, having placed themselves in bondage to "paltry gold."

Notwithstanding its critique of failed Christianity, "The Negro's Complaint" bears a religious overtone that would have been instantly recognizable to Cowper's contemporaries. The poet, himself a famous hymnodist, employs a pattern of alternating rhyme and line lengths (called common meter) shared by many eighteenth-century English hymns and popular songs (at least one copy of the poem is inscribed "to the tune of 'Hosier's Ghost' or 'As near Porto Bello lying,'" the title and subtitle of a popular propaganda ballad from the 1740s). Moreover, the speaker's tone of reasoned formality is in itself a refutation of Eurocentric claims to dominance; toward the end of the poem, a catalog of patiently borne offenses contrasts with the childish delight in gold and sugar displayed by the white people who are being addressed. This is especially striking in light of Cowper's other poems of 1788: "Sweet Meat has Sour Sauce," which adopts the perspective of a down-on-his-luck slave trader, and "Pity for Poor Africans," in which an Englishman stands aghast at the prospect of giving up sugar. In these other poems, speakers who are far less convincing strike poses of crude self-absorption and willful ignorance.

## CRITICAL DISCUSSION

"The Negro's Complaint" was circulated from 1788 onward by the Society for Effecting the Abolition of the Slave Trade, and it soon became, in the words of author Charlotte Sussman, "the motto of the abolitionist campaign of the 1790s." The receptivity of British readers to Cowper's arguments may be assessed by the fact that "The Negro's Complaint" also appeared in three major periodicals: *Scots Magazine* (January 1792), *Town and Country Magazine* (April 1792, reprinted June 1795), and *Gentleman's Magazine* (December 1793). Cowper's poem continued to be cited and excerpted in antislavery tracts and pamphlets, raising awareness among consumers whose purchases supported the slave trade. Sugar cane, which Cowper describes as watered by sweat and tears, provided an early and important target for boycotting campaigns. Pamphleteer William Fox excerpted Cowper's verses in his "Address to the People of Great Britain" (1791),

*Slave Trade*, a print based on a painting created by George Morland in 1788, the same year William Cowper's antislavery poem "The Negro's Complaint" was published. *SLAVE TRADE,* ENGRAVED BY JOHN RAPHAEL SMITH, 1791 (MEZZOTINT), MORLAND, GEORGE (1763–1804) (AFTER)/YALE CENTER FOR BRITISH ART, PAUL MELLON COLLECTION, USA/THE BRIDGEMAN ART LIBRARY.

which advocated a boycott of sugar products due to their origin on slaveholding plantations.

In the wake of partial political successes in 1807, however, Cowper's poetry lost some of its initial impetus. Antislavery coalitions, including the Society that circulated "The Negro's Complaint," retrenched their goals, aiming for the gradual rather than the immediate emancipation of slaves. The definitive victory would come decades after Cowper's death in 1800, with the 1833 passage of the Bill for the Abolition of Slavery in England. Meanwhile, abolitionist campaigns remained in full force across the Atlantic, where divided opinions on the legitimacy of slavery drove the nascent United States apart. Fox's "Address" was reprinted in major American urban centers such as Boston and New York, and "The Negro's Complaint" was also well received among American abolitionists, who adapted, reprinted, and paraphrased the work in their own antislavery tracts (for example, the poem is repeated virtually verbatim in Maria W. Stewart's *Productions of Mrs. Maria W. Stewart presented to the First Africa Baptist Church & Society, of the City of Boston*, 1835).

Contemporary scholarship has remained appreciative of the historic contributions of Cowper's verse while questioning the terms of exoticism and "otherness" in which the poet couches his appeal. Sussman points out that the poem's emphasis on the bodily fluids of "sighs, tears, and sweat" comes disturbingly close to objectifying the enslaved body, a line Cowper indeed crosses in later antislavery poems. Literary critic Joseph Jones speaks more generally of the rhetoric of "The Negro's Complaint," classing it as one of a host of English works that "tell us more about the white men who did the writing than about [those] who did the suffering."

## BIBLIOGRAPHY

### Sources

Bindman, David. "Am I Not a Man and a Brother? British Art and Slavery in the Eighteenth Century." *RES: Anthropology and Aesthetics* 26 (1994): 68–82. Print.

Fox, William. "An Address to the People of Great Britain, on the Propriety of Abstaining from West-India Sugar and Rum." Birmingham: Swinney & Walker, 1791. Print.

Hutchings, W. B. "William Cowper and 1789." *The Yearbook of English Studies* 19 (1989): 71–93. Print.

Isani, Mukhtar Ali. "Far From 'Gambia's Golden Shore': The Black in Late Eighteenth-Century American Imaginative Literature." *The William and Mary Quarterly* 36.3 (1979): 353–372. Print.

Jones, Joseph. "The 'Distress'd' Negro in English Magazine Verse." *Studies in English* 17 (1937): 88–106. Print.

Sussman, Charlotte. "Women and the Politics of Sugar, 1792." *Representations* 48 (1994): 48–69. Print.

### Further Reading

Cowper, William. *Selected Poetry and Prose.* Ed. David Lyle Jeffrey. Vancouver: Regent College Publishing, 2006. Print.

Kitson, Peter J. "'Bales of Living Anguish': Representations of Race and the Slave in Romantic Writing." *ELH* 67.2 (2000) 515–537. Print.

Mayo, Robert. "The Contemporaneity of the *Lyrical Ballads.*" *PMLA* 69.3 (1954): 486–522. Print.

Walvin, James. *The* Zong: *A Massacre, the Law, and the End of Slavery.* London: Yale UP, 2011. Print.

Werkmeister, Lucyle. "Some Whys and Wherefores of Coleridge's 'Lines Composed in a Concert-Room.'" *Modern Philology* 60.3 (1963): 201–205. Print.

Wood, Marcus. *The Poetry of Slavery: An Anglo-American Anthology, 1764–1865.* Oxford: Oxford UP, 2003. Print.

*Media Adaptation*

Cowper, William. *Forc'd From Home and All It's [Sic] Pleasures, For One Or Two Voices.* London, s.n., ca. 1795. Musical score.

*Michael Hartwell*

# ON THE BABYLONIAN CAPTIVITY OF THE CHURCH

*Martin Luther*

## OVERVIEW

Published in 1520, Martin Luther's *On the Babylonian Captivity of the Church* is an extended argument about the nature of religious sacraments and their proper use in a church setting. Intended for an ecclesiastical, academic audience and written in Latin, the document assesses the "Romanist" (or papal) perspective on the seven sacraments of the Roman Catholic Church: communion, baptism, penance, confirmation, marriage, ordination, and extreme unction. Luther concludes that only the first two are sacraments and that all seven have become corrupted by the "Babylonian" and even devilish teachings of the papacy and its adherents. By explaining the proper use of each ceremony, from a perspective based on personal faith and strict adherence to scripture, Luther laid the foundation for the day-to-day practices of the emerging Protestant church—even as he sharply castigated the papal hierarchy and its ideology. Luther's work served as propaganda by promoting an anti-papal mindset and offering an alternative to Romanist practices.

Unlike many of Luther's works, which were written in vernacular German to reach and persuade a wide lay audience, *Babylonian Captivity* was targeted at Luther's fellow intellectuals. However, his adversary Thomas Murner translated it into German almost immediately, exposing the radicalism of its ideas—and highlighting the strong, condemnatory response it received from the Roman faction. *Babylonian Captivity* was the second of three tracts written in 1520 as a response to Pope Leo X's *Exsurge Domine,* which sought to excommunicate Luther for his heretical opinions. In this context, the work attempts to justify Luther's vituperative critiques of standard Romanist ritual, arguing that greed, pride, and flawed human reasoning underpin the approaches to such sacraments. Using detailed scriptural exegesis and engaging directly with his opponents' writings, Luther highlights the corruption characterizing each Roman sacramental procedure. This focus ensured that the work became instantly notorious, galvanizing Roman efforts to brand Luther as a heretic.

## HISTORICAL AND LITERARY CONTEXT

Luther condemned the practices of the Roman Catholic Church hierarchy, which was an extremely powerful, rich, and influential presence in sixteenth-century Europe. Its political and religious opinions influenced the decisions of the French king, the German electors, and the Holy Roman Emperor. Moreover, its titular head—the pope—was almost always aligned by blood with a ruling Italian house, such as the Medici family. With its combined spiritual and political power, the Church hierarchy was able to generate vast amounts of wealth, often by manipulating sacramental procedures. Beginning in 1506, for example, Pope Julius II raised funds to build St. Peter's Cathedral by selling indulgences, which were documents releasing the purchasers from punishment for their sins.

In 1517 the university academic Martin Luther drew attention to the immorality of selling indulgences by publicly posting a set of ninety-five theses giving reasons why the practice should be curbed. Using the new technology of the printing press, Germans began to reproduce this document, taking only a month to spread its ideas throughout Europe. Over the next three years, Luther capitalized strongly on the power of the press to spread his message in propagandistic fashion, creating thirty different documents that sold at least 300,000 copies. Because cheaply printed documents could reach not only the upper classes but also the common people, they were a useful vehicle for Luther's main claims: that anyone who believed in Christ could receive eternal life and that every believer was equally important and useful.

To convey these ideas to every branch of society, reformers like Luther and his companions wrote specifically targeted pieces of literature that could persuade people from different walks of life. For example, Luther's colleague Philip Melanchthon wrote a piece about humanist evangelical education in 1518 and a systematic statement of Lutheran theology in 1521, attempting to convince academics of the rigor and exegetical correctness of the new approach. While *Babylonian Captivity* shared this academic goal, its sarcasm, insults, and bold accusations antagonized intellectuals such as Desiderius Erasmus, who found its theology too radical. Luther and Erasmus would later share a well-publicized literary debate over the question of free will, in which Luther accused Erasmus of hedging and failing fully to embrace the mercy of God toward inevitable human sin.

While it began as an academic tract, *Babylonian Captivity* was received as a vital pastoral document for

✢ *Key Facts*

**Time Period:**
Early 16th Century

**Genre:**
Tract

**Events:**
Protestant Reformation; growing corruption in the Catholic Church

**Nationality:**
German

# LUTHER THE AUGUSTINIAN

Although Martin Luther (1483–1546) would critique the policies of the established Roman Catholic Church, and particularly the idea of taking religious vows at a young age, he started his own career as a monk under papal authority. As the opening of the *Babylonian Captivity* indicates, in 1520 Luther refers to himself as "Martin Luther, Augustinian," three years after he first questioned Roman practice by publishing the Wittenberg theses. By reminding his audience that he had taken monastic vows himself and was a part of the Augustinian order, Luther emphasizes his status as an insider, able to assess the reality of the Roman hierarchy and its devotional practices. In this light, Luther's words on the monastic lifestyle have a special resonance: "I would suggest to those in high places in the church ... that they should do away with all vows and religious orders; or at least not speak of them with approval or praise." Though he still positioned himself as a monk, Luther came to believe that the Church was neglecting biblical models of faith-filled spirituality by promoting the monastic lifestyle and that monks and priests were falling victim to "pride and presumption," viewing themselves wrongly as superior to the laity.

the developing evangelical church. It explained the proper behavior and function of priests and laypeople, demanding that priests preach educational sermons about faith and that laypeople take an active, equal role in the church. Through baptism and communion, laypeople could experience an external sign of God's presence (in water, bread, and wine) as well as the invisible, divine mystery of God's promises. Because it presented specific practical and theological instructions for the new evangelical church, *Babylonian Captivity* was condemned at the pope's Diet of Worms in 1521, when papal representatives asked Luther to recant his anti-Romanist statements. He refused to repudiate his work, however, and its viewpoints on the sacraments still inform practices of worship in Lutheran churches today.

## THEMES AND STYLE

While the main thrust of *Babylonian Captivity* is the argument for reconceptualizing the sacraments, Luther also used the work to promote his beliefs in the salvific power of faith and the straightforward interpretation of scripture. To do this, he employs a blunt and harsh voice, calling the papacy "identical with the kingdom of Babylon and the real Antichrist" because it disagrees with his perspectives. At the same time, Luther wishes to encourage the Roman Catholic Church to change its own practices and emphases. His advice is addressed to any sympathetic reader ("you") within a church hierarchy who is willing to lead the people toward greater faith. The result is a mixed tone that blends earnestness and insults, idealism and cynicism. Luther uses this tone to simultaneously denounce the papacy and

promote a new interpretation of scripture—making his work a piece of thematic propaganda that publicizes his own beliefs about the necessity and efficacy of faith alone.

To promote his own method of scriptural exegesis, Luther targets and argues against specific points raised by Romanist apologists. For example, he castigates the "Leipzig professor" Augustin Alfeld for his loose interpretation of the New Testament, saying that he lacks "proof" for his assertions because they originate in his "own imagination." This style of attack was particularly effective in the humanist culture of the Renaissance, which emphasized a return to original source material as well as responsible, textually rooted strategies of reading. Luther also stressed his own academic qualifications by addressing his text as an open letter to a colleague at the University of Wittenberg and by citing and nuancing the opinions of Church fathers such as Augustine and Thomas Aquinas. Finally, by framing his argument as a response to the abuses of each sacrament in turn, Luther organizes his work in a systematic, university-appropriate way, while allowing room for digressions that provide further instructions about preferable conduct.

Within this academic framework, Luther's language itself is brisk, plain, and earnest. Writing with a strong command of Latin, he nevertheless deploys a colorful, unacademic vocabulary that mimics his usual blunt German: Romanists are "magpies," "toadies," and "wolves," whose scriptural commentaries can be like "sludge" from a "foul drain." This language reinforces Luther's belief that all human expression is both potentially sinful and potentially useful. If insults can alienate listeners, after all, they can also expose ideas plainly and clearly, as Constance Furey argues in her 2005 essay in *Harvard Theological Review*. As a result, the goal of exposing the truth about God, faith, and Christian freedom is threaded throughout the text at the level of vocabulary as well as the level of content. By using plain-spoken, insulting language, Luther equips his academic writing both to denigrate Roman ideas and to galvanize change, pointing out the truth in such an abrupt and jarring way that the reader will be forced to confront it.

## CRITICAL DISCUSSION

In the wake of Luther's intervention, the balance of religious and temporal power in Europe began to shift. On the religious front, reformers such as Huldrych Zwingli and John Calvin debated the specific intricacies of the Lord's Supper, with Luther and Zwingli falling out over the idea of consubstantiation. Meanwhile, Calvin lamented the confusion and disarray caused by this quibbling. A 1567 English translation of his work urges laypeople to "be not troubled out of measure" with the debate over the sacraments. Instead, Calvin states, they should focus on the "right and sincere worship of God," which Luther and his companions also taught. Meanwhile, Luther's books were also causing

An 1870 painting of Luther and Cardinal Cajetan. Martin Luther criticized the Catholic Church in the prefatory letter of his 1520 work *On the Babylonian Captivity of the Church. LUTHER IN FRONT OF CARDINAL CAJETAN DURING THE CONTROVERSY OF HIS 95 THESES,* 1870 (OIL ON CANVAS), PAUWELS, FERDINAND WILHELM (1830–1904)/LUTHERHAUS, EISENACH, GERMANY/THE BRIDGEMAN ART LIBRARY.

political disarray. Holy Roman Emperor Charles V became openly hostile to the evangelical cause. Over the next century, religious warfare would begin across Europe, particularly affecting Switzerland, France, and the Netherlands.

During and after this political upheaval, *Babylonian Captivity* began to be viewed in Protestant nations as a source of practical pastoral advice. Embodying Luther's deeply caring attitude toward parishioners, the work enjoins the clergy to focus on simple acts of service, including preaching and teaching about faith—a focus that is still prioritized today. Still, the *Babylonian Captivity* also exacerbated the schism between reformers and papal supporters. Just as Henry VIII of England strongly denounced the book in print, earning the title of Defender of the Faith from a grateful pope, modern Christians still disagree about its portrayal of the sacraments. In this way, the work holds a mixed legacy among theologians as a pastoral text that has also incited strong divisions between believers.

Recently, scholars have become interested in the way that reformers' language and publication choices helped to shape the path of the Reformation in Europe. As Furey suggests, Luther's aggressive language is an effective rhetorical strategy for two reasons: it "reinforce[s] group cohesion" among anti-Romanists, and it also "expose[s] the truth by piercing through appearances and challenging conventional thought." While language choices are vital to analyze, so are the ways that this language appears in print. As Mark Edwards Jr. points out in *Printing, Propaganda, and Martin Luther* (1994), the widespread dissemination of Luther's work through the printing press "not only conveyed Luther's message but also embodied it"—signaling clearly that all people should have access to religious texts and be able to learn about faith-driven salvation.

## BIBLIOGRAPHY

*Sources*

Bonney, Richard. *The European Dynastic States: 1494–1660.* Oxford: Oxford UP, 1991. Print.

Calvin, John. "A Little Booke of Iohn Caluines Concernynge Offences ..." Trans. Arthur Golding. *EEBO.* London: H. Wykes for William Seres, 1567. Web. 3 Sept. 2012.

Edwards, Mark, Jr. *Printing, Propaganda, and Martin Luther.* Berkeley: U of California P, 1994. Print.

Furey, Constance M. "Invective and Discernment in Martin Luther, D. Erasmus, and Thomas More." *Harvard Theological Review* 98:4 (2005): 469–88. Print.

Luther, Martin. *Martin Luther: Selections from His Writings.* Ed. John Dillenberger. New York: Anchor, 1962. Print.

Spitz, Lewis. *The Protestant Reformation: 1517–1559.* St. Louis: Concordia, 2001. Print.

Steinhaeuser, A. T. W., Frederick C. Ahrens, and Abdel Ross Wentz. "Introduction." *The Babylonian Captivity of the Church.* Trans. A. T. W. Steinhaeuser. *Project Gutenberg.* World Public Library Association, 29 Aug. 2011. Web. 3 Sept. 2012.

*Further Reading*

Oberman, Heiko. "Teufelsdreck: Eschatology and Scatology in the 'Old' Luther." *Sixteenth Century Journal* 19:3 (1988): 435–50. Print.

Osborne, Thomas. "Faith, Philosophy and the Nominalist Background to Luther's Defense of the Real Presence." *Journal of the History of Ideas* 63:1 (2002): 63–82. Print.

Mitchell, Joshua. "Protestant Thought and Republican Spirit: How Luther Enchanted the World." *American Political Science Review* 86:3 (1992): 688–95. Print.

Stadtwald, Kurt. *Roman Popes and German Patriots: Antipapalism in the Politics of the German Humanist Movement from Gregor Heimburg to Martin Luther.* Geneva: Droz, 1996. Print.

Totten, Mark. "Luther on 'unio cum Christo': Toward a Model for Integrating Faith and Ethics." *The Journal of Religious Ethics* 31:3 (2003): 443–62. Print.

Whitford, David. "The Papal Antichrist: Martin Luther and the Underappreciated Influence of Lorenzo Valla." *Renaissance Quarterly* 61:1 (2008): 26–52. Print.

*Nancy Simpson Younger*

# PERICLES'S FUNERAL ORATION
*Thucydides*

## OVERVIEW

The funeral oration of Pericles, recorded by Thucydides during the conflict between Athens and Sparta (431–404 BCE), is a famous speech within Thucydides's masterwork *The History of the Peloponnesian War*. Scholars generally agree that Thucydides wrote down the funeral oration from memory near the end of the war, about twenty-five years after its delivery; how much of it is from the original speech of Pericles and how much Thucydides reinvented is the subject of much debate. The speaker emphasizes Athenian virtues and contrasts these with the rigidity of Spartan institutions. Thucydides, in this way, uses an elaborate antithetical method throughout his entire *History*, particularly within the funeral oration, which promotes democracy, intellectual and spiritual freedom, imperialism, and the overall Athenian way of life. Rather than delivering a typical funeral oration that focuses on the heroic deeds of the dead, the speaker idealizes Athens. The eulogy serves as propaganda because it encourages citizens to protect the greatness of Athens from the invading Spartan foe by adhering to Periclean war policies.

Pericles, the foremost politician in Athens, delivered the famous speech in the winter after the first year of the war in 430 BCE. The Spartans had recently devastated the Attic countryside, while the Athenians passively watched in anger from their protective city walls. The speech appears to have helped morale, and Pericles's war strategies were continued. Years later the publication of Thucydides's *History* went mostly unnoticed. Xenophon—whose works were immensely popular throughout Greece—continued *History* where Thucydides had left off. Others, including Plato and Aristotle, show some awareness of the funeral oration, but the speech was not especially regarded until the age of Cicero three centuries later. It has since been called the greatest speech ever written and has created a portrait of Periclean Athens that still captures popular imagination, portraying it as the most esteemed political and cultural center ever known.

## HISTORICAL AND LITERARY CONTEXT

Under the guidance of Pericles—a prominent statesman—Athens had reached its highest cultural, political, and economic heights. The Parthenon was completed in 438 BCE, and Phidias sculpted both the statue of Athena and the pediments on the Parthenon. Tragedy flourished, with Sophocles and Aeschylus writing their great tragedies during this time. Pericles was a friend of Anaxagoras, the natural philosopher, and Pericles encouraged the traveling sophists to live in Athens to teach rhetorical methods. The Piraeus, the port town just outside Athens, became one of the busiest economic ports in Greece. Democracy was strengthened by making the archonship a paid office and appointed by lot so that every citizen had an equal chance of holding political office. It was the fear and jealousy of the growing power of Athens that hastened the outbreak of the war.

Pericles's war strategy revolved around the simple fact that Sparta was a land power and Athens a naval power. The Athenians rejected battle on land and retreated behind the walls of Athens while they made naval raids against Sparta and its allies along the coast of the Peloponnesus. The Spartan King Archidamus invaded Attica and devastated the land all the way up to the deme Acharnae, from which he could see, in the distance, the Acropolis of Athens. The majority of the Athenians were farmers. They had to watch passively from the cramped quarters of the Acropolis while their houses, crops, vines, and olive trees were destroyed. The Athenians wanted to fight by land, but Pericles's strategy held sway. The offensive naval actions did limited damage to the enemy in the first year. With morale low that first winter, Pericles delivered the inspiring funeral oration.

The Athenians attached great significance to the burial of their dead, and the funeral speech (*epitaphios*) was an age-old cultural custom. Pericles not only delivered his famous funeral oration in 430 BCE but also a previous one in the aftermath of the Samian War in 440 BCE. At public cost the bones of the dead were placed in a tent for three days for friends and relatives to make offerings. Their bones were then put in ten cedar boxes (one for each deme), carried in procession outside the city walls, and buried in the Kerameikos. After the burial, ceremonies traditionally ended with the funeral oration, a speech delivered on a raised platform by the most prominent Athenian. Instead of focusing on the deeds of the heroic soldiers, Pericles's eulogy in 430 BCE—influenced by sophistic rhetoric—praised democratic Athens. The speech served as war propaganda after the demoralizing invasion of Attica.

### ❖ *Key Facts*

**Time Period:**
5th Century BCE

**Genre:**
Speech

**Events:**
Peloponnesian War; growth of tragedy in Athens

**Nationality:**
Greek

## PRIMARY SOURCE

### EXCERPT FROM PERICLES'S FUNERAL ORATION

I shall begin with our ancestors: it is both just and proper that they should have the honour of the first mention on an occasion like the present. They dwelt in the country without break in the succession from generation to generation, and handed it down free to the present time by their valour. And if our more remote ancestors deserve praise, much more do our own fathers, who added to their inheritance the empire which we now possess, and spared no pains to be able to leave their acquisitions to us of the present generation. Lastly, there are few parts of our dominions that have not been augmented by those of us here, who are still more or less in the vigour of life; while the mother country has been furnished by us with everything that can enable her to depend on her own resources whether for war or for peace. That part of our history which tells of the military achievements which gave us our several possessions, or of the ready valour with which either we or our fathers stemmed the tide of Hellenic or foreign aggression, is a theme too familiar to my hearers for me to dilate on, and I shall therefore pass it by. But what was the road by which we reached our position, what the form of government under which our greatness grew, what the national habits out of which it sprang; these are questions which I may try to solve before I proceed to my panegyric upon these men; since I think this to be a subject upon which on the present occasion a speaker may properly dwell, and to which the whole assemblage, whether citizens or foreigners, may listen with advantage.

Our constitution does not copy the laws of neighbouring states; we are rather a pattern to others than imitators ourselves. Its administration favours the many instead of the few; this is why it is called a democracy. If we look to the laws, they afford equal justice to all in their private differences; if no social standing, advancement in public life falls to reputation for capacity, class considerations not being allowed to interfere with merit; nor again does poverty bar the way, if a man is able to serve the state, he is not hindered by the obscurity of his condition. The freedom which we enjoy in our government extends also to our ordinary life. There, far from exercising a jealous surveillance over each other, we do not feel called upon to be angry with our neighbour for doing what he likes, or even to indulge in those injurious looks which cannot fail to be offensive, although they inflict no positive penalty. But all this ease in our private relations does not make us lawless as citizens. Against this fear is our chief safeguard, teaching us to obey the magistrates and the laws, particularly such as regard the protection of the injured, whether they are actually on the statute book, or belong to that code which, although unwritten, yet cannot be broken without acknowledged disgrace.

Xenophon realized the importance of Thucydides's *History* by completing it, and, more than any other speech, the funeral oration had a tremendous impact in the history of speechmaking and rhetoric. Aristotle had Pericles's funeral oration in mind when discussing epideictic speech—speeches of praise and blame—in his famous treatise *Rhetoric*. The funeral oration was highly influential with Cicero and later Roman historians such as Polybius and Plutarch. The historian Garry Wills has shown that the funeral oration inspired President Abraham Lincoln's Gettysburg Address, delivered in 1863, a speech that praised the sacrifice soldiers had made to preserve the union and democracy. Today Thucydides's *History* is considered by many as the most important political history ever written, and the funeral oration—the only epideictic speech in it—as the ultimate statement of democratic theory.

### THEMES AND STYLE

Central to Pericles's funeral oration is the idealization of the Athenian state. In contrast to the oligarchies and monarchies of other Greek city-states, the speaker promotes the democratic and intellectual spirit of Athens. Pericles propounds that "we are rather a pattern to others than imitators ourselves" and concludes that Athens is "the school of all Hellas." He continues by claiming that "our stake in the struggle is not the same as theirs who have no such blessings to lose." In this way Pericles encourages the Athenians to protect their great city-state and its unique institutions. The speech, therefore, serves as propaganda. Rather than praising individual men who died in battle, he glorifies Athenian arête: "You must yourselves realize the power of Athens, and feed your eyes upon her from day to day, till love of her fills your hearts; and then when all her greatness shall break upon you, you must reflect that it was by courage, sense of duty, and a keen feeling of honor in action that men were enabled to win all this." This is a eulogy of Athenian virtue, and the speaker insists that the true Athenian citizens must continue to fight in accordance with the unpopular war strategy.

Thucydides's chief rhetorical device used throughout the funeral oration is antithesis, or the pairing and contrast of ideas, a common sophistic rhetorical strategy. In *The Speeches of Thucydides* (1973), H. F. Harding points out a variety of antitheses in the funeral oration, such as "Words against deeds. Change against status quo. Ideas of leaders of Athens and of Sparta. Idealism against practicality. Written versus unwritten laws. Truth against lies." By means of antithesis the speaker praises Athens at the expense of Sparta: "While in education, where our rivals from their very cradles by a painful discipline seek after manliness, at Athens we live exactly as we please, and yet are just as ready to encounter every legitimate danger." The eulogium remains in Pericles's voice throughout, attempting to rally Athenian morale after the invasion of Attica. But it must be remembered that it is as much Thucydides's voice dictating the general sense of what he remembers and wants to bring across in his *History*.

Stylistically, the funeral oration is epideictic—a speech that praises the glory of Athens—thus functioning as war propaganda. Ceremonial oratory was frequently heard in ancient Athens. Both its language and emotional tenor are that of exhortation and make the hearers feel that they are included in the eulogy. The speaker encourages the pursuit of noble deeds for their own sake and courage in accordance with the law, demonstrating the superiority of Athens over all other states. For example, Pericles expounds, "In short, I say that as a city we are the school of Hellas; while I doubt if the world can produce a man, who where he has only himself to depend upon, is equal to so many emergencies, and graced by so happy a versatility as the Athenian." Thucydides not only uses the declarative sentence for lucidity, but he also employs the periodic sentence, which uses word order to emphasize central ideas and to subordinate minor points—a persuasive style vital to rhetoric.

## CRITICAL DISCUSSION

After the death of Thucydides and throughout the Hellenistic period, there is an almost complete silence about his work. In *Thucydidean Themes* (2011) Simon Hornblower demonstrates how Thucydides's name is scarcely mentioned but how his work was widely read. Xenophon, for example, continued his incomplete history in his famous *Hellenika,* and other continuators include Kratippos and Theopompos. The speeches in *The History of the Peloponnesian War* influenced the great rhetorician Demosthenes, who copied out the work eight times. Aristotle certainly had the funeral oration in mind when he wrote his treatise *Rhetoric.* By the second century BCE Thucydides's work was continuously cited and claimed as a classic. Numerous writers such as Cicero, Dionysios of Halikarnassos, Plutarch, Polybius, and Lucian recognized the immense value of Thucydides's *History.* Quintilian praised his style with the following famous line: "Thucydides is compact in texture, terse and ever eager to press forward."

As part of Thucydides's *History,* Pericles's funeral oration has been regarded as the greatest ceremonial speech ever written. By idealizing the entire Athenian state, the speech not only demonstrates how a leader such as Pericles thought and spoke but also what methods Thucydides believed were necessary to persuade his audience. It reflects the blossoming of rhetoric in classical Athens. Harding writes, "For content, literary style, and historical method we have a book that has been studied for centuries and today captures a reader's attention because its incidents are so startlingly modern and applicable. Its lessons are timeless." In *A History of Greece* (1900), J. B. Bury contends, "The book is in itself a liberal education," thus confirming Thucydides's own statement, "I have written my work, not as an essay which is to win the applause of the moment, but as a possession for all time."

The study of Thucydides's *History* has never been as influential and ubiquitous as it is in the present. Scholarly trends have focused on the military history

# THUCYDIDES

Thucydides, born around 460 BCE, was an Athenian citizen of a wealthy and aristocratic family from whom he inherited gold mines situated in Thrace, or northeastern Greece. His high social position allowed him to travel and gain access to sources that could provide him with information for his *History,* which he began to write around 431 BCE, at the outbreak of the war. He was elected Athenian general in 424 BCE and stationed in Thrace, where he failed to prevent the capture of Amphipolis and was thereafter sent into exile for twenty years. Very little is known about his life during and after exile. He certainly traveled to collect information in order to write his famous work.

Shortly after his return to Athens from exile around 404 BCE, he died and left his work unfinished. His *History* concludes at 411 BCE—seven years before the war ended with the defeat of Athens. The last chapter is less polished than the preceding ones and contains no speeches. Thucydides was a Periclean democrat, admiring Pericles's leadership and political wisdom. He believed that if Pericles had not died in 429 BCE and had continued as leader, Athens would have won the war. The famous nineteenth-century English historian Lord Macaulay once declared, "I have no hesitation in pronouncing Thucydides the greatest historian who ever lived."

of the Peloponnesian War as well as the accuracy and attention to detail of the author Thucydides. Another trend is the comparison of Thucydides's historical methods to those of Herodotus, "the father of history." Most recently, scholars have noted the literary qualities of the work, exploring the elements of tragedy,

Bust of Pericles, marble, Roman copy after a Greek original. SCALA/ART RESOURCE, NY.

rhetoric, and philosophy of human nature. Donald Kagan, Yale professor of classics, has written numerous award-winning works on Thucydides. In *Thucydides: The Reinvention of History* (2010), Kagan points out "the important interpretations" and biases of Thucydides. This has led a few critics to explore the persuasive elements throughout the speeches, particularly the famous funeral oration.

## BIBLIOGRAPHY

*Sources*

Bury, J. B. *A History of Greece.* New York: Modern Library, 1900. Print.

Harding, H. F. *The Speeches of Thucydides.* Lawrence: Coronado, 1973. Print.

Hornblower, Simon. *Thucydidean Themes.* Oxford: Oxford UP, 2011. Print.

Kagan, Donald. *Thucydides: The Reinvention of History.* New York: Penguin Group, 2010. Print.

Thucydides. *The Complete Writings of Thucydides: The Peloponnesian War.* Trans. Richard Crawley. New York: Modern Library, 1951. Print.

Wills, Garry. *Lincoln at Gettysburg. The Words That Remade America.* New York: Simon & Schuster, 1992. Print.

*Further Reading*

Bosworth, A. B. "The Historical Context of Thucydides' Funeral Oration." *Journal of Hellenic Studies* 120 (2000): 1–16. Print.

Carey, Christopher. *Democracy in Classical Athens.* Bristol: Bristol Classical, 2001. Print.

Foster, Edith. *Thucydides, Pericles, and Periclean Imperialism.* Cambridge: Cambridge UP, 2010. Print.

Jaeger, Werner. *Paideia: The Ideals of Greek Culture.* Trans. Gilbert Highet. Vol. 1. Oxford: Oxford UP, 1945. Print.

Ober, Josiah. *Mass and Elite in Democratic Athens: Rhetoric, Ideology & the Power of the People.* Princeton: Princeton UP, 1989. Print.

———. *The Athenian Revolution: Essays on Ancient Greek Democracy & Political Theory.* Princeton: Princeton UP, 1996. Print.

Tritle, Lawrence A. *A New History of the Peloponnesian War.* West Sussex: Wiley-Blackwell, 2010. Print.

Zagorin, Perez. *Thucydides: An Introduction for the Common Reader.* Princeton: Princeton UP, 2005. Print.

*Greg Bach*

# "THROW YOUR BODIES UPON THE GEARS"

*Mario Savio*

## OVERVIEW

On December 2, 1964, Mario Savio delivered a speech—which came to be known as the "Throw Your Bodies upon the Gears" speech—at an outdoor rally moments before roughly one thousand young people entered and occupied the administrative offices in Sproul Hall of the University of California at Berkeley to protest restrictions on free speech rights on the prestigious campus. Savio was a twenty-one-year-old philosophy major from New York City and one of the leaders of Berkeley's Free Speech Movement. He had participated in the 1964 Freedom Summer civil rights campaign in Mississippi, and his exhortatory address drew on the moral fervor of the African American freedom movement. Savio urged the crowd to exert its will through civil disobedience, and, in particular, to oppose the university's bureaucracy, which he likened to a machine: "There's a time when the operation of the machine becomes so odious, makes you so sick at heart, that you can't take part! You can't even passively take part! And you've got to put your bodies upon the gears and upon the wheels, upon the levers, upon all the apparatus, and you've got to make it stop!"

The Sproul Hall sit-in led to 800 arrests. A few days later, a vote of the faculty brought victory to the student demonstrators. The Free Speech Movement was among the earliest and most visible of the radical youth revolts that shook the United States in the 1960s. Savio's speech, captured by television cameras and widely circulated in the press, made him a nationally recognized leader. His call to "put your bodies upon the gears" is now considered one of the decade's most powerful speeches and is indelibly associated with a protest movement of brief duration but lasting historical significance.

## HISTORICAL AND LITERARY CONTEXT

The 1960s were notable for the appearance of many groups advocating for social and cultural change, with young people providing much of the leadership and enthusiasm. The generation that came of age at this time had grown up amid the cold war confrontation between the United States and the Soviet Union, the anticommunist crusades of Senator Joseph McCarthy, and the overall social conservatism that characterized the United States in the 1950s. The movement against racial segregation and discrimination in the South was instrumental in turning the political tide. Young people led many civil rights protests, such as the 1960 lunch counter sit-ins in Greensboro, North Carolina, and the Student Nonviolent Coordinating Committee (SNCC) became one of the key organizations driving the movement. In July 1964, President Lyndon B. Johnson signed federal civil rights legislation into law, handing the movement a major victory at a moment when hundreds of white youths from around the country, including Savio, were working on the Freedom Summer project, an initiative organized principally by the SNCC that aimed to increase the number of registered African American voters in the South.

The controversy on the Berkeley campus arose at the beginning of the 1964 fall semester, when university officials decided that representatives of student organizations could no longer sit at tables, distribute literature, or engage in political advocacy on a piece of university property located at the intersection of Bancroft and Telegraph avenues, the only spot on campus where such activities had previously been permitted. The Free Speech Movement arose spontaneously, and in dramatic fashion, on October 1. On that day, Jack Weinberg, a former student, was arrested by campus police while distributing literature at a table for a civil rights group, but a crowd of students surrounded the police car and kept it immobilized on the spot for more than twenty-four hours. Savio and many others delivered impromptu speeches from the police car's roof. Weinberg was eventually released and the charges against him dropped. Savio viewed the students' demands in starkly moral terms. He linked the conflict to the struggles taking place in the South; in both situations, he argued, the rights to civic participation and due process of law were at stake.

In calling for nonviolent civil disobedience, Savio was invoking a political and literary tradition dating back to Henry David Thoreau and guided by Mohandas Gandhi, Martin Luther King Jr., and other civil rights figures. Savio's critique of the university's bureaucratic administration also revealed the influence of the radical social and educational critic Paul Goodman, particularly his books *Growing Up Absurd* (1960) and *The Community of Scholars* (1962).

Savio's defiant voice injected a new tone of confrontation into the rhetoric of student radicals. Early in

❖ *Key Facts*

**Time Period:**
Mid-20th Century

**Genre:**
Speech

**Events:**
Cold War; Vietnam War; civil rights movement; free speech movement; anti-Vietnam War movement

**Nationality:**
American

# THE PHILOSOPHER OF THE NEW LEFT

Without a doubt, the thinker with whom Mario Savio and his movement colleagues felt the greatest affinity was Paul Goodman. Goodman was fond of them, too. Invited to visit the Berkeley campus just after the students' triumph in the academic senate, Goodman wrote, "Beautifully, a moral struggle has given the students a *habit* of good faith and commitment, and their solidarity has turned into community, like the auroral flush of a good society." Goodman had authored the best-selling book *Growing Up Absurd,* in which he asserted that the problems facing American youth were mostly ways in which society had failed them: "It is desperately hard these days for an average child to grow up to be a man," he wrote, "for our present organized system of society does not want men. They are not safe." His wide-ranging social critique struck a chord among the young, including those who became leaders of the New Left.

Goodman called himself a "community anarchist." He distrusted centralized, bureaucratic institutions and advocated that people act autonomously alongside those around them, using the materials at hand to improve their lives. He applied this thinking to attack educational institutions, from grade schools to graduate schools, in his books *Compulsory Mis-education* and *The Community of Scholars* (both 1962), arguing for decentralization and an emphasis on community values. The documentary *Paul Goodman Changed My Life* (2011) aimed to introduce this nearly forgotten intellectual to a new generation of youth.

1965, just weeks after the Sproul Hall sit-in, President Johnson escalated the nation's military involvement in the Vietnam War. Over the next few years, protests against the war and the draft steadily increased in intensity in cities and on college campuses across the country. Observers now portray the Free Speech Movement in Berkeley as a significant link in joining the civil rights and antiwar movements in the 1960s political left.

**THEMES AND STYLE**

The major theme of Savio's brief address is human freedom and solidarity in the face of oppressive systems of social control. In conveying this theme, Savio alludes obliquely to the ideas of Clark Kerr, president of the University of California system and the Free Speech Movement's most visible antagonist. Kerr's voice is another key influence, albeit a negative one, on Savio's thinking. In speeches and in his book *The Uses of the University* (1963), Kerr expressed his vision of the university (or, as he styled it, the "multiversity") as a kind of "knowledge factory," its functions geared to serve the needs of society and its institutions, including government, industry, and the military. To Savio and his activist comrades, this concept represented precisely what the Free Speech Movement was fighting against. Grounding his appeal for resistance in the movement's values of free speech, active citizenship,

and democratic forms of organization, he argued, "We have an autocracy which runs this university."

Savio's rhetoric dramatizes the students' grievances by portraying the university as a powerful but heartless force, compared metaphorically to a corporation, factory, and machine. If it be a corporation, with President Kerr as its manager, Savio contends that "the faculty are a bunch of employees and we're the raw material! But we're a bunch of raw materials that don't mean to have any process upon us, don't mean to be made into any product.... We're human beings!" The speech aims to stir its listeners to exercise their free will in defense of humane values threatened by the implacable logic of an unresponsive institution: rage against the machine.

The emotional timbre of Savio's speech ranges from mild, conversational notes to peaks of impassioned fury. Savio was known among his fellow students for his distinctive style of public speaking. Those who knew him well were also aware that since childhood he had struggled to overcome a stammer. This effort may partially account for the sense of coiled tension in his lean body and his riveting voice. Despite the intensity and determination in his message, he sprinkles in several moments of lighthearted humor, as when he announces that the demonstrators intend to "conduct our lives for awhile in the second floor of Sproul Hall." They also plan to show movies and hold classes on civil liberties during the sit-in. Savio concludes his speech abruptly by introducing "one last person": the well-known folksinger Joan Baez.

**CRITICAL DISCUSSION**

The direct action that followed Savio's speech, the occupation of Sproul Hall, led to what was then one of the largest mass arrests in U.S. history, a police action ordered by California's governor, Edmund "Pat" Brown. The demonstration brought the campus crisis to a head. Classes were cancelled for days amid a student strike. On December 7, with the conflict roiling in the national press, President Kerr addressed a special meeting at the Greek amphitheater on campus, announcing that regulations on student political advocacy would be relaxed. However, when Savio, who had not been invited to address the meeting, approached the stage, campus police seized and ejected him before he could speak. This show of force enraged the campus community, especially the Berkeley faculty. The next day, the university's Academic Senate voted overwhelmingly to accept the students' demands for the rights to speak and organize on campus.

Despite its victory, though, critical appraisal remained divided about the Free Speech Movement's lasting legacy. Outside campus, opinion polls showed a majority of Californians disapproved of the Berkeley students. Ronald Reagan, in his successful 1966 gubernatorial run in California, capitalized on the backlash against the student dissidents by famously promising to "clean up the mess at Berkeley." Savio's speech, in particular, is widely regarded as one of the oratorical highlights of the 1960s, but as with so many of that decade's events, an ideological fault line runs through critical perspectives on Savio and the demonstrations he helped organize. Defenders of the Free Speech Movement, including many former participants, argue that it achieved its primary objectives, provided a model adopted almost immediately by student activists nationwide, and helped steer the nation's political agenda in a progressive direction. Conservative critics such as Roger Kimball, on the other hand, lament the success of the Berkeley students and the ensuing wave of radical youth-led tumult and "liberal capitulation" to the countercultural left.

Many prominent sociologists, including Nathan Glazer, Goodman, Seymour Martin Lipset, and Sheldon Wolin, debated the Berkeley uprising during the 1960s. A renewal of scholarly interest followed Savio's death in 1996. Robert Cohen and Reginald E. Zelnik edited a volume of essays in 2002 about the Free Speech Movement and its legacy. Cohen followed with the first full biography of Savio, *Freedom's Orator,* in 2009. In the 2012 book *Subversives,* journalist Seth Rosenfeld reveals previously classified material detailing the secret relationships among the Federal Bureau of Investigation and Savio, Kerr, and Reagan. Savio's Sproul Hall speech is also noted as among the first potent critiques of university structures, prefiguring a later strain of debate regarding corporate and military influences on academic life. Several recent academic articles concerning the politics of university life employ Savio's words as a touchstone.

## BIBLIOGRAPHY

### Sources

Cohen, Robert, and Reginald E. Zelnik, eds. *The Free Speech Movement: Reflections on Berkeley in the 1960s.* Berkeley: U of California P, 2002.

Kerr, Clark. *The Uses of the University.* Cambridge: Harvard UP, 1963. Print.

Kimball, Roger. "The Liberal Capitulation." *New Criterion* 16 Jan. 1998: 4. *General OneFile.* Web. 2 Sept. 2012.

Rosenfeld, Seth. *Subversives: The FBI's War on Student Radicals and Reagan's Rise to Power.* New York: Farrar, 2012. Print.

Savio, Mario. "Sit-in Address on the Steps of Sproul Hall." *American Rhetoric Top 100 Speeches.* American Rhetoric, n.d. Web. 2 Sept. 2012. Transcript.

### Further Reading

Cohen, Robert. *Freedom's Orator: Mario Savio and the Radical Legacy of the 1960s.* Oxford: Oxford UP, 2009. Print.

Glazer, Nathan. "'Student Power' in Berkeley." *The Public Interest* 13(1968): 3–21. Print.

Goines, David Lance. *The Free Speech Movement: Coming of Age in the 1960s.* Berkeley: Ten Speed, 1993. Print.

Goodman, Paul. "Berkeley in February." *Dissent* 12.2 (1965): 161–83. Print.

———. *Growing Up Absurd.* New York: Random House, 1960. Print.

Lipset, Seymour Martin, and Sheldon Wolin, eds. *The Berkeley Student Revolt: Facts and Interpretations.* New York: Doubleday, 1965. Print.

Rhoades, Gary, and Robert A. Rhoads. "Graduate Employee Unionization as Symbol of and Challenge to the Corporatization of U.S. Research Universities." *Journal of Higher Education* 76.3 (2005): 243+. *General OneFile.* Web. 2 Sept. 2012.

Saul, Scott. "A Body on the Gears." *The Nation* 29 March 2010. Web. 3 Sept. 2012.

Savio, Mario. "The University Has Become a Factory." *Life* 26 Feb. 1965: 100–01. *Free Speech Movement Archives.* Web. 3 Sept. 2012.

*Roger Smith*

A 2004 reenactment of a 1964 Free Speech Movement rally at the University of California, Berkeley. At the 1964 rally, activist Mario Savio questioned authorities with his "Throw Your Bodies upon the Gears" speech. © ZUMA WIRE SERVICE/ ALAMY.

# "TOTAL WAR" SPEECH

*Joseph Goebbels*

❖ *Key Facts*

**Time Period:**
Mid-20th Century

**Genre:**
Speech

**Events:**
World War II

**Nationality:**
German

## OVERVIEW

Delivered on February 18, 1943, as the Nazi regime was beginning to falter, Joseph Goebbels's speech at the Berlin Sportspalast was a call to the German people to maintain their faith and fight, even as Germany and its allies had suffered major losses at Stalingrad. Rousing in tone, with repeated reminders of the urgency of the situation, the "Total War" speech is a plea for help on the home front. Appealing to the people's nationalist pride in their strength of will and intelligence, Goebbels entreats them to commit fully to the cause, and to accept whatever privations may come, to ensure victory and stop the spread of eastern Bolshevism and "the terror of the Jews" across Europe.

Goebbels had spent the war years waging his own battle to solidify popular support for the war, and this became especially vital following the annihilation of the 6th Army at Stalingrad. His speech, which was staged before a carefully selected crowd of about fourteen thousand, was broadcast twice on national radio and subsequently published in its entirety in newspapers and widely distributed pamphlets. A portion of the speech was also shown in a newsreel on February 24 that preceded the featured film in every theater in Germany. The "Total War" speech was successful for a time, galvanizing citizens throughout the land. It also impressed Adolf Hitler himself, who had ceded his position as the public voice of the Nazi regime to Goebbels as the Reich declined. While some argue that Goebbels's speech prolonged the German war effort, decisive military defeats, food shortages, and increasingly dire living conditions inside the country resulted in the collapse of popular support for the war.

## HISTORICAL AND LITERARY CONTEXT

A steady stream of early victories by the Third Reich made the outcome of World War II a forgone conclusion in the eyes of much of the German public. Hitler's expansion had continued unchecked from his invasion of Poland in 1939 through most of 1941, by which time much of Europe was under Nazi control. In the summer of 1942, Germany launched a bid to capture Stalingrad. Heavy air strikes succeeded in reducing the city to rubble, but the protracted ground fighting, which lasted through the harsh winter of 1942–43, ended in German defeat. News

of this failure was announced to the German people on February 3, 1943, via a special broadcast on state radio, fifteen days before Goebbels's speech at the Sportspalast.

The "Total War" speech, which suggested that victory would only be possible with the people's willingness to engage in a complete mobilization of all human resources in Germany, introduced the possibility that the previously assumed decisive and imminent victory was in jeopardy. With the austerity measures put in place by the Führer after the surrender of forces at Stalingrad, it became doubly vital to maintain public support for the war.

Goebbels, like Hitler, had long been convinced of the importance of persuasion and the power of group sentiment in steering the nation. Indeed, public meetings with speeches as their center were a key part of political life under Hitler. Laying out his philosophy on this point in 1925's *Mein Kampf,* Hitler touted "the magic power of the spoken word, and that alone" in inaugurating all significant political events throughout history. Hitler spoke frequently from his earliest membership in the National Socialist German Workers Party. Further, developing a stable of reliable orators was a cornerstone of his efforts to maintain national unity. Goebbels, Herman Goring, and others made a number of popular speeches that lauded Hitler's vision and the Nazi worldview as an extension of uniquely German values, contributing to the overwhelming support for the government during this time. The Berlin Sportspalast, the largest such venue in the world at the time of its opening in 1910, was a favorite site for party speechmaking, its size a testament to German technical achievement.

Though the "Total War" speech heralded the beginning of the end for the Third Reich, it is generally placed among the most successful of the Nazi propaganda speeches. Following the speech, Goebbels wrote weekly editorials that were published in *Das Reich,* and he has been credited with maintaining morale in the nation as the war dragged to its conclusion. In July 1944 Goebbels was named general plenipotentiary for total war, a title that gave him considerable power to direct war efforts on the home front. With defeat near at hand, however, these efforts were largely for naught and generally considered a footnote to the 1943 speech.

## THEMES AND STYLE

Total war, according to Goebbels, demands the immediate and complete commitment of Germans on the home front in order to prevent "a total Bolshevization of the European continent." Developing his argument, Goebbels outlines three major theses about the necessity of the German effort: first, that without the Third Reich's intercession, Jewish Bolshevism will overtake Europe; second, that Germany and its allies have the strength to defeat the threat and save Europe; and, finally, that the effort must be made immediately or the war will be lost. After outlining these points, Goebbels speaks more specifically about duties citizens should be fulfilling—for instance, women working in factories so that men are freed to fight.

Goebbels's speech draws much of its force from an appeal to the character of the German people and from the enthusiastic response of the crowd, which seems to confirm that consensus has been reached. He therefore is merely expressing the will of the people. Goebbels opens the speech with "my German people's comrades," thereafter making repeated reference to "German people." His plea culminates in a sort of call and response, in which he poses a series of ten rhetorical questions, claiming to represent British statements about Germany, and then makes a response in the name of the people. Having asked and asserted that "you have given me your answers," Goebbels exhorts the crowd to show with actions the sentiments "they" have just put into words.

In the Sportspalast speech, Goebbels delivers his message using an apocalyptic tone to create a sense of the potential for utter destruction of Germany and German values if the people are unwilling to commit to total war immediately. Further, by revealing that Germany is in critical straits, he affects a confessional posture that emphasizes his own position as a truth-teller and realist. Early on Goebbels announces his intention to speak "from the depths of my heart to the depths of yours ... with holy seriousness and openness." He goes on to praise the abilities of the German people to handle an "unvarnished picture of the situation" before revealing that the German army is in danger. Once the revelation has been introduced, Goebbels repeatedly hammers the theme of urgency, referring to the danger as "acute," "immediate," "life-threatening," and the like. Additionally, he makes multiple references to the present moment, underlining the need for immediate acceptance of all of his demands. The famous closing line of "Total War": "People rise up and storm, break loose," is both a dismissal and a rallying cry for the work at hand.

## CRITICAL DISCUSSION

The "Total War" speech was initially popular among the German people as well as being much admired by Hitler himself, who called it a "psychological and propaganda masterpiece." Still, commentators have

# JOSEPH GOEBBELS

Joseph Goebbels was born October 29, 1897, in Rheydt, a small town in the Rhineland area of Germany. A sickly child, he contracted an infection that left him with a clubfoot, a handicap about which he was often reported to be self-conscious. Goebbels studied literature and philosophy at the University of Heidelberg, earning a PhD in 1921.

Goebbels joined the left wing of the Nazi Party in 1924, switching his affiliation to the more conservative anti-Semitic wing after meeting Adolf Hitler in 1926. Due to his close association with Hitler, Goebbels was named district leader of the party for Berlin in 1926 and chief of propaganda starting in 1930. Considered one of the most skillful propagandists of all time, Goebbels used his writing and speaking abilities to gain the coveted minister of propaganda and enlightenment position when the Nazis came to power in 1933. He is credited with constructing the mythology surrounding Hitler as well as being the first to use a full media assault (newspaper, radio, and movies) to disseminate the party's ideology.

Goebbels was the last of the high-ranking Nazi officials to stay with Hitler until the Führer's suicide on April 30, 1945. Goebbels succeeded Hitler as chancellor and held office for one day before he and his wife, Magda, arranged for their six children to be sedated with morphine and killed by cyanide poisoning, after which the couple committed suicide.

noted that it did not succeed in getting Hitler to commit to full mobilization of homeland reserves for the war effort as Goebbels had hoped. On the speech's style, Albert Speer, who was Hitler's war minister, expressed surprise that Goebbels was able to coolly articulate "what had seemed to be a purely emotional outburst" in terms of preconceived rhetorical strategies deployed to obtain specific psychological effects on the audience. Despite the speech's initial effectiveness, by the spring many Germans were skeptical. According to David Welch's *The Third Reich*, for example, many working-class Germans expressed cynicism about the sincerity of the "Total War" message, pointing out the different contributions expected among the classes, particularly in the case of middle-class women and working-class women employed outside the home for the first time. Middle-class women tended to get the lighter jobs in manufacturing, or they avoided the factory floor altogether, which was not the case for their working-class peers.

As one of the most prominent Nazi speeches made during World War II, the "Total War" speech is often used to illustrate propaganda techniques in action. It also marks a turning point in Nazi propaganda strategy. Welch proposes that the failure of the "new realism" of the "Total War" speech pushed Goebbels to stress "the orderly nature of Germany's new

Joseph Goebbels giving his "Total War" speech in the Berlin Sportspalast, 1943. © DIZ MUENCHEN GMBH, SUEDDEUTSCHE ZEITUNG PHOTO/ALAMY.

defensive war," allowing "the accumulating military defeats to be rationalized as 'strategic withdrawals.'" While diverging from the speech on this point, Welch notes Goebbels's continued use of the bogeys from the east—Bolsheviks and Jews—particularly as Goebbels renewed his effort to strengthen resolve through fear of national extermination. The propagandist claim that Jews, if left unchecked, would spread out to exterminate the people of ancient nations is a theme that has been taken up in recent scholarship, particularly as it relates to anti-Semitism in the contemporary world.

Most current research related to Nazi propaganda examines broad trends and their influence on contemporary fundamentalism rather than individual articles such as the "Total War" speech. Jeffrey Herf's *Nazi Propaganda for the Arab World* traces the uneasy alliances between Nazis and the Arab world, discussing the dissemination of Nazi propaganda through the Middle East during World War II. Herf also concludes that anti-Semitism in certain present-day manifestations of radical Islam was shaped in part by the "ideological diffusion" achieved by Nazi propaganda. Some interest also remains in Goebbels's diaries, especially as they shed light on the personal philosophy underpinning his use of propaganda.

**BIBLIOGRAPHY**

*Sources*

Bytwerk, Randall. *Landmark Speeches of National Socialism.* College Station: Texas A & M UP, 2008. Print.

Herf, Jeffrey. *Nazi Propaganda for the Arab World.* New Haven: Yale UP, 2009. Print.

Hitler, Adolf. *Mein Kampf.* Trans. Ralph Manheim. Boston: Houghton Mifflin, 1971. Print.

Welch, David. *The Third Reich: Politics and Propaganda.* London: Routledge, 2002. Print.

*Further Reading*

Bachrach, Susan, and Steven Luckert. *State of Deception: The Power of Nazi Propaganda.* New York: W. W. Norton, 2009. Print.

Bytwerk, Randall. *Bending Spines: The Propagandas of Nazi Germany and the German Democratic Republic.* East Lansing: Michigan State UP, 2004. Print.

Herf, Jeffrey. *The Jewish Enemy: Nazi Propaganda during World War II and the Holocaust.* Cambridge: Harvard UP, 2008. Print.

Manvell, Roger. *Doctor Goebbels: His Life and Death.* London: MBI, 2006. Print.

Read, Anthony. *The Devil's Disciples: Hitler's Inner Circle.* New York: W. W. Norton, 2003. Print.

*Daisy Gard*

# Education and Indoctrination

# THE BOARDING SCHOOL

*Or, Lessons of a Preceptress to Her Pupils*

*Hannah Webster Foster*

## OVERVIEW

Penned by American writer Hannah Webster Foster and published in 1798, *The Boarding School: Or, Lessons of a Preceptress to Her Pupils* is in part a lecture conducted by Mrs. Williams, the respectable widow of a clergyman, to a class of women departing her finishing school and in part a collection of letters exchanged by the women as they embark upon their lives in the outside world. In the novel—a direct descendant of the conduct books popular in the eighteenth century—Mrs. Williams instructs her pupils in academic pursuits considered proper for young middle-class women of the day and, more importantly, imparts a view of the ideal of womanhood to which they should aspire. This ideal is achieved through a gently cultivated intellect, whose critical powers are oriented toward home and family life.

Published during a transitional period in U.S. history, the novel maintains ties with colonial views of women as wives and mothers while embracing a post-Revolutionary War view of the importance of "finished" women who could effectively run a household and raise sons capable of participating fully in the civic life of the new country. Largely ignored by both critics and readers, *The Boarding School* has been reevaluated by contemporary scholars as a transitional work in U.S. literature, helping to span the gap between the dry, didactic texts that preceded it and the more fully realized novels that would come after.

## HISTORICAL AND LITERARY CONTEXT

Women in colonial America led lives centered on home and family, with domestic chores and child rearing considered their proper vocation. They were largely barred from political and economic life, and, with few educational opportunities afforded them, many achieved only minimal literacy. While women were involved in anti-British activities preceding the Revolutionary War, these were mostly in domestic capacities, such as spinning cloth to avoid purchasing British goods. The Revolutionary War saw women assume a broader range of roles, at least temporarily, but the U.S. Constitution and its rhetoric of the equality of persons brought little immediate improvement in the status of women as participants in public political life.

When *The Boarding School* was published, conceptions of the role of education in women's lives in the newly established republic had begun to shift. Increasingly, American women were encouraged to strive toward an ideal that historian Linda Kerber, in her book *Women of the Republic* (1980), terms "Republican Motherhood." It included the notion that women should be educated to be good stewards of the moral and, to an extent, the intellectual development of the sons and future citizens of the republic. To this end, many middle-class girls attended "dame schools," which were small private schools often located in the instructress's home. In addition, as literacy improved, moral instruction was presented through literature. Works such as those of Foster became an important means of transmitting ideas about the evolving place of women.

The eighteenth century saw the rising popularity of conduct books and, later, the seduction novel, both of which provided instruction about achieving ideals of womanhood, as well as avoiding the pitfalls that would lead to moral and social ruin. Books such as Scottish moralist John Gregory's *A Father's Legacy to His Daughters* (1761), representing the former, and English novelist Samuel Richardson's *Pamela* (1740), one of the latter, while originating in Great Britain, were also popular with American women. In her article "Wise and Foolish Virgins" (1990), Sarah Newton discusses *The Boarding School*, along with English-born author Susanna Rowson's *Mentoria, or the Young Lady's Friend* (1794). She describes these two works as "hybrids" of the conduct book and the novel, having "no plot within which a coherent story line develops, but an effective epistolary dramatic frame that ties lesson-giving letters and illustrative anecdotes into a more-or-less coherent whole."

Foster did not write another novel after *The Boarding School*, although she did contribute to the *Monthly Journal or Magazine of Polite Literature* and famously supported the careers of both of her daughters, who became authors in their own right. Foster's own name did not appear on her novels until 1866, twenty years after her death.

**✤ Key Facts**

**Time Period:**
Late 18th Century

**Genre:**
Novel

**Events:**
Aftermath of Revolutionary War; early years of American Republic; shifting conceptions of women's role in society

**Nationality:**
American

# PRIMARY SOURCE

## EXCERPT FROM *THE BOARDING SCHOOL; OR, LESSONS OF A PRECEPTRESS TO HER PUPILS*

Writing is productive both of pleasure and improvement. It is a source of entertainment which enlarges the mental powers more, perhaps, than any other. The mind is obliged to exertion for materials to supply the pen. Hence it collects new stores of knowledge, and is enriched by its own labors. It imperceptibly treasures up the ideas, which the hand impresses. An opportunity is furnished of reviewing our sentiments before they are exposed; and we have the privilege of correcting or expunging such as are erroneous. For this purpose you will find it a good method to collect and write your thoughts upon any subject that occurs; for by repeatedly arranging and revising your expression and opinions you may daily improve them, and learn to think and reason properly on every occasion. By this mean you may like-wise provide yourselves with a fund of matter for future use, which, without this assistance, the memory would not retain. It will be of great service to note down in your common-place book such particulars as you may judge worth remembering, with your own observations upon them. This will be a kind of amusement which will exercise your thinking powers at the time, and by recurring to it afterwards it may afford you many useful hints.

The frequent use of the pen is calculated to refine and enlarge your understandings. Have you any talent at composition? It will be increased by cultivation.

Neglect no opportunity, therefore, which your leisure affords, of delighting your friends, and accomplishing yourselves by the exercise of your genius in this way.

Thrice blessed are we, the happy daughters of this land of liberty, where the female mind is unshackled by the restraints of tyrannical custom, which in many other regions confines the exertions of genius to the usurped powers of lordly man! Here virtue, merit, and abilities are properly estimated under whatever form they appear. Here the widely extended fields of literature court attention and the American fair are invited to cull the flowers, and cultivate the expanding laurel.

But the species of writing, which is open to every capacity, and ornamental to every station, is the epistolary. This, between particular friends, is highly agreeable and interesting. It is a method of

## THEMES AND STYLE

The central theme in *The Boarding School* is the importance to society of stable family life, a life that is founded on the correct behavior of women. Correct behavior for Foster is based on a sound education that instills in girls "such principals of piety, morality, benevolence, prudence and economy, as might be useful through life." The novel opens with Mrs. Williams, the owner and instructor of Harmony Grove, delivering a parting address, which summarizes the principles she has sought to inculcate in the seven young ladies of her class. The remainder of the book consists of a series of letters between Mrs. Williams and her former pupils in which they share news of life after Harmony Grove.

Rather than present basic life instruction to her readers, Foster dresses up her lessons with rudimentary characters and small stories within the larger narrative, contrasting virtuous behavior with its opposite and illustrating the consequences of each for various women. Comparing the stories of two women of similar background who have fallen on hard times, Mrs. Williams points out that the home of Clara, who had wisely learned needlework and practiced it even though she had no need, "was characterized by neatness, cheerfulness and activity," while "negligence, peevishness and sloth" marked Belinda's home. In her lecture, Mrs. Williams touches on a multitude of topics ranging from intellectual pursuits and the importance of avoiding frivolous use of one's talents to the proper conduct with family, friends, and especially suitors. When contemplating marriage prospects, she urges "a rational and discreet plan of thinking and acting," which includes making choices based on good character rather than on appearance, wealth, or gallantry.

*The Boarding School* is characterized by its pedantic tone, which is tempered by the intimations of affection and friendship between teacher and students and among the former students as they write to each other after graduation. Mrs. Williams addresses her students with the authority of their teacher as well as of a woman who has lived by the guidelines she purveys, resulting in a happy and comfortable life for herself and her children. Foster makes clear that Mrs. Williams's attitude toward her students is one of kind regard, thus aligning the preceptress's benign intentions with Foster's own, which she introduces in her preface, dedicating the book "to the young ladies of America, to whom these sheets are affectionately inscribed."

interchanging sentiments, and of enjoying inter-course with those from whom you are far removed, which is a happy substitute for personal conversation. In a correspondence of this sort, all affectation, for-mality, and bombast should be laid aside.

Ease, frankness, simplicity, and sincerity should be its leading traits. Let not your letters he composed of mere sounding terms, and verbose egotism; but intermix sentiment with expression, in such a man-ner as may be improving as well as pleasing. Letters of friendship should conduce no less to the advan-tage than entertainment of the person addressed; and mere cursory letters, of general acquaintance, must, at least, be written with propriety and accu-racy. The formation of the characters, the spelling, the punctuation, as well as the style and sense, must be attended to.

Never omit noticing the receipt of letters, unless you mean to affront the writers. Not to answer a letter, without being able to assign some special reason for the neglect is equally unpardonable as to keep silence when conversation is addressed to you in person.

By habituating yourself to writing, what may at first, appear a task, will become extremely pleas-ant. Refuse not, then, to improve this part of your education, especially by your frequent and dutifully affectionate epistles to your parents, when absent from them. Express your gratitude for their care, and convince them it has not been lost upon you.

Always employ your pens upon something use-ful and refined. Let no light or loose compositions occupy your time and thoughts; but remember that what you utter in this way is in some measure the picture of your hearts. Virtue forbid, that this favorite employment should be disgraced by impurity, indeli-cacy, or the communication of vicious and ignoble sentiments!

One of the sages of antiquity being asked why he was so long in writing his opinion, replied, "I am writing for futurity. "

Your characters during life and even when you shall sleep in the dust, may rest on the efforts of your pens. Beware then how you employ them. Let not the merit of your attainments in this noble art be degraded by improper subjects for its exercise. Suffer not the expectation of secrecy to induce you to indulge your pens upon subjects, which you would blush to have exposed. In this way your characters may be injured, and your happiness destroyed.

## CRITICAL DISCUSSION

*The Boarding School* failed to achieve the critical and popular success of its predecessor, *The Coquette; or, The History of Eliza Wharton* (1797), and received little attention. A review appearing in the *American Review and Literary Journal* (1801) described the novel as unoriginal, lacking even as a model for good letter writing skills, and the critic's prediction that the book could only harm booksellers proved true. After disappointing sales, *The Boarding School* fell into obscurity.

Foster's novels, particularly *The Boarding School*, marked a transition from conduct books, which scholar Newton describes as "a rich source of cultural data," to the early American novel and its portrait of ideal womanhood. Newton calls *The Boarding School* a "hybrid" between the conduct book and the novel, a bridge by which the ideal Republican Mother crossed into American fiction and, by extension, into the consciousness of the U.S. public. Contemporary scholars differ in their views concerning the extent to which Foster's novels critique versus uphold late-eighteenth-century views of women. Commentators agree, however, that the book, recently back in print, provides insight into the daily lives and concerns of American women in the shifting social landscape of post-Revolutionary War America.

*The Boarding School*, along with *The Coquette*, has been of particular interest to feminist scholars. In her article "Sisterhood in a Separate Sphere: Female Friendship in Hannah Webster Foster's *The Coquette* and *The Boarding School*" (1992), Claire Pettengill explores the social function of female friendship in Foster's two novels. Analyzing the epistolary portion of the novel, Pettengill points out how the women use their newfound critical skills to reinforce virtuous behavior, criticizing the frivolity they see in new acquaintances and shap-ing social anecdotes into cautionary tales about women who have gone astray. *The Boarding School*'s portrayal of the importance of friendship, in her view, reinforces the value of female friends, who provided "practical advice for survival in a world marked into separate spheres." Exploring the degree to which *The Boarding School* reflects "the conven-tional bourgeois sexual politics" of the day, scholar W. M. Verhoeven concludes in "American Women Prose Writers to 1820" (1999) that while Foster's

A German illustration from 1886 depicting students at a girls' boarding school. © INTERFOTO/ALAMY.

novel is hardly "the radically subversive novel some have claimed," it does reflect "many of the enlightened and emancipatory views of female education" that were exemplified in texts such as English writer Mary Wollstonecraft's seminal *A Vindication of the Rights of Woman* (1792).

## BIBLIOGRAPHY

### Sources

Foster, Hannah Webster. *The Boarding School.* Boston: Peaslee, 1798. *Google Books.* Web. 4 Oct. 2012.

Newton, Sarah Emily. "Wise and Foolish Virgins: 'Usable Fiction' and the Early American Conduct Tradition." *Early American Literature* 25.2 (1990): 139–67. Print.

Pettengill, Claire C. "Sisterhood in a Separate Sphere: Female Friendship in Hannah Webster Foster's *The Coquette* and *The Boarding School.*" *Early American Literature* 27.3 (1992): 185–203. Rpt. in *Nineteenth-Century Literature Criticism.* Ed. Thomas J. Schoenberg. Vol. 99. Detroit: Gale Group, 2001. *Literature Resource Center.* Web. 2 Oct. 2012.

Verhoeven, W. M. "American Women Prose Writers to 1820." *Dictionary of Literary Biography Vol. 200.* Ed. Carla Mulford, Angela Vietto, and Amy E. Winans. Detroit: Gale Research, 1999. 122–31. Print.

### Further Reading

Armstrong, Nancy, and Leonard Tennenhouse. "The Literature of Conduct, the Conduct of Literature, and the Politics of Desire." *The Ideology of Conduct: Essays in Literature and the History of Sexuality.* Ed. Nancy Armstrong and Leonard Tennenhouse. New York: Methuen, 1987. Print.

Berkin, Carol. *Revolutionary Mothers: Women in the Struggle for America's Independence.* New York: Random, 2005. Print.

Kerber, Linda. *Women of the Republic: Intellect and Ideology in Revolutionary America.* Chapel Hill: U of North Carolina P, 1980. Print.

McMahon, Lucia. *Mere Equals: The Paradox of Educated Women in the Early American Republic.* Ithaca, NY: Cornell UP, 2012. Print.

Richards, Jeffrey H. "The Politics of Seduction: Theater, Sexuality, and National Virtue in the Novels of Hannah Foster." *Essays in Performance and History.* Ed. Della Pollock. U of North Carolina P, 1998. 238–57. Rpt. in *Nineteenth-Century Literature Criticism.* Ed. Thomas J. Schoenberg. Vol. 99. Detroit: Gale Group, 2001. *Literature Resource Center.* Web. 4 Oct. 2012.

Schweitzer, Ivy. *Perfecting Friendship: Politics and Affiliation in Early American Literature.* Chapel Hill: U of North Carolina P, 2006. Print.

Zagarri, Rosemarie. "Morals, Manners, and the Republican Mother." *American Quarterly* 44.2 (1992): 192–215. Print.

*Daisy Gard*

# CHARLOTTE TEMPLE

*Susanna Haswell Rowson*

## OVERVIEW

Written by Susanna Haswell Rowson and first published in 1791, *Charlotte Temple* is a novel about a young English girl seduced by a soldier who takes her to America and abandons her; she dies shortly after bearing their child. While the book was moderately successful in England, where it was first published as *Charlotte: A Tale of Truth,* it became America's first best seller because it appealed to a wide audience, from the well-to-do to blue-collar workers. The story serves as a cautionary warning for young girls and their parents about the dangers of seduction. "Oh my dear girls—for to such only am I writing," states the narrator, "listen not to the voice of love, unless sanctioned by paternal approbation." While young girls and their families are its primary audience, the novel also aims to teach men important lessons. Because the character of John Montraville, the seducing soldier, shows remorse and is somewhat redeemed at the end, the story can also be considered a caveat to men about giving in to desire against their better natures.

*Charlotte Temple* was reprinted more than 160 times and translated into nine different languages. Rowson asserted that her novel was based on a true story, and the public believed her. A grave in a New York churchyard thought to be Charlotte Temple's was a frequently visited site well into the 1800s. Even into the twentieth century, copies of *Charlotte Temple* continued to sell well, making it one of the most enduring books in U.S. literary history.

## HISTORICAL AND LITERARY CONTEXT

While a work of fiction, *Charlotte Temple* reflects the realities of colonial American life. Late eighteenth-century America experienced a sharp rise in premarital pregnancy, and one-third of the weddings in New England alone involved a pregnant bride. While in some ways the tale of Charlotte, a girl abandoned by the man who seduced her, is contrary to the trends occurring in the colonies at the time, it does reflect some of the sexual predation that existed, especially during the Revolution, when rape was a common occurrence.

*Charlotte Temple* was published less than a decade after the end of the American Revolution, and much of its initial popularity was due to the way it reflects the experiences of the newly independent country.

Although victorious, the new government struggled to gain widespread support and create stability. Many citizens were anxious and fearful of a return to chaos. Charlotte herself is an immigrant, albeit a reluctant one, but her own extreme homesickness and nostalgic yearning for a stable past reflect what many Americans of the time were experiencing. One result of these fears was a new emphasis on female virtue: the ideal woman was virtuous and pure, a mother to the new country.

*Charlotte Temple* is firmly within the tradition of the sentimental novel, a genre inaugurated by Samuel Richardson's *Pamela: Or, Virtue Rewarded* (1740) and followed by many other popular works, including Henry Mackenzie's *The Man of Feeling* (1771) and Hannah Webster Foster's *The Coquette* (1797). Because it serves as a cautionary tale, *Charlotte Temple* also has a place within the tradition of conduct books, texts that offer advice to young women on education, marriage, and sexual conduct, such as Mary Wollstonecraft's *Thoughts on the Education of Daughters, with Reflections on Female Conduct in the More Important Duties of Life* (1787).

One of *Charlotte Temple's* most enduring effects was its role in popularizing sentimental novels in the United States and making the genre a primarily female one. By the early nineteenth century, writers such as Susan Warner, Sarah J. Hale, Augusta Evans, and Elizabeth Stuart Phelps dominated the genre. Their books, focusing on the trials of young, innocent girls, were often known as domestic or conduct novels. Yet *Charlotte Temple* has a serious social message about female protection, and Marion Rust argues in a 2003 article in *William and Mary Quarterly* that it can be seen as "causing the aesthetic to be re-conceived in implicitly political terms," a tradition that culminated in Harriet Beecher Stowe's *Uncle Tom's Cabin* (1852), an antislavery sentimental novel.

## THEMES AND STYLE

The central theme of *Charlotte Temple* is the need for young women to protect themselves against their own passion as well as the machinations of unscrupulous men and women. While Montraville seduces Charlotte, it is Madame LaRue, a teacher at Charlotte's school, who arranges for his meetings with her and later, in America, gives Charlotte a bad name. Indeed, Charlotte places the majority of blame on LaRue:

✥ *Key Facts*

**Time Period:**
Late 18th Century

**Genre:**
Novel

**Events:**
Early years of American Republic; sharp rise in premarital pregnancy

**Nationality:**
American

# ROWSON'S MANY CAREERS

Susanna Haswell Rowson was born in 1762 in Portsmouth, England. Her mother died in childbirth, and several years later her father immigrated to the United States, leaving Susanna in the care of relatives. Soon she joined her father and his new wife, and they lived happily and in financial comfort until the Revolutionary War, when, as Loyalists, they were stripped of their property. Susanna's father and stepmother sank into depression at their change of fortune, and fifteen-year-old Susanna assumed a primary role in caring for her parents and two stepbrothers.

In 1778 Susanna and her family were repatriated to England, where she began to write to support her still impoverished family; her first novel, *Victoria,* appeared in 1786. That same year she married William Rowson, a hardware merchant, actor, and trumpeter in the Royal Horse guards. William, however, proved to be inefficient at all of his careers, so Susanna continued to write to support them. In 1792 they joined an acting troupe and moved to Philadelphia at the request of a theater promoter there. In 1797 she decided to open a school for girls, and it became one of the most respected schools in the United States. She also wrote numerous textbooks, novels, plays, patriotic songs, and articles. Susanna died in Boston in 1824.

> That I loved my seducer is but too true! yet powerful as that passion is when operating in a young heart glowing with sensibility, it never would have conquered my affection to you, my beloved parents, had I not been encouraged, nay, urged to take the fatally imprudent step, by one of my own sex, who, under the mask of friendship, drew me on to ruin.

Secondary themes are forgiveness, redemption, and the need for parents to protect and educate their daughters so that they do not fall for "those monsters of seduction." Charlotte's parents forgive her (her father reaches New York just in time to tearfully reunite with her before she dies), and Montraville sees the error of his ways and repents. Years after Charlotte's death, her parents even provide shelter for LaRue.

Perhaps the most remarkable rhetorical feature of *Charlotte Temple* is its narrative form. Most sentimental novels of the time are structured as a series of letters between characters, a form that soon fell out of favor in U.S. novels. The narrative form allows for moments of intrusion by the narrator, who speaks directly to the reader. Such moments generally instruct the reader how to feel and what to think about the events of the story. Halfway through *Charlotte Temple,* when begging sympathy for Charlotte, the narrator implores, "My dear Madam, contract not your brow into a frown of disapprobation. I mean not to extenuate the faults of those unhappy women who fall victims to

guilt and folly; but surely when we reflect how many errors we are ourselves subject to … we surely may pity the faults of others."

*Charlotte Temple* also employs Christian images and themes to develop the story. Charlotte, for example, is similar to the biblical Eve, lured from her Garden of Eden home by the snakelike LaRue; later she undergoes the pangs of childbirth, as does Eve. More broadly, Rowson presents the novel as one intended to instill good values: "If the following tale should save one hapless fair one from the errors which ruined poor Charlotte," she writes, "I shall feel a much higher gratification in reflecting on this trifling performance, than could possibly result from the applause which might attend the most elegant finished piece of literature whose tendency might deprave the heart or mislead the understanding."

## CRITICAL DISCUSSION

*Charlotte Temple*'s popularity was immediate and long lasting. It can perhaps be best demonstrated by the immense popularity of the "grave" of Charlotte Temple in New York. According to literary scholar Cathy N. Davidson in the introduction to a 1986 reprint of *Charlotte Temple,* a gentlemen wrote the following in 1903 in a letter to the *Evening Post*: "In that churchyard are graves of heroes, philosophers, and martyrs…. Their graves, tho marked by imposing monuments, win but a glance of curiosity, while the turf over Charlotte Temple is kept fresh by falling tears." While the majority of critics praised the novel for its morality, good example, and affecting story, an erotic industry arose around the tale, from sensational pictures and retold story lines to a newspaper insert declaring Charlotte to be "The Fastest Girl in New York." Because of this, a 1905 introduction to the book suggests, many who had heard of but not read the book might have had a false or misleading impression of Charlotte's true character.

The popular and critical response to *Charlotte Temple* waned during the twentieth century, when the book was frequently perceived as unsophisticated and overly sentimental. In his 1912 book, *The American Novel,* Carl Van Doren proclaims Rowson's readers to be "housemaids and shopgirls" who were attracted by the author's use of "every device known to the romancer." Critics focused either on the novel's message or on the importance of its narrative form. Davidson sums up the theme as "the fatal consequence of … illicit sexuality."

In the late twentieth century, critics continued to focus on these issues but complicated their implications. Julia Sterne, in a 1993 article for *Arizona Quarterly,* for example, sees the narrator of *Charlotte Temple* as an "emblem of matriarchal power … [whose] symbolic power is felt through the all-pervasive presence of her voice." On the other hand, Blythe Forcey, writing for *American Literature* in 1991, argues that "without the protective boundaries established by a controlling narrative pressure, the epistolary novel leaves the female protagonist exposed, vulnerable, and even invisible." In terms of the novel's treatment of sexuality, Rust argues that "*Charlotte Temple*, despite appearances to the contrary and decades of critical assumption, is not really a novel of seduction, in the sense of being a document that provides sexual titillation under cover of pedagogic censure. Instead, far from depicting Charlotte's overweening desire, the novel portrays the fatal consequences of a woman's inability to want anything enough to motivate decisive action."

Illustration from *Charlotte Temple*, by Susanna Haswell Rowson. © LEBRECHT MUSIC AND ARTS PHOTO LIBRARY/ALAMY.

## BIBLIOGRAPHY

### Sources

Davidson, Cathy N. Introduction. *Charlotte Temple*, by Susanna Haswell Rowson. Ed. Davidson. New York: Oxford UP, 1986: xi–xxxiii. Print.

Forcey, Blythe. "Charlotte Temple and the End of Epistolarity." *American Literature* 63.2 (1991) 225–41. *JSTOR*. Web. 10 Sept. 2012.

Rowson, Susanna Haswell. *Charlotte Temple*. Ed. Cathy N. Davidson. New York: Oxford UP, 1986. Print.

Rust, Marion. "What's Wrong with Charlotte Temple?" *William and Mary Quarterly* 60.1 (2003): 99–118. *JSTOR*. Web. 10 Sept. 2012.

Sterne, Julia. "Working through the Frame: *Charlotte Temple* and the Poetics of Maternal Melancholia." *Arizona Quarterly* 49.4 (1993):1–32. Print.

Van Doren, Carl. *The American Novel*. New York: Macmillan, 1912. Print.

### Further Reading

Anderson, Jill E. "Tomes of Travel and Travesty: The Didactic of Captivity in Susanna Rowson's *Charlotte Temple* and Mary Rowlandson's *The Sovereignty and Goodness of God*." *Women's Studies* 38.4 (2009): 429–48. *MLA International Bibliography*. Web. 10 Sept. 2012.

Baker, Anne. "Tempestuous Passages: Storms, Revolution, and the Status of Women in Rowson's Fiction." *Studies in American Fiction* 38.1–2 (2011): 205–21. *MLA International Bibliography*. Web. 10 Sept. 2012.

Barnes, Elizabeth. *States of Sympathy: Seduction and Democracy in the American Novel*. New York: Columbia UP, 1997. Print.

Barton, Paul. "Narrative Intrusion in *Charlotte Temple*: A Closet Feminist's Strategy in an American Novel." *Women & Language* 23.1 (2000): 26. *Communication & Mass Media Complete*. Web. 10 Sept. 2012.

Davidson, Cathy N. *Revolution and the Word: The Rise of the Novel in America*. Expanded ed. Oxford: Oxford UP, 2004. Print.

Jarenski, Shelly. "The Voice of the Preceptress: Female Education in and as the Seduction Novel." *Journal of the Midwest Modern Language Association* 37.1 (2004): 59–68. *JSTOR*. Web. 10 Sept. 2012.

Rourke, Constance. *The Roots of American Culture and Other Essays*. New York: Harcourt, Brace, 1942. Print.

Ryals, Kay Ferguson. "America, Romance, and the Fate of the Wandering Woman: The Case of *Charlotte Temple*." *Women, America, and Movement: Narratives of Relocation*. Ed. Susan L. Roberson. Columbia: U of Missouri P, 1998. 81–105. Print.

Tuthill, Maureen. "A Medical Examination of Charlotte Temple: Critiquing the Female Healing Community in Susanna Rowson's America." *Legacy* 28.1 (2011): 69–89. *MLA International Bibliography*. Web. 10 Sept. 2012.

Weil, Dorothy. *In Defense of Women: Susanna Rowson, 1762–1824*. University Park: Pennsylvania State UP, 1976. Print.

*Abigail Mann*

# HOW TO WIN
## A Book for Girls
*Frances E. Willard*

⁜ *Key Facts*

**Time Period:**
Late 19th Century

**Genre:**
Pamphlet

**Events:**
Founding of Woman's
Christian Temperance
Union; women's
suffrage movement

**Nationality:**
American

## OVERVIEW

Frances E. Willard's 1886 pamphlet *How to Win: A Book for Girls* urges its audience of young women to use their God-given talents on behalf of the women's rights, women's suffrage, and temperance movements. In a combination of first- and second-person narration, Willard speaks directly to her readers, encouraging them to see themselves as agents of social change. Across the pamphlet's fourteen chapters, Willard argues explicitly that young women's participation in public life in the form of philanthropic, artistic, and journalistic enterprises, alongside their participation in devout Christian home life, will help them to best share their gifts. That this call also urges girls to participate in the Woman's Christian Temperance Union (WCTU), of which Willard was president at the time, solidifies *How to Win* as a propagandist text.

By the mid-1880s women's participation in political circles was gaining traction, and many of their efforts were realized through volunteerism. Because women did not have the right to vote, participation in women's organizations allowed them to share their ideas and agitate for change. *How to Win* is a culmination of many of Willard's efforts as an advocate for women's suffrage and a leader in the temperance movement, and its direct calls to its readers are presented in a logical style; Willard was a frequent orator and journalist. In their book *Let Something Good Be Said: Speeches and Writings of Frances E. Willard* (2007), Carolyn De Swarte Gifford and Amy R. Slagell share that "in 1878, during her brief tenure as editor of the *Chicago Post*, [Willard] wrote a series titled 'Talks for Girls' and published them in the pages of the newspaper. These early speeches and writings laid the groundwork for the more fully developed argument in the 125 pages of *How to Win*."

## HISTORICAL AND LITERARY CONTEXT

The postbellum period in America was one of great social change for women. The Civil War had so decimated the male population that many women found it difficult to find suitors in the ensuing decades. The period also saw the 1870 ratification of the Fifteenth Amendment, which gave African American men the right to vote. This cultural environment helped motivate women to work toward one of the as-yet-unrealized goals of the 1848 Seneca Falls Convention: women's equality. In 1874 the Woman's Christian Temperance Union was founded in Cleveland, Ohio, and Willard was named secretary.

By 1886 Willard had been president of the WCTU for seven years and had traveled widely, lecturing on behalf of the organization. During this time Willard shared with those she met the platform she named "home protection," which she describes in her *Home Protection Manual* (1879) as "the general name given to a movement already endorsed by the W. C. T. Unions of eight states, the object of which is to secure for all women above the age of twenty-one years the ballot as one means for the protection of their homes from the devastation caused by the legalized traffic in strong drink." The home protection ideal is extended in *How to Win* as Willard boosts her readers' resolve for self-betterment within the public sphere and the home simultaneously. In fact, in *How to Win,* Willard shares, "If I were asked the mission of the ideal woman, I would reply: IT IS TO MAKE THE WHOLE WORLD HOMELIKE."

Though much longer than a typical pamphlet, as a guidebook *How to Win*'s structure and focus are in keeping not only with typical WCTU publications but also with other traditional propagandist methods for disseminating information and seeking support. In the tradition of Thomas Paine's *Common Sense* (1776), David Walker's *Appeal* (1826), Angelina Grimké's *Appeal to the Christian Women of the South* (1836), and Frederick Douglass's "Fourth of July" speech (1852), the pamphlet has a storied place in American thinking and political activism. Willard's *Home Protection Manual* is itself a thirty-four-page pamphlet. This genre is one with which Willard was familiar, and while *How to Win* has a greater depth and breadth than the average pamphlet, it is still participating in the genre's conventions.

While itself not the focus of much critical study, *How to Win* proves an awareness of the world from which it springs alongside its direct call to readers to rise above their circumstances. Willard writes, "In this century, when the wage of battle has cost our land an army of her sons, when widows mourn, and unwedded thousands are forced to meet the hard-faced world (from which rose-water theorists would shield them), America is coming to the rescue of her daughters!"

Willard proved to be an encouraging reformer—the WCTU's membership increased by more than 100,000 members during her tenure as president.

## THEMES AND STYLE

Central to *How to Win* is its style of engagement with its readers, an engagement that Willard often presents as a meta-narrative. Throughout the text she muses about her own desires and experiences—including her desire to write *How to Win* and the experience of actually writing it—in order to exemplify the ways that public and home life can be the impetus for women's empowerment. As a main objective, though, she presents the WCTU as the ideal means for women to realize their empowerment. As Willard positions herself as her own example of the ideal activist, she often shares personal stories of her childhood and her education, thereby encouraging her readers to examine their own lives and to seek knowledge and religion. She tells readers, "I might enumerate the societies for Home and Foreign Missions, Indian Reform, Associated Charities, and many other attractive lines of work, but my present object is to win your attention to the Woman's Christian Temperance Union as the most promising field of labor and reward that can be named for women, young or middle-aged or old." This pairing of first- and second-person narration allows Willard to promote the WCTU while still connecting personally with her readers.

Willard's sentence structures also help her to connect with readers, both explicitly and implicitly. Her use of imperative sentences, such as "Cultivate, then, your specialty, because the independence thus involved will lift you above the world's pity to the level of its respect, perchance its honor," helps promote the didactic goals of the text. She also poses questions throughout the text and then answers them in order to encourage her readers to engage in a carefully directed self-searching that will lead them to follow Willard's own model. These direct engagements make clear Willard's ultimate goal: to re-create a generation of young women in her own image by drawing them into the fold.

*How to Win* is also rife with intertextual references to literary, historical, biblical, and mythological figures, which reinforce the kind of professionalism that Willard hoped to foster in her own readers. Citing figures ranging from and including Charlotte Brontë, Margaret Fuller, Ruth, and Diana, she pulls from a variety of female experiences to proffer an image of ideal womanhood. While Willard offers her readers sympathy, acknowledging that "sometimes we wait until a friend's hand leads us up before the mirror of our potential self," she positions herself as the "friend's hand," teaching her readers all they need to know in order to make themselves the winners hinted at in the title.

## CRITICAL DISCUSSION

Tracing Willard's own thoughts regarding *How to Win* is difficult because the once-avid diarist did not maintain a personal journal between 1870 and 1893.

## WELLS AND WILLARD

Frances E. Willard's activism was not without controversy, especially toward the end of the nineteenth century, when Ida B. Wells rose to prominence as an antilynching activist. Willard and Wells clashed over the WCTU's philosophies about African American men's proclivities for alcohol, a clash that came to a head in the 1890s after Willard granted an interview to the temperance publication the *Voice* in which she reinforced the dangerous black male rapist/white female victim stereotype. The piety inherent in the WCTU and in Willard's own writing presupposed the chastity of white middle-class women, thereby marking them as easily victimized by drunken men. Relying on conjecture about African American men's desire for drink, Willard fused them with the other men she deemed menacing to the women she sought to help.

Wells battled Willard until Willard's death in 1898, gaining support from British activists she had swayed during her antilynching tours starting in 1893. This conflict is all the more interesting since Willard wanted for white women what African American men had been granted—the vote—while Wells wanted for all African Americans what white women could often rely on: protection and safety.

Newspaper articles at the time mentioned her various stops on the lecture circuit, but there is virtually no mention of *How to Win* in the popular press or critical literature of the late nineteenth century. The book possibly was eclipsed by Willard's *Woman in the Pulpit* (1888). Ruth Bordin argues, "From the point of view of scholarship, *Woman in the Pulpit* shows considerable mastery of church history and Biblical texts; it was Willard's most ambitious work." After Willard's sudden death in 1898, her personal secretary and companion of twenty-one years, Anna Adams Gordon, published *The Beautiful Life of Frances E. Willard: A Memorial Volume*, a biographical celebration of Willard's long and fruitful career containing remembrances and letters from friends and from Gordon herself.

Broadly speaking, *How to Win*'s impact is in the way it connects Willard's political, social, and personal philosophies with a reader and her own home. No radical feminist, Willard saw women's homes as an important space for social change, especially as women relate to men. Interestingly, she also included men's issues in her call to her readers, noting that "the Ideal of Womanhood, as it exists in the minds of the grandest-natured men, is changing rapidly … the ideal of man is changing—as it must—to keep pace with its blessed correlate." Her thoughts about egalitarian relationships, about the moniker "widower" being adopted as a marker of a man's relationship to his wife, and even about the fallacies of marriage ceremonies that pronounce partners "man and wife" show prescience about the impact her goals could have on both men and women.

Susan B. Anthony (center), Frances Willard (second from right), and other members of the International Council of Women. © CORBIS.

A focus on the home and on traditional gender roles marks *How to Win* as safe reading for Willard's "girls." Speaking generally of Willard's writing, Bonnie J. Dow argues in her 1991 essay for *Southern Communication Journal* that Willard's language and scope "enabled her to reconcile the liberationist goals of woman suffrage with the traditional motivations of conservative audiences. Willard's ideas were always couched in terminology that appealed to the traditional, middle-class values of her audience." Though barely addressed in critical circles, *How to Win* still exemplifies the careful craft of an activist who sees the value in the traditional as a means to the extraordinary.

## BIBLIOGRAPHY

### Sources

Bordin, Ruth. *Frances Willard: A Biography.* Chapel Hill: U of North Carolina P, 1986. Print.

Dow, Bonnie J. "The 'Womanhood' Rationale in the Woman Suffrage Rhetoric of Francis E. Willard." *Southern Communication Journal* 56.4 (1991): 298–307. Print.

Gifford, Carolyn De Swarte. "What about That Twenty-Year Gap?" *Documentary Editing* 20.1 (1998): 18–24. Print.

Gifford, Carolyn De Swarte, and Amy R. Slagell, eds. *Let Something Good Be Said: Speeches and Writings of Frances E. Willard.* Champaign: U of Illinois P, 2007. Print.

Gordon, Anna Adams. *The Beautiful Life of Frances E. Willard: A Memorial Volume.* Chicago: WCTU Publishing Association, 1898. Print.

Willard, Frances E. *Home Protection Manual.* New York: Independent, 1879. Print.

———. *How to Win: A Book for Girls.* New York: Funk & Wagnalls, 1886. Print.

### Further Reading

Donawerth, Jane. "Authorial Ethos, Collaborative Voice, and Rhetorical Theory by Women." *Rhetorical Women: Roles and Representations.* Ed. Hildy Miller and Lillian Bridewell-Bowles. Tuscaloosa: U of Alabama P, 2005. 107–24. Print.

Gifford, Carolyn De Swarte, ed. *Writing Out My Heart: Selections from the Journal of Frances E. Willard, 1855–96.* Champaign: U of Illinois P, 1995. Print.

Marilley, Suzanne M. "Frances Willard and the Feminism of Fear." *Feminist Studies* 19.1 (1993): 123–46. Print.

Parker, Alison M. "Frances Willard: Federal Regulations for the Common Good." *Articulating Rights: Nineteenth-Century American Women on Race, Reform, and the State.* DeKalb: Northern Illinois UP, 2010. 139–76. Print.

Parker, Maegan. "Desiring Citizenship: A Rhetorical Analysis of the Wells/Willard Controversy." *Women's Studies in Communication* 31.1 (2008): 56–78. Print.

Slagell, Amy R. "The Rhetorical Structure of Frances E. Willard's Campaign for Woman Suffrage, 1876–1896." *Rhetoric & Public Affairs* 4.1 (2001): 1–23. Print.

Spain, Daphne. *How Women Saved the City.* Minneapolis: U of Minnesota P, 2001. Print.

*Megan Peabody*

# JOHN HOPKINS'S NOTIONS OF POLITICAL ECONOMY

*Jane Marcet*

## OVERVIEW

Jane Marcet's *John Hopkins's Notions of Political Economy*, published in 1833, collects a number of short stories many of them previously published, to prove that the wealth of the rich actually benefits the poor. John Hopkins, the main character, learns a different economic lesson in each of the book's nine tales. In the first two tales, a fairy grants his wishes to equalize wealth and double wages, with disastrous results in each case. In later tales, Hopkins's ideas about emigration, immigration, and trade are corrected through conversation with family and acquaintances. The tales urge the poor not just to accept the success of the rich but to understand the resulting inequality as crucial to their own interests.

*John Hopkins's Notions* was never a great success commercially. This may have been due, in part, to the fact that its working-class audience could not afford the book, though some wealthy landowners did purchase the book to distribute to their tenants. These landowners and others who were worried about the social and political unrest of the 1830s saw the book as a valuable tool in popularizing their own economic views, which emphasized stable social structures and the universal benefit of concentrated wealth.

## HISTORICAL AND LITERARY CONTEXT

The beginning of the nineteenth century saw a tremendous growth in new economic theories that attempted to make sense of changes in industrial techniques, trade, and geopolitical relations. Public discussion concerning these theories increased as well. David Ricardo's focus on wages, rent, and trade; Thomas Malthus's theory of population; and Adam Smith's ideas about productive and unproductive labor formed the basics of what is now known as classic economics. For the most part, these theorists argued that government policies should be designed to foster the free market as much as possible.

*John Hopkins's Notions* argues for free trade in general and for the repeal of the Corn Laws (the focus of its final tale) in particular. The Corn Laws ("corn" is the generic English term for any grain) were enacted in 1815 when European countries such as France began to export grains at prices significantly lower than those English farmers were able to offer; Parliament imposed tariffs so that the foreign grains did not compete against English-raised ones. Although some working-class people supported repealing the Corn Laws because doing so meant lower costs for essentials, others worried that decreased corn prices would result in employers slashing wages: *John Hopkins's Notions* sought to explain how repealing the Corn Laws and letting the market function on its own would benefit all workers. In doing so, it also attempted to paint such policies as not only better for the economy as a whole but as favorable for workers.

One challenge that political economists faced in the early years of the nineteenth century was accessibility: writers such as Ricardo and Malthus published dense, complicated tracts. Although several later economists did publish summaries of their own work, Marcet stands out as one of the first to present complicated economic ideas in a simple, accessible form. Her most popular work on economic theory, *Conversations on Political Economy* (1816), presents "dialogues" between a governess and her pupil. This dialogic form had its roots in Mary Wollstonecraft's *Original Stories* (1791) and Charlotte Turner Smith's *Rural Walks* (1795), works aimed at "improving" children, women, and the working class; the technique became standard in educational literature of the period. Like Hannah More, a pedagogical writer who authored *Village Politics* in 1792, Marcet wrote in a discursive, animated style that made her popular with both her intended audience and other, more educated readers. The educational literature genre flourished in the nineteenth century, thanks in great part to writers such as Smith, More, and Marcet. Indeed, Marcet's *Conversations* inspired Harriet Martineau to write the tremendously popular *Illustrations of Political Economy* (1832).

*John Hopkins's Notions* did not enjoy the same success as Martineau's *Illustrations of Political Economy*. Although both works used fables to justify free market capitalism to working-class readers, Marcet's tone and her slightly more conservative approach did not endear her to readers. Nevertheless, her emphasis on getting the working class to accept the disparity of wealth and unregulated wages and prices as beneficial

+ *Key Facts*

**Time Period:**
Early 19th Century

**Genre:**
Short Story

**Events:**
Division of wealth; economic theories; Corn Laws

**Nationality:**
English

# JANE MARCET'S CURIOUS NATURE

Perhaps one of the most notable aspects of Jane Marcet was her interest in everything around her. Born into a large family that educated both its boys and girls through private tutors at home, Marcet was exposed to scientists, politicians, and intellectuals from a young age. When, in her late teens, she became interested in painting, her father introduced her to Joshua Reynolds and Thomas Lawrence, prominent artists of the day (Marcet later did sketches for several of her own works).

When Marcet married, her husband, a doctor actively involved in research, introduced her to many of the prominent scientists and thinkers of the day. Most notably, the couple invited Sir Humphry Davy, a popular British chemist and inventor, to their home after attending his popular lectures. Inspired by Davy, Marcet wrote *Illustrations of Chemistry* in 1805, which rapidly became a best seller. This book, in turn, inspired a young Michael Faraday, then a bookbinder's apprentice, who became one of the most prominent physicists of the nineteenth century. He became a friend of Marcet's, and she incorporated his ideas into later editions of her work. Just as her personal relationships with economists such as Ricardo and Malthus shaped her economic writings, her many other notable acquaintances shaped her publications on chemistry, physics, and botany.

to their own interests continues to surface in political debates and policies today.

## THEMES AND STYLE

*John Hopkins's Notions* offers it titular character, a farm laborer, lesson after lesson on the value of free market policies. In the first, most famous tale, John has been granted a wish by a fairy and chooses to remove all luxuries from the world. He explains his choice as a reaction to the inequity of wealth around him: "'I shall no longer,' said he to himself, 'be disgusted with the contrast of the rich and the poor: what they lose must be our gain, and we shall see whether things will not now go on in a different manner.'" Unfortunately, without a market for luxuries, factories close and Hopkins's son loses his job, and without the impetus to buy luxuries, landowners stop cultivating any land beyond that needed for sustenance, and so John, too, loses his job. In the tales that follow, he comes to understand further how seemingly harsh policies and conditions actually directly benefit the working class.

Marcet employs simple tales that emphasize the logical and scientific sense of the economic theory she espouses. Each fable starts with a seemingly beneficial change of policy but walks through its negative consequences step by step. In doing so, Marcet makes political economy seem natural and observable, rather than abstract and theoretical. Additionally, she incorporates actual terms from political economy into the dialogue

of the characters, which again has the effect of naturalizing these ideas. Both techniques can be seen in the words of John's son Dick, who points out that "when wages rise because there is a greater demand for workmen, we are all the better for it, master and man too; but when they rise from a foolish and arbitrary law, it does us all harm instead of good; and it is to be hoped that those who made it will soon see the folly of it, and bring us back to the natural wages." Not only does Dick make the effects seen in the story seem logical, but he incorporates and explains the term "natural wages," one of Ricardo's key concepts.

In "An Unpublished Letter from Malthus to Jane Marcet," Bette Polkinghorn notes the "preaching" tone in *John Hopkins's Notions*, which can be seen both in direct statements, such as Dick's above, and in the tales' insistence that understanding these theories is beneficial to the working-class characters. For instance, Dick, who frequently explains concepts to his father, points out that "Men are sharp witted ... when their interest is at stake." Later, the local landowner praises John for taking an interest in political economy: "I am very far from thinking ... that it is not your business to reflect and consider what is or what is not good for your country.... This, thank God, is not a land in which we are afraid of the people learning to distinguish between right and wrong, even in matters which concern the welfare of the country." These moments suggest that understanding the concepts of political economy as they relate to free trade and unfettered markets is not just a personal virtue but a patriotic necessity.

## CRITICAL DISCUSSION

The immediate reception of *John Hopkins's Notions* was underwhelming. Although Marcet's *Conversations on Political Economy,* aimed at the middle rather than the working class, was a huge commercial and critical success, *John Hopkins's Notions* did not fare as well. Public attention at the time was focused on Harriet Martineau's economic writings, and the debate over the Corn Laws did not really reach fruition until the next decade. One positive review did come from economist Thomas Malthus, who initially supported the Corn Laws as a way to maintain a stable relationship between industry and agriculture but had come to support their repeal by 1833. In a letter to Jane Marcet, Malthus wrote that *John Hopkins's Notions* was "in many respects better suited to the laboring classes than Miss Martineau's Tales which are justly so much admired ... I think your doctrines very sound, and what is a more essential point, you have explained them with great plainness and clearness."

By the end of the nineteenth century, the few commentators who remembered Marcet at all dismissed her work. In part there was a resistance at the time to political writing from earlier in the century, which was often viewed, as Catherine Gallagher writes, "as the direct ideological justification of a particularly

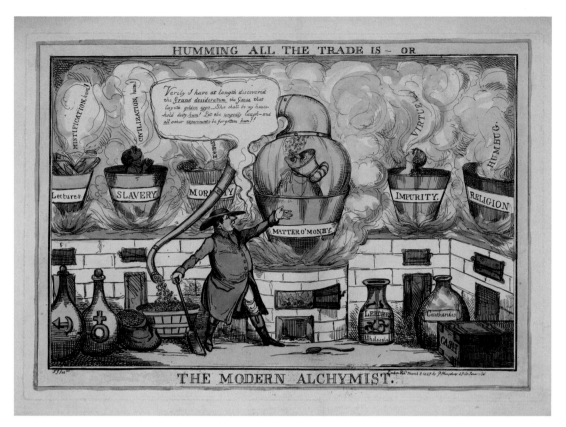

The Modern Alchymist, an 1827 cartoon about English financial matters published by J. Humphrey. English writer Jane Marcet discusses political economy matters in her 1833 work John Hopkins's Notions of Political Economy. SCIENCE & SOCIETY PICTURE LIBRARY/GETTY IMAGES.

rapacious capitalism." Further, economists in particular objected to the "plainness and clearness" Malthus found so attractive: Joseph Schumpeter referred to Marcet's writings as economics for schoolgirls, whereas Alfred Marshall argued that her work did not explain the complexities of economics. However, J. R. Shackleton, writing in 1990, points out that such attacks can be seen as based both in gender discrimination and changing trends in economics. "To some extent," he writes, Marcet "served as [a] scapegoat—conveniently female, from the misogynistic Marshall's perspective—for the failings of classical economics as a whole. He saw [writers like Marcet] as 'parasites' who had warped popular ideas of the scientific core of political economy."

In recent criticism, Marcet's work in general has gained more attention, though there is still little focus on *John Hopkins's Notions* in particular. Critics have reassessed Marcet's role in popularizing political science. Not only did she make ideas accessible, but, as Dorothy Thomson points out, she gave them legitimacy by placing them in a pedagogical and scientific format. More generally, Marcet's role as an educator of adults has gained increasing attention in recent years, with critics noting the sophistication and long-reaching influence of her techniques. *John Hopkins's Notions* offers a chance to further explore Marcet's techniques in educating adults about new, complex economic ideas.

## BIBLIOGRAPHY

### Sources

Gallagher, Catherine. *The Body Economic: Life, Death and Sensation in Political Economy and The Victorian Novel.* Princeton: Princeton UP, 2008. Print.

Marcet, Jane. *John Hopkins's Notions of Political Economy.* Boston: Allen and Ticknor, 1833. Web. 17 Aug. 2012.

Polkinghorn, Bette. "Jane Marcet and Harriet Martineau: Motive, Market Experience and Reception of Their Works Popularizing Classical Political Economy." *Women of Value: Feminist Essays on the History of Women in Economics.* Aldershot: Elgar, 1995. 71–81. Print.

————. "An Unpublished Letter from Malthus to Jane Marcet, January 22, 1833." *The American Economic Review* 76.4 ( 1986): 845–47. *Project Muse.* Web. 16 Aug. 2012.

Shackleton, J. R. "Jane Marcet and Harriet Martineau: Pioneers of Economics Education." *History of Education* 19.4 (1990): 283–97. Print.

Thomson, Dorothy Lampen. *Adam Smith's Daughters.* Jericho: Exposition, 1973. Print.

### Further Reading

Alic, Margaret. *Hypatia's Heritage: A History of Women in Science from Antiquity Through the Nineteenth Century.* Boston: Beacon, 1986. Print.

Cicarelli, James, and Julianne Cicarelli. "Jane Haldimand Marcet (1769–1858)." *Distinguished Women Economists.* Westport: Greenwood, 2003.109–11. Print.

Dimand, Mary A., Robert W. Dimand, and Evelyn L. Forget. *Women of Value: Feminist Essays on the History of Women in Economics.* Aldershot: Elgar, 1995. Print.

Henderson, Willie. *Economics as Literature.* London: Routledge, 1994. Print.

———. "Jane Marcet's *Conversations on Political Economy*: A New Interpretation." *History of Education* 23.4 (1994): 423–37. Print.

Hollis, Hilda. "The Rhetoric of Jane Marcet's Popularizing Political Economy." *Nineteenth Century Contexts* 24.4 (2002): 379–96. *Project Muse.* Web. 17 Aug. 2012.

Marcet, Jane. *Conversations on Political Economy in which the Elements of That Science Are Familiarly Explained.* 5th ed. London: Longman, 1824. Print.

Polkinghorn, Bette. *Jane Marcet: An Uncommon Woman.* Aldermaston: Forestwood, 1993. Print.

*Abigail Mann*

# MOMOTARŌ

## OVERVIEW

Though similar story elements may have been integrated into Japanese folk tales as early as the Muromachi period (1333–1568), most scholars agree that the basic modern version of the folktale *Momotarō* likely dates back to the beginning of the Edo period (1600–1868) and serves as an allegory of the warlord Tokugawa Ieyasu's centralization of power in 1600, which initiated the dynasty bearing his name: the peach-born, heaven-sent Momotarō quested with several subordinate animal companions (usually a dog, a monkey, and a pheasant) to defeat a group of neighboring *oni* (variously translated as "demons" and "ogres") using wit and prowess to bring treasure and security to his home. The tale resurged in popularity and became canonized in textbooks in the nineteenth and twentieth centuries as Japan began to fight international wars, including the Sino-Japanese Wars (1894–1895, 1937–1945), the Russo-Japanese War (1904–1905), World War I (1914–1918), and the Fifteen-Year War (1931–1945) through World War II (1939–1945). As time went on, *Momotarō's* traditional elements were reinterpreted anew, particularly in the films it inspired. Two animated films directed by Mitsuyo Seo during World War II stand out for their celebration of Japanese militarism: *Momotarō no Umiwashi* (*Momotarō's Sea Eagles*) in 1943 and *Momotarō Umi no Shinpei* (*Momotarō's Divine Sea Warriors*) in 1945. *Momotarō*, always a part of Japanese culture, became part of a concerted campaign toward a consolidated Japanese identity in education and entertainment.

Beyond the connection to the Tokugawa dynasty, *Momotarō* may have some historical origins in the legendary Japanese founders of the Okayama prefecture and the town of Kanashi. Both historical figures have been considered models for Momotarō and their exploits against invaders and pirates in the fourth or seventh centuries linked to the tale's origins. Yoshihide Asahina, a thirteenth-century warrior famous for his part in a revolt against the Hōjō clan, has also been tied to the folktale as an inspiration for Momotarō, though this theory flagged in popularity in the twentieth century because of the subversive class dynamic it suggests. Instead, Momotarō was portrayed as a model for Japanese citizens in circulated textbooks and in direct exhortations. Author Sazanami Iwaya implored the Japanese colonial government in Taiwan to develop a strong national character in sync with "Momotarōism" during the Sino-Japanese War, and

the trend spread to the Japanese mainland. Notably, during that war Taiwan was expressly identified as the location of Oni Island in printings of *Momotarō*, though the suggested location of the *oni*, like other details of the narrative, would change during later wars. *Momotarō* is notable for such mutability. It has been adapted to fit changing national allegories for more than three hundred years.

## HISTORICAL AND LITERARY CONTEXT

As Japan entered a more international arena, first through trade and then in war, Japanese folktales such as *Momotarō* that idealized traditional values of family, serving the nation, and cultural superiority gained in popularity, and folktale studies even garnered governmental support. Japan had been fighting and winning wars for decades at the beginning of World War II, and the spirit of war ran high and was incorporated into most elements of Japanese culture. Momotarō, as the face of righteous warfare, was omnipresent in Japanese society until the end of World War II.

When *Momotarō's Sea Eagles* was first viewed in 1943, the Japanese people were confident in a victory against the Allied troops. The Japanese had seen some victories in battle and Japan had not yet faced the devastation of the later war years. By 1945, the spring of their defeat, few children were left in the cities to view *Momotarō's Divine Sea Warriors* in the even fewer remaining theaters. The buoyant expectations of the earlier war years had been replaced by a grim foreboding and horrifying domestic conditions. Yet Seo's *Momotarō's Divine Sea Warriors* still provided a renewed sense of hope for the future and an optimistic perspective on Japan's postwar potential.

As with most Japanese propaganda, *Momotarō's Divine Sea Warriors* was thought destroyed by the American occupying troops. However, a single copy was rediscovered in 1983. Similar cartoons in which characters fight and demonize the enemy sprouted in Western countries as well, featuring well-known figures such as Superman, Donald Duck, and Bugs Bunny. The difference between Japanese and American propaganda cartoons, historian John Dower explains, is that the Japanese propaganda more frequently celebrates an elevated national self rather than a complete bifurcation from the enemy "other," as *oni* are traditionally seen more as outsiders who can be pacified than caricatured as inherently evil, as Western propaganda was wont to do.

❖ *Key Facts*

**Time Period:**
17th-19th Centuries

**Genre:**
Folk Tale

**Events:**
Tokugawa Ieyasu's centralization of power in the shogunate; growth of Japanese internationalism

**Nationality:**
Japanese

# FROM NATIONAL ICON TO LOCAL HERO: MOMOTARŌ IN OKAYAMA

The towns of Inuyama and Kinashi, and the city of Okayama have all claimed to be the birthplace of the folktale hero Momotarō, though Okayama has recently cemented its connection to the folktale most solidly of the three. Both the supposed founder of Okayama and its old name, "Kibi no kuni," ties it strongly to the iconic millet dumplings (*kibi dango*) Momotarō carries. The head of a sweet shop famed for its *kibi dango* even traveled to Hiroshima and, dressed as Momotarō, greeted soldiers returning from the Russo-Japanese war in 1905, appealing to the victorious troops by calling out to them: "You victorious Momotarōs have conquered Oni Island. As a souvenir to take home with you, try the *kibi dango* sold at Okayama station," reports David Henry. Moreover, during the Meiji era (1868-1912), the area was the first in Japan to cultivate peaches, crucial to Momotarō's origin, a link it highlights today. Adding to the prefecture's identification with the folktale, a statue of Momotarō and his three animal companions was erected in Okayama's main train station in 1960, the year of the Tokyo Olympics. Okayama's main street and festival were later renamed for Momotarō by popular consensus. Today, the tale regularly resurges in the local identity of Okayama, capitalizing on its narrative capital to cohere an identity grounded in recast traditions and lore.

*Momotarō's Divine Sea Warriors* spurred Osamu Tezuka, Japan's premier manga artist and animator, to create animated films and series in addition to manga. He went on to produce optimistic allegories of Japanese rebirth in the manga series *Tetsuwan Atomu* (*Astro Boy*, 1952), which became Japan's first televised animated series in 1963, and the manga series *Hi no Tori* (*Phoenix*, 1967), among other now-classic animated films such as *Phoenix 2772* (1980). Rebirth figures strongly in the postwar versions of the tale. Though *Momotarō* was dropped from schoolrooms after the war, new versions of the narrative and its icons arose not as militaristic figures but as representatives of old Japan leading newer nations to peace and wisdom. Several prefectures renewed their identification with the folktale, recasting their local identities in the older, less militaristically nuanced versions of the tale in what some scholars have suggested is a return to traditional values and a rejection of modernity.

## THEMES AND STYLE

The trope of a brave, intrepid, pure, god-sent, and likable hero who easily accrues allies with whom he defeats a demonic enemy threatening his home is central to twentieth-century versions of *Momotarō*. Momotarō was born of a peach and thus born pure, his purity instilling his companions to follow him as a natural leader in defending his homeland from those even more distant to him, the *oni*. The "pure Self" versus the "demonic Other," what Dower calls

the "*Momotarō* paradigm," at the heart of the folktale combined with nationalistic interpretations to produce a sense of moral, racial, and cultural superiority to the many "others" the Japanese fought against in the nineteenth and twentieth centuries. The essential plot points of *Momotarō* translated easily to the ideological pillars of Japanese wartime nationalism, both during World War II and in clashes dating back to the domestic Tokugawa takeover in 1600: central leadership, innate goodness, and homogeneity in a sacred homeland besieged by "demonic enemies."

The versions of *Momotarō* that surfaced at the end of the nineteenth century and into the twentieth century stressed honoring one's father, emperor, and nation in word and deed. In Iwaya's late nineteenth-century version of the folktale, Momotarō begs his father's permission to fight the *oni* who have "not only … chosen not to follow our august majesty but have made themselves enemies of our country, killing the people and taking their valuables." The rhetoric of his request puts the *oni*'s disrespect for the emperor before the slaughter of his countrymen, positioning country above self and individualism. Continuing the emperor's centrality to the developing tale, Momotarō becomes a stand-in for the emperor in some versions of the tale, such as in *Momotarō's Sea Eagles*. In this version, the idea of unification of the Asian nations plays out subtly in the anthropomorphized characters, with the civilized Japanese animals teaching and leading their subordinate allies, all under the guidance of Momotarō. Therefore, during World War II, Momotarō becomes more than the ideal citizen, he becomes a national ideal.

The final *Momotarō* film of World War II still portrays the idealized Momotarō defeating his foe, the horned Anglo-American troops. The devilry of the *oni* played on and played up the idea of "foreign devils" central to Japanese wartime propaganda, in which the word "American" became collocated with "devil." Dower cites a schoolroom poster that incites children to "kill the American devils" as indicative of the widespread demonization of American and British troops. Such polarization of sides is common in war propaganda, though the West tended to caricature or animalize their enemies rather than adding horns to their (sometimes) otherwise human visages.

## CRITICAL DISCUSSION

The cultural power of the tale of *Momotarō* is demonstrated by the appearance of at least a dozen full-length studies and numerous citations of *Momotarō* in the past two hundred years. Kunio Yanagita, considered by Hiroshi Kawamori and many others to be the premier scholar of Japanese folklore, marks the inception of a national Japanese literature in *Momotarō*, both in its content and its role in Japanese education as "local studies" became increasingly integrated. *Momotarō* was also criticized, particularly in the 1930s. One notable parody by Akutagawa Ryūnosuke criticized

*Momotarō's* impact on Japanese notions of hegemony, colonialism, and cultural purity, the very things it would be valued for in the years to follow as it was further reinvented in celebration of Japanese militarism. Such parodies quickly faded as *Momotarō* rose to new heights of popularity through 1945.

Despite its long history of being tied to Japanese warfare, after a period during which it was literally blacked out of Japanese textbooks, *Momotarō* has returned to Japanese and American media as a peaceful symbol of a halcyon past, resurrected in video games, advertisements, and cartoons. Momotarō's militancy has been all but removed from his image, and he has come to represent solidarity through sports, economic growth, and travel. Additionally, the tale became tied to valuing domestic products rather than a questing to gain external groups' lands and goods. Comestibles featured in the folktale, such as *kibi dango* (millet dumplings) and peaches, have come to stand in for the treasures Momotarō gains in traditional versions of the tale, showing a return to appreciating Japanese history and culture more than new, foreign acquisitions.

Although recent scholarship such as Owen Griffith's article on the role of children's print media in Japanese wartime propaganda primarily focuses on the folktale's life from 1890 to World War II, interest in the tale's legacy has sparked additional research into its history. David Henry looks to its shifting sociopolitical meanings from the Meiji era onward in his dissertation "*Momotarō, or the Peach Boy: Japan's Best-Loved Folktale as National Allegory,*" while Klaus Antoni looks at the morphology of *Momotarō* as indicative of a tradition of Japanese militaristic aggression. Antoni finds Momotarō a fairy tale gate to "the Japanese spirit" and "attitude toward that which is foreign" shown in a constellation of Japanese fairy tales that feature uncultivated "devils' islands" being pacified—and often subsequently uplifted—by a "frontier hero." In *War Without Mercy*, which figures Momotarō centrally in discussions of racist wartime propaganda, Dower maintains that Momotarō became the face of Japanese nationalism: a courageous and patriotic hero who, as in a fairy tale, against all odds overcomes a powerful enemy and then, as needed, overcomes its own tropes to help heal Japan in the aftermath of World War II.

**BIBLIOGRAPHY**

*Sources*

Antoni, Klaus. "Momotarō (The Peach Boy) and the Spirit of Japan: Concerning the Function of a Fairy Tale in Japanese Nationalism of the Early Showa Age." *Asian Folklore Studies* 50.1 (1991): 155–88. *JSTOR*. Web. 3 Oct. 2012.

Dower, John. *War without Mercy: Race and Power in the Pacific War*. New York: Pantheon, 1986. Print.

Griffiths, Owen. "Militarizing Japan: Patriotism, Profit and Children's Print Media, 1894–1925." *The Asia-Pacific Journal: Japan Focus*. Japan Focus, 22 Sept. 2007. Web. 14 Oct. 2012.

Henry, David A. "*Momotarō, or the Peach Boy: Japan's Best-Loved Folktale as National Allegory.*" Diss. U of Michigan, 2009. *ProQuest*. Web. 10 Oct. 2012.

Kawamori, Hiroshi. "Folktale Research after Yanagita: Development and Related Issues." *Asian Folklore Studies* 62.2 (2003): 237–56. *JSTOR*. Web. 15 Oct. 2012.

*Further Reading*

Figal, Gerald. *Civilization and Monsters: Spirits of Modernity in Meiji Japan*. Durham: Duke UP, 1999. Print.

Henry, David A. "Japanese Children's Literature as Allegory of Empire in Iwaya Sazanami's *Momotarō* (*The Peach Boy*)." *Children's Literature Association Quarterly* (34.3) 2009: 218–28. *Project Muse*. Web. 13 Oct. 2012.

Kushner, Barak. *The Thought War: Japanese Imperial Propaganda*. Honolulu: U of Hawaii P, 2006. *Ebrary*. Web. 13 Oct. 2012.

Pfoundes, C. "Momotaro." *The Folk-Lore Record* (1) 1878: 123–5. *JSTOR*. Web. 14 Oct. 2012.

Seki, Keigo. "Types of Japanese Folktales." *Asian Folklore Studies* 25 (1966): 1–220. *JSTOR*. Web. 13 Oct. 2008.

*Katherine Bishop*

Illustration of *Momotarō*, from *Wonder Tales of Old Japan* by Alan Leslie Whitehorn, published in 1911. The hero Momotarō travels with a dog, monkey, and bird that he has befriended. © LEBRECHT MUSIC AND ARTS PHOTO LIBRARY/ALAMY.

# "On Seeing England for the First Time"

*Jamaica Kincaid*

✣ **Key Facts**

**Time Period:**
Late 20th Century

**Genre:**
Essay

**Events:**
Antiguan independence
from Britain

**Nationality:**
Antiguan American

## OVERVIEW

"On Seeing England for the First Time" (1991) is an account of Caribbean American writer Jamaica Kincaid's reckoning with her deep anger at growing up colonized—the "iron vice" of the English education system holding her generation of Antiguan school children in thrall of the conquering land so unlike their own. Tracing her encounters with England from the classrooms of her native St. John's, Antigua, to a car tour taken as an adult through Bath, Somerset, Kincaid details the ways in which colonization has affected her view of the world and of herself. Lyrical and angry, the essay is both personal examination and indictment of the indoctrination practices of colonizing cultures.

Written from the perspective of "a grown-up woman" two decades removed from Antigua, "On Seeing England for the First Time" followed ten years of acclaim for Kincaid as a fiction writer and memoirist and was tapped by U.S. writer Susan Sontag for inclusion in *The Best American Essays 1992*. The piece reflects Kincaid's continuing engagement with coming-of-age themes and with questions of cultural identity, both topics of which were in the popular consciousness at the time and became subjects of scholarly consideration at the close of the twentieth century. Powerful in its own right, the essay is also notable as a guide for interpretive work on Kincaid's fiction and a point of entry for encounters with twentieth-century Caribbean literature and other postcolonial literatures more generally.

## HISTORICAL AND LITERARY CONTEXT

Until the seventeen century, Antigua was inhabited by a number of Indian peoples, including the Carib and Arawaks. Sighted by Christopher Columbus in 1493, the island was first colonized by the British in 1632. By the 1680s sugar cultivation by European colonists had begun in earnest, instituting slavery of indigenous peoples and the later practice of bringing slaves from Africa. In addition to building sugar plantations, the British established a large naval base on the island for defense of British trade routes. Although slavery was abolished in 1834, social stratification continued along ethnic and cultural lines, with Europeans controlling the country's wealth, as well as its educational system, churches, and social institutions.

The economic devastation of World War II coupled with a rising tide of anticolonialist sentiment at home and abroad led Britain to disengage from outposts around the world. In Antigua, agitation for decolonization by members of the Antigua Labor Party, among others, helped secure the status of associated state of the Commonwealth in 1968 and independence from Britain in 1981. After independence, Antigua continued to struggle with poverty and political unrest.

Although Kincaid immigrated to the United States in 1966 when she was sixteen years old, much of her writing is concerned with her native Antigua and with the intrusion of English culture on the people living there. For example, *A Small Place,* Kincaid's 1988 memoir, deals with Antigua's complicated history and the author's own reaction to it. Writing in the first person and directing her remarks to white tourists, Kincaid laments the tourists' careless objectification of the natives, describing tourism as a replication or extension of colonialism, the power imbalance between the two groups denying both their humanity. "On Seeing England for the First Time" describes a similar imbalance in the classrooms of Kincaid's childhood and expresses a similar anger at the result—a failure to acknowledge native culture that detrimentally affects those involved.

Occupying a relatively minor spot in Kincaid's oeuvre, "On Seeing England for the First Time" nevertheless distills many of the concerns of her early career, as well as marks a transition to a period of work centering more closely on family, particularly mothers, including the novel *Autobiography of My Mother* (1996) and the memoir *My Brother* (1998). These works, while continuing to reflect Kincaid's preoccupation with her place of birth, also acknowledge the formative influence of family relationships and their power over time, even when family members have grown apart.

## THEMES AND STYLE

"On Seeing England for the First Time" contrasts Kincaid's childhood encounters of England, imposed upon her in almost every facet of daily life, with her very different experience of the country she visits in adulthood. The England of Kincaid's childhood was the "very special jewel" idealized on the map in her classroom. It was the source of her father's brown felt hat, impractical for the sweltering Antiguan climate but "central to his character." It was also the focus of history lessons and celebrations. English literature described a world of "low blue skies and moors over which people took walks for nothing but pleasure," a world where, "when it rained at twilight, wonderful things happened." Kincaid found her own surroundings lacking when compared to these exalted images, and she felt the same about herself when compared to English people. As an adult, Kincaid travels to England and is infuriated by the ordinariness of what she finds. Her anger alienates her from some English friends, bothered by her "prejudice" and unwilling or unable to acknowledge the difference between her hatred of the English and the prejudices underlying colonial practices—"my prejudices have no weight to them, my prejudices have no force behind them."

Kincaid's essay shifts between portraying England from two different vantage points—one imposed on the imagination of an Antiguan child sitting at a desk and the other through the eyes of an educated adult woman traveling freely through the countryside. Encountering the white cliffs of Dover, about which she had "sung hymns and recited poems," she finds them not white at all but "dirty" and "steep." For Kincaid, the difference between these visions underlines the untruth of the first viewpoint, generating rage at all that was lost when this false image was taught in place of content reflecting the real lives of Antiguans.

The language of "On Seeing England for the First Time" moves from the evocative, expressed in a passive voice, to blunt declaration, reflecting Kincaid's own transformation from receptive vessel of foreign culture to angry critic. The first descriptions of the map of England drawn with pink and green "unlike any shadings of pink and green I had seen before" are countered by the later bluntness of her adult assessment—"I find England ugly." The shift in language reflects a crossing of "the space between the idea of something and its reality." The child at the beginning of the essay did not have the knowledge to assess a view of reality based on a country "way, way over there," and Kincaid's descriptions of these early encounters are full of breathless wonder based on distance, as she marvels over the word "rushed" or sausages that come from "up-country"; "imagine, 'up-country.'" Seen in person, the illusory England of her colonial childhood falls away and she says simply, "I hate England."

## CRITICAL DISCUSSION

"On Seeing England for the First Time" was initially published in *Transition,* a magazine based at the W. E. B. Du Bois Institute for African and African-American Research at Harvard University and collected in the 1992 edition of the prestigious *The Best American Essays.* Reviews of the book made passing mention of Kincaid's piece as both highlight and low point, echoing earlier reviews of the similarly themed *A Small Place.* Writing for the *Washington Post* in 1988, David

## JAMAICA KINCAID'S DAFFODILS

Throughout her body of work, Kincaid emphasizes propagandistic aspects of British colonial education. In so doing, she frequently returns to a childhood memory of being forced to memorize William Wordsworth's poem "I Wandered Lonely as a Cloud" (1888). In the poem, considered among the best in British verse, Wordsworth recalls coming upon a field of daffodils and notes the enduring power of the memory to lift his spirits and fill his heart with pleasure. As a symbol of Britain's alleged cultural superiority, Wordsworth's text provoked an intense reaction in the young Kincaid.

In her 1990 novel *Lucy,* the eponymous heroine remembers having been compelled to memorize the poem for a school event. Her praise-winning performance of the poem about an unfamiliar flower becomes a symbol of colonial subjugation for Lucy—of being forced to assume a false and inauthentic standpoint. Kincaid's experience also provides the focus for her 2007 essay "Dances with Daffodils." Kincaid remembers having "had to memorize many things written by British people, since the place I was born and grew up in was owned by the British," but she recalls that Wordsworth's poem provoked particular repulsion. She continues, however, by chronicling her evolving relationship to the daffodil, a flower that she planted by the thousands on her Vermont farm.

Nicholson referred to the memoir as "a bitter little book," which, while commendable in its excoriation of colonialism, contained little beyond a description of the problem in an off-putting "complaining voice."

Although a longtime resident of the United States, Kincaid is often regarded as one of the most prominent voices in Caribbean literature, her body of work providing a starting point for discussion of the impact of colonial practices on subjugated peoples and their literature. "On Seeing England for the First Time" is widely taught in high school and college English courses and is also used as an interpretive guide for Kincaid's fiction, which often centers on themes of personal and cultural identity. Writing in 1990, Leslie Garis in "Through West Indian Eyes" quotes black studies scholar Henry Louis Gates commenting about Kincaid's contribution to the African American tradition: "She never feels the necessity of claiming the existence of a black world or a female sensibility. She assumes them both." Furthermore, "More and more black American writers," he predicts, "will assume their world the way that she does. So that we can get beyond the large theme of racism and get to the deeper themes of how black people love and cry and live and die. Which, after all, is what art is all about."

Most critical interest in the essay focuses on its relation to the themes in Kincaid's longer works, primarily her novels. In an article published in *MELUS* in 1996, Edyta Oczkowicz analyzes Kincaid's novel *Lucy*

A 2009 photograph of a man celebrating Antigua's independence from Great Britain. In her 1991 essay "On Seeing England for the First Time," Jamaica Kincaid discusses the relationship between Antigua and Great Britain. © FINDLAY/ ALAMY.

in terms of the "'space' of complex post-colonial experience" that Kincaid describes in "On Seeing England for the First Time." Much like Kincaid herself, Lucy leaves Antigua as a means of creating a new identity apart from being a colonial subject. Oczkowicz describes this process, which is both destructive and creative, as "translation" and compares Lucy's project to Kincaid's own work as a diasporic writer. Kincaid's dialog with the Western canon is Diane Simmons's subject of interest in her article "Jamaica Kincaid and the Canon" (1998), as she traces the ways in which

Kincaid's English education was both nourishing and diminishing, a duality that informs the novels she herself has written.

## BIBLIOGRAPHY

*Sources*

Garis, Leslie. "Through West Indian Eyes." *New York Times.* The New York Times Company, 7 Oct. 1990. Web. 16 Sept. 2012.

Kincaid, Jamaica. "Dances with Daffodils." *Architectural Digest* Apr. 2007: 78–83. Print.

———. "On Seeing England for the First Time." *Scribd.* Scribd, 2012. Web. 16 Sept. 2012.

Nicholson, David. "The Exile's Bitter Return." *Washington Post Book World* 3 July 1988: 14. Rpt. in *Contemporary Literary Criticism.* Ed. Jeffrey W. Hunter. Vol. 137. Detroit: Gale Group, 2001. *Literature Resource Center.* Web. 22 Sept. 2012.

Oczkowicz, Edyta. "Jamaica Kincaid's *Lucy*: Cultural 'Translation' as a Case of Creative Exploration of the Past." *MELUS* 21.3 (1996): 141–57. Rpt. in *Contemporary Literary Criticism.* Ed. Jeffrey W. Hunter. Vol. 137. Detroit: Gale Group, 2001. *Literature Resource Center.* Web. 20 Sept. 2012.

Simmons, Diane. "Jamaica Kincaid and the Canon: In Dialogue with 'Paradise Lost' and 'Jane Eyre.'" *MELUS* 23.2 (1998): 65. Rpt. in *Literature of Developing Nations for Students: Presenting Analysis, Context, and Criticism on Literature of Developing Nations.* Ed. Elizabeth Bellalouna, Michael L. LaBlanc, and Ira Mark Milne. Vol. 1. Detroit: Gale Group, 2000. *Literature Resource Center.* Web. 16 Sept. 2012.

*Further Reading*

Birbalsingh, Frank. *Jamaica Kincaid: From Antigua to America.* New York: St. Martin's, 1996. Print.

Braziel, Jana Evans. *Caribbean Genesis: Jamaica Kincaid and the Writing of New Worlds.* Albany: State U of Albany P, 2009. Print.

Ferguson, Moira. *Colonialism and Gender Relations from Mary Wollstonecraft to Jamaica Kincaid.* New York: Columbia UP, 1993. Print.

Kincaid, Jamaica. *A Small Place.* New York: Farrar, 1988. Print.

Lang-Peralta, Linda. *Jamaica Kincaid and Caribbean Double Crossings.* Cranbury, NJ: Associated University Presses, 2006. Print.

*The Routledge Reader in Caribbean Literature.* Ed. Alison Donnell and Sarah Lawson Welsh. London: Routledge, 1996. Print.

Said, Edward. *Culture and Imperialism.* New York: Knopf, 1993. Print.

*Daisy Gard*

# THE PILGRIM'S PROGRESS FROM THIS WORLD TO THAT WHICH IS TO COME

*John Bunyan*

## OVERVIEW

Published in two parts (Part I in 1678 and Part II in 1684), John Bunyan's *The Pilgrim's Progress from This World to That Which Is to Come* is a religious allegory that follows Bunyan's protagonist and his family as they journey from the corrupt, sin-filled world toward salvation. The allegory is presented as a dream narrative. In Part I, Christian, an everyman character who represents all Christians, makes a pilgrimage, which Bunyan calls "the way to Glory," from the City of Destruction (this world) to the Celestial City (heaven). In Part II, Christian's wife, Christiana, completes the pilgrimage with her children. The characters the pilgrims meet along the way and the places they visit assume symbolic values that reflect Christian temptations and consolations. As a preacher, Bunyan aims to convert sinners and set them on the path to salvation; he uses the allegory to teach the tenets of Calvinism, declaring that his "dark and cloudy words they do but hold / The Truth."

*The Pilgrim's Progress,* which was composed during a time of religious and political upheaval, met with instant acclaim; twelve editions of the text were published during Bunyan's lifetime. Following the Restoration of the British monarchy in 1660, the Church of England was once again recognized as the official religion of the realm. Nonconformists (i.e., non-Anglican Protestants) were soon prohibited from organizing for religious meetings. Bunyan, a popular Baptist preacher, was jailed for preaching without authorization from the Anglican Church and for refusing to conform to Anglican practices. Part I of *The Pilgrim's Progress* was composed while Bunyan was imprisoned. Since its publication, the allegory has never been out of print and has been hailed as a great work of English literature, as well as one of the most inspired and influential religious texts ever published. Allusions to *The Pilgrim's Progress* abound in the literature of the centuries following, and the allegory has given rise to numerous sequels and retellings, including a twentieth-century opera and several films.

## HISTORICAL AND LITERARY CONTEXT

Religious diversity thrived during the Interregnum (1649–1660), a period of Puritan rule that preceded the Restoration in England. A variety of sects arose, and preachers such as Bunyan were able to teach freely, delivering emotional and sometimes terrifying sermons to convert and motivate their audiences. By the 1670s, however, the Church of England had been restored along with the monarchy, and Nonconformists as well as Catholics were viewed as a threat to the Crown. Parliament passed a number of acts aimed at restricting Nonconformist and Catholic activity. The Conventicle Act of 1664, for example, outlawed conventicles—private religious meetings not authorized by the Church of England. Persons who violated the act, such as Bunyan, were arrested for fear that Nonconformist and Catholic activity would incite a plot to overthrow the monarchy and once again displace Anglicanism as the official state religion.

Bunyan, a well-known Nonconformist who had begun preaching during the Interregnum, was arrested after the Restoration of 1660 and spent several years in jail for preaching without a license from the Anglican Church; he was incarcerated at the time of the allegory's composition. Bunyan might have won his freedom earlier by simply agreeing to desist, but he insisted on continuing to preach Calvinist doctrines. *The Pilgrim's Progress* also reflects the anti-Catholic sentiment prevalent in British society at the time, a trend that reached a fever pitch in 1678, the year in which Bunyan's allegory was first published. That year, Titus Oates, a renegade Anglican priest, fabricated a fictitious conspiracy called the Popish Plot. Oates alleged that Roman Catholics were scheming to assassinate King Charles II and place his brother James, who was openly Catholic, on the throne, effectively reinstating Catholicism as the official religion. Oates's actions fomented anti-Catholic hysteria among Nonconformists and Anglicans alike, and it was in this environment that *The Pilgrim's Progress* was released to the public.

*The Pilgrim's Progress* is steeped in biblical allusion and also bears the imprint of other early Reformation texts. Martin Luther's commentary on the book of Galatians and John Foxe's *Acts and Monuments* (1563), popularly known as the *Book of Martyrs,* had particular power for Bunyan, who was not well educated and whose personal library was limited.

In addition Bunyan draws extensively from his own conversion experience, as recorded in his

**Key Facts**

**Time Period:**
Late 17th Century

**Genre:**
Allegory

**Events:**
Restoration of the Church of England

**Nationality:**
English

# MUCKRAKERS

In John Bunyan's day a muckrake was a tool used for raking manure or dirt. In Part II of *The Pilgrim's Progress,* Christiana witnesses a man with a muckrake who is so obsessed with filth that he is unable to look up, even though he is offered a celestial crown in exchange for his implement. Since Bunyan's time, the term *muckraker* has been used in various contexts. Famously, in a speech delivered on April 14, 1906, President Theodore Roosevelt chastises members of the press for focusing only on "that which is vile and debasing." Roosevelt warns that "the man who never does anything else, who never thinks or speaks or writes, save of his feats with the muck-rake, speedily becomes, not a help to society, not an incitement to good, but one of the most potent forces for evil."

Although the style of journalism that President Roosevelt criticizes had been practiced for several years, the term *muckraker* was not applied to investigative journalists until after the 1906 speech. Muckrakers typically wrote articles exposing corruption and scandal, publishing much of their material in magazines such as *McClure's* and *Collier's Weekly.* Prominent muckrakers included Upton Sinclair, Ida Tarbell, and Lincoln Steffens. Today the term is applied more generally to someone who attempts to expose corruption or misconduct in business or public life.

autobiography, *Grace Abounding to the Chief of Sinners* (1666). In *John Bunyan and English Nonconformity,* Richard Greaves notes that *Grace Abounding* "prefigures the internal struggle allegorically developed in *The Pilgrim's Progress.*"

Bunyan's allegory has had lasting and global influence. The text was often translated by Protestant missionaries, second only to the Bible, and was introduced in the American colonies just a few years after its initial publication. In addition to figuring prominently in subsequent secular publications, Bunyan's work heavily influenced theologians, particularly in the first two centuries following publication. The well-known nineteenth-century preacher Charles Haddon Spurgeon is said to have read *The Pilgrim's Progress* more than one hundred times. In modern culture Bunyan's allegory continues to be discussed and valued for its universal themes as well as for its entertainment value and humor.

## THEMES AND STYLE

One of the major themes in *The Pilgrim's Progress* is that the life of a Christian, particularly a Protestant Christian, is a journey of spiritual growth. Bunyan reveals this process as his protagonist faces and overcomes temptation and evil influences and learns from his mistakes. On his journey Christian encounters difficulties and discouragement, such as in the Slough of Despond, a bog in which travelers are apt to sink in guilt and despair, and in the Valley of the Shadow of Death, a

terrifying and treacherous wilderness. He is also tempted to stray from the path, distracted by such characters as Mr. Worldly Wiseman. As Christian emerges from his trials and learns from his errors, he draws nearer to the Celestial City and thus nearer to God. Bunyan uses his protagonist's example to exhort Christian readers to rely on faith and on the Bible (called "the Book" in the allegory) to reach heaven and dwell with God.

Bunyan develops his allegory through the extended metaphor of the pilgrimage and the Christian quest for salvation. He introduces characters that represent basic human tendencies, both good and evil, personifying abstractions and moral qualities that Christian readers would readily recognize as desirable or undesirable. The names of the characters often reveal their natures—for example, Christian, Evangelist, Help, Faithful, Hopeful, Lord Hate-good, Ignorance, Giant Despair, Obstinate, and Legality. And the everyman protagonist, with his wife and children, leads an ordinary life—one to which readers can draw parallels in their own lives. Bunyan uses their identification to reveal methods for overcoming problems and temptations and to urge readers to stay on the correct path to salvation.

In *The Pilgrim's Progress,* as Cynthia Wall notes in her preface to Bunyan's text, Bunyan uses a "lively, earthy vernacular" that reflects his ability to appeal to a popular, often uneducated audience. The renowned British historian Sir Charles Firth explains that the allegory was successful because "it addressed the unlettered Puritan in a speech which unlettered Puritans could understand. The people for whom Bunyan wrote were illiterate people like his pilgrims themselves." Early in the allegory, for example, as Christian despairs, Evangelist boldly declares, "All manner of sin and blasphemies shall be forgiven unto men; be not faithless, but believing"—a message that would have resonated strongly with Bunyan's intended audience. The language of the allegory is sometimes coarse, even occasionally vulgar, addressed primarily to the middle and lower classes. Wall suggests that another major attraction of the work is its humor, though this is sometimes lost on the modern reader.

## CRITICAL DISCUSSION

With its particular appeal to Nonconformists and eventually to Protestants in general, *The Pilgrim's Progress* was an instant success, and an estimated 100,000 copies of the work were sold during Bunyan's lifetime. Translations began almost immediately. Some of Bunyan's associates had initially discouraged him from printing the allegory, as Bunyan mentions in his apology preceding Part I. Greaves explains in *Glimpses of Glory* that "the colloquial style and the allegorical method troubled some of [Bunyan's] critics, who charged that his approach lacked 'solidness,' blinded readers with metaphors, and couched the message in 'dark' language." Initially, some of the more sophisticated readers in the upper classes dismissed the allegory as base; Bunyan, after all, was a tinker with little formal education, and the language of *The Pilgrim's Progress* contrasts sharply with some of the more refined writings of the era. Nevertheless, its accessibility and universal themes made the book wildly popular. The famed eighteenth-century author and literary critic Samuel Johnson praises the book as having "great merit, both for invention, imagination, and the conduct of the story; and it has had the best evidence of its merit, the general and continued approbation of mankind."

Over the centuries, authors, musicians, and dramatists alike have been inspired by *The Pilgrim's Progress* and have alluded to it or drawn from it for their own creations. The romantic poet Samuel Taylor Coleridge calls it "one of the few books which may be read over repeatedly at different times, and each time with a new and a different pleasure." Allusions to the allegory appear in such novels as Charlotte Brontë's *Jane Eyre* (1847), Louisa May Alcott's *Little Women* (1868), and Mark Twain's *Adventures of Huckleberry Finn* (1884), among numerous others. More modern interpretations include a 1951 opera by Ralph Vaughan Williams as well as several film versions of the allegory, notably *Pilgrim's Progress: Journey to Heaven* (2008), directed by Danny Carrales. It has been translated into more than 200 languages and distributed throughout the world.

Much of modern scholarship focuses on the continued influence of Bunyan's allegory on subsequent literature, particularly literature of the quest, as well as the multicultural appeal of the text. Elizabeth Napier, for example, in "*The Grapes of Wrath*: Steinbeck's *Pilgrim's Progress*," ties the work of John Steinbeck to Bunyan's composition. Some modern scholars, such as Isabel Hofmeyr, have focused on the international impact of *The Pilgrim's Progress,* particularly in non-Western cultures. In *The Portable Bunyan: A Transnational History of* The Pilgrim's Progress, Hofmeyr discusses the effects of Bunyan's work on African culture and literature. And the 2010 publication of the *Cambridge Companion to Bunyan* points to sustained contemporary critical interest.

## BIBLIOGRAPHY

*Sources*

Boswell, James. *Life of Johnson: Unabridged.* New York: Oxford UP, 1998. Print.

Bunyan, John. *The Pilgrim's Progress.* Ed. Cynthia Wall. New York: Norton, 2009. Print.

Coleridge, Samuel Taylor. *Coleridge on the Seventeenth Century.* Ed. Roberta Florence Brinkley. Durham: Duke UP, 1955. Print.

Dunan-Page, Anne. *The Cambridge Companion to Bunyan.* Cambridge: Cambridge UP, 2010. Print.

Firth, C. H. *John Bunyan.* Oxford: Oxford UP, 1911. Print.

Greaves, Richard. *Glimpses of Glory: John Bunyan and English Dissent.* Stanford: Stanford UP, 2002. Print.

———. *John Bunyan and English Nonconformity.* London: Hambledon P, 1992. Print.

In this illustration of a scene from *Pilgrim's Progress,* Christian and his companion near the Celestial City. IMAGE SELECT/ART RESOURCE, NY.

*Further Reading*

Hancock, Maxine. "Folklore and Theology in the Structure and Narrative Strategies of *The Pilgrim's Progress*." *Bunyan Studies: John Bunyan and His Times* 9 (1999–2000): 7–24. Print.

Hofmeyr, Isabel. *The Portable Bunyan: A Transnational History of* The Pilgrim's Progress. Princeton, NJ: Princeton UP, 2004. Print.

Johnson, Barbara A. *Reading* Piers Plowman *and* The Pilgrim's Progress: *Reception and the Protestant Reader.* Carbondale: Southern Illinois UP, 1992. Print.

Newey, Vincent, ed. The Pilgrim's Progress: *Critical and Historical Views.* Totowa, NJ: Barnes and Noble, 1980. Print.

Stachniewski, John. *The Persecutory Imagination: English Puritanism and the Literature of Religious Despair.* Oxford: Clarendon P, 1991. Print.

Swaim, Kathleen M. *Pilgrim's Progress, Puritan Progress: Discourses and Contexts.* Urbana: U of Illinois P, 1993. Print.

*Media Adaptations*

*Pilgrim's Progress.* Perf. Warner Oland. Hochstetter Utility Company, 1912. Film.

*Pilgrim's Progress.* Dir. Ken Anderson. Perf. Peter Thomas, Maurice O'Callaghan, and Liam Neeson. Ken Anderson Films, 1979. Film.

*Harrabeth Haidusek*

# Quotations from Chairman Mao

*Mao Zedong*

✣ *Key Facts*

**Time Period:**
Mid-20th Century

**Genre:**
Handbook

**Events:**
Failure of the Great Leap
Forward; initiation of the
Cultural Revolution

**Nationality:**
Chinese

## OVERVIEW

*Quotations from Chairman Mao,* first published in 1964, sets forth Mao Zedong's Marxist political philosophy, also known as Mao Zedong Thought, as expressed in quotes collected from his writings and speeches. One of the most frequently printed books in history, *Quotations* is made up of thirty-three sections and 427 quotations that are organized into such categories as "The Communist Party," "War and Peace," and "Political Work." New presses were built in China solely for the purpose of printing *Quotations from Chairman Mao* (commonly titled *The Little Red Book* in the West), which was widely distributed between 1966 and 1971 and became emblematic of Mao's Great Proletarian Cultural Revolution.

The Cultural Revolution in China heralded Mao's return to prominence after the failure of his Great Leap Forward and the fracturing of the Chinese Communist Party that occurred as a result. In part to account for the failures of the Great Leap Forward, Mao blamed party leadership and the administration of the state, claiming that these elitist leaders had to "learn from the masses." Mao's attempts to eradicate these elements led to mass detainments in work camps and the persecution of anyone accused of counterrevolutionary thinking. During this period of upheaval, it became vital to be familiar with Mao's directives so as not to violate them. *Quotations,* which had originally been published under defense minister Lin Biao for a government and military audience, became the people's reference on Mao Zedong Thought during the Cultural Revolution. In addition, carrying the book protected citizens to some degree against persecution by the Red Guards and others.

## HISTORICAL AND LITERARY CONTEXT

Between 1958 and 1961, Mao Zedong sought, through a variety of economic and social policies, to replace China's traditional agrarian economy with Marxist-inspired industrialization and collective farming. Rural farms were organized into groups of progressively larger collectives. Many farm workers were not allowed to work their land due to a diversion of resources, and crops rotted. Local officials misrepresented the size of harvests to the government to curry favor, which resulted in miscalculations in grain distribution and exporting and led to widespread food shortages and starvation. Also during this period, "meetings" became the central social activity, replacing local celebrations and religious customs that had traditionally unified communities. By 1961, China's economy was faltering and unrest was widespread. As a result, Mao's methods were criticized by other members of the Chinese Communist Party, and his power waned.

The Cultural Revolution was undertaken, at least in part, to help Mao regain his leadership. Mao had long been critical of the Soviet Union's faulty implementation of Marxism and was keen to delineate his own central principles and position himself as the leader who could make socialism work. At the time, however, there was no definitive statement of Mao Zedong Thought that was widely available. Several years earlier, leaders of the People's Liberation Army had requested a guidebook for their troops, and *Quotations* had been compiled to this end, going through several iterations in response to demands for instruction on multiple subjects. It eventually became clear that *Quotations* could serve a broader purpose; thus, plans were implemented for multiple printings. As a tool of the revolution, *Quotations* was to make Mao's ideas clear and accessible to all of China's citizens.

*Quotations* was unprecedented in the extent of its distribution, with hundreds of millions of copies printed. During one period in the late 1960s, it was the only book authorized by the government to be widely produced and sold in China. Indeed, like other propaganda of the day, such as sloganeering posters and buttons, *Quotations* was extremely thick on the ground.

*Quotations* was largely championed by Mao's defense minister Lin Biao, and after Lin's death in 1971, the importance of book was deemphasized. Nevertheless, the influence of Mao and his *Quotations* came to be felt around the world, in such movements as the Shining Path in South America and the Marxist movement in Nepal. In contemporary Chinese society, as well as elsewhere in the world, the book is largely treated as a collectible, and some rare editions are quite valuable. In 2001, Mao's family members petitioned for royalties on the work, but this bid was unsuccessful: the Chinese Communist Party ruled that Mao's ideas are the intellectual property of the party, not of any single member.

## THEMES AND STYLE

A quote from the first section of the book encapsulates several important themes: "We must have faith in the masses and we must have faith in the Party. These are two cardinal principles. If we doubt these principles, we shall accomplish nothing." As with Karl Marx, Mao emphasizes the masses as the raw source of power, moral and otherwise, with the Chinese Communist Party acting as the means for harnessing this power and building a society that will be good for all. The Party's principles are important in that they enable leaders to "accomplish" goals. Moreover, it is not enough merely to follow party dictates—good communists must have "faith." This sort of language has led some commentators to refer to *Quotations* as a sort of secular bible. All post-1965 editions include an introduction by Lin, who exhorts readers in an almost religious tone to "study Chairman Mao's writings, follow his teachings and act according to his instructions."

*Quotations* derives much of its force from its status as the official word of the venerated leader Mao. While Lin's introduction establishes Mao's importance, the text itself emphasizes the unity between the leader and his people, with repeated references to collective motivations and the collective benefits that accrue to all as a result of correct ideology and behavior. Furthermore, Mao describes a unity defined by common enemies. "People of the world," he writes, should "unite against the U.S. aggressor and all of its running dogs." The unity of purpose Mao promotes is served by the book's format: short quotations that can be easily digested and memorized. The goal is to make the ideas accessible to a great number of "the people." It is worth noting, however, that the book's style is complicated by the fact that all of the quotes are taken from other works and appear out of their original context.

Nevertheless, *Quotations* has a consistent tone of authority, which befits not only the book's origin within the military but also its co-option for the larger purpose of unifying citizens around an ideology and the visionary leader implementing it. The simple strength of the prose is apparent in quotes such as this: "The Chinese Communist Party is the core of leadership of the whole Chinese people. Without this core, the cause of socialism cannot be victorious."

## CRITICAL DISCUSSION

Upon publication, *Quotations from Chairman Mao* was widely and enthusiastically read and studied by most citizens in China, at least according to official accounts. Citizens were required to join study groups to read and discuss the text. Criticism of the book was not tolerated within China, and dissenters remained silent, having learned from the Hundred Flowers Campaign in the mid-1950s. At that time, citizens had been encouraged to present opinions about Mao's regime; however, those who opposed the government were later persecuted. *Quotations* was

## MAO ZEDONG: A BIOGRAPHY

Mao Zedong, sometimes written as Mao Tse-tung, was born in 1893 in Hunan Province. The son of a farmer and grain merchant, Mao was educated in local schools and later attended classes at Beijing University, though he never formally enrolled there because he could not pay tuition. In the early 1920s, Mao helped found the Chinese Communist Party (CCP). Mao took an interest in the 1925 peasant uprisings in Hunan, and in a 1927 party meeting, he delivered his "Report on the Peasant Movement in Hunan," a piece that is widely considered important in the development of his ideas.

After years of on-and-off conflict with the Kuomintang party, the CCP declared victory, and Mao Zedong played a central role in the founding of the People's Republic of China in 1949. Initially allied with the Soviet Union, Mao became disillusioned with Soviet policy; his Great Leap Forward sought to shape his country differently. The Great Leap Forward and the Cultural Revolution that followed are widely considered to have been failures, with millions of Chinese losing their lives due to starvation or political persecution. By the early 1970s, Mao's health was in decline, and he retreated from public life. He died in 1976.

published in numerous other countries, including in the West, where it was greeted with curiosity or hostility, or both. As early as 1968, it had become part of Western pop culture, immortalized in the Beatles song "Revolution."

Since his death in 1976, the Cultural Revolution and the cult of personality surrounding Mao have been widely debated, if not repudiated. In 2010, the *New York Times* reported on a secret document—Politburo document, No. 179—in which top-level Chinese Communist Party officials proposed to purge all references to Mao Zedong Thought from party documents and policy. Still, much of the propaganda dating from that time, including *Quotations,* remains a source of fascination for Chinese and Westerners alike. Furthermore, images of Mao and of the *Little Red Book* are now considered iconic.

Contemporary scholarship most often treats *Quotations* as part of a broader analysis of Mao's propaganda or of the man himself. In her "Popular Propaganda: Art and Culture in Revolutionary China," Barbara Mittler calls representations of Mao "time-resistant semantic units that form important and structuring elements in the collective cultural memory." Mittler sees these elements as being interpreted and reinterpreted to become part of the story of China. In *Mao: A Biography,* Ross Terrill considers *Quotations* in the context of the relationship between Mao and Lin, who was once expected to succeed Mao. Terrill describes Mao as being "irritated" by Lin's promotion of the book and suspecting an ulterior motive related to Lin's own

desire for power. To bolster his point, Terrill quotes a letter from Mao to his wife: "I have never believed that those little books of mine could have such fantastic magic, yet he [Lin] blew them up, and the whole country followed."

## BIBLIOGRAPHY

*Sources*

Leese, Daniel. *Mao Cult: Rhetoric and Ritual in China's Cultural Revolution.* Cambridge: Cambridge UP, 2011. Print.

Levy, Richard. "Mao's Little Red Book." *Guanxi: The China Letter* 2.11 (2008): 10+. *General OneFile.* Web. 8 July 2012.

Mittler, Barbara. "Popular Propaganda: Art and Culture in Revolutionary China." American Philosophical Society Proceedings, Dec. 2008. Web. 8 July 2012.

*Quotations from Chairman Mao Zedong.* San Francisco: China Books, 1990. Print.

Terrill, Ross. *Mao: A Biography.* New York: Harper, 1980. Print.

*Further Reading*

Clark, Paul. *The Chinese Cultural Revolution: A History.* Cambridge: Cambridge UP, 2008. Print.

Cushing, Lincoln. *Chinese Posters: Art from the Great Proletarian Cultural Revolution.* San Francisco: Chronicle, 2007. Print.

Gao, Yuan. *Born Red: A Chronicle of the Cultural Revolution.* Stanford: Stanford UP, 1987. Print.

Lynch, Michael. *Mao.* London: Routledge, 2004. Print.

Mittler, Barbara. A *Continuous Revolution: Making Sense of Cultural Revolution Culture.* Cambridge: Harvard UP, 2012. Print.

*Media Adaptation*

*Quotations from Chairman Mao Tse-Tung.* Dir. Edward Albee. Cast Eileen Burns, Patricia Kilgarriff, Catherine Bruno, et al. New York, © 1979. Videocassette.

*Daisy Gard*

*Opposite page:*
A 1969 poster celebrating the Chinese Communist Party leader Mao Zedong and his "Little Red Book." *LONG LIVE THE THOUGHTS OF CHAIRMAN MAO, SEPTEMBER 1969 (COLOUR LITHO), CHINESE SCHOOL, (20TH CENTURY)/ PRIVATE COLLECTION/ © THE CHAMBERS GALLERY, LONDON/THE BRIDGEMAN ART LIBRARY.*

# SIX NIGHTS WITH THE WASHINGTONIANS

## A Series of Original Temperance Tales

T. S. Arthur

## OVERVIEW

T. S. Arthur's *Six Nights with the Washingtonians: A Series of Original Temperance Tales* was first published in book form in 1842 and had a significant influence on the advancement of the temperance movement. The work is a collection of lightly fictionalized, autobiographical conversion narratives in which men who had ruined their lives with excess drinking—and dragged their families and loved ones down with them—relate how they have reformed themselves and achieved productive sobriety through the fellowship and support of a real-life temperance organization officially named the Washington Temperance Society but popularly known as the Washingtonians. The author's goal was to spread the word about the society, to give hope to the suffering families of drunkards, and to inspire the drunks themselves to join the Washingtonians and "take the pledge." Arthur's prose rarely sings, but he is an effective storyteller with considerable psychological insight.

The Washington Temperance Society, founded in 1840, was one of many—and, initially, among the most successful—anti-alcohol societies that emerged in the United States during the first half of the nineteenth century. While the organization generally took "temperance" to mean abstinence rather than moderation, as the word itself implies, it did not advocate for the criminalization of the sale and consumption of alcohol (prohibition). Instead, it pushed for individuals to take matters into their own hands and refuse to consume alcohol. Most of the stories in *Six Nights* had been previously published as separate pamphlets or in magazines such as *Godey's Lady's Book*. Between 1840 and 1843 the Washington Temperance Society grew from the six reclaimed drunks who founded it one night in a Baltimore, Maryland, tavern to a membership of more than a million men. Such explosive growth was due in no small part to the effectiveness of Arthur's book as a recruitment tool.

## HISTORICAL AND LITERARY CONTEXT

All the reform movements in the antebellum United States can be traced to the Second Great Awakening, a Christian revival campaign that began in the 1790s and reached its apex in the 1820s. The Second Awakening sounded the first systematic attack on alcoholic beverages. It was also democratic, or at least egalitarian, and with its emphasis on individuals saving themselves, it constituted a direct challenge to the pessimistic, predestinarian Calvinism of the established churches. The Second Awakening addressed a country dealing with the first effects of rapid industrialization and urbanization, when social bonds were weakening and drink offered temporary escape from oppressive squalor.

In the United States, the 1840s were years of specific reform movements—abolition, temperance/prohibition, women's rights—that were driven, each at a different speed, by the optimism and idealism of the Second Awakening. During that decade, the two approaches to the control of alcohol—temperance and prohibition—hardened into a do-or-die rivalry. The Washingtonians enjoyed the support of the old, established churches and the new, evangelical ones, and had just been wholeheartedly endorsed by an up-and-coming politician from Illinois named Abraham Lincoln.

In 1842, when *Six Nights* was published, Ralph Waldo Emerson's influential essay "Self-Reliance"—a piece about taking responsibility for the conduct of one's own life—had been out for a year, and it provided strong intellectual support for the Washingtonian project. Nathaniel Hawthorne, meanwhile, had just ended his sojourn at the Fourierist utopian community, Brook Farm, and would later satirize it as "Blithedale" in *The Blithedale Romance* (1852), in which the failure of community efforts implicitly supports a return to "self-reliance." In addition, Harriet Beecher Stowe had published her first work of fiction, *Mark Meridien,* in 1841, and she was already involved in the abolitionist movement that would inspire one of the era's most effective works in influencing public opinion, *Uncle Tom's Cabin* (1852).

*Six Nights with the Washingtonians* brought hundreds of thousands of men to join the eponymous movement, demonstrating the effectiveness of such inspirational tales as propaganda for reform. The success of the book also confirmed Arthur in his vocation as writer. Yet in its emphasis on the self-redemption of the individual drinker rather than the evils of drink, *Six Nights* proved to be a tactical dead end. By the end of the 1840s, with backsliding among its converts and the withdrawal of support from mainline churches in favor of prohibitionism, the Washington Temperance Society had all but disappeared as an effective movement. Nevertheless, history would redeem the society. The support-group format of its meetings and its belief in the perfectibility of humans have since become the models for most contemporary self-help movements, starting with Alcoholics Anonymous in the 1930s.

## THEMES AND STYLE

The primary theme of *Six Nights with the Washingtonians* is that there is no such thing as a "hopeless drunk"—that decency, love, and self-respect are even stronger than the destructive hold of booze. Variations on this theme play out throughout the book, in a series of dramatic—sometimes melodramatic—narratives intended to inspire addicted listeners or readers to "go and do likewise." They are also led to realize how deeply their drinking has wounded the ones who love them most. A clearer connection between the methods and goals of propaganda can scarcely be imagined. The form is that of the Protestant "relation," or conversion narrative: the audience follows the speaker as he drops deeper and deeper into the pit of his addiction, and the suspense builds until he comes across the Washingtonians. Arthur writes, "How often, alas! how often had each made resolutions of reform! How often had each renounced the cup of confusion, only to seek again the bewildering draught, and to sink still lower in the scale of human degradation!"

Arthur employs rhetorical strategies that come straight from the preachers of the Second Great Awakening. The redemption narratives are introduced and reported by a man who is detached but sympathetic and initially skeptical. After a friend has begun to tell him of the society and its founding, the narrator says: "'They did not keep their pledge, of course,' I said, interrupting him, 'Whoever heard of a confirmed drunkard becoming a sober man?'" Despite how convincingly the testifiers proclaim the depths of their degradation, the emphasis of the narratives is on the pain their drinking has inflicted upon their loved ones. The underlying assumption of the entire volume is the democratic notion that we are all sinners together and can help to extricate each other from our traps. There is no authoritarian figure laying down the law—people are persuaded to change their ways through rational argument and pungent example.

Lacking neither melodrama nor hyperbole, *Six Nights with the Washingtonians* nevertheless sustains a tone of reason and optimism. The attitude is always sympathetic and understanding, never scolding: "If I had felt an interest in the old man, I now felt a far deeper interest in that gentle being who, under such painful and trying circumstances, could cling to him, as she evidently did, like a guardian angel." Used as tactics of persuasion, the gentle tone and heartbreaking stories present the reader with the idea that he can save himself if he so chooses. If the reader decides on the

## TIMOTHY SHAY ARTHUR: EDITOR, WRITER, AND REFORMER

T. S. Arthur was born on a farm in Orange County, New York, on June 6, 1809. He was the grandson of Timothy Shay, an officer in the Revolutionary War. The Arthurs were a large family with little money. Arthur initially attended public school, but his teachers deemed him slow, and he was removed from school and apprenticed to a watchmaker. He never completed his apprenticeship due to failing eyesight, yet he became a voracious reader and educated himself.

Working in a Baltimore, Maryland, accounting firm, Arthur used his leisure time to begin writing verse and prose sketches. Edgar Allan Poe was also working in Baltimore during this period as an editor and a journalist. The two met and became friends, and Poe inspired Arthur to write as a profession. At about the same time, Arthur joined the first temperance society in Baltimore; though never a teetotaler, he became convinced that saloons were evil. He became the most successful writer the temperance movement ever produced, perhaps even the most successful writer of all the reform movements, save for Harriet Beecher Stowe. Arthur died at age seventy-five in Philadelphia in 1885.

upward path, the prose suggests, the Washingtonians will help him or her every step of the way.

## CRITICAL DISCUSSION

The immediate reaction to *Six Nights with the Washingtonians* was resounding, with extensive sales of the book and a swelling of society membership to nearly a million people within a year. From then until now, however, there has been virtually no critical discussion of the work as literature. It was considered journalism, and the critical establishment has seldom expressed an interest in journalism. Arthur's friend Edgar Allan Poe chided him in a letter for using overheated language. The few reviews that were written appeared in religious journals; the Evangelicals were enthusiastic and the Calvinists skeptical, though neither group focused on the quality of the writing. Nevertheless, many initial readers claimed the book saved their lives by showing them a way out of drunkenness.

The legacy of *Six Nights with the Washingtonians* is one of remarkably stark contrasts between its immediate influence, its status a decade later, and its present-day oblivion. By 1849 membership in the Washingtonians had dropped so significantly that the organization barely even existed. The established churches withdrew their support—the Calvinists thought the society's message was nearly heretical—and many of those who had enthusiastically taken sobriety pledges had fallen off the wagon. Arthur himself took a darker view of the problem of drinking and began to side with those who would prohibit alcohol altogether. In 1854 he

published a lurid pro-prohibition novel, *Ten Nights in a Barroom and What I Saw There,* about a drunkard who destroys himself and his family. It sold more copies than any American novel before the Civil War except *Uncle Tom's Cabin.* What little scholarly interest there has been in Arthur's work has focused almost exclusively on *Ten Nights in a Barroom.* Van Wyck Brooks's magisterial three-part history of American literature—of which *The Flowering of New England* is the best-known volume—does not even mention Arthur.

Mostly, scholars have examined *Six Nights with the Washingtonians* as an episode in the temperance movement or within a broader survey of antebellum reform movements. Although the proliferating self-help movements of today replicate almost exactly the principles and methods of the Washingtonians, scholars have yet to document a connection, direct or plausibly collateral, between Arthur's book and the founding of any specific movement.

## BIBLIOGRAPHY

### Sources

Arthur, T. S. *Six Nights with the Washingtonians: A Series of Temperance Tales.* New York: Ferrett, 1842. Print.

Brooks, Van Wyck. *The Flowering of New England: 1815–1865.* New York: E. P. Dutton, 1936. Print.

Eiselein, Gregory. "Reform." *American History through Literature 1820–1870.* Vol. 3. Ed. Janet Gabler-Hover and Robert Sattelmeyer. Detroit: Charles Scribner's Sons, 2006. 957–65. *Gale Virtual Reference Library.* Web. 18 Aug. 2012.

"Timothy Shay Arthur." *Dictionary of American Biography.* New York: Charles Scribner's Sons, 1936. *Gale Biography in Context.* Web. 18 Aug. 2012.

"Washingtonians." *Addiction: A Reference Encyclopedia.* Ed. Howard Padwa and Jacob Cunningham. Santa Barbara: ABC-CLIO, 2010. 315–17. *Gale Virtual Reference Library.* Web. 23 Aug. 2012.

### Further Reading

Allen, Hervey. *Israfel: The Life and Times of Edgar Allan Poe.* New York: Farrar & Rinehart, 1934. Print.

Arthur, T. S. *Ten Nights in a Barroom and What I Saw There.* Philadelphia: J. W. Bradley, 1854. Print.

*Drunkard's Progress: Narratives of Addiction, Despair, and Recovery.* Ed. John W. Crowley. Baltimore: Johns Hopkins UP, 1999. Print.

Epstein, Barbara. *The Politics of Domesticity: Women, Evangelism, and Temperance in Nineteenth-Century America.* Middletown: Wesleyan UP, 1981. Print.

Gough, John Bartholomew, *An Autobiography.* Boston: n.p., 1845. Print.

Hawthorne, Nathaniel, *The Blithedale Romance.* Boston: Ticknor, Reed, and Fields, 1852. Print.

"The Temperance Movement and Prohibition." *American Social Reform Movements Reference Library.* Ed. Carol Brennan, et al. Vol. 2: Almanac. Detroit: UXL, 2007. 347–72. *Gale Virtual Reference Library.* Web. 23 Aug. 2012.

*Gerald Carpenter*

*Opposite page:* Depiction of the temperance movement as a heroic battle. T. S. Arthur's greatest literary successes were his writings on the ills of alcohol consumption. © EVERETT COLLECTION INC./ALAMY.

# THINGS FALL APART

*Chinua Achebe*

## OVERVIEW

Chinua Achebe's novel *Things Fall Apart* (1958) is considered a milestone in modern African literature for its retelling of the history of British colonialism from an African perspective. A story describing the encroachment of Western civilization on the native Igbo of eastern Nigeria, *Things Fall Apart* asserts the sophistication of precolonial Igbo society, challenging conventional representations of Africa as primitive and irrational. Achebe chose to redress the historical record using the English language and a Western literary form, and he became the first African novelist to command an international audience. But Achebe was more concerned with restoring pride to Africa. He later stated in the essay "The Novelist as Teacher," "I would be quite satisfied if my novels (especially the ones I set in the past) did no more than teach my readers that their past—with all its imperfection—was not one long night of savagery from which the first Europeans acting on God's behalf delivered them."

The publication of *Things Fall Apart* coincided with the period of decolonization on the African continent, when many nations were agitating against European colonial rule. Conceived as a tool of resistance, the novel was embraced by a generation of young intellectuals in Nigeria for its reflection of an emerging national consciousness that was finally accorded political legitimacy in 1960 when Nigeria gained independence. In 1964 *Things Fall Apart* became the first novel written by a native to be institutionalized as required reading in secondary schools throughout Africa. It has since achieved unparalleled global acclaim as the single most influential African novel written in the twentieth century. Long a fixture on high school and college reading lists all over the world, *Things Fall Apart* has been translated into more than fifty languages and is estimated to have sold more than eleven million copies.

## HISTORICAL AND LITERARY CONTEXT

*Things Fall Apart* records life in the Igbo village of Umuofia at the end of the nineteenth century, when British colonists assumed control of Nigeria and imposed their own social, religious, and political systems in the belief that they were bringing progress and enlightenment to a backward and chaotic people. The story focuses on the character Okonkwo, a great warrior and athlete who refuses the new order and pursues the masculine ideal of the Igbo with a zeal that eventually also brings him into conflict with other members of his clan, many of whom fear that Okonkwo's aggressive nature threatens the survival of their community because of its alienating effects on the Christian missionaries. Okonkwo is in many respects the ideal representative of the vitality of Igbo society and customs. But Achebe also portrays Okonkwo's individualism and resistance to change as forces that signal the extinction of the Igbo.

Before the appearance of *Things Fall Apart*, history and literature about Africa were almost exclusively written from a colonialist perspective, which tended to promote the idea that Western civilization arrived in Africa to deliver the natives from a savage existence. In numerous interviews and essays, Achebe has stated that he wrote *Things Fall Apart* in direct response to the racist portrayal of Africans in Joseph Conrad's *Heart of Darkness* and Joyce Cary's *Mister Johnson,* however critical these novels were of the effectiveness of colonial administration. *Things Fall Apart* was groundbreaking for its use of African characters in a tribal setting to explode the myth of European colonization. In an essay on the social impact of the novel, Claudia Durst Johnson and Vernon Johnson note, "Readers for the first time saw tribal Africans during the time of beginning English colonization as humans with intelligence, families, emotional dimension, and their own religion and culture that were just as sacred to them as Christianity was to the missionaries."

When Achebe wrote *Things Fall Apart*, African storytelling was still very much an oral tradition. Because the artistic and cultural renaissance associated with African nationalist movements was in its infancy, Achebe had just two fictional models: Amos Tutuola's *The Palm Wine Drinkard* (1952) and Cyprian Ekwensi's *People of the City* (1954). Ernest N. Emenyonu reports that the success of *Things Fall Apart* unleashed by 1970 a flood of at least eighty West African novels in English, half of them written by Nigerians. Achebe himself went on to write four more novels that, together with *Things Fall Apart,* document Nigerian history from precolonial times to the uneasy beginnings of democracy.

In addition to establishing the prototype for an emerging canon of African literature written in English, *Things Fall Apart* was highly influential to the development of African literary criticism and academic discourse on the African cultural identity after independence. In the more than fifty years since its publication, the work has generated a voluminous body of critical commentary in a variety of disciplines, and it remains the most widely read and studied of all African novels.

## THEMES AND STYLE

Achebe summarizes the main idea of *Things Fall Apart* in the essay "The Role of the Writer in the New Nation": "The theme—put quite simply—is that African people did not learn of culture for the first time from Europeans; that their societies were not mindless but frequently had a philosophy of great depth and beauty, that they had poetry and, above all, they had dignity." The work is divided into three parts. In the first, Achebe details Igbo social structure and practice, at the same time describing Okonkwo's many successes. The second section concerns Okonkwo's exile from the clan for excessive violence. The conclusion describes Okonkwo's return to Umuofia, now under the influence of the missionaries. When Okonkwo attempts to protect his culture by killing a British messenger, he discovers that he stands alone in his rebellion and hangs himself the following day. Critics have likened the three-part structure to the conventional pattern of classical Greek tragedy, with Okonkwo serving as the tragic hero, noble but flawed.

The first section of *Things Fall Apart*, with its extensive description of day-to-day life in Umuofia—its kinship structures, religious ceremonies, forms of entertainment, dietary practices, and other rituals—has been deemed especially successful in convincing readers of the complexity of tribal ways. But Achebe refuses to romanticize the Igbo. Their worldview is balanced against that of the British, so that neither system of belief is portrayed as all good or all bad. Achebe suggests that, while the arrival of the colonials hastened a rupture in Igbo society, Igbo society cannot remain static if it is to survive. In his essay in *Precolonial Africa in Colonial African Narratives* (2008), Donald R. Wehrs argues that the Igbo's contact with the British was ultimately a testament to their resilience because it encouraged them to reinvest in ancestral principles of survival that had been lost to internal power struggles. Wehrs writes, "Many later African novels, written after the independence of 1960, would draw upon Achebe's model of assessing possibilities for modernization-through-indigenous-roots."

Achebe has been highly praised for his innovations to the Western form of the novel through his sophisticated incorporation of Igbo proverbs, words, and expressions into the English prose of the text. His use of the tribal language reinforces its validity as a method of transmitting knowledge, but it also contributes to the theme of cultural clash and mediation. Critic Francis Abiola Irele, in *African Studies*

# THE MEANING OF THE TITLE

The competing worldviews narrated in *Things Fall Apart*, African and Western, have been discussed with reference to the title, which critics consider exemplary of Chinua Achebe's ambiguity. The title is drawn from "The Second Coming" (1920), a poem by William Butler Yeats envisioning post-World War I apocalypse: "Turning and turning in the widening gyre / The falcon cannot hear the falconer; / Things fall apart; the center cannot hold; / Mere anarchy is loosed upon the world." Scholars have argued that the poem is an apt metaphor for Okonkwo's self-destructive behavior.

On the other hand, the title has been judged ironic commentary on the Igbo community as a whole. According to this view, the dualism inherent in the Igbo spiritual principle of *chi* directs the tribe's accommodation to change, ensuring that they manage to survive by drawing on the best aspects of both belief systems. Achebe's essay "Chi in Igbo Cosmology" confirms the anti-essentialism of the Igbo philosophy and provides context for the individual-community dichotomy embodied in Okonkwo's conflict with his clan: "It is important to stress the central place in Igbo thought of the notion of duality. Wherever Something stands, Something Else will stand beside. Nothing is absolute. The obvious curtailment of a man's power to walk alone and do as he will is provided by another potent force—the will of the community."

*Quarterly*, writes of the "tension produced between what one might call a romanticism of its oral style, which derives from a personal attachment of the writer to his African antecedents, and the realism of the western style, which corresponds to his awareness of their suppression in a new dispensation." Several critics have argued that Achebe's "domestication" of the English language—his use of English to relate stories in the manner of the Igbo and to accurately describe non-English experience—is an even greater rhetorical innovation than his seamless incorporation of the Igbo vernacular.

## CRITICAL DISCUSSION

The earliest reviews of *Things Fall Apart* appeared in Britain and the United States and were virtually unanimous in their praise of its insider's perspective into the intricacies of tribal culture. The criticism tended to focus on the anthropological details of village life, to the exclusion of the literary qualities of the work, including its complex narrative point of view. This type of interpretation persisted among Western critics for more than a decade: in 1967 Martin Tucker confidently wrote that "the novel creates an idyllic picture of pre-Christian tribal life," and in 1972 Charles R. Larson observed that, "in a work such as *Things Fall Apart*, where we are not presented with a novel of character, the anthropological is indeed important. Without it there would be no story."

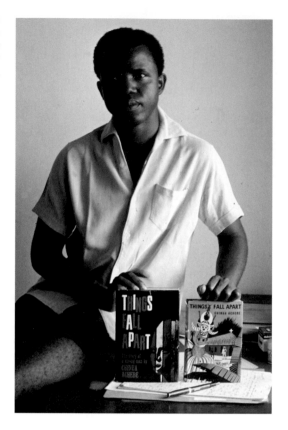

Nigerian writer Chinua Achebe, author of *Things Fall Apart,* in 1960. ELIOT ELISOFON/TIME LIFE PICTURES/GETTY IMAGES.

interpretations of the novel's characterization have reenergized the controversy over its representational authenticity and have been divided over the issue of whether Achebe marginalizes female characters, thus ignoring their important role in the fight for independence, or whether the masculinist creed of Okonkwo is effectively balanced by the designation of feminine attributes, such as tolerance and flexibility, to male characters who appear as his foils, most notably Okonkwo's best friend, Obierike, and eldest son, Nwoye. Critics have for decades occupied themselves with defining the reasons for the tremendous success of *Things Fall Apart.* Speaking of the work's archetypal status and historic intervention in the way African literature was produced, circulated, and interpreted, Simon Gikandi writes in the foreword to *Chinua Achebe Reader,* "Achebe ... shift[ed] the idea of Africa from romance and nostalgia, from European primitivism, and from a rhetoric of lack, to an affirmative culture. It is in this sense that Achebe can be said to have invented, or reinvented, the idea of African culture." In a 2008 introduction to the novel, Kwame Anthony Appiah cites as one of the main sources of the work's appeal its continuing implications for the progress of modern history: "All of us, wherever we live, can share the fascination of watching a culture very different from that of the modern West respond in its local way to the global processes through which all human cultures have become increasingly interconnected."

*Things Fall Apart* became the subject of extensive critical commentary in Africa only in the 1960s, after an affordable paperback edition appeared in Nigeria following independence. Many African critics praised *Things Fall Apart* as pedagogical in its reformulation of the African identity and lauded Achebe's commitment to the social and political realities of his country. Some, however, objected to his decision to write in English, inspiring a debate that still persists on the question of whether a novel written in the language of the colonizer can succeed in subverting stereotypes or merely reinforces them. The debate formed a significant contribution to critical formulations of postcolonial theory in the 1980s. Scholars in the West have generally viewed *Things Fall Apart* as superior to the many African novels in English it inspired by virtue of its skillfully realized hybrid aesthetic, which manages to celebrate Igbo oral forms within the context of a Western literary tradition. The subject of Achebe's strategies of persuasion and rhetoric has in fact gained widespread attention in several books published since the turn of the twenty-first century.

The tendency toward more nuanced readings of Achebe's literary achievement has extended to character analysis as well, generating a variety of interpretations of Okonkwo's suicide—among them, a symbolic execution by the colonists, the will of the gods, or a compelling evocation of the superiority of communal values over an individualistic ethos. Feminist critical

## BIBLIOGRAPHY

### Sources

Achebe, Chinua. "The Novelist as Teacher." *New Statesman* 69 (1965): 161–62. Rpt. *Hopes and Impediments: Selected Essays, 1965–1987.* London: Heinemann, 1988. 27–31. Print.

———. "The Role of the Writer in the New Nation." *Nigeria Magazine* 81 (1964): 157. Rpt. *African Writers on African Writing.* Ed. G. D. Killam. London: Heinemann, 1973. 7–13. Print.

———. *Things Fall Apart.* Ed. Francis Abiola Irele. New York: Norton, 2009. Print.

Appiah, Kwame Anthony. Introduction. *Things Fall Apart.* By Chinua Achebe. New York: Knopf, 2008. ix–xvii. Print.

Emenyonu, Ernest N. Introduction. *The Rise of the Igbo Novel.* Rpt. *Understanding* Things Fall Apart: *A Student Casebook to Issues, Sources, and Historical Documents.* By Kalu Ogbaa. Westport: Greenwood, 1999. 172–79. Print.

Gikandi, Simon. Foreword. *Chinua Achebe Reader.* Ed. M. Keith Booker. Westport: Greenwood, 2003. vii–xv. Print.

Irele, Francis Abiola. "The Crisis of Cultural Memory in Chinua Achebe's *Things Fall Apart.*" *African Studies Quarterly* 4.3 (2000): 1–34. *Literature Resource Center.* Web. 15 Sept. 2012.

Johnson, Claudia Durst, and Vernon Johnson. "*Things Fall Apart,* by Chinua Achebe (Nigeria, 1958)." *The Social Impact of the Novel: A Reference Guide.* Westport:

Greenwood, 2002. 11–12. *Gale Virtual Reference Library.* Web. 16 Sept. 2012.

Larson, Charles R. *The Emergence of African Fiction.* Rev. ed. Bloomington: Indiana UP, 1972. *Literature Resource Center.* Web. 16 Sept. 2012.

Tucker, Martin. *Africa in Modern Literature: A Survey of Contemporary Writing in English.* New York: Ungar, 1967. *Literature Resource Center.* Web. 16 Sept. 2012.

Wehrs, Donald R. "Pre-colonial History and Anticolonial Politics in Achebe's *Things Fall Apart.*" *Pre-colonial Africa in Colonial African Narratives: From "Ethiopia Unbound" to "Things Fall Apart," 1911–1958.* Hampshire: Ashgate, 2008. 133–64. *Literature Resource Center.* Web. 17 Sept. 2012.

*Further Reading*

Achebe, Chinua. "Chi in Igbo Cosmology." *Morning Yet on Creation Day: Essays.* New York: Anchor, 1975. 159–75. Print.

Cary, Peter. *Mister Johnson.* New York: New Directions, 1989. Print.

Conrad, Joseph. *Heart of Darkness.* Minneola: Dover, 1990. Print.

Egar, Emmanuel Edame. *The Rhetorical Implications of Chinua Achebe's "Things Fall Apart."* Lanham: UP of America, 2000. Print.

Ngugi wa Thiong'o. *Decolonising the Mind: The Politics of Language in African Literature.* Nairobi: East African, 1994. Print.

Okechukwu, Chinwe Christiana. *Achebe the Orator: The Art of Persuasion in Chinua Achebe's Novels.* Westport: Greenwood, 2001. Print.

Whittaker, David, ed. *Chinua Achebe's "Things Fall Apart," 1958–2008.* Amsterdam: Rodopi, 2011. Print.

*Media Adaptations*

*Things Fall Apart.* Dir. Hans Jürgen Pohland. Perf. Elizabeth of Toro, Orlando Martins, and Johnny Sekka. Film Three (Germania), 1971. Film.

*Things Fall Apart.* Dir. David Orere. Perf. Funso Adeolu, Fabian Adibe, and Pete Edochie. Nigerian Television Authority, 1987. TV Series.

*Janet Mullane*

# EXPOSÉS

# An Account, Much Abbreviated, of the Destruction of the Indies

*Fray Bartolomé de Las Casas*

## OVERVIEW

Bartolomé de Las Casas published *An Account, Much Abbreviated, of the Destruction of the Indies* (*Brevísima relación de la destrucción de las Indias*) in 1552 to expose colonial Spain's brutal treatment of indigenous peoples in the New World in the decades following Christopher Columbus's arrival in 1492. The work is a series of reflections on island and mainland locales such as what are today Haiti, the Dominican Republic, Cuba, and Florida, lands that had been systematically plundered and ravished in the name of Spanish "conquests." Las Casas gives an unsparing account of the Spaniards and disturbs the reader with graphic depictions of the atrocities they perpetrated against innocent natives. Addressed to Philip II, King of Castile, the *Destruction of the Indies* asks Spain to put an end to the conquests and protect America's native peoples from further harm.

The Americas had been brought to the forefront of the Spanish empire's activities in the so-called "age of discovery" by Columbus's historic voyages, which had been sponsored by the Castilian crown. By the time Las Casas published his *Destruction of the Indies*, the colonization of the Indies—the chain of islands extending from Florida to Venezuela—had become extremely lucrative for Spain. Since much of the literature documenting these and other colonial undertakings was written as propaganda for commercial interests, reports from the New World tended to ignore the harsher realities of the colonial enterprise. Las Casas took it upon himself to break what he called the "conspiracy of silence" over the devastating nature of the Spanish conquests. In doing so, he roused the anger and resistance of those in both Spain and the New World who stood to profit from the colonies. Distinguishing itself as one of the earliest indictments of European colonialism, the *Destruction of the Indies* inadvertently went on to play a critical role in anti-Spanish and anti-Catholic propaganda.

## HISTORICAL AND LITERARY CONTEXT

In asking Philip to stop licensing ventures in the Indies, Las Casas challenged a system of native enslavement and punishment sanctioned by the state since the early 1500s. He knew from firsthand experience what colonial rule meant. As a young man, he

had emigrated from Spain to the island of Hispaniola (now Haiti and the Dominican Republic), where he owned slaves. He supported the *encomienda*, the legal system under which the Spanish crown allocated to certain individuals—mostly conquistadors and soldiers—natives whom they would protect and instruct in the Catholic faith; in return, the *encomenderos* demanded tribute from the natives, usually labor and gold. While potentially fair, the system wound up giving license to the devastating exploitation of entire populations. In 1514, having been ordained as a priest and after participating in several bloody conquests, Las Casas finally realized the unjustness of Spain's colonial ventures.

Though published in 1552, the *Destruction of the Indies* was originally written in 1542, after Las Casas had already made numerous attempts to restore basic human rights to the natives, such as preaching against native mistreatment, helping to draft laws to regulate settlers, and experimenting with model communities in Venezuela and Nicaragua, where settlers and natives might live on equal terms. In the year of writing the *Destruction of the Indies,* he made a successful appeal to Holy Roman Emperor Charles V, who subsequently issued "New Laws" that guaranteed the demise of the *encomienda*. These laws were met with such fierce resistance in the Americas, however, that they were soon repealed. Still, Las Casas continued as an outspoken critic of Spanish colonialism.

Las Casas refers to his *Destruction of the Indies* as an "epitome" of his much larger *History of the Indies* (*Historia de las Indias*), a work in three volumes begun in 1527 and completed in 1561. The *Destruction of the Indies* was given the same task as the *History*—to disclose the brutality of the Spanish colonies—though Las Casas aimed in the former for a plainer, more readable style. Scholars have contrasted the *Destruction of the Indies* with letters written to Spain's King Charles V by Hernán Cortés, the conquistador whose expeditions put an end to the Aztec empire. To be sure, Cortés and Las Casas share rhetorical strategies in their attempts to persuade and to petition royal readers: each emphasizes the value of his own unique testimony, just as each makes it clear that the report he brings of the New World will stretch credulity. However, while Cortés seeks recognition for his own

⊹ **Key Facts**

**Time Period:**
Mid-16th Century

**Genre:**
History

**Events:**
Spanish imperialism in the Americas; plundering of Spanish colonies in the Caribbean

**Nationality:**
Spanish

# THE BLACK LEGEND: A LONG TRADITION OF DEFAMING THE SPANISH

The "Black Legend" is a modern term for a fairly diverse body of propaganda beginning in the late sixteenth century that worked to "blacken" the name and character of Spain at the peak of its political power. Such anti-Spanish texts and images, often originating in the Protestant countries of England and the Netherlands, depicted the Spaniards as a grotesque people given irremediably to superstition and cruelty. *An Account, Much Abbreviated, of the Destruction of the Indies* paved the way for this emerging animosity, especially in later editions printed to carry graphic illustrations by engraver Theodor de Bry.

Between Las Casas and de Bry, ideas and images of the Spanish as butchers of innocent men, women, and children seared the popular consciousness in numerous European countries. Las Casas and de Bry created the impression of what came to be known as the "cruel conquistador," making obvious just how much crueler the Spaniards were than their colonial rivals. Though a product of the early-modern period, the Black Legend was never quite laid to rest: in the United States during the Mexican War of 1846, for example, and in mainland Europe following the Spanish Civil War (1936–1939), detractors resorted to the old images of the Spanish as a brute and bloodthirsty race to diminish their political and religious credibility.

accomplishments, Las Casas puts his life on the line by speaking out about Spain's colonial failings.

Though deeply critical of colonial Spain, Las Casas offered the *Destruction of the Indies* with a view to reforming and redeeming the nation, especially in the eyes of God. He wanted an end to brutality, but by no means did he question Spain's colonial mission. In spite of his intentions, Spain's colonial rivals—Britain, in particular—used the scandalous *Destruction of the Indies* as a political weapon to smear Spain's moral standing and draw attention away from their own colonial misadventures. Consequently, while some modern commentators cite Las Casas as an early advocate of universal human rights, one worthy of beatification, others condemn him for his part in this strategic slandering of Spain that came to be called the "Black Legend."

## THEMES AND STYLE

The *Destruction of the Indies* is built on a fundamental distinction between the virtuous, peaceable indigenes and the wicked, lawless colonials. Time and again, Las Casas observes that the natives are *innocents*: the "simplest people in the world … they are without malice or guile, and are utterly faithful and obedient both to their own native lords and to the Spaniards in whose service they now find themselves." This quality, "which

makes them particularly receptive to learning and understanding the truths of our Catholic faith and to being instructed in virtue," marks them as everything the colonials are not. Hence, if the natives are like "gentle lambs," the Spanish are like "ravening wolves" who "do nothing save tear the natives to shreds, murder them and inflict upon them untold misery." This contrast of gentleness and savagery, of peaceable and murderous, bolsters Las Casas's argument that the natives are redeemable while the colonialists, at least in their present state, are not.

Las Casas assures readers of the truth of his testimony, reminding them at strategic moments that he himself has seen with his own eyes, or at the very least heard from reliable witnesses, all the cruelties he catalogs in the *Destruction of the Indies*. He presents himself "as a man with more than fifty years' experience of seeing at first hand the evil and the harm, the losses and diminutions suffered by those great kingdoms" of the New World. In this relatively unadorned language, Las Casas offers an eyewitness account much more intimate than any conventional history, one perhaps more likely to rouse the audience's sympathy for the Indians and indignation at the Spaniards.

The *Destruction of the Indies* strikes a complex register. On the one hand, Las Casas's language is devout and decorous: respectful of his royal audience, he never forsakes the belief that Spain's imperial mission is ordained by God. On the other hand, he seeks to appall his readers with unforgiving accounts of the Spaniards' crimes. "They forced their way into native settlements," he writes of the first Spanish "Christians" to arrive in the New World, "slaughtering everyone they found there, including small children, old men, pregnant women, and even women who had just given birth"—all while "laughing and joking." With such plain but strong descriptions, Las Casas refuses to glorify or justify the Spanish conquests, describing neither a historic nor a godly mission but an unsettling excess of brute force and a dangerous lack of humanity.

## CRITICAL DISCUSSION

At the time they appeared, Las Casas's writings were met with extreme hostility by rival historians, such as Lopez de Gómara, chronicler of the expedition by Cortés to Mexico, and Gonzales Fernández de Oviedo y Valdés, who had recorded Spain's settling of the Indies. Las Casas denounced both as liars and accused them of sanitizing and romanticizing the conquests. Gómara and Oviedo responded in turn with critiques that demonized Las Casas. Consequently, while rival nations commended Las Casas for the *Destruction of the Indies*'s exposé of Spain's cruelty, he was written off as a traitor and even a heretic throughout his own country's official realm.

The contention surrounding Las Casas continues to this day, with scholars still fiercely divided: there are those who treat the *Destruction of the Indies* as a

Christopher Columbus meets the indigenous people of Hispaniola in this engraving by Theodor de Bry included in *Americae Tertia Pars IV* (1594). Bartolomé de las Casas accompanied Columbus on his voyages and later criticized the explorer's treatment of indigenous peoples in *An Account, Much Abbreviated, of the Destruction of the Indies* (1552). BPK, BERLIN/ART RESOURCE, NY.

genuinely humanitarian work, one yielding a timely yet prescient critique of European colonialism, and others who condemn it as a gross exaggeration, one that only damaged the name of Spain. Anthony Pagden, in his introduction to the Penguin edition of the *Destruction of the Indies,* offers a valuable intervention when he acknowledges that Las Casas does indeed indulge in exaggeration, though not to the detriment of the text's lasting legacy as both a religious and a political document. As Pagden puts it, Las Casas was sometimes creative with so-called facts, but "he was and remains to this day the moral conscience of the 'enterprise of the Indies.'"

Scholarship of the past five decades on the *Destruction of the Indies* has tended to cluster around subject areas including, but not limited to, Spanish imperialism, Western expansion, New World encounters, and indigenous rights. Of particular note is Daniel Castro's 2007 book *Another Face of Empire,* which masterfully puts the *Destruction of the Indies* in context and makes a valuable reappraisal of Las Casas's cultural legacy. Productive time has also been given to historical and biographical inquiry into Las Casas's roles as a priest, bishop (he was the first to be appointed in the New World), and "protector of the Indians." Most recently, scholars have examined his writings—especially the *Destruction of the Indies*—for their rhetorical force, as in the work of Don Paul Abbott and Sarah H. Beckjord, and for their political effects, as in the work of E. Shaskan Bumas and Patricio Boyer.

## BIBLIOGRAPHY

### Sources

Abbott, Don Paul. *Rhetoric in the New World: Rhetorical Theory and Practice in Colonial Spanish America.* Columbia: U of South Carolina P, 1996. Print.

Beckjord, Sarah H. *Territories of History: Humanism, Rhetoric, and the Historical Imagination in the Early Chronicles of Spanish America.* Philadelphia: Penn State Press, 2007. Print.

Boyer, Patricio. "Framing the Visual Tableaux in the *Brevísima relación de la destrucción de las Indias.*" *Colonial Latin American Review* 18.3 (2009): 365–382. Print.

Bumas, E. Shaskan. "The Cannibal Butcher Shop: Protestant Uses of las Casas's *Brevísima relación* in Europe and the American Colonies." *Early American Literature* 35.2 (2000): 107–136. Print.

Castro, Daniel. *Another Face of Empire: Indigenous Rights and Ecclesiastical Imperialism.* Durham: Duke UP, 2007. Print.

Pagden, Anthony. "Introduction." *A Short Account of the Destruction of the Indies.* Ed. Nigel Griffin. New York: Penguin, 1992. Print.

*Further Reading*

Brading, David. "Prophet and Apostle: Bartolomé de las Casas and the Spiritual Conquest of America." *Christianity and Missions, 1450–1800.* Ed. J. S. Cummins. Aldershot: Ashgate Publishing, 1997. 117–138. Print.

Carozza, Paolo G. "From Conquest to Constitutions: Retrieving a Latin American Tradition of the Idea of Human Rights." *Human Rights Quarterly* 25.2 (2003): 281–313. Print.

Orique, David T. "Journey to the Headwaters: Bartolomé de Las Casas in a Comparative Context." *The Catholic Historical Review* 95.1 (2009): 1–24. Print.

Pierce, Brian (1992). "Bartolomé de las Casas and Truth: Toward a Spirituality of Solidarity." *Spirituality Today* 44.1 (1992): 4–19. Print.

Sauer, Elizabeth. "Toleration and Translation: The Case of Las Casas, Phillips, and Milton." *Philological Quarterly* 85.3–4 (2006): 271–291. Print.

Sullivan, Patrick Francis, ed. *Indian Freedom: The Cause of Bartolomé de las Casas, 1484–1566, A Reader.* Kansas City: Sheed and Ward, 1995. Print.

*David Aitchison*

# AND THE BAND PLAYED ON

*Politics, People, and the AIDS Epidemic*

*Randy Shilts*

## OVERVIEW

In his groundbreaking second book, *And the Band Played On: Politics, People, and the AIDS Epidemic* (1987), journalist Randy Shilts presents an exhaustively researched account of the transmission of and response to AIDS in the United States. As the first widely read survey of the epidemic, the book chronologically documents a rapidly growing crisis. Shilts follows public reaction to the disease, from the first reported case—Grethe Rask, a Danish doctor working in Africa—to Rock Hudson's 1985 announcement that he had AIDS, and draws on research performed by the U.S. Centers for Disease Control and Prevention (CDC), as well as his own research on prominent and lesser-known AIDS patients. Throughout the book, hundreds of individual stories converge to create a stark portrait of the inadequate public, medical, and governmental response to the emerging health crisis.

Upon its publication, critics lauded *And the Band Played On,* and it quickly became a best seller. However, as the AIDS epidemic became a polarizing issue, particularly in the gay community, Shilts, an openly gay journalist, became equal parts celebrity and black sheep. Many in the gay community were upset by his assertion that the gay community must take responsibility for the spread of AIDS by making lifestyle changes, and some labeled him a traitor. Medical journals questioned the validity and rigor of his research. Two years after the book's publication, Shilts expressed disappointment about the lack of substantial response to the epidemic despite the amount of attention the book had received. Today, however, the book is considered to have set the standard for contemporary literary whistle-blowing, and it has been a model for numerous other journalistic exposés.

## HISTORICAL AND LITERARY CONTEXT

Scientists made the first clinical observations of AIDS in 1981 when a handful of gay men and IV drug users in Los Angeles, New York, and San Francisco presented symptoms of *Pneumocystis jiroveci* pneumonia (formerly known as *Pneumocystis carinii* pneumonia) and Kaposi's sarcoma—otherwise rare infections that frequently affect individuals with immune deficiencies. The press, exhibiting the homophobia that would come to characterize public response to AIDS, referred to the mysterious new illness as gay-related immune deficiency (GRID). However, in the summer of 1982, the CDC renamed the disease *acquired immunodeficiency syndrome* (AIDS), a more inclusive alternative to GRID, which the CDC deemed fallacious and offensive.

By the time Shilts released *And the Band Played On* in 1987, the public had begun to show some sympathy for people suffering from HIV/AIDS, thanks in no small part to actor Rock Hudson's 1985 announcement that he had AIDS. Nevertheless, activists seeking the expansion of efforts to understand and treat the disease were frustrated by resistance from both politicians who wanted to distance themselves from the gay male population and gay men who refused to modify unsafe behaviors. Shilts stated that as a gay man whose close friends had been affected by the crisis, he felt it was his responsibility to raise awareness about HIV/AIDS and the lack of proper response to the epidemic.

Before publishing *And the Band Played On,* Shilts had established himself as a journalistic champion of gay rights in the United States. In 1981 the *San Francisco Chronicle* hired him as a national correspondent focused almost exclusively on gay rights. As AIDS came to national attention, he devoted himself to covering the unfolding story of the disease and its medical, social, and political implications. His first book—*The Mayor of Castro Street* (1982), a biography of the first openly gay politician in San Francisco, Harvey Milk, who was assassinated in 1978—became the definitive account of Milk's life and of the gay rights movement to that point.

*And the Band Played On* helped to attract attention to the homophobia implicit in the public response to AIDS and led to broader attention to homophobia in U.S. society. Shilts's next book, *Conduct Unbecoming: Gays and Lesbians in the U.S. Military from Vietnam to the Persian Gulf* (1993), examined discrimination against homosexuals in the military, documented in more than a thousand interviews. Although Shilts had attempted to hide his HIV status so that it did not overshadow or color his objectivity as a journalist, his status became public when he developed AIDS. His death in 1994, eight months after publishing *Conduct Unbecoming,* underscored the significance of his work.

✣ *Key Facts*

**Time Period:**
Late 20th Century

**Genre:**
Nonfiction

**Events:**
AIDs epidemic; gay rights movement

**Nationality:**
American

# ROCK HUDSON: HIV-POSITIVE ACTOR

In 1985, two years before the publication of *And the Band Played On*, actor Rock Hudson publicly disclosed that he had AIDS. The announcement generated a media frenzy and made him the first major public figure to openly acknowledge that he had the disease. Some were shocked to learn that the film icon, whose name was synonymous with rugged masculinity, was suffering from the little-understood illness. Many did not understand how the virus that causes AIDS is transmitted, as scientists had identified the virus only a year earlier.

Although Hudson had not come out as a gay man, rumors that he was gay had circulated years before the announcement that he had AIDS. Media speculation not only raised awareness of AIDS but also highlighted the discrimination gays faced. In fact, many credit Hudson's 1985 death with prompting president Ronald Reagan to publicly acknowledge AIDS for the first time. In a telegram Hudson sent weeks before his death, the actor stated, "I am not happy that I am sick. I am not happy that I have AIDS. But if that is helping others, I can at least know that my own misfortune has had some positive worth."

## THEMES AND STYLE

The dominant theme of *And the Band Played On* is the slow social and institutional response to the AIDS epidemic. The book opens on the day of Rock Hudson's death, prior to which AIDS "had seemed a comfortably distant threat to most of those who had heard of it before, the misfortune of people who fit into rather distinct classes of outcasts and social pariahs." Shilts provides a timeline of the emergence of AIDS, depicting numerous instances in which individuals and institutions failed to respond adequately. The book ends with images of an AIDS awareness march to the White House and gay rights advocate Bill Kraus's death from AIDS-related complications in 1986. The author laments, "By the time America paid attention to the disease, it was too late to do anything about it."

The book's rhetorical power derives from the exhaustive research on which Shilts founds his arguments. In addition to citing numerous documents and interviews, he appends nearly a dozen pages of additional sources and explanatory notes. To underscore the rigor of his research, he foregoes section titles in favor of chronological headings reminiscent of archival documentation (e.g., February 22; Centers for Disease Control; Hepatitis Laboratories; Phoenix). The choice supports his effort to present to the medical and political communities a factual record of the epidemic instead of an impassioned plea from a marginalized demographic for which national institutions expressed little sympathy.

The emotional tenor of the book is restrained, with quiet but devastating appeals to Americans' shared humanity. In his acknowledgements, Shilts memorializes scores of his friends and peers who fought to raise awareness about AIDS even as they suffered from it: "if there is an act that better defines heroism, I have not seen it." At the same time, he implicitly denounces the institutions that try to quiet activists' efforts. In one example, he refers to the response to the Irwin Memorial Blood Bank's decision to publicly acknowledge each time it discovered a case of transfusion-related AIDS: "The Irwin policy of candor infuriated other blood bankers who were still clinging to their one-in-a-million rhetoric, if not declining comment on the problem of transfusion AIDS altogether." In the closing paragraphs of the book, he characterizes the stories he has related as tales of "bigotry and what it could do to a nation," noting that "the legacy of the nation's shame could be read in the faces" of those dying from AIDS as the government and public stood by in judgment.

## CRITICAL DISCUSSION

Literary critics generally offered favorable reviews of the book, praising Shilts's investigative and journalistic endeavors. *And the Band Played On* became a Book-of-the-Month Club selection immediately after it was published, which fueled readership and made it an instant best seller. A few critics—mostly members of the scientific and medical communities—resisted Shilts's methodology, stating that he was biased in his assessment of the U.S. response to the AIDS epidemic. In a 1988 review for *Science,* Sandra Panem praises Shilts's efforts to foster public awareness of AIDS but takes issue "with how Shilts arrives at some conclusions, with a simplistic interpretation of events, and with omissions from the story." In a 1986 article for the *American Journal of Law & Medicine,* Wendy Parmet echoes Panem's praise for the power of Shilts's exposé, but she submits that "the weaknesses of Shilts's journalistic technique include his portrayal of the contemporaneous characters," which, she argues, begs the question, "where does fact end and fiction begin?"

Nevertheless, the attention Shilts's work garnered secured his position as an international figure in the AIDS and gay rights movements. Jennifer Warren, in a 1994 obituary for Shilts in the *Los Angeles Times,* writes that he forced Americans "to question the social and political milieu this medical crisis arose within." In her estimation, through his writing, he was "trying to warn us … to have the humility not to repeat history with the next disease that appears among the disenfranchised." Mike Weiss, in a 2004 commemoration of the anniversary of Shilts's death for the *San Francisco Chronicle,* recalls Shilts's "uncanny grasp of history's trajectory" and his "savage irony; disgust with indifference, political cowardice, and selfishness; and passionate anger at injustice … Shilts was many things to many people: an author, an activist, a pioneer, a turncoat. But to himself he was first and foremost a reporter."

Despite its impact, *And the Band Played On* has received little scholarly treatment. The few exceptions, such as Jack Lule's 2005 article in *Critical Studies in Media Communication,* tend to address the news media's inadequacy in times of crisis and journalists who use novel techniques to raise awareness. Lule hails *And the Band Played On* and Shilts's articles for the *Chronicle* as being "years ahead of other media outlets" and as journalism that "can still stand as an exemplar of critical research and media analysis."

## BIBLIOGRAPHY

### Sources

Lule, Jack. "AIDS and the News Media: 1980–2005." *Critical Studies in Media Communication* 22.3 (2005): 256–57. *Academic Search Complete.* Web. 10 Aug. 2012.

Panem, Sandra. "Review: A Drama and Questions." Rev. of *And the Played On: Politics, People and the AIDS Epidemic,* by Randy Shilts. *Science* 239.4843 (1988): 1039–40. Print.

Parmet, Wendy E. Rev. of *And the Band Played On: Politics, People and the AIDS Epidemic,* by Randy Shilts. *American Journal of Law & Medicine* 12.3–4 (1986): 503. *Academic Search Complete.* Web. 10 Aug. 2012.

"Randy Shilts, Journalist, 42, of AIDS." *Telegram & Gazette* [Worcester] 18 Feb. 1994: B7. Web. 10 Aug. 2012.

Shilts, Randy. *And the Band Played On: Politics, People, and the AIDS Epidemic.* New York: St. Martin's, 1987. Print.

Warren, Jennifer. "Randy Shilts, Chronicler of AIDS Epidemic, Dies at 42." *Los Angeles Times* 18 Feb. 1994: 1. Print.

Weiss, Mike. "Randy Shilts Was Gutsy, Brash and Unforgettable." *San Francisco Chronicle* 17 Feb. 2004: D1. Web. 9 Sept. 2012.

### Further Reading

Cohan, A. S. Rev. of *And the Band Played On: Politics, People and the AIDS Epidemic,* by Randy Shilts. *Journal of American Studies* 23.2 (1989): 339. *Academic OneFile.* Web. 10 Aug. 2012.

Greenberg, Daniel S. "Unhealthy Resistance." *Nation* 245.15 (1987): 526. *Academic Search Complete.* Web. 10 Aug. 2012.

Griffin, Gabriele. *Representations of HIV and AIDS: Visibility Blue/s.* Manchester: Manchester UP, 2000. Print.

Manning, Peter K., and Terry Stein. Rev. of *And the Band Played On: Politics, People and the AIDS Epidemic,* by Randy Shilts. *Contemporary Sociology* 18.3 (1989): 422–24. *Academic OneFile.* Web. 10 Aug. 2012.

Miller, Neil. *Out of the Past: Gay and Lesbian History from 1869 to the Present.* New York: Alyson, 2006. Print.

Muraskin, William. Rev. of *And the Band Played On: Politics, People and the AIDS Epidemic,* by Randy Shilts. *Journal of Social History* 23.2 (1989): 421. *Academic OneFile.* Web. 10 Aug. 2012.

Shilts, Randy. *Conduct Unbecoming: Lesbians and Gays in the U.S. Military: Vietnam to the Persian Gulf.* New York: St. Martin's, 1993. Print.

### Media Adaptation

*And the Band Played On.* Dir. Roger Spottiswoode. Perf. Matthew Modine, Alan Alda, and Patrick Bauchau. Home Box Office (HBO), 1993. TV Movie.

*Clint Garner*

A protester in 1988 holding a poster criticizing President Ronald Reagan for his administration's inadequate response to the AIDS epidemic. Journalist Randy Shilts's *And the Band Played On* accuses the U.S. government of failing to take the epidemic seriously. © OWEN FRANKEN/CORBIS.

# THE FEMININE MYSTIQUE

*Betty Friedan*

❖ *Key Facts*

**Time Period:**
Mid-20th Century

**Genre:**
Exposé

**Events:**
Post-World War II
prosperity; middle-class
expansion; start of
second-wave feminism

**Nationality:**
American

## OVERVIEW

*The Feminine Mystique,* a nonfiction exposé written by Betty Friedan in 1963, stemmed from a survey of her former Smith College classmates taken during their fifteen-year reunion and her discovery that many were dissatisfied with their lives as housewives. Marked by its confessional tone and colloquial prose, *The Feminine Mystique* uncovers what Friedan calls "the problem that has no name"—the unhappiness of many white, educated, middle- and upper-class women in the 1950s and 1960s. This problem is both defined and illustrated through a series of interviews with suburban housewives who are happily married with children and living in relative material comfort. Touching on the issue of economic prosperity in the post-World War I 1950s, Friedan exposes the dominant ideologies that preached fulfillment through motherhood and domesticity and critiques the 1950s mindset that forced women to feel abnormal if they were not fully content with a career as a housewife.

Credited with starting the second-wave feminist movement in the United States, *The Feminine Mystique* was originally envisioned by Friedan as an article, but she turned it into a book when no magazine would publish her work. Although the book became an instant best seller and Friedan received hundreds of letters from unhappy housewives who identified with her message, she also felt opposition from both men and women about the divisive gender issues the book raised. Friedan and her husband left the suburbs due to the controversy and moved back to New York City. The book exposed the popular propaganda of the era—what Friedan called the "feminine mystique"—that convinced women they belonged at home instead of in the workplace. Praised as one of the first books to speak from a feminist perspective about popular gender conventions, *The Feminine Mystique* thrust Friedan into the role of spokeswoman for the women's movement and, by the time of her death in 2006, had sold more than three million copies.

## HISTORICAL AND LITERARY CONTEXT

The end of World War II in 1945 marked the beginning of the baby boom and saw many Americans moving to the suburbs and starting families. Young soldiers returned from overseas, ready to settle down, and women were expected to follow suit. To help soldiers integrate back into society, the U.S. government passed the G.I. Bill, which gave low-interest loans to veterans to encourage home ownership and an investment in higher education. With the new benefits for veterans in place and an ever-growing middle class, the country's gross domestic product increased by more than $300 million between 1940 and 1960.

Friedan viewed the postwar economic prosperity as a "failed social experiment," using *The Feminine Mystique* to explore how isolated housewives felt in their new societal roles. She draws attention in Chapter 7 to the change in women's education from the 1940s to the 1960s—specifically how schools for women often offered classes that focused solely on marriage and family issues. She also pinpoints, in Chapter 9, the propaganda perpetuated by advertisers who urged housewives to view themselves as professionals in their new roles and provided specialized, and profitable, household products to do the job.

*The Feminine Mystique* was one of the first cultural critiques of its kind, stemming from Friedan's critical readings of neurologist and psychoanalyst Sigmund Freud—whom she blamed for "elevating the feminine mystique into a scientific religion"—as well as the Kinsey Report and the work of anthropologist Margaret Mead, disagreeing with Mead's statement that anatomy was an inherent destiny. Other cultural critiques from the same era, such as William Whyte's 1956 study of American corporate culture, *The Organization Man,* as well as David Riesman's 1950 study about American social character, *The Lonely Crowd,* discussed the isolation created by suburban growth, but only from a male perspective. Friedan mentioned both of these studies in *The Feminine Mystique,* in addition to identifying Simone de Beauvoir's 1953 book *The Second Sex* as an influence on her work and her desire to illustrate the isolating effects of suburban life on women.

Almost immediately upon its publication, *The Feminine Mystique* garnered Friedan fame and attention, selling 1.4 million copies in its first edition and opening the public's eyes to "the problem that has no name." Friedan's newfound celebrity led her to political activism, and she founded and led the National Organization of Women (NOW) from 1965 to 1970, in addition to teaching nonfiction writing at New York University and the New School for Social Research.

Often referred to as the Mother of the Movement, Friedan's work is said to have influenced modern feminist writers and activists such as Kate Millett and Gloria Steinem.

## THEMES AND STYLE

In keeping with its exposé format, *The Feminine Mystique* focuses on familiar themes such as individual freedom, suburban conformity, and domestic discontent, with a contemporary sense of urgency aimed toward white, middle-class women. Friedan notes, "Each suburban wife struggles with [isolation] alone. As she made the beds, shopped for groceries, matched slipcover material, ate peanut butter sandwiches with her children, chauffeured Cub Scouts and Brownies, lay beside her husband at night—she was afraid to ask even of herself the silent question—'Is this all?'" Friedan's interviews with suburban housewives about their unhappiness and lack of individual freedom exposed the truth behind the media's propaganda-laden agenda, as well as their complicity in perpetuating the trend of suburban conformity.

Friedan takes on her themes with a confessional tone and brings her readers into the world of the suburban housewife using detailed descriptions combined with extensive research about her interview subjects. As a result of her inclusion of the voices of individual women, readers can readily picture the housewives in question and gain a window into their lives, sympathizing with the overwhelming isolation they experience and the lack of opportunities they have aside from completing household chores and raising children. Structured as a collection of personal experiences and insights, *The Feminine Mystique* uses emotional appeals to draw compassion from its readers. Friedan writes:

> In almost every professional field, in business and in the arts and sciences, women are still treated as second-class citizens. It would be a great service to tell girls who plan to work in society to expect this subtle, uncomfortable discrimination—tell them not to be quiet, and hope it will go away, but fight it. A girl should not expect special privileges because of her sex, but neither should she "adjust" to prejudice and discrimination.

Friedan allows her readers to experience the mindset of the suburban housewife and asks them to consider their own response to constant discrimination.

Friedan's writing features a commiserating voice that shows sympathy toward the housewives she interviews. She uses statistics to reflect on the economic prosperity of the baby-boomer generation, noting, for example, that "the proportion of women attending college in comparison with men dropped from 47 percent in 1920 to 35 percent in 1958. A century earlier, women had fought for higher education; now girls went to college to get a husband." Friedan lets hard evidence give credence to the confessional quotes from her subjects that she intersperses throughout the

# NATIONAL ORGANIZATION FOR WOMEN (NOW)

Riding on her success from *The Feminine Mystique,* Betty Friedan founded the National Organization for Women (NOW) on June 30, 1966, in Washington, D.C., along with Reverend Pauli Murray, the first African American female Episcopal priest, and Shirley Chisholm, the first African American woman to run for president of the United States. Written by Friedan and Murray, NOW's statement of purpose pledged to "take action to bring women into full participation in the mainstream of American society now, exercising all privileges and responsibilities thereof in truly equal partnership with men." One of NOW's earliest successes occurred in 1968 when the group issued a bill of rights that called for the passage of the Equal Rights Amendment.

Today, NOW remains active in the feminist community, lobbying on legislative issues and speaking to media outlets. The organization is primarily focused on the following six core issues: abortion rights/reproductive issues, violence against women, constitutional equality, promoting diversity/ending racism, lesbian rights, and economic justice. According to its official website, NOW is the biggest organization of feminist activists in the country, consisting of 500,000 members and 500 chapters across all fifty states and the District of Columbia.

book, stark claims such as "I begin to feel I have no personality" or "You wake up one morning and there's nothing to look forward to."

## CRITICAL DISCUSSION

Upon its publication, *The Feminine Mystique* elicited strong reactions—both positive and negative—from men and women alike. While Friedan was inundated with letters from suburban housewives who related to her message, she was also taken to task by critics who felt her book left out several key cultural factors and was too focused on the behaviors of the middle class. Gerda Lerner, an active member of the trade union movement and the 1960s feminist movement, wrote to Friedan and pointed out that her focus on "the problems of middle-class, college-educated women" could be broadened to include "working women, especially Negro women," who Lerner felt suffered not only from their own feminine mystique, but also from "the more pressing disadvantages of economic discrimination." In his essay in *Betty Friedan and the Making of the Feminine Mystique* (1998), contemporary critic and historian Daniel Horowitz also noted that Freidan failed to address the feeling of celebration that characterized Cold War America.

The lasting legacy of *The Feminine Mystique* remains the way it sparked the second-wave feminist movement, triggering controversial discussions about dominant gender ideologies. In the years that followed Friedan's book, the movement gained momentum

A display of feminist literature, 1970. *The Feminine Mystique*, published by Betty Friedan in 1963, was a highly influential text for second-wave feminism. AP PHOTO.

from the growing political dialogue on and recognition of inequality with the publication of studies such as the Presidential Commission on the Status of Women, President John F. Kennedy's report on gender inequality. Legal rulings such as the Equal Pay Act of 1963, Title VII of the Civil Rights Act of 1964, and the *Griswold v. Connecticut* Supreme Court ruling against the prohibition of contraceptives in 1965 also spurred on the movement. By 2009, with the percentage of women in the American workforce surpassing the percentage of men, it was clear that *The Feminine Mystique* had "played a pivotal role in the rebirth of feminism in the United States," according to Horowitz.

Half a century after its original publication, *The Feminine Mystique* is still considered by critics to be one of the most influential twentieth-century feminist texts. Author Catherine Judd asserts in her overview of the work in *Reference Guide to American Literature* (1994) that the book "became the voice for a generation of women who rejected the conservative values of the 1950s, while [Friedan's] organization NOW embodied the commitment to social change and political activism that characterized the feminist movement of the post-Eisenhower era." Echoing Judd's words, critic Marilyn Elizabeth Perry, writing for *Feminist Writers* in 1996, claims that Friedan revealed "a new way of looking at life to millions of women" and "helped women join forces, find new careers, explore new, more positive images of themselves, and express their true nature in any lifestyle they chose—with pride." *The Feminine Mystique* ushered in both a shift in the popular gender conventions of the 1960s and the women's movement it helped to rekindle.

## BIBLIOGRAPHY

### Sources

Coontz, Stephanie. *A Strange Stirring: The Feminine Mystique and American Women at the Dawn of the 1960s.* New York: Basic, 2011. Print.

Friedan, Betty. *The Feminine Mystique.* New York: W. W. Norton, 1963. Print.

Horowitz, Daniel. "The Development of *The Feminine Mystique*, 1957–63." *Betty Friedan and the Making of the Feminine Mystique: The American Left, the Cold War, and Modern Feminism.* Amherst: U of Massachusetts P, 1998. 197–223. Rpt. in *Nonfiction Classics for Students: Presenting Analysis, Context, and Criticism on Nonfiction Works.* Ed. David M. Galens, Jennifer Smith, and Elizabeth Thomason. Vol. 5. Detroit: Gale, 2003. *Literature Resource Center.* Web. 26 July 2012.

Judd, Catherine. "*The Feminine Mystique*: Overview." *Reference Guide to American Literature.* Ed. Jim Kamp. 3rd ed. Detroit: St. James, 1994. *Literature Resource Center.* Web. 26 July 2012.

Perry, Marilyn Elizabeth. "Betty Friedan: Overview." *Feminist Writers.* Ed. Pamela Kester-Shelton. Detroit: St. James, 1996. *Literature Resource Center.* Web. 21 Aug. 2012.

### Further Reading

Beauvoir, Simone de. *The Second Sex.* New York: Knopf, 1953. Print.

Donadio, Rachel. "Betty Friedan's Enduring 'Mystique.'" *New York Times Book Review* 26 Feb. 2006: 23(L). *Literature Resource Center.* Web. 26 July 2012.

Fermaglich, Kirsten. "'The Comfortable Concentration Camp': The Significance of Nazi Imagery in Betty Friedan's *The Feminine Mystique* (1963)." *American Jewish History* 91.2 (2003): 205+. *Literature Resource Center.* Web. 27 July 2012.

Friedan, Betty. *The Second Stage.* New York: Summit, 1981. Print.

Galens, David M., Jennifer Smith, and Elizabeth Thomason, eds. "Overview: *The Feminine Mystique*." *Nonfiction Classics for Students: Presenting Analysis, Context, and Criticism on Nonfiction Works.* Vol. 5. Detroit: Gale, 2003. *Literature Resource Center.* Web. 26 July 2012.

Menand, Louis. "Books as Bombs." *New Yorker* 24 Jan. 2011: 76. *Literature Resource Center.* Web. 27 July 2012.

Millett, Kate. *Sexual Politics.* Garden City: Doubleday, 1970. Print.

Wolfe, Alan. "The Mystique of Betty Friedan." *Atlantic Monthly* Sept. 1999: 98. *Literature Resource Center.* Web. 27 July 2012.

*Anna Deem*

# HOW THE OTHER HALF LIVES
*Studies Among the Tenements of New York*
*Jacob A. Riis*

## OVERVIEW

The book *How the Other Half Lives: Studies Among the Tenements of New York,* written by Jacob A. Riis and published in 1890, offers a devastating portrayal of the conditions experienced by immigrants living in New York City's slums at the end of the nineteenth century. Riis pairs unsparing descriptions of poverty and hardship with vivid photographs and illustrations to create an affecting exposé of the city's worst neighborhoods. While Riis unequivocally blames many of the problems in these areas on poor law enforcement, he also chastises upper- and middle-class readers, arguing that their ignorance and neglect has caused misery and crime to flourish in impoverished areas. Whether he is appealing to his readers' sympathy, morality, fear, or curiosity, he consistently calls for them to take action to address the problem of the slum.

*How the Other Half Lives* was published at a time when the United States was grappling with social changes such as unprecedented levels of immigration, the explosive growth of cities, and the economic inequities and instability associated with rapid industrialization. The book was enormously successful, garnering enthusiastic national reviews and running through numerous printings in its first decade. In 1902, Riis published *Battle with the Slum,* which he considered a continuation of his first book. *How the Other Half Lives* had an immediate effect on urban reform efforts and continued to inspire generations of reformers throughout the twentieth century. More recently, scholars have raised questions about Riis's use of racist and ethnic stereotypes, as well as his insistent middle-class morality, but the book is still regarded as a groundbreaking exposé that demonstrated the impact photography and journalism could have as a catalyst for change.

## HISTORICAL AND LITERARY CONTEXT

During the last quarter of the nineteenth century, U.S. cities experienced extraordinary social and economic change. More immigrants—11.7 million—came to the United States between 1871 and 1901 than had arrived in the United States and the British North American colonies during the preceding three centuries combined. The population of New York City increased by twenty-five percent in the 1880s alone. These immigrants

arrived in the United States during a period of economic crisis, extreme income inequality, and violent labor unrest. Cities such as New York were ill equipped to provide the jobs, much less the housing and sanitation services, that this exploding population required.

In 1890, when Riis published *How the Other Half Lives,* the problem of New York's slums—specifically, the city's overcrowded tenement buildings—had become the object of some public concern and failed attempts at reform. As the city's population had grown and the demand for housing had increased, landlords had hastily converted single-family homes and small apartment buildings into multifamily dwellings and tenements, with little regard for fire safety or for residents' access to water, light, and ventilation. Riis had spent more than a decade covering New York's poorest neighborhoods for the *New York Tribune,* accompanying police officers and health inspectors as they raided tenement buildings seeking evidence of overcrowding and child labor. In 1887, Riis learned of the invention of flash photography and realized how much greater an impact his writing would have if it was accompanied by images. He began lecturing to New York's Christian aid societies, displaying his photographs as lantern-slide projections and urging his audiences to perform missionary work in the city. His book on "the other half" was the culmination of more than a decade's work to expose the human misery of New York's slums. It reflects and promotes the values of the Progressive Era, which, from its beginnings in the late nineteenth century, was marked by efforts to improve the functioning of modern society through social justice, educational opportunities, positive government, and legal reforms.

Riis's experience in police reporting was the source of the significant innovations he brought to literature that advocated on behalf of the poor. His book also shows the influence of sentimental reform literature, epitomized by Harriet Beecher Stowe's *Uncle Tom's Cabin* (1852), as well as charity writing by authors such as Charles Loring Brace. Riis's work also participated in a larger trend—spearheaded by periodicals such as *Harper's Weekly* and *Frank Leslie's Illustrated Newspaper*—in covering urban poverty and immigration. What distinguishes Riis's book from

**❖ Key Facts**

**Time Period:**
Late 19th Century

**Genre:**
Nonfiction/Photography

**Events:**
Industrialization;
immigration

**Nationality:**
American

# THE PHOTOGRAPHER AND HIS SUBJECTS

The practice of documentary photography, which Jacob A. Riis helped inaugurate, often invites questions about the relationships between photographers and their subjects. A photo might appear to be a straightforward presentation of a scene, but countless factors shape the viewer's interpretation. What occurred in the moments before the shot was taken? What existed or who was present outside the boundaries of the picture? How did the photographer interact with the people in the scene?

Such questions become particularly complicated in the case of Riis's *How the Other Half Lives*. On the one hand, his biography suggests a basis for identification with his subjects, for Riis himself had been a poor immigrant who arrived in the United States from Denmark in 1870 at age twenty-one. On the other hand, the conditions under which Riis took his photographs suggest a different relationship with his subjects. He often entered the tenements in the middle of the night in the company of police and health department inspectors, and his flashlight cartridges had to be fired from a revolver. In his autobiography, *The Making of an American* (1901), he describes the "terror" that tenants expressed at "the spectacle of half a dozen strange men invading a house at the midnight hour armed with big pistols which they shot off recklessly." The expressions of fear and misery in his pictures may be a response as much to the experience of being photographed as to living in the tenements.

these related traditions and publications is his incorporation of social science and photography.

*How the Other Half Lives* was influential on many levels. Three years after *How the Other Half Lives* appeared, Stephen Crane published *Maggie: A Girl of the Streets*, a novel that shocked critics because it immerses readers in the world of the slums and abandons the moralism of earlier reform literature. Riis's book paved the way for such works, offering a gritty, unvarnished image of urban poverty and inviting his readers to "go into … [the] tenements" and observe the "people until you understand their ways, their aims, and the quality of their ambitions." Furthermore, Riis was the first to publish photographs of American slums; for that matter, he was the first to make extensive use of photographs in a book on any subject. As David Leviatin writes in his introduction to the 2011 edition of *How the Other Half Lives*, the book transformed Riis from "an obscure police reporter … [to] a well-connected, nationally known author and lecturer." Riis continued lecturing and writing on poverty, the tenements, and immigration until his death in 1914.

## THEMES AND STYLE

In opening his book with the adage "[O]ne half of the world does not know how the other half lives," Riis makes clear his intention to reveal the world of the urban poor to an audience that is middle or upper class and profoundly ignorant of what it means to live in New York's slums. Riis holds his readers responsible for their ignorance and raises the threat that the misery endured by inhabitants of the ghetto will ultimately affect them: "the sufferings and sins of the 'other half,' and the evil they breed, are but as a just punishment upon the community that gave it no other choice." As early as the introduction, he demands that readers take action. The pressing question, he writes, is "What are you going to do about it?"

At its most basic level, *How the Other Half Lives* is an exposé, and as such, Riis's first concern is to present his information as factual. To do this, he borrows from both the conventions of police reporting and the emerging disciplines of the social sciences (sociology, anthropology, statistics). Riis creates an ethnographic map of the city, carefully including details such as street names as he leads the reader through "Chinatown," "Jewtown," and the Italian and African American neighborhoods. He identifies and examines specific social categories: homeless children (referred to as "street Arabs"), drunks, gangsters, and paupers. Riis also analyzes the work of government and charitable organizations to manage the poor and concludes with an agenda for changing the conditions in the tenements. Finally, he adds an appendix of statistics on immigration, population density, deaths, and arrests.

Despite its meticulous attention to detail, the book is scarcely a dry statement of facts. Alongside the scientific presentation of his information, Riis often employs two other types of language, one of which is sentimental and moral. Riis frames the problem of the tenement as, ultimately, a breakdown of domestic life. The tenements are "nurseries of pauperism and crime. … They touch the family life with deadly moral contagion." The problem is not simply poverty—it is a breakdown of all the barriers that respectable homes require. Eating, working, sleeping, and sex all occur in a single room that is crowded with people of multiple generations. The mark of the tenement is that there are no locked doors: "it is a highway for all the world by night and day. … The Other Half ever receives with open doors." As this passage indicates, Riis's sentimentalism easily metamorphoses into sensationalism, voyeurism, and exoticism. Arguments for the necessity of reform are sometimes superseded by vivid descriptions that draw clear distinctions between Riis's subjects and his readers. This integration of dissonant tones—scientific, sentimental, sensational—no doubt contributed to the impact the book had on readers of the day, even if it complicated his reformist agenda.

## CRITICAL DISCUSSION

Upon its publication, *How the Other Half Lives* was enormously popular and influential. Leviatin has found that hundreds of newspapers and magazines across the country praised the book. A reviewer for the *Chicago Times* found it to be "of immense, shuddering interest."

*New England Magazine* described it as "one of the strongest arraignments of our so-called civilization in the new world which has yet appeared." The book won Riis the attention and friendship of Theodore Roosevelt, who worked with him and other reformers to implement many changes to services and housing for the poor.

Throughout the twentieth century, both urban reformers and documentary photographers regularly cited Riis as an inspiration. Progressive Era and New Deal leaders acknowledged him as a "formative influence" who had brought the problem of urban poverty to the attention of the general public. In the 1960s, when urban poverty again became an important focus of public policy, multiple reprints of Riis's work and biographical accounts of his life were published. Riis is often cited as a pioneer in photojournalism, and his work has been a subject of much critical discussion.

While some recent scholars continue to praise Riis for publicizing the plight of New York's immigrant poor and agitating for reform, many others have criticized him for reproducing racist and ethnic stereotypes. Riis can imagine the assimilation of "hard-working Irish and German immigrants"—"how much farther they might have gone with half a chance"—but the Chinese with their "ages of senseless idolatry" and the Jews with their "queer lingo" are harder to reconcile. As Keith Gandal argues in *The Virtues of the Vicious: Jacob Riis, Stephen Crane, and the Spectacle of the Slum,* "*How the Other Half Lives* offers several conflicting messages. The poor … are just like you and me, but they are deprived of a good home. Alternatively, the poor are [a threat] … so condemn and fear them." Finally, notes Gandal, as a third alternative, "The poor look different from us, they live differently, and they do things in strange ways, so enjoy their peculiarities and thrill to their bizarre conditions of life." Gandal contends that if the first two approaches would solicit different kinds of reform, this third analysis seems to obviate any need for action. It positions the reader as a tourist or flaneur, passively enjoying the spectacle of exotic peoples. Criticism such as Gandal's highlights the degree to which Riis was susceptible to racial and ethnic prejudices, but Riis's simultaneous argument for more progressive social policies is suggestive of a broader shift in the understanding of differences between social groups. As Leviatin notes, Riis wrote *How the Other Half Lives* at a time of ongoing national debate between "those who believed the new immigrant poor were genetically inferior and those who believed them to be materially disadvantaged." Although Riis was not ready to repudiate the view that some groups are inferior by nature, he nonetheless built a powerful argument that all of New York's poor deserved better lives.

Jacob Riis used photographs of New York's tenements to educate readers about the problems of the slum. This photo, taken by Riis circa 1890, shows a necktie workshop in a Division Street tenement. MUSEUM OF THE CITY OF NEW YORK/THE ART ARCHIVE AT ART RESOURCE, NY.

## BIBLIOGRAPHY

### Sources

Daniels, Roger. *Guarding the Golden Door: American Immigration Policy and Immigrants Since 1882.* New York: Farrar Straus & Giroux. 2004. Print.

Gandal, Keith. *The Virtues of the Vicious: Jacob Riis, Stephen Crane, and the Spectacle of the Slum.* New York: Oxford UP, 1997. Print.

Leviatin, David, ed. Introduction. *How the Other Half Lives: Studies Among the Tenements of New York.* By Jacob Riis. New York: Bedford/St. Martin's, 2011. 1–50. Print.

Madison, Charles A. Preface. *How the Other Half Lives: Studies Among the Tenements of New York.* By Jacob A. Riis. New York: Dover, 1971. v–viii. Print.

Riis, Jacob A. *The Making of an American.* New York: MacMillan, 1901. Print.

———. *How the Other Half Lives: Studies Among the Tenements of New York.* New York: Dover, 1971. Print.

Ryan, Susan M. "'Rough Ways Rough and Work': Jacob Riis, Social Reform, and the Rhetoric of Benevolent Violence." *ATQ* 11.3 (1997): 191–212. *America: History & Life.* Web. 26 June 2012.

Yochelson, Bonnie, and Daniel Czitrom. *Rediscovering Jacob Riis: Exposure Journalism and Photography in Turn-of-the-Century New York.* New York: New Press, 2007. Print.

### Further Reading

Buk-Swienty, Tom. *The Other Half: The Life of Jacob Riis and the World of Immigrant America.* Trans. Annette Buk-Swienty. New York: Norton, 2008. Print.

Cosco, Joseph P. "Jacob Riis: Immigrants Old and New, and the Making of Americans." *American Journalism* 20.3 (2003): 13–30. *America: History & Life.* Web. 26 June 2012.

Dougherty, James. "Jacob Riis: Citizenship and Art." *Canadian Review of American Studies* 22.3 (1991): 551–567. *America: History & Life.* Web. 26 June 2012.

Mifflin, Jeffrey. "'The Story They Tell': On Archives and the Latent Voices in Documentary Photograph Collections." *American Archivist* 73 (2010): 250–262. Web. 20 July 2012.

O'Donnell, Edward T. "Pictures vs. Words? Public History, Tolerance, and the Challenge of Jacob Riis." *Public Historian* 26.3 (2004): 7–26. Web. 20 July 2012.

Schocket, Eric. "Undercover Representations of the 'Other Half'; or, the Writer as Class Transvestite." *Representations* 64 (1998): 109–33. Web. 20 July 2012.

Wald, Patricia. "Communicable Americanism: Contagion, Geographic Fictions, and the Sociological Legacy of Robert E. Park." *American Literary History* (2002): 653–85. Print.

Weinstein, Cindy. "How Many Others Are There in the Other Half? Jacob Riis and the Tenement Population." *Nineteenth-Century Contexts* 24.2 (2002): 195–216. Web. 20 July 2012.

*Hana Layson*

# "HOW RAILROADS MAKE PUBLIC OPINION"

*Ray Stannard Baker*

## OVERVIEW

"How Railroads Make Public Opinion," an essay by Ray Stannard Baker that appeared in the March 1906 issue of *McClure's* magazine, sheds light on actions taken by American railroad companies to shape public opinion to be more favorable to their concerns. The fifth installment of a six-part series titled "The Railroads on Trial," Baker's essay is written in a direct, even-handed manner. It discusses how a firm of hired "publicity agents" monitors and generates positive news about the railroads while the railroad industry presses for favorable testimony in congressional hearings. According to Baker, the campaign was undertaken in an effort to thwart pending congressional regulation of the industry. His exposé provides the names of the individuals within the railroad industry and in Congress who are behind these efforts.

Baker's popular series reported on a variety of excesses brought about by a lack of regulation in the railroad industry. A wide audience eagerly awaited each month's installment. The excesses revealed by Baker included the granting of special rates and privileges to preferred industries and individuals. "How Railroads Make Public Opinion" explains why the U.S. Senate refused to pass legislation curbing the railroads in 1905 and why future attempts at reform were in danger as well. Baker does not question the right of the railroads to present their case to the public. Rather, he questions the secrecy and underhanded tactics they adopted to achieve their goals. He portrays these manipulations as an attack on democracy itself.

## HISTORICAL AND LITERARY CONTEXT

At the dawn of the twentieth century, the United States was beginning to see the effects of largely unregulated industries that had sprung up during the industrial revolution. Unchecked industrial expansion had concentrated wealth and power among a small number of individuals, but the general public sensed that this newfound prosperity had not trickled down to the masses. As a reporter for the *Chicago News-Record* in the 1890s, Baker had firsthand experience with the human costs of rampant industrial expansion. By the time he set his sights on the railroad industry, he had already written eye-opening pieces on the Spanish-American War, American imperialism, labor violence, and racial injustice. As Baker saw the railroad industry,

the issues of greatest public concern included unregulated rates; free passes given to select power brokers; joint ownership of alternate shipping methods, such as steamships; and a general disregard for the safety of workers and the general public.

Baker's series on the railroads appeared shortly after the Esch-Townsend Bill, which sought to rein in some of the excesses of the industry but failed to achieve Senate approval in 1905. According to Baker, this close brush with government regulation shocked the railroad industry, convincing it to take actions that would alter public perception of the industry and thus enable it to escape further regulation. As with most of Baker's writings, "How Railroads Make Public Opinion" did not prescribe specific reforms; rather, it sought to bring the industry's antireform activities to light.

Baker was not alone in his crusade against the powerful and wealthy. In the early 1900s, in response to the disparity created by an unchecked industrial landscape, a group of reform-minded journalists, pejoratively called "muckrakers," began to chronicle a variety of industrial abuses. The group included Lincoln Steffens, Ida Tarbell, Mark Sullivan, Samuel Hopkins Adams, and William Hard. Their work was broadranging, shedding light on dangerous foods and drugs, wasted resources, racial inequality, unfair and dangerous labor practices, attacks on freedom of speech and the press, and government corruption at all levels. Perhaps the best-known muckraker was Upton Sinclair, whose novel *The Jungle* described unsanitary and unsafe practices in the meatpacking industry. Through their writings the muckrakers sought to expose and overturn the status quo. These journalists found receptive audiences in *McClure's*, *Collier's*, and other mass-circulation magazines, which had arisen during the 1890s due to advances in the printing process.

By the time Baker wrote his exposé of the railroad industry, his readers included notable public figures such as Senator Robert M. LaFollette of Wisconsin and President Theodore Roosevelt. Baker enjoyed a reputation for fairness, which not all of his muckraking colleagues could claim. His own political beliefs at the time of publication were evolving from an individualist, laissez-faire perspective toward a pragmatic collectivism. By 1908, two years after the publication of his railroad exposé, Baker supported large-scale government involvement in the economy, though he

+ *Key Facts*

**Time Period:**
Early 20th Century

**Genre:**
Essay

**Events:**
Passage of Esch-Townsend Bill; railroad company anti-reform activity

**Nationality:**
American

# BAKER AND ROOSEVELT

Early in his career, Ray Stannard Baker enjoyed a symbiotic relationship with President Theodore Roosevelt. Baker's writings on the exploits of a young Roosevelt and his military campaigns helped to cement the future president's image as a swashbuckling leader. Baker saw Roosevelt as a fellow reformer, dedicated to the cause of rooting out corruption. Roosevelt recognized the utility of cultivating a relationship with the young journalist and even invited Baker to intimate meetings at a seaside resort in New York to celebrate his accomplishments. Roosevelt told Baker that he was impressed with his "earnest desire to be fair," his "freedom from hysteria," and his "anxiety to tell the truth."

In April 1906, however, Roosevelt took umbrage with reform-minded journalists in a highly publicized speech in which he coined the term "muckrakers." Stung by the tone of the speech, Baker asked, "Even admitting that some of the so-called 'exposures' have been extreme, have they not, as a whole been honest and useful?" But it was clear that Roosevelt no longer found his writings to be useful. The relationship had been damaged beyond repair. Eventually Baker became a staunch supporter of Woodrow Wilson, who would go on to defeat Roosevelt for the presidency in 1912.

never subscribed to a purely socialist philosophy. His advocacy would be echoed decades later in a resurgent era of muckraking that arose in the 1960s and 1970s and can most notably be seen in the work of Ralph Nader, whose "Study Group Report on the Interstate Commerce Commission" also called into question the practices of the railroad industry.

## THEMES AND STYLE

"How Railroads Make Public Opinion" focuses on secret mechanisms at work in the service of protecting a well-funded and well-organized industry at the expense of an unwitting public. Baker initially discusses how a group of advertising agents systematically collects and analyzes data from nearly every newspaper in the country and determines the degree to which they are friendly to the railroads. The editors of newspapers deemed not sufficiently friendly then receive passive and active pressure to publish more favorable railroad content. Later in the essay Baker explains how the railroad industry steered testimony at congressional hearings to promote the pro-railroad agenda. He notes that the general public has no idea that these machinations are taking place. "Feeble, unorganized outsiders" have little chance to "register public opinion in the face of such a machine," he concludes.

Baker's essay appeals to his readers' sense of fairness. He admits throughout that "it is no disgrace for a man to favor the railroads either because of honest convictions or for wholly selfish reasons." Yet he maintains that if the general public were privy to the ways they were being manipulated, the railroads would be

less likely to escape regulation. Baker eschews discussing the actual abuses the railroads were accused of committing. Instead the essay uses carefully researched facts and reportage to drive at the notion that the railroad industry is unfairly exerting its influence and money in order to avoid scrutiny, which he maintains makes it impossible for the general public to reach an honest assessment of their practices. He reinforces this sense of unfairness by juxtaposing the machine-like precision of the railroad industry's public relations campaign with the disorganized and overmatched calls for reform.

The essay adopts a decidedly middlebrow tone that is neither erudite nor emotionally overwrought, crafted with the intent to be perceived as informative and impartial. The essay avoids confusing jargon or complex legalistic terms and is meant to be easily understood by a wide and general readership. Still, the author does include rhetorical flourishes that occasionally impress upon the reader the magnitude of the issue, such as when he describes the outcome as "a sort of supreme test of the nation: whether we know enough, whether we are brave enough, to deserve a real democracy." As the essay develops, the tone becomes more conversational, such as when he writes, "One more fact regarding this investigation and I am through with it." This tone bestows an avuncular aura, enabling the author to come across as someone not so different from the reader.

## CRITICAL DISCUSSION

Baker's exposé on the railroad industry came at a time when citizens were primed to suspect the worst of corporate America, and it ignited public sentiment over the tactics employed by the railroad owners. In *The Muckrakers* (2001), historians Arthur and Lila Weinberg posit that the response Baker's essay generated gave leverage to the arguments of reformers, particularly Roosevelt and LaFollette, in their crusade for legislation. In May 1906 Congress passed the Hepburn Act, which regulated rates, forced railroad companies to give up ownership in steamships and coal companies, curtailed the practice of giving free passes, and extended the regulatory jurisdiction of the Interstate Commerce Commission. Shortly before the essay's publication, Roosevelt read the proofs and wrote to Baker: "I haven't a criticism to suggest about the article. You have given me two or three thoughts for my own message."

"How Railroads Make Public Opinion" is an important contribution to the muckraker canon. Collectively these writings helped to create a groundswell of popular support for the reforms of the Progressive period. Muckrakers were often criticized for lacking a coherent or unifying message, especially by critics on the left such as Baker's one-time colleague Steffens. Roosevelt lamented that muckrakers saw "aught that is lofty" and focused too much on that which is "vile and debasing." However, the broader light of history

MUST THE DONKEY DO ALL THE WORK?

Theodore Roosevelt's presidential campaign platform was known as the Square Deal, as he pledged to be fair to all Americans and not bow to special interests. Federal regulation, including railroad regulation, was Roosevelt's priority as president. © MARY EVANS PICTURE LIBRARY/ALAMY.

has largely shown them to be a necessary antidote to the overreach of unchecked industry and government corruption. As historian Harry H. Stein argues in his 1990 essay in *Journalism Quarterly,* "They expounded … an energizing faith that reason plus tractability plus action led to moral promise." Modern readers of Baker's essay will note that many of the tactics he discusses, from coercion of the media to the manipulation of Congress, are still in practice today. In this sense his writing has an air of prophesy.

While much of the writing from the muckraking tradition is viewed today as sensationalistic due to its fevered tones and lurid descriptions, Baker's writing has survived with its reputation largely intact. This is because he seldom relies on titillation to create a response from his audience. Rather, his writing reflects his belief that "the real remedy is … *economic facts* and the dose is to be applied to the people not the legislators." While Baker is less well known today, his writing helped to establish a standard for investigative journalism that continued beyond the Progressive Era and, at various times since then, has exerted an influence on public opinion.

## BIBLIOGRAPHY

*Sources*

Brown, Richard C. "The Muckrakers: Honest Craftsmen." *History Teacher* 2.2 (1969): 51–56. Print.

Buenker, John D. "Ray Stannard Baker." *American Radical and Reform Writers: Second Series. Dictionary of Literary Biography.* Vol. 345. Detroit: Gale, 2009. Web. 19 July 2012.

Chalmers, David M. "The Muckrakers and the Growth of Corporate Power: A Study in Constructive Journalism." *American Journal of Economics and Sociology* 18.3 (1959): 295–311. Print.

Dorman, Jessica. "Where Are Muckraking Journalists Today?" *Nieman Reports* 54.2 (2000): 55. Print.

Roosevelt, Theodore. "The Man with the Muck-Rake." U.S. Capitol, Washington. 14 Apr. 1906. Address. *Voices of Democracy.* Web. 12 July 2012.

Stein, Harry H. "American Muckraking of Technology Since 1900." *Journalism Quarterly* 67.2 (1990): 401–09. Print.

Weinberg, Arthur, and Lila S. Weinberg, eds. *The Muckrakers.* Champaign: U of Illinois P, 2001. 297–99. Print.

*Further Reading*

Baker, Ray Stannard. *American Chronicle, The Autobiography of Ray Stannard Baker.* New York: Scribner's, 1945. Print.

Bannister, Robert C. *Ray Stannard Baker: The Thought and Mind of a Progressive.* New Haven: Yale UP, 1966. Print.

Filler, Louis. *The Muckrakers.* University Park: Pennsylvania State UP, 1976. Print.

Graber, Doris A. *Mass Media and American Politics.* Washington, DC: CQ, 2010. Print.

*Giano Cromley*

# I, Rigoberta Menchú

## An Indian Woman in Guatemala

### Rigoberta Menchú

❖ **Key Facts**

**Time Period:**
Late 20th Century

**Genre:**
*Testimonio*

**Events:**
Guatemalan Civil
War; formation of the
Guatemalan National
Revolutionary Unity

**Nationality:**
Guatemalan

## OVERVIEW

*I, Rigoberta Menchú: An Indian Woman in Guatemala* (1983), told by Quiché Maya leader Rigoberta Menchú and edited by Elisabeth Burgos-Debray, is an example of *testimonio*—a Latin American literary genre that combines memoir and legal testimony—potentially functioning as propaganda. Originally titled *Me llamo Rigoberta Menchú y así me nació la conciencia* ("My name is Rigoberta Menchú and this is how my consciousness was born"), the book presents the story of an indigenous Guatemalan woman, Menchú, and her community during the Guatemalan Civil War (1960–96). Relying on basic vocabulary and a straightforward style, Menchú identifies and denounces the systematic perpetration of violence against Guatemala's indigenous people. As Menchú's work gained international recognition, it generated widespread criticism of the Guatemalan government and encouraged the investigation of its human rights abuses.

At the time of the book's publication, Guatemala was in the midst of a violent civil war, and Menchú's testimonio was a direct response to the atrocities endured by her community throughout the war period. The author accuses the country's Ladinos (nonindigenous Guatemalans and mestizos) of racism that has manifested itself in acts of brutality against the indigenous population—especially during the regimes of General Fernando Romeo Lucas García (1978–82) and General Efraín Ríos Montt (1982–83). *Rigoberta Menchú* immediately gained critical acclaim. In 1999, however, the book sparked controversy after Menchú was accused of inventing or misrepresenting a number of facts. Nevertheless, *Rigoberta Menchú* has had a lasting impact on international human rights discourse as well as on the struggle for indigenous rights in Latin America.

## HISTORICAL AND LITERARY CONTEXT

The Guatemalan Civil War pitted the government and right-wing paramilitary groups against leftist revolutionaries. After coming to power in 1978, General Lucas García initiated a period of increased brutality against the revolutionaries and the indigenous population. In their 1990 book *Literature and Politics in the Central American Revolutions,* John Beverley and Marc Zimmerman describe the Guatemalan state's use

of violence to subdue the indigenous community as "internal colonialism."

Shortly before *Rigoberta Menchú* was published, several revolutionary groups formed the Guatemalan National Revolutionary Unity—an organization with which Menchú and other indigenous leaders were associated. At the time, nationalist and racist propaganda in the Guatemalan media reflected the government's attempt to increase animosity toward revolutionary and indigenous groups. The military state's suppression of any opposition led many indigenous activists to seek refuge abroad, as Menchú did in Mexico in 1981. It was the author's distance from the Guatemalan leadership that enabled her to condemn it so openly.

Menchú's work draws on the Central American literary tradition of the testimonio as a mode of social and political protest. In a 1989 article, Beverley defines testimonio as "a novel or novella-length narrative, told in the first person by a narrator who is also the actual protagonist or witness of the events he or she recounts." Further, it "has to involve an urgency to communicate a problem of repression, poverty, subalternity, imprisonment, [or] struggle for survival." Influential testimonios include Omar Cabezas's *La Montaña es algo más* (*Fire from the Mountain: The Making of a Sandinista*; 1982) and Domitila Barrios de Chungara's *"Si me permiten hablar …": Testimonio de Domitila, una mujer de las minas de Bolivia* (*Let Me Speak! Testimony of Domitila, a Woman of the Bolivian Mines*; 1977). Such recollections inspired Menchú's direct and frank description of her and her family's own suffering.

*Rigoberta Menchú* influenced religious and political leaders to address the widespread human rights violations of the civil war period. Bishop Juan José Gerardi Conedera led the Recovery of Historical Memory project, which documented tens of thousands of cases of murder, torture, rape, and other human rights violations carried out by the state during the war. The report, published in 1988 as "Guatemala: Nunca Más" ("Guatemala: Never Again"), brought about the transparency for which Menchú had continued to advocate. Yet Gerardi's assassination two days after the report's release revealed the continued threat of violence against those seeking justice. Menchú's work also encouraged other survivors to tell their stories, such as *Nunca estuve sola* (*I Was Never Alone*; 1988) by Salvadoran revolutionary Nidia Díaz. In addition, *Rigoberta Menchú* continues to be a foundational text for contemporary fictionalized *novela testimonios* such as Gioconda Belli's *La mujer habitada* (*The Inhabited Woman*; 1988) and *Insensatez* (*Senselessness*; 2004) by Horacio Castellanos Moya.

## THEMES AND STYLE

The central component of Menchú's message is that she does not speak for herself but for her people. The very first lines emphasize the representative nature of her text: "The important thing is that what has happened to me has happened to many other people too: My story is the story of all poor Guatemalans. My personal experience is the reality of a whole people." Menchú tells her story for them, to give voice to all indigenous people who cannot advocate for themselves. From the beginning of the text, it is clear that *Rigoberta Menchú* is intended for a foreign audience. Incredibly detailed descriptions of Mayan culture provide context for readers unfamiliar with the indigenous people of Guatemala. For example, Menchú begins the second chapter with an explanation of power structure: "In our community there is an elected representative, someone who is highly respected. He's not a king but someone whom the community looks up to like a father." Such elementary descriptions make the book relatable to international readers, whose political support Menchú hopes to gain.

In *Rigoberta Menchú*, the testimonial, nonlinear structure gives the book a quality of orality and authenticity, reinforced by a sense of exigency. Menchú represents herself as a "typical" indigenous woman with experiences that could be those of any Quiché Maya woman. The collective narrative perspective Menchú adopts in many parts of the text also emphasizes the representative nature of her testimonio. Her frank descriptions of imprisonments, death threats, and kidnappings lend urgency to the text and emphasize the danger posed by the authoritarian government to her and her family: "My father was away traveling for three months after he got out of prison. Then they kidnapped him and we said, 'They'll have finished him off....'" The text makes it clear that Menchú's family and community will not survive much longer without immediate foreign intervention.

Menchú's voice in the testimonio is naive at first but shifts to indignation and anger as she becomes more politically informed. The humble, straightforward style of her testimonial account is made more prominent by the role of Burgos-Debray as interlocutor. Drawing attention to the unique position of Menchú, Burgos-Debray writes in the introduction, "The voice of Rigoberta Menchú allows the defeated to speak. She is a privileged witness: she has survived the genocide that destroyed her family and community and is stubbornly

## RIGOBERTA MENCHÚ: INDIGENOUS GUATEMALAN LEADER

A member of the Quiché Maya, an indigenous group of Guatemala, Rigoberta Menchú Tum has dedicated her life to raising international awareness about the injustice and adversities faced by indigenous people during the Guatemalan Civil War (1960–96) and afterward. Menchú was born on January 9, 1959, in Laj Chimel, a community in the Quiché region of Guatemala. Her education was limited to the primary level. After leaving school, Menchú became involved in an indigenous campaign against human rights violations committed by the Guatemalan military. Menchú worked under her father, Vicente Menchú, until he was killed by police in 1980.

Menchú was an active member of the revolutionary group the Committee of Campesino Unity until she was forced to escape to Mexico in 1981. It was during her exile that she collaborated with Venezuelan social scientist Elisabeth Burgos-Debray on her *testimonio*, which was published in 1983. Menchú was awarded the Nobel Peace Prize in 1992 for her defense of human rights. Following the Guatemalan Civil War, in 1996 Menchú lobbied for certain political and military leaders to be tried for human rights violations in Spanish courts. In 2006 she helped found the Nobel Women's Initiative, an effort by female Nobel laureates to promote peace, justice, and equality. The next year Menchú formed an indigenous political party in Guatemala. She ran for president in the country's 2007 and 2011 elections but was unsuccessful. Menchú continues to advocate for indigenous rights as a local politician.

determined to break the silence and to confront the systematic extermination of her people. She refuses to let us forget. Words are her only weapons." The combined perspectives of the cultured, educated Burgos-Debray and the oppressed, undereducated Menchú appeal to international readers, who may seek both an "expert" opinion and a sincere personal account. Further, the employment of elementary or uneducated language is clearly a rhetorical tool that serves to underplay the intended persuasive effect of the book. Beverley and Zimmerman reflect on the potential power of persuasion that testimonio affords the author or witness: "In the creation of the testimonial text, control of representation does not just flow one way: someone like Rigoberta Menchú is also in a sense manipulating and exploiting her interlocutor in order to have her story reach an international audience." Readers also experience Menchú's process of politicization alongside her: together, Menchú and her audience "come to consciousness" regarding the reality of her community's situation. Speaking about having to work for cruel landowners, she explains, "The thing was I was fed up with it all.... Slowly I began to see what we had to do and why things were like that." Menchú's indignation is meant to provoke a similar emotion in her audience.

ideological project: the undermining of the legitimacy of the Guatemalan insurgency, in which Menchú was a central actor. Despite the intense media attention she faced as a result of Stoll's accusations, Menchú has continued to be regarded as an important indigenous leader and defender of human rights.

Ultimately, *Rigoberta Menchú* was successful in sparking international outrage over the atrocities in Guatemala and in fueling indigenous movements in other Latin American countries. The negative publicity pressured both the Guatemalan government and the United States—which had provided funding, arms, and training to the Guatemalan military—to bring an end to the civil war. The efforts of human rights defenders and nongovernmental organizations further helped to temper the violence committed by the military state. Outside Guatemala, Menchú's book influenced the Zapatista movement in Mexico, as well as Hugo Chávez's rise to the presidency in Venezuela. *Rigoberta Menchú* continues to inspire testimonios by other victims of torture, rape, and other abuses under authoritarian regimes in Latin America.

*Rigoberta Menchú* has been the subject of a flurry of scholarly publications; most address the issue of authenticity and representation in the Latin American literary genre of testimonio, while some treat the book as a significant work of indigenous feminism. Latin Americanists George Yudice, Misha Kokotovic, Georg M. Gugelberger, and Yajaira Padilla have based their definition and understanding of testimonio on an analysis of Menchú's text. Using *Rigoberta Menchú* as an example, Yudice notes that testimonio tells a "personal story [that] is a shared one with the community to which the testimonialista belongs. The speaker does not speak for or represent a community but rather performs an act of identity-formation that is simultaneously personal and collective." Also regarded as a feminist text, *Rigoberta Menchú* has inspired many Latina and Chicana intellectuals in the United States, according to a 2008 article by Ana Patricia Rodriguez. Sonia Saldívar-Hull devotes the epilogue of her book *Feminism on the Border* to the testimonio genre and to the work of Menchú in particular. Although Menchú may not recognize her testimonio as a feminist statement, Saldívar-Hull asserts that "unlike most academic Western feminisms, this Quiché woman's feminism creates no dichotomy between theory and praxis: 'Women must join the struggle in their own way.'"

Activist and Nobel Peace Prize winner Rigoberta Menchú addressing the crowd. Menchú, an indigenous person of Guatemala, recounts her story in *I, Rigoberta Menchú*. © MARK DOWNEY/ALAMY.

## CRITICAL DISCUSSION

Although *Rigoberta Menchú* received an initial positive reaction from its international audience, it later became the center of a huge controversy. Many early critics praised Menchú for her courage; others found the narrator's realization of the plight of her people inspiring. For instance, a 1984 book review in *Index on Censorship* focuses on the way that "Rigoberta's anger is fuelled by her growing awareness of the precarious nature of the Indians' lives." However, after thoroughly researching Menchú's story, anthropologist David Stoll published *Rigoberta Menchú and the Story of All Poor Guatemalans* (1999), which claims that Menchú falsified or invented certain details to make her testimonio more persuasive. Stoll's book sparked an intense scholarly debate on the importance of authenticity and how it should be defined. Other scholars argued that the anticommunist stance of Stoll's book reflected a larger

## BIBLIOGRAPHY

*Sources*

Beverley, John. "The Margin at the Center: On *Testimonio* (Testimonial Narrative)." *Modern Fiction Studies.* 35.1 (1989): 11–28. Print.

Beverley, John, and Marc Zimmerman. *Literature and Politics in the Central American Revolutions.* Austin: U of Texas P, 1990. Print.

"Book Review: *I, Rigoberta Menchú.*" *Index on Censorship.* Index on Censorship, Oct. 1984: 18–20. 29 July 2012. Web.

Menchú, Rigoberta. *I, Rigoberta Menchú: An Indian Woman in Guatemala.* Ed. Elisabeth Burgos-Debray. Trans. Ann Wright. New York: Verso, 2009. Print.

Rodriguez, Ana Patricia. "The Fiction of Solidarity: Transfronterista Feminisms and Anti-Imperialist Struggles in Central American Transnational Narratives." *Feminist Studies* 34.1–2 (2008): 199–226. Print.

Saldívar-Hull, Sonia. *Feminism on the Border: Chicana Gender Politics and Literature.* Berkeley: U of California P, 2000. Print.

Yudice, George. "*Testimonio* and Postmodernism." *The Real Thing: Testimonial Discourse and Latin America.* Ed. Georg M. Gugelberger. Durham: Duke UP, 1996: 42–57. Print.

*Further Reading*

Arias, Arturo, ed. *The Rigoberta Menchú Controversy.* Minneapolis: U of Minnesota P, 2001. Print.

Grandin, Greg. "It Was Heaven That They Burned." *Nation* 8 Sept. 2010: 2. Print.

Kokotovic, Misha. "Theory at the Margins." *Socialist Review* 27.3–4 (1999): 29–63. Print.

Millay, Amy Nauss. *Voices from the Fuente Viva: The Effect of Orality in Twentieth-Century Spanish American Narrative.* Lewisburg: Bucknell UP, 2005. Print.

Stoll, David. *Rigoberta Menchú and the Story of All Poor Guatemalans.* Boulder: Westview, 1999. Print.

Zimmerman, Marc. "Rigoberta Menchú after the Nobel: From Militant Narrative to Postmodern Politics." *The Latin American Subaltern Studies Reader.* Durham: Duke UP, 2001. Print.

*Katrina White*

# "IN SALVADOR, DEATH"

*Pablo Neruda*

✛ *Key Facts*

**Time Period:**
Mid-20th Century

**Genre:**
Poetry

**Events:**
1932 Salvadoran peasant
massacre; growth of
the Latin American
independence movement

**Nationality:**
Chilean

## OVERVIEW

"In Salvador, Death" ("En Salvador, la muerte") is a short poem by Chilean author and diplomat Pablo Neruda (1904–1973) that speaks out against the 1932 killing of thousands of coffee plantation workers in El Salvador. Characteristically of Neruda, the poem is somber in tone; unusually for the author, however, it is exceptionally brief, compressed, and austere in its use of figurative language. Neruda revisits the massacre as part of a larger political-literary project detailing U.S.-backed suppression of communist activity in Latin America; he dubs Salvadoran president Maximiliano Hernández Martínez, then living in exile, an "assassin" and asserts that his actions have bequeathed decades of violence and martial rule to the Central American nation. Initially published in *Canción de gesta* (1960), the poem became widely available in English only after the author's death, when the volume was translated by Miguel Algarín as *Song of Protest* (1976).

Apart from Algarín's enthusiastic appraisal of Neruda's work, initial reactions to *Song of Protest* in English ranged from dismissive to cautious. Reviewers regarded the new, overtly polemical verse as a departure from such better-known lyric works as *Twenty Love Poems and a Song of Despair* (1924). At length, however, critics came to reassess *Song of Protest* (and with it "In Salvador, Death") as part of Neruda's life-long effort to reconcile his sensuous aesthetic with his political ideals. For students of Neruda's poetry both in Spanish and in translation, "In Salvador, Death" occupies a small but nonetheless significant place among the works of the Chilean laureate.

## HISTORICAL AND LITERARY CONTEXT

"In Salvador, Death" responds directly to the 1932 Salvadoran peasant massacre, itself a consequence of capitalist policy, Neruda writes. Decades of coffee monoculture across much of the Salvadoran landmass had made the nation economically and politically dependent on fluctuations in coffee prices. Thus, when these prices plummeted in 1931, the vast landed estates of western El Salvador became the scene of a brief insurrection among the workers on the coffee plantations, who were encouraged in their efforts by communist leaders. Hernández Martínez, who had recently seized control of the country in a military coup, led the army in a retaliatory attack of tremendous force.

The massacre, known in Spanish as The Matanza ("The Slaughter"), claimed over ten thousand lives (Neruda's poem gives the figure of fifteen thousand).

Neruda's poem, published three decades after the event, may seem too late to have had any propagandistic effect. Yet the poet regarded the Salvadoran massacres as part of a centuries-long process whereby North American interests systematically repressed native efforts at organization and rebellion. *Song of Protest* presents a veritable roll call of such abuses, indicting the military and political leaders of many Central and South American nations as proxies for a U.S. government interested in inexpensive labor and politically cooperative neighbors. Dictators censured in other poems include Rafael Trujillo of the Dominican Republic; Jorge Ubico of Guatemala; and Fulgencio Batista of Cuba, who at the time of publication had just been deposed in the Cuban Revolution of 1959.

*Song of Protest* was not Neruda's first sustained essay in political verse: it was preceded by the 1950 volume *Canto General* ("General Song"), which in 230 poems arrayed over fifteen thematic cantos explores the history of oppression that has haunted Latin America from the time of the conquistadores to the present age. The work was made available in a series of partial English translations but would not be presented in a full English edition until 1993. In 2007 Neruda scholar and translator Martín Espada in an interview for *La Bloga* termed *Canto General* "a history of Latin America in verse, magnificent and sweeping in scale. ... This is not the official history. This is hidden history, history from below, a poet's history."

Printed just a year after Neruda's *Cien sonetos de amor*, *Song of Protest* (and, therefore, "In Salvador, Death") was eclipsed by the earlier work in terms of popular reception, critical study, and literary influence. Despite the connections it draws between historical and contemporary patterns of politically motivated violence (patterns which persisted in Chile well beyond the lifetime of the poet), the poem remains a relatively little-discussed item in Neruda's oeuvre.

## THEMES AND STYLE

The message of "In Salvador, Death," considered as a freestanding poem, is simple: the massacre instigated by Hernández Martínez has created an ongoing legacy of bloodshed in El Salvador, one which time is powerless to counteract and which "rain does not erase … from the roads." Neruda opens the poem by observing that "In Salvador, death still patrols." This assertion has literal and prophetic significance for his contemporaries, who had witnessed a legacy of severely enforced martial law in El Salvador, persisting decades after the 1944 ouster of Hernández Martínez.

The poem attains a greater impact when situated in the larger history described in *Song of Protest*. If "death still patrols" in El Salvador, it also, in the accompanying poems, patrols Guatemala, Honduras, Puerto Rico, and numerous other Latin American nations. In "A Professor Disappears," it even patrols New York City, where in March 1956 a professor compiling a book on Rafael Trujillo suddenly vanished. The historical and geographic continuity of such violence is most evident in Neruda's allusion to the "bloody flavor" which "soaks / the land, the bread and wine in Salvador." The image is of the blood that daubs the figures of Trujillo in the aforementioned poem and U.S. President Dwight D. Eisenhower (in "Le Coubre"). It also recalls, in a striking instance of parallelism, a line from "Treason" in which the assassination of Nicaraguan revolutionary Augusto César Sandino is described as a "feast of bloodied wine."

At just eight lines of rhymed iambic pentameter, "In Salvador, Death" is an exceptionally brief and unornamented work. Within *Song of Protest*, the poem serves as a counterpoint to the numerous longer pieces that, while hardly fanciful by the standards of Neruda's early work, often draw upon satirical allegories or fables. In one poem, "Monarchs," the death of Nicaraguan dictator Anastasio Somoza García spawns "two little fertile frogs" (Somoza's sons) who proceed to adorn themselves in diamonds. In others, a rose comes to symbolize justice and freedom. However, the austerity of "In Salvador, Death" lends grim factuality to what otherwise might be construed as imagistic touches. When Neruda declares Hernández Martínez an "assassin," he is not staging him in a figurative tableau but launching a literal accusation of murder. The fifteen thousand dead to whom he alludes, likewise, assume the air of a reported statistic despite their poetic context (and despite ongoing historical debate as to the precise number killed, which may have been much higher).

**CRITICAL DISCUSSION**

Early reviews of *Song of Protest* expressed reservations about Neruda's move toward political verse. Anglophone readers in particular viewed this as a departure from the well-known, widely translated, and less politically incriminating love poetry of his youth. The 1976 *Kirkus* review of *Song of Protest* regards the book as a disappointment for readers familiar with Neruda's early work. Quoting from "In Salvador, Death," the reviewer suggests that Neruda may be justified in "castigat[ing] the capitalist exploitation of Latin America" but argues that the resulting art is "thoroughly programmatic …

## PABLO NERUDA: WITNESS TO CHILEAN DEMOCRACY

The events of 1973, the year of Neruda's death, add a dimension of foreshadowing to the poems of *Song of Protest*, especially for Anglophone readers to whom the work first became available posthumously. Since 1948 Neruda had written much of his poetry in exile, forced to flee the country when the Communist party was outlawed and leading communist figures (Neruda was then a senator) became subject to detention without trial. Yet during the 1960s, he enjoyed a period of relative freedom, living in a socialist Chile en route to a democratically elected government.

Nominated as a presidential candidate, Neruda instead lent support to Chilean president Salvador Allende, who promoted him as an unofficial laureate. Chile's burgeoning socialist democracy was disrupted, however, in a pattern no doubt familiar to the author of "In Salvador, Death." Unstable economic conditions (in this case, rampant inflation in 1972) presented an opening for U.S. operatives hostile to Marxism to foment social unrest; ultimately, this bore fruit in a CIA-backed military coup d'état on September 11, 1973, led by General Augusto Pinochet. Surrounded by Pinochet's forces, Allende is widely reported to have committed suicide; Pinochet assumed the dictatorship of Chile and ruled for the next seventeen years. Neruda, whose health had been faltering for years, died of heart failure twelve days after the coup.

moving in its agitprop way, but quite lacking in the subtlety, grace, and mystery that once made Neruda a great poet." Rosemary Neiswender, writing for *Library Journal*, takes a somewhat more moderate stance in her November 1976 review of the volume, deeming the contents "abrasive political verse" but acknowledging that "even at its most polemical, Neruda's poetry is supple and sensitive."

"In Salvador, Death" is generally cited as part of wider critical treatments of *Song of Protest* as one instance of the volume's historical and geographic breadth. In his introduction, translator Miguel Algarín (1976) mentions the poem as part of a polemical "tale of United States intervention in the national affairs of Latin American nations," observing that the same pattern "holds for the whole of the continent. It is a story full of violent aggression and deceptions." Algarín proceeds to note that "it is Neruda's personal contact with the history of Latin America that matters here. His involvement in the action is what makes him a purifier of the distorted historical record."

Subsequent critics have reacted to the dichotomy, prevalent among early U.S. reviewers of *Song of Protest*, between personal and political facets of Neruda's poetry. For María Teresa Sicat, writing in 1985 in *Kasarinlan*, "In Salvador, Death" and other *Song of Protest* poems exemplify the interplay between

Pablo Neruda, Chilean writer and winner of the 1971 Nobel Prize in Literature. JEAN-REGIS ROUSTON/ROGER VIOLLET/ GETTY IMAGES.

Matilde Urrutia, which we can note in *Cien sonetos de amor*." Dawes accurately characterizes these two post-1956 volumes as together comprising "a new path in [Neruda's] personal and political lives."

## BIBLIOGRAPHY

*Sources*

Alvarado, Lisa. "Words that Raise the Dead: Interview with Martín Espada." *La Bloga* 1 Mar. 2007. Web. 14 Oct. 2012.

Dawes, Greg. "*Canción de gesta* y la 'Paz furiosa' de Neruda." *Gramma* 21.47 (2010): 128–62. *Universidad del Salvador.* Web. 14 Oct. 2012.

Neiswender, Rosemary. Rev. of *Song of Protest: Poems,* by Pablo Neruda. *Library Journal* 15 Nov. 1976: 2378. Print.

Neruda, Pablo. *Song of Protest.* Trans. Miguel Algarín. New York: Morrow, 1976. Print.

Rev. of *Song of Protest: Poems,* by Pablo Neruda. *Kirkus Reviews* 22 June 1976. Web. 14 October 2012.

Sicat, María Teresa M. "Pablo Neruda's Song of Protest: History as Sensual Delight." *Kasarinlan* 1.3 (1985): 35–46. Print.

*Further Reading*

Agosin, Marjorie. *Pablo Neruda.* Trans. Lorraine Ross. Boston: Twayne, 1986. Print.

Algarín, Miguel. "The Politics of Poetry." *Survival / Supervivencia.* Houston: Arte Público, 2009. Print.

Bizzaro, Salvatore. *Pablo Neruda: All Poets the Poet.* Metuchen: Scarecrow, 1979. Print.

Neruda, Pablo. *Memoirs.* Trans. Hardie St. Martin. New York: Farrar, Straus and Giroux, 2001. Print.

Perriam, Christopher. *The Late Poetry of Pablo Neruda.* Oxford: Dolphin Books, 1989. Print.

*Michael Hartwell*

aesthetics and politics that allowed Neruda to "paradoxically recreate [the] bitterly sad history" of Latin America "into sensually delightful literature." Greg Dawes in a 2010 essay for *Gramma* argues for an even more directly biographical interpretation of the volume as a whole; writing that the political "commitment" evident in *Song of Protest* "is only made viable after having anchored his life in the shared love with

# INSIDE THE COMPANY
## *CIA Diary*
*Philip Agee*

## OVERVIEW

*Inside the Company: CIA Diary,* written by Philip Agee and first published in 1974, was the first book by a former Central Intelligence Agency agent that exposed the organization's undercover personnel and informers. The work is written in the format of a diary but represents Agee's reconstruction of his twelve-year career in the CIA, from his training in the United States to his assignments in Ecuador, Uruguay, and the 1968 Summer Olympics in Mexico City. Alongside copious details of espionage and propaganda campaigns, *Inside the Company* chronicles Agee's growing disillusionment with the CIA and the political role it played in developing nations. By book's end, the author has become a proponent of socialist revolution, committed to neutralizing the CIA by exposing its secrets.

The book was released in the United States in early 1975, a time when the CIA was under intense scrutiny from politicians and the press in the aftermath of the Watergate scandal and the resignation of President Richard M. Nixon the previous August. Agee had first published his book in the United Kingdom to avoid possible censorship or prosecution by the U.S. government. *Inside the Company* attracted wide attention upon its release, much of it devoted to the twenty-page appendix naming more than 200 individuals and organizations allegedly working with or financed by the CIA. Agee became a notorious figure, deported from several nations and reviled by politicians for blowing the whistle on the government's clandestine Cold War interventions abroad. Agee's book and several follow-up works helped reveal the agency's modus operandi to the general public.

## HISTORICAL AND LITERARY CONTEXT

The CIA was officially established in 1947 under the National Security Act, continuing the intelligence coordination and espionage efforts conducted by the Office of Strategic Services during World War II. Starting in the 1950s, the agency played a crucial, though largely secret, role in U.S. foreign policy, especially in combating communist movements around the world. Covert operations were used as a means of exerting strategic influence more robustly than traditional diplomacy but without resort to military intervention. The CIA was directly involved in subverting and overthrowing elected governments in countries such as Iran (1953), Guatemala (1954), and Chile (1973), and it led a major counterinsurgency program during the Vietnam War.

In the early 1970s a number of events brought CIA espionage and other secret government activity into the public spotlight. In 1971 the Supreme Court upheld the right of major newspapers to publish the Pentagon Papers, a set of classified documents exposed by defense analyst Daniel Ellsberg. In December 1974 investigative journalist Seymour Hersh reported that the CIA had illegally engaged in surveillance and infiltrated antiwar organizations inside the United States. Early in 1975 President Gerald Ford and both houses of Congress launched investigations into the alleged wrongdoings of the intelligence community, leading to a flood of disturbing revelations. In this context, Agee, who had left the CIA in 1969, decided to violate his pledge of secrecy and reveal what he knew in order to help expose the agency's techniques and explain its role as "the secret police of American capitalism." Agee told an interviewer in 1974, "I realized that what we were doing on a big scale in Vietnam I had been doing on a lower scale in Latin America."

Agee's work thus contributed to a growing collection of exposés that transformed public perception of the dangers of the abuse of government power. A prior book, *The CIA and the Cult of Intelligence* (1974), cowritten by ex-CIA official Victor Marchetti, had gone to press with many sensitive passages deleted at the CIA's insistence. These sober works of nonfiction provided an antidote of sorts to the best-selling Cold War spy novels such as the James Bond series by Ian Fleming and John Le Carré's *The Spy Who Came in from the Cold* (1963).

Considered the CIA's most dangerous turncoat, Agee persevered and led a small group of researchers, counterspies, and journalists in monitoring and exposing what he believed were the CIA's dirty tricks. Periodicals such as *CounterSpy* and *Covert Action Information Bulletin,* to which Agee contributed, continued well into the 1990s. In the years after the September 2001 terrorist attacks on New York City and Washington,

## ❖ *Key Facts*

**Time Period:**
Late 20th Century

**Genre:**
Nonfiction Account

**Events:**
Cold War; exposure of U.S. government's clandestine interventions in foreign countries

**Nationality:**
American

# THE ABUSE OF COVERT ACTION

Government investigations and investigative reporting of illegal activity by the CIA and the FBI in the mid-1970s revealed many shocking secrets. For example, the CIA attempted to assassinate a number of foreign leaders, including Ngo Dinh Diem, president of South Vietnam; the Dominican dictator Rafael Trujillo; and the leader of Cuba's revolution, Fidel Castro; the organization was successful in its assassination attempt of Patrice Lumumba, the prime minister of the Republic of the Congo. The CIA also launched a paramilitary attack on Cuba in 1961—the failed Bay of Pigs operation.

In Chile the agency intervened in multiple elections to prevent the left-leaning Salvador Allende from winning the presidency. After Allende was elected in 1970, the CIA tried and failed to prevent his inauguration before approaching military officers to suggest they engineer a coup. Ultimately, on September 11, 1973, officers led by General Augusto Pinochet carried out a coup and killed Allende. In addition, the CIA and FBI secretly intercepted and opened hundreds of thousands of pieces of U.S. mail from the 1950s to the 1970s. The CIA ran several programs to spy on, infiltrate, and weaken antiwar and other radical groups inside the United States, although the agency was barred by law from conducting espionage against U.S. citizens. These programs were similar to, but separate from, the FBI's COINTELPRO (Counter-Intelligence Program). In its "MK ULTRA" program, the CIA conducted behavioral research on unwitting U.S. citizens, experimenting with torture, sensory deprivation, and multiple chemicals and drugs, including LSD.

D.C., awareness of and public debate about the covert dimensions of foreign affairs further increased.

## THEMES AND STYLE

The goal of *Inside the Company* was to record with detailed accuracy the typical strategies and clandestine methods the CIA employs in foreign countries. Most of the book's first half chronicles the agency's activity in Ecuador from 1960 to 1963. According to Agee, in order to discredit the political Left and undermine relations between Ecuador and Cuba, the CIA infiltrated political organizations, collaborated with government officials, conducted propaganda campaigns, circulated false stories through the press, and planted phony documents on Communist Party leaders. In July 1963 military leaders in Ecuador collaborating with the CIA deposed the president in a coup, outlawed communism, and arrested dissidents using the agency's list of subversives. By documenting such incidents, Agee seeks to convey the negative impact of CIA activity on the nations affected, not just in regime changes and political battles but also in regard to deeper socioeconomic factors such as poverty, landownership, and inequalities of wealth.

Agee's most significant stylistic choice is to write chronologically in a diary format. Thus, the narrative follows his career in intelligence, beginning with his recruitment while attending college at Notre Dame. Early passages convey his enthusiasm for learning the work and his idealistic belief in liberalism and projects such as President John F. Kennedy's Alliance for Progress. Interspersed with the dense details of daily life in a CIA station are passages revealing the author's growing disaffection and radicalization. Two turning points for him are the U.S. invasion of the Dominican Republic in 1965 and the massacre of student protesters at Tlateloloco, Mexico City, before the 1968 Olympics. By late 1968 Agee has decided to quit the CIA, convinced that U.S. policy is retarding social reform in the developing world and that the agency's true function is "plugging up leaks in the political dam night and day so that shareholders of U.S. companies operating in poor countries can continue enjoying the rip-off." The book's final section covers his efforts to research, write, and publish his exposé while the CIA's spying tactics are now turned against him.

The bulk of *Inside the Company* is written in a fairly dry, informative style. Many sections are overflowing with incidental details about such matters as the bureaucratic structure of intelligence agencies or Uruguayan political parties. Certain anecdotes, however, stand out with stark clarity, such as the moment in December 1965 when Agee, visiting the police chief of Uruguay's capital city, Montevideo, hears the rising moans of a man being tortured in the next room—a man whose name Agee himself had given the police. In the middle sections, the author begins to question the effects and motives of the agency's operations; by the end, the tone shifts to political analysis and overt argumentation from a left-wing viewpoint. Once Agee himself becomes a target of surveillance, the narrative drama increases. These final pages prefigure the fast-paced style of Agee's memoir, *On the Run* (1987). For example, an American "friend" loans him a typewriter that he eventually realizes is bugged. A picture of the typewriter, with the monitoring device revealed in the lining of its case, adorns *Inside the Company*'s hardcover jacket.

## CRITICAL DISCUSSION

With the CIA already reeling from the revelations of the Watergate hearings and Hersh's reporting, *Inside the Company* fell like a bombshell upon its release, becoming a best seller in several countries. Reviewers generally concurred that Agee's case could scarcely be refuted. A former CIA official, Miles Copeland, wrote in the British publication the *Spectator* that "the book is interesting as an authentic account of how an ordinary American or British 'case officer' operates," adding that the substance "is presented with deadly accuracy." A reviewer in an internal CIA journal declassified years later wrote that "the book will affect

Philip Agee's 1974 book *Inside the Company* documents the CIA's long relationship with Latin American politics, a link shown in this billboard in Managua, Nicaragua, depicting Eugene H. Hasenfus, a CIA employee captured in Nicaragua in 1986. © ANDREW HOLBROOKE/CORBIS.

the CIA as a severe body blow as does any living organism." A critical review in the *New York Times* took issue with the author's political conclusions and found Agee's account of his radicalization rather bland but allowed that the book's exhaustive exposition of everyday espionage provided a valuable service.

The book's lasting legacy centers on the author's controversial decision to name names, exposing hundreds of undercover CIA agents and collaborators. Agee and his colleagues, consciously using exposure as a weapon, revealed thousands more names in follow-up works, including *Dirty Work: The CIA in Western Europe* (1978). Agee himself became a political cause célèbre after he was deported from Britain in 1977. He was later forbidden from taking up residence in France, the Netherlands, and West Germany, and his U.S. passport was revoked in 1979. Although Agee had violated his secrecy pledge, his actions broke no existing laws. In 1982 Congress passed the Intelligence Identities Protection Act, making it a federal offense to knowingly reveal the identity of an undercover agent. Agee, according to many, was the prime catalyst and target of this legislation. Former CIA director and U.S. president George H. W. Bush stated publicly in 1997 that he considered Agee a traitor to his country, while some on the political left viewed his actions as heroic and patriotic.

Controversy over the CIA's political role escalated in the run-up to the U.S. invasion of Iraq in 2003. A group of former intelligence professionals, including Ray McGovern and David MacMichael, publicly questioned whether President George W. Bush and his administration had manipulated the intelligence gathering process to buttress its case for going to war. Two Bush administration officials were later suspected of deliberately revealing the identity of covert CIA operative Valerie Plame Wilson to reporters. These events reflected and underscored the legacy of Agee, as was noted in commentary following his death in 2008.

## BIBLIOGRAPHY

*Sources*

Agee, Philip. *Inside the Company: CIA Diary.* New York: Stonehill, 1975. Print.

Agee, Philip, and Louis Wolf, eds. *Dirty Work: The CIA in Western Europe.* New York: Dorset, 1978. Print.

Copeland, Miles. Rev. of *Inside the Company,* by Philip Agee. *Spectator* 11 Jan. 1975: 40. Print.

Eder, Richard. "The Disillusion of a CIA Man: 12 Years from Agent to Radical." *New York Times* 12 July 1974. *New York Times Archive.* Web. 27 Sept. 2012.

Lingeman, Richard. "The Unmaking of a Spy." *New York Times* 31 July 1975. *New York Times Archive.* Web. 27 Sept. 2012.

*Further Reading*

Bloch, Jonathan, and Patrick Fitzgerald. *British Intelligence and Covert Action: Africa, Middle East and Europe Since 1945.* Dingle: Brandon, 1983. Print.

Blum, William. *Killing Hope: U.S. Military and CIA Interventions Since World War II*. Monroe: Common Courage, 1995. Print.

Campbell, Duncan, "The Spy Who Stayed Out in the Cold," *Guardian* (London). Guardian News and Media, 9 Jan. 2007. Web. 27 Sept. 2012.

Karolides, Nicholas J. *Banned Books: Literature Suppressed on Political Grounds*. New York: Facts On File, 1998. Print.

Marchetti, Victor, and John D. Marks. *The CIA and the Cult of Intelligence*. New York: Knopf, 1974. Print.

Weiner, Tim. *Legacy of Ashes: The History of the CIA*. New York: Doubleday, 2007. Print.

*Media Adaptation*

*Inside the CIA*. Dir. Allan Francovich. Perf. Carl Acker, Philip Agee, and Laura Allende. Maljack Productions, 1987. Film.

*Roger Smith*

# "J'ACCUSE"

*Émile Zola*

## OVERVIEW

"J'accuse" ("I accuse"), an editorial by Émile Zola that was published on January 13, 1889, in the Paris newspaper *L'Aurore*, summarizes the drama of the Dreyfus Affair in order to expose the rampant anti-Semitism within France's institutions. "J'accuse" takes the form of a first-person letter to French president Félix Faure, and it outlines the blatantly unjust treatment suffered by army captain Alfred Dreyfus as a direct result of anti-Semitism among the highest-ranking members of the military and justice system. The piece ends with a list of accusations leveled at those individuals directly responsible for the wrongful conviction and imprisonment of Dreyfus. In addition to decrying the "odious antisemitism" of Faure's inaction, Zola implicitly asks his readers—French citizens—to demand tolerance and justice from their politicians, who can no longer be relied upon to uphold the Third French Republic's founding promise to protect rights to fair trials and freedom of religion.

Zola was one of France's best-known writers when he published "J'accuse." A proponent of naturalism and positivism, he was particularly interested in the ways in which morality and biology intersect. As an author, he was fascinated by the novelistic scope of the Dreyfus Affair. The letter's publication created a furor and doubled *L'Aurore*'s circulation overnight. After being tried for libel in February 1898, Zola was fined and sentenced to a year in prison, but he fled the country, spending a year in exile in England. Dreyfus, meanwhile, was freed in 1906, largely because of the public debate that "J'accuse" had stirred. Zola's decision to advocate for Dreyfus's innocence on the basis of his reputation as a well-known author established the role that public intellectuals—notably Jean-Paul Sartre, Albert Camus, and Bernard Henri-Lévy—would play in French politics throughout the twentieth century.

## HISTORICAL AND LITERARY CONTEXT

In late-nineteenth-century France, steadily increasing industrialization and urbanization, along with the bitter and lingering memory of the French defeat in the Franco-Prussian War of 1870, rekindled xenophobic and anti-Semitic discourse among politicians and journalists. As a French-Alsatian Jew who dedicated his life to a career in the French military, Dreyfus was an elite version of the many immigrants who had come to France over the course of the nineteenth century: He was fully assimilated into French culture, and his religion was a private matter that he felt had no bearing on his army career. His troubles began in September 1894, when French intelligence intercepted a letter revealing military secrets to Germany that he had allegedly sent. Despite the shoddy handling of evidence and witnesses, Dreyfus was swiftly tried, found guilty, and sentenced to prison on Devil's Island, a notoriously brutal penal colony off Guyana. The French press, which sold papers based on sensational stories that often sacrificed facts, played a key role in shaping public opinion and explaining away the clearly false evidence used against Dreyfus.

By the time Zola published "J'accuse," the Dreyfus Affair had been dominating political discourse for nearly five years. The case had exacerbated the profound divisions within French society between Catholic, nationalist traditionalists who defended the army and the secularizing, liberal Republicans who proclaimed Dreyfus's innocence. In 1899, as a direct result of Zola's exposé, Dreyfus's family finally succeeded in securing a second trial. Dreyfus was revealed to be innocent in this trial, but it took several more years for him to be definitively exonerated.

Although the Dreyfus Affair had already generated a huge amount of debate, Zola's use of his fame and of the burgeoning medium of journalism in order to deliver his message was remarkable. According to Vanessa Schwartz in *Spectacular Realities* (1998), a law passed in 1881 on the freedom of the press in France "reversed the course of almost a century's limitations" on free speech. Schwartz notes that from 1882 to 1892 the number of periodical titles printed in France nearly doubled from 3,800 to 6,000. Though the press was more often than not a vehicle for tall tales, lurid crime reporting, and vicious political propaganda, Zola's decision to publish "J'accuse" helped legitimize journalism as a powerful tool for justice.

In taking up the mantle for justice, Zola further polarized the French intelligentsia, which had divided into the *Dreyfusard* (those convinced of Dreyfus's innocence) and *anti-Dreyfusard* camps. Many famous writers of the day turned to their craft to make their case for Dreyfus's innocence. Marcel Proust, for example, began work on *Jean Santeuil*, a novel based on the case that he never finished. The affair and Zola's role in it became more broadly emblematic of the modern

### Key Facts

**Time Period:**
Late 19th Century

**Genre:**
Letter

**Events:**
French defeat in the Franco-Prussian War; rapid industrialization and urbanization; Dreyfus Affair

**Nationality:**
French

# PRIMARY SOURCE

## EXCERPT FROM *J'ACCUSE*

Would you allow me, in my gratitude for the benevolent reception that you gave me one day, to draw the attention of your rightful glory and to tell you that your star, so happy until now, is threatened by the most shameful and most ineffaceable of blemishes?

You have passed healthy and safe through base calumnies; you have conquered hearts. You appear radiant in the apotheosis of this patriotic festival that the Russian alliance was for France, and you prepare to preside over the solemn triumph of our World Fair, which will crown our great century of work, truth and freedom. But what a spot of mud on your name—I was going to say on your reign—is this abominable Dreyfus affair! A council of war, under order, has just dared to acquit Esterhazy, a great blow to all truth, all justice. And it is finished, France has this stain on her cheek, History will write that it was under your presidency that such a social crime could be committed.

Since they dared, I too will dare. The truth I will say, because I promised to say it, if justice, regularly seized, did not do it, full and whole. My duty is to speak, I do not want to be an accomplice. …

They delivered an iniquitous sentence that will forever weigh on our councils of war, sullying all their arrests from now with suspicion. The first council of war could have been foolish; the second was inevitably criminal. Its excuse, I repeat it, was that the supreme chief had spoken, declaring the thing considered to be unassailable, holy and higher than men, so that inferiors could not say the opposite. One speaks to us about the honor of the army, that we should like it, respect it. Ah! admittedly, yes, the army which would rise to the first threat, which would defend the French ground, it is all the people, and we have for it only tenderness and respect. But it is not a question of that, for which we precisely want dignity, in our need for justice. It is about the sword, the Master that one will give us tomorrow perhaps. And do not kiss devotedly the handle of the sword, by god!

I have shown in addition: the Dreyfus affair was the affair of the department of war, a High Command officer, denounced by his comrades of

social struggle between, as Jeffrey Mehlman calls it in his essay in *A New History of French Literature* (1994), "the lower intelligentsia over an upper one." This conflict reverberated throughout the twentieth century, most notably in the divisive politics prior to and during World War II.

## THEMES AND STYLE

The main goal of Zola's editorial is to contrast the base anti-Semitism evident in the Dreyfus Affair with the lofty goals of progress and modernization that the French Republic is seeking to embody. He begins with a mention of the "World Fair, which will crown our great century of truth, work, and freedom." He contends that this event, showcasing the benefits of science and reason, is incongruous with the miscarriage of justice in Dreyfus's trial and sentencing and the way in which the "filthy press" has used the affair to "mislay the opinion" of the masses. Furthermore, Zola argues, the reaction to the affair has put the French Republic's place in history at risk: "It is a crime to exploit patriotism for works of hatred … when all the social science is with work for the nearest work of truth and justice."

Zola makes it clear that he is attempting to sway the opinion of none other than the French president, whose duty is to be a beacon for French Republican values. By writing in the first person and publishing the letter in a newspaper, Zola cleverly uses the very press he is criticizing to his advantage. "J'accuse" functions as an example of the engaged action citizens should be taking to protect their Republic instead of passively consuming the scandalous lies published in the press and allowing clearly innocent men such as Dreyfus to suffer as a result. Employing a measured tone, Zola explains how the events leading to Dreyfus's conviction demonstrate behavior at odds with the era of progress and freedom that France would like to believe it has pioneered.

Stylistically, Zola's outrage builds to a crescendo with his appeal to the French president's superior moral compass. At the beginning of the letter, he writes to Faure: "I am sure you are unaware" of the truth of the matter. Zola then outlines the facts of the case against Dreyfus in clear, forceful language, much as a lawyer would in court: "Here then, Mr. President, are the facts which explain how a miscarriage of justice could be made." He reminds the president that he has the power and the mandate to set Dreyfus free and to right the wrongs of a justice system that would deliver such a hateful verdict. Zola concludes his summary by telling Faure that the affair "will remain a stain for your presidency" unless Dreyfus is freed. In *Why the Dreyfus Affair Matters*, Louis Begley notes that, with his repetition of the phrase the High Command, condemned under the pressure of the heads of the High Command. Once again, it cannot restore his innocence without all the High Command being guilty. Also the offices, by all conceivable means, by press campaigns, by communications, by influences, protected Esterhazy only to convict Dreyfus a second time. What sweeping changes should the republican government should give to this [Jesuitery], as General Billot himself calls it! Where is the truly strong ministry of wise patriotism that will dare to reforge and to renew all? What of people I know who, faced with the possibility of war, tremble of anguish knowing in what hands lies national defense! And what a nest of base intrigues, gossips and dilapidations has this crowned asylum become, where the fate of fatherland is decided! One trembles in face of the terrible day that there has just thrown the Dreyfus affair, this human sacrifice of an unfortunate, a "dirty Jew"! Ah! all that was agitated insanity there and stupidity, imaginations insane, practices of low police force, manners of inquisition and tyranny, good pleasure of some non-commissioned officers putting their boots on the nation, returning in its throat its cry of truth and justice, under the lying pretext and sacrilege of the reason of State.

And it is a yet another crime to have [pressed on ?] the filthy press, to have let itself defend by all the rabble of Paris, so that the rabble triumphs insolently in defeat of law and simple probity. It is a crime to have accused those who wished for a noble France, at the head of free and just nations, of troubling her, when one warps oneself the impudent plot to impose the error, in front of the whole world. It is a crime to mislay the opinion, to use for a spiteful work this opinion, perverted to the point of becoming delirious. It is a crime to poison the small and the humble, to exasperate passions of reaction and intolerance, while taking shelter behind the odious antisemitism, from which, if not cured, the great liberal France of humans rights will die. It is a crime to exploit patriotism for works of hatred, and it is a crime, finally, to turn into to sabre the modern god, when all the social science is with work for the nearest work of truth and justice.

This truth, this justice, that we so passionately wanted, what a distress to see them thus souffletées, more ignored and more darkened!

Nineteenth-century French caricature of Émile Zola penning the famous "J'accuse" letter. This letter accused the French government of anti-Semitism in the court-martial of Jewish military officer Alfred Dreyfus. CARICATURE OF 'J'ACCUSE,' ARTICLE WRITTEN BY ÉMILE ZOLA (1840–1902) IN DEFENCE OF ALFRED DREYFUS, 1898 (LITHO), FRENCH SCHOOL, (19TH CENTURY)/BIBLIOTHEQUE HISTORIQUE DE LA VILLE DE PARIS, PARIS, FRANCE/ ARCHIVES CHARMET/THE BRIDGEMAN ART LIBRARY.

# ÉMILE ZOLA AND ALFRED DREYFUS: THE END OF THE AFFAIR

Although "J'accuse" eventually led to Alfred Dreyfus being freed in 1899, the entire affair exacted a serious toll on both him and Émile Zola. Dreyfus spent another seven years in and out of the courts in order to have the original judgment against him formally reversed, while Zola died from smoke inhalation in his apartment on September 29, 1902. Dreyfus attended his funeral despite death threats.

Dreyfus was reintegrated into the army at the rank of major in 1906, but he retired in 1907. While he was attending the transfer of Zola's remains to the Panthéon in 1908, an extremist right-wing journalist shot and wounded him. The assailant was ultimately acquitted of his crime, which was classified as an unpremeditated act of passion. After going on to live a quiet life in Paris with his family, Dreyfus died in 1935. Determined to commemorate the affair, the French government finally commissioned a statue of Dreyfus in 1984, which was defaced with anti-Semitic graffiti in 2002. On the 100th anniversary of Dreyfus's exoneration in 2006, President Jacques Chirac gave a speech at the École Militaire in Paris, where the case first began, denouncing the "extreme violence" of the affair and Dreyfus's betrayal in "a country in which Jews have had civil rights since 1791."

"J'accuse" and use of legal jargon, Zola is effectively "courting prosecution for criminal libel" and testing the impartiality of the French legal system yet again.

## CRITICAL DISCUSSION

Zola's exposé proved to be nothing short of scandalous, as he was charged with libel and brought to court in 1898. The entire episode of "J'accuse" became a favorite subject of French authors for decades to come, most notably in the fiction of Anatole France and Proust. France's novel *Penguin Island* (1908) is an allegory for the history of modern France, including the affair, set in a colony of penguins. Meanwhile, Proust's famous novel *Swann's Way* (1913) threads the affair into the narrative. The case also greatly affected many politicians, such as Léon Blum, a Dreyfusard who would go on to become the first Jewish prime minister of France, and Aristide Briand, whose 1905 law mandated the separation of church and state in France. In the 1942 essay "From the Dreyfus Affair to France Today," German American political writer Hannah Arendt argues that the "Dreyfus Affair was never really settled" and that it left behind a terrible legacy of anti-Semitism and a "mistrust of the Republic itself."

Though Zola wrote dozens of novels, "J'accuse" remains perhaps his best-known work. His use of the phrase "J'accuse!"—arguably the most famous newspaper headline ever published—has entered the popular lexicon as a shorthand rallying cry for writers tackling injustice of all types. In France, "J'accuse" continues to be remembered as the moment the figure of the modern, engaged intellectual first appeared. From the burqa ban in France to the Catholic Church's cover-up of sexual abuse, authors writing about struggles between power and justice still cite Zola's editorial in order to provide historical context.

Today, legal scholars in particular continue to examine the Dreyfus Affair and its implications on the abuse of military power and scapegoating. In her review of Ruth Harris's *The Man on Devil's Island*, Carmen Cahill notes that "the Dreyfus affair is still constantly evoked," most recently in discussions of the legality of detaining suspected terrorists in Guantánamo Bay, Cuba. Additionally, Begley argues that "just as at the outset of the Dreyfus Affair the French found it easy to believe that Dreyfus must be a traitor because he was a Jew, many Americans had no trouble believing the detainees at Guantánamo … were terrorists simply because they were Muslims." Generally, "J'accuse" is more of interest to contemporary historians and political scientists rather than to literary scholars because it stands out as a crossroads in the development of modern French national identity.

## BIBLIOGRAPHY

*Sources*

Arendt, Hannah. "From the Dreyfus Affair to France Today." *Jewish Social Studies* 4.3 (1942): 195–240. *JSTOR.* Web. 15 Sept. 2012.

Begley, Louis. *Why the Dreyfus Affair Matters.* New Haven: Yale UP, 2009. Print.

Burns, Michael. *Dreyfus: A Family Affair, 1789–1945.* New York: Harper Collins, 1991. Print.

Cahill, Carmen. Rev. of *The Man on Devil's Island: Alfred Dreyfus and the Affair that Divided France,* by Ruth Harris. *Guardian.* Guardian News and Media, 25 June 2012. Web. 5 Oct. 2012.

Mehlman, Jeffrey. "1898: Emile Zola Publishes 'J'accuse,' an Open Letter to the President of the Republic in Which He Denounces the Irregularities Leading to Dreyfus' Condemnation." *A New History of French Literature.* Ed. Denis Hollier. Cambridge: Harvard UP, 1994. Print.

Schwartz, Vanessa. *Spectacular Realities: Early Mass Culture in Fin-de-Siècle Paris.* Los Angeles: U of California P, 1998. Print.

Zola, Émile. *The Dreyfus Affair: "J'Accuse" and Other Writings.* Trans. Eleanor Levieux. Ed. Alan Pages. New Haven: Yale UP, 1998. Print.

*Further Reading*

Balakirsky-Katz, Maya. "Émile Zola, the Cochonnerie of Naturalist Literature, and the Judensau." *Jewish Social Studies, New Series* 13.1 (2006): 110–35. *JSTOR.* Web. 10 Sept. 2012.

Blum, Léon. *Souvenirs sur l'affaire.* Paris: Gallimard, 1935. Print.

Caron, Vicky. "The Path to Vichy: Antisemitism in France in the 1930s." United States Holocaust Memorial and Museum Center for Advanced Holocaust Studies, 20 April 2005. Web. 10 Sept. 2012.

France, Anatole. *Penguin Island.* Forgotten Books, 2012. Print.

Harris, Ruth. *The Man on Devil's Island: Alfred Dreyfus and the Affair that Divided France.* London: Penguin, 2011. Print.

*Elizabeth Vitanza*

# THE JUNGLE
*Upton Sinclair*

## OVERVIEW

*The Jungle* (1906), a work of fiction by American journalist and novelist Upton Sinclair, portrays the lives and working conditions of poor, typically immigrant meatpackers in the slaughterhouses of Chicago at the turn of the twentieth century. The narrative focuses on the travails of Jurgis Rudkus, a Lithuanian immigrant to the United States who suffers humiliation and loss in his attempts to achieve the American Dream. In the final chapters, he stumbles on a laborers' gathering and finds salvation in socialism. Sinclair, a member of the Socialist Party of America since 1902, spent weeks in Chicago doing research in order to write about the condition of workers in the industry for the socialist newspaper *Appeal to Reason,* in which the novel was first serialized between February and November 1905. Although his intention was to fight capitalism and promote socialism, audiences largely ignored his depiction of unscrupulous labor practices and the shameful treatment of workers, panicking instead about the unsanitary conditions in which meat was processed.

Although several publishers rejected the novel because of its grimness and violence, *The Jungle* caused an instant sensation upon its publication in book form. While most of the reading public was not sympathetic to Sinclair's political views, readers were horrified by the novel's revelations. Public uproar and personal concerns quickly pushed President Theodore Roosevelt to send inspectors to Chicago, and their official report led to the 1906 passage of the Federal Meat Inspection and Pure Food and Drug Acts. Although Sinclair failed to win many converts to socialism, he raised suspicions about the abuses of capitalism, and *The Jungle* won lasting success as an iconic work of muckraking, or exposé journalism

## HISTORICAL AND LITERARY CONTEXT

From the 1860s to the 1890s, the United States underwent a period termed the Gilded Age, which saw ostentatious growth in the prosperity of a small sector of the population alongside a rapidly growing underclass. Millions emigrated from Europe to fill the need for urban workers, many of whom were poor, non-English speaking, and illiterate. As they crowded into cities to become what some called "wage slaves," living conditions deteriorated, leading to outbreaks of dysentery, cholera, and other deadly diseases. Government implementation of public services, such as sewer systems, was slow, and in these dangerous and unsanitary conditions, workers earned barely enough to survive. Despite the rise of labor unions, rampant corruption hindered the enactment of worker protection laws.

By the time Sinclair's novel was published, the public was already sensitized to the problem of tainted meat. During the 1898 Spanish-American War, Chicago meatpacking companies were commissioned to supply U.S. forces in Cuba; in order to maximize profits, the industry sent adulterated, poorly preserved, and spoiled meat, causing an untold number of deaths. Roosevelt himself had eaten tainted meat while serving during the war. Although a court of inquiry brought no charges, the publicity had done its damage. In the summer of 1904, Sinclair traveled to Chicago to cover a strike of the nascent Amalgamated Meat Cutters and Butcher Workmen of North

✧ *Key Facts*

**Time Period:**
Early 20th Century

**Genre:**
Novel

**Events:**
American Gilded Age; growing economic disparity; rise of socialism

**Nationality:**
American

---

Workers skinning lambs at a Chicago meat-processing plant in 1906, the year Upton Sinclair's *The Jungle* was published. © CORBIS.

## PRIMARY SOURCE

### EXCERPT FROM *THE JUNGLE*

It was only when the whole ham was spoiled that it came into the department of Elzbieta. Cut up by the two-thousand-revolutions-a-minute flyers, and mixed with half a ton of other meat, no odor that ever was in a ham could make any difference. There was never the least attention paid to what was cut up for sausage; there would come all the way back from Europe old sausage that had been rejected, and that was moldy and white—it would be dosed with borax and glycerine, and dumped into the hoppers, and made over again for home consumption. There would be meat that had tumbled out on the floor, in the dirt and sawdust, where the workers had tramped and spit uncounted billions of consumption germs. There would be meat stored in great piles in rooms; and the water from leaky roofs would drip over it, and thousands of rats would race about on it. It was too dark in these storage places to see well, but a man could run his hand over these piles of meat and sweep off handfuls of the dried dung of rats. These rats were nuisances, and the packers would put poisoned bread out for them; they would die, and then rats, bread, and meat would go into the hoppers together. This is no fairy story and no joke; the meat would be shoveled into carts, and the man who did the shoveling would not trouble to lift out a rat even when he saw one—there were things that went into the sausage in comparison with which a poisoned rat was a tidbit. There was no place for the men to wash their hands before they ate their dinner, and so they made a practice of washing them in the water that was to be ladled into the sausage. There were the butt-ends of smoked meat, and the scraps of corned beef, and all the odds and ends of the waste of the plants, that would be dumped into old barrels in the cellar and left there. Under the system of rigid economy which the packers enforced, there were some jobs that it only paid to do once in a long time, and among these was the cleaning out of the waste barrels. Every spring they did it; and in the barrels would be dirt and rust and old nails and stale water—and cartload after cartload of it would be taken up and dumped into the hoppers with fresh meat, and sent out to the public's breakfast. Some of it they would make into "smoked" sausage—but as the smoking took time, and was therefore expensive, they would call upon their chemistry department, and preserve it with borax and color it with gelatine to make it brown. All of their sausage came out of the same bowl, but when they came to wrap it they would stamp some of it "special," and for this they would charge two cents more a pound.

America. The strike failed when the Big Four meat-packing companies employed strikebreakers to man the assembly lines. The acts later passed by Congress fell short of Sinclair's hopes for labor reform. Although the Meat Inspection Act provided for federal oversight of meat production, Sinclair feared inspectors would be easily bribed and business would continue as usual.

Although *The Jungle* was innovative for its choice of subject matter, it followed in the tradition of American naturalism, an extension of the literary realism movement. Naturalism went beyond realism in its insistence on a moral purpose for art and on social determinism, which usually led to a pessimistic outlook. Naturalist writers often linked their work to industrialization and attempts at social reform, numbering Karl Marx among their influences. French author Émile Zola's *Germinal* (1885), a harsh fictional exploration of an 1860s coalminers' strike, provided inspiration for such American writers as Stephen Crane, whose novel *Maggie* (1893) portrays prostitution in the slums of New York; Theodore Dreiser, whose *Sister Carrie* (1900) focuses on consumer culture; and Frank Norris, who wrote *The Pit* (1903) about manipulations in the Chicago wheat trade. Sinclair particularly strove to emulate Harriet Beecher Stowe's *Uncle Tom's Cabin* (1852), the hugely successful novel that was often dubbed as abolitionist propaganda.

*The Jungle* is often also cited as the foundational text of a new style of investigative journalism. Following Sinclair's lead, writers have used the medium to expose various inequalities and injustices, often portraying the individual as powerless. According to journalist and novelist Karen Olsson in a 2006 essay for *Slate*, however, fiction is not these writers' primary vehicle: "Sinclair's heirs today are writers of literary nonfiction, who derive their drama from facts." Muckraking documentary films in this vein include *Nickel and Dimed* (2001), *Fast Food Nation* (2002), and *The Omnivore's Dilemma* (2006). Although much of Sinclair's work is now out of print, the author still lives in the public imagination. Writer and scholar Chris Bachelder's satiric 2006 novel *U.S.!* posits Sinclair's repeated resurrection and murder in the present day, representing the fortunes and undying conviction of the American left alongside right-wing hysterics and violence over a feared Socialist takeover.

### THEMES AND STYLE

The central and unrelenting theme of Sinclair's novel is that capitalism is inherently flawed, even evil, and that socialism, as a more just and legitimate economic and political system, represents a cure for society's troubles. After arriving in a country full of financial promise, Rudkus and his family are systematically torn down by their new life. They are swindled when they buy a house and are surrounded by filth, crime, and exploitation. They endure freezing cold, injury, and illness, and when they can find jobs, they face constant danger at work. The factory owners are "men every bit as brutal and unscrupulous as the old-time slave drivers." The serialized version of *The Jungle* hewed closely to a naturalistic portrayal of the immigrant experience, with Rudkus ending up in prison. The published version, however, cut by five chapters, concludes with the protagonist discovering socialism and regaining his self-respect: "That he should have suffered such oppressions and such horrors was bad enough; but that he should have been crushed and beaten by them ... that was a thing not to be put into words, a thing not to be borne by a human creature, a thing of terror and madness!"

Through unconditional support and sympathy for workers and immigrants, Sinclair works to cultivate the empathy of his audience, gradually creating in the reader the same desperation for change that Rudkus feels. Twenty-seven of the book's thirty-one chapters exhaustively illustrate the problem before the final chapters introduce a resolution that many readers experience as out of place. Despite the critical consensus that the novel's rhetorical strategy is blatantly didactic and overwhelms the development of characters and scenes, *The Jungle* serves the author's purpose of exposing the harsh reality of the lives of immigrant workers.

Stylistically unsophisticated, the novel does little to disguise Sinclair's opinions and intentions. His tone, which varies with the events he recounts, is sometimes unemotional and severe, presenting gruesome incidents and cruel injustices as everyday events. In one scene the narrator relates that the bosses sometimes lie when a worker has been killed: "[I]t was the easiest way out of it for all concerned. When, for instance, a man had fallen into one of the rendering tanks and had been made into pure leaf lard and peerless fertilizer, there was no use letting the fact out and making his family unhappy." Personal experiences are conveyed in simple language, and the participants are rendered almost distant from their pain in the hopelessness of their situation. At one point Rudkus's son is "burning up with fever, and his eyes were running sores; in the daytime he was a thing uncanny and impish to behold, a plaster of pimples and sweat, a great purple lump of misery." When the final chapters introduce the protagonist's revelatory experience at the socialist meeting, the tenor is suddenly sentimental and propagandistic as Rudkus contemplates "the glory of that joyful vision of the people of Packingtown marching in and taking possession of the Union Stockyards!"

## CRITICAL DISCUSSION

*The Jungle*'s popular success spurred its translation into seventeen languages within months. The reactions of critics were mixed, however. Although some considered the novel a masterpiece and an important work of social criticism, it was just as often dismissed as too biased in its politics and its hatred of the rich. Perhaps the most interesting aspect of the novel's early reception was the reaction of Roosevelt. In a 2006 article for *Mother Jones*, Chris Bachelder notes, "Roosevelt's individualism clashed with Sinclair's socialism, but he shared Sinclair's distaste for the 'arrogant and selfish greed on the part of the capitalist.'" In terms of the reception of the book as an exposé of tainted meat production rather than of the mistreatment and suf-

## UPTON SINCLAIR: IDEALIST

Author Upton Sinclair was born in Baltimore, Maryland, to parents who came from wealth, though his family was financially ruined during the Civil War and Reconstruction. He was exposed to two radically different social classes—his own struggling family's and that of his mother's still wealthy parents, whom he frequently visited. Soon after beginning college, he started writing magazine articles and dime-store novels to pay for his education. When he took the assignment to report on the stockyards and workers' strike in Chicago, he reportedly blended in easily with the other workers because of his shabby appearance.

After he published *The Jungle*, he used the proceeds to establish Helicon Hall Home Society, a utopian colony in Englewood, New Jersey—although within a year the colony suffered a fire and disbanded. During the 1920s he became more actively involved in politics, representing the Socialist party for California, first as a candidate for the House of Representatives (1920) and then as a candidate for the Senate (1922); however, both bids were unsuccessful. In 1934, two years after the election of Franklin D. Roosevelt as president, Sinclair ran as the Democratic candidate for governor of California and lost by a slim margin. He returned to his prolific writing career and won a Pulitzer Prize in 1942, publishing more than ninety books by the time of his death in 1968.

fering of the working class, Olsson points out, "in part the book invites this misreading. As a Socialist novel it's unconvincing: The ending, in which Jurgis Rudkus converts to socialism, is the worst part of the book."

Having recently celebrated its centennial, *The Jungle* has been reevaluated and its author has been the subject of new critical biographies. Although the novel has never been considered of literary importance, Anthony Arthur makes a good case in his 2006 biography, *Radical Innocent*, that the opening chapter is among the best in American literature. Olsson describes the work's "seething energy that sweeps you along." Still, Bachelder writes, "structurally it lacks the pleasing symmetries and contrasts, the subtle patterns of imagery and metaphor that we expect from great and lasting works." Nevertheless, most critics agree that Sinclair's novel has lasting value as a vivid portrayal of the immigrant experience and of the clash of ideals that occurred during the Progressive Era.

Continuously in print since 1906, *The Jungle* has been a staple of what Bachelder calls the "muckraking mini-unit in American History." Although the contemporary public considered its revelations as truth, scholar Louise Carroll Wade questions Sinclair's journalistic integrity. In a 1991 article for *American Studies*, she states, "most immigrants were not passive victims of exploitation.... In spite of low wages and often harsh working and living conditions, most established a foothold and in time experienced some upward mobility." Some critics have noted that modern readers may be more inclined to look for social and political ideas and facts in works of nonfiction and that the contemporary use of novels as vehicles for propaganda is usually unsuccessful. Even once-influential explicitly political or moral works such as *Uncle Tom's Cabin* and *The Grapes of Wrath* might not be as well received today. Olsson writes, however, that Sinclair's most famous work is still taught in high schools and colleges across the country partly because it is fiction, pointing out that almost no muckraking nonfiction of the period appears in current curricula.

## BIBLIOGRAPHY

*Sources*

Bachelder, Chris. "*The Jungle* at 100: Why the Reputation of Upton Sinclair's Good Book Has Gone Bad." *Mother Jones.* Mother Jones, Jan. 2006. Web. 8 June 2012.

Gottesman, Ronald. Rev. of *The Autobiography of Upton Sinclair,* by Upton Sinclair. *American Literature* 35.3 (1963): 388–89. Print.

Olsson, Karen. "Welcome to *The Jungle*: Does Upton Sinclair's Famous Novel Hold Up?" *Slate.* Slate Group, 10 July 2006. Web. 8 June 2012.

Sinclair, Upton. *The Jungle.* New York: Penguin, 2006. Print.

Wade, Louise Carroll. "The Problem with Classroom Use of Upton Sinclair's *The Jungle.*" *American Studies* 32.2 (1991): 79–101. Print.

*Further Reading*

Arthur, Anthony. *Radical Innocent: Upton Sinclair.* New York: Random, 2006. Print.

Hicks, Granville. "Fiction and Social Criticism." *College English* 13.7 (1952): 355–61. Print.

Mattson, Kevin. *Upton Sinclair and the Other American Century.* New York: Wiley, 2006. Print.

Meyer, David S., and Deana A. Rohlinger. "Big Books and Social Movements: A Myth of Ideas and Social Change." *Social Problems* 59.1 (2012): 136–53. Print.

Sinclair, Upton. *The Autobiography of Upton Sinclair.* New York: Literary Licensing, 2011. Print.

*Media Adaptation*

*The Jungle.* Dir. George Irving and Jack Pratt. Perf. George Nash, Gail Kane, and Julia Hurley. All Star Feature Film Corp, 1914. Film.

*Colby Cuppernull*

# MY LAI 4

*A Report on the Massacre and Its Aftermath*

*Seymour Hersh*

## OVERVIEW

In *My Lai 4: A Report on the Massacre and Its Aftermath* (1970), journalist Seymour Hersh delves into the My Lai massacre and its subsequent cover-up, a story that he first broke on November 12, 1969. His original reporting—which several news outlets initially rejected—was eventually picked up by the Dispatch News Service and subsequently published in more than thirty newspapers, garnering him the Pulitzer Prize for international reporting in 1970. Told from an objective, journalistic point of view, *My Lai 4* builds on Hersh's original articles by delving deeper into the efforts to conceal events surrounding the massacre, which involved U.S. troops killing hundreds of Vietnamese, many of them civilians. Instead of simply reporting on the massacre, Hersh exposes problems within "the Army as an institution" and describes how the military was able to whitewash its atrocities and send pro-Vietnam War messages to the American public.

The public was outraged to learn about the mass murder and torture, as well as the cover-up by the U.S. military, whose report at the time of the massacre was that "U.S. infantrymen had killed 128 Communists in a bloody day-long battle." Military leaders did not acknowledge that any innocent citizens had been killed. Hersh's reporting on the massacre led to increased opposition to U.S. involvement in the Vietnam War and fueled the U.S. peace movement, which called for the withdrawal of troops. Many of Hersh's journalist colleagues reacted with anger at his bold message, although they gradually came to see the importance of his reporting to fomenting public opposition to the war. Today Hersh's book is known as one of the most powerful military exposés in U.S. history.

## HISTORICAL AND LITERARY CONTEXT

Opposition to U.S. involvement in the Vietnam War had been growing since 1964, with various groups participating in either peaceful demonstrations or violent protests. The bulk of antiwar sentiments stemmed from opposition to the draft, arguments against U.S. intervention in Vietnam, and reaction to graphic media portrayals of the war. Antiwar protests were especially common across college campuses, where negative opinions of the war encouraged student activism and participation in a variety of political and social organizations. Mainstream support for the war began to decline after the Viet Cong-led Tet offensive in early 1968, which stunned Americans, who began to doubt that the war was winnable.

Although the My Lai massacre occurred on March 16, 1968, it was not made public knowledge until Hersh reported on the atrocities in 1969 following a tip he received from *Village Voice* reporter Geoffrey Cowan. According to Cowan, an army lieutenant named William Calley had been court-martialed for killing innocent Vietnamese citizens. Hersh published his original articles and the subsequent book on the My Lai massacre on the heels of demonstrations held October 15, 1969, called the Moratorium to End the War in Vietnam. The demonstrations were the first major protests against the involvement of the administration of U.S. President Richard Nixon in the war, and they engaged millions of Americans nationwide.

Anti-Vietnam War literature was popular even before the publication of *My Lai 4,* with writers such as Allen Ginsberg and Denise Levertov setting the stage for Hersh's revealing articles and book. Like Hersh, Ginsberg was public about his antiwar feelings, participating in a 1965 protest at the Oakland-Berkeley city line in California and refusing to pay taxes by signing the Writers and Editors War Tax Protest pledge in 1968. Levertov's war-inspired poetry—which touched on themes of the individual versus the government, community change, and social reform—was published in several books, including 1971's *To Stay Alive* and 1975's *The Freeing of the Dust.*

After its publication, *My Lai 4* spurred examination of how the U.S. military was able to cover up the massacre for eighteen months. Journalists pointed to the Pentagon's culture of concealment, a defense strategy often called a second war between the government and the media. Critical acclaim ignited Hersh's career, catapulting him from freelance writer to full-time reporter at the *New York Times.* He went on to become one of most trusted journalists in the United States, garnering attention again in 2004 when he reported on mistreatment of detainees at the Abu Ghraib prison in Iraq. *My Lai 4* continued to be relevant in light of the unpopular wars led by the United States in Iraq

+ **Key Facts**

**Time Period:**
Late 20th Century

**Genre:**
Nonfiction

**Events:**
My Lai massacre;
Vietnam War; military
corruption

**Nationality:**
American

U.S. troops killed these and other citizens of My Lai 4, South Vietnam (Republic of Vietnam) in the 1968 My Lai Massacre. This incident, and the cover-up following the killings, is described in Seymour Hersh's *My Lai 4: A Report on the Massacre and Its Aftermath* (1970). © WORLD HISTORY ARCHIVE/ALAMY.

and Afghanistan, and in 2009 Italian director Paolo Bertola produced a movie based on the seminal book.

## THEMES AND STYLE

The primary themes of *My Lai 4* are American injustice and military corruption. Hersh discusses the killing of innocent Vietnamese civilians using details from his interviews with Lieutenant Calley, who led the massacre. The author describes the soldiers' thoughts in order to explore the psychology behind the torturing and killing of innocent civilians. He writes, "Everything became a target ... Gary Garfolo borrowed someone's M79 grenade launcher and fired it point-blank at a water buffalo ... Others fired the weapon into the bunkers full of people." However, Hersh saves his harshest criticism for the military for its corruption and cover-up of the massacre, essentially using the events at My Lai to delve into the larger problems of the U.S. military, the broader effects of American policy in Vietnam, and the corrupt nature of the U.S. government. By the end of the book, the massacre becomes a single piece in a larger portrait of corruption and malfeasance.

Hersh employs various rhetorical strategies in his writing, such as the use of asides to expand on his main points and the use of vivid details culled from his interviews with the soldiers involved in the massacre. The details serve to present a full picture of the twisted individuals who instigated the massacre. In one aside, Hersh mentions how George S. Patton III, the son of the famous general who was a colonel in Vietnam, "celebrated Christmas in 1968 by sending cards reading: 'From Colonel and Mrs. George S. Patton III—Peace on Earth.' Attached to the cards were color photographs of dismembered Viet Cong soldiers stacked in a neat pile." The jarring details allude to the notion that the events at My Lai were more than a massacre: they were symptoms of deep, systemic problems within the military as an institution.

Like Hersh's original articles about the massacre, *My Lai 4* is expository and objective in tone, allowing the reader to draw conclusions from the facts and interviews presented. However, Hersh expands on the idea of traditional reportage by drafting a highly detailed, riveting account of the events at My Lai and their subsequent concealment by the military. The vivid details and personal interviews appeal to readers' emotions by putting readers at the scene. Hersh quotes one sergeant's recollection: "The whole thing was so deliberate. It was point-blank murder and I was standing there watching it." The decision to give soldiers a strong voice in the book serves to humanize them, emphasizing the culpability of the institutions that placed them in the center of the conflict.

## CRITICAL DISCUSSION

Hersh's reports were widely read, in part because they tapped into Americans' growing disillusionment with the Vietnam War. Although the public welcomed Hersh's exposé, many journalists were turned off by his bold investigative style. One *Washington Post* reporter called Hersh to ask, "Where do you get off writing a lie like that?" However, as more details about the massacre surfaced and Hersh published *My Lai 4,* reporters began to see Hersh as a hero. After winning the Pulitzer Prize for his reporting on the massacre, he was hailed by *New York Times* managing editor A. M. Rosenthal as "the hottest piece of journalistic property in the United States." As Hersh's career blossomed, the United States drew down its presence in Vietnam, eventually ending the unpopular war.

In the years following its publication, *My Lai 4* has been revered as an essential book about the Vietnam War for exposing the truth behind one of the most horrific wartime cover-ups in U.S. military history. The majority of critics have praised Hersh's writing and investigative style. Reporter David Jackson of the *Chicago Tribune* wrote in 2004, "Hersh's 1969 disclosure of the My Lai massacre [was] pivotal in turning the tide of public opinion against the Vietnam War." Jackson also quotes Bill Kovach, Hersh's editor at the *New York Times* during the 1970s, as saying that

Hersh "exposed some of the most despicable behavior on the part of public officials" and "made Americans aware when our leaders don't measure up to the values expressed in all the songs we sing and pledges we make." Hersh's intrepid style paved the way for future investigations into the war in Iraq and the 2004 Abu Ghraib prison scandal.

Today critics celebrate *My Lai 4* as an exemplar of investigative reporting and praise Hersh as a quintessential muckraker. Scott Sherman notes in a 2003 essay for *Columbia Journalism Review* that Hersh "seems most content when he's exhaling fire, revealing what he considers to be the secrets behind the secrets, and rousing the ire of his targets." Hersh's close friend, author David Wise, in a 2004 interview with Rupert Cornwell for the *Independent,* lauds Hersh's "bulldog" work ethic: "He's the tops at what he does; no one can dig up a story like Sy. He's fiercely independent; he's always stood outside the establishment."

## BIBLIOGRAPHY

### Sources

Cornwell, Rupert. "Seymour Hersh: The Reporter Who's the Talk of the Town." *London Independent* 22 May 2004: 40. Web. 6 Sept. 2012.

Hersh, Seymour M. *My Lai 4: A Report on the Massacre and Its Aftermath.* New York: Random, 1970. Print.

Jackson, David. "The Muckraker." *Chicago Tribune.* Chicago Tribune. 25 June 2004. Web. 6 Sept. 2012.

Kirchick, James. "The Deceits of Seymour Hersh: Chronicling a Singular Career in Meretricious Journalism." *Commentary* Mar. 2012: 16. *Literature Resource Center.* Web. 1 Aug. 2012.

Robson, Seth. "Clemency Is Last Hope for a More Normal Life." *Stars and Stripes.* Stars and Stripes. 12 May 2009. Web. 6 Sept. 2012.

Sherman, Scott. "The Avenger Sy Hersh, Then and Now." *Columbia Journalism Review* 42.4 (2003): 34–44. Web. 1 Aug. 2012.

### Further Reading

Belknap, Michal R. *The Vietnam War on Trial: The My Lai Massacre and the Court-Martial of Lieutenant Calley.* Lawrence: UP Kansas, 2002. Print.

Greiner, Bernd. *War without Fronts: The USA in Vietnam.* New Haven: Yale UP, 2009. Print.

Hersh, Seymour M. *Cover-Up: The Army's Secret Investigation of the Massacre at My Lai 4.* New York: Random, 1972. Print.

Levertov, Denise. *The Freeing of the Dust.* New York: New Directions, 1975. Print.

O'Brien, Tim. *In the Lake of the Woods.* Boston: Houghton/Seymour Lawrence, 1994. Print.

### Media Adaptations

*Massacre at My Lai Four.* Story and screenplay by Gianni Paolucci and Stefano Pomilia. Dir. Ed. Daniele Campbelli. [U.K.]: Scanbox Entertainment, © 2011. DVD.

Hersh, Seymour. *My Lai 4: CBS, Inc.; Executive Producer, Don Hewitt; Correspondent, Mike Wallace.* New York, NY: CBS News New Archives, 2012. DVD.

*Anna Deem*

# SECRETS
## *A Memoir of Vietnam and the Pentagon Papers*
### Daniel Ellsberg

✛ *Key Facts*

**Time Period:**
Early 21st Century

**Genre:**
Exposé

**Events:**
Vietnam War; run-up to the wars in Iraq and Afghanistan after 9/11

**Nationality:**
American

## OVERVIEW

Daniel Ellsberg's *Secrets: A Memoir of Vietnam and the Pentagon Papers* (2002) is an autobiographical exposé warning the American public about the nature, depth, and magnitude of government collusion in the administration of war efforts. The book chronicles Ellsberg's time as an advisor to both the U.S. Department of Defense and the State Department, paying particular attention to the periods just before and after he leaked to several media outlets in 1971 the Pentagon Papers—a 7,000-page top-secret Pentagon study of U.S. government decision making in Vietnam from 1945 to 1967. Seeing parallels between the war in Vietnam and the two preemptive wars on the horizon in Afghanistan and Iraq, Ellsberg in his autobiography offers insight into mistakes in the military past of the United States and warns against repetition of those mistakes in the immediate future.

The book could do little for Ellsberg's legacy that had not been accomplished via the leak itself. For his efforts to end the war and elevate public consciousness, he had received the Gandhi Peace Award in 1978 and would later (in 2004) win the inaugural Ron Ridenhour Courage Prize. But both critics and the public recognized the power of Ellsberg's detailed account and the significance of its release on the precipice of another preemptive war. What the book lacked in novelty it more than made up for in timeliness and gravity, encouraging Americans—public servants and civilians alike—to take an honest look at the conduct of the executive and legislative branches during foreign conflicts.

## HISTORICAL AND LITERARY CONTEXT

Ellsberg's experiences during his time as an advisor to the U.S. government made him increasingly frustrated with the bureaucratic machinations and deceit with which the federal government was handling the Vietnam War. He felt that his loyalty should be to his country, not to individuals in government, and he decided that the best way to defend the nation's integrity was to inform its citizens of their leaders' secret dealings by stealing the Pentagon Papers in 1969 and releasing them in 1971. The extra pressure placed on President Richard M. Nixon following the leak, Ellsberg hoped, would precipitate the same results as his and others' earlier whistle-blowing (in 1967), which had helped to stop Lyndon Johnson from enacting a plan to escalate the war.

Ellsberg was hardly alone among the foreign-policy elite in believing that the United States, not Soviet and communist expansion, had become the leading threat to international relations before, and especially following, Vietnam; indeed, long before the U.S. retreat from Saigon, the idea that anticommunism had crippled U.S. foreign policy had become the presiding axiom of the Democratic Party. Ellsberg simply went further than most, eschewing the tradition of Cold War liberalism in favor of the antiwar radicalism of his own day. In releasing *Secrets* in 2002, during the buildup to what many had come to see as an inevitable war in Iraq, he hoped to elucidate foreign policy errors of the past in order to avert their repetition.

Many had worked to expose subversive government behavior surrounding operations in Vietnam. Phil Caputo's memoir, *A Rumor of War* (1977), examines the impact of ineffectual foreign policy on the soldiers on the ground in Vietnam; he supplemented this scrutiny of federal collusion as part of a Pulitzer Prize-winning group of journalists covering election fraud in the 1970s. In 1967, just a few years prior to Ellsberg's leak, the *New York Times* printed an anonymous leak revealing Johnson's intention to increase troop levels in Vietnam without notifying the American public. However, these efforts only provided a precursory, outsider assessment of the forces at work behind the policies, and most scholarly treatments of the Pentagon Papers and their public release looked more at the minutiae of the document than at the nuance of the political climate implicit therein.

Dissatisfied with how long the document's significance had been glossed in this manner, and troubled by the foreign policy directions taken by George W. Bush's administration following the terrorist attacks of September 11, 2001, Ellsberg wrote and released *Secrets*. The book not only recounts in great detail the ways in which Ellsberg came to possess the Pentagon Papers and his reasons for releasing them but also alerts readers to disturbing parallels between the secretive practices of the Johnson and Nixon administrations and that of Bush. Taking up Ellsberg's cause, Julian

Assange in 2006 founded WikiLeaks, an international online organization that publishes submissions of private, secret, and classified media from anonymous sources. The organization is purported to have published more than 1.3 million documents within the first year of its launch.

## THEMES AND STYLE

The central concern of *Secrets* is alerting the public to the long-standing and continued secretive practices of the federal government, particularly in military and foreign affairs. Recounting his first trips to Vietnam as part of a Pentagon task force in 1961, Ellsberg remembers being allowed access to top-secret advisory folders and staying "up half the night several nights in a row reading plans and reports and analyses," stating that "the smell of rot, of failure, lay all over them" and that the colonel serving as his liaison "made no attempt to pretend otherwise." Ellsberg hoped that the book would create for readers this same type of revelatory, disillusioning moment and that they would then begin demanding more transparency from their government.

The power of the book lies in Ellsberg's candor and humility. Rather than pretending he was not a part of the very mechanisms he is decrying, he details the ways in which he became complicit and at what point he had had enough. In response to an attack in Qui Nhon, for instance, Ellsberg is asked to "gather 'atrocity' details" and compile a list of "other terrorist actions" to build the case for the first large-scale bombing campaign in 1964. He describes his trepidation: "For the first time I was being drawn into the process of directly persuading the president on a course I considered disastrous.... I was asked to gather data directly for [Secretary of Defense Robert] McNamara for a use I deplored." In assessing his decision to comply with his orders, he says only, "That's the memory I have to deal with."

It is this quiet remorse that colors most of the book and that serves as the foundation of his warning to incumbent public servants. Speaking later about the efficacy with which he followed his orders from McNamara, he says matter-of-factly, "I didn't disappoint him." Adding to the power of these admissions is his refusal to make excuses for his action. He concedes at one point that "given my foreboding about the bombing campaign, I have never been able to explain to myself—so I can't explain to anyone else—why I stayed in my Pentagon job after the bombing started." The only assessment Ellsberg can offer is that "that night's work was the worst thing I've ever done."

## CRITICAL DISCUSSION

While a few critics, believing Ellsberg and his leak were no longer novel or relevant, were disenchanted by the book, most lauded the exposé. David Rudenstine, writing for the *Nation* in 2002, recognizes some of the logistical shortcomings of the book but deems it "a

# ELLSBERG AND CONTEMPORARY WHISTLE-BLOWERS

In May 2010, U.S. Army private Bradley Manning was arrested for releasing more than a quarter million classified military files to Julian Assange's controversial whistle-blowing website, WikiLeaks. Manning was serving as an intelligence analyst in Iraq at the time, and the materials he released included video footage of air strikes in both Iraq and Afghanistan and 260,000 diplomatic cables to and from military leaders in Iraq and Afghanistan. Manning claimed that the files—which came to be known as the Iraq War Logs and Afghan War Logs—revealed criminal back dealings between major military leaders and numerous ambassadors.

While a House committee decided what charges could legally be brought against Manning and Assange, former inside whistle-blower Daniel Ellsberg held a press conference to speak in support of their actions. He argued that by releasing the documents, Manning and Assange were performing an invaluable service for their country, offering a reminder that the charges leveled against him for releasing classified documents in Vietnam had been thrown out by several judges. Offering mostly praise for the pair, Ellsberg had but one criticism—that Assange could do a better job of protecting his sources' anonymity, as Manning's name had reportedly been linked to the leak by a hacker.

brave act," adding that both the initial leak and the memoir make a "notable contribution to American democracy." These sentiments were echoed by reviews in other national outlets, including the *Washington Post*. Nicholas Lemann agreed but also saw the parallels Ellsberg hoped to draw between Vietnam and the impending war in Iraq. Writing for the *New Yorker* in 2002, Lemann posits that "in the case of Vietnam (and, by extension, Iraq) there is another explanation for the failure of accurate information to produce a single, rational outcome: the decision-makers are making value judgments about how important the goal is and how high a price they are willing to pay to achieve it."

As evidenced by his decision to publish *Secrets,* and by the timing thereof, Ellsberg has made executive transparency his life's work, using the Pentagon Papers as the case study supporting his arguments. The effects of his efforts have been wide ranging. Others have taken up the cause as individuals, leading to the formation of organizations such as WikiLeaks and OpenLeaks (founded as a more transparent alternative by former WikiLeaks employee Daniel Domscheit-Berg). More significant, though, is the increasing frequency with which the government declassifies secret documents, as happened with the 9/11 Commission report, which revealed the extent to which the federal government was aware of possible attacks prior to their

## BIBLIOGRAPHY

### Sources

Appy, Christian G. *Patriots: The Vietnam War Remembered from All Sides.* New York: Viking, 2003. Print.

Barakat, Matthew. "Daniel Ellsberg Defends Julian Assange, Bradley Manning." *Huffington Post.* TheHuffingtonPost.com, 16 Dec. 2010. Web. 23 Oct. 2012.

Ellsberg, Daniel. *Secrets: A Memoir of Vietnam and the Pentagon Papers.* New York: Viking, 2002. Print.

Lane, Jonathon. "Loyalty, Democracy and the Public Intellectual." *Minerva: A Review of Science, Learning & Policy* 43.1 (2005): 73–85. *Academic Search Complete.* Web. 27 July 2012.

Lemann, Nicholas. "Paper Tiger." *New Yorker* 4 Nov. 2002. *Academic OneFile.* Web. 27 July 2012.

Poulsen, Kevin, and Kim Zetter. "U.S. Intelligence Analyst Arrested in WikiLeaks Video Probe." *Wired* 6 July 2010. Web. 23 Oct. 2012.

Rudenstine, David. "Who Will Tell the People?" *Nation* 275.22 (2002): 33. Print.

Schrag, Peter. *Test of Loyalty: Daniel Ellsberg and the Rituals of Secret Government.* New York: Simon, 1974. Print.

### Further Reading

Ehrlich, Judith, et al. *The Most Dangerous Man in America: Daniel Ellsberg and the Pentagon Papers.* Harriman: New Day Films, 2009.

Engelhardt, Tom. *The End of Victory Culture: Cold War America and the Disillusioning of a Generation.* New York: BasicBooks, 1995. Print.

Freedman, Lawrence D. "Secrets (Book)." *Foreign Affairs* 82.1 (2003): 162–63. *Academic Search Complete.* Web. 27 July 2012.

Halloran, Richard. Rev. of *Secrets: A Memoir of Vietnam and the Pentagon Papers,* by Daniel Ellsberg. *Parameters* Spring 2003: 149+. *Academic OneFile.* Web. 27 July 2012.

Heilbrunn, Jacob. "The Leaker." *Commentary* 114.4 (2002): 75+. *Academic OneFile.* Web. 27 July 2012.

*The Pentagon Papers: The Defense Department History of United States Decisionmaking on Vietnam.* Boston: Beacon, 1971. Print.

Ungar, Sanford J. *The Papers & the Papers: An Account of the Legal and Political Battle over the Pentagon Papers.* New York: Dutton, 1972. Print.

### Media Adaptation

*The Most Dangerous Man in America: Daniel Ellsberg and the Pentagon Papers.* Dir. Judith Ehrlich and Rick Goldsmith. First Run Features, 2009. DVD.

*Clint Garner*

Daniel Ellsberg protesting the war in Iraq (2006). Ellsberg, a former Defense Department worker, has been similarly critical of American involvement in Vietnam and released the Pentagon Papers in 1971. He discusses these developments in *Secrets: A Memoir of Vietnam and the Pentagon Papers* (2002). BRENDAN SMIALOWSKI/ GETTY IMAGES.

enactment. While still offering only hindsight, the 9/11 Commission's release by the government itself represents a step toward the transparency for which Ellsberg has fought.

While becoming the subject of a plethora of critical attention, *Secrets* has yet to garner a substantial body of scholarly treatment. One notable exception is Jonathon Lane's "Loyalty, Democracy, and the Public Intellectual," written for the *Essay Review* in 2005. The essay places *Secrets* in conversation with two other titles released in 2002—*Public Intellectuals: A Study of Decline* by Richard Posner and *The Public Intellectual* by Helen Small—for the purpose of examining the obligation of individual intellectual figures to their respective communities and to the global community. It is through this lens that Ellsberg's own contentions find their most concise expression, as Lane submits that it is "the failure of the specialists in positions of influence to become public intellectuals—their prolonged loyalty to a closed and corrupted institution—that led to their heinous mistakes" and to the resultant policy failure.

# SILENT SPRING

*Rachel Carson*

## OVERVIEW

Published to a storm of controversy in 1962, biologist Rachel Carson's nonfiction book *Silent Spring* helped initiate the environmental movement. The work became immediately popular, in part because of Carson's unique ability to couch complex scientific research in readable, often lyrical, language. The author's obvious ecological passion inspired generations of readers to view the natural world not as something alien and separate but as a living, dynamic system of which human beings are an integral part. In her book, Carson argues that humans are obligated to steward the earth ethically and safely. Her topic, contentious at the time, concerned the rampant and largely unregulated use across the United States of pollutants and pesticides, in particular the insecticide DDT. *Silent Spring* questions society's blind confidence in industrial development and imagines a grim future in which human, plant, and animal life is blighted, if not altogether destroyed, by toxic substances.

*Silent Spring,* first serialized in the *New Yorker* magazine, sparked one of the first productive (if notably heated) national conversations about the environment. Chemical companies as well as some scientists and government agencies rejected Carson's arresting findings—namely, that the unchecked employment of toxic substances causes myriad and unforeseen damages for entire ecosystems—but the general public responded strongly to her call to action. *Silent Spring*'s sweeping influence cannot be overstated: thanks to Carson's work, Americans became increasingly environmentally savvy, calling on policy makers to maintain, protect, and restore the natural world from harmful chemicals and unbridled industrialization. Even President John F. Kennedy came out in support of *Silent Spring*'s warnings, although not until after the President's Science Advisory Committee substantiated Carson's conclusions. The subsequent passage of watershed legislation, including the Endangered Species Act and National Environmental Policy Act, and the creation of the Environmental Protection Agency were made possible in part by the influence of Carson's best seller.

## HISTORICAL AND LITERARY CONTEXT

Throughout World War II, DDT was considered a veritable godsend: the potent substance allowed soldiers in the Pacific to escape malaria and typhoid that were spread by flies and mosquitoes, and it helped soldiers in Europe to stay free of head lice. In 1945 DDT was marketed to the public as a general panacea for all insect woes, and the insecticide made its way onto not only farmlands and orchards but also front yards and flower gardens. During the economic boom years that followed the war, environmental concerns were low or nonexistent on the list of civic concerns of the average politician or citizen. It took Carson's description of DDT's extensive poisonous effects to shock the country into environmental consciousness.

In the early 1960s, Americans began to grow increasingly alarmed by the harmful effects of poorly regulated industrialization. Indeed, Carson's once idyllic hometown of Springdale, Pennsylvania, was polluted by coal-fired electric plants that sprang up along the Alleghany River. Certain groups (for the most part chemical companies and affiliates) rejected Carson's assertions in *Silent Spring,* going so far as to question her sanity. Although *Silent Spring* would top best-seller lists and be chosen for the Book-of-the-Month Club, one company intimidated Carson's publishers with talk of lawsuits before the book was even printed. Another, soon after her book was published, distributed "The Desolate Year," a backlash brochure that parodied the first chapter of *Silent Spring,* contending that a world without DDT would be rife with disease and disaster. *Silent Spring* stirred up a fiery and impassioned dialogue about pesticide use, with both sides vehemently endorsing their differing perspectives.

*Silent Spring,* one of the foundational works of contemporary environmentalism, is certainly not the first text to engage with ecology and environmental concerns: Carson counted American essayist Henry David Thoreau and English novelist Henry Williamson as inspirations. American environmentalist Aldo Leopold's *A Sand County Almanac* (1949) and Scottish-born naturalist John Muir's *Studies in the Sierra* (1950; originally published in seven parts in *Overland Monthly* magazine in 1874–1875) paved the way for writing that presented scientific inquiry and naturalist observations in readable, flowing language. In fact, Carson's books on ocean life—*The Sea around Us,* among others—followed in the footsteps of such earlier naturalist writers, and, unlike *Silent Spring,* they did not have an activist or potentially inflammatory tone. A note from a friend regarding DDT-caused bird

✛ **Key Facts**

**Time Period:**
Mid-20th Century

**Genre:**
Nonfiction

**Events:**
Environmental
degradation; revelation
of DDT's toxicity

**Nationality:**
American

# THE POWER OF A SKETCH

For a long time, the United States was blessed with seemingly limitless wilderness. By the early 1960s, however, the effects of hundreds of years of development and industrialization were starting to become apparent to the average American. Many realized, for the first time, that nature, once taken for granted, must be treasured and protected or else permanently lost. *Silent Spring* tapped into these concerns and fears, offering a vision of a world without songbirds and wildflowers, without clean rivers and oceans.

Louis Darling's illustrations—now iconic—are an essential aspect of *Silent Spring*'s argument. The simple sketches of baby robins, curious bunnies, budding trees, and patchwork farm fields hearken back to a pre-DDT era, one of health and simplicity. Each chapter begins with a sketch: Chapter 2, for instance, offers a blooming dogwood halfway obscured by a DDT hose. A closer look reveals that the flowers and leaves are dripping with pesticide. Chapter titles such as "Needless Havoc" and "And No Birds Sing" are at odds with the nearby images of birds' nests, raccoon babies, and grazing does. Darling's artwork coupled with Carson's chilling data and emotional appeals create a forceful case against DDT and other chemicals.

deaths on Cape Cod, Massachusetts, however, coupled with Carson's growing knowledge of the effects of unregulated pesticide use, incited her to write *Silent Spring,* a vigorous denunciation of toxic chemicals.

*Silent Spring* brought environmental concerns to the forefront of the national conversation, where they have remained, more or less, into the twenty-first century. Although a handful of writers and scientists had spoken out against pesticide use before Carson, their worries were largely ignored. Although many groups attacked the veracity of *Silent Spring,* Carson's elegantly argued and thoroughly researched book, along with the book's prestigious supporters, rebuffed most challengers. The legacy of *Silent Spring* is broad: since the book's publication, most Americans have become aware that unchecked industrialization and development have myriad repercussions. Equally telling, books that take up Carson's issues are routinely published to little fanfare—a testament to how deeply *Silent Spring* has pervaded popular culture.

### THEMES AND STYLE

*Silent Spring*'s epigraph from English poet John Keats—"The sedge is wither'd from the lake, / And no birds sing"—epitomizes the central equation that drives the book: if the utilization of toxic chemicals continues unabated, then the world will be a place free of songbirds, flowers, trees, and, by implication, healthy people. In particular, Carson was interested in debunking industrialized nations' blithe confidence in technological progress, and she dared citizens to learn more about the chemicals on their lawn and the smoke puffing from power plants. Far from reading like a tedious scientific report, though, *Silent Spring* plumbs the minutiae of pesticides in a personal, journalistic tone, crafting a comprehensive argument against their unstudied application. Carson knew that in order for her message to reach the widest audience possible, her writing style would have to be readily accessible to all, not just to scientists.

The accessibility of *Silent Spring* stems from Carson's choice to employ storytelling techniques found more often in fiction than in scientific writing. Vignettes, likable characters, suspenseful chapters, storybook illustrations, and other creative writing tactics make the book's complicated information palatable to the average reader. Moreover, *Silent Spring* is written not from the personal perspective of Carson herself but from a collective "we." In regards to combating DDT, Carson asserts that "we should no longer accept the counsel of those who tell us we must fill our world with poisonous chemicals." This first-person perspective immediately implicates the reader in the global pesticide story. Throughout *Silent Spring,* Carson compares the effects of pesticides to the effects of nuclear radiation, an analogy to which her contemporary readers, living through the Cold War, could certainly relate.

Carson's engaging, often lyrical, language coupled with her prudent, well-researched findings create an inspiring argument against toxic chemicals. The book is littered with distressing descriptions of familiar plants and animals harmed by rampant pesticide use: "Few [robins] were seen in their normal foraging activities ... few nests were built; few young appeared." The reader cannot help but be affected—troubled, even—by such moribund accounts. Carson argues that humans cannot separate themselves from the health of the natural world, and she pointedly appeals both to the reader's intellect and emotions to make this point. Nowhere is this strategy clearer than in "A Fable for Tomorrow," the first chapter of *Silent Spring,* in which Carson imagines a town devoid of birdsong and haunted by the mysterious deaths of several constituents, a town utterly ruined by the overuse of pesticides: "On the morning that had once throbbed with a dawn chorus of robins, catbirds, doves ... [now] silence lay over the fields." Carson trusts her readers to react to the fable with sorrow, fear, and anger; she counts on them, thus incensed, to fight against DDT and similar toxins.

### CRITICAL DISCUSSION

Even before *Silent Spring* landed on bookstore shelves in late summer 1962, Carson received an onslaught of critical interest. The *New York Times* was one of the first publications to endorse the book's case, going so far as to declare: "If [Carson's] series helps arouse enough public consciousness ... the author will be as deserving of the Nobel Prize as was the inventor of DDT." Indeed, most major publications' response was

A man fumigating trees before the ban of DDT. Carson's *Silent Spring* took on the largely unregulated use of pesticides and pollutants across the United States. © WILLIAM GOTTLIEB/CORBIS.

laudatory. Some reviewers even expressed gratitude to Carson for exposing the public to the dangers of pesticides. The chemical industry, however, fought back, as did some writers for scientific journals. Some took umbrage with Carson's flowery language and emotional tone. In "Silence, Miss Carson!," a review published in the magazine *Chemical & Engineering News,* professor William Darby attacked *Silent Spring* as a "high-pitched sequences of anxieties."

Many scholars believe that *Silent Spring* single-handedly brought environmental concerns to the forefront of American consciousness. Craig Waddell, in his article "The Reception of *Silent Spring,*" writes that "The modern environmental movement—with its emphasis on pollution and the general degradation of the quality of life on the planet—may fairly be said to have begun with … *Silent Spring.*" Outside her legacy as an anti-DDT crusader, Carson is also remembered as one of the first to argue that technological progress without regulation would ultimately damage the earth (and, by implication, humanity) beyond recognition. *Silent Spring* has not lost its timeliness: in the twenty-first century, the book is still discussed, studied, and referenced in various sources ranging from newspapers and magazines to academic journals and books.

Carson and *Silent Spring* has received ample critical attention, especially from feminist and eco-critical scholars. Carson's life and words are the focus of a handful of biographies and critical anthologies, and she is studied by both scientists and scholars of the humanities—a testament to the breadth of her influence. In addition, scholars have become interested in the negative, gendered reactions to *Silent Spring.* Michael B. Smith notes in his article "'Silence, Miss Carson!' Science, Gender, and the Reception of *Silent Spring*" that in the early 1960s many people were threatened by Carson, "a woman, an independent scholar whose sex and lack of institutional ties placed her outside the nexus of the production and application of conventional scientific knowledge." Smith argues that inciting the ire of large companies continues to keep environmentalist writers—often corporate outsiders—cowed and silent. Most critics agree that *Silent Spring* still inspires generation after generation of environmental activists.

## BIBLIOGRAPHY

*Sources*

Carson, Rachel. *Silent Spring.* New York: Mariner, 2002. Print.

Garb, Yaakov. "Rachel Carson's *Silent Spring.*" *Dissent* Fall 1995: 539–46. Rpt. in *Nonfiction Classics for Students: Presenting Analysis, Context, and Criticism on Nonfiction Works.* Ed. David M. Galens, Jennifer Smith, and Elizabeth Thomason. Vol. 1. Detroit: Gale, 2003. *Literature Resource Center.* Web. 21 June 2012.

Quetchenbach, Bernard. "Rachel Louise Carson." *Twentieth-Century American Nature Writers: Prose.* Ed. Roger Thompson and J. Scott Bryson. Detroit: Gale, 2003. *Dictionary of Literary Biography* Vol. 275. *Literature Resource Center.* Web. 20 June 2012.

"Rachel Carson's Warning." *New York Times* 2 July 1962. *ProQuest Historical Newspapers: The New York Times (1851–2008).* Web. 26 June 2012.

THE LITERATURE OF PROPAGANDA ❖ VOLUME 1 ❖ APPROACHES

**139**

Smith, Michael B. "'Silence, Miss Carson!' Science, Gender, and the Reception of *Silent Spring*." *Feminist Studies* 27.3 (2001): 733+. *Literature Resource Center*. Web. 26 June 2012.

Waddell, Craig, ed. "The Reception of *Silent Spring*: An Introduction." *And No Birds Sing: Rhetorical Analyses of Silent Spring*. Carbondale: Southern Illinois UP, 2000. Web. 20 June 2012.

*Further Reading*

Brooks, Paul. *The House of Life: Rachel Carson at Work*. Boston: Houghton, 1972. Print.

Carson, Rachel. *Under the Sea-Wind; A Naturalist's Picture of Ocean Life*. New York: Simon, 1941. Print.

——. *The Edge of the Sea*. Boston: Houghton, 1955. Print.

——. *The Sea around Us*. New York: Simon, 1958. Print.

Graham, Frank. *Since Silent Spring*. Boston: Houghton, 1970. Print.

Hynes, H. Patricia. *The Recurring Silent Spring*. New York: Pergamon, 1989. Print.

Lear, Linda. *Rachel Carson: Witness for Nature*. New York: Holt, 1997. Print.

Lutts, Ralph H. "Chemical Fallout: Rachel Carson's *Silent Spring*, Radioactive Fallout, and the Environmental Movement." *Environmental Review: ER* Autumn 1985: 210–25. *JSTOR*. Web. 28 June 2012.

Matthiessen, Peter, ed. *Courage for the Earth: Writers, Scientists, and Activists Celebrate the Life and Writing of Rachel Carson*. New York: Houghton, 2007. Print.

Sterling, Philip. *Sea and Earth: The Life of Rachel Carson*. New York: Crowell, 1970. Print.

*Media Adaptation*

*Rachel Carson's Silent Spring*. Writ. and prod. Neil Goodwin. Ed. Michel Chalufour. Music by Sheldon Mirowitz. Host David McCullough. WGBH Boston Video, 2007. DVD.

*Claire Skinner*

# THIS BLINDING ABSENCE OF LIGHT

*Tahar Ben Jelloun*

## OVERVIEW

*This Blinding Absence of Light* (2001), a novel by Tahar Ben Jelloun, explores the effect on the individual psyche of the physical and psychological torture practiced from 1973 to 1991 at the secret detention center of Tazmamart in Morocco. Ben Jelloun writes that the novel is "based upon real events drawn from the testimony of a former inmate of Tazmamart Prison," Aziz Binebine. The story is told by a first-person narrator, Salim, giving it the authority of an eyewitness account—although Binebine's experience is fictionalized and the novel's meditations on suffering and spirituality originate with Ben Jelloun. The novel makes important corrections to the historical record through its personal and powerful testimony to the human rights abuses that took place under King Hassan II.

Although *This Blinding Absence of Light* became a best seller in France and its 2002 English translation was enthusiastically received, the novel's impact has been lessened somewhat by controversy surrounding Ben Jelloun. Nearly one-third of the twenty-eight survivors of Tazmamart published memoirs or testimonies, creating a distinct corpus within the broader tradition of Moroccan prison literature. Ben Jelloun was accused of producing an inauthentic account and profiting when it was safe to do so, while failing to speak out against Tazmamart when the prisoners were still incarcerated. Nevertheless, as a beautifully written literary text and the only Tazmamart account translated into English, *This Blinding Absence of Light* remains an important contribution to the reconciliation and healing process.

## HISTORICAL AND LITERARY CONTEXT

The period of King Hassan II's rule (1961–1999), known in Morocco as the "Years of Lead," was characterized by widespread oppression, repression, and human rights abuses, including the capture and torture of dissidents. Outrage over endemic corruption eventually led to an aborted coup d'état on July 10, 1971, when one thousand Moroccan soldiers descended on a party celebrating Hassan's forty-second birthday. Although the soldiers succeeded in killing close to one hundred guests, the coup d'état failed, and the officers, many of whom later claimed to be unwitting rebels, were tried and imprisoned at Kenitra prison. In 1973, after a second coup attempt also failed, fifty-eight of these prisoners were taken in the middle of the night to Tazmamart, one of a dozen secret prisons in Morocco. Located on the edge of the Sahara Desert, the former barracks stood over two blocks of underground cells filled with scorpions and cockroaches, absent of light and too low for a person to stand. The prisoners were refused medical attention and were given only enough food and water to keep them alive.

In 1991, the twenty-eight survivors, only three of whom were from Cell Block B, where *This Blinding Absence of Light* is set, left Tazmamart. During their thirteenth year of internment, the prisoners managed to notify the outside world of the detention center's existence and their survival by smuggling notes through sympathetic, or at least well-bribed, guards. After five additional years of campaigning by the prisoners' families, Amnesty International, and French journalists, the prisoners received royal pardons. They had been secretly hospitalized prior to release in an attempt to mask the physical evidence of malnourishment and torture, and Tazmamart was destroyed. However, before being set free, the prisoners were explicitly instructed not to speak publicly about their experiences. Works such as *This Blinding Absence of Light* seek to expose the existence of Tazmamart as well as the atrocities committed there during the rule of Hassan II.

Following the surviving prisoners' release from Tazmamart, testimonies and fictionalized accounts of their experiences added to an already sizeable tradition of Moroccan prison literature written in both Arabic and French. Political prisoners of the 1970s and 1980s had already documented the harsh conditions at Kenitra, and the 1990s saw the publication of texts exposing the existence of other secret detention centers. French journalists such as Gilles Perrault and Christine Daure-Serfaty, whose Moroccan activist husband Abraham Serfaty was imprisoned at Kenitra from 1974 until 1991, began to write about Tazmamart in the early 1990s, when the prison was still in operation. Several testimonies by former inmates of Tazmamart were published prior to the appearance of *This Blinding Absence of Light*. In 1993, former prisoner Ahmed Marzouki's "Le Pigeon de Tazmamart" (The pigeon of Tazmamart) appeared in the Moroccan journal *L'Opinion,* and between 1999 and 2000 Mohammed Raiss's testimony of events was published in serialized form in the newspaper *al-Itihad*

***Key Facts***

**Time Period:**
Early 21st Century

**Genre:**
Novel

**Events:**
Serious human rights abuses under King Hassan II during "Years of Lead," causing thousands of dissidents to "disappear" or be jailed, tortured, killed, or exiled

**Nationality:**
Moroccan

# BLACK SITES

Although Tazmamart and other secret Moroccan prisons were closed in the 1990s, reports of new secret and illegal detention facilities in the country emerged in the early 2000s. These reports allege the involvement of not only Moroccan security agencies but also the U.S. Central Intelligence Agency (CIA) in the clandestine operations. According to an ABC News report that was later withdrawn, one of these "black site" prisons is located just southeast of Rabat, the Moroccan capital, in Ain Aouda. Locals described a hidden construction site in a restricted and wooded area, but officials have denied the prison's existence. It is believed that the facility was built to detain suspected members of Al Qaeda after the exposure of a secret CIA prison in Poland.

The CIA is also purported to have held terrorists in another secret prison, the Temara Detention Facility, located in a secluded area south of Rabat. Operated by the Direction de la Sécurité du Territoire (DST), Morocco's internal security agency, the Temara prison is allegedly a primary site for torture and interrogation by the DST. A current Guantánamo Bay detainee has charged that CIA interrogators tortured him at Temara when he refused to answer questions. These Moroccan facilities are part of a worldwide network of black sites that the CIA has used to conduct "enhanced interrogations" as part of the U.S. War on Terror.

*al-Ishtiraki,* and the newspaper saw a marked increase in its readership as a result. Marzouki's full-length testimony, *Tazmamart Cellule 10* (Tazmamart Cell 10), became a best seller in France and Morocco the same year *This Blinding Absence of Light* was published.

Many of the surviving prisoners denounced Ben Jelloun for not speaking out while they were still incarcerated, arguing that as the winner of the prestigious 1987 French Goncourt Prize and an internationally known novelist, he could have quickly brought attention to their suffering. In time, he admitted that fear had silenced him. He was also widely criticized for profiting from a fictionalized report of Tazmamart. Although he claims that Binebine's brother, author and artist Mahi Binebine, requested that the novelist write *This Blinding Absence of Light,* Ben Jelloun was later accused of stealing Binebine's story. Binebine himself has said that while he may have been the inspiration for the novel, the story belongs to Ben Jelloun. Despite the controversy, the novel remains the only account that has been translated into English; thus it succeeded in exposing the horrors of the prison to a wider audience. In an effort to combat the accusations leveled against him, Ben Jelloun wrote *The Last Friend* (2004), which draws on his own years in prison.

## THEMES AND STYLE

Central to *This Blinding Absence of Light* is the narrator's struggle to keep his mind sound and to maintain his humanity even while physical and psychological torture destroys his body and slowly dehumanizes him. The cells at Tazmamart are designed to keep the prisoners in prolonged agony, so even death is withheld as long as possible. Salim relies on spiritual exploration and storytelling—inspired by novels, films, and his own imagination—for his survival. To Salim, the eighteen years spent at Tazmamart represent a discrete life characterized by constant suffering. He tells his readers, "I was born and died on July 10, 1971." Upon his release on October 29, 1991, he experiences his third beginning: "I had just been born." The novel's title is drawn from Salim's meditation on the different kinds of silence, "the hardest, most unbearable" of which is the absence of light. The text itself represents a resistance to a different kind of silence. Elsewhere Salim indicates his intention to fill this absence with his story "not for revenge, but for the record, to add a document in our history file." Thus, *This Blinding Absence of Light* underlines the necessity of bearing witness to the horror of Tazmamart, not just in the form of a collective record of names and facts but also through storytelling that illuminates an individual life.

The novel is written in the first person, which gives the illusion of testimony even though the narrative voice does not belong to Binebine. The text participates in the experience of collective witnessing, which includes the naming of those responsible for the atrocities at Tazmamart. However, Ben Jelloun's novel largely favors the exploration of its narrator's personal encounter with suffering and spirituality over the careful documentation of other Tazmamart writings. The novel places a great deal of emphasis on storytelling, both thematically by stressing its life-sustaining and curative power in the prison and through the actual narrative, which frequently follows Salim's retelling of popular novels and films. At the same time, this approach introduces another form of testimony, suggesting that while accounts firmly rooted in reality are necessary, the fictionalization of reality provides an alternative means of coping with trauma and rewriting Tazmamart back into the collective historical imagination.

Stylistically, *This Blinding Absence of Light* is, as Maureen Freely writes in *The Guardian* in 2004, "a novel stripped, like its subject, of all life's comforts." Reflecting the bareness of Salim's surroundings and the darkness that deprives him of sight, the novel's sparse prose contrasts sharply with Ben Jelloun's usual lyricism. Salim's meditations on the black stone of the Kaaba in Mecca and the spiritual journeys he takes to leave behind the physical suffering of his body are related in the language of Islamic mysticism, although the darkness he seeks to escape is real rather than metaphorical.

## CRITICAL DISCUSSION

Although the English translation of *This Blinding Absence of Light* was warmly received, the French original was sharply criticized in France and Morocco.

Despite this criticism, the English translation of the novel won the 2004 International Impac Dublin Literary Award. In a 2002 review for *Booklist,* Donna Seaman calls it a "wrenching yet exquisite tribute to the 'supreme light' of the human spirit in the face of 'infinite cruelty.'" Freely similarly notes that the novel "makes revelations of grave importance, but never gravely. It is, despite its dark materials, a joy to read." She asserts that "in Tahar Ben Jelloun the authorities have an enemy more formidable than 1,000 foreign journalists."

In the years since the novel's translation into English, debate over its authenticity has often overshadowed other scholarly concerns. In a 2006 article for *The Journal of the Midwest Modern Language Association,* Johanna Sellman raises the issue during her comparison of *This Blinding Absence of Light* with other Tazmamart narratives. She asks, "[H]ow does one accurately convey these years, and who has the right to do so?" ultimately concluding that Ben Jelloun's deviance from eyewitness documentation firmly identifies *This Blinding Absence of Light* as fiction rather than testimony.

Apart from widespread interest in the testimonial role of *This Blinding Absence of Light* and the moral implications of its publication, scholarship has largely focused on the text's literary qualities. In *Narratives of Catastrophe: Boris Diop, Ben Jelloun, Khatibi* (2009), Nasrin Qadar explores the challenges faced by authors of Tazmamart accounts, whether testimony, memoir, or fiction, given "the inability of language to narrate this experience and the necessity for language to narrate this experience." She addresses in particular Ben Jelloun's treatment of time and the methods he employs to narrate its impact on language as well as its physical and psychological effects on Salim. Simona Livescu expresses similar concerns in an essay in *Human Rights, Suffering, and Aesthetics in Political Prison Literature* (2011) with the ways in which suffering in prison narratives influences the individual. Through a comparison of several prison narratives, Livescu observes that there is a "*modus felicitatis*—a state of happiness or bliss—experienced by prisoners of conscience as victims of systemic human rights abuse." She argues that in addition to its function as a survival mechanism, this "epiphanic experience," born of a sense of community, uniquely affects the prisoner's level of political and social engagement following his or her release.

Moroccan troops search for suspects in 1971 following an alleged coup and assassination attempt on Morocco's King Hassan II. Those arrested for this incident endured brutal imprisonment for decades; their experiences form the basis of Tahar Ben Jelloun's novel *This Blinding Absence of Light.* © BETTMANN/CORBIS.

## BIBLIOGRAPHY

*Sources*

"Extraordinary Rendition: Mapping the Black Sites." *Frontline/World.* WGBH Educational Foundation, 4 Nov. 2007. Web. 4 Dec. 2012.

Freely, Maureen. "Into the Darkness." Rev. of *This Blinding Absence of Light,* by Tahar Ben Jelloun. *The Guardian* 23 July 2004: 21. Print.

Lalami, Laila. "Exile and the Kingdom." *The Nation.* The Nation, 20 Mar. 2006. Web. 27 Sept. 2012.

Livescu, Simona. "Deviating from the Norm?: Two Easts Testify to a Prison Aesthetics of Happiness." *Human Rights, Suffering, and Aesthetics in Political Prison Literature.* Ed. Yenna Wu and Simona Livescu. Lanham: Lexington Books, 2011. 185–205. Print.

Qadar, Nasrin. *Narratives of Catastrophe: Boris Diop, Ben Jelloun, Khatibi.* New York: Fordham UP, 2009. Print.

Seaman, Donna. Rev. of *This Blinding Absence of Light,* by Tahar Ben Jelloun. *Booklist* 98.18 (2002): 1573. Print.

Sellman, Johanna. "Memoirs from Tazmamart: Writing Strategies and Alternative Frameworks of Judgment." *Journal of the Midwest Modern Language Association* 39.2 (2006): 71–92. Print.

*Further Reading*

Ben Jelloun, Tahar. *The Last Friend.* Trans. Kevin Michel Capé and Hazel Rowley. New York: New Press, 2006. Print.

Hughes, Stephen O. *Morocco under King Hassan.* Reading: Ithaca, 2001. Print.

Orlando, Valérie. *Francophone Voices of the "New" Morocco in Film and Print: (Re)presenting a Society in Transition.* New York: Palgrave Macmillan, 2009. Print.

Oufkir, Malika, and Michele Fitoussi. *Stolen Lives: Twenty Years in a Desert Jail.* Trans. Ros Schwartz. New York: Hyperion, 2001. Print.

Slyomovics, Susan. *The Performance of Human Rights in Morocco.* Philadelphia: U of Pennsylvania P, 2005. Print.

*Media Adaptation*

*This Blinding Absence of Light.* Dir. Alessandro Olla. Perf. Massimo Zordan. SDNA, 2010. Video.

*Allison Blecker*

# WikiLeaks Manifesto

*Julian Assange*

❖ *Key Facts*

**Time Period:**
Early 21st Century

**Genre:**
Manifesto

**Events:**
Foundation of WikiLeaks group; September 11th attacks; U.S. War on Terror

**Nationality:**
Australian

## OVERVIEW

Written by Julian Assange and posted online in 2010, *WikiLeaks Manifesto* provides justification for the activities of WikiLeaks, a nonprofit organization founded by Assange in 2007 that reports classified information and news leaks, often from anonymous sources. The manifesto emphasizes technology's role as a populist check on authoritarian regimes and on the hidden maneuvering of the political elite. Comparing the secrecy of U.S. government directives to that of the covert terrorist organizations it fights, *WikiLeaks Manifesto* suggests a worldview wherein governments represent, in a quote from Theodore Roosevelt, "an unholy alliance between corrupt business and corrupt politics," an alliance that is supported by the practices that keep much information secret.

WikiLeaks' visibility increased steadily from its inception in 2006. By 2010 the group was the subject of significant debate, and Assange himself was under scrutiny by a number of corporate and government entities. Published in August of that year, *WikiLeaks Manifesto* generated a large amount of online commentary, but the traditional media largely ignored it. At first, the release of a large number of U.S. diplomatic cables dominated coverage, followed by accounts of the sexual assault allegations against Assange. While much in online culture has a notoriously short shelf life, the ideas set forth in the manifesto—that transparency limits corruption and that technology can and should be used to expose the abuses official statements belie—continue to resonate for many. *WikiLeaks Manifesto* exemplifies twenty-first-century skepticism of large institutions as self-serving and deceptive, as well as the contemporary belief in technology as an investigative tool of the people.

## HISTORICAL AND LITERARY CONTEXT

In the late 1980s and early 1990s, computer use was just becoming common and the Internet was in the early stages of development. As the Internet evolved, concerns about online privacy and security grew, and computer hackers were frequently arrested. As a teenager and young adult, Assange was involved in hacking and in its attendant subculture, much of which is characterized by anti-authoritarian views and a tendency to place a premium on freedom of information. At the same time, message boards, social media, and collaborative online projects proliferated together with a sense of the potential for free expression and participation in culture, including untrammeled political and social critique not present elsewhere.

*WikiLeaks Manifesto,* published four years after the organization's formation, reflects growing anger across the globe after an extended period of unrest. The United States and its allies were embroiled in unpopular conflicts in both Afghanistan and Iraq that to many seemed divorced from their original War on Terror justifications following the terrorist attacks on the United States on September 11, 2001. Corporate misdeeds were also in the news, with the collapse of Enron in the United States occurring just months after 9/11 and contributing to a general attitude of distrust of profit-over-people practices. In this political climate, WikiLeaks attracted growing support but was also subject to criticism and litigation, especially by entities whose documents had been leaked to and published at wikileaks.org. For example, the organization was sued by Swiss bank Julius Baer in 2008 and threatened by the Church of Scientology with a lawsuit that same year. It was also clear that the U.S. government was closely following Assange and his organization. Indeed, in 2010, WikiLeaks posted a U.S. government report dating back to 2008, which dealt with WikiLeaks deterrence.

Commentators note that *WikiLeaks Manifesto* bears a great similarity to two of Assange's essays from 2006, *State and Terrorist Conspiracies* and *Conspiracy as Governance,* both of which deal with technology's potential to counteract government secrecy. These essays share a good deal of text with *WikiLeaks Manifesto,* including use of the same quotations from other works, such as Lord Halifax's adage, "The best party is but a kind of conspiracy against the rest of the nation." *Conspiracy as Governance* is notable in that it makes Assange's contempt for mainstream media and media ties to government explicit. He writes, "Modern communications states provide their populace with an unprecedented deluge of witnessed, but seemingly unanswerable injustices." This sort of communication is detrimental because "those who are repeatedly passive in the face of injustice soon find their character corroded into servility."

Shortly after the publication of *WikiLeaks Manifesto,* Assange was arrested on charges of sexual assault,

*Opposite page:*
A banner showing support for *WikiLeaks Manifesto* author Julian Assange outside the Ecuadorian Embassy in London, 2012. Assange had many supporters in the wake of his arrest in the United Kingdom after allegedly committing sex crimes in Sweden. © MATTHEW ASLETT/DEMOTIX/CORBIS.

## PRIMARY SOURCE

### EXCERPT FROM *WIKILEAKS MANIFESTO*

#### TERRORIST CONSPIRACIES AS CONNECTED GRAPHS

Pre and post 9/11 the Maryland Procurement Office (National Security Agency light cover for academic funding, google for grant code "MDA904") and others have funded mathematicians to look at terrorist conspiracies as connected graphs (no mathematical background is needed to follow this article).

We extend this understanding of terrorist organizations and turn it on the likes of its creators where it becomes a knife to dissect the power conspiracies used to maintain authoritarian government.

We will use connected graphs as way to harness the spatial reasoning ability of the brain to think in a new way about political relationships. These graphs are easy to visualize. First take some nails ("conspirators") and hammer them into a board at random. Then take twine ("communication") and loop it from nail to nail without breaking. Call the twine connecting two nails a link. Unbroken twine means it is possible to travel from any nail to any other nail via twine and intermediary nails. Mathematicians say that this type of graph is connected.

Information flows from conspirator to conspirator. Not every conspirator trusts or knows every other conspirator even though all are connected. Some are on the fringe of the conspiracy, others are central and communicate with many conspirators and others still may know only two conspirators but be a bridge between important sections or groupings of the conspiracy.

#### SEPARATING A CONSPIRACY

If all links between conspirators are cut then there is no conspiracy. This is usually hard to do, so we ask our first question: What is the minimum number of links that must be cut to separate the conspiracy into two groups of equal number? (divide and conquer). The answer depends on the structure of the conspiracy. Sometimes there are no alternative paths for conspiratorial information to flow between conspirators, other times there are many. This is a useful and interesting characteristic of a conspiracy. For instance, by assassinating one "bridge" conspirator, it may be possible to split the conspiracy. But we want to say something about all conspiracies.

#### SOME CONSPIRATORS DANCE CLOSER THAN OTHERS

Conspirators are discerning, some trust and depend each other, others say little. Important information flows frequently through some links, trivial information through others. So we expand our simple connected graph model to include not only links, but their "importance."

Return to our board-and-nails analogy. Imagine a thick heavy cord between some nails and fine light thread between others. Call the importance,

and he distanced himself from WikiLeaks while in the process of appealing extradition to Sweden and subsequently seeking asylum in Ecuador. However, the ideas expressed in his manifesto remain guiding principles of WikiLeaks, which has continued to leak documents in his absence, including U.S. government files related to Guantánamo Bay detainees; internal e-mails from the private security firm Stratfor; and the Syria Files, thousands of e-mails between Syrian officials.

#### THEMES AND STYLE

*WikiLeaks Manifesto* argues that authoritarian governments are analogous to terrorist organizations, requiring conditions of secrecy to develop and enact their exploitive policies. It also states that such governments contain the seeds of their own destruction, because once people are aware of the nefarious plans of the "power elite," they will resist. In addition, Assange asserts that contemporary technology provides a particularly effective tool in the fight against government conspiracies, presumably as both a means of acquiring information and as a means of disseminating it once acquired. Assange exhorts his audience to "develop a way of thinking … that is strong enough [to] carry us through the mire of political language" that governments and corporations produce. Such clarity can "inspire within us and others a course of ennobling, and effective action."

*WikiLeaks Manifesto* is vague about the conspiracies that it discusses, but it does refer to the U.S. government's commission of a project to analyze terrorist conspiracies as connected graphs, noting that this analysis can be turned "on the likes of its creators where it becomes a knife to dissect the power conspiracies used to maintain authoritarian government." Thus, the work co-opts the connected-graphs metaphor for his own purposes, while indicting the United States, and possibly other governments, for being the equivalent of terrorist organizations. The thickness or heaviness of a link its weight. Between conspirators that never communicate the weight is zero. The "importance" of communication passing through a link difficult to evaluate a priori, since it its true value depends on the outcome of the conspiracy. We simply say that the "importance" of communication contributes to the weight of a link in the most obvious way; the weight of a link is proportional to the amount of important communication flowing across it. Questions about conspiracies in general won't require us to know the weight of any link, since that changes from conspiracy to conspiracy.

## CONSPIRACIES ARE COGNITIVE DEVICES. THEY ARE ABLE TO OUT THINK THE SAME GROUP OF INDIVIDUALS ACTING ALONE

Conspiracies take information about the world in which they operate (the conspiratorial environment), pass it around the conspirators and then act on the result. We can see conspiracies as a type of device that has inputs (information about the environment) and outputs (actions intending to change or maintain the environment).

## WHAT DOES A CONSPIRACY COMPUTE? IT COMPUTES THE NEXT ACTION OF THE CONSPIRACY

Now I we ask the question: how effective is this device? Can we compare it to itself at different times?

Is the conspiracy growing stronger or weakening? This is a question that asks us to compare two values.

## CAN WE FIND A VALUE THAT DESCRIBES THE POWER OF A CONSPIRACY?

We could count the number of conspirators, but that would not capture the difference between a conspiracy and the individuals which comprise it. How do they differ? Individuals in a conspiracy conspire. Isolated individuals do not. We can capture that difference by adding up all the important communication (weights) between the conspirators, we will call this the total conspiratorial power.

## TOTAL CONSPIRATORIAL POWER

This number is an abstraction. The pattern of connections in a conspiracy is unusually unique. But by looking at this value which in independent of the arrangement of conspiratorial connections we can make some generalizations.

## IF TOTAL CONSPIRATORIAL POWER IS ZERO, THERE IS NO CONSPIRACY

If total conspiratorial power is zero, there is no information flow between the conspirators and hence no conspiracy.

A substantial increase or decrease in total conspiratorial power almost always means what we expect it to mean; an increase or decrease in the ability of the conspiracy to think, act and adapt.

---

remainder of the work extends the graph metaphor, likening the graph to a board filled with nails, representing various parties to the conspiracy and connected by twine, which signifies "communication." Through this visual description, *WikiLeaks Manifesto* illustrates the complexity of conspiracies, as well as the many points at which they might be vulnerable to interference.

Although many of the leaks Assange has published deal with subjects such as war crimes and corporate fraud, which could inflame readers' emotions, Assange avoids treating the subjects as a polemic and instead opts for the cool tones of formal argument. He does not avoid the suggestion of violence entirely, however, referring to the "knife" of analysis and to the body of a conspiracy, whose "blood may be thickened and slowed till it falls." The general tone of *WikiLeaks Manifesto* makes clear that Assange is taking the moral high ground, intending no "traditional attacks on conspiratorial power groupings … assassinations

… killings, kidnapping, blackmailing." However, it is also clear that he intends decisive action and that he considers this action justified.

## CRITICAL DISCUSSION

Following the appearance of *WikiLeaks Manifesto*, Assange supporters and detractors engaged in debate online, with supporters lauding the work's boldness and fresh use of metaphor and detractors pointing out Assange's vagueness, particularly in being out of step with the demands of the manifesto as a political tool for inciting action. In a 2011 article in *Technology Review*, Jason Pontin, the magazine's editor in chief, describes Assange's work as "strange, epigrammatic, abstracted prose." Mainstream journalists largely ignored the document, or they mentioned it only in passing. In a 2011 article for the *New York Times*, author Robert Wright calls it "grandiose," adding that it "ranges from the undeniably plausible … to the eccentrically metaphorical … to the flat-out opaque."

Even if, as critics suggest, *WikiLeaks Manifesto* is destined for obscurity, the ideas it enshrines, such as the importance of institutional transparency and the role of technology in achieving this transparency, will likely remain part of public and scholarly debate about privacy, security, and free speech. Following the release of thousands of classified cables in 2010, U.S. officials introduced the SHIELD Act to amend the Espionage Act of 1917, making it a crime to disseminate classified intelligence information or details about the identity of U.S. informants. Although the bill did not pass, its introduction raised issues about First Amendment protections weighed against the safety of American troops. Analyzing the constitutionality of the SHIELD Act, author Geoffrey R. Stone argues in a 2012 article in *Federal Communications Law Journal* that First Amendment protection should be extended to dissemination of leaked documents except when it would "result in likely, imminent, and grave harm to national security" and "the publication would not significantly contribute to public debate." Much of the current research related to WikiLeaks and its practices takes up these issues, considering the legal and social consequences of leaks and the costs of trying to control information in a free society.

While little has been written about the manifesto as a stand-alone document, scholars have engaged with the ethical questions that follow from the work's promotion of transparency of information. In a 2012 article in the *Yale Law Journal,* Patricia Bellia discusses the U.S. Supreme Court's treatment of the Pentagon Papers case as it has been interpreted by Assange defenders as a vindication of WikiLeaks. While Bellia notes that the Pentagon Papers case ultimately supported the publication of classified documents by the *New York Times* and others, she suggests that judicial opinion in the case assumed that news outlets such as the *New York Times* would be constrained by ethical as well as legal considerations. She adds that it is unclear whether WikiLeaks or other organizations, operating under different principles, would show the same restraint. Bellia's argument gets at the heart of the debate about what constitutes journalism in the technological and political climate of the early twenty-first century. In a 2012 article for the *New Yorker,* Raffi Khatchadourian writes, "[Assange] said that some leaks risked harming innocent people—'collateral damage, if you will'—but that he could not weigh the importance of every detail in every document."

## BIBLIOGRAPHY

### Sources

Assange, Julian. *Conspiracy as Governance. AsPDF.* AsPDF, 3 Dec. 2006. Web. 12 Sept. 2012.

———. *WikiLeaks Manifesto. The Comment Factory.* The Comment Factory, 1 Aug. 2010. Web. 12 Sept. 2012.

Bellia, Patricia L. "WikiLeaks and the Institutional Framework for National Security Disclosures." *Yale Law Journal* (2012): 1448+. *General OneFile.* Web. 13 Sept. 2012.

Khatchadourian, Raffi. "No Secrets: Julian Assange's Mission for Total Transparency." *New Yorker.* Condé Nast, 7 June 2012. Web. 12 Sept. 2012.

Pontin, Jason. "Transparency and Secrets." *Technology Review* 114.2 (2011): 70–73. *Academic Search Elite.* Web. 13 Sept. 2012.

Stone, Geoffrey R. "WikiLeaks and the First Amendment." *Federal Communications Law Journal* (2012): 477+. *General OneFile.* Web. 12 Sept. 2012.

*WikiLeaks.com.* Web. 29 Sept. 2012.

Wright, Robert. "Is Julian Assange Helping the Neocons?" *New York Times.* The New York Times Company, 11 Jan. 2011. Web. 13 Sept. 2012.

### Further Reading

Beckett, Charlie. *WikiLeaks: News in the Networked Era.* Cambridge: Polity, 2012. Print.

Birchall, Clare. "Transparency, Interrupted: Secrets of the Left." *Theory Culture Society* 28.7–8 (2011): 60–84. Print.

Leigh, David, and Luke Harding. *Wikileaks: Inside Julian Assange's War on Secrecy.* New York: Public Affairs, 2011. Print.

MacKinnon, Rebecca. *Consent of the Networked: The World-wide Struggle for Internet Freedom.* New York: Basic Books, 2012. Print.

Sifry, Micah L. *Wikileaks and the Age of Transparency.* Berkeley: Counterpoint, 2011. Print.

*Daisy Gard*

# Formal Innovations

# AMERICAN PICTURES
## A Personal Journey through Black America
*Jacob Holdt*

## OVERVIEW

Published in 1977 by Danish photographer Jacob Holdt, *American Pictures: A Personal Journey through Black America* is a nonfiction book of photography showcasing the hardships faced by lower classes in the United States. Using only a cheap pocket camera while hitchhiking across the country for more than five years, Holdt traveled 100,000 miles and shot more than 15,000 photos, selling his blood plasma twice a week so he could afford to buy film. He stayed in more than 400 households and photographed a diverse range of families, from migrant workers to the Rockefellers, but he focused his lens primarily on the plight of black Americans. Holdt compiled a slideshow depicting the disparities between the rich and the poor and displayed it at more than 300 college campuses throughout the United States. This caught the attention of the KGB, the intelligence agency of the Soviet Union, which allegedly planned to use his book to start a campaign that would show the United States was guilty of human rights violations against its own citizens.

Frustrated with Denmark's support of the Vietnam War, Holdt originally planned to travel to Chile in the spring of 1970 to support Salvador Allende, the presidential candidate of the socialist-communist Popular Unity Party, and to fight for socialism. He began his trip in Canada, made his way to the United States, and abandoned his plans to go to Chile after being startled and fascinated by the injustice and poverty that he encountered in such a seemingly prosperous country. Since its publication in 1977 *American Pictures* has stood as evidence of the importance of the fight for human rights around the world. Holdt has spearheaded a movement through his work with the Cooperative for Assistance and Relief Everywhere (CARE) and his continued documentation of U.S. poverty.

## HISTORICAL AND LITERARY CONTEXT

Political, social, and economic unrest spread around the world during the late 1960s and early 1970s. This unrest was largely the outcome of a growing global conflict between capitalist, communist, imperialist, and independence forces in the wake of World War II. As the United States and Soviet Union rose to become increasingly antagonistic superpowers during the 1950s and 1960s, the world became increasingly polarized along capitalist and communist lines. Perhaps the most significant manifesto of this polarization occurred in Vietnam. Beginning in the mid-1950s, the United States and other foreign anticommunist forces allied with South Vietnam to combat the communist North Vietnam. As this conflict dragged on and became increasingly bloody, a protest movement against the war erupted in the United States in Europe and was led largely by students and the young. As Holdt became involved in this movement in the 1960s, he became increasingly committed to radical left-wing causes.

When Holdt began taking the photographs that would become *American Pictures,* he believed he was merely passing through the United States on his way from working on a Canadian farm to join in Allende's effort to implement socialist change in Chile. While in the United States, however, Holdt became fascinated by the antiwar effort and by the dramatic social, economic, and racial injustice he encountered. Though his documentary effort was at first random, he soon decided to focus his project and document African American poverty. His aim was not merely to expose the injustice of the U.S. capitalist system but also to communicate his findings to his Danish compatriots. This latter aim became more urgent when, on November 25, 1971, Denmark established diplomatic relations with the Republic of Vietnam (South Vietnam), thereby demonstrating its support for the Vietnam War. Holdt's dissatisfaction with his native country's political stance fueled his interest in showcasing class disparity in the United States. In 1975, after five years in the United States, he returned to Denmark and toured with a slideshow of his photos. Two years later the work was published in book form. As the scholar Ole Bech-Petersen writes in his 2000 essay in *American Studies International,* "Through a combination of photography, personal anecdotes and agitprop sociology, Holdt's book portrayed the United States as a violently oppressive and polarized society of injustice, racism and inequality."

By opening the eyes of many Americans to the gap between the poor and the rich in the United States, Holdt joined a group of social realist artists who did similar work throughout the twentieth century. Photographer Tom Stone, born in the same decade that Holdt hitchhiked across the United States, also documented poverty in the United States, capturing images of those

+ **Key Facts**

**Time Period:**
Late 20th Century

**Genre:**
Nonfiction/Photography

**Events:**
End of Vietnam War; Cold War; oil crisis; economic recession

**Nationality:**
Danish

# BEHIND THE CAMERA: THE LIFE OF JACOB HOLDT

Born in 1947, Jacob Holdt was the son of a pastor and spent most of his childhood in Fåborg, Denmark, a small village near Esbjerg in western Jutland. After being kicked out of his first high school, he ended up at Krogerup Folk High School, north of Copenhagen, in 1965. Later Holdt was also thrown out of the Royal Palace Guard after only serving eight months. Before deciding to travel to Chile via Canada and the United States, Holdt participated in Vietnam War protests in Denmark.

After the success of *American Pictures* Holdt focused his work on white supremacist groups, specifically the Ku Klux Klan, following local chapters of the group and documenting their daily lives. He has also adapted the material included in his *American Pictures* slideshow and book into a movie and an online picture book, both of which are available on Holdt's website, american-pictures.com. In 2008 Holdt was one of four photographers short-listed for the Deutsche Börse Photography Prize.

on the fringes of society and exhibiting his work in Los Angeles, San Francisco, and Miami. Chilean writer and photographer Camilo José Vergara followed in Holdt's footsteps as well, photographing U.S. slums and dilapidated urban environments in the 1980s. Esther Bubley, who took photos of ordinary people in their everyday lives, and Walker Evans, the famed Great Depression documenter, paved the way for photographers such as Holdt to turn their cameras on ordinary citizens and document their stories for the world.

In addition to raising awareness of economic, social, and racial injustice in the United States, *American Pictures* left a significant cultural and literary legacy. In his short story "A Voice Foretold," for example, the American writer John Edgar Wideman writes of a character much like Holdt, a radical, foreign photographer who is compelled to witness and document the grimmest instances of racial injustice. Holdt's project of traveling around the United States and documenting the American experience was taken up in 1973 by Stephen Shore. The photographs Shore took over a six-year period and later collected as the book *Uncommon Places* lacked the political and social agenda of *American Pictures* but were influenced by Holdt's method of photographing the overlooked aspects of American life.

## THEMES AND STYLE

The focal point of *American Pictures* is the social and economic disparity and racial division and tension that existed in the United States in the 1970s. Holdt writes that "traveling in such a deeply divided society inevitably was a violent experience," and he describes how he was attacked numerous times by robbers and police and was once almost killed by a mob that had surrounded him in a dark alley. Haunting passages

about Holdt's travels are interspersed between his stark images, drawing attention to the disparities of living conditions in the United States. Although he had only intended to depict the social injustices he had encountered, his project became more expansive than he imagined, especially as he turned the social commentary of his art into a tour of college campuses.

Holdt eschews lengthy prose and extraneous details in the captions and passages about his travels, writing instead in a poetic, free-verse style that reads like a stream of consciousness. He does not recount every detail of his experience; he presents key information that either corresponds to a photo or sheds light on the family or city he was visiting. In chapter three, for example, he writes about experiencing gun violence:

> When you come from Europe and have never seen a pistol before, to hear the tone of this language for the first time gives you a shock you'll never forget. After only two days in this new country I was held up by gun men—a type of people I had never met before. The fear I felt was a fear I had never experienced before: the fear of another human being.

In addition to explicating the context of a certain set of photos, this text offers an implicit critique of U.S. society through observational commentary. Throughout the text, Holdt employs this kind of outside perspective to exhume the injustice concealed within the prosperous veneer of American culture.

Holdt writes reflectively about his travels, presenting an inquisitive take on his encounters instead of a biased viewpoint. After picking cotton in the South, Holdt wonders, "How can these people be called free, when everything around them reminds them of the old master/slave relationship?" When writing again about gun violence, he describes his take on fear and the lower class: "Even such questions were beyond my imagination, but from the day when I faced that cold 'piece' of American reality I began to understand how fear locks us up in behavior patterns which daily force millions of people into ghettos and eventually into an underclass." While there is certainly an emotional appeal in most of Holdt's writing, he stands back from his experiences and questions everything, allowing readers to, in turn, ask themselves the same questions and make their own determinations.

## CRITICAL DISCUSSION

Initial reviews of Holdt's traveling show of *American Pictures* applauded his brave attempt to capture the disparity between American social classes. Then, when he published those photos as *American Pictures: A Personal Journey through Black America*, it was universally hailed by critics and reviewers in Denmark. The praise for Holdt's work was largely a result of the revelatory view it offered of the United States. As Danish reviewer Bech-Petersen wrote, "Many will probably deny that this is real. What Holdt is telling stands in so complete contrast to the conventional view of the United States that it is not hard to imagine how the psychological defense mechanisms will be activated." The book was not reviewed as extensively in the United States. Still, because the book is often taught in college courses, there has been ample critical discussion of it. In the *Oxford History of Art: American Photography,* author Miles Orwell agrees with the early positive reviews of the traveling show: "*American Pictures* is one of the most powerful indictments of racism, but it is also a work that refuses to take a scolding tone, as Holdt discovers in himself the grounds of white racism, implicating the reader as well, white or black, in the complex violence of our racist society."

Since its publication, *American Pictures* has left a decisive mark upon Danish impressions of the United States. Bech-Petersen writes that the book "was a comprehensive national intervention with massive repercussions on how Danes have viewed the United States in the past almost quarter-century." While *American Pictures* undermined the prevailing Danish perception of the United States as a land of freedom and opportunity, Holdt intended his photographs to offer a broader critique of the capitalist West and of Denmark, in particular. Though he has made this case in subsequent writings, *American Pictures* remains best known for razing the idea of American exceptionalism in the minds of many Danes and other Europeans.

Other artistic works have since offered social commentary on economic disparities in the United States, but *American Pictures* remains one of the foremost statements on the differences between the classes in the last half of the twentieth century. Some critics have taken issue with Holdt's role in his subjects' lives. J. Hoberman writes in the *Village Voice*: "The paradox of *American Pictures* is how forcibly one's attention is drawn from the conditions photographed to the condition of the photographer. And while it would be unjust to accuse Holdt of exploiting his subjects, he certainly offers no insight into how he appeared in the context of their lives." Nina Berman and Richard Martin also comment on this issue in the *Chicago Reader,* using Holdt's own inquisitive approach: "Is he simply another white male from a middle-class background exploiting minorities, putting them under a microscope and dissecting them? Is *American Pictures* just like so many other black or socially critical art productions paraded at the Museum of Modern Art? Is it, in the end, only passive escapism?"

**BIBLIOGRAPHY**

*Sources*

Bech-Petersen, Ole. "The Fatalistic Hobo: Jacob Holdt, Touring, and the Other Americans." *American Studies International* 38.1 (2000). *JSTOR.* Web. 16 Nov. 2012.

Berman, Nina, and Richard Martin. "Moving Pictures: Jacob Holdt's Mirror on America." *Chicago Reader* 6 Nov. 1981. Print.

Hoberman, J. "Annals of the Poor." *Village Voice* 11 Sept. 1984. Print.

Holdt, Jacob. *American Pictures: A Personal Journey through the American Underclass.* Copenhagen: American Pictures Foundation, 1985. Print.

Van Gelder, Lawrence. "Film: 'Pictures,' a View of Poverty in America." *New York Times.* The New York Times Company, 5 Sept. 1984. Web. 13 Sept. 2012.

*Further Reading*

Evans, Walker. *Walker Evans.* New York: Museum of Modern Art, 1971. Print.

Roddick, Anita. "Anita Roddick on Racism, Poverty and Oppression, Class Diversity and Ethnic Conflict." *American Pictures.* American Pictures. Web. 17 Aug. 2012.

Tuchman, Mitch. "American Pictures." *Film Comment.* Film Society of Lincoln Center, Feb. 1983. Web. 17 Aug. 2012.

*Media Adaptation*

Holdt, Jacob. *Jacob Holdt's American Pictures.* Freshman Seminar Speaker Series, No. 2. 1992. VHS.

*Anna Deem*

In this 2010 photograph, Oscar Otzoy of the Coalition of Immokalee Workers holds chains used in modern slavery. Jacob Holdt discusses modern slavery in his 1977 book *American Pictures.* AP PHOTO/THE NEWS PRESS, ANDREW WEST.

# American Slavery As It Is

*Testimony of a Thousand Witnesses*

*Theodore Dwight Weld*

## OVERVIEW

*American Slavery As It Is: Testimony of a Thousand Witnesses,* compiled in 1838–1839 by American abolitionist Theodore Dwight Weld with assistance from his wife, Angelina Grimké Weld, and her sister, Sarah Grimké, seeks to indict slavery through firsthand accounts of its effects. Presented as a court case against the slave system, with the "reader … empanelled as a juror," the book offers evidence for the harm slavery does both to individual slaves and to the overall moral tenor of slaveholding society. Weld solicited eyewitness accounts from abolitionists, former slaveholders, and visitors to the South, then added editorial arguments to weave them together with what are, for many readers, the most persuasive elements of the book: excerpts from Southern newspapers, including advertisements for runaway slaves and accounts of violence perpetrated by slaveholders on both slaves and each other. The result—at least as far as abolitionist readers were concerned—was a compendium of verified facts that could be used to construct an irrefutable case against slavery.

Although Americans had debated the acceptability of slavery since before the founding of the Republic, the movement for immediate abolition began in earnest in the early 1830s. The nation's most famous antislavery paper, William Lloyd Garrison's *The Liberator,* began publication in 1831, and the American Anti-Slavery Society, which published *American Slavery As It Is,* was founded in 1834. At the time of the book's publication, many Northerners, including those who opposed slavery, had little concept of what the day-to-day lives of slaves were like. Weld's book provided them with that information, together with a long final section that includes refutations of common "objections" to antislavery arguments. With sales reaching 100,000 within a year, *American Slavery* was the most widely read abolitionist tract of its day and continued to influence antislavery arguments in the decades that followed.

## HISTORICAL AND LITERARY CONTEXT

By the 1830s, American abolitionists had reason to hope that their goals were achievable: both Britain and the United States outlawed the Atlantic slave trade in 1807 and 1808, respectively; the Missouri Compromise limited expansion of slavery into new U.S. territories in 1820; and slavery was abolished by the British Parliament in 1833. The bloody rebellion led by Virginia slave Nat Turner in 1831, coupled with the ensuing violence against slaves and free blacks, intensified the slavery debate in the United States. Abolitionists cited the rebellion as proof that slavery was neither a safe nor a just system, whereas others agitated for Southerners to defend slavery and argued for stricter control of slaves' movements.

Proposed solutions to the slavery issue varied even among those who agreed that slavery should end. One well-established antislavery tradition, embraced by some slaveholders, called for gradual emancipation and colonization: the deportation of freed slaves to Africa or to territories of the United States separate from those inhabited by Americans of wholly European descent. However, the 1830s saw the rise of a more radical abolitionist movement, with leaders—including Garrison, Weld, and the Grimké sisters—advocating for immediate emancipation and full citizenship for former slaves. Both Weld and the Grimké sisters, members of a South Carolina slaveholding family who had moved to Philadelphia in part because of their abhorrence of slavery, spent the mid-1830s traveling through the Northeast and near West, giving speeches in support of the abolitionist cause. Weld's voice began to fail from these efforts, and soon after his marriage to Angelina, they sought to reach an even larger audience with *American Slavery As It Is.*

Theodore, Angelina, and Sarah were all experienced authors of polemical literature. Weld had turned parts of his antislavery lectures into *The Bible Against Slavery,* which was published in 1837. Angelina Grimké made similar biblical arguments in her *Appeal to the Christian Women of the Southern States* in 1836, followed by her *Appeal to the Women of the Nominally Free States* in 1837. Both sisters had used their writing to refute the arguments of those who believed women should not speak in public or otherwise participate in civic life. In creating *American Slavery,* they could also draw on the example of Thomas Clarkson, whose gathering and publication of voluminous factual materials, including the now-familiar drawing showing how African captives were packed into the hold of a slave ship, had played a vital role in the British abolitionist movement.

*American Slavery As It Is* played a similar role in the American abolitionist movement, providing material for antislavery speakers who followed Weld and the Grimkés and for abolitionist writers including Harriet Beecher Stowe. Many of the book's rhetorical strategies, including its incorporation of such Southern materials as advertisements for runaway slaves and its emphasis on extreme violence—especially whipping—are echoed in later antislavery fiction and nonfiction. Even after the Thirteenth Amendment outlawed slavery in the United States in 1865, these themes continued to shape representations of American slavery.

## THEMES AND STYLE

*American Slavery* emphasizes the violence perpetrated on slaves and the deprivations they experienced. Both the personal narratives (written in response to questions provided by Weld) and the subject headings for thematic sections emphasize masters' failure to provide for their slaves' basic human needs and the cruelty with which slaves were treated. Sections and subsections include "privations of the slaves" in the areas of "food," "labor," "clothing," "dwellings," and "treatment of the sick," as well as "punishments," including "floggings," "slave driving," "cruelty to slaves," and "tortures of slaves" using devices such as "iron collars, chains, and hand-cuffs." The "objections considered" section—especially the final discussion of "objection VII—public opinion is a protection to the slave"—broadens the focus of the work to the moral degradation of the community as a whole, suggesting that the violence and callousness with which slaves are treated spill over into interactions among whites. This section identifies several criminal and antisocial behaviors, from murder to dueling to violent sports involving animals, and asserts that such deeds occur more frequently in the slaveholding states and are indirect effects of the slave system.

The strength of the book's argument derives from the sheer volume of the material it presents, its repetition of key points (such as the violence of physical punishments inflicted on slaves, which is mentioned in the majority of personal narratives as well as in several of the thematic sections), and the verifiability of the information. Personal narratives are often accompanied by affidavits from neighbors, clergymen, and other leading citizens of the towns in which the eyewitness resides, attesting to his (or, in a few cases, her) character. Extracts from newspapers, laws from Southern states, and speeches in state legislatures and the U.S. Congress are cited with precision. Weld describes the present location of his sources with the same exactness, assuring the reader that the "recent newspapers, published in the slave states" from which "a majority of the facts ... contained in t[he] work" were "taken" would be "deposited at the office of the American Anti-Slavery Society, 143 Nassau Street, New York City. ... Those who think the atrocities, which they describe, incredible," he continues, "are invited to call and read for themselves."

## WHO WROTE *AMERICAN SLAVERY AS IT IS*?

Although usually attributed to Theodore Dwight Weld, *American Slavery As It Is* includes no author's name on the title page. We know from letters written by members of and visitors to the Weld-Grimké household that Sarah and Angelina did much of the work of identifying, extracting, and arranging material from the recently outdated newspapers Weld bought at reading rooms in New York. We also know that the Grimké sisters were experienced authors and that they, like others who contributed to the "personal narratives" sections of the book, signed their individual eyewitness accounts of slavery. We do not know who wrote the editorial portions of the book, including the introduction and the sections that weave together the personal narratives and the extracts from newspapers, laws, and legislative speeches. These sections may, as has traditionally been assumed, be the work of Weld alone; they may also be the product of a collaboration between Weld and the Grimké sisters. We cannot be sure. We do know that Weld, a strong advocate of the abilities and rights of women, and an early believer in egalitarian marriage, would have been distressed to see a collaborative work attributed to him alone.

Although for the most part the book is designed to allow the accumulated facts to speak for themselves, the voice of the editorial sections joining the eyewitness narratives and extracts ranges from coolly objective to bitterly satirical. When setting out principles for selecting accounts of white-on-white crime from the slaveholding states, the editorial voice is neutral. By contrast, in answering the objection "public opinion is a protection to the slave," it sardonically summarizes the argument it is about to refute: "It was public opinion that *made man a slave* ... and now, forsooth, this same public opinion will see to it, that these *chattels* are treated like *men!*"

## CRITICAL DISCUSSION

Abolitionists read and praised *American Slavery,* but its impact on the broader public was mostly indirect, accomplished through later authors who borrowed its tactics and some of its materials. The Antislavery Society distributed free copies to legislators and other leaders, as well as to each of the Southern newspapers on which the book drew. In 1842, as Ellen Gruber Garvey relates, parts of *American Slavery As It Is* received a wider, if unknowing, readership when Charles Dickens presented some of the ads extracted by Weld and the Grimkés in his *American Notes* "as though he had come across [them] himself" during his Southern travels.

The most important reuse of the book's strategies and material was by Harriet Beecher Stowe, whose 1852 best seller *Uncle Tom's Cabin* captured the

Photograph of a slave family in a Georgia cotton field, c. 1860. A SLAVE FAMILY IN A GEORGIA COTTON FIELD, C. 1860 (B/W PHOTO), AMERICAN PHOTOGRAPHER, (19TH CENTURY)/PRIVATE COLLECTION/PETER NEWARK AMERICAN PICTURES/THE BRIDGEMAN ART LIBRARY.

attention of many hitherto indifferent Northern readers in a way that *American Slavery* had not. As Thomas Leonard notes, "Stowe said that she slept with *American Slavery As It Is* under her pillow while writing *Uncle Tom's Cabin,* and in *A Key to Uncle Tom's Cabin* (1853) she recycled Weld-Grimké clippings" and added some of her own. The association of *American Slavery* with Stowe's sentimental novel has also influenced scholarly conversations about the earlier work, with critics debating whether the Weld/Grimké volume is essentially factual and realistic, essentially sentimental and sensationalistic, or, perhaps, both.

Most modern critics emphasize the book's focus on extreme violence and on the sexual vulnerability of slave women. Some argue that its emphasis on arousing emotion, a hallmark of sentimental literature, undermines its ability to spur action. Thomas Browne, for instance, believes that "by virtue of its style and the sentimentalism it encouraged, the text could at least provide the satisfactions of moral exhaustion" while allowing readers to "retain allegiance to the [capitalist] system which made [slavery] possible." Karen Halftone proposes a more sympathetic interpretation of abolitionists' emphasis on physical suffering, arguing that "the reformers' purpose was not to exploit the obscenity of pain but to expose it, in order to redefine a wide range of previously accepted social practices as cruel and unacceptable." Garvey approaches *American Slavery As It Is* from a twenty-first-century angle, pointing out that the book "was the product of a new way of using media," noting that "the Grimkés

and Weld reconceptualized the press and mined it as a database."

## BIBLIOGRAPHY

*Sources*

Browne, Stephen. "'Like Gory Spectres': Representing Evil in Theodore Weld's *American Slavery As It Is.*" *Quarterly Journal of Speech* 80 (1994): 277–292. *Communication & Mass Media Complete.* Web. 10 July 2012.

Garvey, Ellen Gruber. "Nineteenth-Century Abolitionists and the Databases They Created." *Legacy: A Journal of American Women Writers* 27.2 (2010): 37–366. Print.

Halftone, Karen. "Humanitarianism and the Pornography of Pain in Anglo-American Culture." *The American Historical Review* 100.2 (Apr. 1995): 303–334. *JSTOR.* Web. 9 July 2012.

Leonard, Thomas C. "Antislavery, Civil Rights, and Incendiary Material." *Media and Revolution.* Ed. Jeremy D. Popkin. Lexington: U of Kentucky P, 1995. *Google Books.* Web. 13 July 2012.

[Weld, Thomas.] *American Slavery As It Is: Testimony of a Thousand Witnesses.* New York: American Anti-Slavery Society, 1839. Web. *Google Books.* 21 June 2012.

*Further Reading*

Abzug, Robert H. *Passionate Liberator: Theodore Dwight Weld & the Dilemma of Reform.* New York: Oxford UP, 1980. Print.

Grimké, Angelina E. *Appeal to the Christian Women of the South.* New York: American Anti-Slavery Society, 1836. Web. *Uncle Tom's Cabin & American Culture: A Multi-Media Archive.* University of Virginia, 2009. 13 July 2012.

Itis, R. S. "Figuration of Moral Reform in the Rhetoric of Theodore Dwight Weld." *Rhetorical Democracy: Discursive Practices of Civic Engagement: Selected Papers from the 2002 Conference of the Rhetoric Society of America.* Eds. Gerard A. Hauser and Amy Grim. Mahwah: Lawrence Erlbaum, 2004. Print.

Lasser, Carol. "Voyeuristic Abolitionism: Sex, Gender, and the Transformation of Antislavery Rhetoric." *Journal of the Early Republic* 28.1 (Spring 2008): 83–114. *Project Muse.* Web. 12 July 2012.

Lerner, Gerda. *The Grimké Sisters from South Carolina: Pioneers for Women's Rights and Abolition.* New York: Oxford UP, 1998. Print.

McGill, Meredith L. *American Literature and the Culture of Reprinting, 1834–1853.* Philadelphia: U of Pennsylvania P, 2003. Print.

Perry, Mark. *Lift Up Thy Voice: The Grimké Family's Journey from Slaveholders to Civil Rights Leaders.* New York: Penguin, 2001. Print.

Weld, Theodore Dwight. *The Bible Against Slavery, or, An Inquiry into the Genius of the Mosaic System, and the Teachings of the Old Testament on the Subject of Human Rights.* Pittsburgh: United Presbyterian Board of Publication, 1864. Repr. Ithaca: Cornell University Library Digital Collections, n.d. Print.

*Catherine E. Saunders*

# THE COMPLETE MAUS

*Art Spiegelman*

## OVERVIEW

One of the most influential and celebrated of graphic novels, Art Spiegelman's *Maus: A Survivor's Tale* was initially serialized in the magazine *Raw* from 1980 to 1991. The first six chapters were collected and published as a book with the subtitle *My Father Bleeds History* in 1986, and the final five sections appeared in book form as *Maus II: A Survivor's Tale: And Here My Troubles Began* in 1991. Together, the two volumes tell the story of the author's experiences interviewing his father, Vladek, a Holocaust survivor. Spiegelman's troubled relationship with his father and his own struggles to write the novel are central to the story. *Maus*'s simple structure and minimalist drawings disguise its complexity; it employs multifaceted symbols and experiments with several postmodern techniques, such as metafiction, or fiction that reflects on its own processes. One of the most notable, and sometimes controversial, features of the novel is Spiegelman's decision to depict the Nazis as cats, the Jews as mice, and the Poles as pigs. In using animals to represent human characters, the work echoes Nazi propaganda, which dehumanized races that were deemed inferior and often depicted Jews as rats or mice.

Published during a lull in the popularity of comic books, *Maus* instantly revitalized and revolutionized the form, introducing the graphic novel to adult mainstream audiences. Besides being a huge popular success, it also brought the genre into the world of academia, where it gained respect. It was the first work of its kind to win a Pulitzer Prize. Spiegelman's masterpiece continues to command scholarly and critical attention in diverse fields, including Jewish and oral history, historiography, cultural and comics studies, and feminist and psychoanalytic theory. The work has also inspired many writers to adopt the comic or graphic novel medium.

## HISTORICAL AND LITERARY CONTEXT

From the Nazi Party's initial development in early 1920s Germany, it demanded a simplistic categorization of human beings and used various methods of propaganda to exalt or vilify these populations. The Nazis focused foremost on Jews, whom they saw as the cause of all suffering and shame. During World War II they used anti-Semitic propaganda in support of extermination policies designed to create a dominant master race. The United States and the USSR, after temporarily allying to defeat the Nazis, turned their profound philosophical differences into the Cold War, similarly classifying individuals broadly and oversimplifying the complexity of human culture and political thought. Members and suspected members of the Communist Party, other leftists, homosexuals, union members, educators, and entertainers were among those tried and sometimes convicted of treason or "un-American activities" by the U.S. Senate and the private business sector in the early 1950s. Published near the end of the Cold War, *Maus*'s depiction of the Nazis' dehumanization of the Jews explores the ways in which prejudice and intolerance continue to dehumanize individuals and separate people along racial, cultural, national, and political lines.

Traditional superhero comic books date from the late 1930s, beginning with Marvel Comics' *Fantastic Four* and DC Comics' *Superman* and *Batman,* which reached their peak popularity in the 1940s and 1950s. Their format was embraced in the introduction of "comix," underground (1960s) and alternative (1970s) adult-oriented comic books, many overtly criticizing American social and political values. The later 1970s found the traditional medium wallowing. Soon, however, a new group of writers and artists began approaching comics from a different angle, creating stories that took on a more realist style. Refusing to categorize themselves, these artists saw their work as a new form of literary expression. In 1978 Will Eisner popularized the term "graphic novel" when he used it on the cover of *A Contract with God, and Other Tenement Stories.* Spiegelman has stated that he was more directly influenced by the work of Frans Masereel, a Belgian woodcut artist who produced *Mon Livre d'Heures,* a wordless "autobiography of the spirit," in 1919; Harvey Kurtzman, American cartoonist and founding editor of the satirical serial *Mad* magazine in 1952; and Bernard Krigstein, *Mad* contributor and author of the celebrated graphic short story "Master Race" (1955), a rare early popular media treatment of the Holocaust.

Spiegelman's work raised the status of the genre to that of the novel and short story; graphic novels are now considered literary works worthy of study and critical analysis. *Maus* not only spawned abundant scholarship but also inspired inventiveness in

### + Key Facts

**Time Period:**
Late 20th Century

**Genre:**
Graphic Novel

**Events:**
World War II;
Holocaust; Cold War

**Nationality:**
American

## COMIC BOOKS VERSUS HITLER

*Maus* is hardly the first comic to deal with World War II, the Nazis, and the Holocaust. During the late 1930s, when it became clear that war in Europe was inevitable, American comic books began to take on the subject. The most important character was Superman, and *Superman* comics of the time reveal a propagandistic political agenda. In early issues the caped crusader visits Washington, D.C., to root out corrupt politicians. As America entered the war, Superman began to appear on comic book covers with the American flag and American soldiers. One famous cover depicts Superman holding Adolf Hitler and Hirohito, the emperor of Japan, off of the ground, singlehandedly taking on the two dominant figures of the Axis powers.

Comics served as an important distraction and escape for American troops during the war. The idea of heroes battling and defeating blatantly evil villains not only comforted the combatants but also reinforced the notion that the United States was engaged in a war against an archvillain. The 1940s saw a rise in more overtly patriotic characters who fought for and represented the "American Way," most notably Captain America and Wonder Woman. These early examples deal with their subjects in explicitly patriotic ways and are less morally complex than *Maus,* but without them *Maus* may not have been written.

varied forms. Many graphic novels have found their way into classrooms and have been adapted for the screen (Frank Miller's 1991–92 graphic novel *Sin City* was released as a film in 2005, and Alan Moore and David Gibbons's 1986–87 *Watchmen* premiered on the big screen in 2009), and canonical literary works have been turned into graphic novels (*Macbeth* in 2008 and *The Odyssey* in 2010), making them available and relevant to a new generation of readers. One of the most important graphic novels to date is the 2006 reworking of the U.S. government-contracted *9/11 Commission Report* under the title *The 9/11 Report: A Graphic Adaptation,* by Sid Jacobson and Ernie Colon. This creative work brought the underread findings on the terrorist attacks of September 11, 2001, to a much wider audience, becoming a best seller. Critically acclaimed graphic novelists such as Daniel Clowes, Jason (the pen name of Jason Sæterøy), Craig Thompson, and David Mazzucchelli have also followed in Spiegelman's footsteps; the popularity of the graphic novel and its continued and growing impact owe much to the influence of *Maus.*

### THEMES AND STYLE

The central themes of *Maus* are racism and its dehumanization of the individual, familial guilt, and the relationship between the past and present. In one scene Vladek, who has suffered unspeakable horrors because of his race, becomes upset with the character Artie's wife, Françoise, for picking up an African American hitchhiker. When Françoise points out the hypocrisy in Vladek's racism, he replies, "It's not even to compare, the schwartsers [blacks] and the Jews!" Also central to the text is the relationship between Art and Vladek, which is weighed down by the guilt the two men feel; they have never gotten along, Art admits, conscience-stricken about not having been a better son to his father and mother, who committed suicide. Besieged with survivor's guilt, Vladek vents much of his angst on Art. Neither is able to let go of the past and find peace.

The difficulty of facing the truth and finding a way to fairly, accurately, and artistically present it runs throughout the novel, creating a need for various rhetorical strategies. The metaphoric use of animal species to represent human characters begins as a strong persuasive technique. The predatory Nazi cats are almost entirely uniform and without distinguishing characteristics, while their victims, the Jewish mice (vermin) and the Polish pigs (swine), are individualized, each a unique character. Although it is a racist rendering—ironically so—this rhetorical inversion of Nazi propaganda emphasizes the absurdity of the generalizations racism requires. One of Spiegelman's struggles, both in creating the novel and within its pages, is to facilitate the continued and intentional deconstruction of the parallels between animals and humans. He wonders, for example, how to depict his French wife, who has converted to Judaism. Should she be drawn as a mouse or as a frog?

The emotional tenor of the novel is one of struggle. Vladek writhes with guilt and is beset by memories. Art grapples with filial remorse and with the practical and ethical difficulties of his work as an artist: he says to Françoise, "I mean, I can't even make any sense out of my relationship with my father.... How am I supposed to make sense out of Auschwitz? ... of the Holocaust?" Spiegelman struggles to make the metaphor of the animals work while also struggling with his obligations to his father and how they relate to his work as a storyteller. The other characters in the novel wrestle with their emotions, their pasts, and their stories. Each of *Maus*'s two structural strands has a unique tone. In the melancholic and self-reflective metafictional present, Spiegelman interviews his father and prepares to write the story; here he examines the effects of the very serious trauma of the Holocaust on its survivors and its impact on their relationships with their children, spouses, and the world around them. The segments set in the past, documentarian and straightforward in tone and diction, depict the experiences Vladek recalls from World War II and the Holocaust, emphasizing the debasement of Jews and others at the hands of the Nazis and in Nazi propaganda and policy. For example, in almost matter-of-fact language, Vladek says, "We knew the stories—that they will gas us and throw us in the ovens. This was 1944 ... we knew the stories. And here we were."

## CRITICAL DISCUSSION

Spiegelman had difficulty finding a publisher willing to print his installments in book form, but the eventual novel received ecstatic reviews in high-ranking periodicals. Lawrence L. Langer of the *New York Times* wrote, "Perhaps no Holocaust narrative will ever contain the whole experience. But Art Spiegelman has found an original and authentic form to draw us closer to its bleak heart." In spite of the positive reviews, booksellers were reluctant to stock *Maus* because of problems in categorizing the text, which was variously shelved under history, biography, autobiography, memoir, or fiction. The publisher lobbied for "graphic novel," though Spiegelman himself rejected the term on the grounds that his book was a work of nonfiction. Winning the 1992 Pulitzer Prize Special Award cemented *Maus*'s critical reputation.

*Maus* has remained a vital work in its medium. In 1999 the *Comics Journal* named it the fourth-greatest comic book of the twentieth century, and in 2002 *Wizard* magazine awarded it first place on its list of the 100 greatest graphic novels. The work is regularly taught in a range of courses, including history, psychology, language arts, and social studies. More scholarship has been written on *Maus* than on any other graphic novel. Most negative reactions to the novel come not from critics but from survivors of the Holocaust, some of whom feel that the novel makes light of the tragedy by rendering it in comic form. The animal metaphor, because of its close ties to Nazi philosophy and propaganda, is a particularly significant issue for many readers. Despite these critiques, the work has been translated into more than thirty languages and has become an international best seller.

Because no scholarly tradition of analyzing comics existed, early critical study of *Maus* worked at placing the material in a literary or historical context. One of the earliest considerations of the novel, however, written in 1988 by social historian Joshua Brown for the *Oral History Review*, examines the emotional circumstances under which it was written—in particular, the complex dynamic Spiegelman navigated in telling the story of his father's life. Another important critical strain has analyzed *Maus* from a sociological perspective, emphasizing the impact tragic events can have on succeeding generations. Diverse perspectives continue to inform twenty-first-century commentaries. In "Reading Art Spiegelman's *Maus* as Postmodern Ethnography" (2011), Rosemary V. Hathaway, a specialist in ethnicity and folklore, approaches the text as an analysis of storytelling. For Hathaway, the novel simultaneously articulates the inherent imperfection and crowning asset of the act of storytelling: its powerlessness to be completely accurate in recreating identity and history. Ultimately, the enduring strength of *Maus* is that it defies classification, leading scholars from almost every field to consider the work and broaden its implications.

Art Spiegelman, author of *Maus,* at his studio in New York in 2008. © AURORA PHOTOS/ALAMY.

## BIBLIOGRAPHY

*Sources*

Brown, Joshua. "Of Mice and Memory." Review of *Maus,* by Art Spiegelman. *Oral History Review* 16.1 (1988): 91–109. *JSTOR.* Web. 12 July 2012.

Hathaway, Rosemary V. "Reading Art Spiegelman's *Maus* as Postmodern Ethnography." *Journal of Folklore Research* 48.3 (2011): 249–67.

Hirsch, Marianne. "Family Pictures: *Maus,* Mourning, and Post-Memory." *Discourse: Journal for Theoretical Studies in Media and Culture* 15.2 (1992–93): 3–29. *JSTOR.* Web. 12 July 2012.

Langer, Lawrence L. "A Fable of the Holocaust." Rev. of *Maus: A Survivor's Tale II: And Here My Troubles Began,* by Art Spiegelman. *New York Times* 3 Nov. 1991: n. pag. Print.

Spiegelman, Art. *The Complete Maus: A Survivor's Tale.* New York: Pantheon, 1996. Print.

*Further Reading*

Ewert, Jeanne C. "Reading Visual Narrative: Art Spiegelman's *Maus.*" *Narrative* 8.1 (2000): 87–103. Print.

Geis, Deborah R., ed. *Considering* Maus: *Approaches to Art Spiegelman's "Survivor's Tale" of the Holocaust.* Tuscaloosa: U of Alabama P, 2007. Print.

Harvey, R. C. *The Art of the Comic Book: An Aesthetic History.* Jackson: UP of Mississippi, 1996. Print.

Hirsch, Marianne. *Family Frames: Photography, Narrative and Postmemory.* Cambridge: Harvard UP, 1997. Print.

———. *The Generation of Postmemory: Visual Culture after the Holocaust.* New York: Columbia UP, 2012. Print.

Jacobson, Sid, and Ernie Colon. *The 9/11 Report: A Graphic Adaptation.* New York: Hill, 2006. Print.

Smith, Graham. "From Mickey to *Maus*: Recalling the Genocide through Cartoon." *Oral History* 15.1 (1987): 26–34. Print.

Witek, Joseph. *Comic Books as History: The Narrative Art of Jack Jackson, Art Spiegelman, and Harvey Pekar.* Jackson: UP of Mississippi, 1989.

*Colby Cuppernull*

# A GAME AT CHESSE

*Thomas Middleton*

## OVERVIEW

*A Game at Chesse,* a play written by Thomas Middleton during the Palatinate phase of the Thirty Years' War (1624), allegorizes the political and religious tensions between Protestants and Catholics. Written with Middleton's typical flair for irony and often mean-spirited if not obscene humor, the characters of the White House, representing England and the Protestants, square off against the characters of the Black House, representing Spain and the Catholics—specifically, the Jesuits. Spain's envoys in London at the time were most offended by the characterizations of the Black Knight (who represented Spain's ambassador emeritus, Count Gondomar) and the Fat Bishop (who represented the clergyman Marcus Antonius de Dominis). National antipathy toward Spain ran strong, and the previous year had seen the failure of the Spanish Match—an effort to get the heir to the English throne, Charles, to marry the daughter of the Spanish king. The play dramatizes pamphlets such as Thomas Scott's *Vox-Populi* and John Gee's *Foote Out of the Snare* (1624) that described both Spain and Catholicism as morally bankrupt and invested in the destruction of Britain.

Middleton wrote many plays during his lifetime, but *A Game at Chesse* was extraordinary in that it was quite profitable and so well loved that it ran for nine days straight at a time when most troupes showed a new play at each performance. It would have run longer had it not been shut down by the king. The Spanish ambassador to England, Don Carlos Coloma, who also served as commander in the Palatinate, wrote a letter to King James expressing his outrage at the play. King James had been away from London, a fact not lost on the King's Men, who had mounted the play.

## HISTORICAL AND LITERARY CONTEXT

Tensions between Spain and England had existed for some time before the play was written. In the 1550s Spain's King Philip II was also King of Britain and Ireland, having married Queen Mary I. When Mary died the firmly Protestant Elizabeth I ascended to the throne, and Britain and Ireland's Catholics were left without a leader. Philip II offered to marry Elizabeth, but she refused. Piracy and privateering in the New World between British and Spanish ships was one source of tension; Elizabeth's backing of Dutch Protestant rebels in their revolt against Spanish rule was

another. Complicating the situation was the increasing hostility between Catholicism and Protestantism. The Anglo-Spanish War, though never officially declared, lasted from 1585 to 1604. Mistrust between the two countries remained after the war, and the notion of Empresa de Inglaterra (the Enterprise of England, or the dismantling of the new Protestant regime) crystallized in the Catholic world as a political imperative.

In 1614 Gondomar had come to London with the proposal to marry Charles, King James I's son, to the King of Spain's daughter, Infanta Maria Anna. In exchange for a generous dowry and Spanish help with England's ongoing difficulties in Ireland (a vexed element of the offer, since in 1580, during the second Desmond Rebellion, English troops massacred 400 Papal troops, Spanish soldiers among them), Gondomar hoped to secure an English promise of cessation of hostilities toward the Spanish in the New World. Negotiations dragged. In 1613 James's daughter had married Frederick V, Elector Palatine, head of the forces that opposed Spain's forces in the Thirty Years' War. In 1623 Prince Charles, along with the king's favorite, George Villiers, Duke of Buckingham, went to Madrid. When they found out that Charles would be forced to become a Catholic in order to marry Maria, they returned to England, to massive popular joy—the moment thought to have inspired the play. Charles eventually married Henrietta Maria of France, a Catholic, but he never converted.

As *A Game at Chesse* suggests, the British as a nation saw themselves as quite distinct from the rest of Europe. Although pamphleteers such as Scott were officially reprimanded and sent into exile, tracts denouncing Catholic hostility toward Protestantism and making fun of such figures as Gondomar and de Dominis—who switched from the Catholic Church to the Protestant and back again—continued to circulate. The second installation of Scott's *Vox Populi* (1624) featured on its title page an illustration of Gondomar alongside the special chair he had built to accommodate his anal fistula, a particularity Middleton exploits in the play.

British drama in 1623 and 1624 featured several plays that may be seen as propaganda for the faction of King James's court that opposed the Spanish Match and James's pacifist attitude toward Spain. For Twelfth Night 1623–24, Ben Jonson and Inigo Jones wrote a

+ **Key Facts**

**Time Period:**
Early 17th Century

**Genre:**
Play

**Events:**
Thirty Years' War; Catholic-Protestant Conflict

**Nationality:**
English

# LOST LEGENDS

In 1616 Sir Walter Raleigh led a second British expedition to find *El Dorado,* the legendary city of gold. The Spanish believed it to exist in what is now Colombia, among the Chibcha-speaking Muisca tribes that lived there, whom the Spanish first encountered in 1537. Raleigh, having failed to find it on his first attempt in 1594, was determined to redeem himself. As failure again seemed imminent, his team violently disposed of a Spanish encampment in South America, and Raleigh was imprisoned upon his return. Gondomar agitated for his execution, and King James eventually conceded, perhaps having not quite forgotten Raleigh's earlier arrest and imprisonment for his alleged involvement in the Main Plot, an attempt, backed by King Philip III of Spain and the Pope, to kill King James and replace him with his cousin Arabella, to whom the Pope was trying to marry off his brother, in hopes of regaining a Catholic foothold in Britain. Raleigh, though a favorite of James's predecessor Queen Elizabeth, was held thirteen years in the Tower of London. Only the promise of gold convinced the financially strapped King James to set him free. Meanwhile, the Spanish were methodically killing as many Muisca as they could.

masque, *Neptune's Triumph for the Return of Albion,* in which Neptune (King James) sends Albion (Prince Charles) to a distant land to see about his future bride. Thomas Drue's *The Life of the Duchess of Suffolk,* licensed by the Master of Revels on January 2, 1624, was about a Protestant duchess persecuted by Catholic bishops during the reign of Mary Tudor. Middleton's play, written in response to political events—some argue that the play was as relevant to the loss of the Palatine by James's daughter and son-in-law as to Charles's marriage negotiations—did not alter events as such but did flatter the British Protestant population in their continued resistance to Catholic influence. Don Carlos complained to his colleague and countryman Duke Olivares that "there were more than 3000 persons there on the day that the audience was smallest."

## THEMES AND STYLE

Central to *A Game at Chesse* is the continued urgency of Britain's political and religious situation in relation to the rest of the Continent and its problems—both internal, with Ireland, and with Europe, in terms of Catholicism and Protestantism. James I's difficulties with Philip IV and the Pope were fodder for endless rounds of debate, and the public's appetite for the type of commentary Middleton was so adept at providing was insatiable. Its timeliness was equally irresistible: "Next news you hear expect my books against you / Printed at Douay, Brussels, or Spalato," says the Fat Bishop, while de Dominis was at that very moment imprisoned in Rome, accused by the Pope of heresy for his writings. Audiences clearly welcomed the chance

to condemn his vacillations by laughing heartily at Middleton's characterization.

The playwright frames the complex political-religious conflict within the trope of the popular game of chess, enjoyed by noblemen and less wealthy citizens alike. Gioachino Greco, one of the first celebrated chess masters, lived in London from 1622 to 1624. The plot involving the White Queen's Pawn is thought to be modeled on the Queen's Gambit, a device mentioned in an early chess manual, the Göttingen manuscript (ca. 1500). The "new chess" in which the queen enjoyed a greater range of motion than any other piece originated around that time, and it was a Spanish author, Lucena, who noted the change in 1497, just as Queen Isabella was enjoying unprecedented powers as monarch of Spain. The play's action is not constrained by the chess theme so much as leavened by it every so often, and the black-and-white set and costumes are pleasing onstage. "Yonder's my game, which, like a politic chess-master, / I must not seem to be," says the lustful Black Bishop's Pawn, underscoring the cynical machinations the Catholic establishment was thought to be deploying against Protestantism. In Middleton's play *Women Beware Women* (1621), which also incorporates the game of chess, the character Isabella is killed by gold on fire.

Stylistically, the play draws on Middleton's already near-perfect appropriation of the smartest dialogue likely to be heard in London's ordinaries, at court, and at fashionable cathedrals. Sly allusions to bodily functions abound, prompting comparisons to Rabelaisian scatology, with ample fodder provided by the Black Bishop Pawn's insatiable lust—analogous to de Dominis's greed in taking lucrative appointments and gifts from King James while continuously asking for more—and the Black Knight's loquacious, cynical ambition mirroring Gondomar's slick diplomatic style. "There's a foul flaw in the bottom of my drum," the Black Knight says in reference to Gondomar's fistula and to the agenda behind his constant presence in international affairs. The Black Knight, insulted by the Fat Bishop's unkind joke, vows to expose the Fat Bishop to both the King and the Pope, which Gondomar did to de Dominis in 1622.

## CRITICAL DISCUSSION

Middleton's play sparked immediate controversy. Spanish diplomats voiced their indignation and had its license revoked, and a warrant was issued for Middleton's arrest on August 30, 1624. The first written critique may have been his own plea for clemency: "A harmless Game coyned only for delight, / Was play'd betwixt the black house and the white. / The white house won. Yet still the black doth brag, / They had the power to put me in the bag," he reportedly wrote in his petition to King James. Middleton editor A. Dyce (1840) believed that John Milton borrowed from the play's "opening eyelids of the morn" for his *Lycidas,* in which "the high lawns appear'd / Under the opening eyelids of the morn." A. C. Swinburne (1904) concurred, and he praised *A Game of Chess* for "its complete and thorough harmony of execution and design."

J. W. Harper, editor of the Mermaids edition (London, 1966), notes that "Middleton had found the perfect formula for popular success. However, his example was not followed and *A Game of Chess* remains unique." Appointed City Chronologer in 1620, Middleton was, as T. S. Eliot describes him in his 1927 essay, "a 'great recorder' who, having 'no point of view' or 'message,' was 'merely the name associated with six or seven great plays." Nevertheless, it continues to offer up a fascinating combination of history and dramatic craftsmanship that has been continuously mined by scholars of Spanish and British politics. Its function in the actual diplomacy of the time is part of what made it remarkable—not least because it was technically illegal to depict a sitting monarch onstage, which was the officially given charge against the play, that the Black and White Kings represented Spain's King Philip IV and Britain's King James I.

*A Game at Chesse* is frequently discussed within the context of the court intrigues involving the Spanish Match and Frederick V's loss of the Rhine Palatinate and Bohemia as well as in light of its engagement with chess. Jerzy Limon sees the play as being part of the Duke of Buckingham's project of demonizing the Spanish while parrying other critics' doubts as to Middleton's understanding of chess. Paul Yachnin agrees that "Middleton ignores the technical side of chess in order to concentrate on its allegorical significance," while participating in a tradition of chess allegories that includes the fifth book of Rabelais's *Gargantuaet Pantagruel.* Leticia Álvarez Recio takes Eliot's stance that the play reflects existing opinion regarding anti-Catholic and anti-Spanish sentiment in Britain. *A Game at Chesse* exists at a crossroads between art and politics, exploiting the very set of circumstances that led to its suppression.

Portrait of Maria Anna of Spain. *A Game at Chesse* is an allegorical play based on the proposed marriage between Prince Charles I of Great Britain and then-Princess Maria Anna of Spain in 1623. *THE INFANTA MARIA OF AUSTRIA (1606–46) QUEEN OF HUNGARY, 1630* (OIL ON CANVAS), VELAZQUEZ, DIEGO RODRIGUEZ DE SILVA Y (1599–1660)/ PRADO, MADRID, SPAIN/ THE BRIDGEMAN ART LIBRARY.

## BIBLIOGRAPHY

*Sources*

Limon, Jerzy. *Dangerous Matter: English Drama and Politics in 1623/4.* Cambridge: Cambridge UP, 1986. Print.

Middleton, Thomas. *A Game at Chess.* Ed. J. W. Harper. London: The New Mermaids, 1966. Print.

———. *A Game at Chess.* Ed. T. H. Howard-Hill. Manchester: Manchester UP, 1993. Print.

Recio, Leticia Álvarez. "The White House en *A Game at Chess*: El Ataque de Thomas Middleton a la Politica Real." *Atlantis* 22.2 (2000). Print.

Reed, Isaac, and Octavius Gilchrist, eds. *A Select Collection of Old Plays, In Twelve Volumes.* Vol. V. London: Septimus Prowett, 1825. 278–79. Print.

Swinburne, Algernon. *The Age of Shakespeare. The Complete Works of Algernon Charles Swinburne.* Ed. Edmund Gosse and Thomas James Wise. Vol. 11. London: Heinemann, 1926. Print.

Taylor, G., and T. T. Henley, eds. *The Oxford Handbook of Thomas Middleton.* Oxford: Oxford UP, 2012. Print.

Yachnin, Paul. "*A Game at Chess* and Chess Allegory." *Studies in English Literature, 1500–1900* 22.2 (1982). Print.

*Further Reading*

Bawcutt, N. W. "Was Thomas Middleton a Puritan Dramatist?" *The Modern Language Review* 94.4 (1999). Print.

Cogswell, Thomas. "Thomas Middleton and the Court, 1624: *A Game at Chess* in Context." *Huntington Library Quarterly* 47.4 (1984). Print.

Dyce, A., ed. *The Works of Thomas Middleton.* London, 1840. Print.

Eliot, T. S. "Thomas Middleton." *Times Literary Supplement* 30 June 1927, 445–6. Print.

Fuller, Thomas. *The Church History of Britain from the Birth of Jesus Christ until 1648.* Ed. J. S. Brewer. Oxford: Oxford UP, 1845. Print.

Heller, Jennifer L. "Space, Violence, and Bodies in Middleton and Cary." *Studies in English Literature, 1500–1900* 45.2 (2005). Print.

Simons, Patricia. "(Check)Mating the Grand Masters: The Gendered, Sexualized Politics of Chess in Renaissance Italy." *Oxford Art Journal* 16.1 (1993). Print.

Taylor, Gary, and John Lavagnino, eds. *The Collected Works of Thomas Middleton.* Oxford: Clarendon Press, 2007. Print.

———. *Thomas Middleton and Early Modern Textual Culture.* Oxford: Clarendon Press, 2007. Print.

Tricomi, Albert H. "Middleton's *Women Beware Women* as Anticourt Drama." *Modern Language Studies* 19.2 (1989). Print.

Yalom, Marilyn. *Birth of the Chess Queen: A History.* New York: Harper Collins, 2004. Print.

*Rebecca Rustin*

# HALFWAY TO FREEDOM

## A Report on the New India

### Margaret Bourke-White

## OVERVIEW

In 1949 photojournalist Margaret Bourke-White published *Halfway to Freedom: A Report on the New India,* a book of photographs and text that offers a sustained examination, from a distinctly American perspective, of the social, political, and cultural situation in India and Pakistan soon after the two nations achieved independence from Britain. When *Halfway to Freedom* was published, Bourke-White was already a renowned photojournalist, known particularly for her photographs documenting the fighting and aftermath of World War II. She first visited the Indian subcontinent on assignment for *Life* magazine in 1946; she returned in 1947 and 1948. There Bourke-White found a region on the brink of widespread transformation. Unyoked from British rule, the subcontinent had divided into two countries, India and Pakistan— a division known historically as Partition. In keeping with the stated aim of *Life* magazine's editor Henry Luce, Bourke-White's pictures and text perpetuate the notion that the spread of American ideals—in particular, freedom, democracy, and capitalism—could help lead India and Pakistan out of turmoil, inequality, and poverty in the postindependence era.

*Halfway to Freedom* was originally published to wide acclaim as a series of essays and photographs in *Life.* When the images and text were collected in book form in 1949, the work was a critical and popular success. Hailed for its deep look into a region that had not been widely covered by American journalists, *Halfway to Freedom* helped to cement Bourke-White's reputation as one of the most important documentary photographers of the time. It also enhanced her standing as a writer of penetrating nonfiction. Though not as well known as some of her other works, *Halfway to Freedom* is notable for offering a brand of journalistic "realism" that portrays the suffering and unrest in developing nations as part of a larger human struggle to achieve the American version of liberty, one that necessarily exists within the framework of liberal democracy and a capitalist economy.

## HISTORICAL AND LITERARY CONTEXT

From 1858 to 1947 Great Britain ruled the Indian subcontinent, which comprises modern-day India, Pakistan, and Bangladesh. British rule, known as the Raj, united the various peoples of South Asia, including Hindus, Muslims, and Sikhs. Under the Raj, India experienced pronounced economic development and became more closely tied to the West. However, the era of British rule also saw crushing poverty, famine, and disease. The period culminated in a powerful Indian movement for independence. At the forefront of that movement was the Indian National Congress (INC). Beginning in the early 1920s, Mohandas Gandhi led the INC to embrace a nonviolent approach to overthrowing the Raj. Over the next several years, the struggle for a free India united the nation's Hindu and Muslim factions. However, in the 1940s, when the British finally began to negotiate independence for India, there was a rift in the Indian movement, and Mohammed Ali Jinnah, leader of India's Muslim League, announced his aim to create a separate, Muslim state called Pakistan.

Two years before *Halfway to Freedom* was published in 1949, the Indian subcontinent had achieved independence but had broken into two states, India and Pakistan. Gandhi refused to accept Partition, and so Jawaharlal Nehru became the first prime minister of independent India. Meanwhile, Jinnah was sworn in as the first governor-general of Pakistan. With independence came newly drawn borders that separated the largely Hindu population of India from the largely Muslim population of Pakistan. Yet millions of members of each religious group remained on the "wrong" side of the borders, resulting in panic, rioting, and mass migrations. Violence erupted as millions of Muslims in India fled to Pakistan and millions of Hindus and Sikhs in Pakistan rushed toward India. Between 250,000 and 500,000 people died in the chaos. In *Halfway to Freedom* Bourke-White portrays this violent unrest and political upheaval as the awful but inevitable cost of moving out of the darkness of tradition and toward the redeeming light of Western conceptions of freedom, equality, and prosperity. As she writes in her preface, "The seething conflicts, the ferment and growth, the powers of medievalism clinging to ancient privilege while the people struggle upward to reach the light—this to me was the drama of India."

Bourke-White's conception and depiction of the situation in India and Pakistan was deeply influenced by the writing of Luce, the founder of *Life,* whose

+ *Key Facts*

**Time Period:**
Mid-20th Century

**Genre:**
Nonfiction/Photography

**Events:**
Partition of India;
Indian independence;
founding of Pakistan

**Nationality:**
American

# MARGARET BOURKE-WHITE AND THE AESTHETICS OF SUFFERING

Though widely admired and published, Margaret Bourke-White was not without her critics, the preeminent of whom was her colleague and contemporary Walker Evans. During the Great Depression, Evans and Bourke-White both recorded the suffering of the poor in the American South. The clear-eyed and candid pictures taken by Evans were included in *Let Us Now Praise Famous Men,* a work of nonfiction that also features the prose of James Agee. For Evans, it was the "objectivity" of written and photographic accounts that lent them not only authority but also ethicality. Artfulness, he argued, was antithetical to empathy.

Bourke-White, on the other hand, collaborated with the writer (and her future husband) Erskine Caldwell on their own documentary account of the Great Depression. After traveling through the South for two months in 1936, the couple produced *You Have Seen Their Faces.* While the work was a huge popular success, it drew charges that her posed and professional photographs aestheticized suffering. Unlike Evans, Bourke-White intended her images to catalyze viewers to feel sympathy and act for justice. In an article, she wrote, "We are only hoping that the book may do some good." Critics have argued that such an intention invariably backfires, as it forces the viewer to notice the artfulness of the photographer at the expense of her suffering subject.

editorial "The American Century" argued that the United States had a mission to lead the world to "freedom and democracy." First published in 1941, five years before Bourke-White began *Halfway to Freedom,* Luce's essay advocated an American-led "transnationalism" that "would be grounded neither in politics nor mere military might, but on a more subtle level—on the culture of consumption." As one of *Life*'s original photographers, Bourke-White had an important role in putting Luce's vision into action. The influence of Luce's conception of Americans' role in the world is apparent in the ways in which *Halfway to Freedom* depicts traditional Indian political, economic, and social systems as "inhumanities" to be "corrected" by the arrival of Western progress.

Bourke-White's portrait of postindependence India is radically different from those produced by native Indian and Pakistani authors, for whom Partition was a wrenching national trauma—not a momentous, though difficult, stage in the forward march of progress. Pakistani writer Saadat Hasan Manto's short story collection *Siyah Hashiye* ("Black Margins"; 1948) depicts Partition as an absurd and grotesque act that had devastating consequences for millions of innocent people. The Indian writer Khushwant Singh offers a similarly grim vision of Partition in his novel *Train to Pakistan.* Originally published in 1956, *Train to Pakistan* focuses on the fighting that erupted between

Sikhs and Muslims living on the new border between India and Pakistan. Still, in spite of the unmistakably Western perspective that informs *Halfway to Freedom,* Bourke-White's work remains a singular contribution to the historical record of India's independence and the birth of Pakistan. It is noteworthy that a 2006 reissue of *Train to Pakistan* contains sixty-six of Bourke-White's photographs—indicating, it seems, the enduring legacy of Bourke-White as a documentarian without whom the human faces of this historical moment would remain unknown.

## THEMES AND STYLE

The central theme of *Halfway to Freedom* is that India, despite the political upheavals and social unrest, is on the path to progress and prosperity. In photographs and text, Bourke-White documents the fraught and nascent independence of India and Pakistan. In addition to depicting the suffering and struggle of the Indian people, she also documents the country's economic and political development. As she seeks to capture this drama in all its human dimensions, she suggests that India and Pakistan are on a positive trajectory, away from the senseless suffering brought on by traditional ways of life and toward the liberation and prosperity of Westernization. Though not an explicit work of propaganda, the text and photographs betray Bourke-White's belief that the modernization of these new nations is part of the "whole forward march of the world."

Though she attempts to maintain an attitude of detached observation, Bourke-White's Western bias asserts itself in the form, tone, and structure of the book. She portrays the situation in India as the "rising tide of democracy sweeping through India with independence and threatening to wash away the ancient bulwarks of feudalism." In this kind of triumphalist language, she perpetuates the notion that the arrival of American values will cleanse and repair this foreign land. Even her depiction of Gandhi in a flattering, almost reverential light is indicative of her belief that Western-style democracy and liberty will be India's salvation. This can be seen in the book's final lines, which come just after Gandhi is gunned down by an assassin: "His supreme sacrifice in the cause for tolerance and unity could mean the turning point for India. He had given his life to light the way."

Stylistically, Bourke-White's text and photographs are distinguished by their combination of humanity and humility. She is careful throughout the book to depict herself as deeply invested in the lives of the Indians and Pakistanis she encounters while also attempting to refrain from judgment. Even her unflattering depiction of Jinnah is tempered by an attempt at understanding the complexity of her subject's struggle to do the right thing: "Analytical, brilliant, and no bigot, he knew what he had done. Like Doctor Faustus, he had made a bargain from which he could never be free." In this way, she demonstrates her

Indian leader Mohandas Gandhi in a 1948 photograph by Margaret Bourke-White. Bourke-White's *Halfway to Freedom: A Report on the New India* contains photographs and writings about India and the surrounding region. MARGARET BOURKE-WHITE/TIME & LIFE PICTURES/GETTY IMAGES.

evenhandedness, even as she makes clear her indictment of Jinnah's behavior. In her prose and her photos, Bourke-White employs a kind of detached sympathy in order to convince her audience that her view of the situation is realistic and therefore right.

## CRITICAL DISCUSSION

Bourke-White's longstanding reputation at *Life* magazine, where she had been employed as a photographer since 1936, lent authority to *Halfway to Freedom* when it was published in 1949. She had recently completed an assignment at Germany's Buchenwald concentration camp, which had been liberated in the spring of 1945. The public's fascination with her disturbing photos from World War II gave Bourke-White the momentum to compile her photographs and writings about India and Pakistan's independence and publish them as *Halfway to Freedom*. Although the book was generally well received by critics, some questioned Bourke-White's methods. Lee Eitington, a journalist who went to Punjab with Bourke-White in August 1947, described his horror at seeing her ask scared refugees to repeat their action of flight multiple times until she got the perfect photo: "That's why she was such a good photographer. People were dying under her feet. She thought herself a great humanitarian, but when it came to individual people. ..." Eitington's remark indicates the clear difference between a photographer on assignment and a humanitarian whose job is to help others.

Nevertheless, as *Halfway to Freedom* boosted Bourke-White's professional reputation, it also showed other photojournalists that their work could have a lasting social and political legacy. A piece in *Kirkus Reviews* speaks to the book's influence: "Margaret Bourke-White has distilled the essence of two years' study, and two extensive trips through India, in a determination to present all aspects of the face of the new India. She shows the tortuous steps by which the sacredness of feudal privilege is giving way to the 20th-century concepts of human equality." Biographer and critic Vicki Goldberg argues that Bourke-White successfully manipulated her subjects into attitudes that seemed natural but were in fact determined by the photographer. Goldberg writes that with *Halfway to Freedom,* Bourke-White mastered this technique of "the posed candid." Today, Bourke-White is remembered as a groundbreaking photojournalist who documented Soviet industry, Nazi concentration camps, U.S. poverty, and many other vital subjects.

Not as well known or studied as some of Bourke-White's other works, *Halfway to Freedom* has garnered a small body of scholarly and critical attention since its initial publication. In a 2006 article, *New York Times* writer Somini Sengupta notes the power of the *Halfway to Freedom* photographs: "[They] are gut-wrenching, and staring at them, you glimpse the photographer's undaunted desire to stare down horror." Goldberg pinpoints the legacy of *Halfway to Freedom*: "Americans saw India's complex and terror-filled progress to independence chiefly through Margaret Bourke-White's magisterial photographs."

## BIBLIOGRAPHY

*Sources*

Bourke-White, Margaret. *Halfway to Freedom: A Report on the New India in the Words and Photographs of Margaret Bourke-White.* New York: Simon, 1949. Print.

Goldberg, Vicki. *Margaret Bourke-White: A Biography.* New York: Harper, 1986. Print.

———. "Photography Review; Looking at India's Upheaval From the Inside (and the Side)." *New York Times.* The New York Times Company, 21 Aug. 1998. Web. 14 Sept. 2012.

Karlekar, Malavika. "On Freedom's Trail." *Telegraph.* Telegraph India, 21 Nov. 2010. Web. 14 Sept. 2012.

Rev. of *Halfway to Freedom,* by Margaret Bourke-White. *Kirkus Reviews.* Kirkus Reviews, 1949. Web. 14 Sept. 2012.

Sengupta, Somini. "Bearing Steady Witness to Partition's Wounds." *New York Times.* The New York Times Company, 21 Sept. 2006. Web. 14 Sept. 2012.

Silverman, Jonathan. *For the World to See: The Life of Margaret Bourke-White.* New York: Viking, 1983. Print.

Vials, Chris. *Realism for the Masses: Aesthetics, Popular Front Pluralism, and U.S. Culture, 1935–1947.* Jackson: UP of Mississippi, 2009. Print.

*Further Reading*

Bourke-White, Margaret, and Sean Callahan. *The Photographs of Margaret Bourke-White.* New York: Bonanza, 1972. Print.

———. *Margaret Bourke-White: Photographer.* Boston: Little, Brown, 1998. Print.

Gandhi, Mahatma. *Hind Swaraj.* Ahmedabad: Navjivan, 1922. Print.

Khushwant, Singh. *Train to Pakistan.* New York: Grove, 1956. Print.

"Margaret Bourke-White." *Contemporary Authors Online.* Detroit: Gale, 2002. *Literature Resource Center.* Web. 9 Sept. 2012.

*Anna Deem*

# LET US NOW PRAISE FAMOUS MEN

*James Agee, Walker Evans*

## OVERVIEW

Writer James Agee and photographer Walker Evans published their unique masterpiece, *Let Us Now Praise Famous Men,* in 1941, five years after they visited rural Alabama on assignment for *Fortune* magazine. At first glance, the text presents itself as documentary nonfiction. This genre, popular during the Great Depression of the 1930s, aimed to reveal the plight of those impoverished by the worldwide economic downturn to middle-class readers who would, hopefully, feel empathy and take some action to help those less fortunate than themselves. Agee and Evans's text, however, breaks with its literary kin through Agee's self-consciousness and minutely detailed prose and through Evans's disconcerting, captionless photographs. Through its formal experimentation, Agee and Evans created a book that complicated prominent political positions of the time, thereby elevating the work to an intriguing piece of literary propaganda.

*Let Us Now Praise Famous Men* details the lives of three white tenant farmer families—the fictitiously named Gudgers, Ricketts, and Woods. The book features extensive passages that elaborate Agee's complicated, ambivalent response to being what he called "a spy, traveling as a journalist" along with Evans, "a counter-spy, traveling as a photographer." Agee declares early on that it seemed "obscene and thoroughly terrifying … to pry intimately into the lives of an undefended and appallingly damaged group of human beings." *Praise* thus deliberately diverges from seemingly similar texts, such as photographer Margaret Bourke-White and journalist Erskine Caldwell's *You Have Seen Their Faces* (1937), a popular work that also focuses on the lives of Depression-era tenant farmers. In contrast, *Praise* rejects a sentimental tradition of liberal propaganda aiming to help "the poor" and, instead, insists on the complicity of the book's creators, and its readers, in the problematic viewing of other human beings.

## HISTORICAL AND LITERARY CONTEXT

The Great Depression in American history spanned the 1930s, beginning with the stock market crash of 1929 and concluding with the advent of World War II in 1939. The Dust Bowl, an environmental catastrophe that affected most of the Great Plains region and contributed to the drought- and Depression-induced poverty in the country's Southeast, worsened economic conditions. As a result, many people abandoned their homes, seeking (but rarely finding) better work elsewhere. Even more stayed, battling for survival in subsistence conditions. In the South, tenant farmers tilled their landlord's property and lived lives of hard work and extreme poverty.

Under assignment from *Fortune,* Agee and Evans went to rural Alabama to conduct research and take photos for an article on the plight of tenant farmers. Against Agee's inclinations, *Fortune* insisted that the article feature only white families, even though a majority of tenant farmers were black. Agee also felt uncomfortable both with *Fortune*'s overt celebration of capitalism and the tendency for such pieces to sentimentalize their subjects. After several false starts, Agee and Evans found three families willing to let the pair record their lives. Upon returning to New York after the research was complete, however, Agee was not able to create a usable article for *Fortune,* and the magazine eventually relinquished its claim to the material. Agee decided to expand the project into a book, but the continued difficulties he faced in writing delayed the publication date by several years.

Agee wrestled with the ethical implications of his project, which led him to create a work that transcends other propagandistic works of the time, particularly those emphasizing either communist or liberal politics. The rhetoric of these ideologies tended to emphasize a universal "we" that Agee believed denied the singularity of the tenant farmers. As Jeanne Follansbee Quinn contends in her 2001 article in the scholarly journal *Novel: A Forum on Fiction,* "Agee experimented with an alternative rhetoric that could confound sentimental identification by representing the sharecroppers as *both* human like us *and* utterly different from us." Evans's candid, haunting images that open the book combine with Agee's extensive use of detail about the tenants' lives—including appearances, clothes, food, homes, and schedules—and style of expressing his own impressions as an interloper. With these strategies, *Praise* insists upon the humanity of its subjects. Because of this approach, *Praise* aligns as well with one of the Depression's greatest works of fiction, John Steinbeck's *The Grapes of Wrath* (1939).

*Praise* appeared at the outbreak of World War II and, therefore, faced a readership preoccupied with

*Key Facts*

**Time Period:**
Mid-20th Century

**Genre:**
Nonfiction/Photography

**Events:**
The Great Depression

**Nationality:**
American

# A COUNTERMELODY: RICHARD WRIGHT'S *TWELVE MILLION BLACK VOICES*

In 1941, the same year that *Let Us Now Praise Famous Men* was published, a countertext appeared. Like *Praise,* Richard Wright's *Twelve Million Black Voices* mingled text with photographs to shed light on the hardships facing a group of people. The people Wright depicted, however, faced even more than poverty and class inequality; they also faced the oppression of institutional racism in the United States. Because such bigotry extended throughout most of the United States, Wright's text focuses on both rural and urban African Americans, struggling against the poverty that was made even more acute by the Great Depression.

Like Agee, Wright aims to alienate the (white and/or elite) reader, declaring in the first paragraph that "our history is far stranger than you suspect, and we are not what we seem." Yet, unlike Agee, Wright uses the communal "we" throughout his text, thereby making a different political move. Whereas Agee and Evans sought to salvage the specificity of each tenant farmer from the homogeny of a vague, universal humanity, Wright orated for the entire African American population, particularly the impoverished and uneducated who lacked a voice in American society. The confluence of powerful images and eloquent text in *Black Voices* adds an important addition to the aesthetic and political project of *Praise.*

war rather than conditions in the rural South. It sold slightly more than 1,000 copies and quickly went out of print. In the 1960s, however, the work gained cult status among activists doing work for the civil rights movement. *Praise* has subsequently been hailed as an American classic that expanded the boundaries of journalism and propaganda writing. Further, critics argue that the work bridged the gap between the formal experimentation of modernism and the fracture and hybridity that characterize postmodernism. Thus, *Let Us Now Praise Famous Men* remains important not only for its complex portrait of a historical moment but also for its resonance in ongoing political and aesthetic conversations.

## THEMES AND STYLE

*Let Us Now Praise Famous Men* grapples with acknowledging the dignity of every human being and how to maintain that dignity while representing—in prose and pictures—real people. The text opens with Evans's photographs—straightforward, unsentimental portraits of people and things presented without captions. The images overshadow the whole book as Agee's text acts, in a sense, as their captions. In so doing, Agee and Evans emphasize the impossibility of understanding an image through a handful of words. Further, they question whether any number of words

or any collection of images can do justice to an actual life. The silent images and effusive, fractured text serve to discomfort and discombobulate the reader, deliberately failing to provide a "complete portrait" of any of the tenant farmers and, thereby, insisting upon each person's individual dignity.

Agee felt compelled to interrogate his motivations as deeply as he did the lives of his farmer subjects, and this impulse led to the book's experimental form. Agee and Evans are both characters in *Praise,* with Agee as the narrator of the book's scenes and events. The text is presented in nonchronological order and includes outside quotes that interrupt the main text, long reflections by Agee on his experiences and limitations, and attempts to render verbally scenes in photographic detail. Agee emphasizes the minutiae of the farmers' lives, focusing on excruciating detail coupled with soaring prose, both moves an attempt to uphold his subjects' dignity. For example, Agee's multipage description of the men's overalls and workshirts includes an exegesis on their color: "a region and scale of blues, subtle, delicious, and deft beyond what I have ever seen elsewhere approached except in rare skies, the smoky light some days are filmed with, and some of the blues of [French postimpressionist painter Paul] Cézanne." Agee uses precision and imagery to imbue simple overalls with the import they deserve as the primary garment of the farming men. Such moves make the book a propagandistic argument for the need to engage ethically and cautiously with every person.

Stylistically, Agee's prose swings between confidence and uncertainty. He uses both tones to argue that he and the readers are trespassers rather than saviors. Agee emphasizes that each of his subjects "*exists,* in actual being, as you do and as I do, and as no character of the imagination can possibly exist. His great weight, mystery, and dignity are in this fact." The irrefutable presentation of this passage shows Agee's confidence in his ethical revision to other political perspectives. Yet in Agee's description of accidentally terrorizing a young African American couple as he runs up to speak to them, he relates, "I could not bear that they should receive from me any added reflection of the shattering of their grace and dignity, and of the nakedness of depth and meaning of their fear, and of my horror and pity and self-hatred." Agee pours out his agonized uncertainty, insisting that he is the element that does not belong and that, as he and Evans do not belong, neither do the readers for whom they write and photograph. This tonal tightrope between assertiveness and precariousness underscores the text's commitment to its subjects' specificity.

## CRITICAL DISCUSSION

*Let Us Now Praise Famous Men* initially met with mixed reviews. With the American preoccupation with the war in Europe, little interest was left for what seemed like yet another book about impoverished people. Further, many critics disliked Agee's convoluted,

Sharecropper Bud Fields and his family at home in Hale County, Alabama, in 1936. Photographed by Walker Evans and published in the book *Let Us Now Praise Famous Men.* © EVERETT COLLECTION INC./ALAMY.

self-flagellating style. For example, Ralph Thompson of the *New York Times,* as quoted in John Hersey's introduction to *Let Us Now Praise Famous Men,* wrote that Agee was "arrogant, mannered, precious, gross." Other critics, however, celebrated the text, including Lionel Trilling, who wrote in the *Kenyon Review* that "Agee has a sensibility so precise, so unremitting, that it is sometimes appalling." He added that Agee's sensibility "never wearies us" because "it is brilliantly normal and because it is a moral rather than a physical sensibility." Despite such praise, the book was a critical and commercial failure.

*Let Us Now Praise Famous Men* found an audience in the 1960s among white civil rights workers and African Americans fighting for their voting rights in the South, and the book was seen as a catalyst for cross-cultural, political engagement. Unfortunately, Agee died of a heart attack in 1955 at the age of forty-five, so he did not live to see his text hailed as a masterpiece. Evans, however, contributed an introduction to a subsequent edition of the book. *Praise*'s rise in popularity led inevitably to its canonization, and it is often read in college classrooms. As the fervor of the civil rights movement waned, readers and scholars returned to debating the merits and effectiveness of Agee's style as a means to representing his subjects—a conversation that continues in the twenty-first century.

After its return to print in the 1960s, *Let Us Now Praise Famous Men* enjoyed much critical discussion. Certain scholars still object to Agee's approach, but most recognize the text's radical formality and honest attempt at ethical representation. Quinn argues that Agee and Evans used modernist techniques and pragmatist philosophies to modify the political ideologies of both liberalism and communism, whereas T. V. Reed in the 1988 article "Unimagined Existence and the Fiction of the Real" claims that *Praise* lays the groundwork for the innovations and preoccupations of postmodernism. Fittingly for a work such as *Praise,* many critics take a hybrid approach in their readings of the text. In late-twentieth-century scholarship, John Hersey, Paula Rabinowitz, and Bruce Jackson all mingle personal experiences with academic engagement in their readings of *Praise.*

### BIBLIOGRAPHY

*Sources*

Agee, James, and Walker Evans. *Let Us Now Praise Famous Men.* Boston: Houghton Mifflin, 1988. Print.

Hersey, John. Introduction. *Let Us Now Praise Famous Men.* By James Agee and Walker Evans. Boston: Houghton Mifflin, 1988. v–xl. Print.

Jackson, Bruce. "The Deceptive Anarchy of *Let Us Now Praise Famous Men.*" *Antioch Review* 57.1 (1999): 38–49. *JSTOR.* Web. 14 Aug. 2012.

Quinn, Jeanne Follansbee. "The Work of Art: Irony and Identification in *Let Us Now Praise Famous Men*." *Novel: A Forum on Fiction* 34.3 (2001): 338–68. *JSTOR*. Web. 14 Aug. 2012.

Rabinowitz, Paula. "Voyeurism and Class Consciousness: James Agee and Walker Evans, *Let Us Now Praise Famous Men*." *Cultural Critique* 21 (1992): 143–70. *JSTOR*. Web. 14 Aug. 2012.

Reed, T. V. "Unimagined Existence and the Fiction of the Real: Postmodernist Realism in *Let Us Now Praise Famous Men*." *Representations* 24 (1988): 156–76. *JSTOR*. Web. 14 Aug. 2012.

### Further Reading

Agee, James, Michael A. Lofaro, and Hugh Davis. *James Agee Rediscovered: The Journals of* Let Us Now Praise Famous Men *and Other New Manuscripts*. Knoxville: U of Tennessee P, 2005. Print.

Allred, Jeff. *American Modernism and Depression Documentary*. Oxford: Oxford UP, 2009. Print.

Caldwell, Erskine, and Margaret Bourke-White. *You Have Seen Their Faces*. Athens: U of Georgia P, 1995. Print.

Gilles, Mora, and John T. Hill. *Walker Evans: The Hungry Eye*. New York: Abrams, 1993. Print.

Humphries, David T. "Returning South: Reading Culture in James Agee's *Let Us Now Praise Famous Men* and Zora Neale Hurston's *Mules and Men*." *Southern Literary Journal* 41.2 (2009): 69–86. *Project Muse*. Web. 14 Aug. 2012.

Lofaro, Michael A. *James Agee: Reconsiderations*. Knoxville: U of Tennessee P, 1992. Print.

Maharidge, Dale, and Michael Williamson. *And Their Children after Them: The Legacy of* Let Us Now Praise Famous Men, *James Agee, Walker Evans, and the Rise and Fall of Cotton in the South*. New York: Pantheon, 1989. Print.

Schultz, William Todd. "Off-Stage Voices in James Agee's *Let Us Now Praise Famous Men*: Reportage as Covert Autobiography." *American Imago* 56.1 (1999): 75–104. *Project Muse*. Web. 14 Aug. 2012.

Stott, William. *Documentary Expression and Thirties America*. Chicago: U of Chicago P, 1973. Print.

Wright, Richard. *Twelve Million Black Voices: A Folk History of the Negro in the United States*. New York: Thunder Mouth's Press, 2002. Print.

### Media Adaptation

*Let Us Now Praise Famous Men: Alabama Forty Years On*. Prod. Alan Yentob. Dir. Carol Bell. Phot. Colin Munn and Bob Perrin. Ed. Gregory Harris. Sound by Ron Crabb and Alan Dykes. Great Britain: British Broadcasting Corporation [production company], 1979. VHS.

*Sarah Stoeckl*

# "OF CANNIBALS"

*Michel de Montaigne*

## OVERVIEW

"Of Cannibals," Michel de Montaigne's ironic exploration of native culture in the New World, was published in French in 1580 in a volume of collected works titled *Essays*. The French word *essais* means "attempts," and Montaigne's essays represent his deeply personal reflections on a variety of topics and their relationships to society and philosophy. The collection was translated into English in 1603 by John Florio. Supposedly based upon Montaigne's conversations with an acquaintance who had lived in an early French colony in South America, "Of Cannibals" details the author's perceptions of the peoples of recently discovered lands and his comparisons between their way of life and that of the "civilized" societies of Europe. While portraying the cannibals of his narrative as exotic and outlandish specimens of humanity, Montaigne repeatedly makes the point that their lives are more pure, content, and authentic than those of his Renaissance readers.

Montaigne's influential portrait of native innocence emerged during the Renaissance, a period of intellectual and physical exploration. The era was characterized by intense interest in the internal human experience and critiques of society, which developed alongside an avid curiosity about the boundaries of the physical world. During the fifteenth and sixteenth centuries, a revival of interest in the Greek and Roman classics led to a literary humanism that identified people as part of the natural world rather than as beings apart from nature. In addition, the exploration of unknown parts of the globe began to expand European horizons. Montaigne's essays introduce a genre that combines objective analysis with subjective commentary in a way that exemplifies the development of the Renaissance viewpoint. His writing in "Of Cannibals" reflects an admiration of simplicity and nature that would remain influential in French philosophy for centuries.

## HISTORICAL AND LITERARY CONTEXT

The period generally called the Renaissance, which marked a rebirth of European culture, began in the late fourteenth century in Italy and was characterized by an expansive spirit of exploration and discovery. As early as the twelfth century, soldiers returning home from the crusades brought exotic goods from the East and broadened awareness of unfamiliar customs, art, and literature. This cultural exchange intensified after the conquest of Constantinople, the cosmopolitan center of the Byzantine Empire, by the Ottoman Turks in 1453. Following the fall of Constantinople, a number of scholars and artists fled west to Italy, where they became part of burgeoning intellectual movements. Additionally, the Renaissance was fostered by economic growth in Europe, increased international trade, and the development of humanism, with its focus on classical antiquity. The spread of this new culture of ideas and art was aided by advancements in printing technology. The introduction of Johannes Gutenberg's movable-type printing press in 1440 made books more widely and inexpensively available than ever before, encouraging the spread of literacy. In the early sixteenth century, the Renaissance spread to France as Francis I brought Italian artists and writers to his court. These developments would influence the type of education someone like Montaigne might have received later in the century.

The years of the Renaissance have also been dubbed the Age of Exploration, as the search for new trade routes to Asia led to the discovery and colonization of previously unknown lands west and south of the European continent. Portugal and Spain launched the earliest explorations into unfamiliar seas, redrawing the global map and discovering and laying claim to inhabited areas of the West Indies and the Americas by the turn of the sixteenth century. The French hastened to claim their share of New World lands and wealth, and in 1555 the Frenchman Nicholas Durand de Villegaignon established a colony called Antarctic France in what is now Brazil. French explorers brought a number of Brazilians back to France, and though the French colony was destroyed by the Portuguese after only five years, it was the native people of Antarctic France who inspired Montaigne's musings about the dubious advantages of civilization.

The new passion for travel and the increased availability of printed books inspired a Renaissance literature that glorified human perfectibility while casting a skeptical eye on many institutions of human society. In his *In Praise of Folly* (1511), the Dutch philosopher Desiderius Erasmus satirizes the church, the government, and human foibles, and in *Utopia* (1516) the British humanist Thomas More couches his critique of war and oppression in the seminal description of an ideal state. The British playwright Christopher Marlowe

## Key Facts

**Time Period:**
Late 16th Century

**Genre:**
Essay

**Events:**
European Renaissance and Age of Exploration; introduction of the Gutenberg press

**Nationality:**
French

## EMBRACING LIFE FROM THE IVORY TOWER

Although Montaigne would become one of the most respected writers of one of the most influential periods in history, he did not begin his writing career until he was thirty-eight, an advanced age in the sixteenth century. Born Michel Eyquem in Gascony in 1533, the young Frenchman was the first in his family to adopt the name "de Montaigne," a title of modest nobility that had been conferred to his great-grandfather. Educated at home, where he spoke only Latin until the age of six, Montaigne later attended college and studied law, gaining a position in the *parlement* of Bordeaux, a regional supreme court, in 1557. He became one of the highest-ranking judges in the Guyenne region.

Montaigne was unenthusiastic about the law, but while serving as a judge in the Bordeaux *parlement,* he became close friends with the writer and philosopher Étienne de la Boétie. Montaigne was heartbroken upon La Boétie's death in 1563, and many scholars believe that the author began writing his essays to continue the wide-ranging philosophical discussions he had enjoyed with his friend. In 1571 Montaigne, by then comfortably married to Françoise de la Chassaigne, retired to Chateau de Montaigne outside Bordeaux. There he began to write in earnest, publishing his *Essays* in 1780. Although he considered himself withdrawn from society, he traveled and corresponded with friends, worked as a translator and an editor, and continued to serve as an advisor to the government as well as mayor of Bordeaux.

employs a supernatural device to showcase the price of human vanity in *The Tragical History of Doctor Faustus,* written during the late 1500s.

Montaigne's idealized depiction of the uncorrupted purity of primitive peoples was one of the earliest articulations of a theme that would fascinate writers and scholars into the Romantic period of the early nineteenth century. In the early seventeenth century, playwright William Shakespeare borrowed lines from "Of Cannibals" to describe a primordial utopian vision in his comedy *The Tempest* (1611). Writers such as Jonathan Swift (*Gulliver's Travels*; 1726) and Voltaire (*Le Mondain*; 1736) echo Montaigne's use of satire and irony to challenge conventional definitions of good and evil, and by the eighteenth century, Jean Jacques Rousseau's concept of an uncorrupted "state of nature" had elevated the image of the "noble savage" to an archetype. Some scholars believe it is possible that Montaigne's ideas also influenced Herman Melville's paean to cannibal culture, *Typee* (1846).

### THEMES AND STYLE

The tendency to demonize the different is one of the major themes of the work. Montaigne begins his essay by noting that the Greeks used the word *barbarian* to describe all people of other nations: "Every one gives the title of barbarism to everything that is not in use in his own country … we have no other level of truth and reason, than the example and idea of the opinions and customs of the place wherein we live." Montaigne reveals his central skepticism about his society in his comparison of the barbarism of the native peoples with that of modern Renaissance Europeans: "We may then call these people barbarous, in respect to the rules of reason: but not in respect to ourselves, who in all sorts of barbarity exceed them." "Of Cannibals" was written against the backdrop of the French Wars of Religion, which pitted Catholics and Huguenots (Calvinists) against one another and which led to massacres and widespread, often brutal, violence. The Saint Bartholomew's Day Massacre, for example, took place only eight years before the composition of Montaigne's *Essays*. Montaigne approaches with frankness the scandalous fact that the indigenous people are indeed cannibals who ritually eat the bodies of their own, comparing the custom to accepted European practices of torture: "I conceive there is more barbarity in eating a man alive, than when he is dead; in tearing a body limb from limb by racks and torments … than to roast and eat him after he is dead."

Such unexpected comparisons give Montaigne's essay its persuasive power by forcing readers to view their own society from the outside. For example, Montaigne describes the visit of three South American Indians who met King Charles IX at Rouen: "They had observed, that there were among us men full and crammed with all manner of commodities, while, in the meantime, their halves were begging at their doors, lean, and half-starved with hunger and poverty." In contrast, in the Indians' own society, "they have no want of anything necessary, nor of this greatest of all goods, to know happily how to enjoy their condition and to be content." In addition, Montaigne employs epigram to strengthen his argument, declaring, for example, that "the estimate and value of a man consists in the heart and in the will: there his true honor lies."

Although Montaigne's condemnation of societal hypocrisy and corruption is often strongly worded, the author's playful ironic tone eases his message, as when he describes the European lust for conquest of distant lands: "I am afraid our eyes are bigger than our bellies, and that we have more curiosity than capacity; for we grasp at all, but catch nothing but wind." His style is rhythmic and poetic, and he describes the life of native South Americans with engaging detail: "Their drink is made of a certain root, and is of the colour of our claret, and they never drink it but lukewarm. It will not keep above two or three days; it has a somewhat sharp, brisk taste, is nothing heady, but very comfortable to the stomach."

### CRITICAL DISCUSSION

The probing skepticism of Montaigne's essays typifies the Renaissance spirit of inquiry and reflection. His work was an influential part of the developing modernist thinking that led to the Enlightenment of the 1700s. Joseph Addison, writing in 1714, describes the intensely personal nature of Montaigne's explorations. In an essay republished in *The Works of the Right Honourable Joseph Addison* (1854), he states, "The title of an essay promises, perhaps, a discourse upon Virgil or Julius Caesar; but when you look into it, you are sure to meet with more upon Monsieur Montagne [sic] than either of them." "Of Cannibals" in particular sparked further meditations on the intersection of innocence and corruption in such works as Voltaire's controversial 1759 satire *Candide, ou l'Optimisme* (Candide, or Optimism).

Montaigne's greatest contribution to literature is the essence of the essay form—the personal analysis of the self in relation to the world. "Of Cannibals," with its sly social satire combined with Renaissance wonder at the marvel of undiscovered lands and people, is often seen as one of Montaigne's most representative works and has become one of his most frequently anthologized essays. The influence of his complex portrayal of the noble primitive can be seen in later works, from Jean Jacques Rousseau's *Discourse on the Origin of Inequality* (1754) to James Cameron's blockbuster film *Avatar* (2009).

Montaigne's writing has been the subject of scholarly analysis since its publication, with each subsequent generation positing new perspectives on the essays. Hugo Friedrich's study *Montaigne* (1949) represents a common view of the author as a moralist bent upon improving his readers, while Jean-Yves Pouilloux's *Lire les "Essais" de Montaigne* (1970) transforms scholarship on the essays by suggesting that it is the form of the writing and the manner of expression that give Montaigne's work enduring value. In a 1992 essay for *The Atlantic,* Phyllis Rose makes a case for viewing Montaigne as one of the originators of jazz, the "inventor of the verbal riff, the man who … first made art by letting one thing lead to another." Twenty-first-century critics continue to explore the author's intent in "Of Cannibals." In *Montaigne and the Ethics of Skepticism* (2005), Zahi Anbra Zalloua asserts that the essay was never meant as a portrait of a distant culture, but rather "the essayist manipulates the figure of the cannibal in service of a political end … to express his critique of Christian fanaticism." In a 2012 essay for *Rhetorica,* Eric MacPhail points out the author's intention to challenge readers' assumptions: "Montaigne praises precisely what is best calculated to repel his audience and thereby to reveal the unstable foundations of consensus."

## BIBLIOGRAPHY

### Sources

Addison, Joseph. *The Works of the Right Honourable Joseph Addison.* Ed. Richard Hurd. London: Henry G. Bohn, 1854. Web. 22 Oct. 2012.

MacPhail, Eric. "Philosophers in the New World: Montaigne and the Tradition of Epideictic Rhetoric." *Rhetorica* 30.1 (2012): 22–36. Print.

Portrait of Michel de Montaigne by Étienne Martellange (1569–1641). MICHEL EYQUEM DE MONTAIGNE (1533–92) (OIL ON PANEL), MARTELLANGE, ÉTIENNE (1569–1641)/ PRIVATE COLLECTION/THE BRIDGEMAN ART LIBRARY.

Montaigne, Michel de. *The Complete Essays of Michel de Montaigne.* Trans. Charles Cotton. Ed. William Carew Hazlitt. Stanford: Stanford UP, 1958. Web. 22 Oct. 2012.

Rose, Phyllis. "Michel de Montaigne, Father of Jazz." *Atlantic* Aug. 1992: 93–94. *Literature Resource Center.* Web. 1 Oct. 2012.

Zalloua, Zahi Anbra. *Montaigne and the Ethics of Skepticism.* Charlottesville, VA: Rookwood, 2005. Print.

### Further Reading

Beauchamp, Gorman. "Montaigne, Melville, and the Cannibals." *Arizona Quarterly* 37.4 (1981): 293–309. *Literature Resource Center.* Web. 27 Sept. 2012.

Boucher, Philip P. "Revisioning the 'French Atlantic.'" *The Atlantic World and Virginia, 1550–1624.* Ed. Peter C. Mancall. Chapel Hill: U of North Carolina P, 2007. 274–306. Print.

de Léry, Jean. *History of a Voyage to the Land of Brazil.* Trans. Janet Whatley. Berkeley: U of California P, 1990. Print.

De Lutri, Joseph R. "Montaigne on the Noble Savage: A Shift in Perspective." *French Review* 49.2 (1975): 206–11. Print.

Hamlin, William M. "Florio's Montaigne and the Tyranny of *Custome*: Appropriation, Ideology, and Early English Readership of the *Essayes*." *Renaissance Quarterly* 63.2 (2010): 491–544. Print.

———. *The Image of America in Montaigne, Spenser, and Shakespeare: Renaissance Ethnography and Literary Reflection.* New York: St. Martin's, 1995. Print.

Kirsch, Arthur. "Virtue, Vice and Compassion in Montaigne and *The Tempest*." *Studies in English*

*Literature, 1500–1900* 37.2 (1997): 337–52. *Literature Resource Center.* Web. 1 Oct. 2012.

La Blanc, Michael L., ed. *Image of the Noble Savage in Literature.* Literature Criticism from 1400 to 1800, 79. Detroit: Gale, 2002. *Literature Resource Center.* Web. 1 Oct. 2012.

Lestringant, Frank. *Cannibals: The Discovery and Representation of the Cannibal from Columbus to Jules Verne.* Berkeley: U of California P, 1997. Print.

MacKenzie, Scott R. "Breeches of Decorum: The Figure of a Barbarian in Montaigne and Addison." *South Central Review* 23.2 (2006): 99–127. *Literature Resource Center.* Web. 27 Sept. 2012.

Popkin, Richard. *The History of Skepticism: From Savonarola to Bayle.* New York: Oxford UP, 2003. Print.

Rendall, Steven. "Dialectical Structure and Tactics in Montaigne's 'Of Cannibals.'" *Reading Montaigne.* Ed. Dikka Berven. New York: Routledge, 1995. 32–40. Print.

*Tina Gianoulis*

# PALE FIRE

*Vladimir Nabokov*

## OVERVIEW

*Pale Fire,* a novel written in English by Russian-American novelist Vladimir Nabokov and published in 1962 in the United States, consists of a 999-line poem written after the death of his daughter Hazel by the fictional poet John Shade and, by fictional scholar Charles Kinbote, a foreword, a commentary, and an index. Writing in the style of an academic study, Kinbote interjects his own narrative through his detailed notes about Shade's poem. These notes often diverge from their ostensible poetic subject to focus on details of Kinbote's own life; his friendship with and influence on his scholarly subject; and Kinbote's "true" identity as King Charles II, the deposed ruler of a remote northern kingdom called Zembla. The structure of the novel, which is constructed like an elaborate puzzle of hidden meanings and invites nonlinear reading, calls into question the authority of its narrator, of critical discourse, and of the traditional realist novel.

At the time of *Pale Fire*'s composition, Nabokov was a noted author of literary novels in Russian and in English. When the book was published in 1962, response was divided between critics who praised Nabokov's formal experiments and linguistic brilliance and those who found the book's subject slight and its satire weak. The novel is a continuation of earlier preoccupations and motifs for Nabokov: the language of the university, the implementation of verbal games and puzzles, and the exploration of deeply humanistic themes cloaked in aesthetic experiment. The author also returns to themes arguably drawn from his own life: exile from privilege, revolution and assassination, and academia as an imperfect refuge. As a work of allusion and intertextuality, *Pale Fire* makes the question of authorial stability its central subject. The book reflects a notable advancement in formal experiments for Nabokov and for the literature of metafiction; the novel's structure has had a continuing influence on experimental writers today and is considered an anticipation of the Internet's hypertext structure.

## HISTORICAL AND LITERARY CONTEXT

Since the novel's beginnings with Miguel de Cervantes's *Don Quixote,* writers have questioned the definition and domain of the novel. Two eighteenth-century works of fiction, Laurence Sterne's *Tristram Shandy* and Denis Diderot's *Jacques le fataliste,* conceive the novel as a grand game. During the nineteenth-century, according to Milan Kundera in *The Art of the Novel* (1986), fictional prose became tied to verisimilitude, realistic settings, and a discernible chronological order. At the beginning of the twentieth century, modern writers as diverse as James Joyce and Franz Kafka proposed alternative approaches to plot and character. Then, in the 1950s a group of French novelists—including Robbe-Grillet, Marguerite Duras, Natalie Sarraute, and Julio Cortazar—wrote experimental novels latterly called the *nouveau roman* (new novel). Their fiction challenged novelistic traditions by offering linear and non-linear readings and open-ended structures.

As *Pale Fire*'s ostensibly academic format suggests, in mid-twentieth-century America, the university and scholarly discourse were preeminent in assessing the legitimacy of a work of literature. By contrast, Nabokov's former homeland, Russia (then a part of the Soviet Union), forged its own literary template with the Joseph Stalin-approved mode of socialist realism, stylized fiction that promoted an idealized picture of the Stalinist society. Nabokov rejected all forms of totalitarian "regimentation of thought, governmental censorship, racial or religious persecution," notes Natasa Kovacevic in *Narrating Post/Communism: Colonial Discourse and Europe's Borderline Civilization* (2008). He also resisted realist regimentation in his work and famously compared writing fiction to a game of chess: "competition in chess … is between composer and hypothetical solver, just as in a first-rate work of fiction the real clash is not between the characters but between the author and the world."

Nabokov did not admit to many influences, but his work arguably sprang from his early Russian and English literary encounters—such as the linguistic virtuosity and neologisms of William Shakespeare and the aesthetics and experiments of Aleksandr Pushkin—and from elegiac memories of his former homeland. His commentaries on Pushkin's hundred-page novel *Eugene Onegin* filled two volumes and seemed to have informed *Pale Fire* narrator Kinbote's elaborate notes on Shade's poem. The mode of discovery within *Pale Fire* guides the reader through a complex narrative that otherwise might burden the reader (as in James Joyce's *Finnegans Wake*) or become an endless intricacy (as in Georges Perec's *Life: A User's Manual*). Indeed, according to Brian Boyd in *Nabokov's "Pale*

### ✤ Key Facts

**Time Period:**
Mid-20th Century

**Genre:**
Novel

**Events:**
Rise of totalitarianism in the Soviet Union; growth of socialist realism in communist countries

**Nationality:**
Russian

# VLADIMIR NABOKOV—
# ECSTATIC STYLIST

Vladimir Nabokov was born in 1899 to a wealthy noble family in St. Petersburg, Russia. He grew up trilingual, speaking English before he spoke French and Russian. After the Russian Revolution in 1917, Nabokov began a lifelong exile that he elegized in fiction and autobiography. He entered Trinity College at Cambridge University in 1919 to study zoology and modern and medieval languages. After his father died protecting a Russian Democratic party leader from an assassin's bullet in 1922, Nabokov moved to Berlin and published his first poems and novels under the pseudonym V. Sirin. There, he married his Russian Jewish wife, Vera, who became his secretary and translator.

The couple left Berlin for Paris in the 1930s and escaped the invading German army for the United States in 1940. Nabokov began his career as an academic at Wellesley College in 1941, teaching comparative literature, studying lepidoptery, and later leading the school's one-man Russian department. In 1948 Nabokov accepted a teaching position at Cornell University. The notoriety and success of his novel *Lolita* allowed him to retire from lecturing and to move to Montreux, Switzerland, so that he could pursue writing full-time. Though criticized for his often amoral narrators, Nabokov was a masterful stylist who returned to several themes, particularly the desire to revive the past through imagination and the search for what he called "aesthetic bliss."

Fire": *The Magic of Artistic Discovery* (1999), Nabokov's writing might be viewed to be more strongly influenced by philosophic ideas of the early twentieth century, such as philosopher Karl Popper's *Logic of Scientific Discovery*, which rejects all claims for certainty through traditional methods but asserts a possibility of exponential growth of knowledge without a defined path of achieving it.

While *Pale Fire* polarized critical audiences when it was published, the novel has a far-reaching legacy among experimental novelists and linguistic scholars. Nabokov's own life and career were transformed when his earlier work, *Lolita* (1955), was filmed by Stanley Kubrick, allowing Nabokov to give up his work as a professor and to move to Switzerland to devote his time to writing. The critic James Wood asserts that Nabokov's gorgeous prose and relentless aesthetic impulses are hard to resist: "his style is contagious; after a day of re-reading Nabokov I am imitating him." *Pale Fire* has influenced writers as disparate as Martin Amis, Jeffrey Eugenides, W. G. Sebald (in whose novel *The Emigrants* Nabokov appears as an unnamed character), David Mitchell, Shelley Jackson, and Zadie Smith.

**THEMES AND STYLE**

Central to *Pale Fire* is the interplay between the various texts and authorial voices that constitute the work, a confrontation that forces character, author, and

reader to determine their own truths. Shade's poem establishes the novel's preoccupations with mortality, truth, and hidden meanings:

> I suspected that the truth
> About survival after death was known
> To every human being: I alone
> Knew nothing, and a great conspiracy
> Of books and people hid the truth from me.

But commentator Kinbote wrests the book away from his deceased subject: "Let me state that without my notes Shade's text simply has no human reality at all." In Kinbote's discursive commentary, he claims to have inspired the work of his neighbor Shade: "I saturated him with my vision." Nabokov's book regularly asserts multiple realities. According to Kinbote, a Zemblan assassin mistook Shade for Kinbote and murdered the poet—another occasion in the text where the identities of the two authors are conflated. And though there are references that can be read as allusions to Nabokov's own history (Kinbote's homeland Zembla, "a remote northern country," shares some traits with Russia), the book suggests a slippery relationship between author, narrator, and textual meaning.

Nabokov exploits weaknesses in the tradition of academic work by presenting a primary text of heightened aesthetic value (the poem) that is followed by commentary that has a tangential relation to the source text. Kinbote quickly diverges from a scholarly third-person voice to reveal a fallible and imbalanced first-person narrator, who makes assumptions about his readers ("Canto Two, your favorite") and interjects comments about his own reality ("There is a very loud amusement park right in front of my lodgings"). The reader's experience is disrupted by the unconventional form of the novel, which, as noted by Stephen Jan Parker in *Understanding Vladimir Nabokov* (1987), "precludes a direct linear experience" by encouraging the reader to move back and forth between poem, notes, and index. Moreover, Kinbote often makes a tenuous connection between text and commentary. For example, he extracts the phrase "a great conspiracy" from Shade's line "a great conspiracy of books" in order to describe the selection of an assassin for the Zemblan king. Kinbote's voice is a parody of scholarship, challenging the reader to find an authority within the text.

Stylistically, Nabokov's novel affects a number of voices that compete for control over the novel. Influenced by Shakespeare and Alexander Pope, Shade's poem favors high aestheticism over emotion. Even Shade's heightened meditations on mortality ("*Life is a message scribbled in the dark.*") and on the suicide of his daughter ("It is the writer's grief.") suggest his own experience is mere fodder for creative work ("*Man's life as commentary to abstruse / Unfinished poem. Note for further use.*"). Meanwhile, Kinbote acknowledges Jonathan Swift's

A bronze statue of *Pale Fire* author Vladimir Nabokov, located in front of the Palace Hotel in Montreux, Switzerland, where he resided for nearly two decades. © E. J. BAUMEISTER JR./ALAMY.

satirical sway ("I notice a whiff of Swift in some of my notes. I too am a desponder in my nature … although I have my moments of volatility and *fou rire*."), evoking a comically critical stance. While Nabokov often depicted morally assailable narrators, Kinbote's instability renders *Pale Fire* a fanciful and experimental work. It also serves as counterpoint to Nabokov's more obviously autobiographical campus novel, *Pnin* (1957), about a refugee expatriate professor from Russia.

## CRITICAL DISCUSSION

In the context of the Cold War, Nabokov's aesthetic values were, according to Anthony Burgess in a review of the work for *Yorkshire Post*, a "deliberate naughty perversion of literature," assuredly out of step with the Soviet regime. Critics found in Nabokov's brilliance a new hope for the modern novel. In her review for the *Atlantic*, Mary McCarthy wrote that *Pale Fire* "is one of the very great works of art of this century, the modern novel that everyone thought was dead and that was only playing possum." In contrast, Dwight MacDonald, writing for *Partisan Review*, thought it was "high class doodling," and, according to Norman Page in *Vladimir Nabokov: Critical Heritage* (1997), Alfred Chester called it a total wreck. Burgess also extolled the book, saying Nabokov's "love affair with the English language achieved prolonged consummation."

In the context of Nabokov's oeuvre, *Pale Fire* has been regarded as a masterpiece, a culmination of the author's aesthetic and stylistic concerns that expanded the definition of and possibilities for the novel.

Nabokov's book also heralded an era of metafiction: fiction that took on the novel, the writer, and acts of reading as subjects. Other such works include Kurt Vonnegut's *Slaughterhouse Five* and *The Crying of Lot 49* by Thomas Pynchon, Nabokov's former student at Cornell. Even critics who disliked the work acknowledged that Nabokov was attempting to solve the problems of the twentieth-century novel. Chester wrote "[In] *Pale Fire*, [Nabokov] tells us there is no novel at present, and he offers this book in its place." Written as a rejection of Nabokov's work, this comment highlights the utility of Nabokov's experiment: *Pale Fire* releases the novel from realism's grip.

*Pale Fire*'s most widely divisive subject is perhaps the matter of internal authorship. In "Shade and Shape in *Pale Fire*," Boyd notes, "The comedy and pathos of its disintegratedness, so essential to [the novel's] effect, derive from the absurd breach between Shade's contribution and Kinbote's." René Alladaye suggests a third potential author: "Hazel may be a more valid option than Shade and Kinbote as internal author of the whole book." In *Nabokov's "Pale Fire,"* Boyd explains the novel as a double ghost story, with Hazel's spirit appearing to offer her father succor and Shade's shade "infiltrat[ing] and animat[ing] Kinbote's imagination." Other commentators have approached Nabokov's elusive literary work according to perceived biographical elements. Boyd, in *Stalking Nabokov*, notes that *Pale Fire* "juxtapose[s] a closely observed real world (an émigré's alien capital) and an imagined, romantic elsewhere (Zembla) that has persistent tones of the beyond."

BIBLIOGRAPHY

*Sources*

Alladaye, René. "Through the Looking-Glass—*Pale Fire* as Anamorphosis: An Alternative Theory of Internal Authorship." *Nabokov Online Journal* VI. Dalhousie Electronic Text Centre, 2012. Web. 19 Nov. 2012.

Boyd, Brian. *Nabokov's "Pale Fire": The Magic of Artistic Discovery.* Princeton: Princeton UP, 1999. Print.

———. "Shade and Shape in *Pale Fire*." *Nabokov Studies* 4 (1997): 173–224. Rpt. in *Twentieth-Century Literary Criticism.* Ed. Linda Pavlovski and Scott T. Darga. Vol. 108. Detroit: Gale Group, 2001. *Literature Resource Center.* Web. 13 Nov. 2012.

———. *Stalking Nabokov: Selected Essays.* New York: Columbia UP, 2011. Print.

Burgess, Anthony. Rev. of *Pale Fire,* by Vladimir Nabokov. *Yorkshire Post.* 15 Nov. 1962. Print.

Connolly, Julian W. "Vladimir Vladimirovich Nabokov." *Twentieth-Century Russian Emigre Writers.* Ed. Maria Rubins. Detroit: Gale, 2005. *Dictionary of Literary Biography.* Vol. 317. *Literature Resource Center.* Web. 10 Oct. 2012.

Duncan Morris, Paul. *Vladimir Nabokov: Poetry and the Lyric Voice.* Toronto: U of Toronto P, 2010. Print.

Kundera, Milan. *The Art of the Novel.* New York: Grove, 1986. Print.

MacDonald, Dwight. Rev. of *Pale Fire,* by Vladimir Nabokov. *Partisan Review* Summer 1962. Print.

McCarthy, Mary. "A Bolt from the Blue." Rev. of *Pale Fire,* by Vladimir Nabokov. *New Republic.* 4 June 1962. Print.

Nabokov, Vladimir. *Speak, Memory.* New York: Vintage, 1989. Print.

Page, Norman, ed. *Vladimir Nabokov: Critical Heritage.* Oxford: Taylor, 1997. Print.

Parker, Stephen Jan. *Understanding Vladimir Nabokov.* Columbia: U of South Carolina P, 1987. Print.

*Vladimir Nabokov: Critical Heritage,* ed. Norman Page. Oxford: Taylor, 1997. Print.

Wood, James. "Discussing Nabokov." *Slate.* The Slate Group, 26 Apr. 1999. Web. 2 Oct. 2012.

*Further Reading*

Edelstein, Marilyn. "*Pale Fire*: The Art of Consciousness." *Nabokov's Fifth Arc: Nabokov and Others on His Life's Work.* Ed. J. E. Rivers and Charles Nicol. Austin: U of Texas P, 1982. 213–23. Rpt. in *Twentieth-Century Literary Criticism.* Ed. Thomas J. Schoenberg. Vol. 189. Detroit: Gale, 2007. *Literature Resource Center.* Web. 10 Oct. 2012.

Gold, Herbert. "The Art of Fiction, No. 40. Interview with Vladimir Nabokov." *Paris Review* Summer-Fall 1967. *theparisreview.org.* Web. 2 Oct. 2012.

Haegert, John. "The Author as Reader as Nabokov: Text and Pretext in *Pale Fire.*" *Texas Studies in Literature and Language* 26.4 (1984): 405–24. Rpt. in *Twentieth-Century Literary Criticism.* Ed. Thomas J. Schoenberg. Vol. 189. Detroit: Gale, 2007. *Literature Resource Center.* Web. 10 Oct. 2012.

Karshan, Thomas. *The Presence of Pope in Vladimir Nabokov's "Pale Fire."* Oxford: U of Oxford, 2002. Print.

Knapp, Shoshana. "Hazel Ablaze: Literary License in Nabokov's *Pale Fire.*" *Essays in Literature* 14.1 (1987): 105–15. Rpt. in *Twentieth-Century Literary Criticism.* Ed. Thomas J. Schoenberg. Vol. 189. Detroit: Gale, 2007. *Literature Resource Center.* Web. 10 Oct. 2012.

Wright, Austin M. "Creative Plot: *Pale Fire.*" *The Formal Principle in the Novel.* Ithaca: Cornell UP, 1982. 260–87. Rpt. in *Twentieth-Century Literary Criticism.* Ed. Thomas J. Schoenberg. Vol. 189. Detroit: Gale, 2007. *Literature Resource Center.* Web. 10 Oct. 2012.

*Karen Bender*

# PALESTINE

*Joe Sacco*

## OVERVIEW

Joe Sacco's *Palestine* (1993–95), a groundbreaking work of journalism in comics form, depicts the author's experiences visiting the Israeli-occupied West Bank and Gaza Strip in the early 1990s. The narrative of the graphic novel is largely autobiographical, detailing Sacco's experiences and reactions, but it is driven by interviews with the Palestinians who have suffered under Israeli occupation. These conversations cultivate a sense of intimacy, even as they posit the stories in relation to the large sweep of history. Although the narrative draws from real locations, real individuals, and real accounts, the visuals of the book are markedly stylized, amplifying the idea that this is truth as conveyed through the personal perspective and sensibility of the author. *Palestine* has been lauded for its efforts to shed light on the Palestinian conflict, peering behind the official narrative embraced by the governments and media of Israel and the United States. However, some critics have remarked that more than offering objective truth, it proselytizes its own point of view at the expense of others.

*Palestine* was first published as a nine-issue comic book series from 1993 to 1995. It can be seen as a part of the decade's new wave of alternative and autobiographical comics, a movement largely spearheaded by Sacco's publisher, Fantagraphics. But even within this movement *Palestine* stood out as something pioneering, something that would come to be called "comics journalism." The book certainly tells the author's own story, but it approaches the much larger issue of territorial dispute with an eye for reporting underrepresented viewpoints. Although the work served as an inspiration for contemporary and future comic artists to explore new nonfiction uses for comics, Sacco's distinctive style of storytelling makes *Palestine* utterly unique in comics and in literature in general.

## HISTORICAL AND LITERARY CONTEXT

The Israeli-Palestinian conflict began to some degree in the late nineteenth century with the rise of Zionism, and it intensified with the British Mandate for Palestine of 1923 and the creation of the state of Israel in 1948. The displacement of Palestinians that resulted was further exacerbated by the 1967 war between Israel and its Arab neighbors, in which Israel captured the Gaza Strip from Egypt and the West Bank from Jordan. The territories were occupied by the Israeli military and saw an influx of civilian settlers. In the mid-1980s the spread of Israeli settlements in these areas increased, such that the Jewish population of the West Bank, for example, nearly quadrupled in a decade. Palestinian fears of being fully evicted from the territories led to an increase in Palestinian nationalism.

Malta-born Sacco visited the disputed territories during the Palestinian uprising known as the First Intifada, which lasted from roughly 1987 to 1993. Palestinian resistance was primarily nonviolent, but more radical elements within the population took an increasingly aggressive stance, leading to crackdowns on the territories by the Israeli army. At least 2,000 Palestinians were killed by the army or by other Palestinians persecuting alleged collaborators. The U.S.-backed Oslo Accords of late 1993 offered some initial promise of peace, and for many people the accords marked the official end of the First Intifada. The agreements established the Palestinian Authority and granted it control of the disputed areas, though they remained Israeli territories. Sacco's portrait of the region, then, comes as the Intifada was winding down. For most Americans, the media portrait of the conflict had largely been controlled by Israel and the United States. Consequently, Sacco saw his own role as documenting the results of the conflict from the perspective of the Palestinians from ground level.

When *Palestine* appeared there had been ample writing about the Israeli-Palestinian conflict, but relatively little of it published in the United States had addressed the conflict from the Palestinian point of view. Edward Said's controversial *The Question of Palestine* (1979) is an important exception. It represents perhaps the most direct precedent to *Palestine,* since both works attempted to counter the prevailing narrative surrounding the conflict. This narrative, according to Said in his introduction to the 2001 edition of *Palestine,* was the product of "a media-saturated world in which a huge preponderance of the world's news images are controlled and diffused by a handful of men sitting in places like London and New York." *Palestine* is also a product

⚜ *Key Facts*

**Time Period:**
Late 20th Century

**Genre:**
Graphic Novel

**Events:**
First Intifada

**Nationality:**
Maltese-American

## PRIMARY SOURCE

### EXCERPT FROM *PALESTINE*

Do we need to talk about 1948? It's hardly a secret how the Zionists used rumors, threats, and massacres to expel the Arabs and create new demographics that guaranteed the Jewish nature of Israel.

Of course, it's more comfortable to think of refugees as some regrettable consequence of war, but getting rid of the Palestinians has been an idea kicking around since Theodor Herzl formulated modern Zionism in the late 1800s. "We shall have to spirit the penniless population [sic] across the border," he wrote, "by procuring employment for it in the transit countries, while denying it employment in our own country."

After all, some Zionists reasoned, Palestinians were less attached to their ancestral homeland than the Jews who hadn't lived there for centuries. According to Israel's first prime minister, David Ben-Gurion, a Palestinian "is equally at ease whether in Jordan, Lebanon or a variety of places." With war imminent, Ben-Gurion had no illusions about "spiriting" or inducing the Palestinians away. "In each attack," he wrote, "a decisive blow should be struck, resulting in the destruction of homes and the expulsion of the population." When that was basically accomplished he told an advisor, "Palestinian Arabs have only one role left—to flee."

But if 1948 is no secret, it's all but a non-issue, dismissed entirely by Prime Minister Golda Meir: "It was not as though there was a Palestinian people considering itself as a Palestinian people and we came and threw them out and took their country away from them. They did not exist."

But they <u>did</u> exist and they <u>do,</u> and here they are … and their children, and their children's children … and <u>still</u> they are refugees … stale ones, maybe, in the nightly new scheme of things, but, nonetheless, refugees … which I suppose means they're waiting to go back…

But back to what? Close to 400 Palestinian villages were razed by the Israelis during and after the '48 war … fleeing Palestinians were declared "absentees" … their homes and lands declared "abandoned" or "uncultivated" and expropriated for settlement by Jews.

You say refugee camp and I picture tents, people lying on cots … but somewhere along the line Balata's residents figured they' be here for the long haul, and the camp took on a sort of shabby permanence. … People live here, they watch T.V., they shop, they raise families. … On first glance, sloshing down a main road, what sets Balata apart is the mud. The snows have melted and the road is mud. Everywhere, mud.

SOURCE: Fantagraphics Books, August 2001, pp. 37, 41–2. Copyright © 2001 by Fantagraphics Books. All rights reserved. Reproduced by permission.

others—an intimacy that is missing even from Said's treatment of the conflict.

Just as there had been nothing quite like *Palestine* before its publication, there has been nothing that looks quite like it since. Unquestionably the book helped to propel the status of nonfiction graphic novels, and many have followed in its path, but none has imitated Sacco's narrative approach or idiosyncratic visual style. *Palestine* certainly established Sacco as a significant talent, and he continued to produce cornerstone works in the genre of comics journalism, which he virtually created, including *Safe Area Gorazde* (2000), *The Fixer* (2003), and *Footnotes from Gaza* (2009).

### THEMES AND STYLE

Aside from serving as an exposé of conditions in which Palestinians live under Israeli rule, *Palestine* also examines broader questions of perspective, both personal and "official," and of how opinions are formulated and conditioned. Although Sacco's illustrations convey a sense of chaos and energy, the focus is on quiet conversations. Everyone, it seems, has a story to tell, and they are usually eager to tell it. Sacco often depicts what his interview subjects are describing, and he thereby attempts to illustrate experiences that the world at large does not see, but he also calls his own role as documentarian into question. Critical of the media though Sacco may be, he acknowledges himself as a part of that media. He, the author-as-character, becomes a device for examining the bloodlust of popular media, as when he refers to himself as a "vulture" and when he declaims, "Man, I wish I'd seen the soldiers firing tear gas."

It is Sacco's role as a character in the story that brings the story to life. Sacco judges others, sometimes sympathetically, sometimes harshly, and he judges himself. "It's very clear I'm subjective," he has said. "I'm not trying to pretend I'm objective." As he interviews his subjects, Sacco remains largely neutral, letting them have their say, but as an artist Sacco uses captions to register his internal reactions to what people are saying—often with empathy, sometimes with frustration. In a generally grave book, given its subject matter, these captions allow for a bit of humor to lighten the tone, as with Sacco's running commentary on how much tea he is forced to drink in the name of courtesy.

All of this is embodied in Sacco's illustrative style, one of the most distinctive in comics. His figures often have a surreal quality to them, less due to their anatomy than as a result of the perspectives of Sacco's "camera": dramatic overhead and ground-level angles, extended foreshortening, extreme deep focus, and chaotic page layouts. Likewise, as Mark Binelli points out in his 2004 article in *Rolling Stone,* "Joe Sacco" the character departs from Joe Sacco the artist: "Though Sacco draws himself as slouching and awkward in his books, in reality he is much more confident and put-together than the cartoon model." This self-caricature matches

of the alternative comics movement of the late 1980s and early 1990s and has the intimacy of autobiographical comics such as those of Art Spiegelman, Harvey Pekar, Joe Matt, Chester Brown, and the self-deprecating, self-criticizing commentary that Sacco laces liberally through the story, just as his dramatic contorting of reality captures the turmoil of life in the occupied territories. There is one area, however, where Sacco's visual distortions are abandoned: his highly detailed settings. Sacco wants his readers, without influence, to evaluate for themselves every muddy tire track, every coil of barbed wire, every pile of refuse.

## CRITICAL DISCUSSION

The initial critical reception of *Palestine* was limited by its format and the circumstances of its publication. Not only was it published serially in a traditional comic book format—limiting the attention it received in the mainstream press—but also, as an alternative comic, it was ignored by most of the fan press. Nevertheless, a number of critics praised *Palestine* for its stylistic and subject-matter innovations. When it was published in book form in 1994, critics outside of the rarified world of small press comics largely echoed previous sentiments. *Publishers Weekly* hailed the book as a "fascinating you-are-there-with-me comics account as impressive for its idiosyncratic personal tone as for its scrupulous documentation of human-rights abuses" and reiterated that "there is nothing else quite like this in alternative comics."

Upon reaching a larger audience, *Palestine* courted praise and controversy. The controversy was not completely fabricated by the book; instead, Sacco had waded directly into the ongoing debates about the Israeli-Palestinian conflict. *Palestine* clearly throws its sympathies toward the Palestinians, which has led some to condemn the book as anti-Israel propaganda. The preponderance of criticism, however, recognized the work as far more complex and nuanced in its point of view than is typical of propaganda, suggesting, as Said does, that "there's no obvious spin, no easily discernible line of doctrine." Indeed, even Sacco draws attention to the question of sympathies, late in the book depicting his conversation with two Israeli women who ask him, "Shouldn't you be seeing *our* side of the story, too?" Sacco's response is "I've heard nothing but the Israeli side most all my life."

Additionally, much of the critical attention directed at *Palestine* has discussed its role as a pioneer in comics journalism. In his essay in *The Rise and Reason of Comics and Graphic Literature: Critical Essays on the Form* (2010), Benjamin Woo has argued that *Palestine* ought not be considered journalism, having "abandoned the traditional indices of newsworthiness," suggesting that the form itself prevents it from passing the journalistic litmus test. Others, including Amy Kiste Nyberg and Rocco Versaci, believe that, even though the work is a different kind of journalism, it adds a valuable alternate voice to coverage of world events. In discussing both Sacco's work and comics journalism in general, Nyberg, in her piece in *Critical Approaches to Comics: Theories and Methods* (2012),

## NONFICTION COMICS

Although the popular image of comic books continues to evoke the superheroes who have dominated the market for five decades, comics have a respectable history of works that engage with national and global issues, historical and contemporary. In the early days of the form, these were often rather dry affairs, produced as educational supplements. Only in the last decades of the twentieth century did nonfiction comics develop in such a way as to increase the respectability of the form as a whole. Art Spiegelman's *Maus* (1986), documenting his father's experiences in Nazi concentration camps during World War II, is one of the most recognized examples, and in many ways it set the stage for Sacco to take the comics form in his own direction.

Other important books of this new movement are Joe Kubert's *Fax from Sarajevo* (1996); Marjane Satrapi's *Persepolis* (2000); Guy Delisle's *Pyongyang: A Journey in North Korea* (2003) and *Burma Chronicles* (2007); Josh Neufeld's *A.D.: New Orleans after the Deluge* (2009); and Emmanuel Guibert, Didier Lefèvre, and Frederic Lemercier's *The Photographer: Into War-torn Afghanistan with Doctors without Borders* (2009). Many of these works have found their way into classroom courses and have created a new way of accessibly understanding events that have shaped the world. Like Sacco's work, these comics have much to say about the place of the individual creator in relation to sweeping global events.

notes that drawings "do not possess the same documentary quality as photographs" and consequently they "convey a sense of the constructed nature of news in a way that is unique to the form."

## BIBLIOGRAPHY

*Sources*

Binelli, Mark. "Joe Sacco's Cartoon Violence." *Rolling Stone* 22 Jan. 2004: 40–41. Print.

Nyberg, Amy Kiste. "Comics Journalism: Drawing on Words to Picture the Past in *Safe Area Gorazde*." *Critical Approaches to Comics: Theories and Methods.* Ed. Matthew J. Smith and Randy Duncan. New York: Routledge, 2012. Print.

Rev. of *Palestine,* by Joe Sacco. *Publishers Weekly.* PWxyz, 4 July 1994. Web. 23 Oct. 2012.

Sacco, Joe. *Palestine.* 1996. Seattle: Fantagraphics, 2001. Print.

Versaci, Rocco. *This Book Contains Graphic Language: Comics as Literature.* New York: Continuum, 2007. Print.

Woo, Benjamin. "Reconsidering Comics Journalism: Information and Experience in Joe Sacco's *Palestine*." *The Rise and Reason of Comics and Graphic Literature: Critical Essays on the Form.* Ed. Joyce Goggin and Dan Hassler-Forest. Jefferson: McFarland, 2010. 166–77. *Academia.edu.* Web. 15 Sept. 2012.

*Further Reading*

Blincoe, Nicholas. "Cartoon Wars." *New Statesman* 6 Jan. 2003: 26–27. Print.

A refugee camp in Gaza, 1992. Joe Sacco's graphic novel *Palestine* records his experiences as an American visiting Gaza and the West Bank in 1991 and 1992. © PETER TURNLEY/ CORBIS.

Crain, Liz. "An Interview with Joe Sacco." *Progressive* July 2011: 33–37. Print.

Doughty, Dick. "Palestine with Attitude." *Journal of Palestine Studies* 27.2 (1998): 99–100. Print.

Gilson, David. "The Art of War: An Interview with Joe Sacco." *Mother Jones.* Mother Jones and the Foundation for National Progress, July/Aug. 2005. Web. 15 Sept. 2012.

Thrill, Scott. "Joe Sacco on Comics, the Arabs and the Jews." *LA Weekly.* LA Weekly, 16 Jan. 2008. Web. 15 Sept. 2012.

*Marc Oxoby*

# PERSEPOLIS

*Marjane Satrapi*

## OVERVIEW

In the introduction to her autobiographical graphic novel *Persepolis* (2000), Marjane Satrapi presents one of her most important themes: "I believe that an entire nation should not be judged by the wrongdoings of a few extremists." Opening on the heels of the Islamic Revolution, *Persepolis*'s coming-of-age story scrolls forward through a shifting cultural landscape, backgrounded by the Iran-Iraq War and the lives of several generations of the author's family, who are living in a complicated political situation. The novel, which takes its name from the ancient Persian city, is an indictment of Iran's totalitarian government, as well as a child's-eye view of a beloved country in turmoil.

*Persepolis* documents changes in Iranian society resulting from the Islamic Revolution in 1979. Years of dissatisfaction with secular, Westernizing forces in the Iranian monarchy led to Shah Mohammad Reza Pahlavi's exile in 1979. In the vacuum created by his absence, Islamic leader Ruhollah Khomeini seized power, instituting a cleric-directed government, the Islamic Republic of Iran. That same year the Iranian hostage crisis, in which fifty-two employees in the American Embassy were held for 444 days, served to make Iran's new government highly unpopular with Westerners, especially those in the United States. Relations between the two countries have remained difficult in the years since and were further strained following the terrorist attacks of 9/11, which cast a wide net of suspicion on fundamentalist Islam. *Persepolis* evokes sympathy for everyday Iranians and is notable for making a complex portrait of Iranian life accessible to a broad Western audience.

## HISTORICAL AND LITERARY CONTEXT

The 1970s were years of unrest in Iran. The shah's regime faced opposition from conservative Islamic groups that were outraged by his secularization of the country, such as prohibitions on the hijab and other traditional Muslim dress. Middle-class, left-leaning intellectuals were angered by violations of the 1906 constitution, including acts of brutality inflicted by the shah's secret police. Further, the oil boom of the 1970s contributed to rising inflation and the institution of unpopular austerity measures while the royal family continued to live lavishly and profited from their lucrative oil dealings with the West. Years of

mounting protests led to a regime change in 1989, after which conditions in Iran changed dramatically. Public spaces became segregated by gender. Women, who had recently been marching bareheaded to protest the shah, were required to wear a hijab and were subject to detainment by roving morality police. Universities were closed down, as were the presses. Emigration began in earnest.

*Persepolis* was part of a wave of autobiography published by female Iranian expatriates in the early twenty-first century. The novel, which appeared as two volumes in its original French, was translated into English and published in the United States under the single title *Persepolis* in 2003, the same year in which the best-selling *Reading Lolita in Tehran* by Azar Nafisi appeared. Interest in the experience of people, and especially women, living under Islamist regimes was high following the September 11, 2001, terrorist attacks, and articles and news reports responded to this interest. However, U.S. media portrayals of Muslim women were often one note, painting them as cultural and religious victims with little agency of their own. Satrapi's account of her life in Iran is, in a sense, an argument against homogenized Western portrayals of Iranian people, especially women.

Art Spiegelman's *Maus,* which won the 1992 Pulitzer Prize, legitimized the graphic format as a medium equal to, or perhaps even especially suited to, the task of drawing attention to culturally significant topics such as fanatic nationalism and the fracturing of families during wartime and beyond. *Maus* layers a "present-day" narrative of an estranged father and son with the father's reluctant recounting of his experience as a Polish Jew during World War II. Similarly, *Persepolis* examines the difficult choices families face when living under totalitarian rule. Although the Satrapi family is loving and connected, the novel ends with the physical separation of Marjane from her parents when she is sent to live in Vienna for fear that her continued questioning of authority will have dire consequences. Like Spiegelman, Satrapi uses an accessible format as a means to gain a wider audience for her explorations.

Like *Maus* before it, *Persepolis* served to increase the cultural cachet of the graphic novel. It also transformed the career of its author, who was already successful in her adopted country of France. Satrapi went

**✦ Key Facts**

**Time Period:**
Late 20th-Early 21st Century

**Genre:**
Graphic Novel

**Events:**
Islamic Revolution in Iran; Iran-Iraq War

**Nationality:**
French-Iranian

## READING LOLITA IN TEHRAN

Published in 2003, the same year that *Persepolis* appeared in the United States, Azar Nafisi's *Reading Lolita in Tehran* chronicles the author's experiences as a university professor under the Islamic Republic government, as well as the book club she formed and directed until her emigration in 1997. On the best-seller list for more than 100 weeks, *Reading Lolita in Tehran* provides an interesting counterpoint to *Persepolis*.

Nafisi, who is a generation older than Marjane Satrapi, returned to Iran after studying in Switzerland and the United States and began teaching literature at the University of Tehran in 1979, the year of the revolution. Angered by the increasingly restrictive rules being applied to women, Nafisi refused to wear a hijab and was fired from several posts before finally resigning permanently from teaching. Her book club, which ran from 1995 to 1997, included works by Henry James, Jane Austen, and the infamous Vladimir Nabokov novel *Lolita*. *Reading Lolita in Tehran* documents Nafisi's attempts to grapple with her options as a woman under an oppressive regime, as well as with her students' attempts to grapple with some of the classics of the Western literary canon.

Although Nafisi's book received much positive attention, she was also criticized for perpetuating negative stereotypes about Muslim women and for placing herself in the privileged position of purveyor of culture—and Western high-brow culture at that. Columbia professor Hamid Dabashi, for example, compared her book to "the most pestiferous projects of the British in India."

on to produce a sequel, published in the United States as *Persepolis 2*, that deals with her time abroad and her subsequent return to Iran. She codirected the film version of *Persepolis*, which was released in 2007 to critical acclaim despite failing at the box office. Satrapi also wrote *Chicken with Plums* (2004), an acclaimed graphic novel that was made into a movie in 2011.

### THEMES AND STYLE

*Persepolis* explores the complexity of the coming-of-age experience, which is both universal and particular: relatable to her Western readers and specific to the Iran she experienced throughout childhood and into adolescence. Satrapi's experience is not typical, however, of Western media portrayals of growing up in Iran, which might perhaps be more in line with what is described in the chapter "The Key." The Key depicts scenes from a typical school day, during which Marji and her classmates are lined up twice a day to beat their breasts and mourn war martyrs. By contrast, the novel's first chapter, "The Veil," depicts Marji and her peers as they are forced to don the hijab after years of not wearing it. Rebelling, they do what most children would do with something they do not want to wear— repurpose it as a jump rope or a scary monster mask.

As the novel progresses, the hijab becomes a part of daily life, and the consequences for being caught without it—or for being caught with the Western tapes Marji buys on the black market—are far worse than the grounding a Western teenager might receive. Somewhat paradoxically, the child who resents the veil aspires to be a prophet and has nightly conversations with God.

As many critics have noted, Satrapi's use of a child narrator allows her to approach a broad audience with a narrative that contains elements both familiar and alien. The story is more nuanced than reporting on Iran might suggest. In a sense, many readers are positioned relative to events in Iran much the same way ten-year-old Marji is. She is uninitiated and trying to make sense of a host of contradictions; for instance, her father and mother are agitating to overthrow a king who is lauded by schoolbooks as "chosen by God" despite the fact that they also value her education and have chosen a good school. Marji herself is a bundle of contradictions, as illustrated by the veiled child on the book's front cover and the Westernized woman smoking a cigarette on the back inside flap.

In keeping with Satrapi's use of a child's-eye view, commentators have noted that the emotional tone of *Persepolis* is established by her simple, almost childlike illustrations. Similar to a child's perception of strange events, these images have a startling intensity, depth, and humor. Meanwhile, the dialogue, which has the rhythms of workaday family conversations and the bright curiosity of a child's questions, is often darkened by the heavy black-and-white drawings. The emotions of Marji's parents—her father's anger as he listens to stories of their friends' experiences as political prisoners or her mother's fear as she scolds Marji for arguing with her fundamentalist teachers—are visually unmistakable. Of course, Marji's mother also scolds her for cutting class and lying about it, to which Marji cheekily replies, "Dictator! You are the guardian of the revolution in this house!" This type of humor, which is often associated with some of the more universal elements in Marji's experience, is present throughout *Persepolis* and is also a key part of Satrapi's approach. The adult Marjane is often depicted as laughing at herself as a teenager or child, especially in frames where she draws her younger self meeting the reader's gaze directly.

### CRITICAL DISCUSSION

*Persepolis* was well received in both France and the United States. Writing for the *New York Times,* critic Fernanda Eberstadt calls the novel "delectable" and adds that *Persepolis* "dances with drama and insouciant wit." An early critical treatment of *Persepolis* by Nima Naghibi and Andrew O'Malley unpacks images of East and West in the novel and discusses the ways in which the treatment of these categories is subversive. The authors argue that *Persepolis* "upsets the easy categories and distinctions that it appears to endorse," for instance, between the secular West and religious East and between veiled and unveiled women. Satrapi herself told Michelle Goldberg, a writer for *Salon,* "The world is not divided between East and West. You are American, I am Iranian, we don't know each other, but we talk together and we understand each other perfectly."

*Persepolis* has become a work of significance in Western discourse about Iranian culture and, more generally, about the Western relationship with other peoples of the world. The novel was named one of *Newsweek*'s ten best fiction books of the decade and was made into an award-winning movie released in 2007, broadening its audience even further. Although traditional literature courses have tended to avoid the graphic novel as outside the canon, works such as *Persepolis* have gained traction as worthy objects of critical attention, perhaps helping to expand the criteria used to develop literature courses. Further, *Persepolis* is often taught at the high school level as its deceptively simple text lends itself to discussion of literary strategies and to teaching visual literacy, as well as to broader discussions of cultural difference as constructed in art and the media and as experienced in life.

Since its publication, *Persepolis* has been the subject of a variety of scholarship. Replying to Naghibi and O'Malley, *French Forum*'s Typhaine Leservot analyzes Satrapi's construction of the West in her novel as an example of Iranian Occidentalism, but an Occidentalism that rejects the "view that western influences in Iran are necessarily imperialistic" or "always used against the West." Leservot views Satrapi's "nuanced" reading of the appropriation of Western images by people too repressed to produce their own "counterdiscourse" as a valuable addition to postcolonial literary theory. Meanwhile, in examining both the novel and the film for *Forum for World Literature Studies* in 2011, Megan Gilbride focuses on Satrapi's use of visual storytelling to "close the gap between viewer and viewed, and between personal memory and official history." Similarly, in a 2007 issue of *symploke,* Babak Elahi uses theories of framing from the social sciences and from art criticism to examine Satrapi's use of mirrors "as a motif that doubly frames the self and allows for a deconstruction and reconstruction of Iranians as individuals who matter."

## BIBLIOGRAPHY

### Sources

Eberstadt, Fernanda. "God Looked Like Marx." *New York Times Book Review* 11 May 2003: 8. *Literature Resource Center.* Web. 3 July 2012.

Elahi, Babak. "Frames and Mirrors in Marjane Satrapi's *Persepolis.*" *symploke* 15.1-2 (2007): 312+. *Literature Resource Center.* Web. 4 July 2012.

Gilbride, Meghan. "Perceiving *Persepolis*: Personal Narrative, Sense Memories, and Visual Simplicity in Marjane Satrapi's Animated Autobiography."

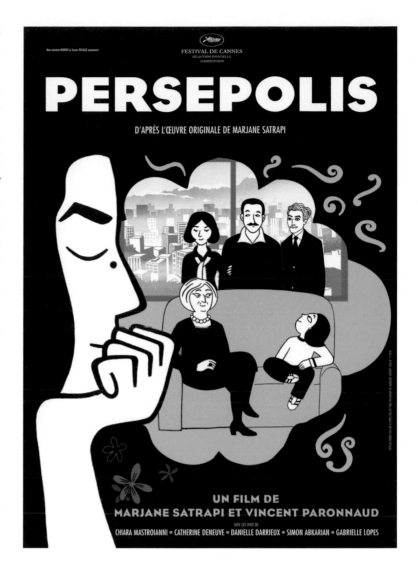

*Forum for World Literature Studies* 3.1 (2011): 137+. *Literature Resource Center.* Web. 3 July 2012.

Goldberg, Michelle. "Sexual Revolutionaries." *Salon* 24 Apr. 2005. Web. 4 July 2012.

Leservot, Typhaine. "Occidentalism: Rewriting the West in Marjane Satrapi's *Persepolis.*" *French Forum* 36.1 (2011): 115+. *Literature Resource Center.* Web. 3 July 2012.

Nafisi, Azar. *Reading Lolita in Tehran: A Memoir in Books.* New York: Random House, 2003. Print.

Naghibi, Nima, and Andrew O'Malley. "Estranging the Familiar: 'East' and 'West' in Satrapi's *Persepolis* (1)." *English Studies in Canada* 31.2–3 (2005): 223+. *Literature Resource Center.* Web. 3 July 2012.

Satrapi, Marjane. *Persepolis.* New York: Pantheon, 2003. Print.

Spiegelman, Art. *Maus/1, My Father Bleeds History.* New York: Pantheon Books, 1986. Print.

### Further Reading

Chun, Christian W. "Critical Literacies and Graphic Novels for English-Language Learners: Teaching *Maus*: Using Graphic Novels in the Classroom

A poster for the 2007 animated film based on Marjane Satrapi's graphic novel *Persepolis.* © SONY PICTURES CLASSICS/ COURTESY EVERETT COLLECTION.

Can Help Explain How Language Works Both for and against People and Enable Students to Acquire an Appreciation for Critical Literacy." *Journal of Adolescent & Adult Literacy* 53.2 (2009): 144+. *Literature Resource Center.* Web. 3 July 2012.

Chute, Hillary L. *Graphic Women: Life Narrative and Contemporary Comics.* New York: Columbia UP, 2010. Print.

Gooch, S. C., and Juan Meneses. "Political Engagements: Thinking Inside the Frame." *Forum for World Literature Studies* 3.1 (2011): 147+. *Literature Resource Center.* Web. 3 July 2012.

Malek, Amy. "Memoir as Iranian Exile Cultural Production: A Case Study of Marjane Satrapi's *Persepolis* Series." *Iranian Studies* 39.3 (2005): 353–80. Print.

Notkin, Debbie. "Growing Up Graphic." *Women's Review of Books* 20.9 (2003): 8. Rpt. in *Contemporary Literary Criticism.* Ed. Janet Witalec. Vol. 177. Detroit: Gale, 2004. *Literature Resource Center.* Web. 3 July 2012.

Satrapi, Marjane. *Persepolis 2.* New York: Pantheon, 2004. Print.

*Media Adaptation*

*Persepolis.* Dir. Vincent Paronnaud and Marjane Satrapi. Perf. Chiara Mastroianni, Catherine Deneuve, and Gena Rowlands. France 3 Cinéma, 2007. Film.

*Daisy Gard*

# THE POLITICAL HOUSE THAT JACK BUILT

*William Hone, George Cruikshank*

## OVERVIEW

*The Political House That Jack Built* is a satirical political pamphlet published in 1819 that was written by the English satirist William Hone and illustrated with woodcuts by George Cruikshank. Hone parodies the form of a popular British nursery rhyme in order to mock the repressive nature and venality of the Regent and to defend the freedom of the press and the rights of the common man. The pamphlet begins with an illustration of a treasure chest containing the Magna Carta, the Habeas Corpus Act, and the Bill of Rights, which together are the "Wealth that lay in the house that Jack built." As the narrative proceeds, this wealth is threatened by plundering "vermin," including the military, members of the government, and the Prince Regent. Ultimately it is the printing press that provides the poison to the vermin, and the tale concludes with a call for political reform. In this and other political satires by Hone, he works to expose the hypocrisy and bring attention to the abuses of power in the government.

In 1817 Hone was charged with libel for three political squibs that parodied religious texts. Despite—or, perhaps, because of—these charges, for which he was eventually acquitted, he became a national hero and continued to publish works that engaged with corrupt government officials. His acquittal meant de facto immunity from further libel prosecution, enabling him to continue creating his political parodies. *The Political House That Jack Built* sold more than 100,000 copies and reputedly ran to more than fifty editions. The power of the pamphlet lay in its ability to quickly disseminate a radical interpretation of contemporary politics to a broad group of the English public, many of whom were only semiliterate. Hone and Cruikshank repeated the format of their illustrated pamphlet in a series of highly successful publications over the next two years.

## HISTORICAL AND LITERARY CONTEXT

After the Napoleonic Wars ended in 1815, economic markets contracted, leaving many returned soldiers and citizens out of work or severely underemployed. In an attempt to protect British farmers, the government passed a series of laws known as the Corn Laws, which imposed tariffs on foreign grain and effectively made the cost of food higher for residents. As famine and unemployment rates rose, many individuals expressed interest in political reform, and a growing number turned to the radical press, mass petitioning, and trade unions, which were illegal, to protect the rights of the poor. Parliament failed to represent England's shifting demographics: the lower classes were marginalized economically and politically disenfranchised. For example, many industrial towns, such as Manchester, boasted large populations but had little to no representation in Parliament.

On August 16, 1819, the Manchester Political Union organized a gathering to address parliamentary reform and asked radical speaker and agitator Henry Hunt to speak at the event. The assembly drew a crowd of an estimated 60,000 people to a field just outside Manchester. Magistrates issued arrest warrants for Hunt and other organizers and, to disperse the gathering, sent cavalrymen, who charged into the crowd with their weapons drawn. In the resulting confusion, fifteen (sometimes reported to have been eleven or eighteen) people were killed and hundreds were injured in what became known as the Peterloo Massacre. This event gave rise to government attempts to suppress political reform through the passing of the Six Acts, which labeled any meeting for radical reform as "an overt act of treasonable conspiracy." *The Political House That Jack Built* celebrates the power of the free press and its ability to keep a repressive government in check.

Various forms of literature at the time took on the bourgeoning political discussion and became a key method of disseminating political ideas. Poets such as Percy Bysshe Shelley and Samuel Bamford offered literary responses to the Peterloo Massacre. Shelley's "Mask of Anarchy" was deemed too radical to be published because of the government crackdown following Peterloo, whereas Bamford's *Passages in the Life of a Radical* is largely considered to be the best account of Peterloo. William Cowper's lengthy 1785 poem *The Task* provides the epigraphs to each section of *The Political House That Jack Built*. Because of its melancholic sense of a bygone honorable social order as well as its social commentary on the foolishness of public life, *The Task* was an influential text on reform-minded individuals in the nineteenth century, especially during the later Regency period. After the success of *The Political House That Jack Built*, Hone and Cruikshank continued to create

✧ *Key Facts*

**Time Period:**
Early 19th Century

**Genre:**
Pamphlet

**Events:**
Peterloo Massacre; growing social unrest; passage of the Six Acts

**Nationality:**
English

# WILLIAM HONE'S TRIAL AND CONTRIBUTION TO PRINT CULTURE

William Hone (1780–1842) greatly shaped British popular print culture in the early part of the nineteenth century. Early in his career, print culture was primarily the realm of wealthy, upper classes; by his death in 1842, it had expanded to include a mass reading public. In January 1817 Hone published three popular squibs—*The Late John Wilkes's Catechism of a Ministerial Member; The Political Litany, Diligently Revised*; and *The Sinecurist's Creed, or Belief*—that were parodies of well-known passages from the Book of Common Prayer of the Anglican Church. Their rapid circulation caught the attention of Lord Sidmouth, who notified the attorney general Samuel Shepherd that the pamphlets were both blasphemous and seditious and were the catalyst of political and religious disaffection among those exposed to their ideas. On May 3, 1817, Shepherd had Hone arrested and imprisoned on three charges of blasphemous libel.

Hone, representing himself at trial, argued that his parodies did not bring the original liturgical texts into disrepute and that the originals only provided a serviceable form for his satiric attack on the government. To support his argument, he cited a collection of biblical parodies written by notable individuals, such as Martin Luther and then-cabinet minister George Canning. Hone argued that if he was guilty of blasphemy, then Canning should be tried for similar charges. His defense strategy worked, and the jury brought back not-guilty verdicts on all three charges. Hone printed the transcripts of the trial, and they were frequently reprinted throughout the nineteenth century, becoming a notable work in the history of the English press.

political squibs, including *The Man in the Moon* (1820), a dreamlike poem parodying the Prince Regent's 1820 address to Parliament; *The Queen's Matrimonial Ladder* (1820), which traces Queen Caroline's unfortunate marriage to the prince; and *The Political Showman—At Home!* (1821), which adopts the parlance of a carnival barker to display a series of unflattering caricatures of prominent political figures.

Wildly popular due to its ideas and its accessibility, *The Political House That Jack Built* provoked a number of imitations and adversary mimicries. One of the most interesting of these is *The Palace of John Bull, Contrasted with the Poor "House That Jack Built,"* which represented the wealthy constituents of Loyalist England through eight hand-painted copper engravings. The pamphlet sought to publicly denounce the prospects of radical reform by paralleling it with the cheap and plebian appeal of its propaganda. Illustrations in the pamphlet depicted that reform would leave crumbled buildings, burning hillsides, and roving gangs of "ruffian assemblies." Hone's political pamphlets and the growing tradition of radical writing also influenced writers such as Charles Dickens. In her book *Dickens*

*and the Popular Radical Imagination*, Sally Ledger argues that Dickens's choice of themes, his frequent use of the satiric and melodramatic modes favored by radical writers, and the political positions he takes in his novels reflect a deep relationship with the tradition of radical writing that can be traced back to the early pamphlets produced by Hone and Cruikshank. In Hone's unique multimedia approach to representing contemporary politics, his pamphlets anticipated the genre of illustrated political journalism.

## THEMES AND STYLE

Hone's central point in *The Political House That Jack Built* is a portrayal of the ways in which governmental figures undermine the popular liberties that constitute the wealth of England and how such abuses of power must be checked. With the clarity of a cartoon, his words mimic a nursery rhyme, while Cruikshank's woodcuts crystallize Hone's intention. Beginning with the "wealth that lay in the house that Jack built," which is represented by the Magna Carta, the Habeas Corpus Act, and the Bill of Rights, Hone incrementally introduces the "vermin" that threaten the wealth; the "thing" that will poison the vermin (the free press); the "public informer" who tries to silence the press; the "reason for lawless power" (government officials who seek to uphold the status quo); the "Dandy of Sixty" (the Prince Regent who Hone sees as responsible); the people "all tatter'd and torn" under attack by the yeomanry of Peterloo; and, finally, the "word"—*reform*—emblazoned on a flag in Cruikshank's woodcut, that will bring hope to England's political future.

The author makes these political ideas accessible to the average Englishperson by combining elements of different media to thoroughly represent the contemporary political situation. Hone's doggerel verse parodies the cumulative style and authoritative tone of an old nursery rhyme. In combination with Cruikshank's remarkable woodcuts as well as epigraphs taken from *The Task, The Political House That Jack Built* is a complex work of striking irony in which the whole is greater than the sum of its parts. While the illustrations work to clarify meaning and make the work accessible even to illiterate civilians, the epigraphs that are included on each page are often used ironically. For instance, describing the Regent, Hone uses the epigraph "Great offices will have Great talents," which comes from book IV of *The Task*. What follows, however, is a description of the "Dandy of Sixty," who has become more concerned with his private pleasures than his political alliances or the welfare of the state. The satirical mosaic created by Hone and Cruikshank creates a piece of political commentary that challenges the status quo and is widely accessible to a large swath of individuals.

Stylistically the pamphlet re-creates the simplistic quality of a nursery rhyme while providing biting irony and deep political ideas. Utilizing incremental repetitions typical of nursery rhymes that accumulate

George Cruikshank addresses political controversy in his 1819 illustration *Loyal Addresses and Radical Petitions*. Cruikshank also illustrated William Hone's antigovernment *The Political House That Jack Built* that same year. 'LOYAL ADDRESSES AND RADICAL PETITIONS,' 1819, CRUIKSHANK, GEORGE (1792–1878)/ GUILDHALL LIBRARY, CITY OF LONDON/THE BRIDGEMAN ART LIBRARY.

at the end, Hone calls attention to the "vermin"-like behavior of government officials that threaten to "plunder the wealth" and undermine the rights of citizens. His tone is scathing, boldly calling the Prince Regent a "Dandy of Sixty," while Cruikshank's picture depicts a portly man squeezed into a decorated military uniform that barely covers his bulging midsection. The closing lines of the section suggest that the Regent may be more dangerous than just a foppish embarrassment to the nation; in an "evil hour" this Regent takes into counsel "friends of the Reasons lawless power," suggesting that the Peterloo Massacre may have been carried out from the Regent's direct orders. Hone's text is defiant and tests the limits of free speech after the events of Peterloo. In his introduction Hone offers the epigraph "A straw—thrown up to show which way the wind blows," indicating his desire to see whether or not the pen will outweigh the combined force of legal and military oppression.

## CRITICAL DISCUSSION

The general reaction to Hone and Cruikshank's pamphlet was favorable, although the satire left certain members of the government feeling uneasy. While the public snapped up copies of the pamphlet in a whirlwind, according to Robert L. Patten in *George Cruikshank's Life, Times, and Art. Volume I: 1792–1835* (1992), the Regent wanted to prosecute Hone but could not because of the author's immunity garnered

from earlier acquittals. Much of the pamphlet's initial success can be attributed to Cruikshank's entertaining woodcuts, especially the caricatures of government officials. The depiction of the Prince Regent as the "Dandy of Sixty" was enlarged and sold separately with excerpts of Hone's verse, much to the chagrin of the prince and to the delight of the people.

The topical, political squibs produced by Hone and Cruikshank were written to expose what Hone felt to be abuses of power by the government, sentiments that resonated with the people of nineteenth-century England. His use of simple and straightforward language as well as easily recognizable cultural texts made his work instantly accessible to a wide variety of readers. As Kyle Grimes notes in *British Reform Writers, 1789–1832*, Hone's genius was not based on outstanding political or economic theory but rather on his "unsurpassed ability to publicize radical interpretations of contemporary political events to extremely large audiences." His radical pamphlet helped consolidate widespread antigovernment sentiment in order to push England toward the social ideals of free press and an equitable representative government.

Although Hone was a prolific writer and publisher in his time, his works respond to specific events that seem to today's readers as dated, and his pamphlets are not often ranked highly among works of great literature. Ben Wilson argues in his biography of Hone that the author deserves wider recognition for his role in creating a climate in which it was more difficult for politicians to silence the voice of the people. Similarly, Marcus Wood provides an illuminating analytic framework for radical satire in the Regency period in his book *Radical Satire and Print Culture, 1790–1822* (1994), in which he gives detail on the cultural context surrounding Hone's works. Wood's contribution also sheds light on the way in which Hone fused the literary inheritance of eighteenth-century satire with modern developments in advertising and mass marketing in a way that "demands breaking down genre distinctions and notions of high and low art." Hone's career as a humorist and his innovative embracing of mass marketing offer an example of how the tools of satire and parody can galvanize public opinion to initiate real social change.

## BIBLIOGRAPHY

### Sources

Grimes, Kyle. "William Hone." *British Reform Writers, 1789–1832. Dictionary of Literary Biography.* Vol. 158. Ed. Gary Kelly and Edd Applegate. Detroit: Gale, 1996. Web. 3 Aug. 2012.

Hone, William. *The Political House That Jack Built.* 1819. Ed. Kyle Grimes. *Romantic Circles.* U of Maryland, 1998. Web. 3 Aug. 2012.

Patten, Robert L. *George Cruikshank's Life, Times, and Art. Volume I: 1792–1835.* New Brunswick: Rutgers UP, 1992. *Google Books.* Web. 6 Aug. 2012.

Wilson, Ben. *The Laughter of Triumph: William Hone and the Fight for the Free Press.* London: Faber, 2005. Print.

Wood, Marcus. *Radical Satire and Print Culture, 1790–1822.* Oxford: Clarendon, 1994. Print.

### Further Reading

Bowden, Ann. *William Hone's Political Journalism, 1815–1821.* PhD Dissertation. U of Texas at Austin, 1975. Web. 6 Aug. 2012.

Kent, David A., and D. R. Ewen, eds. *Romantic Parodies, 1797–1831.* Rutherford: Fairleigh Dickinson, 1992. Print.

Marsh, Joss. *Word Crimes: Blasphemy, Culture and Literature in Nineteenth-Century England.* Chicago: U of Chicago P, 1998. Print.

McElligott, Jason. "William Hone (1780–1842), Print Culture, and the Nature of Radicalism." *Varieties of Seventeenth- and Early Eighteenth-Century English Radicalism in Context.* Ed. Ariel Hessayon and David Finnegan. London: Ashgate, 2011. 241–60. Print.

Rickword, Edgell, ed. *Radical Squibs and Loyal Ripostes: Satirical Pamphlets of the Regency Period, 1819–1821.* Bath: Adams, 1971. Print.

*Elizabeth Orvis*

# THE SILVER TASSIE

*Seán O'Casey*

## OVERVIEW

*The Silver Tassie*, a four-act play by Irish political play-wright Seán O'Casey that was first produced in 1929, tells the story of a group of working-class Dubliners during World War I. The first act is set in a Dublin tenement in the hours before a group of friends are to board a troopship that will take them to fight in the British army on the battlefields of France. The vigor of the young men is embodied in Harry Heegan, a talented young amateur soccer player, who helps his local team to win the cup, the "silver tassie," three times before going off to war. The manic, stylized second act is set on the battlefield, and in the postwar third act, we find Simon and Sylvester, who celebrated Harry's athleticism in Act One, at the hospital visiting Harry, who is paralyzed from the waist down. In the fourth act, Harry watches helplessly from a wheelchair as his pal Barney seduces his girlfriend, Jessie. This play, an expressionist piece of antiwar propaganda, attacks not only the pointlessness of war but also the callous disregard of those unaffected by war for its victims, a theme that had special resonance in the context of Irish nationalism in the 1920s.

Before *The Silver Tassie*, O'Casey was known for naturalistic dramas—in particular, the three plays that became known as his Dublin Trilogy: *The Shadow of a Gunman* (1923), *Juno and the Paycock* (1924), and *The Plough and the Stars* (1926). These radical plays, which dramatize the lives of working-class Dubliners, were performed at Dublin's Abbey Theatre, which was managed by the poet W. B. Yeats. In 1926, Yeats defended O'Casey when *The Plough and the Stars,* which is set in Dublin during the 1916 Easter Rising, triggered a riot because of its ambivalence regarding nationalist heroes. In 1928, however, Yeats rejected *The Silver Tassie,* and it was first produced in London, where O'Casey was then living.

## HISTORICAL AND LITERARY CONTEXT

As a young man, O'Casey was a supporter of the Irish nationalist cause and a member of the Irish Citizen Army until 1914. Following the failed 1916 Easter Rising, the subsequent executions by the British, and the signing of the Anglo-Irish Treaty in December 1921, Ireland was divided between those who supported the treaty that established the Irish Free State and those, including future Irish president Eamon de Valera, who advocated independence from the crown. O'Casey had a further complaint about the effects of the dispute over Ireland's autonomy: that nationalist causes had drawn attention away from more pressing issues of poverty and workers' rights.

*The Silver Tassie* is an explicitly antiwar play, but perhaps equally important is its treatment of World War I as an event in Irish history that was, by the late 1920s, becoming overshadowed by the Easter Rising in republican narratives. Although, as literary historian Jim Haughey points out, "Armistice Day services in Dublin drew huge crowds" even in the 1920s, a growing number of republican nationalists saw Irish involvement in the Great War as "a thinly disguised celebration of Ireland's imperial past." World War I was progressively erased from Irish historical narratives in the mid-twentieth century to the extent that it came to be described by Irish historians as the "Great Oblivion," a gap in Irish nationalist memory. While republican nationalism is not explicitly O'Casey's target in *The Silver Tassie,* the working-class soldiers, their lives destroyed by war, are, as Eamonn Hughes argues, the victims of "militarism in all its forms."

Many Irish writers, including George Bernard Shaw, James Joyce, and later Samuel Beckett, found that the political and religious atmosphere in their native country stifled artistic freedom. Although O'Casey moved to London in 1926 to oversee the production of *Juno and the Paycock,* he had firsthand experience with the difficulties of working in a divided nation. As described by the playwright in an exchange of letters with Yeats that was published in an August 1928 issue of the *Literary Digest, The Silver Tassie* reflects O'Casey's close acquaintance with working-class "wounded men fresh from the front ... the armless, the legless, the blind, the gassed, and the shell-shocked." The play is consistent with O'Casey's interest in documenting the war, in tracking its effects as he had done with Ireland's civil war in previous plays. In the letter that initiated the exchange, Yeats remarked, "You were interested in the Irish Civil War, and at every moment ... wrote out of ... your sense of its tragedy ... and you moved us as Swift moved his contemporaries." Such commentary places the work in the context of other contemporary antiwar plays, including Allan Monkhouse's *The Conquering Hero* (1923) and R. C. Sherriff's *Journey's End* (1928).

⁜ *Key Facts*

**Time Period:**
Mid-20th Century

**Genre:**
Play

**Events:**
World War I; Easter Rising; Irish struggle for independence

**Nationality:**
Irish

# SEÁN O'CASEY

Seán O'Casey (1880–1964) was born in Dublin, left school at age fourteen, and worked in various manual jobs, including as a railwayman, while developing an interest in amateur theater. He became involved in the trade union movement and was both a socialist and a nationalist before becoming increasingly disillusioned with nationalism after 1914. Though O'Casey did not serve in World War I, his brothers were soldiers, and he spent time in hospitals visiting the wounded. He started writing plays in 1917, and *The Shadow of a Gunman* was first performed at the Abbey Theatre in Dublin in 1923. By the time *The Silver Tassie* was performed in London in 1929, O'Casey was celebrated as a dramatist in Ireland and England, his adopted home.

O'Casey traveled to England in 1926 to receive the Hawthornden Prize for his play *Juno and the Paycock,* and in 1949 he also accepted an award from the Newspaper Guild of New York. He was a principled and determined man, however, who never gave up his socialist and republican views, and he would not accept the rule of the monarchy in Britain. In 1963 he turned down the honor Commander of the British Empire, as well as honorary degrees from Durham University and from Trinity College Dublin, because of changes he was required (but refused) to make to his play *The Drums of Father Ned* in 1958.

O'Casey's experiment with expressionism in the second act of *The Silver Tassie* was a new and ambitious approach to dramatizing the trenches.

Yeats's rejection of *The Silver Tassie* for performance at the Abbey Theatre angered O'Casey and signaled the end of his relationship with the theater. It also separated the play from the plays that make up the Dublin Trilogy. As a result, Hughes suggests, the critique of nationalism in the earlier works has become detached from the explicitly antiwar message of *The Silver Tassie,* to the detriment of all four plays. *The Silver Tassie* relates less specifically to the context of Irish republicanism than the earlier plays, and its more universal antiwar message made it suitable for adaptation in 1999 in an acclaimed opera by composer Mark-Anthony Turnage.

## THEMES AND STYLE

The four-act structure of *The Silver Tassie* emphasizes the contrast between pre-war and postwar societies by focusing on the transition of Harry from athlete to invalid, of Susie Monican from Bible-wielding moralizer to flirtatious good-time girl, and of Teddy from violent husband to blind dependent who must be led around by the wife he once abused. The physical destruction of the men's bodies parallels the transformation of their families and community. Lives shattered by war are being remade, and the past is being erased by a new narrative when, in the final act, the silver tassie is crushed. Harry declaims from his wheelchair: "Mangled and bruised as I am bruised and mangled. Hammered free from all its comely shape. Look, there

is Jessie writ, and here is Harry, the one name safely separated from the other. (*He flings it on the floor.*) Treat it kindly. With care it can be opened out, for Barney there to drink with Jess, and Jess to drink with Barney."

O'Casey presents his four acts in three distinct styles, beginning with the boisterous, comedic naturalism of Act One. He portrays the characters as people unconscious of their condition: Harry Heegan is described in the stage directions as "sensible by instinct rather than by reason. He has gone to the trenches as unthinkingly as he would go to the polling booth." The expressionistic Act Two, set in the trenches but without the sound of bombardment, represents the moment at which Harry and his friends might see what is happening to them. A corporal sings a litany to a gun, "Hail cool-hardened tower of steel emboss'd," to which the soldiers reply, as if to a priest before an altar, "We believe in God and we believe in thee." In the third act, set in a hospital, Susie Monican, now a nurse, conspires in the dehumanization of the injured men, referring to them only by their bed numbers, but the tragedy thus symbolized is leavened by an absurd humor. After Harry has railed against the world, the Sister enters, and she responds to Harry as though his anger was merely a childish tantrum:

> Sister: (*to Harry*) Keeping brave and hopeful, twenty-eight?
>
> Harry: (*softly*) Yes, Sister.
>
> Sister: Splendid. And we've got a ukelele, too. Can you play it, my child?

Harry's isolation on his return to society, as Declan Hiberd has argued, represents "an eerie continuation of his condition in the war zone, where each soldier stood on a spookily silent set and 'only flashes are seen. No noise is heard.'" In the fourth act, Harry, in his diminished position, is cut off from the festivities and left behind by his girlfriend, Jessie, and her new lover, the hero Barney. Barney saved Harry's life but has taken away the thing that made it worth living.

The play turns on the second act, and the tone evoked in this jarring, disorienting interruption in the lives of the characters—in a war zone in which "every feature of the scene seems a little distorted"—is key. The features of this scene—the unseen enemy, chanted Latin liturgy from a ruined monastery, staccato exchanges between the soldiers, and a grim depiction of the injured being taken away on stretchers—create a bleak and frightening representation of the battlefield. Rather than recreating the scene naturalistically, however, O'Casey renders it, perhaps for the first time, as a felt experience for his audience.

## CRITICAL DISCUSSION

With *The Silver Tassie,* Yeats thought that O'Casey had stepped across a line between political theater and propaganda. In the aforementioned letter published in the *Literary Digest,* Yeats wrote to the dramatist, "But you

Gwynne Howell plays "The Croucher" in Mark-Anthony Turnage's 2000 opera adaptation of *The Silver Tassie.* © ARENAPAL/ THE IMAGE WORKS.

arc not interested in the Great War; you never stood on its battlefields or walked its hospitals, and so write out of your opinions." Yeats instructed him: "Among the things that dramatic action must burn up are the author's opinions." George Bernard Shaw, who shared O'Casey's political views, attributed Yeats's uneasiness to his unwillingness to face reality. In *Rose and Crown,* O'Casey recalls Shaw's letter: "If Yeats had said 'It's too savage; I can't stand it' he would have been in order." *The Silver Tassie* was eventually performed in London in October 1929, and the *Times* of London gave it a positive review, remarking that in the play "we move in a new plane of imagination" and calling it "extravagant" while also pointing out that it "fails sometimes with a great stumbling failure. But it is a method with a future." When the play was performed in Ireland in 1935, as noted in Keith Jeffery's *Ireland and the Great War,* people rioted because of its blasphemy and bad language. Brinsley Macnamara, one of the directors of the Abbey Theatre, wrote a long diatribe to the *Irish Independent* against the play and subsequently resigned from the theater, according to Richard Cary.

Perhaps because of the coherence of the Dublin Trilogy, *The Silver Tassie* is not often discussed in isolation from the earlier plays. As John Countryman points out, the play has often been misinterpreted, particularly in regard to Susie's final speech, in which she says, "Come along and take your part in life!" Some critics have interpreted this as an optimistic conclusion. The play's second act, however, belies such an interpretation and marks a significant change, not only in O'Casey's dramatic technique, but perhaps also in his artistic vision. James R. Scrimgeour outlines this shift: "[I]n the second act of *The Silver Tassie,* O'Casey shows us the horrors of war by creating a mood of sadness, waste, and desolation. After watching *The Plough and the Stars,* we feel sorry for Lieutenant Langon and Bessie Burgess, but after watching the second act of *The Silver Tassie,* we feel a world-sorrow, a sorrow for all the waste of life in this world."

Largely because of Yeats's intervention, *The Silver Tassie* has been seen as separate from the Dublin Trilogy and as a lesser work. In addition, the difficulty of putting on a play with such a large cast and four complete changes of scene has contributed to its being performed less often than the earlier plays. But it is perhaps more useful to consider *The Silver Tassie* as part of O'Casey's struggle to produce political plays about the working class at a time when nationalism, rather than life at the sharp end of capitalism, was the pressing issue in Ireland. By the late twentieth century, critics and scholars better understood this aspect of O'Casey's work. As Ben Levitas writes, O'Casey "garrulously contemplated" the "great gap" between rhetoric and politics. *The Silver Tassie* can thus be viewed as part of an artistic movement toward finding a new mode of expression that discarded the old mannerisms of political theater. O'Casey was an overtly political writer, but he wrote in his autobiography that he was "a voluntary exile from every creed, from every party, and from every literary clique."

## BIBLIOGRAPHY

*Sources*

Cary, Richard, "Two Casey Letters." *Colby Quarterly* 9.10 (1972): 547–55. Print.

"A Dublin Tempest." *Literary Digest* 4 Aug. 1928: 24–25. Print.

Haughey, Jim. *The First World War in Irish Poetry.* Lewisburg: Bucknell UP, 2002. Print.

Hughes, Eamonn. "'…What's far worse, it'll have two mothers': Rhetoric and Reproduction in Sean O'Casey's Dublin Quartet." *Journal of Irish Studies* (2005): 148. Print.

Jeffery, Keith. *Ireland and the Great War.* Cambridge: Cambridge UP, 2000. Print.

Kiberd, Declan. *Inventing Ireland: The Literature of the Modern Nation.* London: Vintage, 1995. 244. Print.

Levitas, Ben. "Plumbing the Depths: Irish Realism and the Working Class from Shaw to O'Casey." *Irish University Review* 33.1 (2003): 133. Print.

O'Casey, Sean. *Plays 2.* London: Faber, 1988. Print.

Scrimgeour, James R. *Sean O'Casey.* Boston: Twayne, 1978. 111–38. *Gale Virtual Reference Library.* Web. 11 July, 2012.

*Further Reading*

Countryman, John. "It's a hell of a play!" *Irish Literary Supplement* 31.2 (2012): 14. *General OneFile.* Web. 11 July 2012.

Kenneally, Michael. *Portraying the Self: Sean O'Casey & the Art of Autobiography.* Gerrards Cross: Smythe, 1998. Print.

Krause, David. *Sean O'Casey and His World.* New York: Scribner, 1976. Print.

McAteer, Michael. *Yeats and European Drama.* Cambridge: Cambridge UP, 2010. Print.

Murray, Christopher. *Sean O'Casey, Writer at Work.* Dublin: Gill, 2004. Print.

O'Casey, Sean. *Innisfallen Fare Thee Well.* London: Macmillan, 1948. Print.

———. *Rose and Crown.* London: Macmillan, 1950. Print.

Sternlicht, Sanford. *Masterpieces of Modern British and Irish Drama.* Westport: Greenwood, 2005. Print.

*Media Adaptation*

*The Silver Tassie.* Dir. Bill Bryden. Perf. Gerald Finley, Sarah Connolly, Vivian Tierney, et al. Designer William Dudley. Conductor Paul Daniel. BBC2, 2002. VHS.

*Chris Routledge*

# U.S.A.

*John Dos Passos*

## OVERVIEW

Written by John Dos Passos and comprising the novels *The 42nd Parallel* (1930), *1919* (1932), and *The Big Money* (1936), the *U.S.A.* trilogy paints an elaborate portrait of the United States during the first three decades of the twentieth century. The novels alternate between four distinct narrative techniques—straightforward third-person narration of the lives of twelve characters; biographical sketches of prominent American figures; "Newsreel" sections of actual newspaper headlines, song lyrics, advertising slogans, and government propaganda; and stream-of-consciousness "Camera Eye" segments that present the author's personal reactions to the narrative. In the trilogy, Dos Passos presents a vision of a nation in decline, torn apart by class divisions and political conflict. This overarching tone of disillusionment becomes more pronounced as the trilogy progresses, leading ultimately to a refutation of the notion of America as the land of "liberty and justice for all" with the oft-repeated phrase "alright we are two nations."

As a member of the so-called Lost Generation of American writers—authors known for their depictions of the destruction of idealism by the horrors of World War I—Dos Passos in his previous works had explored both antiwar themes and questions of the role of the individual in a modern society characterized by mass communication, political fragmentation, and widespread alienation. In the *U.S.A.* trilogy, he incorporates these themes into the formal structure of the work itself, reflecting the fragmentation and chaos of the postwar period in a fragmentary, multiperspectival work. This technique of making the nation as a whole, and not any single character, the focus of the trilogy has led critics to deem Dos Passos a pioneer of the collectivist novel.

## HISTORICAL AND LITERARY CONTEXT

The *U.S.A.* trilogy is a work of the American Lost Generation, which was profoundly shaped by World War I and its repercussions, including the growing gap between the wealthy and the poor, and increased control over information by the government as socialism and communism came to be seen as direct threats to American capitalism. Many labor unions, influenced by socialist ideals, formed to combat economic inequality and poor working conditions, leading to violent clashes between unionized workers and the police, who represented the interests of wealthy industrialists and the state. Along with political upheaval and social dissatisfaction, the early decades of the twentieth century were also marked by the rise of public relations and advertising, two disciplines that utilized newly invented mass communications techniques to influence political and economic decisions and to combat dissent from political activists in America and around the world.

The government's blatant manipulation of public opinion to manufacture consent for what many believed to be a senseless war was seen by Dos Passos and others as the beginning of a dangerous collusion between mass media and the state. The murder trial and 1927 execution of Italian anarchists Nicola Sacco and Bartolomeo Vanzetti seemingly confirmed their worst fears. Dos Passos reported on the highly charged trial and was among many leading artists who vehemently decried what they believed to be an unfair process based not on a desire for justice but rather on government-sponsored antiradical politics and the abuse of the poor, largely influenced by biased journalism and governmental paranoia. The execution of Sacco and Vanzetti, along with the war and various other historical events, like a 1931 coal miners' strike in Harlan County, Kentucky, that left eleven people dead, are depicted in the *U.S.A.* trilogy as the events that define modern America and leave significant portions of the country feeling marginalized and ultimately defeated by forces outside of their control.

Dos Passos designed his trilogy to reflect his generation's disillusionment with previously held ideals such as individualism, freedom, and democracy, and attempts to fill the void with something other than petty materialism and nationalist rhetoric. In this way, the trilogy stands alongside F. Scott Fitzgerald's *The Great Gatsby* (1925), Ernest Hemingway's *The Sun Also Rises* (1926) and *A Farewell to Arms* (1929), and T. S. Eliot's groundbreaking poem "The Waste Land" (1922) as a vital work of the lost generation and a critical assessment of American idealism. As in "The Waste Land," Dos Passos does not provide any resolution to the alienation of the individual in the *U.S.A.* trilogy, but instead depicts a world in which the individual is subject to the whims of an authoritarian government and a myopic ruling class, adrift in a sea of historical

❖ *Key Facts*

**Time Period:**
Early 20th Century

**Genre:**
Novel

**Events:**
World War I; rise of advertising and public relations; murder trial and execution of Italian anarchists Nicola Sacco and Bartolomeo Vanzetti

**Nationality:**
American

# DOS PASSOS AND HEMINGWAY

Perhaps no single time period has produced as many important literary figures as the years following World War I. John Dos Passos was one of the most important members of the group now referred to as the Lost Generation. As World War I began, Dos Passos found himself in Europe volunteering with friends and future Lost Generation artists E. E. Cummings and Robert Hillyer for the Ambulance Corps. He also would see action as an ambulance driver in Paris and Italy.

Another famous American writer, Ernest Hemingway, worked as an ambulance driver during World War I. Later, he and Dos Passos would become close friends, eventually traveling to Spain to report on and fight in the Spanish Civil War. However, their friendship unraveled. Dos Passos grew disillusioned with the socialist cause when his friend, photographer José Robles, was killed by socialist fighters and the murder was covered up. The incident was among the first events that pushed Dos Passos away from socialism and toward a more conservative political viewpoint. Hemingway would go on to refer insultingly to Dos Passos as a "pilot fish"; however it seems more likely that Dos Passos was simply the most critically invested and politically sensitive member of the Lost Generation.

forces outside of his or her control. This dejection is often seen as a counterpoint to the inclusiveness and optimism of Walt Whitman, the nineteenth-century "poet of democracy."

In the twenty-first century, the *U.S.A.* trilogy is best remembered not for its politics but for its stylistic innovations and the accuracy and poignancy of its depiction of the United States during the early twentieth century. The montages of newspaper headlines and songs, as well as the brief personal reminiscences, bring the conflict between individual experience and mass culture into concrete focus. The trilogy remains an important piece of American literature as well as Dos Passos's best-known work, and its stylistic explorations have influenced countless writers to push the boundaries of traditional realism.

### THEMES AND STYLE

The themes of the *U.S.A.* trilogy center on the threat to democracy posed by industrialization, mass media, and government-sponsored manipulation of public opinion in the early decades of the twentieth century. As Matthew Stratton argues in a 2008 essay for *Twentieth Century Literature,* "Continually reminding his readers how susceptible public opinion actually was to the manipulation of language, [Dos Passos] reveals the notion of a rationally formed and informed public opinion not just as hopelessly naive but as actively harmful." As such, the trilogy features a number of characters who partake in and are ultimately disheartened by the dissemination of

information to the public. Jerry Burnham, a war correspondent, complains that "a newspaperman had been little more than a skunk before the war, but … now there wasn't anything low enough you could call him." Mary French, a reporter who writes stories sympathizing with striking coalminers, has her work rejected by the newspaper editor, who complains that her depiction of the miners does not fit into the national narrative about union members being dangerous and subversive communists. Fainy "Mac" McCreary is reprimanded by the police for attempting to distribute prounion pamphlets and eventually abandons his socialist beliefs in disgust. Perhaps the most powerful indictments of the media environment in the early twentieth century are the swirling newsreel sections, which juxtapose patriotic lyrics with manipulative headlines and jingoistic slogans such as "REDS WEAKENING WASHINGTON HEARS" and "MACHINEGUNS MOW DOWN MOBS IN KNOXVILLE."

Part of Dos Passos's rhetorical strategy for depicting the divide between those who "control the means of information production" and those who are subject to its influence is to emphasize the alienation, anonymity, and impotency of the common citizen in modern America. In contrast to the biographical sketches of powerful Americans like J. P. Morgan, Thomas Edison, Henry Ford, and Andrew Carnegie (each of whom made enormous profits in the years surrounding World War I), Dos Passos famously describes the body of an unknown soldier returned from the war in a pine box "containing what they'd scraped up of Richard Roe and other person or persons unknown." That the soldier's body parts are interchangeable with those of other anonymous soldiers while Ford, Edison, and the like are portrayed as distinct, larger-than-life public figures underscores the theme that common individuals have become less important to society as the United States has grown.

The language and tone of "The Body of an American," the final section of *1919,* are emblematic of the pessimistic attitude of the trilogy as a whole and contribute to the image of America as "two nations." Dos Passos plays with language in the section, leaving no spaces between the words when speaking in the voice of Congress to accentuate the hollowness of the official-sounding words as they zoom past. He describes the life of the dead soldier as a pastiche of all soldiers' lives ("John Doe was born and raised in Brooklyn, in Memphis, near the lakefront in Cleveland, Ohio, in the stench of the stockyards in Chi, on Beacon Hill, in an old brick house in Alexandria Virginia, on Telegraph Hill, in a halftimbered Tudor cottage in Portland the city of roses"), emphasizing the commonness of his life and death in contrast to the privileged position of "the diplomats and the generals and the admirals and the brasshats and the politicians and the handsomely dressed ladies out of the society column of the *Washington Post.*"

## CRITICAL DISCUSSION

According to the critic Daniel Aaron, the *U.S.A.* trilogy immediately "secured Dos Passos's place in American literary history." The overwhelming reaction to the works as they were published was both immediate and positive. Dos Passos's literary and political reputation led to his being featured on the cover of *Time* magazine in 1936. Perhaps the most notable quotation regarding the author and his place in American and international letters came from the French philosopher and writer Jean-Paul Sartre, who in 1936 declared Dos Passos "the greatest writer of our time." Lauded for his prescient and thoughtful politics and stylistic innovations, the author would later find himself more popular in Europe than in the United States.

The *U.S.A.* trilogy has remained immensely popular and critically esteemed. Aaron, one of the leading Dos Passos critics, has remarked, "[N]o other novelist of his times had so ingeniously evoked the scope and variety of the United States." While some critics like Malcolm Cowley have found the work excessively pessimistic ("for all their scope and richness, they fail to express one side of contemporary life—the will to struggle ahead, the comradeship in struggle, the consciousness of new men and new forces constantly rising"), Dos Passos has remained a vital American writer, his name tied inexorably to the experimental forms of literary modernism and the existential soul-searching of American letters at the turn of the twentieth century.

In recent years, Dos Passos' reputation has somewhat declined, a phenomenon that some attribute to his gradual turn toward right-wing politics and abandonment of his earlier convictions. Others suggest that his white-male-centric depiction of the early twentieth century is too narrow to be applicable to contemporary understandings of American history. Critic Townsend Ludington in a 1996 essay for *Virginia Quarterly Review* notes that Dos Passos is "regularly anthologized" but "rarely is he eulogized." In other words, there remains broad recognition of the writer's talent and the importance of his best works, but he has not retained the fame of some of his less politically minded contemporaries. Ludington also writes, "[A]nyone wishing to dismiss Dos Passos should remember that he was an intelligent, thoughtful man of letters who agonized about his politics." Because of Dos Passos's changing political beliefs, the *U.S.A* trilogy is remembered less for its political stance and more for its stylistic experimentation and its detailed depiction of the United States after World War I.

## BIBLIOGRAPHY

*Sources*

Aaron, Daniel. "U.S.A." *American Heritage* 47.4 (1996): 63. Print.

Cowley, Malcolm. "John Dos Passos: The Poet and the World." *Dos Passos: A Collection of Critical Essays.* Ed. Andrew Hook. New Jersey: Prentice Hall, 1974. 76–86. Print.

John Dos Passos in the late 1930s. © EVERETT COLLECTION INC./ALAMY.

Dos Passos, John. *U.S.A.* New York: Library of America, 1996. Print.

Ludington, Townsend. "John Dos Passos, 1896–1970: Modernist Recorder of the American Scene." *Virginia Quarterly Review* Autumn 1996: 565–80. Print.

Sartre, Jean-Paul. *Literary and Philosophical Essays* New York: Criterion, 1955. Print.

Stratton, Matthew. "Start Spreading the News: Irony, Public Opinion, and the Aesthetic Politics of *U.S.A.*" *Twentieth Century Literature* 54.4 (2008): 419–47. Print.

*Further Reading*

Beach, Joseph Warren, "Dos Passos 1947." *Sewanee Review* Summer 1947: 406–18. Print.

Carr, Virginia Spencer. *Dos Passos: A Life.* Chicago: Northwestern UP, 2004. Print.

Dos Passos, John. *Manhattan Transfer.* New York: Mariner, 2003. Print.

———. *One Man's Initiation—1917.* New York: Nabu, 2010. Print.

———. *Three Soldiers.* New York: Nabu, 2010. Print.

Landsberg, Melvin. *Dos Passos' Path to U.S.A.: A Political Biography: 1912–1936.* Boulder: Colorado Assoc. UP, 1972. Print.

Luddington, Townsend. *John Dos Passos: A Twentieth-Century Odyssey.* New York: Carroll and Graf, 1998. Print.

Nanney, Lisa. *John Dos Passos Revisited.* New York: Twayne, 1998. Print.

Rosen, Robert C. *John Dos Passos: Politics and the Writer.* Lincoln: U of Nebraska P, 1981. Print.

*Colby Cuppernull*

# HISTORIES

# THE BROKEN SPEARS
## The Aztec Account of the Conquest of Mexico
*Miguel León-Portilla*

## OVERVIEW

*The Broken Spears: The Aztec Account of the Conquest of Mexico,* originally *La visión de los vencidos: Relaciones indígenas de la conquista,* by Miguel León-Portilla with Ángel María Garibay Kintana, was published in Spanish in 1959 and in English in 1962. León-Portilla's book compiles the accounts of indigenous peoples of Aztec descent describing the sixteenth-century Spanish conquest of Mexico. *Broken Spears* is notable as one of the earliest scholarly texts to publish in Spanish (and later in English) Mesoamerican indigenous documents originally written in Nahuatl, the native language of the indigenous people. León-Portilla's arrangement of the documents is roughly chronological, and his introduction and conclusion to each account construct a specific historical narrative that reflects his authorial perspective. León-Portilla's work serves as propaganda by sympathetically presenting the "vision of the defeated/conquered." His translations give voice to a population traditionally marginalized and subordinated in Mexico's history.

In *Broken Spears,* León-Portilla follows in the footsteps of his academic mentor, Fray Angel María Garibay K., who translated and published numerous Nahuatl documents beginning in the 1930s. *Broken Spears* enjoyed a warm reception among English-language scholars, who saw it as an invaluable resource providing insight into the perspective of the "other side" of the Spanish conquest. León-Portilla contributes a unique timeline of the reactions of native inhabitants, from the arrival of the Spanish conquerors through the aftermath of the conquest and the survivors' attempts to adapt to life as a conquered people. The work is notable in the way that its chronological structure and the author's historical commentary place different indigenous accounts in dialogue with each other. Since its publication, *Broken Spears* has been regarded as a significant historical document and is often referenced in scholarly discussions of the Spanish conquest.

## HISTORICAL AND LITERARY CONTEXT

The political and economic crisis that began in Mexico in the 1950s culminated in 1968 with the massacre of protesters associated with the Mexican Student Movement. Mexico was struggling to maintain its autonomy in the international political arena while floundering economically in the world market. The state's myth of national populism and its attempts to forge unity with massive state-promoted cultural projects were faltering, and unrest was going among long-oppressed indigenous, mestizo, student, and lower-class groups. Secret police and military forces used coercion and force to maintain the hegemony of the state—a good example being the suppression of the Railroad Workers Union's strikes during 1958 and 1959 and the imprisonment of union leaders by the government.

While pursuing his doctoral studies at the Autonomous University of Mexico (UNAM) in Mexico City, León-Portilla was conscious of the growing unrest, and his work was in part an attempt to contribute to the national and international understanding of indigenous culture and history. During this period, the *indigenismo* movement—a component of the cultural nationalist movement left over from former President Álvaro Obregón's post-revolutionary project that idealized and romanticized indigenous culture as a central part of the nation's past, but not its present—was prominent. *Indigenista* promoted *mestizaje* (race-mixing), which encouraged indigenous peoples' assimilation into Mexican society. Garibay and León-Portilla contested this essentialist understanding of indigenous culture, advocating a more profound appreciation and comprehension of the indigenous community.

One of the central works of *indigenismo* was Manuel Gamio's *Forjando patria: pro nacionulismo* (1916), which urged indigenous Mexicans to completely assimilate into the nation's racially mixed society. By contrast, *Broken Spears* carries on the tradition of Garibay, who published, among other things, a Spanish translation of the 1528 Aztec document *Anales de Tlatelolco* (1956), which provided new insights into the conquered indigenous community. In 1953 scholars Adrian Recinos, Delia Goetz, and Jose Chonay published *The Annals of the Cakchiquels (Title of the Lords of Totonicapan),* translated from the original Mayan. These works reflect the interest of Latin American scholars in recovering the history and cultural legacy of Mesoamerican prehispanic civilizations.

León-Portilla's seminal work in *Broken Spears* clearly influenced his successors in the sphere of Mesoamerican, and particularly Nahuatl, studies.

✣ **Key Facts**

**Time Period:**
Mid-20th Century

**Genre:**
History

**Events:**
Growing struggle for indigenous peoples' rights; Spanish conquest of Mexico

**Nationality:**
Mexican

# THE MEXICAN STUDENT MOVEMENT OF 1968

The Mexican Student Movement was a product of the same political and cultural changes that produced *Broken Spears*: the mounting public awareness of and struggle against government oppression. Often compared to roughly contemporaneous movements around the globe, it was enabled by a growing middle class whose prosperity fueled university enrollment and, with it, increased political dialogue. By the summer of 1968, student political groups were gaining momentum. Like their counterparts in the United States and elsewhere, these students rejected what they saw as outdated political and social ideologies. The immediate impetus for a unified student movement was the police crackdown on protestors before the 1968 Summer Olympics, scheduled to begin in Mexico City on October 12.

On October 2 thousands of students assembled in Mexico City's Tlatelolco Plaza. After shots were fired at soldiers who were attempting to arrest movement leaders, the soldiers opened fire on the crowd. Although official reports claimed that only four people had died, many witnesses maintained that hundreds were killed. Following the massacre, then-president Ernesto Zedillo's government propaganda labeled the movement's leaders Communist subversives and insisted that they had initiated the violence. After the election of President Vicente Fox in 2000, new attempts were made to uncover the truth about the massacre. Although much about the incident remains unknown, investigators revealed evidence that the initial shots were fired not by protestors but by snipers from Mexico's elite Presidential Guard who hoped to quash the student movement by inciting violence.

For example, his influence is apparent in the scholarship of Fernando Horcasitas, whose works include *De Porfirio Díaz a Zapata. Memoria Náhuatl de Milpa Alta* (1965) and *The Aztecs Then and Now* (1979). Other works that followed the work of León-Portilla and Garibay include *Beyond the Codices* (1976), compiled and edited by Arthur Anderson, Frances Berdan, and James Lockhart, and *Nahuatl in the Middle Years: Language Contact Phenomena in Texts of the Colonial Period* (1976), edited by Frances Karttunen and Lockhart. These works expanded the field of Nahuatl studies, bringing to light significant historical sources that had previously been discarded or marginalized. Current scholars of indigenous Mexican history and Mesoamerican culture continue to turn to *Broken Spears* as an important historical source.

## THEMES AND STYLE

As a compilation of multiple historical documents related to the history of the indigenous Mexican community, *Broken Spears* reconstructs the reactions and experiences of members of these communities during the sixteenth-century Spanish conquest and its immediate aftermath. Despite the fact that the majority of the text incorporates the voices of these very communities, the text also reflects León-Portilla's sympathetic position, evident in the introductions and conclusions to the different sections. In the book's introduction, the author states, "On November 8, 1519, the Spanish conquistadors first entered the great city of Mexico, the metropolis the Aztecs built on a lake island … It was the first direct encounter between one of the most extraordinary pre-Columbian cultures and the strangers who would eventually destroy it." León-Portilla's emphasis on the grandeur of Aztec civilization and the destructive aims of the conquistadors in this passage is exemplary of the incorporation of his authorial perspective and opinion, which sides with and advocates for the conquered.

León-Portilla elucidates the advanced nature of Aztec culture in his praise for the eloquence and lyricism of the indigenous texts he presents in *Broken Spears*: "We have chosen two different accounts of the massacre, both written originally in Nahuatl. They describe it with a realism comparable to that of the great epic poems of classical antiquity." The direct parallel constructed between the classic epic poems and the Nahuatl accounts presented in the text and the direct authorial intervention in the book exemplify León-Portilla's sympathetic representation of these indigenous documents. It is also important to note that the author's decision to organize the text in chronological order, despite certain discrepancies and contradictions, which the author himself admits, was critical to the construction of a dramatic and powerful narrative of the indigenous community's experiences of the conquest.

León-Portilla conveys his authorial perspective by employing an emotional tone in his introduction to indigenous passages that further dramatizes their experiences. Discussing the experiences of Aztec leader Motecuhzoma (for whose name Léon-Portilla uses the original Nahuatl spelling), the author explains, "Both he and his people lived through days of intense fear. … The informants offer what could almost be called a psychological portrait of Motecuhzoma as he struggled with his fears and uncertainties." By highlighting Motecuhzoma's fear and uncertainty, Léon-Portilla engages readers, enabling them to sympathize with the Aztec witnesses and survivors. In his presentation of a later passage, Léon-Portilla writes, "It describes how Cortes bullied and even tortured the Aztec lords in order to obtain the gold and other valuables that the Indians had treasured since ancient times." The use of verbs like "bully" carry out the task of interpreting the passage for readers before they have contemplated the account itself, further contributing to *Broken Spears*' sympathetic representation of the experiences of the Aztec community.

## CRITICAL DISCUSSION

Expressing an opinion shared with the majority of scholars, Carl Compton notes about *Broken Spears*, "Never before has a connected account of the coming

Statue of Tlaloc, a Pre-Columbian Nahuan deity, outside a museum in Mexico City. In *The Broken Spears: The Aztec Account of the Conquest of Mexico* (1962), Miguel León-Portilla portrays how Nahuan speakers viewed the Spanish conquerors. © PRISMA ARCHIVO/ ALAMY.

of the Spaniards to Mexico and the conquest of Tenochtitlan been put together from native accounts." D. B. Quinn warns of the problems of translating the Nahuatl texts into Spanish, then English, before praising the work: "Precisely what has been gained and lost in this double [translation] process is a highly technical question to which this book ... does not give, in itself, the material for the answers, but on its merits it provides a most illuminating view of a notable physical and cultural conflict." Historian Camilla Townsend finds *Broken Spears* problematic because the indigenous accounts were written after the Spanish conquest and their creation was supervised by Spaniards.

*Broken Spears* has attained iconic status and is one of the best-known sources on the Nahuatl accounts of the conquest. The book is one of the predecessors of the New Philology, which Matthew Restall describes as "a school within ... the ethnohistory of colonial Mesoamerica," made up of "scholarship based on native-language sources." Lockhart is the most notable New Philologist; his work has continually engaged with that of León-Portilla. León-Portilla published other scholarly studies—including *Los antiguos mexicanos a través de sus crónicas y cantares* (1961), *Literaturas indígenas de México* (1992), and *Quince poetas del mundo náhuatl* (1994)—some of which have been translated into English. *Broken Spears* has been acclaimed worldwide, with several new editions published in recent years and translations issued in German, French, Polish, and Catalan.

*Broken Spears* has been discussed extensively by scholars. One issue that has received much attention is the possible mistranslation of "broken spears." Lockhart claims in *We People Here* (1993) that Garibay, who translated the text for *Broken Spears,* confused the Nahuatl word for "bone" (*omitl*) with the word for "spear" (*mitl*); thus, Lockhart concludes that the phrase should actually be "broken bones." Other researchers have accepted this conclusion and have treated it as a cautionary tale in scholarly translation, but León-Portilla, writing in 2009 in *The Americas*, defends Garibay's translation, noting that Garibay used an earlier manuscript in which *o* and *mitl* were two separate words. Other scholars have discussed how *Broken Spears* has brought more attention to Nahuatl/Aztec literature. For example, G. R. Coulthard observes, "A final but most important point about the re-creations of Aztec literature by Garibay and León-Portilla is that both have popularized their work. ... the *Vision de los vencidos* ... [is] aimed at a wide-reading public, and [is], in fact, highly readable."

**BIBLIOGRAPHY**

*Sources*

Compton, Carl. Rev. of *The Broken Spears: The Aztec Account of the Conquest of Mexico,* by Miguel León-Portilla. *Hispanic American Historical Review* 43.2 (1963): 281. Print.

Coulthard, G. R. "Parallelisms and Divergencies between 'Negritude' and 'Indigenismo.'" *Caribbean Studies* 8.1 (1968): 31–55. Print.

León-Portilla, Miguel, ed. *The Broken Spears: The Aztec Account of the Conquest of Mexico.* Boston: Beacon, 1962. Print.

Lockhart, James, ed. and trans. *We People Here: Nahuatl Accounts of the Conquest of Mexico.* Berkeley: U of California P, 1993. Print.

Quinn, D. B. Rev. of *The Broken Spears: The Aztec Account of the Conquest of Mexico,* by Miguel León-Portilla. *English Historical Review* 80.315 (1965): 391–92. Print.

Restall, Matthew. "A History of the New Philology and the New Philology in History." *Latin American Research Review* 38.1 (2003): 113–34. Print.

*Further Reading*

Anderson, A., F. Berdan, and J. Lockhart, eds. *Beyond the Codices: The Nahua View of Colonial Mexico.* Berkeley: U of California P, 1976. Print.

Horcasitas, Fernando. *The Aztecs Then and Now.* México: Editorial Minutiae Mexicana, 1979. Print.

Karttunen, Frances, and James Lockhart, eds. *Nahuatl in the Middle Years: Language Contact Phenomena in Texts of the Colonial Period.* Berkeley: U of California P, 1976. Print.

León-Portilla, Miguel. *Aztec Thought and Culture: A Study of the Ancient Nahuatl Mind.* Trans. Jack Emory Davis. Oklahoma City: U of Oklahoma P, 1963. Print.

———. "Response to John F. Schwaller." *The Americas* 66.2 (2009): 252–54. *Project MUSE.* Web. 11 Sept. 2012.

Schwaller, John F. "Broken Spears or Broken Bones: Evolution of the Most Famous Line in Nahuatl." *The Americas* 66.2 (2009): 241–52. Print.

Townsend, Camilla. "Burying the White Gods: New Perspectives on the Conquest of Mexico." *American Historical Review* 108.3 (2003). *History Cooperative.* Web. 11 Sep. 2012.

*Katrina White*

# BURY MY HEART AT WOUNDED KNEE

*Dee Brown*

## OVERVIEW

*Bury My Heart at Wounded Knee* (1970) by Dee Brown presents the American Indian perspective of the injustices that Native Americans experienced at the hands of the U.S. government in the late nineteenth century. In the book Brown portrays the government's actions as continued attempts to destroy the culture and way of life of the Native American tribes. Titled after the final line of the 1927 poem "American Names" by Stephen Vincent Benét, *Bury My Heart at Wounded Knee* is also a tribute to the Wounded Knee Massacre in South Dakota on December 29, 1890—one of the last battles between Native Americans and the U.S. army. Told primarily from an American Indian viewpoint, Brown's history of Native American relations is often viewed as propaganda because it acknowledges only the perspective of the Native American victims without also accounting for other points of view.

The book was published during a period of increased American Indian awareness and activism in the United States and remained on the best-seller list for more than a year. Reviewer R. Z. Sheppard, writing for *Time* in 1971, touches upon the awareness Brown raised: "With the zeal of an IRS investigator, he audits U.S. history's forgotten set of books. Compiled from old but rarely exploited sources plus a fresh look at dusty Government documents, *Bury My Heart at Wounded Knee* tallies the broken promises and treaties, the provocations, massacres, discriminatory policies and condescending diplomacy." The book has been translated into at least seventeen different languages and has never gone out of print, selling nearly four million copies. Its reputation persists as one of the most influential twentieth-century works about the American West.

## HISTORICAL AND LITERARY CONTEXT

In the late 1960s the United States was fighting the Vietnam War, which many felt was unjustified and for which they blamed the government. During that time, Americans' concerns also extended to another group: Native Americans. With the formation of the National Congress of American Indians in 1944, Native American rights were becoming a much-discussed topic in the United States. In the 1960s a key issue regarding Native American rights emerged, as many Native Americans began speaking out against what they viewed as offensive and racist depictions of their culture among sports teams and their mascots, such as the Washington Redskins, the Cleveland Indians, and the Atlanta Braves.

In 1970, when *Bury My Heart at Wounded Knee* was published, Americans had witnessed several high-profile injustices of the Vietnam War, including the 1968 My Lai Massacre, in which innocent Vietnamese civilians had been murdered. In his work Brown gives voice to American Indian victims, who like the murdered Vietnamese citizens never had the opportunity to tell their story. As the first author of his kind to write purely from a Native American perspective, however, he writes only one side of history in an attempt to persuade his audience of the injustices perpetrated on Native Americans.

Because of the praise Brown garnered for writing from the American Indian perspective, many critics initially thought that he was of Native American ancestry. Although he was not Native American, he had maintained contact with American Indians since his childhood in Arkansas. This multicultural upbringing inspired his early writings, such as his fictionalized account of Davy Crockett in *Wave High the Banner* (1943), as well as other fiction and nonfiction works focused on the American West, including *Settlers' West* (1955), *Yellowhorse* (1956), *The Gentle Tamers: Women of the Old Wild West* (1958), and *Calvary Scout* (1958).

Since its publication, *Bury My Heart at Wounded Knee* has influenced many other writers of the American West, such as writer Peter Matthiessen, author of *In the Spirit of Crazy Horse* (1983), a nonfiction work about the clashes between the Sioux tribe and the U.S. government. The influence of Brown's work has also extended to film: In 2007 HBO Films released a made-for-television version of *Bury My Heart at Wounded Knee*, starring Aidan Quinn, Adam Beach, and Anna Paquin. The adapted film, which treats the last two chapters of Brown's book, received several Emmy Awards and a Broadcast Film Critics Award for Best Movie Made for Television.

## THEMES AND STYLE

The majority of *Bury My Heart at Wounded Knee* focuses on the displacement of various tribes and their forced relocation onto reservations by the U.S. government. Starting with the arrival of Christopher

✢ *Key Facts*

**Time Period:**
Late 20th Century

**Genre:**
History

**Events:**
Wounded Knee Massacre; forced relocation of American Indians by the U.S. federal government

**Nationality:**
American

# DEE BROWN: WRITER AND LIBRARIAN

Before he stirred up controversy among critics, Dorris Alexander "Dee" Brown was just another small-town kid. Born on February 29, 1908, in Alberta, Louisiana, he spent most of his formative years in Ouachita County, Arkansas. He later relocated to Little Rock with his family so that he and his siblings could attend a better high school. Seeking refuge in his local public library, Brown began reading such authors as Sherwood Anderson and John Dos Passos, who would later be influential to his writing. After studying education at the Arkansas State Teachers College, and later library sciences at George Washington University, he worked as a librarian in Washington DC while he wrote some of his early novels.

From 1948 to 1972, Brown lived in Illinois, where he and his wife raised their two children. He worked as an agriculture librarian at the University of Illinois at Urbana-Champaign. After the success of *Bury My Heart at Wounded Knee,* he and his wife retired to Little Rock in 1973. On December 12, 2002, Brown died at the age of ninety-four. A branch of the Central Arkansas Library System in Little Rock was named in his honor.

Columbus in the Americas and moving chronologically through U.S. history, Brown mainly focuses on the relations between the tribes and the U.S. government from 1860 to 1890. Instead of explaining why the government felt it necessary to relocate the tribes, however, he explores Native Americans' perspectives, detailing their attempts to save their people through war, peace, or retreat. Brown writes of key Native American figures, "During the following thirty years these leaders and many more would enter into history and legend. Their names would become as well known as the names of the men who tried to destroy them." In its discussion of important Native American leaders and omission of the government officials on the opposing side, Brown's statement reveals an intent to give the names of Native Americans more prominence than those of government officials.

The Native American viewpoint from which Brown explores the displacement of tribes in *Bury My Heart at Wounded Knee* is perhaps the book's most effective rhetorical strategy. By downplaying the viewpoint of the U.S. government, Brown influences the reader's opinion about the events described in the book. This strategy occurs throughout the text, as when Brown describes a Navajo counterattack on Fort Defiance: "The United States Army … considered the attack a challenge of the flag flying over Fort Defiance, an act of war." Brown goes on to describe how the army stalked the Navajo tribe until the army finally gave up. In relating the story, he largely avoids quoting from the army or using a source that gives the army's point of view.

While *Bury My Heart at Wounded Knee* is written in a straightforward manner typical of nonfiction, Brown allows the reader to connect with the emotion of the atrocities that he details. Using facts and first-person accounts to draw his audience into a specific period, he uses the history itself to inject emotion into his language. When he allows the voice of the U.S. military to enter into the book, it is only to describe the atrocities the soldiers witnessed, such as in the following excerpt from a soldier's first-person account: "The Navahos, squaws, and children ran in all directions and were shot and bayoneted … I saw a soldier murdering two little children and a woman." Brown refrains from using his own words to explain the atrocities committed by the U.S. government; instead he allows the witnesses of the events to speak for themselves.

## CRITICAL DISCUSSION

When Brown's text was published in 1970, most critics applauded his attempt to write from a marginalized perspective. However, many spoke out against *Bury My Heart at Wounded Knee* for its one-dimensional view of history. Francis Paul Prucha (1972) notes in the *American Historical Review* that Brown lacked sources for most of his material. Prucha also takes aim at Brown for not presenting a balanced view of history and for failing to acknowledge other events that occurred during the same period within the government and across the United States. Such sentiments were echoed by other critics, including Helen McNeil, who argues in a 1971 essay for the *New Statesman* that the book is a "deliberately revisionist history" that portrays the "westward march of the civilised white men, 'like maggots,' according to a Sioux commentator, as a barbaric rout of established Indian culture."

In presenting only one side of history, Brown sends a message to other nonfiction authors struggling with how to accurately write about history and how to incorporate overlooked viewpoints. In 1980 American historian and political scientist Howard Zinn published *A People's History of the United States* in an effort to present American history through the eyes of ordinary people rather than from the view of the elite ruling classes. Unlike Brown, however, Zinn offers both sides of every topic he covers, such as a discussion of both Christopher Columbus and the eventual displacement of Native American tribes. Thus, Zinn attempts to give readers all available facts so that they can draw their own conclusions about history.

Although *Bury My Heart at Wounded Knee* faced intense scrutiny from critics when it was published, it became one of the most revered books about the American West. Critic Douglas Dupler (2003) writes in an essay for *Nonfiction Classics for Students: Presenting Analysis, Context, and Criticism on Nonfiction Works,* "by so intricately researching and assembling his history, Brown is able to show how the forces of cultural imperialism were so devastating, and brings the individuals and tragedy in this history alive for the reader." Praise for *Bury My Heart at Wounded Knee* continues. An adaptation of the book, titled *Saga of the Sioux: An Adaptation from Dee Brown's* Bury My Heart at Wounded Knee, was published by Dwight Jon Zimmerman in 2011. In the book Zimmerman also writes from a Native American viewpoint, detailing battles, discrimination, and broken treaties from the Sioux tribe.

## BIBLIOGRAPHY

### Sources

Brown, Dee Alexander. *Bury My Heart at Wounded Knee: An Indian History of the American West.* New York: Bantam, 1972. Print.

Dupler, Douglas. "Critical Essay on *Bury My Heart at Wounded Knee.*" *Nonfiction Classics for Students: Presenting Analysis, Context, and Criticism on Nonfiction Works.* Vol. 5. Ed. David M. Galens, Jennifer Smith, and Elizabeth Thomason. Detroit: Gale, 2003. *Literature Resource Center.* Web. 17 Aug. 2012.

McNeil, Helen. "Savages." *New Statesman* 1 Oct. 1971: 444–45. *Literature Resource Center.* Web. 17 Aug. 2012.

Prucha, Francis Paul. Rev. of *Bury My Heart at Wounded Knee,* by Dee Brown. *American Historical Review* 77.2 (1972): 589–90. Print.

Sheppard, R. Z. "Books: The Forked-Tongue Syndrome." *Time* 1 Feb. 1971: n.p. Web. 17 Aug. 2012.

### Further Reading

Brown, Dee Alexander. *Wave High the Banner: A Novel Based on the Life of Davy Crockett.* Albuquerque: U of New Mexico P, 1999. Print.

Matthiessen, Peter. *In the Spirit of Crazy Horse.* New York: Viking, 1983. Print.

Momaday, Scott. "A History of the Indians of the United States." *New York Times* 7 Mar. 1971: BR46. Print.

Richardson, Heather Cox. *Wounded Knee: Party Politics and the Road to an American Massacre.* New York: Basic Books, 2011. Print.

Zimmerman, Dwight Jon, and Dee Alexander Brown. *Saga of the Sioux: An Adaptation from Dee Brown's* Bury My Heart at Wounded Knee. New York: Holt, 2011. Print.

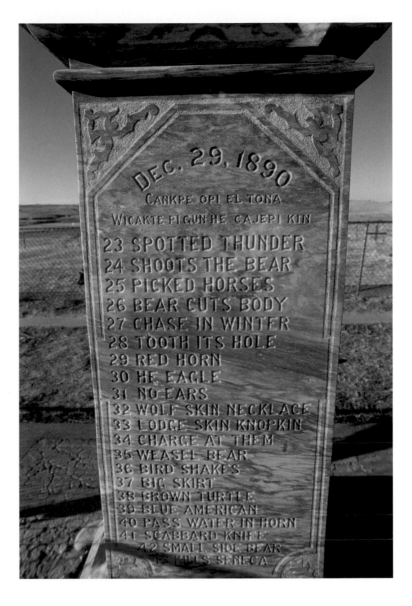

### Media Adaptation

*Bury My Heart at Wounded Knee.* Dir. Yves Simoneau. Perf. Aidan Quinn, Adam Beach, and August Schellenberg. HBO Films, 2007. TV Movie.

***Anna Deem***

Gravestone commemorating the 1890 massacre at Wounded Knee, South Dakota. © LAYNE KENNEDY/CORBIS.

# THE CRUSADES THROUGH ARAB EYES

*Amin Maalouf*

❖ *Key Facts*

**Time Period:**
Late 20th Century

**Genre:**
History

**Events:**
Christian crusades
against Muslims in the
11th and 12th centuries

**Nationality:**
Lebanese-born French

## OVERVIEW

Amin Maalouf's *The Crusades through Arab Eyes,* published in French in 1983 and translated into English in 1984, tells the history of the Crusades from the perspective of the invaded Islamic countries. Written for general readers with little or no knowledge of Muslim history, Maalouf's work is based on accounts of medieval Muslim historians and chroniclers who experienced firsthand what they described as the "Frankish invasions." *The Crusades through Arab Eyes* is explicitly intended as a response to standard Western historical accounts of the Crusades. As Maalouf writes in the forward to the text, "The basic idea of this book is simple: to tell the story of the Crusades as they were seen, lived, and recorded on 'the other side'—in other words, in the Arab camp."

Despite the book's popular appeal, its academic reception was mixed. Many scholars acknowledged the value of Maalouf's ideas but wanted more analysis and less storytelling. An Arab Christian from Lebanon, Maalouf began his writing career as a journalist with the leading Beirut daily *An-Nahar.* In 1976 he emigrated to Paris to escape the violence of the Lebanese Civil War. Once there, he continued working as a journalist, first as the director of the international edition of *An-Nahar* and later as the editor in chief of *Jeune Afrique. The Crusades through Arab Eyes* is Maalouf's first book-length work. It became a best seller in France and was soon translated into Italian, Spanish, German, Dutch, and English. Although a handful of later works have covered the same material in a more scholarly way, *The Crusades through Arab Eyes* remains the most accessible—and popular—account of the Crusades from the Muslim perspective for the general reader.

## HISTORICAL AND LITERARY CONTEXT

In 1095 Pope Urban II called on Christian knights to stop fighting each other and to take up arms to free the Holy Lands from Muslim control. These warriors described themselves as crusaders, after the cross-shaped red patch that was the emblem of their mission. Over the course of two hundred years, at least eight campaigns of crusaders invaded the region of modern Palestine with the goal of bringing Christian holy places, especially Jerusalem, under Christian control. It was 1187 before the Kurdish leader Saladin united the divided Islamic states and reconquered

Jerusalem. Muslim forces finally expelled Europeans from Acre, the last Crusader stronghold, in 1291.

At the time *The Crusades through Arab Eyes* was published, little international attention had been paid to the perspective of the invaded peoples. The Crusades occurred at a time when Muslim homelands were under attack by political and sectarian divisions and by foreign invaders. The Muslim chroniclers and historians on whose accounts Maalouf draws saw the Crusades simply as another set of wars against foreign invaders, not as holy wars fundamentally different from the attacks of Berber tribes in North Africa or the waves of Turks and Mongols from the west. Although Muslim historians of the period recorded the history of the Crusader invasions, the Crusades were never treated as an isolated topic. As Islamicist Carole Hillenbrand points out in *The Crusades: Islamic Perspectives* (2000), modern historians must piece together "their reflections on the events of the Crusading period ... like a jigsaw from stray references, anecdotes and comments tucked away in universal or dynastic histories of the Islamic world and the chronicles of cities—in other words, works with quite other emphases and historiographical aims."

The Crusades are the subject of an extensive body of historical writing in the West, beginning as early as the late twelfth century. Most of these accounts are written from a Western perspective using Western sources. Crusade specialist Jonathan Riley-Smith argues that this is in large part because few medieval scholars learn Arabic and few Islamicists study the Crusades. Whatever the reason, the result is what Hamid Bahri and Francesca Canadé Sautman describe in *Medievalisms in the Postcolonial World: The Idea of the "Middle Ages" Outside Europe* (2009) as "a history of Western endeavor and of Western politics, in which those subject to attack and conquest were passive victims, ineffectual adversaries or, perhaps, picturesque characters."

Maalouf breaks new ground in *The Crusades through Arab Eyes,* giving Western readers access to another perspective on the topic for almost the first time. In the years following its publication, Maalouf moved from history to historical fiction, writing novels that Justin Cartwright in a 2011 article for *The Guardian* describes as based on "a rich appreciation of the history of the Middle East, and its endlessly competing empires and civilizations." In works such as *The Rock of Tanios* (1993), for which Maalouf won the Goncourt Prize; *Leo Africanus* (1986); and *Balthazar's Odyssey* (2002), he continues to reinterpret the Arab past through the lens of the present, to explore how historical sources are used, and to refuse to be defined by what he terms "lethal identities."

## THEMES AND STYLE

In *The Crusades through Arab Eyes*, Maalouf explicitly sets out to write the story of the Crusades from "a hitherto neglected point of view." Underlying his stated intent is a less explicit theme: the parallels between the world of the Crusaders and the Middle East of the 1980s. In particular he compares the four small kingdoms the Crusaders carved out around Jerusalem to modern-day Israel because of their shared status as religiously defined, non-Muslim territories within a larger Muslim region. Maalouf refers directly to this secondary theme only in the brief epilogue; nonetheless the idea reappears throughout the book, particularly through the use of modern descriptors and anachronistic terms, such as *Palestinians, Lebanese, Syrians, permanent occupation,* and *settlements.* Driven by the combination of stated and unstated themes, Maalouf occasionally veers into partisanship, transposing the traditional heroes and villains of Eurocentric Crusade histories.

Maalouf's work succeeds not simply because of the new viewpoint it offers, but also because of the strength of his storytelling. He describes his work as a "true-life novel of the Crusades," and in fact uses devices more common to novelists—or nineteenth century historians such as Thomas Babington Macaulay—than to academic historians. In particular, academic reviewers object to what James Brundage in a 1988 essay for *Journal of Near Eastern Studies* decries as Maalouf's habit of "telling us things that neither he nor anyone else knows," including his characters' thoughts and emotions. Although Maalouf does not simply accept what his sources report without question, he avoids analysis of the events he relates. Instead, he gives the reader what Mahmood Ibrahim in a 1988 review for *International Journal of Middle East Studies* describes as "an almost endless series of military encounters interspersed with intrigues, assassinations, alliances, counteralliances, battles lost and won, sieges raised and lifted, thus concentrating on the leaders and what they said and did and what they suffered and enjoyed."

Stylistically, Maalouf balances his own prose with the formal, formulaic language of the medieval historians whom he quotes and Arabic names and terms unfamiliar to many Western readers. Even his critics agree that his writing is smooth, pleasant, and lively—a position summed up in Brundage's grudging assessment that Maalouf "has a story to tell, and he tells it with a good deal of gusto." To move the story forward, Maalouf often uses flowing sentences with repetition and interlocking phrases rather than

## AMIN MAALOUF AND *LOVE FROM AFAR*

In 1999 Amin Maalouf returned to the topic of the Crusades, writing a libretto for Finnish composer Kaija Saariaho for the opera *L'Amour de Loin* (*Love from Afar*), which premiered in 2000 at the Salzburg Festival, where it received standing ovations and critical praise. Set during the Crusades, the opera is loosely based on a legendary episode from the life of twelfth-century troubadour Jaufré Rudel, prince of Blaye. Jaufré dreams of an idealized and distant love but does not believe such a woman exists until a pilgrim from the Crusader kingdom of Outre-mer arrives at his court and tells him of Clémence, the Christian ruler of Tripoli. Jaufré begins to extol her in his songs as his "love from afar." Clémence, too, begins to dream of a faraway love. Increasingly obsessed, Jaufré decides to travel to Tripoli to meet Clémence. The voyage is rough, and he arrives only to die in her arms.

Although both main characters are Christian, the Crusades and the question of Christian rule in an Islamic land are never far from the surface. In the libretto Maalouf evokes the cultural distances at the heart of the period through metaphors of distance and unrequited love and by inserting Arabic words into the speech of the chorus.

the short, expository sentences of modern journalism. When commenting on a sonorous quotation from one of his medieval sources, his prose becomes crisper, almost taking the form of asides to his reader: "These Franj are crazy, the Mosul historian seems to be saying." The result is what Bahri and Sautman describe as "a suspenseful and spry narrative."

## CRITICAL DISCUSSION

*The Crusades through Arab Eyes* was immediately popular with students and general readers but received a mixed response from the academic community. Even the most critical reviewers acknowledged that Maalouf's well-written work fills a gap in available studies on the Crusades. However, many felt the work was too journalistic in style and concentrated on storytelling at the expense of much-needed analysis. Brundage, by far the most negative reviewer of Maalouf's work, dismissed the book as "superficial, anecdotal, and oversimplified." Even relatively positive reviewers shared the criticism. For example, Ibrahim complains that Maalouf does not provide "any analysis of the ideology of the Crusades, of the contemporary conditions in the Middle East and of the Crusaders' final failure to establish a permanent presence in the area."

At the time of its publication, and for many years after, *The Crusades through Arab Eyes* stood virtually alone in its presentation of a Muslim view of the Crusades. Since 2000, as the field of medieval studies has increasingly adopted postcolonialism, gender studies, and other postmodern critical approaches,

Saladin, pictured here on horseback, was a leader of Muslim forces during the Third Crusade. © NORTH WIND PICTURE ARCHIVES/ALAMY.

## BIBLIOGRAPHY

### Sources

Bahri, Hamid, and Francesca Canadé Sautman. "Crossing History, Dis-Orienting the Orient: Amin Maalouf's Uses of the 'Medieval.'" *Medievalisms in the Postcolonial World: The Idea of the "Middle Ages" Outside Europe*. Ed. Kathleen Davis and Nadia Altschul. Baltimore: Johns Hopkins UP, 2009. Print.

Brundage, James A. Review of *The Crusades through Arab Eyes,* by Amin Maalouf. *Journal of Near Eastern Studies* 47.2 (1988): 149–50. *JSTOR.* Web. 7 Oct. 2012.

Cartwright, Justin. "Amin Maalouf: Profile." *London Guardian* 30 Mar. 2011. Web. 7 Oct. 2012.

Hillenbrand, Carole. *The Crusades: Islamic Perspectives.* New York: Routledge, 2000. Print.

Ibrahim, Mahmood. Review of *The Crusades through Arab Eyes,* by Amin Maalouf. *International Journal of Middle East Studies* 20.4 (1988): 559–60. *JSTOR.* Web. 7 Oct. 2012.

Maalouf, Amin. *The Crusades through Arab Eyes.* Trans. Jon Rothschild. London: Al Saqi Books, 1984. Print.

### Further Reading

Al-Azm, Sadik J. "Western Historical Thinking from an Arab Perspective." *Western Historical Thinking: An Intercultural Debate.* Ed. Jören Rüsen. New York: Berghahn Books, 2002. 119–27. Print.

Bourget, Carine. "The Rewriting of History in Amin Maalouf's *The Crusades through Arab Eyes.*" *Studies in Twentieth and Twenty-First Century Literature* 30.2 (2006). *General One File.* Web. 8 Oct. 2012.

Constable, Giles. "The Historiography of the Crusades." *The Crusades from the Perspective of Byzantium and the Muslim World.* Ed. Angeliki E. Laiou and Roy Parviz Mottahedeh. Washington, DC: Dumbarton Oaks, 2001. 1–22. Print.

Daniel, Norman. *The Arabs and Medieval Europe.* London: Longman, 1975. Print.

Finucane, Ronald C. *Soldiers of the Faith: Crusaders and Moslems at War.* New York: St. Martin's, 1983. Print.

Gabrieli, Francesco, ed. *Arab Historians of the Crusades: Selected and Translated from the Arabic Sources.* Trans. E. J. Costello. London: Routledge and Kegan Paul, 1969. Print.

Holt, P. M. *The Age of the Crusades: The Near East from the Eleventh Century to 1517.* New York: Longman, 1986. Print.

Nicholson, Helen J. "Muslim Reactions to the Crusades." *Palgrave Advances in the Crusades.* Ed. Helen J. Nicholson. New York: Palgrave Macmillan, 2005. Print.

Nicolle, David. *Crusader Warfare.* Vol. 2. New York: Continuum, 2007. Print.

Riley-Smith, Jonathan. *What Were the Crusades?* 3rd ed. New York: Palgrave Macmillan, 2002. Print.

### Media Adaptation

*Cabaret Crusades: The Path to Cairo.* Dir. Wael Shawky. Alcimé, 2012. Film.

scholars have produced a small but growing body of work focused on what is now often referred to as the "counter-crusade." The most influential of these works is Hillenbrand's *The Crusades: Islamic Perspectives* (1999). In a bibliographical essay, Hillenbrand explicitly acknowledges both the importance and the limitations of *The Crusades through Arab Eyes*: "It came as a breath of fresh air into this field … [but] is unashamedly general in its approach, is not comprehensive or academic, and furnishes little new information."

Despite the fact that more scholarly treatments of the subject are now available, *The Crusades through Arab Eyes* has been continually in print since 1984 and still holds a place on lists of recommended introductory books on the Crusades. In recent years, *The Crusades through Arab Eyes* has begun to receive scholarly attention, most of which considers Maalouf's work using the same postmodern critical approaches that fuel studies of the counter-crusade. The most extensive piece of scholarship dealing with Maalouf's work is Bahri and Sautman's "Crossing History, Dis-Orienting the Orient: Amin Maalouf's Uses of the 'Medieval,'" a critical essay on the role of the medieval in Maalouf's work as a whole, published as part of a collection considering the topic of medievalism in places outside Europe.

*Pamela Toler*

# AN ECONOMIC INTERPRETATION OF THE CONSTITUTION

*Charles Austin Beard*

## OVERVIEW

In *An Economic Interpretation of the Constitution,* historian Charles Austin Beard seeks to revise previous historical understandings of the Founding Fathers as men motivated by patriotic ideals. Publishing the work in the midst of the Progressive era in 1913, Beard instead asserted that the men who drafted and supported the Constitution had a vested interest in protecting their investments in what Beard called "personalty" (securities, bonds, and related business investments)—as opposed to those who owned "realty" (land and agricultural interests, including slaves). Beard's study fit well into the Progressive school of historical writing that saw monied interests as often conspiring against genuine democratic forces and viewed economic motives as the engines of history.

Beard was born in Indiana into a farming family, and his progressivism was rooted in his Quaker background. As a student at Indiana's DePauw University, he visited the Hull House settlement house in Chicago in 1896. As professor of history at Columbia University, he published a lecture titled *Politics* (1908), in which he notes that the basis of the state is "conquest" by a ruling class. Government does not operate upon theories of the common good but instead upon "the will of the group of persons actually in control at any one time" or upon an "equilibrium" established by conflicts between groups seeking control. Applying this theory to the Constitution, Beard in *Economic Interpretation* establishes his reputation as a leading historian of his time.

## HISTORICAL AND LITERARY CONTEXT

During the 1890s, when Beard was a student, many reform-minded individuals feared that large conglomerations of capital were compromising individuals' freedom but believed that problems could be solved with study. Some of the problems that northern progressives confronted were urban slums (the result, in part, of the influx of immigrants from southern and eastern Europe), working conditions in factories, trusts and monopolies, and corruption of urban political machines. Among these reformers were Theodore Roosevelt from New York; Jane Addams, who had founded Hull House; and muckraking journalists Lincoln Steffens and Ida Tarbell.

The year before Beard's *Economic Interpretation* was published, Americans in the election of 1912 faced a choice between two versions of progressivism: one represented by Theodore Roosevelt's New Nationalism in his third-party Bull Moose campaign and the other by Democrat Woodrow Wilson's New Freedom. Roosevelt in the New Nationalism envisioned a strong executive who would guide large organizations of labor and capital toward serving society justly and efficiently, while Wilson's program emphasized limited legislative acts toward the encouragement of competition among smaller businesses. In a three-way race with Republican William Howard Taft, Wilson won the election, ushering in several years of unprecedented reforms, including antitrust, banking, and tariff legislation. Beard embraced Wilson in 1912 and again in 1917 when he supported U.S. involvement in World War I.

Beard quickly became a leading member of the Progressive school of historiography, dating back to the publication of Frederick Jackson Turner's "frontier thesis" in 1893. Turner proposed that the existence of a frontier and the abundance of land contributed to a democratic American character more than ideas transplanted from Europe, a theory, which like Beard's, stressed material interests over ideas. A third member of this school was one of Turner's students at Wisconsin, Carl L. Becker, who argues in his influential *Political Parties in the Province of New York from 1766–75* (1908) that the Revolution had two battles: one against Britain for home rule and one to see who would rule at home. The year before *Economic Interpretation* was published, Beard released a thin volume titled *The Supreme Court and the Constitution* (1912), in which he praises the precedent of judicial review as a check to possible "legislative tyranny." But *Economic Interpretation* gained far more attention. Beard expands his thesis in *The Economic Origins of Jeffersonian Democracy* (1915) and *The Rise of American Civilization* (1927), the latter of which he cowrote with his wife, Mary Ritter Beard.

The triumph of Progressive history would become clear as Turner, Becker, and Beard each became president of the American Historical Association (AHA) in 1910, 1931, and 1933, respectively. Beard influenced

**⁘ Key Facts**

**Time Period:**
Early 20th Century

**Genre:**
History

**Events:**
Progressive era; election of Woodrow Wilson as U.S. president

**Nationality:**
American

# THE BEARDS' COMMITMENT TO HISTORY EDUCATION

While Charles Beard made a name for himself with *An Economic Interpretation of the Constitution,* he and his wife, Mary Beard, were more successful publishing collections of primary documents and more general American history surveys. By publishing primary document readers, the Beards were pioneers in a part of history pedagogy that is now taken for granted, as many textbook publishers devote a significant part of their catalogs to such readers.

In 1909 he published the textbook *American Politics and Government,* which went through ten editions. Along with it, he published a collection of writings titled *Readings in American Politics and Government.* With longtime educator and Columbia colleague William Bagley, he cowrote public school textbooks in the 1920s, including *History of the American People,* which sold more than 657,000 copies. Beard believed so much in a "usable past" that he wanted to stress values of service and humanitarianism rather than wars and strife. He and his wife went on to cowrite *American Citizenship* (1914); *The History of the United States* (1920); *The Rise of American Civilization* (1927), which sold more than 130,000 copies of its two volumes in its early editions; and finally *The Basic History of the United States* (1944).

others, such as James Harvey Robinson, a colleague at Columbia, who also served as president of the AHA (in 1929) and coauthored two books with Beard: *Outlines of European History* (1914) and *History of Europe: Our Own Times* (1921). One reason Beard was so influential was his optimism that the study of history could be used to reform society. As such, he was part of a wider intellectual movement in which literary critic Van Wyck Brooks called on American writers to evoke a "usable past." Yet years later, in his 1933 presidential address to the AHA, Beard appeared to undermine this mission, describing history as "a noble dream" and an "act of faith"—an attack on "objectivity" that drew criticism then and later. Beard's dismissal of objectivity also laid the seeds of the Progressive movement's decline. By the early 1930s, the shocks of World War I and the Great Depression had compromised beliefs in progress. In his 1931 AHA presidential address titled "Everyman His Own Historian," Becker reduces history to interpretations relative to writers' individual experiences: "The history which he [the historian] imaginatively recreates as an artificial extension of his personal experience," he argued, "will inevitably be an engaging blend of fact and fancy."

## THEMES AND STYLE

Beard saw the American Revolution as a genuinely democratic movement; however the framers of the Constitution, the majority of whom controlled personalty such as investments and securities, moved to reform the weak government of the Articles of Confederation at a time when financial instability loomed among the mass of debtors. Even the planter interests represented at the Constitutional Convention, the wealthiest owners of realty, or landed property, were often debtors. As those who compromised Revolutionary democracy, the wealthy personalty-owning founders, in Beard's view, were not villains but, as Pope McCorkle points out, Machiavellian realists acting on the interests of their class.

Beard describes the landed interests as men on the decline, while the business-oriented founders were aggressive and confident asserters of power. He writes as though clear evidence supports his conclusions even though James Madison's minutes of the Constitutional Convention do not provide individual delegates' votes on key clauses on such matters as currency and contracts. Instead he relies on the backgrounds of those delegates who made the motions for important economic-related clauses and articles and those who seconded the motions. Even before the Convention, delegates took advantage of property requirements for voting to take their places in Philadelphia to advance their class interests.

The stark contrast between the assertive personalty-holding class and the defensive landholding class becomes clear in Beard's description of Virginia governor Edmund Randolph and his characterization of the change in government framework as a coup d'état. Beard notes that Randolph, "apparently never very prosperous" and "burdened with debt," long considered his slaves an "encumbrance." Referring to the ratification process, which bypassed the unanimity of each state required under the Articles of Confederation, Beard comments, "The revolutionary nature of the work of the Philadelphia Convention is correctly characterized by Professor John W. Burgess when he states that had such acts been performed by Julius or Napoleon, they would have been pronounced coup d'état." (Burgess, Beard's colleague at Columbia, taught political science and law.) Historian Forrest McDonald later pointed out that Beard often understated the property holdings of some of the planters he examined, perhaps because of a lack of better data.

## CRITICAL DISCUSSION

Initial reaction to Beard's book from prominent conservatives was fiercely negative, although the firestorm of protest helped to establish Beard's national reputation. Former president William Howard Taft conceded that the facts of the book were accurate but asked, "Why did the damn fool print it?" Fellow Constitutional scholar E. S. Corwin dismissed the book as an attempt to prove socialist determinism, and Harvard historian Albert Bushnell Hart called it "little short of indecent." For his part, Beard denied that he was a Marxist, but even Columbia University president Nicholas Murray Butler, when asked if he had read Beard's last book, replied, "I hope so." By the time the Great Depression struck the world economy,

A 1937 photo showing tourists standing below *The Constitution of the United States,* a 1936 mural by Barry Faulkner depicting American founders and the Constitution. Charles Austin Beard, in *An Economic Interpretation of the Constitution* (1913), argues that the founders wrote the Constitution in order to protect their own economic interests. © J. BAYLOR ROBERTS/ NATIONAL GEOGRAPHIC SOCIETY/CORBIS.

however, Beard's work was considered a bible to many young scholars who believed, as one student of Beard's recalled, that "democratic constitutionalism" could equal "jobs and bread" for the masses. The book went through seven printings through 1935. In the 1938 *New Republic* survey of intellectuals titled "Books That Changed Our Minds," *Economic Interpretation* received the most votes, tied with Thorstein Veblen's *The Theory of the Leisure Class.*

During the 1950s Beard's reputation went into decline. In *President Roosevelt and the Coming of the War* (1948), a controversial account of the Pearl Harbor attack that brought widespread criticism, Beard argues that president Franklin Delano Roosevelt deliberately created a situation in which the Japanese had no alternative but to attack. Meanwhile, his *Economic Interpretation* thesis came under stricter scrutiny, and many of his conclusions were challenged. McDonald in *We the People* (1958) provides his own analysis of the founders and their implied votes to show that there were numerous, not simply two, competing interests, at the Constitutional Convention. Meanwhile the Progressive school was eclipsed more generally by so-called consensus history, which reemphasized the importance of American ideas, specifically an underlying agreement on the values of democracy and capitalism. Richard Hofstadter commented by 1968 that Beard's reputation stood as "an imposing ruin in the landscape of American historiography." Still, one of the most prominent scholars

of southern history, C. Vann Woodward, embraced a Beardian approach in such works as *Origins of the New South, 1877–1913* (1951).

The debate over Beard's thesis has continued into the late twentieth and early twenty-first centuries. One scholar in 2007 called *Economic Interpretation* "the most important work ever written on the American founding." In the 1980s and 1990s, prominent historians Bernard Bailyn and Gordon Wood stressed the importance of ideas behind the Constitution, arguing that the framers voted impartially. In 1986 McDonald introduced a new study on the Convention, emphasizing the political experience and wisdom among the founders as key explanations to their behavior. More recently, Wake Forest University economist Jac C. Heckelman and University of Georgia political scientist Keith L. Dougherty, using revised statistical analysis, have concluded that delegates with personalty interests did not vote in a significantly different way than those with realty interests, although ownership of securities was a key variable in the votes on important clauses on contracts, currency, and debts.

## BIBLIOGRAPHY

*Sources*

Beard, Charles Austin. *An Economic Interpretation of the Constitution.* New York: Macmillan, 1913. Print.

Gibson, Alan Ray. *Understanding the Founding: The Crucial Questions.* Lawrence: UP of Kansas, 2007.

Heckelman, Jac C., and Keith L. Dougherty. "Personalty Interests at the Constitutional Convention: New Tests of Beard's Thesis." *Cliometrica* 4 (2010): 207–28. Print.

McCorkle, Pope. "The Historian as Intellectual: Charles Beard and the Constitution Reconsidered." *American Journal of Legal History* 28.4 (1984): 314–63. Print.

McDonald, Forrest. "Charles A. Beard and the Constitution: Forrest McDonald's Rebuttal." *William and Mary Quarterly* 17.1 (1960): 102–110. Print.

———. *Novus Ordo Seclorum: The Intellectual Origins of the Constitution.* Lawrence: UP of Kansas, 1986. Print.

———. *We the People: The Economic Origins of the Constitution.* Chicago: U of Chicago P, 1958. Print.

Soderbergh, Peter A. "Charles A. Beard and the Public Schools, 1909–1939." *History of Education Quarterly* 5.4 (1965): 241–52. Print.

### Further Reading

Bailyn, Bernard. *The Ideological Origins of the American Revolution.* Cambridge: Harvard UP, 1992. Print.

Brown, David S. *Beyond the Frontier: The Midwestern Voice in American Historical Writing.* Chicago: U of Chicago P, 2009. Print.

Collier, Christopher. *Decision in Philadelphia: The Constitutional Convention of 1787.* New York: Random House, 1986. Print.

Egnal, Marc. "The Beards Were Right: Parties in the North, 1840–1860." *Civil War History* 47.1 (2001): 30–56. Print.

Farrand, Max, ed. *The Records of the Federal Convention of 1787.* 4 vols. New Haven: Yale UP, 1966. Print.

Hofstadter, Richard. *The Progressive Historians.* New York: Knopf, 1968. Print.

Jillson, Calvin C. *Constitution Making: Conflict and Consensus in the Federal Convention of 1787.* Flemington: Agathon, 2008. Print.

McGuire, Robert A. *To Form a More Perfect Union: A New Economic Interpretation of the United States Constitution.* New York: Oxford UP, 2003. Print.

Nore, Ellen. *Charles A. Beard: An Intellectual Biography.* Carbondale: Southern Illinois UP, 1983. Print.

Strout, Cushing. *The Pragmatic Revolt in American History: Carl Becker and Charles Beard.* New Haven: Yale UP, 1958. Print.

*Wesley Borucki*

# THE ETHNIC CLEANSING OF PALESTINE

*Ilan Pappe*

## OVERVIEW

*The Ethnic Cleansing of Palestine,* a 2006 work of historiography by Israeli historian Ilan Pappe, approaches the forced expulsion of Arabs from Palestine between 1947 and 1949 as an act of ethnic cleansing. Pappe challenges dominant narratives that describe the mass exodus of the Arab population as an act of voluntary migration or lament it as an unfortunate and unplanned outcome of the 1948 Arab-Israeli War, also called the Israeli War for Independence. Relying on careful documentation, Palestinian sources and oral histories, and close portraits of individual Palestinian villages in addition to official Israeli archives, Pappe is able to confront the myth of Jewish victimhood during the period, revealing the military and bureaucratic atrocities committed by Israel in the process of establishing a Jewish state.

Published after the end of the Second Intifada, a period of intensified Palestinian-Israeli hostility and aggression from 2000 to 2005, *The Ethnic Cleansing of Palestine* builds on the work of a group known as the New Historians. Emerging in Israeli academia in the late 1980s, these scholars confronted the official Israeli narrative of the 1948 war. Pappe's work provides a counter narrative that challenges even these earlier attempts at revision. Speaking directly to the contemporary despair in the peace process, the book raises controversy by calling on Israel to recognize the Palestinian right to repatriation and to admit that the expulsion of the Palestinians represented an ethnic cleansing operation. The book received mixed reactions within and outside of Israel, and although it is often cited, it has been the subject of only limited scholarly attention.

## HISTORICAL AND LITERARY CONTEXT

The massive expulsion of Arabs from Palestine before, during, and after the war is referred to as the *nakba,* meaning catastrophe. The first waves of refugees were driven from their land before the end of the British Mandate for Palestine, a period of British governance over the area from 1922 until after World War II. In 1947 the United Nations adopted Resolution 181, which outlined a plan for partitioning Palestine between the Jewish and Arab populations. Both sides considered the plan unacceptable, but whereas the Palestinians rejected it outright, the Jewish leadership decided to "accept and ignore" it. Fighting between the two sides began within days. Pappe records that the majority of the rural population was still Palestinian and that "within the borders of their UN-proposed state, [Jews] owned only eleven per cent of the land, and were the minority in every district." The desire to create a favorable balance, expand their allotted territory, and secure a Jewish identity for it motivated the Jewish leaders to formulate Plan Dalet (or Plan D), which called for the expulsion of Arabs from Palestine. The plan was finalized in March 1948, and the Jewish leadership declared the establishment of the state of Israel in May, which led to the Arab-Israeli War. The last major exodus of Palestinians occurred during the months after the war ended. By then, according to Pappe, "more than half of Palestine's native population, close to 800,000 people, had been uprooted, 531 villages had been destroyed, and eleven urban neighbourhoods emptied of their inhabitants." In December 1948 the United Nations passed Resolution 194, which asserts the right of first-generation Palestinian refugees and their descendants to return to properties they were forced to leave during the exodus.

In July 2000 U.S President Bill Clinton met with Israeli prime minister Ehud Barak and Palestinian Authority president Yasser Arafat at Camp David as part of the continuing Middle East peace process, hoping to come to a final resolution of the Arab-Israeli conflict. Two months after the collapse of negotiations, the Second Intifada began. A 2005 ceasefire brought a temporary end to the fighting, but the atmosphere of animosity persisted, and the concurrent completion of a large portion of the West Bank barrier, which the Israelis built ostensibly to protect areas inside Israel from Palestinians, further diminished hopes for peace. *The Ethnic Cleansing of Palestine* charges that the unrelenting Israeli refusal to honor the UN-declared Palestinian right of return and the denial of the ethnic cleansing of Palestine are the major stumbling blocks to the negotiation of a lasting peace.

In the 1980s the New Historians began to challenge the foundational myth of the 1948 War of Independence as the struggle of a "Jewish David against the Arab Goliath." Scholars such as Benny Morris (in his 1987 book *The Birth of the Palestinian Refugee Problem, 1947–1949,* for instance) studied Israeli archival materials and revealed a series of atrocities and human rights violations committed by the Jews. This included

**Key Facts**

**Time Period:**
Early 21st Century

**Genre:**
History

**Events:**
Forced expulsion of Arabs from Palestine; 1948 Arab-Israeli War

**Nationality:**
Israeli

# A PALESTINIAN REFUGEE'S FICTIONALIZATION OF 1948

Ghassan Kanafani was born in 1936 in Acre, in what was then Mandatory Palestine. In 1948 he and his family were expelled to Lebanon, and they later settled in Damascus, Syria. An active member of the Palestinian Liberation Organization, Kanafani was assassinated in 1972. During his life he wrote a number of short stories and novels that drew on his experiences as a refugee.

Kanafani's novella *Returning to Haifa* (1969) tells the story of a Palestinian couple who are exiled from Haifa to the West Bank in 1948 and, in the chaos, inadvertently abandon their infant son. When they are finally able to return twenty years later, they find their house occupied by a Jewish refugee from World War II and discover that he and his wife found their son and raised him as an Israeli Jew. Whereas Pappe highlights the right of return as a necessary precondition to peace in *The Ethnic Cleansing of Palestine, Returning to Haifa* underlines the inherent psychological and moral complications of this seemingly simple demand. Even if physical repatriation becomes possible one day, the systematic alteration of Palestine's demographic reality, geography, and even history make return in any true sense an impossibility.

the terrorizing, slaughter, or forced transfer of the majority of the native Arab population. The exclusion of Palestinian sources and oral histories limited the revisionist scope of the first wave of New Historians, however. Pappe had written several books and articles on the subject, beginning with his 1988 analysis *Britain and the Arab-Israeli Conflict, 1948–1951,* before publishing *The Ethnic Cleansing of Palestine.*

Following its publication, *The Ethnic Cleansing of Palestine* was the subject of a large number of review articles, which tended to either heroize or demonize Pappe. He later researched the plight of Israeli-Palestinians in *The Forgotten Palestinians* (2011), which examines the long-term effects of the ethnic-cleansing operation, studying the status of the Palestinians who avoided slaughter and forced expulsion only to become second-class Israeli citizens. Also in 2011 Pappe published *Out of the Frame: The Struggle for Academic Freedom in Israel,* a personal narrative that describes his departure from Zionism, as well as his subsequent ostracism from Israeli academia as a result of his controversial views. *The Ethnic Cleansing of Palestine* remains one of the most radical revisionist histories about the formation of the state of Israel available in English today, and it has helped popularize a vocabulary of ethnic cleansing in contemporary scholarship on the nakba.

## THEMES AND STYLE

The central argument of *The Ethnic Cleansing of Palestine* is that the 1947 to 1949 expulsion of hundreds of thousands of Arabs from Palestine represents a calculated act and that the Jewish leadership considered it a necessary precondition to the establishment of the Jewish state. While the policies considered most effective in achieving the goal of "de-Arabisation" changed as the struggle progressed, neither was the displacement of the Palestinians the result of circumstances that developed during the conflict nor was it voluntary, as other historiographical narratives have asserted. According to Pappe, Plan D made it clear that "the Palestinians had to go"; "the aim of the plan was in fact the destruction of both the rural and urban areas of Palestine." A sophisticated bureaucracy accompanied by military power aimed at "not only dispossession of the people but also the repossession of the spoils." The examination of events within the "paradigm of war" that so many scholars have adopted avoids assigning blame and must be replaced with a "paradigm of ethnic cleansing" that acknowledges the premeditated crimes committed by such individuals as David Ben-Gurion (first prime minister and defense minister of Israel) and Yigael Yadin (early chief of staff of the Israeli Defense Forces and later deputy prime minister), "the heroes of the Jewish war of independence." The text also condemns Britain, the United Nations, and the surrounding Arab states for their failure to intervene in the unfolding operation. By writing the events of the 1948 ethnic cleansing into world history, Pappe's goal was to counteract the "ideological memoricide" that has kept the Palestinian right of return off the table during attempts to negotiate a lasting peace.

Pappe makes his case for adopting a paradigm of ethnic cleansing through detailed documentation of events and the remapping of Israeli geography. Using both Israeli and Palestinian sources, Pappe creates a historical record of military actions, important players, bureaucratic procedures, and war crimes, such as massacres and cases of rape and looting. During this accounting, he lists the villages that, after being demolished or renamed in an attempt to "de-Arabise the terrain" and "Hebraize Palestine's geography," were erased from official maps. In this way *The Ethnic Cleansing of Palestine* disputes the Israeli narrative that conceals the physical landscape of the nakba in its efforts to paint a picture of Palestine as an "'empty' and 'arid' land before the arrival of Zionism." Pappe is anxious to reclaim the geography of remaining built spaces as well, indicating that evidence of the area's former Palestinian inhabitants is often hidden in plain sight: "The Israelis turned the mosques of Majdal and Qisarya into restaurants and the Beersheba mosque into a shop. The Ayn Hawd mosque is used as a bar." Using these techniques, the author gradually undermines the dominant narratives.

Stylistically, the book applies the language of victimhood that has traditionally been used to describe the Jews in their struggle for statehood to the Arab population of Palestine. The text charges Ben-Gurion and his advisors with almost unilateral aggression against the Arab population, since "rural Palestine showed no desire to fight or attack, and was defenseless." Pappe opens several chapters by juxtaposing at least two quotes, one or more discussing the nakba and another addressing the ethnic cleansing of Kosovo in similar language, drawing emotional power from the evoked comparisons although rarely discussing the similarities in a direct manner. The inclusion of nostalgic written portraits of pre-1948 Palestinian village life, demonstrating how in each one "a whole community disappeared, with all its intricate social networks and cultural achievements," further emphasizes the sympathetic tone of the text. In his recounting of local history and exceptional characteristics of these villages, Pappe shows that many were cleansed or destroyed at a time of economic prosperity. His snapshots humanize the Palestinian population even as they dehumanize the Jewish forces that expelled it.

## CRITICAL DISCUSSION

When *The Ethnic Cleansing of Palestine* was first published in 2006, assessments varied. In "The Liar as Hero" (2011), Benny Morris denounces the book, asserting, "At best, Ilan Pappe must be one of the world's sloppiest historians; at worst, one of the most dishonest." A 2006 review in the *Economist* compares the book to other works by New Historians that have "the defect of treating the Palestinians only as victims, not as actors in their own right" and questions the relevance of the debate altogether, arguing that Israel's admission of ethnic cleansing would do little to change the current reality. Uri Ram's 2008 commentary in the *Middle East Journal* praises the text for openly confronting "Israeli historiography and collective memory and even more importantly Israeli conscience"; he also similarly faults Pappe's "simplistic" insistence that "if Israel would only admit its crimes and repent them by letting the refugees return, everybody would be able to sit secure under their vine and fig trees."

As part of Pappe's larger body of work, *The Ethnic Cleansing of Palestine* has contributed to the gradual transformation of the vocabulary used to discuss the nakba. Although he was not the first to refer to the Palestinian exodus as an "ethnic cleansing," scholars have in the years since the publication of his text increasingly employed the phrase in their own discussions of the relationship between the foundation of the State of Israel and the expulsion of the Palestinians. Whereas in his 2006 book *The Iron Cage: The Story of the Palestinian Struggle for Statehood,* Rashid Khalidi uses the term "ethnic cleansing" with the caveat that it "is rarely applied to what happened in 1948," Lebanese novelist Elias Khoury's 2012 article "Rethinking the Nakba" asserts, albeit not entirely accurately, that "ethnic cleansing as incarnated by Plan Dalet is no longer a matter of debate among historians."

Apart from numerous reviews, *The Ethnic Cleansing of Palestine* has received little critical attention, although it is often cited in scholarly works as an extreme example of the revisionist trend in Israeli

Jewish Haganah troops in Palestine in 1948. In *The Ethnic Cleansing of Palestine,* Ilan Pappe claims that Jewish leaders and Haganah members massacred Arab Palestinians in a system of ethnic cleansing. © BETTMANN/CORBIS.

historiography. In their preface to *The War for Palestine: Rewriting the History of 1948* (2007), Eugene L. Rogan and Avi Shlaim argue that Pappe's provocative use of the ethnic cleansing paradigm effectively excludes him from the public conversation and severely limits his influence on Israeli academia. Even so, aspects of the historical narrative Pappe presents are repeatedly referenced by later historiographers and scholars, especially outside of Israel. In *Palestine Inside Out: An Everyday Occupation* (2008), American literary critic Saree Makdisi refers to *The Ethnic Cleansing of Palestine* in his discussion of Plan D, quoting Pappe extensively. Makdisi also echoes Pappe's ethnic cleansing paradigm in his argument for a one-state solution, asserting that "the sense that there is an inherently Jewish land cluttered up with a non-Jewish population that needs to be dealt with somehow or other drove Zionist planning all through the 1930s and through the ethnic cleansing of Palestine in 1948, and it has prevailed ever since."

## BIBLIOGRAPHY

*Sources*

Khalidi, Rashid. *The Iron Cage: The Story of the Palestinian Struggle for Statehood.* Boston: Beacon, 2006. Print.

Khoury, Elias. "Rethinking the Nakba." *Critical Inquiry* 38.2 (2012): 250–66. Print.

Makdisi, Saree. *Palestine Inside Out: An Everyday Occupation.* New York: Norton, 2008. Print.

Morris, Benny. "The Liar as Hero." *New Republic* 242.5 (2011): 29–35. Print.

"Nations and Narratives." Rev. of *The Ethnic Cleansing of Palestine,* by Ilan Pappe. *Economist* 4 November 2006: 108–09. Print.

Ram, Uri. "Arab-Israeli Conflict." Rev. of *The Ethnic Cleansing of Palestine,* by Ilan Pappe. *Middle East Journal* 62.1 (2008): 150–52. Print.

Rogan, Eugene L., and Avi Shlaim. Preface. *The War for Palestine: Rewriting the History of 1948.* 2nd ed. Ed. Rogan and Shlaim. Cambridge: Cambridge UP, 2007. xvii–xxiv. Print.

*Further Reading*

Khalidi, Walid, ed. *All That Remains: The Palestinian Villages Occupied and Depopulated by Israel in 1948.* Washington, D.C.: Institute for Palestine Studies, 1992. Print.

Khoury, Elias. *Gate of the Sun.* Trans. Humphrey Davies. New York: Archipelago, 2005. Print.

Masalha, Nur. *Expulsion of the Palestinians: The Concept of "Transfer" in Zionist Political Thought, 1882–1948.* Washington, D.C.: Institute for Palestine Studies, 1992. Print.

Morris, Benny. *The Birth of the Palestinian Refugee Problem, 1947–1949.* New York: Cambridge UP, 1987. Print.

Pappe, Ilan. "The Vicissitude of the 1948 Historiography of Israel." *Journal of Palestine Studies* 39.1 (2009): 6–23. Print.

*Allison Blecker*

# THE GALLIC WAR

*Gaius Julius Caesar*

## OVERVIEW

*De Bello Gallico,* or *The Gallic War,* consists of seven books written by Gaius Julius Caesar during his military command in Gaul from 58 to 50 BCE and an eighth book composed by his friend Aulus Hirtius. Caesar's firsthand account describes not only the battles and ultimate conquest of Gaul but also geography and Gallic culture. Caesar wrote *Gallic War* in the third person with both clarity and artful language. He published his military achievements for his contemporaries—the Roman literate and the listening public—in order to elevate his political career and his *dignitas,* or reputation. Thus, *Gallic War* served as propaganda for Caesar.

Some scholars maintain that Caesar wrote and published the seven books around 52 BCE, while others more convincingly assert that he composed and published them individually in the winters following each campaign. There has also been debate over the audience. It was once thought that Caesar's writings were intended for select senators, but recent scholarship has demonstrated that the works were also prepared for large-scale oral performances. Once published, *Gallic War* served to reinforce Caesar's status as not only one of the world's greatest generals but also as a refined rhetorician and popular leader. *Gallic War* helped to make Caesar the most widely known figure in Roman history. The text is still used as an introduction to Latin because of its lucid prose, and it has inspired countless individuals, including William Shakespeare, who furthered the mythos surrounding Caesar by penning the play *Julius Caesar.*

## HISTORICAL AND LITERARY CONTEXT

Coming from a declining patrician family, Caesar relied on his skills as orator for political advancement. After holding the positions of pontifex maximus and praetor, he obtained the governorship of Further Spain in 61 BCE, during which time he became aware of his military talents. The senate's most important duty was to hold military adventurers in check, and it therefore stubbornly refused him further campaigns. Caesar responded by forming the First Triumvirate in 59 BCE. This was an unofficial and private coalition between Caesar, Pompey, and Crassus, three ambitious and powerful men who worked together for their mutual political advantage. Caesar introduced a land

act in 59 BCE that, among other things, relieved overcrowding in Rome and was popular with average citizens. The act faced opposition in the senate because its members, conservative aristocrats, perceived Caesar to be acting as a demagogue and, therefore, viewed him as a threat to their political power. However, Caesar overcame this resistance by physical force and secured the passage of the law. The incident demonstrates the impotence of the republican senate and the growing power of Caesar.

By means of the First Triumvirate, Caesar realized his main objective by becoming governor and military commander of Gaul. From 58 to 50 BCE, he led military campaigns against the numerous tribes of Gaul, a province that included modern France, Belgium, Holland, Switzerland, and Germany west of the Rhine River. Gallic civilization was more advanced than any other European societies beyond the Mediterranean border, and intertribal feuds frequently led to the invocation of Roman aid. In 58 BCE, the Helvetii traversed the land of the Aedui, who implored Rome for help. Caesar engaged in a fight against the Helvetii, thus beginning eight years of war against several Gallic tribes. All the while, Caesar maintained close ties to Rome, where he could purchase political services, and his propagandist *Gallic War* kept the public mindful of his achievements.

The extant writings of Caesar were titled *C. Iuli Caesaris commentarii rerum gestarum,* or *Julius Caesar's Memoirs of His Achievements.* The *commentarius* had been a form of composition with a long history but was further developed by Roman writers to suit their own purposes. Originally, the *commentarius* was an official or private letter not intended for publication. It was not a polished art but rather a statement of facts for their own sake that aided a person's memory. Alexander the Great and his successors employed it as war diaries. The format served Caesar's purposes because it enabled him to give the impression that he had a disinterested desire to tell the truth, making his incredible achievements undeniable.

Caesar's *Gallic War* has had a tremendous cultural influence. In ancient Rome, he had many continuators of his work, such as Hirtius, and the Augustine poets frequently connected Caesar to the divine. Honorific statues such as the Demigod Statue attest to his influence. During the Middle Ages, Caesar was

### ✛ *Key Facts*

**Time Period:**
First Century BCE

**Genre:**
History

**Events:**
Roman conquest of Gaul

**Nationality:**
Roman

## THIS RISE AND FALL OF JULIUS CAESAR

Julius Caesar was born into a patrician family in 100 BCE, and his formative years occurred during Sulla's dictatorship and proscriptions. Caesar received the finest education, learning rhetoric from M. Antonius Gnipho and Apollonius Molon. At the age of twenty-three, he made his debut in the courts with much success. He took part in the Catiline Conspiracy, casting doubts on the constitutional propriety of executing Catiline and his associates without trial. After holding various political offices, he proved himself a man of action after conquering the whole of Gaul by 50 BCE. When the senate ordered Caesar's early recall on January 7, 49 BCE, he responded by crossing the Rubicon with his legions and declared, "The die is cast." Civil war ensued.

In victory, Caesar proved to be clement toward his enemies and an efficient administrator. He instituted the Julian calendar and granted the franchise to provincials. He assumed a new dictatorship in 44 BCE with widespread popularity and was granted many honors, such as coins bearing his image. In the conspiracy of Brutus and Cassius on March 15, 44 BCE, Caesar was assassinated under a rain of daggers. He left behind many notable written works, including *Gallic War*, *Civil War*, *Spanish War*, and *De Analogia*.

considered an exemplary military leader and was placed in Limbo among the virtuous heathens by Dante. There was humanist enthusiasm for Caesar's *Gallic War* during the Renaissance, which culminated with Shakespeare's play *Julius Caesar* in 1599. In addition, many military figures—including Pope Julius II, Napoleon Bonaparte, and Benito Mussolini—were compared to Caesar for propagandist means. Today, television and cinema dramatize and perpetuate the mythos of Caesar; an example of this is HBO's acclaimed series *Rome* (2005–07).

### THEMES AND STYLE

Central to Caesar's *Gallic War* are his *res gestae*, or accomplishments. His swift campaigns against the Gallic tribes, his descriptions of geography and native customs, and the threat of the Germanic tribes to Gaul and Rome are major themes. The most famous episode is the invasion of Britain in 55 BCE, which Caesar justifies because the Britons had given military aid to the Gauls. In actuality, Caesar invaded Britain because of its reputed riches and to secure the glory of leading his legions to victory on a distant and unknown island. Focusing on exotic elements, he writes that the charioteers—vehicles no longer used in Gaul—of Britain "unnerved our men and that his support was most timely." The reaction in Rome was one of excitement, and the senate decreed a public thanksgiving of twenty days. With a second invasion in 54 BCE, Caesar took hostages and imposed an annual tribute.

His imaginative descriptions drew the Roman people to his writings.

The rhetorical strategies employed by Caesar are designed to legitimatize conquest and increase his popularity. He maintains his third-person objectivity—ostensible though it may be—throughout the work, which makes his accomplishments seem indisputable. Caesar omits many facts, such as his desire for and his acquisition of plunder, instead claiming that the giving of aid to Roman allies is his foremost imperative. In this way, the Republic appears to take precedence over personal interests. Caesar also describes the Gallic enemy in detail, thereby strengthening his credibility. In "Noble Gauls and Their Other in Caesar's Propaganda," Jonathan Barlow writes, "The impression implanted is of a reporter who is unconcerned with the imperative of propaganda, who is anxious to balance the merits of his own case against those of the other side." Caesar contrasts his own noble attributes with Gallic savagery, such as human sacrifice, in order to justify his conquests: "Some weave huge figures of wicker, and fill their limbs with live humans, who are then burned to death when the figures are set afire." Ultimately, Caesar tells the people what they want to hear. According to recent studies in propaganda, this strategy is more effective than an attempt to convert them.

Stylistically, *Gallic War* is lucid and economical, never theoretical and interpretive. Caesar's word choices are precise; for example, he uses the word "flumen" for river instead of the alternatives "fluvius" or "amnis." For Caesar, a particular thing was best described by one particular word. "The choice of words," he writes, "is the fountainhead of eloquence," and he avoids "the unusual and extravagant word." Since Caesar was an orator whose works were read aloud, he placed importance on clarity. In *Institutio Oratoria,* Roman rhetorician Quintilian says, "Such force dwells in him, such sharpness, and such passion that it seems that he spoke with the same vigor with which he fought." Moses Hadas sums up Caesar's approach in the 1957 translation of *The Gallic War and Other Writings of Julius Caesar*: "His credibility is enhanced by a style at once lucid and precise."

### CRITICAL DISCUSSION

Ascertaining the initial reaction to *Gallic War* is a matter of guesswork, though the public most likely responded with enthusiasm at large-scale oral performances. It was certainly admired for its clear prose and recognized as valuable primary source material. In *Brutus* (46 BCE), Cicero claims that it was written so that "others might have material to their hand if they composed a history." A century later, Plutarch wrote *Caesar* and Suetonius *Divus Iulius,* in which the authors emphasize Caesar's military prowess and lucid writing style, qualities best illustrated in *Gallic War*. Moreover, ancient historians such as Tacitus, Appian, and Cassius Dio highlighted his historical importance, viewing him as a pivotal figure. Cassius Dio, in particular, realized the equivocal nature of Caesar's achievements.

Fifteenth-century miniature depicting Julius Caesar's troops and Germanic forces battling at the Rhine River. In *The Gallic War,* (58 to 50 BCE), Caesar describes his military exploits in the ancient region of Gaul. ALBUM/ ART RESOURCE, NY.

Caesar is perhaps the most controversial figure in world history. In *Natural History,* written in the first century CE, Pliny the Elder reflects that Caesar's Gallic campaigns were "so great a wrong to the human race, even if a necessary one." Centuries later, George Washington inspired his soldiers with the example of Cato the Younger—the famous statesman, politician, defender of the republic, stoic philosopher, great-grandson of one of Rome's most famous war heroes, and greatest antagonist of Caesar. Cato was known for his moral integrity and stubborn self-assertiveness, frequently rallying the senate in opposition to Caesar's acts. In her essay in *Julius Caesar in Western Culture* (2006), Margaret Malamud writes, "Cato embodied the qualities most admired in the eighteenth century America: moral virtue, unselfish patriotism, and courage. Julius Caesar stood for their opposites: unchecked ambition and tyrannical ambition." Moreover, several contemporary critics have compared U.S. president George W. Bush's agenda in Iraq in the early 2000s to Caesar's imperialism in Gaul.

There have been predominant trends in recent scholarship about *Gallic War,* as academics have attempted to discover and explain both its composition and publication dates. In "The Publication of *De Bello Gallico,*" T. P. Wiseman provides the most convincing evidence that the seven books were composed and published at intervals. Understanding Caesar's true intentions is another scholarly trend. In her essay in *Julius Caesar as Artful Reporter* (1998), Catherine Torigian dissects the famous first line—"The whole of Gaul is divided into three parts"—in order to illustrate Caesar's overall purpose. She writes, "Cutting up Gaul, Caesar, in effect, cuts it down to a more manageable size and renders it a less formidable obstacle to Roman, and his own, expansionist ambitions." Caesar stands as an equivocal figure. Some label him a popular leader condemned by aristocratic judgments, while others criticize him as a megalomaniacal tyrant. *Gallic War* has not entirely defined Caesar, but it has certainly perpetuated his legacy.

## BIBLIOGRAPHY

*Sources*

Barlow, Jonathan. "Noble Gauls and Their Other in Caesar's Propaganda." *Julius Caesar as Artful Reporter.* Ed. Katheryn Welch and Anton Powell. London: Gerald Duckworth, 1998. Print.

Caesar, Julius. *The Gallic War and Other Writings of Julius Caesar.* Trans. Moses Hadas. New York: Modern Library, 1957. Print.

Malamud, Margaret. "Manifest Destiny and the Eclipse of Julius Caesar." *Julius Caesar in Western Culture.* Ed. Maria Wyke. London: Blackwell, 2006. Print.

Pliny. *Natural History.* Trans. H. Rackham. Cambridge: Harvard UP, 1938. Print.

Quintilian. Institutio Oratoria. Vols. 1–3. Trans. H. E. Butler. Cambridge: Harvard UP, 1980. Print.

Torigian, Catherine. "The *Logos* of Caesar's *Bellum Gallicum,* Especially as Revealed in Its First Five Chapters." *Julius Caesar as Artful Reporter.* Ed. Katheryn Welch and Anton Powell. London: Gerald Duckworth, 1998. Print.

Wiseman, T. P. "The Publication of *De Bello Gallico.*" *Julius Caesar as Artful Reporter.* Ed. Katheryn Welch and Anton Powell. London: Gerald Duckworth, 1998. Print.

*Further Reading*

Adcock, F. E. *Caesar as Man of Letters.* Cambridge: Cambridge UP, 1956. Print.

Garcea, Alessandro. *Caesar's De Analogia.* Oxford: Oxford UP, 2012. Print.

Griffin, Miriam. *A Companion to Julius Caesar.* London: Blackwell, 2009. Print.

Grillo, Luca. *The Art of Caesar's Bellum Civile.* Cambridge: Cambridge UP, 2012. Print.

Parenti, Michael. *The Assassination of Julius Caesar: A People's History of Ancient Rome.* New York: The New Press, 2004. Print.

Riggsby, Andrew. *Caesar in Gaul and Rome: War in Words.* Austin: U of Texas P, 2006. Print.

*Media Adaptation*

Caesar, Julius. *Gallic Wars.* St. Laurent, Quebec, Canada: Madacy Entertainment Group, [1997], © 1995. VHS.

*Greg Bach*

# THE HISTORY AND TOPOGRAPHY OF IRELAND

*Gerald of Wales*

## OVERVIEW

*The History and Topography of Ireland* (Latin title: *Topographia Hibernica*), an ethnographical treatise written by the Norman-Welsh clergyman Gerald of Wales (Latin name: Giraldus Cambrensis) and completed around 1188, is a lengthy description of the geography, fauna, and people of Ireland. (Despite the word "history" in the English title, the work contains relatively little actual history.) Written in Latin, the book is split into three distinct sections: the first part details Ireland's landscape and natural life, the second discusses a number of miracles and "wonders"—often supernatural in nature—that Gerald ascribes to Ireland, and the third describes the history and culture of the Irish people as Gerald saw them. As one of the most comprehensive and widely read works on Ireland from the Middle Ages, it substantially influenced public perception of that country and its inhabitants, whom Gerald largely depicted as barbarous and deceitful, thus implicitly justifying the then-recent Anglo-Norman invasions of Ireland in 1169 and 1171.

The first of several ethnographical and historical works Gerald composed throughout his life—his next book was about the invasion of Ireland, and two more were about Wales—Gerald's *History and Topography* (which Gerald revised several times throughout his life, mostly adding material extraneous to Ireland itself) was well received upon its completion. It soon became the standard medieval overview of Ireland, and it was used as a source for numerous subsequent English writings on Ireland and Irish society. Its condescending portrayal of the Irish helped to propagate Norman and English views of Ireland as a fertile but uncivilized backwater, a stereotype that served as part of the cultural ambience throughout centuries of colonialist ventures in Ireland. Gerald's text remains important as one of very few original sources of twelfth-century information about Ireland, despite its frequent naïveté and its obvious anti-Irish, pro-colonialist bias.

## HISTORICAL AND LITERARY CONTEXT

The latter half of the twelfth century was marked by a great deal of Norman colonial activity in the British Isles. In 1169 the Anglo-Norman king of England, Henry II, allowed a number of his subjects to be recruited for a military campaign in Ireland, ostensibly to restore Dermot MacMurrough, the ousted Irish

king of Leinster, back to his throne. Then, in 1171, Henry himself brought a much larger fleet to Ireland in order to consolidate Norman political control in the country, in addition to consolidating his own control over the Normans already present. By 1172 most of the Irish kings had pledged fealty to him.

In 1185 Gerald of Wales—many of whose relatives had been personally involved in the invasion of Ireland, which Gerald had first visited in 1183—was sent there as part of the entourage of King Henry's eighteen-year-old son, John, who had been appointed as lord of Ireland in 1177. It was during this excursion that Gerald began composing his *History and Topography*. Gerald's close familial involvement with the Norman invasion and occupation—which provided the background for his next book, *The Conquest of Ireland*—is likely reflected in his work's negative portrayal of the Irish. In contrast, in his later surveys of Wales, Gerald wrote a condescending but relatively sympathetic depiction of Welsh culture (which Gerald shared to some extent, being partly Welsh). In addition, he had professional reasons to flatter Henry and create a text complimentary to the king's actions.

Historiography was a crowded and vibrant literary genre throughout the twelfth century, and Gerald made use of some of this work, both as models and as sources. However, the type of book-length ethnographical survey Gerald engaged in was fairly unique in English literature at the time, since expositional portraits of cultural groups tended to take the form of digressions within longer texts rather than being the focus of a text. The closest analogue within twelfth-century literature to Gerald's writings on the Irish is perhaps the work of the Saxon historian Helmold of Bosau, whose *Chronicle of the Slavs* depicts the history and culture of the Polabian Slavic tribes as well as their military conquest and religious conversion. Like Gerald, Helmold depicted the subjects of his work as barbarous and primitive, thereby implicitly justifying the intervention of others.

In addition to inaugurating an influential series of similar writings by Gerald himself, his *History and Topography* was a profound influence on English opinion of Ireland and was sometimes used uncritically as a source in subsequent histories, especially in the sixteenth century, when its impact on other texts became especially pronounced. Later Irish-written

+ *Key Facts*

**Time Period:**
Early 12th Century

**Genre:**
Treatise

**Events:**
Anglo-Norman invasions of Ireland; Middle Ages; Irish history and culture

**Nationality:**
Latin

# GERALD AND THE SEE OF ST. DAVID'S

The effusive praise with which Gerald lavishes Henry II in *The History and Topography of Ireland* can perhaps partly be attributed to professional ambition: throughout much of his career, Gerald hoped to be appointed as archbishop to the See of St. David's. Indeed, he had been nominated for the position in 1176, but Henry objected, largely because Gerald's Welsh background (he was one-quarter Welsh and three-quarters Norman) gave Henry pause about granting him a Welsh see, especially since the chapter of St. David's already seemed to have plans for independence from the ecclesiastical authority of Canterbury.

Gerald's writings as a rule tended to be caustic and biting, sometimes even to Henry and his sons. Therefore, *History and Topography*'s atypically fawning treatment of Henry (who died in 1189) can be seen partly as an exercise in flattery carried out by Gerald in the hope of receiving his coveted appointment in the future. Gerald never achieved his career goal, though his vigorous pursuit of it eventually led him to make several trips to Rome, come into conflict with the pope, and be briefly imprisoned in France. His later years were occupied largely with scholarship, and he died in 1223.

histories, such as Geoffrey Keating's *History of Ireland* (c. 1634), often took an adversarial stance toward Gerald's work and presented themselves as redressing the damage it had caused. Contemporary histories of Ireland continue to use it as a unique source of rare information but also tend to emphasize its biased and often unreliable nature.

## THEMES AND STYLE

Central to Gerald's *History and Topography* is a portrait of Ireland as a wondrous, almost enchanted land inhabited by uncivilized savages. Much of Gerald's topographical description depicts Ireland as something of a paradise, sometimes bringing in spurious notions of magic, as when Gerald asserts that not only nothing in Ireland is poisonous but also "if poison be brought in, no matter what it be, from elsewhere, immediately it loses all the force of its evil." Gerald tends to suggest that such a glorious country is wasted on the Irish themselves, however; hence his assertion that the Irish are failing through laziness to take advantage of their fertile soil: "the nature of the soil is not to be blamed, but rather the want of industry on the part of the cultivator." This type of rhetoric combines with some straightforward attacks on the Irish populace—whom Gerald refers to as "a filthy people, wallowing in vice"—to create the impression that allowing the island to remain unconquered would have been a tragically missed opportunity.

A frequent rhetorical maneuver Gerald uses to convey his themes is his tendency to follow a straightforward recounting of supposed facts with a moralistic miniature sermon. For example, his report of an Irish woman having sexual intercourse with a goat (bestiality being, in Gerald's estimation, "a particular vice of that people") is followed by much hand-wringing and excoriation: "How unworthy and unspeakable! How reason succumbs so outrageously to sensuality!" Likewise, Gerald's description of Ireland's regal history and eventual conquest by Henry II is followed by a lengthy encomium on the greatness of Henry and his achievements: "truly you are a king and conqueror, ruling your courage by your virtue, and conquering your anger with your temperance." Gerald's final sentence, a quotation from the Roman poet Horace asserting that "he has won every point who has joined the useful to the sweet," perhaps sums up his rhetorical approach of coupling interesting information with sententious didacticism.

The emotional tenor of Gerald's language tends toward a curious mixture of blasé credulity and pompous sermonizing. The reader is assured that "I have put down nothing in this book the truth of which I have not found out either by the testimony of my own eyes, or that of reliable men found worthy of credence," and even when Gerald describes the most outlandish events (many of them evidently derived from rumor and legend), he generally maintains a steadfastly credulous tone of address, describing Ireland's supposed wonders and miracles in an amiably prosaic fashion as if their veracity were beyond dispute. His language becomes more vigorous and emphatic not when describing fantastic events but when imparting the moral lessons to be extracted from those events, as when he attributes the cataclysmic sinking of an inhabited landmass to Godly retribution against the inhabitants' "filthy crimes against nature."

## CRITICAL DISCUSSION

Gerald's *Topography and History* was apparently popular upon its completion, notwithstanding some negative appraisals. Gerald reported a positive reception at Oxford and praise from Baldwin of Forde, the archbishop of Canterbury, though Gerald himself is the only source of this information. He also apparently believed, perhaps mistakenly, that the prominent clergyman and belletrist Walter Map strongly approved of the book. Meanwhile, Gerald's own bitter complaints about attacks on his work indicate that not everyone thought highly of it, but James F. Dimock points out in the preface to his Latin edition that the large number of early manuscript copies testifies to its popularity in Gerald's time, and that "no doubt he speaks far too strongly, as always when his feelings were touched, of the ill reception of these treatises by his contemporaries." It was not until the seventeenth century, when Irish writers such as Stephen White and John Lynch excoriated it for its obvious biases, that the work began to meet with enduring, recorded disapprobation.

Monorbier Castle in Pembrokeshire, Wales. Built in the twelfth century, it was home to Gerald of Wales. © KRISTY DURBRIDGE/ALAMY.

*The Topography and History of Ireland* became a key part of the ideological background of England's centuries of colonial involvement in Ireland. In his 1999 analysis of English perceptions of Ireland in the Early Modern period, Andrew Hadfield observes that "it is generally agreed that most Tudor representations of Ireland and the Irish owed a great deal to [Gerald]," who "was indeed the 'ghost in the machine' of English representations of Ireland for at least four-and-a-half centuries." The relationship between Gerald's writing and English colonialism remains a subject of considerable interest among scholars.

Modern scholarship of Gerald's text often focuses on its antagonistic portrayal of the Irish, frequently discussing the responses of later Irish writers and placing the work into the ideological context of its milieu. An example of this approach is John Brannigan's 1998 postcolonial analysis, which observes that "in defining the Irish as barbarous and savage, [Gerald] was confirming what earlier Greek and Roman authors had written, and so, in the circular system of authentication which pervaded the European intellectual climate of the middle ages, the weight of intellectual authority behind the work was established." Other criticism considers his works on Ireland in combination with those on Wales, an example being Robert Bartlett's 1982 monograph on Gerald, which compares his overall approach to that of other outside observers of "barbaric" cultures, such as Helmold and Adam of Bremen, and makes a case for Gerald's innovativeness as a twelfth-century ethnographer.

## BIBLIOGRAPHY

*Sources*

Bartlett, Robert. *Gerald of Wales, 1146–1223*. Oxford: Clarendon, 1982. Print.

Brannigan, John. "'A Particular Vice of that People': Giraldus Cambrensis and the Discourse of English Colonialism." *Irish Studies Review* 6.2 (1998): 121–30. *Academic Search Complete*. Web. 18 Aug. 2012.

Dimock, James F. Preface. *Giraldi Cambrensis Opera*. Vol. 5. By Giraldus Cambrensis. Ed. Dimock. London: Longman, Green, Reader, and Dyer, 1867. ix–lxxxix. Print.

Gerald of Wales. *The History and Topography of Ireland*. Trans. John J. O'Meara. Harmondsworth: Penguin, 1982. Print.

Hadfield, Andrew. "Rethinking Early-Modern Colonialism: The Anomalous State of Ireland." *Irish Studies Review* 7.1 (1999): 13–27. *Academic Search Complete*. Web. 18 Aug. 2012.

*Further Reading*

Cain, James D. "Unnatural History: Gender and Genealogy in Gerald of Wales' *Topographia Hibernica*." *Essays in Medieval Studies* 19 (2002): 29–43. Print.

Cambrensis, Giraldus. *Expugnatio Hibernica: The Conquest of Ireland*. Ed. and Trans. A. B. Scott and F. X. Martin. Dublin: Royal Irish Academy, 1978. Print.

Duggan, Anne J. "The Making of a Myth: Giraldus Cambrensis, Laudabiliter, and Henry II's Lordship of Ireland." *Studies in Medieval and Renaissance History* 19.4 (2007): 107–70. Print.

Gerald of Wales. *The Journey Through Wales; and, The Description of Wales.* Trans. Lewis Thorpe. Harmondsworth: Penguin, 1978. Print.

Helmold, Priest of Bosau. *The Chronicle of the Slavs.* Trans. Francis Joseph Tschan. New York: Columbia UP, 1935. Print.

Knight, Rhonda. "Werewolves, Monsters, and Miracles: Representing Colonial Fantasies in Gerald of Wales's *Topographia Hibernica.*" *Studies in Iconography* 22 (2001): 55–86. Print.

Mittman, Asa Simon. "The Other Close at Hand: Gerald of Wales and the 'Marvels of the West.'" *The Monstrous Middle Ages.* Ed. Bettina Bildhauer and Robert Mills. Cardiff: U of Wales P, 2003. 97–112. Print.

Roberts, Brynley F. *Gerald of Wales.* Cardiff: U of Wales P, 1982. Print.

Rollo, David. "Gerald of Wales' *Topographica Hibernica*: Sex and the Irish Nation." *Romanic Review* 86.2 (1995): 169–90. Print.

*James Overholtzer*

# HISTORY OF THE KINGS OF BRITAIN

*Geoffrey of Monmouth*

## OVERVIEW

The *History of the Kings of Britain* (Latin: *Historia Regum Britanniae*), a pseudohistorical chronicle written by Geoffrey of Monmouth and completed in or around 1136, purports to tell the complete history of the British monarchy, beginning with the legendary founding of Britain by the Trojan hero Brutus late in the second millennium BCE and ending with Britain's domination by Anglo-Saxons in the seventh century CE. Written in Latin and claiming to be a translation of a (likely fictitious) Welsh-language chronicle, the *History* is now given little credence as a factual account, as it is replete with verifiable inaccuracies, heroic legends presented as truth, and, occasionally, outright supernatural content. It was, nonetheless, tremendously influential as a history and as a source of legendary material, especially in its popularization of King Arthur as a mythic figure and national hero. Geoffrey's presentation of an idealized, glorious British past was implicitly flattering to the Anglo-Norman aristocracy that ruled England at the time, and his book was a foundational text in the construction and promulgation of a sense of British historical and cultural identity.

Geoffrey's *History* emerged from a vibrant tradition of historical writing in England during the High Middle Ages (1000–1300), a period when historical accounts of England's past were numerous and popular, though Geoffrey's specific purview, the Britons' rule of England, had been relatively ignored. These histories were of highly variable quality in terms of accuracy, but even by the standards of the time, Geoffrey's work was devoted more to legend than to fact. It was occasionally condemned for this reason, but before the seventeenth century, most readers accepted its veracity without question. This acceptance, coupled with the book's massive popularity, allowed it to shape, directly and indirectly, much of subsequent British literature, folklore, and national self-perception.

## HISTORICAL AND LITERARY CONTEXT

In 1066 the Norman monarch William I (commonly known as William the Conqueror) invaded England, bringing to an end the period of Anglo-Saxon domination, which had itself begun with the defeat of the Britons in the seventh century, as documented in the conclusion of Geoffrey's *History*. The new rulers and their Anglo-Norman descendants profoundly altered English politics and culture, establishing French as the new language of the aristocracy and Latin as the language of official transactions and introducing an ideal of courtly life that shaped later English conceptions of "chivalry."

By the twelfth century there was a great deal of aristocratic interest in pre-Anglo-Saxon British history, much of which had, in the popular imagination, accumulated narrative embellishment and assumed the status of legend, even as the disempowered Britons themselves had long since fragmented into the relatively discrete Welsh, Cornish, and Breton peoples. Given this interest, Geoffrey's *History* served as a means of ingratiating the author with his Anglo-Norman rulers, especially since its depiction of the chivalrous and imperialistic court of King Arthur was modeled at least as much on the Anglo-Norman present as on the British past. Likewise, the book's codification of a common history for the now-dispersed Britons served as a cultural rallying point for them and, eventually, for England in general.

English historiography in the twelfth century was a thriving literary genre, with such authors as William of Malmesbury and Henry of Huntingdon composing popular historical chronicles that drew heavily on the seminal English histories of previous centuries, including those of Bede, Nennius, and Gildas, the last of whom was actually more of a polemicist than a historian. Geoffrey shared his contemporaries' indebtedness to past chroniclers, but he compounded his use of historical record with material drawn from myth, legend, and (probably) his own imagination, producing a far more fanciful account than a strict adherence to facts would have generated. In contrast to his colleagues' more down-to-earth narratives, Geoffrey's work is less a straightforward history than a literary paean to a mythical British past.

The *History of the Kings of Britain* was a seminal influence in subsequent English historiography as well as in English (and French) literature in general. Its frequent acceptance as truth led to its use as a source for numerous subsequent histories, which were themselves massively influential. For example, Geoffrey's description of the reign of King Leir was used as a source for Raphael Holinshed's 1577 *Chronicles,* which then became Shakespeare's historical source for his play *King Lear.* Likewise, the *History*'s dissemination of

**⁘ Key Facts**

**Time Period:**
Mid-12th Century

**Genre:**
Pseudohistorical Chronicle

**Events:**
William the Conqueror's capture of England; change of British culture under Anglo-Norman rule

**Nationality:**
English

# THE MATTER OF BRITAIN

*The History of the Kings of Britain* was a central text in what later came to be known as the "Matter of Britain," a large body of literature and folklore concerned with the events of a mythical, idealized British past and in particular with the reign of King Arthur. Influenced in part by Celtic mythology, Christian beliefs, and pre-Norman historical chronicles, the Matter of Britain eventually came to encompass a vast cycle of legends, of which the most well known are probably the chivalric idyll of Camelot and the quest for the Holy Grail.

An early approximation of Camelot can easily be discerned in Geoffrey's *History,* but the Grail legend was actually introduced into Arthurian literature much later in the twelfth century by the French poet Chrétien de Troyes. Indeed, for several centuries it was France, rather than England, that made the most lasting literary contributions to the Matter of Britain. With the exception of the anonymous late-fourteenth-century poem *Sir Gawain and the Green Knight,* it was arguably not until the very end of the Middle Ages, with Thomas Malory's *Le Morte d'Arthur* (1485), that an English writer after Geoffrey produced an Arthurian work whose literary merit is generally accepted today.

various legends about Merlin, King Arthur, and other legendary British figures made it a direct and indirect source of much French and English Arthurian literature, from Marie de France's *Lanval* to Thomas Malory's *Le Morte d'Arthur.* Its legacy of idealized British pseudohistory can be seen today (albeit without claims of factuality) in more modern Arthurian works such as T. H. White's *The Once and Future King* and Mary Stewart's Arthurian novels.

## THEMES AND STYLE

A recurring theme in Geoffrey's *History* is the glorification of British military conquest and imperialism. Throughout the narrative, the British monarchy's aggressive campaigns in the British Isles, as well as in Gaul and Rome, are presented in unambiguously heroic and positive terms. In describing the aftermath of King Arthur's defeat of the Romans, for example, Geoffrey writes that "the Britons pursued them as fast as they could go, putting them to death miserably, taking them prisoner and plundering them…. All this was ordained by divine providence." Although many of Britain's kings are depicted negatively—Vortigern, in particular, is castigated for abetting the Anglo-Saxon invasion through his friendship with a Saxon ruler—their ruthless expansionism is never presented as a flaw. Geoffrey's celebration of British conquest thus serves as both a patriotic reminder of the now-displaced Britons' past glories and as an implicit endorsement of the current Anglo-Norman rulers' imperialistic ventures.

Throughout his *History,* Geoffrey tends to alternate between straightforward historical chronicle and a more inventive and literary approach to suit his rhetorical aims. Many kings' reigns are summarized within a brief space; for example, a single sentence—"after the death of Cunedagius, his son Rivallo succeeded him, a peaceful, prosperous young man who ruled the kingdom frugally"—is fully half of Geoffrey's historical coverage of Rivallo's reign. Accounts of other reigns are given far more attention, often turning into miniature stories with fabricated dialogue and detailed description, as when King Uther conspires with Merlin to magically disguise himself as the lady Ygerna's husband, a ruse that leads to Arthur's conception. These latter, more sensationalistic sections no doubt contributed to the book's enduring popularity. The more straightforward passages, meanwhile, give the work a patina of historical legitimacy, a façade further supported by Geoffrey's occasional explicit references to other historical works, by means of which he implicitly positions his own work as a factual account, despite the implausible nature of some of his claims.

Stylistically, Geoffrey's *History* is for the most part fairly unadorned, with relatively few figures of speech and a largely plain, prosaic tenor, but it reaches occasional heights of emotional intensity during its treatment of especially patriotic subjects. Battle scenes, in particular, are described with great vigor and detail, as are heroic speeches: "A great flood-tide of joy boiled up within him and he shouted at the top of his voice: 'God has granted my prayer! Now, men, down with what is left of the Ambrones! Victory is in your hand!'" What stylistic embellishment the text contains is usually deployed for the purpose of emphasizing British might and glory, as befits Geoffrey's general interest in presenting an idealized portrait of his subject.

## CRITICAL DISCUSSION

Upon its completion, Geoffrey's text quickly became one of the most popular accounts of English history. Although some of Geoffrey's fellow historians, including William of Newburgh and Gerald of Wales, derided the *History* as wildly inaccurate—an accusation that persisted through the centuries and has now become the standard view—a much larger proportion of its readers enjoyed it and accepted it unquestioningly. As Geoffrey Ashe points out in his 1985 study of the historical foundations of Arthurian legends, the positive reception of Geoffrey's depiction of King Arthur encouraged that depiction to be historically sanctioned: "among serious chroniclers, many were doubtful and one or two were hostile, but quite a number succumbed to popular belief by including [King Arthur] in their histories." It was not until the seventeenth century that doubt of the accuracy of Geoffrey's history became truly widespread.

As a seminal document in the literary consolidation of a sense of British national identity, Geoffrey's *History* profoundly shaped nationalistic thought in the centuries after it was published. Its glorified portrait of British rule was eventually claimed not just by the displaced Britons who were its ostensible subjects but also by England as a whole, making it part of the country's ideological fabric. As J. S. P. Tatlock observes in his 1938 discussion of Geoffrey's motives for writing his *History,* "Geoffrey again and again exalts his Britons by showing them … as European if not world conquerors," which led to his text being "much used as affording precedents for English rule of other countries." The *History's* influence on British political thought has since been the subject of much scholarship.

Modern critical work on *The History of the Kings of Britain* often explores the complexities of its dubious status as a history, debating the possible sources of Geoffrey's various assertions about the British past and situating the work in relation to English historiography in general. Christopher Brooke's 1976 article "Geoffrey of Monmouth as a Historian" is an example of this trend; Michael J. Curley's 1994 monograph on Geoffrey, which closely considers Geoffrey's inspirations for specific passages, is another. Also common is the tendency to analyze the text in relation to colonialism, as in Michael A. Faletra's article "Narrating the Matter of Britain: Geoffrey of Monmouth and the Norman Colonization of Wales" (2000), which concludes that Geoffrey's history was deliberately constructed in order to please his Anglo-Norman rulers and give support to their imperial designs in Wales.

Sir Galahad is presented to King Arthur and the Knights of the Round Table. According to legend, Arthur was king of Britain during the Anglo-Saxon invasion. © IVY CLOSE IMAGES/ALAMY.

## BIBLIOGRAPHY

*Sources*

Ashe, Geoffrey. *The Discovery of King Arthur.* Garden City: Anchor-Doubleday, 1985. Print.

Brooke, Christopher. "Geoffrey of Monmouth as a Historian." *Church and Government in the Middle Ages.* Ed. Brooke et al. Cambridge: Cambridge UP, 1976. 77–91. Print.

Curley, Michael J. *Geoffrey of Monmouth.* New York: Twayne, 1994. Print.

Faletra, Michael A. "Narrating the Matter of Britain: Geoffrey of Monmouth and the Norman Colonization of Wales." *Chaucer Review* 35.1 (2000): 60–85. *JSTOR.* Web. 8 Aug. 2012.

Geoffrey of Monmouth. *The History of the Kings of Britain.* Trans. Lewis Thorpe. Harmondsworth: Penguin, 1966. Print.

Tatlock, J. S. P. "Geoffrey of Monmouth's Motives for Writing His *Historia.*" *Proceedings of the American Philosophical Society* 79.4 (1938): 695–703. *JSTOR.* Web. 8 Aug. 2012.

*Further Reading*

Crick, Julia. "Geoffrey and the Prophetic Tradition." *The Arthur of Medieval Latin Literature: The Development and Dissemination of the Arthurian Legend in Medieval Latin.* Ed. Siân Echard. Cardiff: U of Wales P, 2011. 67–82. Print.

Curran, John E., Jr. "Geoffrey of Monmouth in Renaissance Drama: Imagining Non-History." *Modern Philology* 97.1 (1999): 1–20. Print.

Echard, Siân. *Arthurian Narrative in the Latin Tradition.* Cambridge: Cambridge UP, 1998. Print.

Jankulak, Karen. *Geoffrey of Monmouth.* Cardiff: U of Wales P, 2010. Print.

Jones, Timothy. "Geoffrey of Monmouth, *Fouke le Fitz Waryn,* and National Mythology." *Studies in Philology* 91.3 (1994): 233–49. Print.

Ingledew, Francis. "The Book of Troy and the Genealogical Construction of History: The Case of Geoffrey of Monmouth's *Historia regum Britanniae.*" *Speculum* 69.3 (1994): 665–704. Print.

Tatlock, J. S. P. *The Legendary History of Britain: Geoffrey of Monmouth's Historia Regum Britanniae and Its Early Vernacular Versions.* Berkeley: U of California P, 1950. Print.

Warren, Michelle R. "Making Contact: Postcolonial Perspectives through Geoffrey of Monmouth's *Historia regum Britannie.*" *Arthuriana* 8.4 (1998): 115–34. Print.

Wood, Juliette. "Where Does Britain End?: The Reception of Geoffrey of Monmouth in Scotland and Wales." *The Scots and Medieval Arthurian Legend.* Ed. Rhiannon Purdie and Nicola Royan. Cambridge: Brewer, 2005. 9–24. Print.

*James Overholtzer*

# "HISTORY WILL ABSOLVE ME"

*Fidel Castro*

✛ *Key Facts*

**Time Period:**
Mid-20th Century

**Genre:**
Testimonial

**Events:**
Dictatorial rule of
Cuba by Batista; failed
revolution of 1952

**Nationality:**
Cuban

## OVERVIEW

"History Will Absolve Me" is the last sentence and the ultimate title of a lengthy testimonial statement (as much as four hours long) given by Fidel Castro before a Cuban court on October 16, 1953, when he was being tried for attempting to overthrow the government of Cuba led by Fulgencio Batista. Rather than a legal defense, Castro's speech is a passionate and melodramatic indictment of the Batista regime and a blueprint for a new and better Cuba. Castro spoke without notes and no court record was kept, so "History Will Absolve Me" was reconstructed by the author after he had been convicted and sent to prison on the Isle of Pines. The speech, a brilliant propaganda coup, turns the tables on the Batista government, accuses *it* of illegal seizure of power, and in highly charged language makes an eloquent plea for its overthrow.

Batista had overthrown the presidency of Carlos Prío Socarrás in March of the preceding year, dissolving the national congress, cancelling the presidential election then in progress, and making himself president. Fidel Castro, a young activist lawyer, then organized and led a spectacularly unsuccessful attack on the Moncada Army Barracks in Santiago, Cuba. His speech at his subsequent trial effectively made him the leader of the movement to overthrow Batista, provided the resistance with its greatest recruiting tool, and gave drive and focus to the revolution that eventually took power in Cuba in 1959. In a global sense, the speech marks Castro's first step onto the stage of international politics, where he was to become a hero of the anticolonial movements then sprouting around the world.

## HISTORICAL AND LITERARY CONTEXT

Cuba became an independent nation following the Spanish-American War (1898–1901). From 1902 to 1933, governance in Cuba was turbulent and uncertain, with presidents elected and overthrown and repeated military interventions by the United States. In 1933 a junta of army sergeants, including Batista, overthrew the corrupt and increasingly dictatorial presidency of Gerardo Machado. Batista then made himself head of the army and ruled Cuba through a string of puppet presidents. In 1940 Batista himself was elected president, and he served until 1944, when a mildly progressive national constitution was instituted. He then went to live in the United States, but

he returned to Cuba in 1952 to run for another presidential term. When it was obvious that he would lose the election, Batista led a military coup and again took power as president.

Fidel Castro was 25 in 1952, and he had been politically engaged since studying law at the University of Havana in 1945. Immediately following Batista's coup d'état, Castro and his brother Raúl began to organize and train resistance movements, operating in the environs of the university. On July 26 the Castro brothers led approximately 125 rebels—chiefly intellectuals like themselves—in an armed attack on the Moncada Barracks in hopes of obtaining armaments and a symbolic victory. One-half of the rebels were killed and others, fleeing, were hunted down and shot. The remainder, including Fidel and Raúl, were captured and charged with attempting to overthrow the lawful government. They were put on trial together, and Fidel served as their defense attorney. Ultimately, however, Fidel was tried by himself after the others had been found innocent or guilty in a separate venue. It was during this second trial that he delivered the "History Will Absolve Me" speech.

Castro made deft modern use of an ancient tradition. For more than two-thousand years, the accused have used their "day in court" to justify their actions and proselytize their views. The most famous instance in the ancient world was the trial of Socrates (399 BCE), which was described by Plato in *The Apology* and by Xenophon in his *Memoirs of Socrates*. In the late Middle Ages, the simple eloquence of Joan of Arc at her trial (1431) put to shame her English accusers. In both these cases, however, the testimony of the accused was turned into propaganda by others after the fact, whereas Castro conceived, planned, delivered, and later reconstructed his own speech for use as propaganda.

The speech's propagandistic effect, however, is based entirely on Castro's subsequent reconstruction and publication of the speech, not on his actual delivery of it. Had an audio or video recording been made of the speech it might not have had nearly the impact that the printed document had. One might argue, in fact, that Castro was able to generate the influential work through miscalculations on the part of the Batista regime. Tyrants since have been careful not to offer their opponents such a golden opportunity.

## THEMES AND STYLE

In "History Will Absolve Me," Castro plays variations on five major themes: (1) Castro's relationship to the court trying him; (2) the chain of events culminating in the attack on the Moncada Barracks; (3) what the success of the attack would have meant to the political and social regeneration of Cuba; (4) the brutality of the Batista regime's treatment of captured rebels; and (5) the factors that drove Castro and his comrades from opposition into open rebellion. Cleverly, he makes scarcely any reference and attaches no blame to the United States—although, on many other occasions, he makes it plain that slavish subservience to U.S. interests constitutes one of his chief criticisms of all Cuban governments from 1902 to 1952. His immediate aim is to convince the Cuban people to join his movement—without, if possible, provoking the United States to intervene.

Castro begins his oral argument as he intends to continue, with a burst of hyperbole: "Never has a lawyer had to practice his profession under such difficult conditions; never has such a number of overwhelming irregularities been committed against an accused man." His strategy throughout is to switch the role of defendant for that of prosecutor. Batista is the criminal, the usurper; Castro and his fellow insurgents want only to restore Cuba's constitutional, legal government. From his entry into the courtroom for the first trial—when he raised his manacled hands and shouted "Mr. President … I want to call your attention to this incredible fact … not even the worst criminals are held this way in a hall that calls itself a hall of justice"—until he uttered the final declaration ("History will absolve me!") at the second trial, Fidel Castro set the tone and direction of the entire proceeding.

Since it is not the judges whom he addresses, Castro seldom makes recourse to logic or rational argument. He piles vivid assertion ("The accused, who is now exercising this right to plead his own case, will under no circumstances refrain from saying what he must say") upon passionate denunciation ("My most important mission in this trial [is] to totally discredit the cowardly, miserable and treacherous lies which the regime had hurled against our fighters") upon emotional outcry ("the infinite misfortune of the Cuban people who are suffering the cruelest, the most inhuman oppression of their history!"). He knows his conviction is pre-ordained, and he is already turning the military disaster and legal defeat into moral and political victories.

## CRITICAL DISCUSSION

The immediate reaction to "History Will Absolve Me" by those who heard Castro deliver it has not been recorded in any detail, but he was found guilty as charged and sentenced to thirteen years in prison. After Castro's reconstruction of the speech was smuggled from the prison—and 10,000 copies printed and distributed—the majority of first readers, who were all

# FIDEL CASTRO—REVOLUTIONARY BREEDING

Although Fidel Castro's father was wealthy, it is misleading to paint Fidel as the typical son of the ruling class, spoiled and rebellious. Fidel's father, Ángel Castro y Argiz (1875–1956), was hardly a typical Cuban bourgeois and still less an aristocrat. Born in Spain to a poor peasant family, he was drafted into the Spanish army and sent to Cuba, then a Spanish colony, to fight against rebels. When Cuba gained independence, Ángel Castro stayed on and became a prosperous farmer. He married but after a few years separated from his wife. He then took up with one of his household servants, thirty years his junior, who bore him seven children, but he never married her.

Fidel, the third child, was thus born out of wedlock. Fidel's father had him raised among the poor and illiterate workers on the plantation, but when Fidel was eight years old he was baptized a Roman Catholic, which made it possible for him to be educated by the Society of Jesus. He was a noisy and boisterous student, more interested in sports than in learning, but he managed to graduate and to get himself accepted to the University of Havana Law School. There he immediately became immersed in left-wing politics and began the political engagement that led to the toppling of Batista.

more or less sympathetic to the project of overthrowing Batista, were moved to join the July 26 movement and to proclaim Fidel Castro its rightful leader. The initial and continuing response of the Batista regime was that the speech was a tissue of treasonous lies. Because it was not published as a book until two years after Castro's forces had driven Batista out of Cuba and had set up their own government, there was minimal critical or scholarly reaction to the speech for at least nine years after it was delivered.

"History Will Absolve Me" carries a cultural and political legacy of considerable magnitude. It not only served as the founding document and manifesto of the Cuba-wide popular movement to oust Batista that enabled the Castro forces to install a government that has survived more than fifty years but also gave Castro elevated status among earnest revolutionaries in left-wing insurgencies across the globe. In 1976, following the aftermath of the kidnapping of Patricia Hearst by the Symbionese Liberation Army, the group's remnants published a pamphlet called "History Will Absolve Us." Scholarly interest in Castro's speech has grown steadily, chiefly among Marxists and establishment students of U.S.-Cuban relations.

Most of the scholarship concerning "History Will Absolve Me" deals with the speech's place in the narrative of the Cuban Revolution, not with the its merits as a work of rhetoric—that is, persuasive writing. Among the scholars who view the work as an episode in the revolution, the Chilean sociologist Marta Harnecker

Fidel Castro, right, during the 1953 trial during which he delivered his speech "History Will Absolve Me."
© PHOTOS 12/ALAMY.

time 'absolute priority to the speech,'" while the exiled lawyer Mario Lazo faults Batista for handing Castro his golden opportunity.

**BIBLIOGRAPHY**

*Sources*

Castro, Fidel. "History Will Absolve Me." Secaucus, N.J.: Lyle Stuart, 1961. Web. 12 Aug. 2012.

"Fidel Castro Trial: 1953." *Great World Trials*. Detroit: Gale Research, 1994. World History in Context. Web. 12 Aug. 2012.

Harnecker, Marta. *Fidel Castro's Political Strategy: From Moncada to Victory*. New York: Pathfinder, 1987. Web. 12 Aug. 2012.

Jayatilleka, Dayan. *Fidel's Ethics of Violence, the Moral Dimension of the Political Thought of Fidel Castro*. Ann Arbor, MI: Pluto, 2007. Web. 12 Aug. 2012.

Lazo, Mario. *Dagger in the Heart: American Policy Failures in Cuba*. New York: Funk & Wagnall's, 1968. Print.

Perez, Louis A. *Cuba: Between Reform and Revolution*. New York: Oxford UP, 1995. Print.

*Further Reading*

Benjamin, Jules R. *The United States and the Origins of the Cuban Revolution*. Princeton, NJ: Princeton UP, 1990. Print.

Bourne, Peter G. *Fidel: A Biography of Fidel Castro*. New York: Dodd, Mead, 1986. Print.

Brenner, Philip, et al., eds. *The Cuba Reader: The Making of a Revolutionary Society*. New York: Grove, 1989. Print.

Castro, Fidel. *Speeches*. Ed. Michael Taber. New York: Pathfinder, 1981. Print.

*Cuban Revolution Reader: A Documentary History of Fidel Castro's Revolution, 2d ed.* Ed. by Julio Garcia Luis. New York: Ocean. 2008. Print.

De la Cova, Antonio Rafael. *The Moncada Attack: Birth of the Cuban Revolution*. Columbia: U of South Carolina P, 2007. Print

Mencia, Mario. *El Grito del Moncada*. Havana: Editora Política, 1985. Print.

Merle, Robert. *Moncada: Premier Combat de Fidel Castro*. Paris: Robert Laffont, 1965. Print.

notes that it was a deliberate decision on the part of the rebel leadership, following the disastrous Moncada attack, that an "'immediate plan for violent action' must be cast aside in order to assign at that

*Gerald Carpenter*

# THE INFLUENCE OF SEA POWER UPON HISTORY

*1660–1783*

*Alfred Thayer Mahan*

## OVERVIEW

Alfred Thayer Mahan's *The Influence of Sea Power upon History: 1660–1783* (1890) is perhaps the most significant book on naval strategy ever written. Its concepts not only were immediately implemented by navies around the world but also are generally believed to have instigated the frantic naval weapons buildup that led to World War I. President of the U.S. Naval War College in Newport, Rhode Island, from 1886 to 1889, Mahan was a thorough and well-respected historian, but his true talent was as a propagandist. During the twenty-four years between the publication of his book and his death at the beginning of World War I, he succeeded in convincing such world powers as Britain, Germany, Japan, and the United States that military supremacy lay in developing a naval fleet comprised of massive fighting ships with huge guns.

Mahan's theories were shaped by the dramatic advances in naval military techniques and strategy of the seventeenth and eighteenth centuries, when England, France, Holland, and Spain fought for control of the seas and international trade routes. Upon its publication *The Influence of Sea Power* was quickly translated into German, French, Spanish, Italian, Russian, and Japanese, and it gained much more immediate attention and support throughout the rest of the world than it did in the United States. Significant tensions already existed among the great European powers, and many military and political leaders used Mahan's ideas to channel their resources toward more specific purposes. By the time Thayer died in 1914, however, his country had achieved the major goals he had set for it. Although the United States demobilized its forces after World War I, its navy remained powerful with bases in the Caribbean and throughout the Pacific. In addition, the United States had nearly finished building the Panama Canal, opening a quick route between the two oceans. In his 1939 biography *Mahan,* W. D. Puleston quotes an obituary asserting that Mahan had "profoundly modified in his own lifetime the history of the age in which he lived."

## HISTORICAL AND LITERARY CONTEXT

The years 1840 to 1914 constitute the Age of Imperialism (or New Imperialism), when empire-building efforts focused on carving up Africa and increased the need for naval power in order to project influence around the world. American colonization of other territories happened slowly until nationalism and competition for resources prompted the government to emulate Europe's expansionist aspirations. In the second half of the nineteenth century, the United States amassed territories in the Western Hemisphere and the Pacific, where missionaries had paved the way for Americans to pursue commercial interests. In 1867 the U.S. government purchased Alaska from Russia and claimed Midway Atoll; Hawaii, Guam, the Philippines, Puerto Rico, and Samoa were annexed by 1900.

During the War of the Pacific (1879–83), in which Chile opposed Peru and Bolivia, the United States sent ships to protect its interests and its foreign nationals. In 1884 Mahan was in command of the steam sloop *Wachusett,* anchored off Callao, the main seaport of Lima. The postwar assignment was tedious, and he passed the time reading German classicist Theodor Mommsen's multivolume *History of Rome* (1854–56). During the next few years, he developed a thesis on the importance of naval power to a country's military and economic well-being. As the major European powers struggled for domination by increasing the volume and firepower of their militaries, Mahan's book not only validated European paranoia but also furnished it with structure, rules, and goals. However, when the work was published in 1890, the United States was still dismissive of the possibility of foreign invasion, believing that the buffer of two enormous oceans adequately protected American coasts. During the following decade, a combination of outdated ships, advances in naval technologies, and the 1898 Spanish-American War prompted a decision to modernize the fleet, and Mahan's theories became crucial.

Mahan's studies, lectures at the Naval War College, and eventually *The Influence of Sea Power* drew heavily on standard military classics, in particular the writings of Mommsen and the French general Antoine-Henri Jomini, one of the most celebrated writers on the Napoleonic wars. Whereas Jomini's greatest competitor, Prussian soldier and military theorist Carl von Clausewitz, treated war in psychological and political terms, Jomini focused on practical subjects and strategy, and importantly embraced sea power.

### Key Facts

**Time Period:**
Late 19th Century

**Genre:**
History

**Events:**
Lead-up to World War I; increased nationalism; naval arms race among European powers

**Nationality:**
American

# ALFRED THAYER MAHAN: NAVAL STRATEGIST

Alfred Thayer Mahan was born in West Point, New York, on September 27, 1840. His father, Dennis Hart Mahan, was a professor at the military academy there. After attending the Naval Academy at Annapolis, Mahan graduated second in his class in 1859. He was commissioned as a lieutenant in 1861 and served as an officer on various Union Army ships during the Civil War. In 1872 he was promoted to commander of his own ship. According to British military historian John Keegan in his 2009 book *The American Civil War,* Mahan's *The Influence of Sea Power upon History, 1660–1783*—which took form as a series of lectures at the Naval War College in 1886—thrust the author onto the world stage and earned him the title of "most important American strategist of the nineteenth century."

He followed with more books and articles at a prodigious pace. In 1902 he was credited with coining the term "Middle East" in an article he wrote for the *National Review* titled "The Persian Gulf and International Relations." He was promoted to rear admiral in 1906 but died of a heart attack on December 1, 1914. During the last few months of his life, he suffered great mental anguish and guilt, believing that he had stimulated the development and utilization of the German navy, which had then used its massive battleships and U-boats to sink Allied commercial cargo ships during World War I.

His analysis of war as an exact science rather than an art transformed prevailing views of military theory. His first book, *The Gulf and Inland Waters* (1883), coupled naval tactics with historical events during the Civil War in an effort to determine a basis for important future decision making.

Mahan's work inspired other historians, politicians, and military strategists to write their own treatises on the best ways to establish military dominance. In 1921 Italian Giulio Douhet published *The Command of the Air,* promoting strategic bombing. Others who pleaded the case for the superiority of air power over other forms of warfare included Sir Hugh Trenchard, who helped establish the Royal Air Force after World War I; Billy Mitchell, whose tested strategies of bombing warships significantly influenced American air tactics from the 1920s on; and German Luftwaffe commander Walther Wever, who advanced theories of strategic bombing in the early 1930s. Wolfgang Wegener, a vice admiral in the German navy, published a series of influential works between 1915 and 1929 (collectively known as the Wegener Thesis) that criticized World War I German naval strategies in favor of a variation of those used by the British. Admiral Raoul Castex, a French classical naval theorist, foresaw the increased roles of aircraft and submarines in naval warfare in his *Théories Stratégiques* (1929–39). And in 1892 Mahan further applied his theories in

*The Influence of Sea Power upon the French Revolution and Empire, 1793–1812.*

## THEMES AND STYLE

Mahan's statement that "whoever rules the waves rules the world" embodies his overarching theme. *The Influence of Sea Power* explores the interrelationship between naval and political history to demonstrate that the "economic power which went with control of the sea gave its possessor a dominant position in world affairs." According to his interpretation, "sea power is far more than naval power, comprising not only a military fleet but commercial shipping and a strong home base … navies, campaigns, and battles are only a means to an end. Neither a flourishing merchant marine nor a successful navy is possible without the other." For a nation to be prosperous, Mahan maintains, it needs a robust and successful maritime commerce to generate money and resources to build a navy; for maritime commerce to be successful, it needs a strong navy to control the shipping lanes, protect commercial operations, and prevent other nations from building up their naval powers. Mahan's detailed historical accounts provide many examples of maritime prowess, which helped Rome destroy Carthage in the second century BCE, made Spain a world power beginning in the late 1500s, and subsequently helped the Dutch and the British achieve the same goal. Mahan concludes that if the United States were to embrace his philosophy, it could assert its proper supremacy over other world powers.

Mahan developed the rhetorical format and strategies for his book long before he began writing it, specifically in his research for lectures to young officers at the U.S. Naval War College. By outlining the rise and fall of the great naval powers throughout history, he discovered six common elements necessary to achieving dominance: geographical position, abundant natural resources, extensive territory, a population large enough to defend that territory, a society based on maritime commerce, and a government with the character and policy to rule the sea. Mahan begins by presenting and explaining the six conditions then illustrates them with dozens of examples from the history of naval conflict during the years his book covers.

Mahan's language in *The Influence of Sea Power* is both cautious and calculating. For instance, Charles Carlisle Taylor, in his biography *The Life of Admiral Mahan, Naval Philosopher* (1920), explains at length how Mahan decided on the 1890 title. The term "sea power" was carefully chosen "to compel attention and to receive currency." Mahan states, "I deliberately discarded the adjective 'maritime' as being too smooth to arrest men's attention or stick in their minds."

## CRITICAL DISCUSSION

*The Influence of Sea Power* rapidly became a worldwide success. Published during an especially competitive phase of imperialistic rivalry, it offered reasons and

U.S. warships bombarding San Juan, Puerto Rico, May 12, 1898. In *The Influence of Seapower upon History*, Alfred Thayer Mahan argues that countries with superior naval power will have greater worldwide influence. © NIDAY PICTURE LIBRARY/ALAMY.

strategies for initiating new military programs or expanding those already under way. A reviewer for an 1898 issue of the British publication *Blackwood's Edinburgh Magazine* refers to the book as "oil to the flame of colonial expansion everywhere leaping into life." Mahan was considered a hero in England and was invited as guest of honor to two state dinners given by Queen Victoria. The Germans were no less enthusiastic. Taylor quotes German Kaiser Wilhelm II's statement, "I am just now not reading but devouring Captain Mahan's book. It is on board all my ships. … Our future lies upon the water; the trident must be our fist." The Japanese also made sure that Mahan's book was required reading on every naval vessel. Eager to learn even more specifics, top members of the Imperial Japanese Navy began an extensive correspondence with Mahan on numerous maritime military topics. Because the United States had yet to embark on serious imperialistic policies, it was slower to adopt the book, but with its annexation of Puerto Rico in 1898 and the Philippines in 1899, the United States expanded its influence much more rapidly, and Mahan's theories became important.

Although *The Influence of Sea Power* was both persuasive and valuable at the time of its publication, its importance lessened as technology advanced. Today

it has ceded its place to discussions of predator drones, killer robots, and cyber attacks. In a 2006 article for the *Naval War College Review,* Jon Sumida summarizes Mahan's book as follows: "the applicability, if not the validity, of even 'immutable principles of strategy' may be affected critically by technological change … The complexity, difficulty, and above all, inconstancy of strategic problems are likely to upset plans based upon either adherence to sanctified principles or the creation of technological panaceas."

Today's scholarship views Mahan's work from a historical perspective. Critics point to *The Influence of Sea Power* as an inspiration for the naval arms race that led to World War I, including Japan's attempts to curtail Russian naval expansion in the Far East, which led to the Russo-Japanese War of 1904–5; the 1906 British launch of the super-battleship HMS *Dreadnought*; and concurrent German innovations in submarine technology. Various scholars over the years have questioned whether Mahan's classic would have been as wildly popular or influential had it been published at an earlier period in history. The greatly increasing tensions among nations in the years leading up to World War I fed the interest in Mahan's work and gave military leaders the confirmation they needed to build their naval arsenals. The advent of air power at the beginning of the twentieth century and its application in World War I, however, diminished the perception of naval power as an all-encompassing solution, and critical interest in naval warfare became secondary.

## BIBLIOGRAPHY

### Sources

Ferreiro, Larrie D. "Mahan and the 'English Club' of Lima, Peru: The Genesis of *The Influence of Sea Power upon History.*" *Journal of Military History* 72.3 (2008): 901–6. Web. 25 Aug. 2012.

Keegan, John. *The American Civil War.* New York: Knopf, 2009. Print.

Mahan, Alfred Thayer. *From Sail to Steam: Recollections of Naval Life.* 1907. New York: Da Capo, 1968. Print.

Puleston, W. D. *Mahan: The Life and Work of Captain Alfred Thayer Mahan.* New Haven: Yale UP, 1939. Print.

Rev. of *The Influence of Sea Power upon History, 1660–1783,* by Alfred Thayer Mahan. *Blackwood's Edinburgh Magazine* 163.4 (1898): 564. *Google Books.* Web. 25 Aug. 2012.

Sumida, Jon Tetsuro. "Geography, Technology, and British Naval Strategy in the Dreadnought Era." *Naval War College Review* 59.3 (2006): 89–102. Web. 25 Aug. 2012.

Taylor, Charles Carlisle. *The Life of Admiral Mahan, Naval Philosopher.* New York: Doran, 1920. Print.

### Further Reading

Hattendorf, John B., ed. *The Influence of History on Mahan: The Proceedings of a Conference Marking the Centenary of Alfred Thayer Mahan's* The Influence of Sea Power upon History, 1660–1783. Newport: Naval War College P, 1991. Print.

Mahan, Alfred T. *Armaments and Arbitration, or The Place of Force in the International Relations of States.* New York: Harper, 1912. Print.

Mahan, Alfred T., and Allan F. Westcott. *Mahan on Naval Warfare: Selections from the Writing of Rear Admiral Alfred T. Mahan.* Boston: Little, 1941. Print.

Paret, Peter. *Makers of Modern Strategy: From Machiavelli to the Nuclear Age.* Princeton: Princeton UP, 1986. Print.

Sadao, Asada. *From Mahan to Pearl Harbor: The Imperial Japanese Navy and the United States.* Annapolis: Naval Institute P, 2006. Print.

Seager, Robert. *Alfred Thayer Mahan: The Man and His Letters.* Annapolis: Naval Institute P, 1977. Print.

Sumida, Jon Tetsuro. *Inventing Grand Strategy and Teaching Command: The Classic Works of Alfred Thayer Mahan Reconsidered.* Baltimore: Johns Hopkins UP, 1997. Print.

———. "New Insights from Old Books: The Case of Alfred Thayer Mahan." *Naval War College Review* 54.3 (2001): 100–111. Web. 25 Aug. 2012.

Turk, Richard W. *The Ambiguous Relationship: Theodore Roosevelt and Alfred Thayer Mahan.* New York: Greenwood, 1987. Print.

Zimmermann, Warren. *First Great Triumph: How Five Americans Made Their Country a World Power.* New York: Farrar, 2002. Print.

*Jim Mladenovic*

# THE IRISH REBELLION

*Sir John Temple*

## OVERVIEW

*The Irish Rebellion,* a historical account written by Sir John Temple and first published in 1646, details the events leading to the Irish uprising of 1641 and the legislation that was passed as a result. The piece is based on Temple's eyewitness evidence and testimonies from Protestants who had been captured by the rebels. Addressing his English Protestant country-men, Temple denounces the atrocities committed by the Irish Catholics and paints a visceral image of the violence that occurred. He characterizes this rebellion as unfounded, thus contradicting a pamphlet titled *A Remonstrance of Grievances* that had been distributed in 1642 in which Irish Catholics defended the upris-ing and argued that it was because the English govern-ment was confiscating their lands and criminalizing their religion.

Temple's work was released at a time when many pamphlets and firsthand reports by Irish Protestants were being printed in London. This was a politically charged atmosphere that contributed to the popular-ity of *The Irish Rebellion,* and the text's authoritative reputation was furthered by the multiple reprintings of Temple's synthesis. Later generations were influ-enced by his characterization of the Irish Catholics as ethnically distinct from the Protestants. To Temple the former were "barbarians" whom the Kings of Eng-land had been attempting to pacify or subdue since the year 1172. Temple's influence also extended to younger generations of authors, who took up his man-ner of presenting their treatises as objective historical accounts; these writers also borrowed the victims' testimonies presented in his original work.

## HISTORICAL AND LITERARY CONTEXT

When the English colonized Ireland, they redistrib-uted much of the arable land and rendered the practice of Catholicism punishable by law. In 1640 the King of England, Charles I, and the English Parliament were locked in reformation debates, destabilizing the gov-ernment and its control over the Irish colony. Thus the Irish rebels were able to plot an in-depth strategy to seize power in relative secrecy.

*The Irish Rebellion* details the rebels' maneuvers beginning on October 23, 1641, as well as the meas-ures taken by English governmental figures to defend the Castle of Dublin. Temple's account contradicts

any cause for Irish Catholic unrest, claiming that "the exercise of all their Religious Rites and Ceremo-nies was freely enjoyed by them." He writes from his perspective as a government official whose intent is to preserve the national identity of the English as benevolent settlers. The undoubtedly heinous crimes committed by the rebels are therefore characterized as "a barbarous stripping and despoiling" treacher-ously executed against "the present government most sweetly tempered."

The uprising was followed by a period of nation-alist fervor on the part of the English, as their litera-ture attests. John Booker's *A Bloody Irish Almanack* (1646) maintains that "God would be right to punish the whole nation, for the Irish have ever beene most rebellious and treacherous to the English Nation." Edmund Borlase's *The Reduction of Ireland* (1675) presents an equally subjective account and is heavily indebted to Temple's rendition. Apart from Temple's treatise, other firsthand accounts to come out of this period were the depositions, or sworn testimonies, that Temple incorporated and popularized in *The Irish Rebellion.* These documents, now compiled in thirty-one volumes and referred to collectively as the 1641 depositions, furthered the nationalist cause in 1649 when Oliver Cromwell used them to garner support for his military campaign in Ireland. Very few contem-poraries supported Ireland's right to self-govern, and works that did so, such as George Wharton's "Bellum Hybernicale: or Ireland's Warre Astrologically," have fallen into obscurity.

Published after the rebellion had been subdued, Temple's piece served to construct an identity for the Protestants of Ireland and England that was based on persecution and righteousness. His style also influ-enced the genre of martyrology, then a popular subset of historical writing. Contemporary martyrologists attempted to demonstrate the plight of the faithful and the inevitable triumph of good over evil. Samuel Clarke's second edition of *A General Martyrologie* (1651) was revised to include some of the depositions in *The Irish Rebellion.*

## THEMES AND STYLE

*The Irish Rebellion* effectively portrays well-intentioned Protestant victims subjected to a violent upheaval administered by the Irish Catholics. Temple first

+ **Key Facts**

**Time Period:**
Mid-17th Century

**Genre:**
History

**Events:**
Irish uprising of 1641;
English suppression
of Irish independence
movement

**Nationality:**
Irish

# CROMWELL'S RETALIATION

Sir John Temple retained government posts through Oliver Cromwell's rise to power. During England's Civil Wars (1642–48), Cromwell positioned himself as a leading Parliamentarian who favored lower taxes and more oversight of the monarch. King Charles I's ineffectual rule was demonstrated by the political insurgencies of his Catholic subjects. However, his progressive ideas did not extend to the Irish colony. Cromwell took up the view, shared by many of his countrymen and proliferated by Temple, that Catholicism was mere idolatry that threatened the civilized world. As a pious military leader, Cromwell claimed to fight in the name of God to subdue the "barbarous wretches."

Using the atrocities of 1641 as grounds for reinvading Ireland in 1649, Cromwell set about to conquer the colony anew. He first took the town of Drogheda, north of Dublin, killing all of the Catholics he encountered. The Irish resisted Cromwell's military until 1652, at the expense of 20 percent of the Irish population. Lands that had been seized by the rebels were once again redistributed, and practice of the Catholic faith was criminalized. These draconian measures served to bolster Irish resentment toward the English in the ensuing generations.

presents a brief history of English and Irish relations leading up to the rebellion, demonstrating how initially the Irish "who considered even the most gentle means of Reformation as sharp, corrosive medicine ... began desperately to struggle for their liberty." By 1640 Temple claims that the "two Nations had now lived together 40 years in peace ... knit and compacted together with all those bonds and ligatures of Friendship, Alliance, and Consanguinity." What follows this section is his interpretation of the rebellion, punctuated by his introduction into the text of official documents and depositions.

Temple intentionally depicts the years leading up to the rebellion as a "great calm" to dramatize the contrast between purportedly peaceful times and "a *most desperate* and formidable *Rebellion*." An uprising that was portrayed as illogical and ahistorical would have been more fully appreciated by the London audience as "so odious to God and the whole world, that no age, no kingdom, no people, can parallel the horrid cruelties" experienced by the British. The Protestants are variously represented as refugees, or as benevolent landlords who lack the means to raise an army of defense. The Irish, on the other hand, had come from "the Scythians, Gauls, Africans, Goths, or some other more eastern nation," and their plans had been "laid in the dark." Temple's characterization of his work as "An History" is an attempt to lend authority to his conjecture that the rebellion involved two ethnically and morally distinct populations and to convince any audience of readers that all claims therein were made with absolute verisimilitude.

The treatise appeals to the sympathy of its readers by employing the rhetoric of the historian, the beleaguered citizen, and the Lords. The presentation of these documents together is meant to paint a holistic picture of harrowing events. To this end, the tone ranges from one of shock in testimonies of "Rebels who wounded and stabbed men with their Pikes ... then buried them alive" to somber heroism in which Lords resolve that they "shall and will, to their uttermost power, maintain the rights of his Majesty's Crown, and Government of this realm, and peace and safety thereof."

## CRITICAL DISCUSSION

While the rhetorical strategies set forth by Sir John Temple were imitated in his day, he and others were later criticized for relying on the depositions to convey facts. Historian James Morgan Read, in his 1938 article for *Public Opinion Quarterly*, illustrates their fallibility, referring to one "which claimed that a certain Irish woman had grown fat from the eating of many Protestants." Read goes on to say that while *The Irish Rebellion* "was destined long to remain a standard work," it was mostly due to "goriness" that the text enjoyed "a sizable circulation." Temple is also accused by Read of distilling the depositions to such a degree that the testimonies are taken out of context; thus what was hearsay is presented by Temple as eyewitness accounts.

The dissemination of Temple's ideas helped to shape Irish Protestant identity, through his text's multiple reprintings and through his tropes that were taken up by other propagandists. Kathleen Noonan writes in 2004 for *Albion*, "[E]ven when Temple's work was discredited as mere polemic," the public was exposed to his version of the Protestant-as-martyr "through authors they had come to trust." Noonan also argues that political relations between England and Ireland were marred by Temple's lasting assertion "that portrayed the Irish as immune to reformation and incapable of coexistence with the English."

Contemporary scholarship assesses Temple's piece not in terms of fact but in order to gauge the national reaction to events that took place more than three and a half centuries ago. The depositions that he presents, and that were long discredited by scholars for their overly passionate tones, have been revisited to present a less biased view of the rebellion. Joseph Cope reveals positive relations between neighbors that led to the safety of both parties in a 2003 article for *Historical Journal*. Similarly, Nicholas Canny utilizes the depositions to present a less biased view of Irish history, representative of more classes than the literary elite who were its usual authors. Canny, in a 1993 essay for *History Ireland*, concedes that the testimonies cannot be expected to be factually "reliable," or even "plausible," but they are useful "if only to explain the terror of the settlers and why so many of them fled their homes even when they were not obliged to do so."

## BIBLIOGRAPHY

### Sources

Canny, Nicholas. "The 1641 Depositions: A Source for Social & Cultural History." *History Ireland* 1.4 (1993): 52–55. *JSTOR*. Web. 13 Oct. 2012.

Cope, Joseph. "The Experience of Survival during the 1641 Irish Rebellion." *Historical Journal* 46.2 (2003): 295–316. *JSTOR*. Web. 13 Oct. 2012.

Noonan, Kathleen M. "'Martyrs in Flames': Sir John Temple and the Conception of the Irish in English Martyrologies." *Albion* 36.2 (2004): 223. *Literature Resource Center*. Web. 13 Oct. 2012.

Read, James Morgan. "Atrocity Propaganda and the Irish Rebellion." *Public Opinion Quarterly* 2.2 (1938): 229–44. *JSTOR*. Web. 16 Oct. 2012.

Temple, John. *The Irish Rebellion*. London: R. Wilks, 1812. Print.

### Further Reading

Capp, Bernard. "George Wharton, 'Bellum Hybernicale,' and the Cause of Irish freedom." *English Historical Review* 112.447 (1997): 671–77. *Gale World History in Context*. Web. 16 Oct. 2012.

Love, W. D. "Civil War in Ireland: Appearances in Three Centuries of Historical Writing." *Emory University Quarterly* 22 (1966): 57–72. *JSTOR*. Web. 16 Oct. 2012.

McElligott, Jason. "English Newsbooks and Irish Rebellion, 1641–1649." *Canadian Journal of History* 43.1 (2008): 140. *Gale World History in Context*. Web. 16 Oct. 2012.

Russell, Conrad. Rev. of *The Outbreak of the Irish Rebellion of 1641*, by M. Perceval-Maxwell. *Albion* 28.1 (1996): 179–81. *JSTOR*. Web. 13 Oct. 2012.

*Caitie Moore*

Illustration depicting Irish Catholics drowning English Protestants during the Irish Rebellion of 1641. © CLASSIC IMAGE/ALAMY.

# MANINBO

## Ko Un

✣ *Key Facts*

**Time Period:**
Late 20th to Early 21st
Century

**Genre:**
Poetry

**Events:**
Division of Korea; Korean
War; political repression
in North and South
Korea; gradual rise of
dissident movements

**Nationality:**
Korean

## OVERVIEW

The poet Ko Un began writing *Maninbo*, or *Ten Thousand Lives*, in 1986 after a particularly arduous time in solitary confinement. As an active political dissident since the 1970s, Ko had been in jail many times, and in 1980 he was arrested again for protesting the military dictatorship of Chun Doo-Hwan. In this instance, the poet was sentenced with life imprisonment. Between 1980 and 1982 he was tortured and left in solitary confinement so dark that he could not see. Ko began to hallucinate—or be "visited by," as he put it—all of the friends, relatives, and public figures in his memory, and he composed poems in his head to each of them. In 1986 he began to set these poems to paper and compile them into volumes. All thirty of his anticipated volumes were completed in 2010, and a selection from the first ten volumes was collected in an English version published in 2005.

The text as a whole has been praised for its massive scope, and its individual poems have been lauded for their witty insights and political understanding. Breaking with the Chinese tradition of depicting nature—as well as with Western modernism, which had made its way to Korea in the 1930s—Ko's collection of 4,001 poems seeks to explicitly address the political situation in Korea.

## HISTORICAL AND LITERARY CONTEXT

*Maninbo* came out of an experience of life in a country controlled by various colonial regimes. In 1910 Japan annexed Korea, using its land for a military base and its people for cheap labor and eventually, in 1937, prohibiting the use of the Korean language in public schools. At the end of World War II, in the face of Japan's defeat by the Allied nations, Korea gained liberation. The United States and the U.S.S.R., then allies, agreed to steward the country and divided it arbitrarily along the 38th parallel. Soon thereafter, tensions arose, with the beginnings of the Cold War. North Korea was being governed by a communist regime and South Korea by a capitalist one, and between the two were many varying political views. During the ensuing Korean War (1950–53), Ko Un witnessed the murder of many communist sympathizers who were his family and friends. As punishment for "spying" on these killings, he was forced to bury his relatives and neighbors in mass graves. After the war the border was closed,

leaving the two countries completely secluded from each other. Leftist or communist ideas were violently suppressed in South Korea by U.S.-backed leadership.

Against the silencing of his language and repression of his culture, Ko created *Maninbo*, which has been called both a litany and a prayer. North Korea and South Korea teach different versions of their shared history in schools, denying collective memory between the two countries. Ko hoped to suggest in *Maninbo* that memory and individual lives transcend the power of governmental parties and censorship. He became political when he read about a garment worker's self-immolation outside of a factory. By the 1980s Ko had developed the idea of *minjung munhak*, or "people's literature," in opposition to aesthetic tendencies in literature that he viewed as nationalistic.

As Ko became politically active in the 1970s, his poems slowly became that way as well. He had lived as a Buddhist monk for ten years after the trauma of the war and a suicide attempt. His poems had the quality of zen (*sŏn* in Korean) koans, or paradoxes. In the 1970s they became more directly critical of government policy. *Maninbo* asserts a definition of Korea through its people, individually and from the inside. As a catalog of mundanity as well as triumph in life, it disrupts facile definitions of Korea as communist or capitalist, as a dictatorship, or as an emerging global power.

In 1988 the Olympic Games were held in Seoul, South Korea, an event that had been in the making since the vote was passed by the Olympic tribunal in 1981. The government endeavored to portray the country as a legitimate, moderate nation stable enough to house hundreds of thousands of visitors. Ko's poetry belies this stability by relating events that had occurred during nearly a century of colonialism. He employs a style that recalls the rich tradition of oral history in Korea. This documentary style continues to influence poets, as well as extend to protesters who held demonstrations calling for his release the numerous times he was jailed throughout the 1980s. His reputation as a political poet has also gained him several nominations for the Nobel Prize.

## THEMES AND STYLE

The number 10,000 in Korean is also used to designate *all*, so *Maninbo* could alternatively be translated as "All the People." Ko's strategy of demonstrating the universal versus the individual experience is clear from the beginning. In these volumes the poet uses every life to show the effects of different regimes and occupations. He makes clear that it is the policies of the governments of Japan, China, the United States, and North and South Korea that are generalizable—not the effects of those policies and not the individuals through which those policies are carried out. Taken together, the stories of people from all sectors of society have the effect of affirming daily life and culture in Korea. Ko believes that "the poet should be a shaman who can build a bridge between the spirits of different people." Building bridges between people accurately describes both Ko's political and aesthetic aims.

As he recounts stories of migration and refuge, the poet simultaneously contradicts the idea that North and South Korea should remain cut off from one another. In the opening lines of "Yi Jŏng-yi's Family" he says, "They walked all the way from Chinnamp'o in North Korea / to Hongsŏng in South Korea's Ch'ungch'ŏng Province." In this poem, neither country is safe; the people are presided over in both places by a dangerous authoritarian military. The poem continues, "They dreaded the American troops" prompting the family to cover themselves with excrement and ash. Ko's attempt to portray the similarities in the North Korean and South Korean experiences occurs across both space and time. In another poem, "DDT," Americans are again the cause of humiliation. First during liberation, "All the Koreans working in Hodge's headquarters / and the Koreans in the streets / outside his headquarters / were liberally doused with DDT." Later, when the Korean War began, "Korea again became a land of DDT" as the soldiers behave as if "fleas, bugs, and the plentiful lice and nits about their bodies, / even invisible microbes, / were uncivilized Koreans / so the Americans drenched the Koreans / in plentiful quantities of DDT."

Ko is known for his easy, colloquial style, typical of a populist poet. He has refused formal strictures of rhythm and does not employ regular meter or stanzaic length. This makes the work accessible to farmers and activists as well as academics. He calls the poems in *Maninbo* his "other-centered poems" and views them as "somehow transcending the self." In the name of accessibility, however, Ko has not eschewed lyricism completely. In order to maintain his humanist outlook, the political qualities of his poems are balanced by metaphysical concerns. At the end of "Traveler," for example, he describes a man who has "drifted here and there / his stories had no end. Tired as he was sleepless, he told stories until dawn." The traveler's earthly struggle elicits "cries of joy from that sky of stars."

## CRITICAL DISCUSSION

*Maninbo* has been consistently praised in both Korea and the United States. In Korea, Ko is respected as the leader of his literary movement, but he is also derided for his casual style by more formal poets. The poet has,

## KO UN'S REUNIFICATION STRATEGY

Ko Un was raised in a farming community with very little money. He recounts being a toddler and wanting to be fed the stars, which he mistook for fruit. Later, after the traumatic loss of many of his family members, he attempted to take his own life in a way that left him almost completely deaf. It was then that he entered monkhood, only to become disillusioned with it after a decade of study and promotion to respected positions. In the 1990s he married and moved to the country, where he found stability, perhaps due also to the newfound stability of South Korea.

In keeping with his aesthetic theory that poetry and language can do much to further diplomatic relations, as of 2012 Ko is compiling a dictionary with a coalition of writers from both sides of the border between North Korea and South Korea. The two sides have developed markedly different speech patterns and grammatical usage since liberation in 1945. Their hope is that the dictionary will be both a record of what definitions the two languages have in common as well as a communication aid for those working to unify the nations.

however, consistently and effectively rejected the idea that a poem should be restricted to a set of rules that might not be appropriate to its purpose. Prominent U.S. poets Robert Hass and Gary Snyder have both acknowledged Ko's contribution to global literature. Snyder, who read with Ko Un in California in the early 1990s, believes the poems' "purity, their nervy clarity, and their heart of compassion" render them as more than just the poetry of Korea. Instead, he says, "they belong to the world." Due to both censorship and lack of reliable translations, the Western world was not exposed to *Maninbo* until twenty years after it was begun.

In the interim Ko's work has done much to further the goal of unification shared by many Korean poets. Traveling with President Kim Dae Jung, with whom he had once been imprisoned, Ko went to North Korea in 2000 for diplomatic purposes and sang the "Reunification Song" with delegates from both sides of the 38th parallel. In 2005 a coalition of writers from both countries issued a call for reconciliation. Brother Anthony of Taizé, who has translated much of Ko Un's work, remarks that Ko's poetry is successful because it strikes a balance between the "two poetic poles of the Korean life experience," namely "rejoicing and suffering," by portraying these opposites as "virtually inseparable."

Scholarship in the early twenty-first century tends to highlight how integral Ko's poetry has been to shaping perceptions of Korea. Having rejected the grammatical structures of Chinese and Western literature, Ko is able to display a more authentically Korean experience in his poems. Katie Peterson notes in the *Boston Review* (2006) that "*Maninbo* is an uncanny testament

Buddhist monks at Tongdosa, a Buddhist temple in South Korea. The Korean poet Ko Un, author of *Maninbo,* was once a Zen Buddhist monk. © PIEDER/ALAMY.

to the brutalities of history and a nervy attempt to remind us that individuals are worth dignifying." Roland Bleiker and David Hundt demonstrate in their important essay "Ko Un and the Poetics of Post-Colonial Identity" (2010) how the poems convince readers of their "underlying idea … that a nation consists of its people, not the state." Bleiker and Hundt further argue that Ko has freed poetry from state confines while also redefining citizenship and state relations.

## BIBLIOGRAPHY

*Sources*

Bleiker, Roland, and David Hundt. "Ko Un and the Poetics of Post-Colonial Identity." *Global Society* 24. 3 (2010): 331–49. *JSTOR*. Web. 8 Oct. 2012.

Ko, Un. "Memory of the Graves." *The Columbia Anthology of Modern Korean Poetry.* Ed. David R. McCann. New York: Columbia UP, 2004. Print.

———. *Ten Thousand Lives.* Trans. Brother Anthony of Taize, Young Moo Kim, and Gary G. Gach. Los Angeles: Green Integer, 2005. Print.

Peterson, Katie. Rev. of *Ten Thousand Lives,* by Ko Un. *Boston Review.* Boston Review, May/June 2006. Web. 8 Oct. 2012.

*Further Reading*

Kim, Hyesoon, ed. *Anxiety of Words: Contemporary Poetry by Korean Women.* Brookline: Zephyr, 2006. Print.

———. *Mommy Must Be a Fountain of Feathers.* Notre Dame: Action, 2008. Print.

Ko, Un. "The Sky." *Contemporary Korean Poetry.* Ed. Kim Jaihun. Buffalo: Mosaic, 1994. Print.

———. *The Three Way Tavern.* Trans. Claire You and Richard Silberg. Berkeley: U of California P, 2006. Print.

Lee, Peter H., ed. *Anthology of Korean Literature: From Early Times to the Nineteenth Century.* Honolulu: U of Hawaii P, 1981. Print.

———. *The Silence of Love: Twentieth Century Korean Poetry.* Honolulu: U of Hawaii P, 1980. Print.

*Caitie Moore*

# MY GRANDMOTHER

*A Memoir*

Fethiye Çetin

## OVERVIEW

First published in Turkish as *Anneanem* (2006), *My Grandmother: A Memoir* (2008), written by lawyer Fethiye Çetin's, recounts the experiences of Çetin's maternal grandmother, Seher, during the Armenian genocide in the early twentieth-century Ottoman Empire. The book is the result of a shocking admission made by Seher, a Turkish Muslim woman: although she was born into a Christian Armenian family, she was made to hide her identity as a child to avoid persecution. Written nearly twenty years after her revelation and almost ninety years after the genocide, Çetin's text is nevertheless controversial for its depiction of the atrocities perpetrated on Armenians by Turks, details of which have long been suppressed from official accounts of Turkish history. The compassion and humanity of the text strive to transcend long-held rivalries and animosity between the two groups in hopes of reconciliation and mutual understanding.

Despite dealing with taboo subjects, Çetin's book sold well in Turkey and was translated into several other languages, including Eastern and Western Armenian, soon after its original release. The popularity of *My Grandmother* has been attributed in part to the fact that Seher's experience is not uncommon. She and many like her, Christian orphans adopted and raised as Muslims, were termed the "remains of the sword." The broad diasporic Armenian population and an estimated two million Turkish citizens recognize in Çetin's account their own experiences and family stories. The memoir has become an important part of a larger literary movement grappling with the legacy of the genocide and the fact that Turkish officials vehemently deny it happened. Since *My Grandmother* was published, dialogue about the genocide and about the struggle to regain lost identity among Armenians and Turks has become more observable, and reconciliation efforts have been made at all levels, from grassroots apology campaigns to an agreement to reopen the Armenian-Turkish border.

## HISTORICAL AND LITERARY CONTEXT

The Armenian Genocide (1915–18) has been attributed to increasing nationalism in the Ottoman Empire. As officials moved to solidify the nation of Turkey, they sought to establish a singular Turkish identity, excluding ethnic Armenians and Christians as well as other minorities. Systematic massacres and death marches caused an estimated 1.5 million Armenian deaths and the relocation of many more. Until the late twentieth century, discussion of the genocide was strictly prohibited in public, and younger Turks were largely unaware of it. *My Grandmother* responds to Turkish politics and policies that denied recognition of, or responsibility for, the human tragedy associated with the Armenian genocide in the years since the religious and ethnic minority group was eradicated.

Throughout the memoir, Çetin focuses on the alienation of culture and identity, highlighting the pain that stems from omissions in Turkey's cultural history. Since the 1915 genocide, Turkey has steadfastly held the position that Armenians were removed from the region for allying with Russia during World War I. The government maintains that a mere 300,000 people died during evacuations. Official policies such as the new Latinate language and the prohibition against "insulting Turkishness"—which made public statements about genocide punishable—obscured the atrocities from later generations. However, by the time *My Grandmother* was published in 2006, opposition to this silence had grown as a result of the assassination of Hrant Dink, an Armenian journalist and vocal critic of Turkey's denial, and because many Turks had made discoveries similar to Çetin's.

Çetin's book is part of a large body of works on the Armenian Genocide, but *My Grandmother* stands out as a memoir by a Turkish author. Other diasporic Armenians have written similar memoirs of family members' escape and survival. Among the most well-known include Armenian American authors Michal J. Arlen, whose National Book Award-winning *Passage to Ararat* (1976) is a memoir about connecting with his Armenian heritage, and David Kherdian, who recreates his mother's childhood experience in *The Road from Home: A True Story of Courage, Survival, and Hope* (1979). Çetin's book also appeared alongside several Turkish texts that indirectly approach the issue in fiction, including Orhan Pamuk's novel *Snow* (2002), which depicts Turkey's complex contemporary

⁂ *Key Facts*

**Time Period:**
Late 20th Century

**Genre:**
Memoir

**Events:**
Turkish denial of Armenian genocide

**Nationality:**
Turkish

# THE DEBATE OVER OFFICIAL RECOGNITION OF ARMENIAN GENOCIDE

Armenians were expelled from the Ottoman Empire nearly a century ago, but the international community continues to passionately debate the event's designation. Genocide and Holocaust scholars aver that the expulsion does indeed fit the definition of genocide. However, disputes over the facts of the event have been overshadowed by concerns of political allegiance. Twenty-one nations worldwide officially recognize the Armenian Genocide and Turkey's role in the mass killing. Yet, Turkey's staunch denial of the genocide means that nations wishing to ally themselves with the Eastern European power must remain silent on the issue at the risk of alienating Armenians. Such is the position taken by the United States, although forty-three states have independently ratified recognition of the genocide.

Within Turkey, debates are equally fraught: admitting culpability to the systematic massacre of Armenians could engender costly reparations but continuing to deny its responsibility may hinder Turkey's coveted acceptance into the European Union. The EU demands admission to the genocide as a term of Turkey's accession in order to demonstrate the nation's commitment to human rights, which has been questionable both in the past and in its present treatment of Kurds and other minority groups. Although Turkey refuses to renege its official position, grassroots efforts among Turks have attempted to inspire individual action. One petition, called "We Apologize," gathered signatures online but was soon outmatched by an opposing petition endorsed by government officials. As the centennial anniversary approaches, neither Turkey nor the international community is any nearer agreement on the events of 1915–1918.

tensions, and Elif Shafak's *The Bastard of Istanbul* (2006), which details the country's violent past.

In the years following *My Grandmother*'s publication, the body of literature about the Armenian genocide has grown unabated. Although Çetin's text does not include the term "genocide," later works are less careful to avoid political discussion. Among the most notable works is the seminal historical tome, *A Shameful Act: The Armenian Genocide and the Question of Turkish Responsibility* (2006) by Taner Akçam, which has been called "a landmark assessment of Turkish culpability," the first such work by a Turkish historian. Çetin later coedited a collection of stories, published in 2011 as *Torunlar* (*Grandchildren*), from Turks who had similarly discovered their own Armenian lineage.

## THEMES AND STYLE

The central theme of *My Grandmother* is the cost of the Armenian genocide, both the immediate loss of life and the loss of culture and identity during the atmosphere of oppression and secrecy that followed. Çetin endeavors to give the political struggle a face through Seher's

young eyes and through Çetin's memories of her grandmother. In interviews, Çetin asserted that her project in *My Grandmother* was to "reconcile us with our history; but also to reconcile us with ourselves." To foreground the emotional context of the event rather than its brutality, the book opens with Seher's funeral, where Çetin announces her grandmother's true heritage: "I fall silent, anxious that I might make those around me cry even more if I repeat my accusations or stand by my words. I bow my head as I cry inside, ashamed that even here we have to carry on pretending." The family tragedy is more heartrending because Seher's true identity is dishonored even in death.

The memoir achieves it rhetorical effect by suggesting that the importance of family transcends the deep animosity dividing Turks and Armenians. *My Grandmother* demonstrates that those believed to be the enemy may in fact be one's own flesh and blood. Çetin's primary audience is Turkish, necessitating a diplomatic portrayal of the events. The deliberate omission of the word "genocide" reveals the careful balance at stake in the memoir. *My Grandmother* prioritizes Seher's and Çetin's emotional journeys, appealing to universal values such as family connections and the search for identity, which underscores the similarities between Turks and Armenians and Muslims and Christians, rather than emphasizing their differences. The text opens with a depiction of Seher's funeral, then shifts to a description of the young girl's idyllic youth before the genocide. Both scenes elicit a sense of compassion for the protagonists rather than alienating readers by accusing or attacking.

Stylistically, *My Grandmother* generally adheres to the genre conventions of memoir; however it diverges when narration shifts from Çetin's present-day perspective to that of Seher as a child and a young woman. The tone of the text remains compassionate despite dealing with controversial political topics. A lawyer by profession, Çetin creates prose that is unembellished and has been called "sober and heartbreaking." Critics have said that the matter-of-fact descriptions "cast a horrifying light on the atrocities committed on a million and a half Armenians," amplifying the terrible images witnessed by young Seher. *My Grandmother* achieves its rhetorical force through understated language that communicates the experience of the genocide without sensationalism or accusation.

## CRITICAL DISCUSSION

When *My Grandmother* was first released in 2006, it was a best seller among Turkish readers, reaching its seventh printing within two years. The book was popular among general readers and was soon translated into several languages, expanding the readership of the text. Many welcomed Çetin's heartfelt portrait of her family's struggle, and despite her attempts to avoid the use of overt invocation of genocide, the memoir renewed heated discussions of national identity and the secrecy surrounding the events. Maureen

This photo from 1915 features a group of Armenian children who became refugees in the wake of genocide by the Ottoman Turks. Fethiye Çetin's grandmother witnessed the mass killings of women and children in the wake of the genocide. APIC/GETTY IMAGES.

Freely, translator of the 2008 English language version asserts, "Readers of *My Grandmother* are now well equipped to question what they were taught at school about Turkish identity." The memoir also resonates among English language readers and has been called "powerful" and "earnest" by reviewers. In both English and Turkish classrooms, the slim volume has been used to teach about the end of the Ottoman Empire and about the experience of genocide, though such activism is countered by the government's consistent denial of the genocide, which includes popular demonstrations to this end.

Since the publication of *My Grandmother,* Turkish citizens have more openly grappled with the Armenian Genocide and the resulting "history of denial, nationalism, and fears of political consequences." The body of Turkish literature attempting to fill the gap in Turkish history and culture left by Armenians has continued to grow. And increasing numbers of Turks have uncovered their own Armenian heritage, forcing a reconsideration of what it means to be "Turkish." Meanwhile, communication between Turkey and Armenia has been reestablished. In 2009, after more than a year spent in negotiations, representatives from both nations signed an accord that would, among other things, reopen the border between the two countries, closed since 1993. However, this move was opposed by people in both Turkey and Armenia, for whom the wounds of the past remain raw, and was delayed.

*My Grandmother* has been singled out by scholars as an exemplary depiction of the Armenian Genocide and has been invoked in a variety of scholarship looking at the event's effects. Popular publications focus on the text's illumination of historical events and use the book as an example of the questions many Turks face today. Predominant trends in scholarship have focused on identity formation among diasporic and "secret" Armenians, and have looked at the effects of trauma on the group. Several scholars have combined these themes to understand how Armenians created new identities while haunted by the past. Arlene Avakian writes about identity construction among Armenian Americans and the lack of women's voices in contemporary Armenian scholarship in a 2010 essay for *New Perspectives on Turkey.* She posits that a refusal to deal with the psychological effects of genocide has limited the group's ability to address contemporary issues such as gender roles. She also identifies Çetin's text as a work that foregrounds the female experience of the genocide.

## BIBLIOGRAPHY

### Sources

Avakian, Arlene Voski. "A Different Future? Armenian Identity through the Prism of Trauma, Nationalism, and Gender." *New Perspectives on Turkey* 42 (2010): 203–14. Print.

Bilefsky, Dan. "A Family Tree Uprooted by a 60-Year-Old Secret." *New York Times.* New York Times, 5 Jan. 2010. Web. 5 Sept. 2012.

Çetin, Fethiye. *My Grandmother: A Memoir.* Trans. Maureen Freely. London: Verso, 2008. Print.

Fisk, Robert. "A Voice Recovered from Armenia's Bitter Past." *London Independent* 23 Aug. 2008: 38. Print.

Pope, Hugh. Rev. of *My Grandmother,* by Fethiye Çetin. *Today's Zaman* 2 June 2008. Web. 8 Sept. 2012.

Watenpaugh, Keith David. "The League of Nations' Rescue of Armenian Genocide Survivors and the

Making of Modern Humanitarianism, 1920–1927." *American Historical Review* 115.5 (2010): 1315–39. Print.

*Further Reading*

Danielian, Jack. "A Century of Silence." *American Journal of Psychoanalysis* 70 (2010): 245–64. Print.

Emcioglu, Fikret Erkut. "Turkey in Books." *Middle East Quarterly* 14.2 (2007): 51–55. Print.

Freely, Maureen. "Secret Histories." *Index on Censorship* 39.1 (2010): 14–20. Print.

Geerdink, Fréderike. "Lawyer and Writer Fethiye Çetin: 'My Identity Has Never Been Purely Turkish.'" *Journalist in Turkey.* Journalist in Turkey, 20 May 2006. Web. 5 Sept. 2012.

Göle, Nilüfer. "Europe's Encounter with Islam: What Future?" *Constellations* 13.2 (2006): 248–62. Print.

Singer, Amy, Christopher K. Neumann, and Selcuk Aksin Somel, eds. *Untold Histories of the Middle East: Recovering Voices from the 19th and 20th Centuries.* New York: Routledge, 2011. Print.

Üngor, Ugur Ümit. "Orphans, Converts, and Prostitutes: Social Consequences of War and Persecution in the Ottoman Empire, 1914–1923." *War in History* 19.2 (2012): 173–92. Print.

*Elizabeth Boeheim*

# "NATIONAL LIBERATION AND CULTURE"

*Amílcar Cabral*

## OVERVIEW

First presented in 1970, "National Liberation and Culture" by Amílcar Cabral, the leader of Guinea's fight for independence, describes the importance of understanding the totality of a nation's culture in furthering the aims of a national, anticolonial movement. Cabral delivered the text as a lecture at Syracuse University in New York on February 21, 1970, as part of the Eduardo Mondlane Memorial Lecture Series. Written in an academic, theoretical style, Cabral's text depicts the fight against colonialism as the struggle for a nation to have its own independent culture, with anticolonial movements needing to "embody the mass character, the popular character of the [colonized] culture" in all its complexity. Although scholar Patrick Chabal, in *Amílcar Cabral: Revolutionary Leadership and People's War* (1983), points out that "the majority of [Cabral's] writings are party documents and reflect the very specific purpose and audience for which they are intended," "National Liberation and Culture" represents part of the larger project in which Cabral was engaged: striving for a theory of national liberation malleable enough to be transplanted to other struggles in the Third World. This aim corresponds with his earlier claim from "The Weapon of Theory" (1966), where he states that "nobody has yet made a successful revolution without a revolutionary theory."

Although there appears to be no documentary account of the reception that "National Liberation and Culture" received when first presented as a lecture, the legacy of the text is clear. Its eventual publication, various translations, and inclusion in multiple anthologies helped to build Cabral's status as a leading thinker on anticolonial politics in the second half of the twentieth century. Along with a remarkable body of writing, ranging from poetry and technical papers on agriculture to political and economic theory, "National Liberation and Culture" would, according to Robert Benewick and Philip Green in *The Routledge Dictionary of Political Thinkers* (1998), "place [Cabral] at the forefront of black intellectuals like Frantz Fanon, Julius Nyerere, Kwame Nkrumah, and Patrice Lumumba."

## HISTORICAL AND LITERARY CONTEXT

Following the weakening of the colonial powers of Europe during World War II, the rise of African anticolonial movements succeeded in securing a wave of new independent African states through the 1950s and 1960s. Michael R. Hall, however, in his 2010 article on Cabral, states that under the deeply authoritarian Estado Novo ("New State") regimes of António de Oliveira Salazar and (from 1968) Marcelo Caetano, "while most European colonial powers were considering dismantling their colonial empires, the Portuguese were determined to strengthen their hold over their colonial empire in Africa." Cabral was the leader of the liberation movements of Guinea-Bissau and Cape Verde against Portuguese colonialism, cofounding the Partido Africano da Independência da Guiné e Cabo Verde (PAIGC; African Party for the Independence of Guinea and Cape Verde) in 1956.

Presented in 1970, "National Liberation and Culture" was produced while Cabral was leading a revolutionary war in Guinea-Bissau (one that did not achieve its twin aims of independence for Guinea-Bissau and Cape Verde until 1973 and 1975, respectively). As such, the text can be seen as a working party document for the PAIGC. As a valued figure in the international anti-imperial struggle, however, Cabral was in a unique position to bridge the gap between the specific situation in Guinea-Bissau and Cape Verde and a general theory of national liberation and culture. In aligning the Guinea-Bissau people working on plantations with the more elite merchant class of Cape Verdeans, whom he hoped would fight alongside the peasant classes and then become the cultural and political leaders, Cabral was seeking a unified identity in which to propel the two nations into a successful postcolonial life. His work creating alliances within the Portuguese colonies encouraged other countries seeking liberation to acknowledge his process of defining culture and identity through mutual cooperation and therefore molding self-determination.

As a student in Lisbon in the late 1940s and early 1950s, Cabral was exposed to antifascist groups in Portugal, including those involved in what Benewick and Philips term "the Portuguese Marxist underground and radical African nationalism." Cabral's work as a revolutionary and theorist can be seen broadly as an attempt to marry these sometimes complementary and sometimes contradictory viewpoints. Although he was not a declared Marxist and is recorded as having been unimpressed by the need of others to classify his thought as specifically Marxist, his work, like that

+ *Key Facts*

**Time Period:**
Mid-20th Century

**Genre:**
Speech

**Events:**
Growth of anticolonial effort in Africa; Independence struggles in Guinea-Bussau and Cape Verde

**Nationality:**
Guinea-Bissauan and Cape Verdean

# AFTER LIBERATION

In "National Liberation and Culture" (1970) and elsewhere, Amílcar Cabral argued that the revolution would not end when Guinea-Bissau and Cape Verde were liberated from Portuguese colonial control. He was proven correct: independence only exacerbated the strife and conflict within the new country, and the struggle for peace and prosperity continued unabated.

Immediately after the Portuguese left, the Partido Africano da Independencia da Gunié-Bissau e Cabo Verde (PAIGC), which Cabral had founded in the mid-1950s, established one-party control over the state with Cabral's brother Luis as the first Guinea-Bissaun president. Factionalism and corruption ensued, as the revolutionary apparatus became entrenched in military and governmental positions. Elections were held in 1976, but they were marred and delegitimized by fraud. In 1980 Joao Bernardo Vieira overthrew Cabral's regime. Although Vieira's leadership was characterized by authoritarianism and factionalism, he did attempt to institute democratic and economic reforms during his nearly two-decade-long reign. The country remained unstable and corrupt, however, despite efforts to create a constitution and hold multiparty elections. Then, in 1998, an army commander named Ansumane Mané ousted Vieira. The civil war that followed ended in 1999. Mané subsequently allowed free elections, and in 2005 Vieira returned from exile in Portugal and reclaimed the presidency.

of Fanon, is broadly an effort to integrate a Marxist understanding of social relations with a specifically nationalist struggle for liberation. Like Fanon, Cabral was also initially deeply impressed by the *négritude* movement, with his concept of the "return to source," according to Chabal, owing much to his exposure to the ideas of the creators of négritude, Léopold Senghor and Aimé Césaire. As well as other works that follow Vladimir Lenin's "Imperialism, the Highest Stage of Capitalism" in seeking to apply Marxist ideas to the imperial situation and the key texts of the négritude movement, Cabral's "National Liberation and Culture" can be profitably read against *The Wretched of the Earth* (1961), in which Fanon elucidates his own theories of national consciousness and national culture.

Although mapping the specific impact of the text is extremely difficult, Cabral's "National Liberation and Culture" remains an important historical document as a testament not only to the importance of the cultural factor in the Guinea-Bissau and Cape Verde national liberation movement but also to similar movements of the twentieth century. The text has a contemporary significance, however, in its discussion of the nation-building politics of the postcolonial and neocolonial world. Indeed, this is a point Cabral makes clear in "The Weapon of Theory" when he claims that "the liberation struggle is a revolution [that] does not finish at the moment when the national flag is raised and the national anthem played."

## THEMES AND STYLE

In Cabral's "The Weapon of Theory," the author outlines the key battle in a revolutionary anticolonial movement to be an "expression of the internal contradictions in the economic, social, cultural (and therefore historical) reality of each [oppressed] country." In "National Liberation and Culture," Cabral offers a discussion of the specific importance of the cultural factor in this battle, seeing the movement's understanding of this factor as of central importance to national liberation and social revolution. Since the domination of a people "can be maintained only by the permanent, organized, repression of the cultural life of the people concerned," Cabral argues that to ensure national solidarity "the liberation movement must ... embody the mass character, the popular character of the society" in all its complexity. Crucially, Cabral's vision is not essentialist in that it advocates the preservation of "the positive cultural values of every well defined group, of every category, and to achieve the confluence of these values in the service to the struggle, giving it a new dimension—the national dimension." Despite broad likenesses between individual cases of anticolonial struggle, these factors are specific to the country in question. One of the evident aims of "National Liberation and Culture" is to bridge this gap by creating a theory of the centrality of culture to the struggles of the oppressed by an oppressor broad enough such that it can be somehow exportable.

Although the tenor of the piece is largely academic, "National Liberation and Culture" contains moments of striking rhetoric that hint at Cabral's reputation as an accomplished multilingual speaker. These include the memorable and oft-quoted metaphor of the simultaneousness of culture and history as that of the flower and the plant. Within this model, Cabral advocates that those colonized who have become culturally alienated by their adoption into a petite bourgeoisie should be "reconverted," ultimately through "daily contact with the popular masses in the communion of sacrifice required by the struggle." This reflects, of course, Cabral's own personal position as a figure who himself undertook a lifetime of—as he puts it in "The Weapon of Theory"—"class suicide" from a relatively privileged, highly educated graduate of the Instituto Superior de Agronomia in Lisbon to the militant leader of the popular liberation movements of Guinea-Bissau and Cape Verde.

The form of language follows from this idea. In its demanding academic style, couched in theoretical and technical terminology and assuming a great deal of sophistication in its audience, "National Liberation and Culture" is clearly not a propaganda piece intended for mass consumption. Academic Jock McCulloch has argued in his book *In the Twilight of Revolution: The Political Theory of Amilcar Cabral* (1983) that "Cabral's analysis of culture is essentially an account of the situation, experience and aspirations of the petty bourgeoisie," with "National Liberation and Culture" directed toward the culturally alienated intelligentsia, including a call to these groups within African liberation movements to commit to the process of "re-Africanization."

## CRITICAL DISCUSSION

Determining the specific influence of "National Liberation and Culture" on the liberation movements of Guinea-Bissau and Cape Verde and beyond is extremely difficult, and there was little early academic criticism on Cabral's work. Although Cabral was assassinated immediately before the liberation of Guinea-Bissau in 1973, through his works he was to emerge as one of the most successful thinkers and theoreticians during the late twentieth century.

The impact of Cabral's writings in the political sphere of anticolonialism was immediate: Hall claims that "Cabral's writings and ideas contributed to the development of a national liberation strategy in an all-African context." As well as being a key text in academic studies of postcolonialism, "National Liberation and Culture" is, according to Tamara Sivanandan in her article "Anticolonialism, National Liberation, and Postcolonial Nation Formation" (2004), now understood as "a blueprint for any society seeking liberation."

Cabral's position as a key thinker of imperialism and culture is largely attributed to the rise of postcolonial studies in the Western academy in the 1970s and 1980s. This resurgence included the reappraisal and establishment of certain of Cabral's works, including "National Liberation and Culture," as canonical within academic discourses on postcolonial politics and culture. Despite the trend toward elevating Cabral's work to the status of academic "theory"—a direction that the specific text of "National Liberation and Culture" seems to invite—Chabal has argued persuasively that in a broad sense Cabral's writings "were essentially analyses of the events in which he was involved; they were not theories about, or inquiries into, abstract social or political questions."

Monument in Cape Verde honoring Amílcar Cabral, author of "National Liberation and Culture."
© DIRK RENCKHOFF/ALAMY.

## BIBLIOGRAPHY

### Sources

Benewick, Robert, and Philip Green. *The Routledge Dictionary of Political Thinkers.* London: Routledge, 1998. Print.

Cabral, Amílcar. "The Weapon of Theory." *Revolution in Guinea: Selected Texts.* Trans. and ed. Richard Handyside. New York: Monthly Review, 1969. 90–111. Print.

———. "National Liberation and Culture." *Colonial Discourse and Post-Colonial Theory: A Reader.* Ed. Patrick Williams and Laura Chrisman. New York: Columbia UP, 1994. 53–65. Print.

Chabal, Patrick. *Amílcar Cabral: Revolutionary Leadership and People's War.* Cambridge: Cambridge UP, 1983. Print.

Hall, Michael R. "Amilcar Cabral." *Oxford Encyclopedia of African Thought.* Ed. F. Abiola Irele and Biodun Jeyifo. Vol. 2. Oxford: Oxford UP, 2010. 200–02. Print.

McCulloch, Jock. *In the Twilight of Revolution: The Political Theory of Amilcar Cabral.* London: Routledge, 1983. Print.

Sivanandan, Tamara. "Anticolonialism, National Liberation, and Postcolonial Nation Formation." *Cambridge Companion to Postcolonial Literary Studies.* Ed. Neil Lazarus. Cambridge: Cambridge UP, 2004. 41–65. Print.

### Further Reading

Chilcote, Ronald H. *Amílcar Cabral's Revolutionary Theory and Practice: A Critical Guide.* Boulder: Rienner, 1991. Print.

Davidson, Basil. *No Fist Is Big Enough to Hide the Sky: The Liberation of Guinea-Bissau and Cape Verde.* London: Zed, 1981. Print.

Fanon, Frantz. *The Wretched of the Earth.* Trans. Richard Philcox. New York: Grove, 2005. Print.

Fobanjong, John, and Thomas K. Ranuga. *The Life, Thought, and Legacy of Cape Verde's Freedom Fighter Amilcar Cabral (1924–1973): Essays on His Liberation Philosophy.* Lewiston: Mellen, 2006. Print.

Rudebeck, Lars. *Guinea-Bissau: A Study of Political Mobilization.* New York: Africana, 1974. Print.

*Franklyn Hyde*

# Native Life in South Africa, Before and Since the European War and the Boer Rebellion

*Solomon Tshekeisho Plaatje*

✣ *Key Facts*

**Time Period:**
Early 20th Century

**Genre:**
Nonfiction

**Events:**
South African War; Boer
War; escalation of racial
segregation

**Nationality:**
South African

## OVERVIEW

Written between 1914 and 1916 and published in London in 1916, Solomon Tshekeisho Plaatje's *Native Life in South Africa, Before and Since the European War and the Boer Rebellion* draws attention to the plight of blacks during a period of escalation in racial segregation in South Africa. In a style that is distinctly personal yet soberly political, the text describes the origins and catastrophic effects of the 1913 Natives Land Act, a law instituted by the all-white parliament of South Africa that introduced territorial segregation restricting black ownership of land to approximately 7 percent of the country. Although the work is now regarded as a classic of South African protest literature, *Native Life in South Africa* was initially intended for a non-South African audience.

Within the context of its stated purpose—Plaatje wrote with the specific purpose of eliciting British sympathy and support in addressing the injustice of the Natives Land Act—*Native Life in South Africa* was unsuccessful. The Natives Land Act is seen as a major step toward apartheid, which was fully implemented following the rise of the Nationalist Party in 1948 and remained the basis for the tribal reserve system until it was repealed by the F. W. de Klerk government in 1991. Though the act was repealed, the provisions of a 1994 constitutional settlement, particularly one in which land restitution claims can only apply if the land was expropriated after 1915, have ensured an ongoing legacy of displacement and poverty. However, *Native Life in South Africa* has significant legacies in both the political and literary protest traditions in South Africa: as the first piece of major protest literature written by a black South African, *Native Life in South Africa* marks the emergence of an authentically black voice in its political vision and rhetorical and aesthetic strategies.

## HISTORICAL AND LITERARY CONTEXT

Following the South African War of 1899–1902 in which the Afrikaner republics of the Transvaal and Orange Free State were annexed by the British, the Union of South Africa established the country as a British dominion in 1910. In the process, the British prioritized political and economic unity in a way that offered significant concessions to Afrikaner nationalists. The black intelligentsia of South Africa—including Plaatje—had to a certain extent placed their faith in the moderating influence of the British but were sorely disappointed by the British acceptance of a whites-only franchise following the South African War and the ceding of power to Afrikaner-led political interests in 1910.

Plaatje was inspired to complete his work on *Native Life in South Africa* after a trip to Britain failed to gain support for his cause. He was part of the South African Native National Congress (later the ANC), a group that was pressed into action by the 1913 Natives Land Act. With several other members, Plaatje traveled to Britain to lobby the British government. The delegation received a cold welcome from Herbert Asquith's Liberal Party government, which had supported the Boers in the South African War as victims of aggression but failed to recognize that, once in power, the Boers themselves became oppressors of black South Africans.

Plaatje's written works are regarded as foundational to black South African literature. *Native Life in South Africa* is considered the first great work of protest literature produced by a black writer in South Africa, and his *Mhudi* (1930) was the first novel written by a black South African in English. Plaatje was influenced by Olive Schreiner's *Trooper Peter of Mashonaland* (1897), but his central model for *Native Life in South Africa* was not South African but American, specifically W. E. B. Du Bois's *The Souls of Black Folk* (1903). According to Laura Chrisman in *Postcolonial Contraventions: Cultural Readings of Race, Imperialism, and Transnationalism* (2003), "Like *Souls*, *Native Life* is a travelogue in which the writer chronicles the lives of black people under white racism [and in which] both writers use a first person narrative to explore their own relationship to the black communities they represent." *Native Life in South Africa* garnered an immediate response from other black South African writers keen to further demonstrate the injustices of segregation, notably D. D. T. Jabavu in *The Black Problem* (1920) and *Criticisms of the Native Bills* (1935).

*Native Life in South Africa* can be seen as the inception point of far broader traditions. Plaatje's work as an artist, a political activist, and a theorist—including his contributions to the Setswana language, culture, and values, and his translations of two Shakespearean plays into Setswana—as well as his exploration of his complex identification as a Motswana, an African, and a subject of the British Empire, have informed subsequent generations of literary and political figures who sought to overthrow apartheid in South Africa and to deal with the lasting impacts on black South Africans of the Natives Land Act.

## THEMES AND STYLE

*Native Life in South Africa* is part objective history and part personal travelogue. As promised in the full title of the text, Plaatje gives a broadly historical account of native life "before and since the European War and the Boer Rebellion." However, the text centers most importantly on the historical origins and enactment of the Natives Land Act and an account of a journey lasting several weeks made by Plaatje through the Afrikaner-dominated territories of the Transvaal and Orange Free State, as well as through the Province of the Cape of Good Hope. The text is self-identified as propaganda: in his prologue, Plaatje describes the work as an endeavor "to describe the difficulties of the South African Natives under a very strange law, so as most readily to be understood by the sympathetic reader." *Native Life in South Africa* was written with the specific purpose of garnering British support in addressing issues associated with the Natives Land Act, and, in light of the advent of World War I, plays "to the patriotic sentiment so strong in Britain at the time." In *Empire, the National, and the Postcolonial 1890–1920* (2003), author Elleke Boehmer notes that, despite this, Plaatje "remained throughout mindful of a wider audience, the Natives, whose rights and interests had impelled him to speak out in the first place."

The text is deeply personal, contrasting the experience of the author, dispossessed blacks, and sympathetic whites with the impersonal rhetoric of the Afrikaner nationalists. *Native Life in South Africa* develops this contrast, according to Boehmer, "through an accretion of eye-witness reports of native suffering, case studies of white 'disloyalty,' and official quotations placed in ironic or critical juxtaposition with one another." This personal element is most clearly demonstrated by Plaatje's account of the death of his own son in chapter 7 of the text—a death made emblematic of the struggle for life and freedom for the native peoples of South Africa by way of contrast with the ad hoc funeral of the black child of a displaced family witnessed by Plaatje in the veld.

*Native Life in South Africa* shows a broad array of reference such that Boehmer claims that the work is "interdiscursive, where … interdiscursivity refers to the interaction between literary and cultural discourses including orature and oral resources." He goes

## SOUTH AFRICA'S NATIVES LAND ACT

Passed by the government of Louis Botha, the first prime minister of the Union of South Africa, the Natives Land Act (No. 27 of 1913) was the founding legal basis for apartheid's tribal reserve system. Under the provisions of the act, 93 percent of the country was reserved for fewer than 400,000 whites, with the remaining 7 percent reserved for five million black Africans. Black ownership of land both inside and outside of the reserve system was tightly prohibited, and sharecropping was outlawed, with the effect that profitable farming became impossible for black South Africans.

Although contemporary scholarship shows that many of the intended effects of the act did not materialize due to the weakness of the white power during this period, the results were—as Plaatje shows—immensely damaging to the black population. As part of the broader process of segregation, the Natives Land Act can be seen helping to create a politically disenfranchised underclass that was subsequently dependent upon wage labor for white employers to survive. The act was finally repealed by the government of F. W. de Klerk in 1991, during the early stages of the transition of South Africa from the apartheid to postapartheid era, though its impacts continue to be felt across the country.

on to say the text is a "layered verbal collage … [a] function of [Plaatje's] mission education combined with a powerful oral heritage." The former is most obvious when analysis in *Native Life in South Africa* is predicated upon or at least illustrated by scriptural example, with the author himself stating, "When one is distressed in mind there is no greater comforter than an appropriate Scriptural quotation." *Native Life in South Africa* demonstrates a broad emotional register, from lighter touches of irony and humor used by the author in satirizing the hypocrisies surrounding the Natives Land Act, to the great pity, deep sorrow, and searing anger evident in Plaatje's personal accounts of the suffering of black South Africans.

## CRITICAL DISCUSSION

When measured against its stated aim of garnering British support for black South Africans, the initial reception of *Native Life in South Africa* was poor. The British liberal elite to whom the text was directed were noncommittal in their response, and there was no British intervention to repeal the Natives Land Act. The text was, however, impressive enough to be taken up by American activist and Pan-Africanist Du Bois. Plaatje had met Du Bois and Marcus Garvey on a lecture tour of the United States in the early 1920s, and *Native Life in South Africa* was published by the former in the National Association for the Advancement of Colored People's journal the *Crisis* in 1922.

By 1934 the immediate political impetus of *Native Life in South Africa* was already somewhat blunted,

A native woman grinds corn on a stone mortar in Transkei, South Africa, in 1942. Solomon Plaatje wrote *Native Life in South Africa* to expose the devastating effects of the Native Lands Act on South Africa's native people, who were largely deprived of their right to own land. NGS IMAGE COLLECTION/THE ART ARCHIVE AT ART RESOURCE, NY.

Du Bois, contrasting *Native Life in South Africa* with *The Souls of Black Folk* and rebuilding Plaatje as a specifically South African nationalist. Boehmer has sought to place Plaatje within the broader context of his willingness to be a specifically British colonial subject, ultimately showing Plaatje as something of an indeterminate figure, "caught up in all the contradictory *agon* of being 'civilized' and articulate by Western standards, but from a colonial point of view never quite adequately so because of his Africanness."

though the text was already becoming regarded as a classic: Jabavu refers to the text as "a distressing book doomed to remain a monumental indictment of South African native policy." Although the specific issues *Native Life in South Africa* sought to address no longer have the same immediacy in contemporary South Africa, the text has a lasting importance as a unique response to the injustices of racial discrimination. The text also provides a background document by which continuing struggles over land reform in postapartheid South Africa can be better understood.

Critics of the *Native Life in South Africa,* including Brian Willan in *Sol Plaatje: South African Nationalist 1876–1932* (1984), continue to place it as "one of South Africa's great political books," with an emphasis on integrating the text into the greater narrative of Plaatje's political life and his role in the inception and development of the protest movement in South Africa. Contemporary scholarship on Plaatje's work is scarce, but Chrisman recently sought to demonstrate Plaatje's relationship to the Pan-Africanism of

## BIBLIOGRAPHY

### Sources

Boehmer, Elleke. *Empire, the National, and the Postcolonial 1890–1920: Resistance in Interaction.* Oxford: Oxford UP, 2003. Print.

Chrisman, Laura. *Postcolonial Contraventions: Cultural Readings of Race, Imperialism, and Transnationalism.* Manchester: Manchester UP, 2003. Print.

Jabavu, D. D. T. "Bantu Grievances." *Western Civilization in Southern Africa.* Ed. L. Schapera. New York: Routledge, 2004. 285–99. Print.

Parsons, Neil. "Introduction." *Native Life in South Africa, Before and Since the European War and the Boer Rebellion.* Solomon Plaatje. New Haven: Yale UP, 1993. 2–5. Print.

Plaatje, Solomon T. *Native Life in South Africa, Before and Since the European War and the Boer Rebellion.* New Haven: Yale UP, 1993. Print.

Willan, Brian. "Introduction." *Native Life in South Africa, Before and Since the European War and the Boer Rebellion.* Solomon Plaatje. Athens: Ohio UP, 1993. 1–14. Print.

### Further Reading

Chrisman, Laura. *Rereading the Imperial Romance: British Imperialism and South African Resistance in Haggard, Schreiner, and Plaatje.* Oxford: Oxford UP, 2000. Print.

Heywood, Christopher. *A History of South African Literature.* Cambridge: Cambridge UP, 2004. Print.

Plaatje, Solomon T. *Mafeking Diary: A Black Man's View of a White Man's War.* Ed. John Comaroff. Athens: Ohio UP, 1990. Print.

———. *Sol Plaatje: Selected Writings.* Ed. Brian Willan. Athens: Ohio UP, 1996. Print.

———. *Mhudi.* Ed. Stephen Gray. London: Penguin, 2005. Print.

Rall, Maureen. *Peaceable Warrior: The Life and Times of Sol T. Plaatje.* Kimberly: Sol Plaatje Educational Trust, 2003. Print.

Willan, Brian. *Sol Plaatje: South African Nationalist, 1876–1932.* Los Angeles: U of California P, 1984. Print.

Worden, Nigel. *The Making of Modern South Africa: Conquest, Segregation, and Apartheid.* Oxford: Blackwell, 2000. Print.

*Franklyn Hyde*

# A PEOPLE'S HISTORY OF THE UNITED STATES

*Howard Zinn*

## OVERVIEW

In *A People's History of the United States,* first published in 1980, Howard Zinn sketches a lively chronicle of the nation from a perspective that is sympathetic to ordinary people such as workers and minorities, whose views and voices are frequently absent from history books. From the arrival of Columbus in the New World—and the resulting genocide of Native Americans—through centuries of slavery to the rise of modern capitalism, the book depicts U.S. history as a series of confrontations between powerful elite groups and oppressed masses. Zinn sets out to construct an alternative to what he views as the phony "official story" found in social studies textbooks. Avowedly subversive, *A People's History* aims for the opposite of the patriotic, celebratory tone associated with sanitized history, instead casting the nation's exploits in an unrelentingly harsh light.

Zinn's work arose from the cultural conflicts the United States underwent during the 1960s and 1970s. The initial impact of *A People's History* was modest, but its populist, antiauthoritarian spirit had lasting appeal, especially among the young. By the early twenty-first century, nearly two million copies of the book had been sold and it was required reading in many high school and college classrooms. *A People's History* and other works of its ilk have had a polarizing effect on historical and educational debates. Zinn, who died in 2010 at age eighty-seven, was widely lauded for influencing attitudes toward both the United States and the study of history, but critics on the right attacked him as a peddler of Marxist, anti-American propaganda.

## HISTORICAL AND LITERARY CONTEXT

The social movements of the 1960s shattered the ethos of consensus and conformity that had characterized the previous decade. The struggle for African American civil rights brought millions of white-skinned Americans face to face with the reality of bigotry not only in the South but nationwide. Student activists formed the New Left, questioning how well the country was living up to its principles of liberty and democracy and seeking a broad-based counterculture based on dissent from the status quo. Their activities helped sow the seeds of the women's and gay liberation movements. At the same time, a growing, youth-led antiwar movement helped turn public opinion against U.S. military involvement in Vietnam. Coming amid this social discord, the Watergate scandal, which led to the resignation of President Richard Nixon in 1974, appeared to confirm widespread doubts about the legitimacy of powerful institutions in American life.

Though the effects of these developments were still playing out as the 1970s ended, a conservative resurgence was also gaining steam, as evidenced by the Republican Ronald Reagan's landslide victory in the 1980 presidential race. The curtain was rising on an era of intense partisanship and politicized "culture wars" between liberals and conservatives over social issues such as abortion and welfare. Zinn's project of challenging conventional concepts of U.S. history was in keeping with the increasingly ideological cast of academic and educational debates. Zinn himself was a committed activist who had been involved in civil rights battles while teaching at Spelman College, a historically black women's school in Atlanta, and had, in 1967, published a book-length argument for withdrawal from Vietnam. In *A People's History,* Zinn aimed to expose and contest what he perceived as the nationalistic bias in standard presentations of U.S. history. The facts selected or omitted by historians, he contended, invariably reflect the historians' own values and interests.

Zinn can be counted among those who spearheaded a revisionist trend in historical studies and historiography. Adherents to the view he called "history from the bottom up," such as C. L. R. James, Slaughton Lynd, and E. P. Thompson, often deliberately downplayed the role of elites and the powerful and instead shifted the emphasis to the lives of ordinary people and voices from disenfranchised groups. Similar inclinations drove the development of academic departments focused on women's history, black history, and other ethnic and cultural studies.

Ironically, *A People's History,* intended as an implicit attack on the textbook field, has itself become a quasi-standard textbook in certain educational quarters. Its historical narrative is structured like that of other works in the genre, with chapters roughly representing historical periods and events such as the Civil War and the Great Depression. However, several of the events and issues emphasized—Native American removal and the labor and socialist movements, for example—indicate a viewpoint informed by the struggles of the 1960s.

### ✤ *Key Facts*

**Time Period:**
Late 20th Century

**Genre:**
History

**Events:**
Cold War; rise of the New Left; end of the Vietnam War; election of Ronald Reagan

**Nationality:**
American

# HOWARD ZINN AND MATT DAMON

Actor and screenwriter Matt Damon was born and raised in Cambridge, Massachusetts. In his youth, he came to know his neighbor, Howard Zinn, who taught nearby at Boston University. Zinn even accepted Damon's invitation to speak to his fifth-grade class about the legacy of Christopher Columbus. Damon and another friend and neighbor, Ben Affleck, wrote the screenplay for the film *Good Will Hunting* (1997), which starred Damon, Affleck, and Robin Williams. When Damon's character, a brilliant and troubled young man named Will, first meets his new therapist, Sean Maguire (played by Williams), Will criticizes the professional's choice of reading matter: "You wanna read a *real* history book," he says, "read Howard Zinn's *People's History of the United States.* That book'll knock you on your ass."

Damon went on to collaborate with Zinn, serving as executive producer of *The People Speak,* a documentary film that aired on the History Channel in December 2009. The film features dramatic performances based on the letters, diaries, and public speeches of ordinary Americans from different historical periods; the documents are read by many well-known actors and musicians, including Bruce Springsteen and Bob Dylan. Damon has also appeared in live stage performances of *The People Speak.*

Many students and teachers have gravitated toward the viewpoint expressed in Zinn's counter-history, and numerous "People's History" products have been released since his book was published, such as *Voices of a People's History of the United States* (2004, coedited with Anthony Arnove) and *A Young People's History of the United States* (2007, adapted by Rebecca Stefoff).

**THEMES AND STYLE**

In contrast to mainstream textbooks whose themes can be gleaned from such titles as *Triumph of the American Nation, The American Pageant,* and *The Challenge of Freedom, A People's History* centers on the idea of conflict between groups. The most important conflicts are those of race, gender, and, especially, social and economic class. Zinn repeatedly offers sympathetic portrayals of downtrodden groups (such as West African slaves and rioting prison inmates at the Attica state prison in New York) and dissidents (such as members of Shays' Rebellion and the Industrial Workers of the World). Arrayed against these representatives of "the people" are the forces of "the system": the nation's power structure, whether represented by plantation owners, robber barons, or corporate interests, with the police or military at the ready. The disputes between these forces are frequently resolved through violence and suppression. A related theme is that the nation's development was achieved at a brutal cost, paid by Native Americans, African Americans, poor whites, factory and farm laborers, and the families of young men shipped off to war.

The book's rhetorical effect flows naturally from its commitment to the bottom-up viewpoint on history and the pitched battles between dominant interests and radical underdogs that appear in many of its chapters. When Zinn zeroes in on prominent politicians and economic elites, he often perceives the profit motive to be driving their decisions. Zinn tends to portray social change as the combined result of pressure from below, created by social movements, and accommodation from above. For hardheaded reasons of self-interest, he argues, elites occasionally implement modest reforms, as in the Progressive era and the New Deal, in order to forestall more thoroughgoing or revolutionary change. The text expresses skepticism toward unifying sentiments conveyed by political leaders, as in references to "we the people" from the Revolutionary era or to the "national interest" during World War I. In Zinn's view, elites truly seek "to create an artificial community of interest between rich and poor, supplanting the genuine community of interest among the poor that showed itself in sporadic movements." Class conflict, it is implied, is the prevailing state of affairs.

The vivid, engaging style of *A People's History* is crucial to its persuasive appeal. Zinn's text is neither dry nor disinterested, and his voice is that of a storyteller. Describing the U.S. war in the Philippines in 1899, for example, Zinn writes, "Dead Filipinos were piled so high that the Americans used their bodies for breastworks. A British witness said: 'This is not war. It is simply massacre and murderous butchery.' He was wrong; it was war." Through anecdotes, vignettes, and primary source material, he invites the reader to identify with his protagonists and their struggles of resistance. He focuses on dramatic events such as strikes, demonstrations, and insurrections, rarely overlooking violent incidents and entertaining details. The book's ideological framework remains consistent and grows ever clearer from chapter to chapter.

**CRITICAL DISCUSSION**

Upon its initial appearance, *A People's History* was not widely recognized as a breakthrough in the field. Reviewers praised the book's lively tone, and some appreciated the scope of the author's ambitions. However, several reviewers chastised Zinn for the relative thinness of his research and for committing sins of omission. For example, the *Washington Post Book World* pointed out the short shrift given to religion, a major force in the life of the American people, and concluded that Zinn had offered an imbalanced, "singleminded, simpleminded history, too often of fools, knaves and Robin Hoods." Even the *Nation,* a liberal bastion, charged that *A People's History* "suffers the defects of the textbook genre," most notably a lack of nuance and sophistication. Despite the uneven reviews, the book was a runner-up for the 1980 National Book Award.

Over time, and with the publication of several updated editions covering events through 2005, the

A diverse gathering in Times Square, New York City, during the 2009 inauguration of U.S. president Barack Obama. Howard Zinn's *A People's History of the United States* discusses the role of different Americans throughout the nation's history. © AURORA PHOTOS/ALAMY.

book has acquired a devoted following and etched a unique place in American society. Many students find it far easier to relate to and learn from Zinn's writing, with its pungent tone and accessible moral template, than more conventional textbook fare. Progressive-minded teachers and "alternative" secondary schools have also embraced the book, often assigning its chapters to supplement or balance the perspective of texts that more closely follow state learning standards. Its approach has been justly cited—notably, by fellow historians such as Eric Foner, journalists including Bill Moyers, and artists such as novelist Alice Walker and rapper Talib Kweli—for popularizing the idea that poor people and social movements constitute valuable subjects and sources in the study of history.

As is to be expected, however, the legacy of this polemical book is highly politicized. Among conservatives, Zinn and his work have been roundly denigrated. Roger Kimball typifies this view in a 2010 *National Review* article, lamenting that "most American students are battened on a story of their country in which Blame America First is a cardinal principle." On the other hand, many liberals and radicals have lionized Zinn. His defenders often assert, however, that he presents history from the bottom rather than the left. In his original *Nation* review, Bruce Kuklick presciently anticipates the book's political value, saying it is "designed to give the left a usable past." In the *Chronicle of Higher Education,* Christopher Phelps calls *A People's History*

a successful "effort to synthesize a widely shared shift in historical sensibilities."

**BIBLIOGRAPHY**

*Sources*

Kammen, Michael. "How the Other Half Lived." *Washington Post Book World* 23 Mar. 1980: 7. Rpt. in *Contemporary Literary Criticism.* Ed. Jeffrey W. Hunter. Vol. 199. Detroit: Gale, 2005. *Literature Resource Center.* Web. 4 Aug. 2012.

Kimball, Roger. "Professor of Contempt: The Legacy of Howard Zinn." *National Review* 22 Feb. 2010: 29. *Gale U.S. History in Context.* Web. 14 Aug. 2012.

Kuklick, Bruce. "The People? Yes." *Nation* 24 May 1980: 634–636. Rpt. in *Contemporary Literary Criticism Select.* Detroit: Gale, 2008. *Literature Resource Center.* Web. 4 Aug. 2012.

Phelps, Christopher. "Howard Zinn, Philosopher." *Chronicle of Higher Education* 1 Feb. 2010. Web. 17 Aug. 2012.

Zinn, Howard. *A People's History of the United States: 1492—Present.* New York: Perennial Classics, 2001. Print.

*Further Reading*

Bobb, David J. "The Future of Patriotism." *Claremont Review of Books* Spring 2005: 23+. *Literature Resource Center.* Web. 17 Aug. 2012.

Kazin, Michael. "Howard Zinn's History Lessons." *Dissent* Spring 2004. Web. 17 Aug. 2012.

Handlin, Oscar. "Arawaks." *American Scholar* 49 (1980): 546–50. Web. *Contemporary Literary Criticism.* Web. 17 Aug. 2012.

Loewen, James W. *Lies My Teacher Told Me: Everything Your American History Textbook Got Wrong.* New York: New, 1995. Print.

Zinn, Howard. *You Can't Be Neutral on a Moving Train: A Personal History of Our Times.* Boston: Beacon, 1994. Print.

Zinn, Howard, and Anthony Arnove, eds. *Voices of a People's History of the United States.* New York: Seven Stories, 2004. Print.

*Media Adaptation*

*The People Speak.* Writ. Anthony Armove and Howard Zinn. Dir. Anthony Arnove, Chris Moore, and Howard Zinn. Perf. Matt Damon, Josh Brolin, Sean Penn, et. al. History Channel, 2009. TV.

*Voices of a People's History of the United States.* Read by Howard Zinn, Lili Taylor, Paul Robeson, et al. Intro. Amy Goodman. New York, NY: Seven Stories Press, 2004.

*Roger Smith*

# POLITICAL ACTIONS

# THE BOMB

*Frank Harris*

## OVERVIEW

An expression of American anarchist ideas, Frank Harris's *The Bomb* (1908) presents a fictionalized account of the Haymarket Affair of 1886—a peaceful organized labor rally that turned violent when a bomb was thrown at police attempting to disperse the crowd. To narrate the story, Harris creates a fictionalized version of the real-life Rudolph Schnaubelt, a young man suspected as the thrower of the bomb, who was arrested briefly before fleeing the country. Harris's depiction of the hardships Schnaubelt, an immigrant from Germany, endures as a workman in New York and Chicago paints a startling picture of the suppressive squalor imposed on the working class from above. In the novel, after enduring many ordeals, Schnaubelt meets Louis Lingg—a German American anarchist not present at Haymarket Square but suspected of making the bomb that was thrown. Throughout the rest of the novel, Lingg is presented as a nearly Christ-like figure and the workers, as innocent victims. The end of the work, which includes almost verbatim testimony of the real defendants in the Haymarket Trial, represents a fictionalized and dramatized version of some of the most clearly articulated American anarchist ideology in twentieth-century literature.

Harris's fellow left-wing authors openly praised *The Bomb*. Writer Emma Goldman called it the bible of anarchism, while playwright George Bernard Shaw, for whom Harris had been a biographer, labeled it the Homer of anarchism. Unfortunately, the few critics who afforded it any attention expressed less enthusiasm. Part of the book's challenge was its timing, as much of the public interest in labor issues was already invested in Upton Sinclair's *The Jungle* (1906), a wildly popular exposé of unhealthy standards in the meatpacking industry. Therefore, despite its political bent, *The Bomb* was popular mostly among readers of melodrama, who lionized the novel's sexual candor and violence—traits that would later become synonymous with Harris's name. Despite the novel's traction among anarchist literati, it did little to invigorate the second-wave labor movement as a whole. Today, *The Bomb* is seen as the creative expression of an impassioned journalist frustrated with the vilification of anarchists' personal and political beliefs.

## HISTORICAL AND LITERARY CONTEXT

Shortly after arriving in the United States in 1882, German anarchist Johann Most published a manifesto titled *Science of Revolutionary Warfare: A Handbook of Instruction Regarding the Use and Manufacture of Nitroglycerine, Dynamite, Gun-Cotton, Fulminating Mercury, Bombs, Arsons, Poisons, etc.* (1885). The text changed the face of American anarchism, previously embodied in the civil disobedience professed by Henry David Thoreau, Ralph Waldo Emerson, and Walt Whitman. Nowhere was this shift more apparent than in Chicago, where industrial relations were acrid, police were brutal, and armed resistance was heavily advocated. About half the nation's approximately 6,000 anarchists were in Chicago, most belonging to either the Socialist Labor Party (SLP) or to the International Working People's Association (IWPA). The Haymarket Affair occurred in May 1886 when the McCormick Harvester Factory locked out 1,400 workers without warning after unions began calling for an eight-hour workday. Fighting broke out in front of the factory, and police fired on the workers, killing several and wounding dozens more.

Released amid renewed tension surrounding the labor movement in 1908–09, Harris's first novel, *The Bomb*, retells the events that unfolded the day following the McCormick lockout. A protest meeting that was held at Haymarket Square was breaking up peacefully when police advanced in formation on the gatherers. A bomb was thrown, killing seven of the policemen, and an exchange of gunfire afterward killed four civilians and wounded as many as seventy more. Although the true identity of the bomber may never be known, in the novel Harris posits the bomber as a lone radical acting on a desire not shared by the majority of anarchists and labor activists. The real-life events at Haymarket Square had tainted public perceptions of the SLP and IWPA for years, and Harris—an Irish-born naturalized American with a personal interest in anarchist labor movements in both the United States and United Kingdom—attempted to recast them as sympathetic victims of systemic vilification by making the bomber the novel's narrator.

Harris was not the first author to express compassion for those executed following the Haymarket Affair. William Dean Howells's *A Hazard of New Fortunes* (1888) and Robert Herrick's *Memoirs of an American*

# THE EIGHT-HOUR MOVEMENT

On May 1, 1886, a few days before the Haymarket Square bombing in Chicago, unionized workers around the United States walked off the job in an orchestrated effort to secure an eight-hour workday. The movement for a limited and regulated workday had been ongoing in the United States and Europe for half a century, ever since factory employment became common in the 1820s and 1830s. Despite strikes, petition drives, and the organization of workingmen's parties, however, the crusade had been unsuccessful. Then, in the 1880s, the Noble and Holy Order of the Knights of Labor joined with the new American Federation of Labor, as well as various other labor groups, to organize an intensified effort. The result was the May 1 walkout. That action led many employers to meet their workers' demands, and the movement seemed to be gaining traction. When the Haymarket Affair happened just a few days later, opponents used the violence in Chicago to dismiss labor's demands.

The struggle for an eight-hour day was checked but not stopped. The goal was not achieved, however, until the Great Depression, when reduced hours were implemented to allow new job creation and alleviate the nation's extreme unemployment rates. Eventually, in 1938, Congress passed the Fair Labor Standards Act, which not only established a forty-hour workweek but also restricted child labor and created a federal minimum wage.

*Citizen* (1905) both deal with public responses to the Haymarket Affair, albeit in drastically different ways. Howells, a former editor of the *Atlantic Monthly*, indirectly protests public demonization of the protestors by presenting a story in which a working-class man refuses to vilify and alienate an anarchist friend and colleague despite pressure from his employer. Herrick, on the other hand, addresses the events at Haymarket Square, telling his story from the perspective of a member of the jury ultimately responsible for executing the men. Through the juror, Herrick reflects on the public hysteria following the bombing, the haste with which the men were convicted and hanged, and the enthusiasm with which the American public supported the decision.

In *The Bomb* Harris goes a step further, adopting the point of view of the culprits. By following Schnaubelt and Lingg so closely, the author comments on the subpar working conditions that gave rise to the anarchist movement and hypothesizes a scenario in which the actions of the bomb thrower were not representative of the movement's overall character. After Harris's text was published, the Haymarket Affair almost entirely disappeared from American letters, resurfacing only once, in Howard Fast's *The American* (1946). The novel tells the story of John Peter Altgeld, the Illinois governor who pardoned three of the executed men and decries the conduct of both the state and its citizens immediately following the Haymarket Affair.

## THEMES AND STYLE

Harris would later become notorious for both the sexually explicit and sometimes graphically violent scenes he first displayed in *The Bomb*. John Dos Passos, in his introduction to the 1963 Chicago edition of the novel, quotes Harris as saying, "Kissing and fighting were the only things I cared for at thirteen or fourteen and these are the things the English public desires and enjoys today." The clearest examples of this approach can be found in passages where an almost Christ-like version of anarchist Louis Lingg describes to the narrator his sexual exploits: "our lips clung together. Feeling her yield, and overpowered by desire … her supple, warm beauty gave itself … the blood was rioting through my veins … I taste life's ecstasy again at the springing fount." In the riot scenes, "women and children attacked the patrol wagons and threw stones at the policemen. Men, women, and even children were savagely clubbed in return … in a sort of frenzy of rage." The mixture of sexual and political seduction in the novel functions as a method of winning over the reader and propagandizing the anarchist movement.

Harris's main rhetorical strategy in the novel is to cast anarchists in a sympathetic light and to paint big business as despotic. He frequently describes Albert Parsons—one of four men hanged for the Haymarket Affair—calling "on American workmen to stand by their foreign brothers and resist the tyranny of the employers" and the police. Harris's most expressive pleas, however, come from his characterization of Lingg, as in Lingg's courtroom speech near the end of the book: "I had intended … to defend myself; but the trial has been so unfair, the conduct of it so disgraceful, the intent and purpose of it so clearly avowed, that I will not waste words. Your capitalist masters want blood; why keep them waiting?"

Regarding compassion as a foregone disposition, Harris avoids emotional evocations in favor of reasoned arguments colored at times by the melodrama typical of popular fiction of the period. In response to a harrowing story told by a worker at a socialist gathering, the narrator begins "to understand that resignation was a badge of servitude, that such sheepish patience was inherited … my blood boiled, and pity shook me." The young man telling the story is described as "blind at six and twenty, and turned out to starve, as one would not turn out a horse or a dog." Although Harris's prose in *The Bomb* is at times melodramatic, it is also lucid and direct, avoiding the ambiguity and esoteric wordplay of many of the novelist's modernist contemporaries.

## CRITICAL DISCUSSION

*The Bomb* elicited mixed responses in the few reviews that were published. The *New York Times* (1909) held that while the novel's characters were readable and its speculation plausible, "in its fictional expression it breaks down in some places and moves clumsily in others." The review further criticizes Harris's

Frank Harris's novel *The Bomb* discusses the bombing at an 1886 labor event at Chicago's Haymarket Square, an event captured in this engraving by T. de Thulstrup. © BETTMANN/ CORBIS.

violence and sexual frankness, concluding, "chapters upon chapters of mere lovemaking reduced to its primal elements become ridiculous when not offensive. Many of Mr. Harris's are both." Meanwhile, the *Saturday Review* (1908) hails the novel as a "thoroughly fine piece of work." The reviewer is convinced by Harris's depiction of the anarchists and the bomber, proclaiming that in the confession that concludes the book, "Mr. Harris *is* Schnaubelt, with an amazing vividness, with an absolute translation of himself into the soul of this simple, emotional, painstaking, ordinary young German."

*The Bomb* was eventually overshadowed in Harris's body of work by his more successful, if scandalous, autobiography, *My Life and Loves* (1922–27). Among literary treatments of the Haymarket Affair, the novel is generally considered the most accurate depiction of the events. Everett Carter, writing for *American Quarterly* in 1950, concludes that the novel in its political moment also represents "the potpourri of 'Socialism, Christianity, anarchy, and hero-worship' … typical of American radicalism in the first ten years of the 20th century." As such, scholarly interest in the novel lies more in its value as a window into the political moment of the Haymarket Affair than as either a modernist novel or as a twentieth-century anarchist tract.

Contemporary views of *The Bomb*'s importance are perhaps best summarized in Dos Passos's introduction to the 1963 reprinting. He writes that the book "was very much of a precursor" of the "proletarian novels" that followed it. Although he admits the writing is mediocre and will stand "with Wells's or Kipling's as an example of the limpid English style of the period," he maintains that "half a century after the book was first printed the reader will find the re-creation" of the social and political climate surrounding the Haymarket Affair "singularly convincing." Attributing the book's accuracy to Harris's close personal experiences in the social labor movement of the 1870s and 1880s, Dos Passos sees *The Bomb* as invaluable to understanding the early anarchist movement's character, which in the 1960s appears "as naively alien as the Children's Crusade. The oppressions and injustices that [the anarchists] protested against were real, but the notion that society could be shocked into justice and charity by the blowing up of a few policemen ranks with delusions relegated to the psychiatric ward."

## BIBLIOGRAPHY

### Sources

Carter, Everett. "The Haymarket Affair in Literature." *American Quarterly* 2.3 (1950): 270–78. *JSTOR.* Web. 31 Oct. 2012.

Harris, Frank. *The Bomb: A Novel.* Chicago: U of Chicago P, 1963. Print.

"Haymarket Tragedy." *New York Times Saturday Book Review* 27 Feb. 1909, 118. Rpt. in *Twentieth-Century Literary Criticism.* Ed. Dennis Poupard. Vol. 24. Detroit: Gale, 1987. *Literature Resource Center.* Web. 2 Aug. 2012.

"Mr. Frank Harris' New Story." *Saturday Review* 106.2770 (1908): 674. Rpt. in *Twentieth-Century Literary*

*Criticism.* Ed. Dennis Poupard. Vol. 24. Detroit: Gale, 1987. *Literature Resource Center.* Web. 2 Aug. 2012.

Tobin, A. I., and Elmer Gertz. *Frank Harris: A Study in Black and White.* New York: Haskell House, 1970. *Google Books.* Web. 31 Oct. 2012.

*Further Reading*

Boston, Richard. "Anarchy Unloosed." *New Statesman* 126.4318 (1997): 48. *Academic Search Complete.* Web. 2 Aug. 2012.

David, Henry. *The History of the Haymarket Affair: A Study in the American Social-Revolutionary and Labor Movements.* New York: Russell & Russell, 1958. Print.

Green, James R. *Death in the Haymarket: A Story of Chicago, the First Labor Movement, and the Bombing That Divided Gilded Age America.* New York: Pantheon, 2006. Print.

Krutch, J. W. "The Case of Frank Harris." *Nation* 115.2974 (1922): 19–20. *Academic Search Complete.* Web. 2 Aug. 2012.

Longa, Ernesto A. *Anarchist Periodicals in English Published in the United States (1833–1955): An Annotated Guide.* Lanham, MD: Scarecrow, 2010. Print.

Messer-Kruse, Timothy. *The Trial of the Haymarket Anarchists: Terrorism and Justice in the Gilded Age.* New York: Palgrave Macmillan, 2011. Print.

Nelson, Bruce. *Beyond the Martyrs: A Social History of Chicago's Anarchists, 1870–1900.* Rutgers: Rutgers UP, 1988. Print.

*Clint Garner*

# THE COMING INSURRECTION

*Invisible Committee*

## OVERVIEW

Written in 2007 by an anonymous French group called the Invisible Committee—allegedly members of the leftist organization the Tarnac 9—*The Coming Insurrection* is an anarchistic book that details the shortcomings of capitalist culture and calls for an end to capitalism altogether. The first of the work's two parts identifies the "seven circles of alienation" that have resulted from modern capitalism: the self, social relations, work, the economy, urbanity, the environment, and civilization. The second part seeks to thwart capitalism by forming communes that will function as underground communities and will attack the capitalist structure when it is weakened by political, social, or environmental crises. *The Coming Insurrection* serves as propaganda because it only discusses the negative aspects of capitalism and selectively fails to mention that eradicating the system would put international trade and the world economy at great risk.

*The Coming Insurrection* is very much a product of the period in which it was written, as it points to issues such as the economic crisis of the late 2000s and environmental decline as leading to the failure of capitalism. Upon its publication, it garnered attention from the *New York Times* and *Adbusters* magazine, as well as liberal documentary director and activist Michael Moore. Anarchists in the United States also took an interest in the work. The profile of the book was further raised when conservative commentator Glenn Beck first mentioned it on his talk show, *The Glenn Beck Program,* in July 2009. Since then, Beck has pointed to the work many times as an example of leftist radicalism and has even conducted panel discussions on its topics.

## HISTORICAL AND LITERARY CONTEXT

Anarchism has a long history in France, dating back to the French Revolution in the late 1700s. The Tarnac 9 took an interest in anarchy after one of its members, Julien Coupat, cofounded *Tiqqun,* a French radical journal that was published from 1999 to 2011 and aimed to "recreate the conditions of another community." The writers behind *Tiqqun* were influenced by a long line of French intellectuals, including Michel Foucault, George Bataille, Giorgio Agamben, and Alain Badiou.

The publication of *The Coming Insurrection* in 2007 came on the heels of two years of student-led protests in France against labor laws that made it easier for companies to fire new employees. Amid the civil unrest, further action by the work's alleged authors followed. On November 11, 2008, they were charged in the village of Tarnac, France, with "criminal association for the purposes of terrorist activity" for delaying the French train rail system by disabling more than 160 trains.

While writing *The Coming Insurrection,* the Invisible Committee looked to situationist and lettrist works such as the French journal *Internationale Situationniste* (which reached its apex in the late 1960s), Guy Debord's *On the Poverty of Student Life* (1966) and *Society of the Spectacle* (1967), and Raoul Vaneigem's *The Revolution of Everyday Life* (1967). These works address topics such as Marxist critical theory and anti-authoritarianism. The poetic style of *Tiqqun* was inspired by the situationist and lettrist movements. Not surprisingly, the writings published in *Tiqqun* helped frame the thoughts of the Invisible Committee, including a piece titled "Introduction to Civil War," which was published in book form in 2010. Inspired by Foucault, the work calls for a civil war, or rebellion, to reclaim "the workings of the soul."

Since its publication, *The Coming Insurrection* has heavily influenced anarchist and radical leftist movements, and it has also forced individuals in the mainstream to consider the power of underground direct-action groups. Sorbonne criminologist Alain Bauer—who brought the Tarnac 9 to the attention of the French government—was quoted in the *Observer* as saying that "with Action Directe and the Red Brigades [earlier radical groups], there was a first intellectual phase, followed by a radicalization and then a transition to physical action. Books like *The Coming Insurrection* are strongly reminiscent of the first phase." The intellectual nature of *The Coming Insurrection* was captured on the stage in September 2010 when Coline Struyf adapted it for the National Theatre of Belgium.

## THEMES AND STYLE

*The Coming Insurrection* focuses on an eventual rebellion that will center on "the local appropriation of power by the people, of the physical blocking of the economy and of the annihilation of police forces." This theme of a society led by its citizens and free of police and government control ties directly to the

### ✣ Key Facts

**Time Period:**
Early 21st Century

**Genre:**
Treatise

**Events:**
Global economic crises; Seattle protests against the World Trade Organization; student protests in France

**Nationality:**
French

## JULIEN COUPAT: THE FACE BEHIND TARNAC 9

Although the Invisible Committee is still viewed as an anonymous group, French political activist Julien Coupat emerged as one of its key figures following the arrest of the Tarnac 9 in 2008 for disrupting the French rail system. Born on June 4, 1974, in Bordeaux, France, Coupat was raised in a well-educated family and went on to study business and social sciences. In 1999 he founded the radical journal *Tiqqun*. Six years later he set up a commune in Tarnac, France, where he lived and worked with his friends.

Coupat's first brush with the law came shortly thereafter when the FBI discovered that he and his girlfriend had crossed the border illegally from Canada to New York City. Later, they were involved in a protest outside an army recruitment center, which later became the site of a bomb attack. From then on the FBI monitored Coupat's dealings, and he was arrested as one of the leaders of a plot to disrupt train lines in France in November 2008. Coupat was charged with "criminal association for the purposes of terrorist activity" and was released on May 28, 2009. After that, he kept a relatively low profile.

Invisible Committee's plan to persuade its readers that an anticapitalist system is necessary. Until capitalism is eradicated, power will not flow back to the citizenry. The Invisible Committee writes, "Governing has never been anything other than postponing by a thousand subterfuges the moment when the crowd will string you up, and every act of government is nothing but a way of not losing control of the population."

To make its points, the Invisible Committee uses several rhetorical strategies, including placing blame on capitalist organizations and slanting issues so that they support the group's aims. Offering examples such as the student protests in France, the mayhem following Hurricane Katrina in 2005, and the 2006 Oaxaca protests, the Invisible Committee attempts to convince its audience that a "breakdown in the modern social order" is a means through which a revolt can take place. In doing so, however, the group glosses over all other opinions, specifically those of a pro-capitalist nature.

*The Coming Insurrection* utilizes emotion—in the form of an angry voice—to make dramatic appeals to its audience. Painting government as an organization with "mechanisms of power that preventively and surgically stifle any revolutionary potential in a situation," the group indignantly conveys that its message is the right message and that anyone who does not agree with it is not only foolish but also in danger of being suffocated by a capitalist society that does more harm than good. The passionate tone of the Invisible Committee's language gives the text a sense of urgency. There is, the book boldly states, no choice but to take

immediate and direct action: "To put it bluntly, Paris now stands out only as a target for raids, as a pure terrain to be pillaged and ravaged. Brief and brutal incursions from the outside strike at the metropolitan flows at their point of maximum density."

### CRITICAL DISCUSSION

When it was first published, *The Coming Insurrection* made a relatively small cultural impact. Before Beck was made aware of the text, various radical groups passed around bootlegged copies of it and actively discussed its content, which they felt had been written expressly for them. Although most of these groups lauded the essay, several others were critical. For example, the zine *Anarchist News* published a negative write-up that criticized the Invisible Committee for its "ridiculous insurrectionist bullshit" and for ignoring the feminist and antiracism movements. Nevertheless, the power of *The Coming Insurrection* could not be denied. In his essay "Back to Meinhof," Daniel Miller writes, "*The Coming Insurrection* is without a doubt the most thought-provoking radical text to be published in the past ten years. It deserves to be read and discussed."

Following its publication, *The Coming Insurrection*'s push for direct action not only aligned with the Tarnac 9's 2008 attempt to disable more than 160 trains in France—causing many people to believe that the group was responsible for the manifesto—but it also frightened the mainstream media into thinking that the "insurrection" in question would result in an onslaught of major terrorist action. After Beck first mentioned *The Coming Insurrection* on his show in 2009, he told his viewers that they should read this "crazy" and "evil" text, as he referred to it, so that they could better understand the thoughts of leftist radicals. Since then, Beck has referenced the book as a way to try to make sense of various incidents of unrest, including 2011 revolution in Egypt, the 2010–11 protests in Greece, and the Occupy Wall Street demonstrations.

Though *The Coming Insurrection* has not led to any large-scale social or political changes, it is regarded as an influential work that pinpoints the anticapitalist concerns of underground radical and anarchist groups. In his 2011 essay in *Anarchist Studies*, Iain McKay addresses what he sees as the work's distorted reality: "Reading *The Coming Insurrection* on my way to work made me wonder at times whether it was an elaborate satire. One thing is true, it does not describe the world as I, or many others, know it." Despite his misgivings, McKay goes on to find worthwhile aspects in the text: "Still, good points are often made, with the usual striking and imaginative turn of phrase we come to expect of French protesters." McKay's commentary sums up the view of many contemporary critics toward *The Coming Insurrection*: they are realistic enough to know that capitalism will not be wiped out, but they admire the bold language and strong convictions of the Invisible Committee.

**BIBLIOGRAPHY**

*Sources*

*Introduction to Civil War.* Trans. by Alexander R. Galloway and Jason E. Smith. Cambridge: MIT P, 2010. Print.

Lopez, Andrew, and Phillip Mahoney. "Know the Enemy." *Criticism* 53.3 (2011): 495+. *Literature Resource Center.* Web. 10 Aug. 2012.

McKay, Iain. "The Coming Insurrection." *Anarchist Studies* 19.1 (2011): 124+. *Literature Resource Center.* Web. 10 Aug. 2012.

Miller, Daniel. "Back to Meinhof." *New Statesman* [1996], 19 Oct. 2009: 52+. *Literature Resource Center.* Web. 10 Aug. 2012.

*The Coming Insurrection.* Los Angeles: Semiotext(e), 2009. Print.

*Further Reading*

"Brief Excerpts…" *Libcom.org.* Libcom.org, 26 Dec. 2009. Web. 10 Aug. 2012.

Galloway, Alexander R., and Jason E. Smith. *Introduction to Civil War.* Los Angeles: Semiotext(e), 2010. Print.

Moynihan, Colin. "Liberating Lipsticks and Lattes." *New York Times.* The New York Times Company, 16 June 2009. Web. 11 Aug. 2012.

Nardi, Sarah. "The Coming Insurrection." *Adbusters.* Adbusters, 14 July 2009. Web. 11 Aug. 2012.

"Why She Doesn't Give a Fuck about Your Insurrection." *Anarchist News Dot Org.* Anarchist New Dot Org, 18 July 2009. Web. 11 Aug. 2012.

***Anna Deem***

This 2008 photograph shows protestors criticizing the American government's financial aid to Wall Street firms. According to the authors of *The Coming Insurrection* (2007), capitalism is on the verge of collapse. © ANDREW LICHTENSTEIN/THE IMAGE WORKS.

# GREEN BOOK

*Irish Republican Army (IRA)*

✣ **Key Facts**

**Time Period:**
Late 20th Century

**Genre:**
Training Manual

**Events:**
Struggle for Irish Home
Rule; the Troubles;
militarization of the Irish
Republican Army

**Nationality:**
Irish

## OVERVIEW

The Irish Republican Army's (IRA's) *Green Book* (1977), the training manual provided to new members of the organization, contains both practical instruction regarding security and an introduction to the history and philosophical underpinnings of the IRA. Penned by members imprisoned during the Provisional Irish Republican Army campaign of the mid-1970s, the *Green Book* makes the argument that the provisional IRA—or Provos, as the group was sometimes known during this period—is "the legal representatives of the Irish people" and as such is "morally justified in carrying out a campaign of resistance against foreign occupation forces and domestic collaborators." Stressing the importance of being politically educated and secure in its convictions about the justness of a unified Ireland, the *Green Book* also stresses the importance of public image in the ongoing campaign.

The history of the development and dissemination of the *Green Book* remains somewhat obscure, because the work was a secret document of an organization on the British Home Office's list of proscribed terrorists. It is fairly certain that the *Green Book* was considered a cornerstone of volunteer training during the late 1970s and early 1980s, particularly the sections dealing with police interrogation tactics and the importance of remaining silent following arrest. Indeed, in the years immediately after the document's appearance a number of murders were allegedly carried out by the IRA against members who were suspected of leaking IRA secrets. In the years following the 1998 Good Friday Agreement, the IRA demilitarized and the manual fell into disuse. Nevertheless, the document remains important historically and provides a view of the philosophy and culture of militant secrecy that characterized the IRA of the late twentieth century.

## HISTORICAL AND LITERARY CONTEXT

The first English invasion of Ireland dates to 1170, when Richard de Clare, also known as Strongbow, advanced into Leinster. Henry II followed in 1171, subjecting Ireland to the papal bull of Laudabiliter, which instituted reforms to the Church of Ireland. Over the next eight centuries, English influence in Ireland underwent a number of shifts. The English Reformation, in which the Church of England rejected papal authority and broke from the Roman Catholic Church, was particularly significant, marking a religious divergence that would play a role in later conflicts. The two countries were joined in the United Kingdom of England and Ireland, which was instituted in 1801 with the Act of Union. By the early twentieth century, mounting tensions led to the 1916 Easter Rising by Irish republicans seeking an end to English rule and, ultimately, in the Anglo-Irish War (1919–21). Confronted with British casualties and growing antiwar sentiment at home, the British government sought to establish a system of home rule in Ireland by partitioning the country into two distinct parts via the Government of Ireland Act (1920). In the following year, the Anglo-Irish Treaty declared both the predominantly Protestant counties in the northern section of the island and the largely Catholic counties in the south as part of the Irish Free State. The government in Northern Ireland quickly opted out of the new state, electing to remain part of the United Kingdom. The resulting dissatisfaction among Northern Ireland's Catholic minority would lead to a protracted period of unrest known as the Troubles.

The Provisional Irish Republican Army split from the older group of the same name in 1969, following rioting that centered on complaints of discrimination against Catholics and nationalists in Northern Ireland by the Protestant unionist majority and the English government. This newer group favored violent resistance as a means of expelling the English from Northern Ireland and began recruiting and training volunteers in tactics of guerilla warfare. The earliest operations were small scale, involving sniper attacks and small bombs, and the group's activities received little public support. The events of Bloody Sunday, in which British forces shot twenty-six unarmed civil rights protesters, turned the tide of public opinion, and as recruitment for the new organization grew the vestiges of the older organization disappeared. Over the next five years, several attempts at a cease-fire failed and violence escalated. IRA leaders such as Gerry Adams, who was imprisoned on and off during this period, committed themselves to a "long war" strategy, accepting that it might take years to meet their objectives. The *Green Book* demonstrates the IRA leadership's recognition of the need to justify this strategy and to secure the cooperation of army members, many of whom would likely face interrogation and long jail sentences at some point in their careers.

The 1977 *Green Book* bears some similarity to *A Handbook for Volunteers of the Irish Republican Army Notes on Guerilla Warfare,* also called the *Green Book,* which appeared in 1956. Although these two books share a title, they are clearly products of different eras. The 1956 book is a product of an organization with a different, more militant face, and it focuses less on political propaganda and more on the practical aspects of guerilla warfare broadly defined as "the resistance of all people to enemy power." While the section "Our History" makes it clear that the "enemy" referred to throughout the book is England, there are few overt references to England in the rest of the book, and little attempt is made to justify IRA operations. Moreover, the book contains somewhat detailed information about bombs and other weapons, but the focus is on "destruction and breakdown of enemy communications, administration and supplies" rather than violence against persons. The 1977 edition, which deals with guerilla strategy in a short section of the same name, advocates "causing as many casualties and deaths as possible."

After its production, the *Green Book* became an important part of the initiation process for new members of the IRA, with all members required to read the document before admittance. The anti-interrogation techniques outlined in the manual and the admonishment "loose-talk costs lives" became IRA gospel, with members suspected of revealing information suffering harsh reprisals, including torture and death.

**THEMES AND STYLE**

The *Green Book* casts the IRA as "the legal representatives of the Irish people," imbuing army objectives with a moral weight that justifies violence and commands complete loyalty. Indeed, the book warns potential volunteers about joining out of "emotionalism, sensationalism or adventurism." According to the *Green Book*'s analysis, the IRA has a legitimate history and a military structure, which engages in guerilla warfare by virtue of its small size and minority status but has clear goals and a chain of command that must be obeyed. The ultimate goal is a peaceful and unified Ireland, but volunteers are encouraged to reflect on the means that will be used to achieve this peace and their willingness to participate in dangerous operations. In addition to being willing to kill, volunteers must vow never to speak of the IRA, either in their civilian lives or on arrest. Although army members are sworn to secrecy and silence, the *Green Book* advocates using prorepublican propaganda techniques as a "defensive precaution," attempting to create public sympathy for the cause before striking. Having set forth the basis for the IRA's actions and the demands made of members, the bulk of the remainder of the document details anti-interrogation practices that should be employed if one is arrested or jailed.

## STAKEKNIFE

Although the *Green Book* (1977) initiated an era in which the IRA ruthlessly dealt with informants, one of the group's most significant turncoats was not found out until after the group demilitarized in the late 1990s. Among the British intelligence agents he supplied with information, the man was identified only by his code name, Stakeknife. He was Alfredo "Scap" Scappaticci to members of the IRA's internal security department. Both groups knew him to be a vicious and violent man who was in charge of finding—and killing—moles within the IRA. According to one IRA source, "He was the bogeyman of the IRA: judge, jury and executioner. He didn't have to attend brigade meetings. He didn't get involved in the politics or talking. But whenever something went wrong, Freddy Scappaticci was sent for."

In charge of enforcing the IRA's internal security, Scappaticci was thoroughly undermining it. In exchange for eighty thousand British pounds a year, he handed over information that led to many of the most crucial arrests and disruptions in the course of the IRA's downfall. He was also granted immunity for some forty murders, including those of his fellow informants, who the British feared might expose him. After Scappaticci's true role in the "dirty war" in Northern Ireland was revealed, he was hidden away in Britain to protect him from reprisals.

The *Green Book* contests the authority of the English in Ireland, stating that the English have "no moral or historical justification for being here in the first place," and claims that the IRA is "the direct representative of the 1918 Dáil Éireann Parliament." This distinction is further elaborated by contrasting the IRA volunteer who "receives all of his support voluntarily from his people" against the English citizens, whose taxes support the government but who have not approved by ballot their government's colonization of Ireland. Further, while the goal of the volunteer is "political freedom and social and economic justice for his people," the average English citizen has no such personal goals or noble stake in the struggle, and the motivation of the English government is explained largely in terms of economic exploitation.

The first and second parts of the *Green Book,* labeled Volumes I and II, both carefully manage their portrayals of the English. In the first part, which discusses the army's underlying philosophy, the English are referred to politely, if diminutively, as "Brits," which contrasts with inflammatory names for the Irish attributed to the English: "Paddy," "Musck Savage," and "Bog-Wog." The second part, which details both anti-interrogation techniques and the court-martial proceedings that result from revealing IRA secrets, casts imprisoned IRA members as "victims." It also associates "British police stations" with Nazi concentration camps, implying that the British government is as villainous and brutal, at least in its interrogation methods, as the Nazi regime.

An IRA member wears a hood to conceal his identity during the Troubles in Northern Ireland, 1981. © HOMER SYKES ARCHIVE/ALAMY.

were mercilessly sniffed out by a newly instituted internal security force. Later, as part of the peace process between the United Kingdom government and the government of Ireland, a 1999 treaty established the Independent Commission for the Location of Victims' Remains to search for the bodies of executed informants who had never been found. With the advent of the Good Friday Agreement of 1998 and the Troubles seemingly part of history, a number of books dealing with the *Green Book* and the IRA began to appear.

The *Green Book* is generally discussed in histories of the IRA and has not attracted significant scholarship as a stand-alone document. Timothy Shanahan, in his *Provisional Irish Republican Army and the Morality of Terrorism,* quotes David George's more general analysis of the republican argument advanced by the *Green Book*'s claim to be heir to the original Irish Republic. According to George, the "Irish Republic proclaimed in 1916, reaffirmed in 1919 by the Dáil Éireann and the object of allegiance of militant Republicans ever since, was, and is, a legal nonentity" and therefore could not confer on the Provisional IRA the authority to wage war. Discussing the IRA as a terrorist group, Joseph Tuman remarks on the *Green Book*'s use of a military framework to legitimize IRA activities and to quash dissent from individual members.

## BIBLIOGRAPHY

*Sources*

George, David. "The Ethics of IRA Terrorism." *Ethics in International Affairs: Theories and Cases.* Ed. Andrew Valls. Lanham, MD: Rowman & Littlefield, 2000. 81–97. Print.

*A Handbook for Volunteers of the Irish Republican Army Notes on Guerilla Warfare.* Irish Republican Army General Headquarters, 1956. Web. 18 Aug. 2012.

*Irish Republican Army "Green Book."* 1977. Web. 18 Aug. 2012.

Moloney, Ed. *A Secret History of the IRA.* New York: Norton, 2002. Print.

Shanahan, Timothy. *The Provisional Irish Republican Army and the Morality of Terrorism.* Edinburgh: Edinburgh UP, 2009. Print.

*Further Reading*

Collins, Eamon. *Killing Rage.* London: Granta, 1997. Print.

Coogan, Tim Pat. *The IRA.* New York: Palgrave, 2000. Print.

Dillon, Martin. *The Dirty War.* London: Random, 1991. Print.

English, Richard. *Armed Struggle: The History of the IRA.* Oxford: Oxford UP, 2003. Print.

Toolis, Kevin. *Rebel Hearts: Journeys within the IRA's Soul.* New York: St. Martin's, 1995. Print.

Tuman, Joseph. *Communicating Terror: The Rhetorical Dimensions of Terrorism.* Thousand Oaks: Sage, 2010. Print.

## CRITICAL DISCUSSION

The early dissemination and use of the *Green Book* remains obscure, given the content of the book and the IRA's culture of secrecy. Ed Moloney's *A Secret History of the IRA* describes the 1977 *Green Book* as part of the reorganization scheme championed by Gerry Adams and Ivor Bell, who strategized during their incarceration at Long Kess in the 1970s. In his account, being "Green-Booked" meant that a volunteer had been trained in anti-interrogation, a practice that became widespread in late 1978 to early 1979. After this period, according to Maloney, "the only defense that an IRA member could make to a proven accusation of informing was that he or she had not been Green-Booked."

As an exemplar of IRA thought and practices, the *Green Book* ushered in an era in which informants

*Daisy Gard*

# GUERRILLA WARFARE

*Ernesto "Che" Guevara*

## OVERVIEW

Ernesto "Che" Guevara an Argentina-born leader of Cuba's socialist revolution, wrote a brief introduction to unconventional revolutionary insurrection titled *La guerra de guerrillas* (1960; *Guerrilla Warfare*, 1961). This straightforward manual was intended as a tool to encourage dissidents across Latin America to take up the armed struggle against dictatorial governments and ruling elites. The author cited the success of Cuba's guerrilla war as evidence for his thesis that a small group of devoted combatants in the remote countryside can defeat a nation's army.

Guevara, a physician, had played a prominent role alongside communist revolutionary leader Fidel Castro in the movement that toppled General Fulgencio Batista's Cuban regime in January 1959. Guevara then went on to serve a number of key roles in Castro's government, even overseeing hundreds of executions at Havana's La Cabaña fortress in the revolution's first months. The success of the Cuban rebels came as a surprise to many around the world, including the leaders of the Soviet Union and Latin American communists, who had believed conditions in the Americas were not ripe for Marxist revolution. In *Guerrilla Warfare*, Guevara argues that a skillful guerrilla campaign can sometimes bring about revolutionary conditions within a country. The slim volume is a basic primer in the tactics of armed revolt, but devotees of the subject do not view it as innovative in its structure or content. The book, however, does demonstrate Cuba's efforts to foment armed uprisings in other states in the region. Guevara was captured and killed while leading such an effort in Bolivia in October 1967.

## HISTORICAL AND LITERARY CONTEXT

Since ancient times, undercover wars of resistance have often been waged by small bands against more powerful, better-armed adversaries. The word *guerrilla* comes from the Spanish diminutive of *guerra* ("war"). In the modern era, the Russian Bolsheviks under Vladimir Lenin and Chinese communists following Mao Zedong made extensive use of guerrilla tactics in their paths to power. In fact, Lenin and Mao each wrote a book on guerrilla warfare. While Guevara was penning his rendition of the topic, another significant guerrilla war was taking place in Vietnam, orchestrated by the Viet Minh under Ho Chi Minh

and Vo Nguyen Giap against Japanese, French, and later U.S. occupation.

Guevara, who traveled the length of Latin America as a young man, became a committed revolutionary in 1954 when he visited Guatemala and witnessed a coup d'état instigated by the U.S. Central Intelligence Agency against that country's elected leader, Jacobo Arbenz Guzmán. The next year in Mexico City, Guevara met the exiled Cuban brothers Fidel and Raúl Castro. Joining their scheme to oust the reviled dictator, Batista, the doctor undertook training in guerrilla fighting and became the only foreign-born member of Cuba's revolutionary vanguard. In late 1956 Guevara, along with Castro's troops, landed in Cuba, only to be nearly destroyed by Batista's forces. The survivors, made up of Guevara and only a dozen comrades, took refuge in the Sierra Maestra mountain range for two years, staging guerrilla attacks against Batista's forces and recruiting new members. In early 1959 Guevara triumphantly led the rebel forces into Havana. Thus, *Guerrilla Warfare* has value both as an indirect account of the Cuban victory and as a handbook on the principles other guerrillas might follow to replicate that success.

Despite the fact that Guevara makes virtually no references to earlier texts in *Guerrilla Warfare*, the book builds upon a tradition of martial literature including Sun Tzu's ancient Chinese classic, *The Art of War*, and Prussian military strategist Carl von Clausewitz's *On War* (1832). Guevara's understanding of his subject was shaped by Alberto Bayo, a Cuban-born veteran of the Spanish Civil War and the author of *150 preguntas a un guerrillero* (1955; *150 Questions to a Guerrilla*, 1963), who helped train the Cuban rebels in Mexico. Guevara's political perspective strongly reflects the influence of Karl Marx, Vladimir Lenin, and Mao Zedong. He seems in particular to have adopted Marx's dictum that "the philosophers have only interpreted the world, in various ways; the point is to change it."

Guevara's model of revolution spearheaded by a disciplined cadre (or *foco*) was later deemed the foco theory. In later writings, he expanded his notion of the circumstances under which political dissidents may legitimately undertake armed struggle. Through the Cuban government's Department of Liberation, Guevara trained and indoctrinated guerrillas from many

**⁜ *Key Facts***

**Time Period:**
Mid-20th Century

**Genre:**
Manual

**Events:**
Cuban revolution; Latin American independence movement

**Nationality:**
Argentinian

# CHE'S IMAGE: RADICAL CHIC

One of the most famous photographs of all time shows Che Guevara wearing a black beret, staring intensely into the distance, his wavy hair blowing in the breeze. Called *Guerrillero Heroico* ("Heroic Guerrilla Fighter"), the shot was taken in Havana on March 5, 1960, at a memorial service for scores of Cubans killed in a suspicious explosion. The photographer, Alberto Korda, was working for *Revolución* magazine. The publication did not print the image, but Korda kept it and made an enlargement. Just before Guevara's death in 1967, Korda let an Italian publisher use the shot for a poster. European anarchists circulated the photo, and it was widely seen during the 1968 student revolt in Paris. Within a few years, that image was ubiquitous, found on T-shirts, billboards, tattoos, bikinis, jewelry, and other trinkets: a universal icon of resistance to capitalism, bought and sold daily in mass quantities. Korda, a committed Marxist, never sought or received payment for his work. The photo has been the subject of many art exhibitions, of books such as *Che's Afterlife: The Legacy of an Image* (2009) by Michael Casey, and of the documentary film *Chevolution* (2008).

*Opposite page:*
A tee shirt emblazoned with a portrait of Argentine revolutionary Che Guevara. © ROBERT JOHN/ALAMY.

Latin American countries. Others studied his book to prepare for warfare on their own. After leaving Cuba in 1965, Guevara became one of the world's most notorious freelance communist agitators, surfacing amid revolutionary movements in the Congo and Bolivia. His death at the age of thirty-nine, and the dissemination of an iconic photograph taken by Alberto Korda, helped ensure that Guevara would became a legend and a symbol of rebellion to scores of nationalists and leftists around the world.

## THEMES AND STYLE

Thematically, the most important content in *Guerrilla Warfare* is found in the book's opening chapter on general principles, in which Guevara argues that the Cuban victory proves that popular forces can prevail through guerrilla tactics and that "it is not necessary to wait until all conditions for making revolution exist; the insurrection can create them." Additionally, Guevara states that guerrilla bands in Latin America should organize in the countryside rather than in the cities so that they can hide in remote areas beyond the enemy's reach. These controversial theories all depart from the prevailing communist doctrine of the time. Tactically, Guevara contends, guerrilla combat requires great mobility, secrecy, nocturnal movement, economy in the use of ammunition, and intimate knowledge of the terrain. In order to succeed, guerrilla groups must rely on the support of the local peasant population and come to be seen as the armed vanguard of a popular uprising. (Indeed, the lack of response from the peasants proved fatal to the Bolivian mission and led to Guevara's capture and execution.) Guevara maintains that guerrilla warfare represents only an early phase of

a liberation struggle; if successful, the guerrilla militia will gradually expand into a regular army capable of waging and winning a conventional "war of positions."

The power of Guevara's text lies chiefly in the unsparing pragmatism of its instructions on how to mount an insurgency. Its practical advice on martial matters such as choice of weapons, combat maneuvers, and techniques of sabotage is occasionally interspersed with broader observations about revolutionary objectives or management issues such as methods of discipline within guerrilla squadrons. Throughout the work, the author invariably derives authority from the Cuban experience, providing frequent reminders that the ultimate goal of victory can be achieved and that "victory of the enemy against the people is finally impossible. Whoever does not feel this undoubted truth cannot be a guerrilla fighter." Guevara's descriptions of the ideal character traits of the guerrilla warrior, such as idealism, cunning, endurance, and asceticism, are presented so that prospective guerrilla recruits can identify with and be inspired by them.

The tone of *Guerrilla Warfare* is primarily didactic, as befits a basic training manual. Lengthy sections are filled with detailed descriptions of relatively minute matters such as the articles a combatant should carry in his backpack. The details are instructive and often convey some of the flavor of daily life in combat. For example, Guevara writes, "The vital necessities of the guerrillas are to maintain their arms in good condition, to capture ammunition, and, above everything else, to have adequate shoes." The text occasionally veers into strident or soaring Marxist rhetoric. More often, however, the language invokes a steely, matter-of-fact approach to the topics of death and killing, as when the author notes, "A wounded enemy should be treated with care and respect unless his former life has made him liable to a death penalty, in which case he will be treated in accordance with his deserts [sic]."

## CRITICAL DISCUSSION

First released in May 1960, Guevara's manual was translated into English and published in the United States as *Guerrilla Warfare* the following year. The Cold War and the revolution in Cuba were of grave concern to U.S. leaders at the time, and thus the book received considerable attention. Some critics perceived it as a curious artifact of communist culture. One academic reviewer, Professor Renzo Sereno, found it noteworthy that "the work belongs to that genre in which politics and warfare are inextricably enmeshed," adding that "its ideology is Marxian to an almost childish point." Scholar Joseph S. Roucek, in a terse review, commented that "this little volume should be placed high on the required reading list of the Chiefs of Staff and President [John F.] Kennedy's advisers." Indeed, the military and intelligence operatives studied *Guerrilla Warfare* with great care—and still do—in order to refine their capabilities in counterinsurgency techniques. Partially for this reason, however, Guevara's text quickly became outdated from a tactical standpoint.

Away from the centers of capitalist power, Guevara's words achieved some of their intended effect, inspiring hundreds if not thousands of people in several countries to take to the jungles with weapons. Many of them were killed, and no guerrilla campaigns succeeded in capturing state power until Nicaragua's Sandinista revolution of 1979. *Guerrilla Warfare* remained influential after its author's death, more for its arguments on armed struggle than as a practical primer. The Cuban government has continued to perpetuate the legacy of Guevara as a revolutionary hero. According to James Petras, a noted academic and writer, in his article "Che Guevara and Contemporary Revolutionary Movements" (1998), Guevara's imprint can be found in the twenty-first century in militant unions, popular movements, and direct action-oriented peasant and indigenous organizations across Latin America. The most well known of these organizations is the Zapatista National Liberation Army in Chiapas, Mexico, whose spokesperson, the masked Subcomandante Marcos, evokes something of Guevara's charismatic mystique.

New English editions of *Guerrilla Warfare* appear periodically, although the text is often derided as anachronistic. The figure of Guevara remains the subject of polarizing debate, with some viewing him as an ideal of principled radicalism and others as a bloodthirsty ideologue. In 1999 *Time* magazine included Guevara on its list of the one hundred most influential people of the twentieth century. Electoral victories for leftists in Venezuela, Bolivia, Ecuador, and other Latin American countries, as well as the outbreak of anticapitalist movements in the global north—such as Occupy Wall Street in the United States, where the revolutionary's image was displayed—appear to testify to Guevara's ongoing relevance.

## BIBLIOGRAPHY

### Sources

Guevara, Che. *Guerrilla Warfare.* New York: Monthly Review, 1961. Print.

Lewis, Steve. "Che Guevara and *Guerrilla Warfare*: Training for Today's Nonlinear Battlefields." *Military Review* 81.5 (2001): 98–101. *JSTOR.* Web. 12 Oct. 2012.

Petras, James. "Che Guevara and Contemporary Revolutionary Movements." *Latin American Perspectives* 25.4 (1998): 9+. *Gale Biography in Context.* Web. 12 Oct. 2012.

Roucek, Joseph S. Rev. of *Guerrilla Warfare,* by Che Guevara. *Western Political Quarterly* 15.1 (1962): 180–81. *JSTOR.* Web. 12 Oct. 2012.

Sereno, Renzo. Rev. of *Guerrilla Warfare,* by Che Guevara. *Annals of the American Academy of Political and Social Science* 340 (1962): 132–33. *Sage Publications.* Web. 12 Oct. 2012.

### Further Reading

Anderson, Jon Lee. *Che Guevara: A Revolutionary Life.* New York: Grove, 1997. Print.

Dorfman, Ariel. "Che Guevara: The Guerrilla." *Time.* Time, 14 June 1999. Web. 17 Oct. 2012.

Dosal, Paul J. *Comandante Che: Guerrilla Soldier, Commander, and Strategist, 1956–1967.* University Park: Pennsylvania State UP, 2003. Print.

Fontova, Humberto. *Exposing the Real Che Guevara: And the Useful Idiots Who Idolize Him.* New York: Sentinel, 2007. Print.

Galloway, George. "A Very Modern Icon: Che Guevara Represents What Today's Politicians Conspicuously Lack." *New Statesman* [1996] 12 June 2006: 44+. *Gale Biography in Context.* Web. 12 Oct. 2012.

Lavan, George, ed. *Ché Guevara Speaks.* New York: Merit, 1967. Print.

Sinclair, Andrew. *Guevara.* London: Fontana, 1970. Print.

*Roger Smith*

# HIND SWARAJ

*Mohandas Gandhi*

## OVERVIEW

Mohandas Gandhi's *Hind Swaraj*, published in 1909, is generally considered the seminal statement of the political ideas that Gandhi developed over the course of his career. The short political tract was originally serialized in *Indian Opinion*, the weekly newspaper that Gandhi published in South Africa. It was subsequently issued as a booklet first in Gujarati and later in English under the title *Indian Home Rule*—the only one of his works that Gandhi translated himself. Although he had expressed most of the ideas previously, *Hind Swaraj* was the first time that he articulated them in a fully formed philosophy.

Gandhi was inspired to write *Hind Swaraj* after a trip to London, where he had traveled as part of a delegation lobbying the British government to intercede with the colonial government in South Africa to rescind legal discrimination against its South Asian residents. The trip was a failure; Britain declined to help its British Indian citizens in their struggles for civil rights in South Africa. While there, Gandhi spent time in conversation with young Indian expatriates who advocated violence as a means of freeing India from English rule—the opposite approach Gandhi had pioneered in South Africa. He left England determined to involve Indian nationalists in the Indian struggle in South Africa, which he saw not only as part of the same battle the nationalists were waging but also as an example of how the battle should be fought. He wrote a 276-page manuscript that would later be seen as a manifesto for his life's work on the ship's stationary on the journey back to South Africa.

## HISTORICAL AND LITERARY CONTEXT

In 1909 the Indian nationalist movement was at a crossroads. The partition of Bengal province in 1905 by the British viceroy Lord Curzon had unleashed a nationalist protest, known as the *Swadeshi* (self-sufficiency) movement. Protestors boycotted British goods and institutions and called for *swaraj,* or home rule. As the movement went on, peaceful protests had given way to violence and terrorism. By 1909 the nationalist movement was divided. The "moderates" wanted to continue their longstanding policy of working within the British constitution, a policy Gandhi described as "prayer, petition, and protest." The growing number of "extremists" believed the only way to gain India's

liberation was through violence, specifically acts of individual terrorism. When Gandhi landed in England in July 1909, London was still in shock following the assassination nine days earlier of Sir William Curzon Wyllie, aide-de-camp to the secretary of state for India, by Indian engineering student Madan Lal Dhingra.

Gandhi offered an alternative to what Gandhi specialist Anthony Parel has described as the "uncreative constitutionalism and violent extremism" of the moderates and extremists: the technique of nonviolent noncooperation he called *satyagraha* ("force in truth"). Gandhi had developed his ideas about nonviolent noncooperation in South Africa, not in India. In 1893 Gandhi took a job as an attorney in the South African province of Natal. Once there, he was shocked to find himself subject to a degree of anti-Indian discrimination worse than anything he had experienced as a student in London, and he began to fight for Indian rights in South Africa. He led his first satyagraha campaign in 1906, when the colonial Transvaal government passed a law requiring the Indian population to file their fingerprints with the government. Led by Gandhi, Indians held a mass protest meeting in Johannesburg, where they took a vow to disobey the ordinance and accept the penalties for their actions. In 1914 the South African government conceded most of Gandhi's demands. Soon thereafter, he returned to India, where he organized campaigns on behalf of workers on indigo plantations and in steel plants. It was not until 1919 that he became involved in the nationalist movement in response to the oppressive Rowlatt Acts, which allowed political cases to be tried without juries and suspects to be held without trial.

Gandhi developed his philosophy of nonviolent noncooperation after studying widely in both Eastern and Western thought, a fact he readily acknowledged. In the preface to *Hind Swaraj,* he discusses his debt to "Tolstoy, Ruskin, Thoreau, Emerson and others, besides the masters of Indian philosophy." The appendix lists twenty important works, from Plato to Leo Tolstoy, that he recommends "for perusal to follow-up the study of the foregoing." His ideas about social protest are rooted both in the Jain religion's tenet of *ahimsa* (nonviolence) and in Tolstoy's discussions of Christianity as an ethical system. His most well-known Western influence is Henry David Thoreau,

+ *Key Facts*

**Time Period:**
Early 20th Century

**Genre:**
Tract

**Events:**
Growth of Indian independence movement; anticolonialism; passive resistance

**Nationality:**
Indian

## PRIMARY SOURCE

### EXCERPT FROM *HIND SWARAJ*

#### PASSIVE RESISTANCE

Reader: Is there any historical evidence as to the success of what you have called soul-force or truth-force? No instance seems to have happened of any nation having risen through soul-force. I still think that the evil-doers will not cease doing evil without physical punishment.

Editor: The poet Tulsidas has said: "Of religion, pity, or love, is the root, as egotism of the body. Therefore, we should not abandon pity so long as we are alive." This appears to me to be a scientific truth. I believe in it as much as I believe in two and two being four. The force of love is the same as the force of the soul or truth. We have evidence of its working at every step. The universe would disappear without the existence of that force. But you ask for histori-

cal evidence. It is, therefore, necessary to know what history means. The Gujarati equivalent means: "It so happened." If that is the meaning of history, it is possible to give copious evidence. But, if it means the doings of the kings and emperors, there can be no evidence of soul-force or passive resistance in such history. You cannot expect silver ore in a tin mine. History, as we know it, is a record of the wars of the world, and so there is a proverb among Englishmen that a nation which has no history, that is, no wars, is a happy nation. How kings played, how they became enemies of one another, how they murdered one another, is found accurately recorded in history, and if this were all that had happened in the world, it would have been ended long ago. If the story of the universe had commenced with wars, not a man would have been found alive today. Those people who have been warred against have disappeared as, for instance,

from whom he borrowed the term "civil disobedience" as a meaningful English equivalent for satyagraha. Gandhi was equally indebted to John Ruskin and a handful of other sociopolitical writers less well known to modern readers, whose writings shaped his critique of industrial civilization.

Today, *Hind Swaraj* is considered the place to start any serious study of Gandhi's writings. Parel has described it as "the seed from which the tree of Gandhian thought has grown to its full stature." Similarly, Judith Brown claims that *Hind Swaraj* is "the closest he came to producing a sustained work of political theory."

#### THEMES AND STYLE

In *Hind Swaraj*, Gandhi grapples with three inter-related ideas: the true nature of swaraj, the corrosive influence of modern civilization, and the path to swaraj through satyagraha. He takes the position that nationalists, including him, have "used the term 'Swaraj' without understanding its real significance." The popular concept of swaraj, or self-rule, is political independence or home rule. Gandhi argues that swaraj in fact means self-control. Because of this misconception, most people felt that the British were the primary obstacle to self-rule in India. Gandhi argues that the true obstacle to swaraj is "modern western civilization," as he believes that all evils from which India suffers, from plague and poverty to lawyers, are the result of modern civilization. He suggests that if the British left India but their institutions remained, it would not be true self-rule: "[Some people think]

that we can have English rule without the Englishman. That is to say, you want the tiger's nature, but not the tiger; you would make India English. And when it becomes English, it will be called not *Hindustan* but *Englishstan*. This is not the *Swaraj* that I want." Because his goal is not simply the removal of British rule, Gandhi concludes that neither moderates nor extremists are correct. Instead the only path to swaraj is a combination of passive resistance, which he describes as "love-force," and "*Swadeshi* in every sense." Only when Indians give up English goods, English institutions, and the English language will they truly win home rule.

The book is written in the form of a dialogue between the Editor, presumably Gandhi himself, and the Reader, an Indian nationalist with openly extremist views. The Editor is equally eager to see an end to British rule in India but is opposed to armed resistance and terrorism, ideas that he condemns as borrowed from the West. Parel points out that it is significant that Gandhi chose the role of a newspaper editor for himself—a very modern figure—rather than that of a traditional figure, the guru. This is a dialogue between members of the class of westernized Indians who made up the nationalist movement. At the same time, the dialogue draws on a primary model. Gandhi claims that he chose the dialogue form to make the book easy to read, but in fact there is a long tradition of the dialogue in Indian religious and philosophical texts. In an analysis of the work in *Exploring* Hind Swaraj (2009), M. P. Mathai identifies a strong resemblance between the dialogue format of *Hind Swaraj* and that used in the natives of Australia of whom hardly a man was left alive by the intruders. Mark please, that these natives did not use soul force in self-defense, and it does not require much foresight to know that the Australians will share the same fate as their victims. "Those that take the sword shall perish by the sword." With us the proverb is that professional swimmers will find a watery grave.

The fact that there are so many men still alive in the world shows that it is based on the force of arms but on the force of truth or love. Therefore, the greatest and most unimpeachable evidence of the success of this force is to be found in the fact that, in spite of the wars in the world, it still lives on.

Thousands, indeed tens of thousands, depend for their existence on a very active working of this force. Little quarrels of millions of families in their lives

disappear before the exercise of this force. Hundreds of nations live in peace. History does not and cannot take note of this fact. History is really a record of every interruption of the even working of this force of love or of the soul. Two brothers quarrel; one of them repents and re-awakens the love that was lying dormant in him; and the two again began to live in peace; nobody takes note of this. But if the two brothers, through the intervention of solicitors or some other reason take up arms or go to law which is another form of brute force, their doings would be immediately noticed in the press, they would be the talk of their neighbors and would probably go down to history. And what is true of families and communities is true of nations. There is no reason to believe that there is one law for families and another for nations. History, then, is a record of an interruption of the course of nature. Soul-force, being natural is not noted in history.

the Indian spiritual classic the *Bhagavad Gita*. In the *Bhagavad Gita*, Lord Krishna liberates Arjuna from his delusions and motivates him to perform his duty; in *Hind Swaraj*, the Editor similarly leads the Reader away from his attachment to violence and toward his duty to true swaraj.

The style of *Hind Swaraj* has been described as "deceptively simple." Gandhi himself, in the 1939 edition, describes it as an "incredibly simple book, so simple as to be regarded foolish." In fact, Gandhi's simple style, colloquial language, and vivid metaphors make complex philosophical arguments accessible.

## CRITICAL DISCUSSION

On its initial publication, *Hind Swaraj* met with hostility from Indian nationalists and the British government alike. The British banned the original book within three months of its publication because it "contain[ed] matter declared to be seditious." Indian nationalists of all stripes attacked the book, some for its embrace of Christian values, some for its leanings toward anarchism, others for its sheer impracticality. In his *Autobiography*, Gandhi reports that the nationalist Gopal Krishna Gokhale told him "after you have stayed a year in India, your views will correct themselves." One important exception to the generally unfavorable reception was Tolstoy, who praised the work, saying, "I think the question you have therein dealt with is important not only for Indians but for the whole of mankind."

Gandhi's political ideas as outlined in *Hind Swaraj* and developed over the course of forty years have inspired others who sought to affect political and social

change through peaceful resistance, including the civil rights movement led by Martin Luther King Jr., the American peace movement of the 1960s and 1970s, and the antiapartheid movement in South Africa under the leadership of Nelson Mandela in the 1950s.

Mohandas Gandhi c. 1910, around the time he authored *Hind Swaraj*. IMAGNO/ GETTY IMAGES.

# SATYAGRAHA AFTER INDEPENDENCE

In *Hind Swaraj* Mohandas Gandhi argued that one man who had mastered the true *swaraj* of self-control could force a government to listen. In 1948, he put his words into action. When India gained its independence in 1947, British India was split into two states: the Republic of India, which had a Hindu majority, and Pakistan, which had a Muslim majority. Gandhi had fought bitterly against the division, known as partition. After partition, he was unhappy to find Muslims subject to persecution in New Delhi in India. On January 13, 1948, he began a fast in protest. Anti-Muslim protestors gathered in the street outside and chanted, "Let Gandhi die." Inside, India's new prime minister, Jawaharlal Nehru, and his cabinet gathered around Gandhi's bed and promised cooperation with Pakistan if he would end the fast.

It was Gandhi's last use of *satyagraha*. On January 30, as Gandhi walked to a prayer meeting, he was assassinated by a young Hindu fanatic named Nathuram Godse, who shot him three times in the chest at point-blank range.

Most recently, Gandhi's influence has appeared in the Occupy Wall Street movement and its imitators.

Despite the furor with which it was greeted on its initial publication, *Hind Swaraj* received less attention than Gandhi's later works for many years. Although all serious studies of Gandhi recognize its importance, for many years only a handful of studies dealt specifically with *Hind Swaraj*. The first serious appraisal of the work appeared in 1938, when Sophia Wadia published a special issue of the theosophical journal *Aryan Path* devoted to *Hind Swaraj*. In 1973 *Gandhi Marg,* the journal published by the Gandhi Peace Foundation, organized a scholarly symposium on the book. Both sets of essays combined reverence for the author with respectful criticism of the work itself, which was seen as utopian rather than a practical political philosophy. In 1985 the Gandhi Peace Foundation produced *Hind Swaraj: A Fresh Look,* which reviewed the book's effect on modern Indian politics and attempted to update it for the modern world. Only at the centenary of its publication, in 2009, did *Hind Swaraj* become the focal point of sustained serious discussion.

## BIBLIOGRAPHY

*Sources*

Brown, Judith M. *Gandhi: Prisoner of Hope.* New Haven: Yale UP, 1989 Print.

Gandhi, Mohandas K. *Indian Home Rule (Hind Swaraj).* New Delhi: Promilla, 2009. Print.

Gandhi, Mohandas K., and Mahadev H. Desai. *Gandhi's Autobiography: The Story of My Experiments with Truth.* Washington, D.C.: Public Affairs, 1949. Print.

Mathai, M. P. "*Hind Swaraj*: A Very Short Introduction." *Exploring Hind Swaraj.* Ed. M. P. Mathai and John Moolakkattu. New Delhi: Gandhi Peace Foundation, 2009. Print.

Parel, Anthony J. "Editor's Introduction." *Hind Swaraj and Other Writings,* by Mohandas K. Gandhi. Cambridge: Cambridge UP 1997. xiii–lxii. Print.

Tolstoy, Leo. "Letter to Gandhi Dated 8 May 1910." *Hind Swaraj and Other Writings,* by Mohandas K. Gandhi. Cambridge: Cambridge UP, 1997. Print.

*Further Reading*

Brown, Judith M. *Gandhi and Civil Disobedience: The Mahatma in Indian Politics, 1928–1934.* Cambridge: Cambridge UP. 1977. Print.

Brown, Judith M., and Anthony Parel, eds. *The Cambridge Companion to Gandhi.* Cambridge: Cambridge UP, 2011. Print.

Coward, Harold, ed. *Indian Critiques of Gandhi.* Albany: SUNY P, 2003. Print.

Erikson, Erik H. *Gandhi's Truth: On the Origins of Militant Nonviolence.* New York: Norton, 1969. Print.

Mathai, M. P. and John Moolakkattu, eds. *Exploring* Hind Swaraj. New Delhi: Gandhi Peace Foundation, 2009. Print.

Rao, K. Raghavendra. "Communication against Communication: The Gandhian Critique of Modern Civilization in *Hind Swaraj*." *Political Discourse: Explorations in Indian and Western Political Thought.* Ed. Bikhu Parek and Thomas Pantham. New Delhi: Sage. 1987. 266–76. Print.

Seal, Anil. *The Emergence of Indian Nationalism.* Cambridge: Cambridge UP, 1968. Print.

*Anna Deem*

# MANIFESTO FOR ARMED ACTION

*Ulrike Meinhof*

## OVERVIEW

First appearing on June 5, 1970, in a German newspaper and presumably written by Ulrike Meinhof, *Manifesto for Armed Action* (also known as *Build the Red Army!*) is a communiqué that implores the proletariat of West Germany to join in a violent struggle against the government. The first public statement from a West German terrorist group popularly known as the Baader-Meinhof gang (later the Red Army Faction), the manifesto uses informal, colloquial language to appeal to the "potentially revolutionary section of the people." Published just three weeks after Meinhof and other members of the group helped their leader, Andreas Baader, make a violent escape from prison, the communiqué defends "counter-violence" as a means to an end and demands that the oppressed people of West Germany rise up against their government.

Although Meinhof was not one of the leaders of the Red Army Faction, she was one of its most famous members, having left a very successful journalistic career to serve its cause. She is believed to be the writer of most of the group's statements to the press, many of which were released during the early 1970s. The violent freeing of Baader horrified West Germany, and the manifesto, which serves as a bitter defense of the shooting as a means to an end, continued to incite controversy. Today *Manifesto for Armed Action* is known as one of the formative texts of the Red Army Faction, a group that continued to terrorize and fascinate West Germany for decades.

## HISTORICAL AND LITERARY CONTEXT

The Red Army Faction, which arose from the student protest groups that formed in the 1960s in West Germany and all over the world, became disillusioned with peaceful protest and embraced violence against the state. The recent legacy of Nazism, as well as the merging of the two major political parties into one, was a major source of discontent for young West Germans. Other key issues for student movements were ending the Vietnam War and the treatment of youth in state-run group homes. The protest movements of West Germany gradually became more violent on both sides, and in the late 1960s two watershed events occurred: in 1967 police shot and killed a German student who was participating in a peaceful protest, and in 1968 a right-wing fanatic shot and injured a student leader of the leftist movement.

On May 14, 1970, Baader, who was serving time in prison for arson, was on an approved, guard-escorted trip to a library located near the prison, under the guise of conducting research for a book. Members of a terrorist group that would become the Red Army Faction entered the library bearing guns, shot and wounded a sixty-four-year-old librarian, and successfully freed Baader, who escaped by jumping out of a window. *Manifesto for Armed Action* appeared just three weeks later, expressing scorn for the group's critics and justifying the group's actions in the context of a global movement taking place "in Vietnam, in Palestine, in Guatemala, in Oakland and Watts, in Cuba and China, in Angola and in New York."

Meinhof and the other members of the Red Army Faction were influenced by international extreme left-wing thinkers, and they explicitly rejected the more moderate rhetoric of the West German left. They were also influenced by activists such as Che Guevara and the American Black Panther Party, as well as by Frantz Fanon's book *The Wretched of the Earth* (1961). *Manifesto for Armed Action* echoes many of the themes found in Meinhof's columns for the newspaper *Konkret,* as well as in her film *Bambule* (1970), which sharply condemns the state as an institution of organized violence. The manifesto is significant for its informal tone and for serving as Meinhof's first interaction with the press as a wanted terrorist.

Meinhof continued to be the scribe of the Red Army Faction until her death in 1976. As a call to action, the *Manifesto for Armed Action* established some of the organization's future vocabulary of revolution. However, it is most significant for creating an image and a brand for the group, which continued to fascinate audiences for decades after Meinhof's death. Stephen Aust's 1985 book *The Baader-Meinhof Complex* became a best seller and in 2008 was made into a popular film.

## THEMES AND STYLE

*Manifesto for Armed Action* serves as a defense for the liberation of Baader and an aggressive call for action against the state. Meinhof sharply criticizes the "petit-bourgeois intellectuals" of the left as "chatterers" who talk without acting. She addresses her cry to disenfranchised youth, who are already "prisoners" of the state and "those who have realized that the future promised to them by their teachers and professors and

## ✦ Key Facts

**Time Period:**
Mid- to Late 20th Century

**Genre:**
Manifesto

**Events:**
Rise of the Red Army Faction; Vietnam War; revolutionary movements in United States, Cuba, Guatemala, Angola, Palestine, and other countries

**Nationality:**
German

# THE CASE OF ULRIKE MEINHOF'S BRAIN

Many have wondered why Ulrike Meinhof would abandon a successful journalism career and two daughters to become a terrorist. Some have speculated that the answers might be found in the chemistry of her brain. Authorities found her dead in her prison cell in 1976 after she was found guilty of multiple counts of murder and of forming a criminal organization. The circumstances of her death point to suicide by hanging, although many speculate that prison guards murdered her in her cell. The doctor who performed her autopsy removed her brain without her family's consent and sent it to neurologists for study because federal prosecutors wanted to know if there was a neurological basis for her decision to become a left-wing terrorist.

Neurologists found damage in Meinhof's brain, which was caused by surgery she had in 1962 for an enlarged blood vessel. Her brain remained in a cardboard box for twenty years, until Bernhard Bogerts studied it in 1997. He concluded that a brain illness was the cause of Meinhof's decision to become a terrorist, claiming that the part of her right brain that dealt with emotional response was damaged in 1962. This explanation remains unproven, however, and has been called into question by other scientists. In 2002 Meinhof's family was finally able to bury her brain with the rest of her body.

landlords and social workers and supervisors and foremen and union representatives and city councilors is nothing more than an empty lie." Meinhof juxtaposes taunting of readers—calling them "numbskulls" and "shitheads"—with appeals to camaraderie and understanding: "the army we are building is [your] army."

The manifesto uses confrontational and aggressive language in order to make the text feel immediate and urgent. To emphasize the collective, Meinhof is not identified as the author, and the actions of the Red Army Faction are referred to as something "we" committed. The manifesto is addressed as a letter to the "comrades of 883" and is full of commands to readers. It demands that readers "explain the liberation of Baader" to the disenfranchised groups of West German youth and at times almost childishly taunts readers, telling them to "stop lounging on the sofa … counting up your love affairs" and not to "complain that it's too hard" to join the movement. The text culminates in a series of commands written in capital letters, telling readers to

DEVELOP THE CLASS STRUGGLE

ORGANIZE THE PROLETARIAT

BEGIN THE ARMED STRUGGLE

BUILD THE RED ARMY!

Thus, the fanatical enthusiasm of the text reinforces the urgency for action.

The diction of *Manifesto for Armed Action* is informal and crude, readily employing words like "assholes" and "shitheads" and exclamations such as "whatever" and "damn it!" Although Meinhof was university educated and a trained journalist, she uses low-register language in an attempt to appeal to a less-educated demographic. In fact, after the manifesto was published, the Red Army Faction stopped using capital letters in its communications, emphasizing the idea that language is meaningless chatter whereas action is essential.

## CRITICAL DISCUSSION

The violence of Baader's escape shocked political figures on the right and the left, and Meinhof's manifesto did little to allay their fears. Coverage in the media was mainly negative, and sensationalistic headlines about the Red Army Faction abounded in West Germany, accusing the group of a plot to kidnap Willy Brandt, the chairman of the Social Democratic Party. In *The New York Times*, Meinhof's manifesto was alluded to in the condescending headline "Tiny West German Group Vows to Overthrow State." In spite of the Red Army Faction's violence, many Germans saw members of the group as romantic or tragic figures in the style of Bonnie and Clyde, an American couple who went on a murderous crime spree in the early 1930s.

Today *Manifesto for Armed Action* serves as an introduction to the aims of the Red Army Faction, a group that became an integral part of the fears and imagination of German society. The text identifies the audience that the Red Army Faction intends to court and excludes the wealthy, comfortable members of the left. It also introduces some of the language of the future organization. At the time of the manifesto's publication, the Red Army Faction did not have its name, but the term "Red Army" appears extensively, as does the notion of meaningless *geschwätz* (chatter). Meinhof later dismissed *Manifesto for Armed Action* as a vague statement of purpose, while critics dismissed it and future Red Army Faction writings as posthoc justifications of senseless violence. Nevertheless, Meinhof's columns and film show the transformation of a woman who was becoming increasingly comfortable with violence as a means to an end.

Critical discussion of *Manifesto for Armed Action* is rare in the English language. Recent scholarship has focused on Meinhof's relationship with language as an oppressive structure. In the 2005 book *Ulrike Meinhof and West German Terrorism,* author Sarah Colvin argues against scholars who "dismiss the manifesto as an adolescent-sounding explosion" and states that Meinhof's use of subversive language "is a significant act" that "expresses a will to occupy a position of authority rather than submitting (in a childlike way) to authority." Other scholarship focuses on the relationship between the Red Army Faction and West German media, a relationship that seems in many ways contrary to the group's stated beliefs. In the 2011 book *Ulrike Meinhof and the Red Army Faction,* author Leith Passmore writes about how Meinhof's manifesto "made vast concessions to the way the capitalist media operated" and "even borrowed techniques from advertising to begin developing a logo and a brand." Essentially, *Manifesto for Armed Action* works within the system in order to work against it.

## BIBLIOGRAPHY

### Sources

Aust, Stefan. *The Baader-Meinhof Group: The Inside Story of a Phenomenon.* London: Bodley, 1985. Print.

Colvin, Sarah. *Ulrike Meinhof and West German Terrorism: Language, Violence, and Identity.* Rochester: Camden House, 2009. Print.

Huffman, Richard. "Baader-Meinhof Source Documents." *Baader-Meinhof.com.* Baader-Meinhof.com, 2011. Web. 11 Sept. 2012.

Passmore, Leith. *Ulrike Meinhof and the Red Army Faction: Performing Terrorism.* New York: Palgrave-Macmillan, 2011. Print.

Smith, J., and Andre Moncourt. *The Red Army Faction: A Documentary History.* Montreal: Kersplebedeb, 2009. Print.

### Further Reading

Bauer, Karen, ed. *Everybody Talks about the Weather ... We Don't: The Writings of Ulrike Meinhof.* New York: Seven Stories, 2008. Print.

Becker, Jillian. *Hitler's Children: Story of the Baader-Meinhof Terrorist Gang.* New York: Harper, 1979. Print.

Colvin, Sarah. "Wir Frauen haben kein Vaterland: Ulrike Marie Meinhof, Emily Wilding Davison, and the 'Homelessness' of Women Revolutionaries." *German Life & Letters* 64.1 (2011): 108–21. *Academic Search Complete.* Web. 11 Sept. 2012.

Fanon, Frantz. *The Wretched of the Earth.* New York: Grove, 1963. Print.

Preece, Julian. *Baader-Meinhof and the Novel.* New York: Palgrave-Macmillan, 2012. Print.

Varon, Jeremy. *Bringing the War Home: The Weather Underground, the Red Army Faction, and Revolutionary Violence in the Sixties and Seventies.* Berkeley: U of California P, 2004. Print.

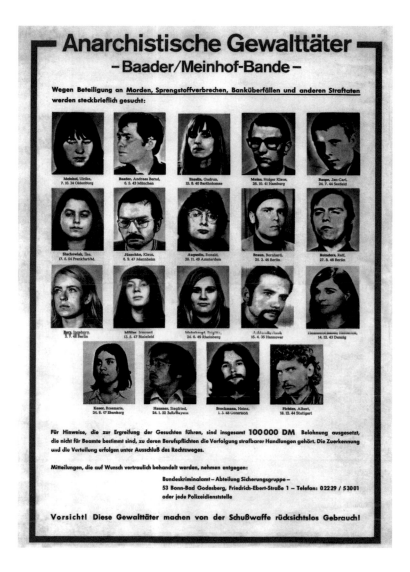

### Media Adaptation

*Der Baader-Meinhof Complex.* Dir. Uli Edel. Perf. Martina Gedeck, Moritz Bleibtreu, and Johanna Wokalek. MPI Home Video, 2010. DVD.

*Emily Jones*

1970s criminal poster featuring the Red Army Faction, a group of German terrorists who wrote the *Manifesto for Armed Action* (1970). © INTERFOTO/ALAMY.

# Minimanual of the Urban Guerrilla

*Carlos Marighella*

✧ *Key Facts*

**Time Period:**
Late 20th Century

**Genre:**
Manual

**Events:**
Cuban Revolution;
Brazilian military
government establishing
"Doctrine of National
Security" to justify
censorship and
repression of political
dissent; violent
suppression of student
protests spurring growth
of the urban guerrilla
movement

**Nationality:**
Brazilian

## OVERVIEW

The *Minimanual of the Urban Guerrilla* (1969), written by Carlos Marighella, is a training manual for waging guerrilla warfare in urban environments. Marighella, a Brazilian communist revolutionary, presents the ideological underpinnings of his approach to guerrilla combat and offers readers strategic and tactical instruction. The slim volume, first written in Portuguese, was published in the midst of widespread political battles throughout Latin America, many of which included extensive guerrilla engagements. The *Minimanual* reveals the influence of important Latin American revolutionary thinkers such as Che Guevara, whose own tome, *Guerrilla Warfare,* was published in 1960. Primary to such texts' objectives is the ousting of oppressive governments through small, clandestine organizations working to "systematically inflict damage on authorities and on the people who dominate the country and exercise power," in order to inspire revolution. Marighella's text, however, stands out as the first among these to theorize guerrilla warfare in a specifically urban context. In both encouraging a belief in the communist cause and fostering a methodology for effective political revolution, the book aims to galvanize revolutionaries in Brazil's cities.

First distributed among Brazilian communist radicals, the volume had a circulation that quickly increased and its value was soon recognized by numerous international terror organizations, such as the American Weathermen and the German Baader-Maeinhof Gang, who adopted and put into practice many of Marighella's suggestions. The first English translation appeared in the June 7, 1970, edition of the underground counterculture periodical *Berkeley Tribe* and was completed by the North American Congress on Latin America (NACLA). Concurrently, government officials and counterrevolutionaries attempted to block the influence of the text by banning the work; they also studied the text carefully to anticipate and prepare to oppose guerrilla-style conflict.

## HISTORICAL AND LITERARY CONTEXT

The *Minimanual of the Urban Guerrilla* responds to reactionary militaristic regimes and international intervention to quell the spread of communism during the Cold War. Latin America was a site of particularly unstable political relations, due to unrest and repressive government action. The Brazilian military government in power between 1964 and 1985 exemplified the tensions between authoritarian regimes and left-wing dissidents. When the *Minimanual* was first published, the military regime had been in place for four years. Citing a doctrine of national security as justification, the dictatorship limited personal liberties (such as freedom of speech), heavily censored media outlets, and violently punished dissenters.

As indicated by the *Minimanual,* Marighella, a former member of the Brazilian Communist Party, vocally supported armed resistance to the regime, which prompted his departure from the moderate party and provided the foundations for the *Minimanual.* Resistance began with nonviolent student protests, but by 1969 numerous organizations were engaging in guerrilla-style armed conflict, following the precedent set by the Cuban Revolution. The book builds upon communist and socialist theories of popular resistance, combining these with a previously unexplored approach to guerrilla warfare: relocating these tactics from the rural mountainsides to the city centers of São Paolo and Rio de Janeiro. Marighella's text functions as a guide for those protesters and dissenters in search of more extreme measures for resisting and overthrowing the authoritarian regime with hopes of establishing a communist state.

The *Minimanual of the Urban Guerrilla* follows the precedent set by several tracts by communist thinkers and leaders. These include Vladimir Lenin's *Partisan Warfare* (1906), which insists that to be successful, guerrilla efforts must be endorsed by the working class; and Mao Zedong's *On Protracted War* (1938), influential for its prioritization of small attacks over traditional, large-scale armed confrontation. In addition to laying important theoretical groundwork, both texts offer practical advice for engaging in guerrilla battles. Marighella's Latin American contemporary Guevara also published a manual for the execution of guerrilla combat: *Guerrilla Warfare,* based largely on Guevara's involvement in the Cuban Revolution. Unlike its predecessors, however, Marighella's text asserts that successful resistance will be achieved in the cities. Before the *Minimanual,* Marighella mused on guerrilla warfare, in less instructional ways, in his texts *The Brazilian Crisis* (1966) and *Some Questions about the Guerrillas in Brazil* (1968).

In the years following its publication, the *Minimanual of the Urban Guerrilla* became an important text for left-wing revolutionaries, who soon began to take their cues from the text. Marighella went on to write *For the Liberation of Brazil* (1971), published posthumously in France, consisting of a timeline of the Brazilian resistance and a collection of essays written prior to Marighella's resignation from the official Communist Party. The lasting legacy of the *Minimanual* ultimately lies less in subsequent literary works but instead in its widespread adoption by terror groups throughout the world. The *Minimanual* has informed numerous insurgencies into the twenty-first century and has enabled counterrevolutionary forces, including the U.S. military, to combat guerrilla warfare.

## THEMES AND STYLE

The central theme of the *Minimanual of the Urban Guerrilla* is the effective overthrow of authoritarian regimes by means of unconventional, small-scale armed opposition in urban environments. The text offers readers the definition of a guerrilla and of the perceived value of guerrilla tactics in fighting oppressive governments. As Marighella stated in an interview, the purpose of guerrilla warfare is "the expulsion of United States imperialism and the total destruction of dictatorship and its military forces in order, in consequence, to establish the power of the people," which represents the end goal of the *Minimanual.* Marighella's conviction that revolution would be accomplished in Brazil's cities is illustrated through discussion of how tactics such as ambush, occupation, and explosives can be adapted to urban areas and of the unique advantages and challenges a metropolis presents to guerrillas: "It is an impossible problem for the police, in the labyrinthine terrain of the urban guerrilla, to catch someone they cannot see, to repress someone they cannot catch, and to close in on someone they cannot find."

The text achieves its rhetorical effect through appeals to the character of an effective guerrilla and through appeals to the righteousness of his cause. Marighella's targeted audience includes individuals already interested in overthrowing their government, but needing practical advice and suggestions for how to best do so. Opening with a definition of the urban guerrilla and his characteristics, Marighella emphasizes bravery, decisiveness, and cleverness in addition to proficiency with weapons and technology. In a didactic maneuver, Marighella repeatedly invokes a general and impersonal "urban guerrilla," who serves as a model of what to do and not to do in guerrilla combat: "The urban guerrilla must have a great ability for observation." The exemplary figure also functions to differentiate Marighella's city-based guerrilla from the more traditional rural fighter. This model fighter stands as a paragon for readers to strive to imitate in their own armed conflicts.

Stylistically, the *Minimanual of the Urban Guerrilla* follows genre conventions for a training manual. Throughout the book, Marighella maintains an

## CARLOS MARIGHELLA: FAILED POLITICAL REVOLUTIONARY

Before writing the *Minimanual of the Urban Guerrilla,* Carlos Marighella was a prominent member of the Brazilian Communist Party, a well-respected political group that opposed the strict military regime in place during the 1960s and 1970s. Yet Marighella's adherence to violent resistance alienated him from his party and eventually led to his expulsion. Aiming to incite radical armed conflict, he founded the communist-socialist guerrilla organization Ação Libertadora Nacional (ALN; National Liberating Action) in 1968. The ALN quickly earned notoriety in Brazil and throughout Latin America as a leading example of urban guerrilla warfare for their efforts in Rio de Janeiro and São Paolo. At its height, the group claimed 200 members acting to overthrow the military dictatorship and executed infamous acts of terror, including overtaking the national radio station to read the ALN manifesto on the air; attacking police stations; and kidnapping the U.S. ambassador, Charles Burke Elbrick. Although the ambassador was later exchanged for political prisoners, this last act sealed Marighella's fate.

Soon after the kidnapping, the Brazilian government ceased negotiations with all guerrilla groups and increased its brutality. Covert officers assassinated Marighella in Uruguay in 1969, signifying the end of the ALN, which disbanded less than a year later. The unsuccessful fate of the ALN prefigures the failure of most Latin American resistance groups to depose authoritarian regimes.

instructive and official tone, dispassionately presenting philosophy and strategies yet communicating concrete and applicable advice. The text attempts to comprehensively cover every facet of guerrilla warfare in thirty-seven brief chapters, highlighting topics such as armed propaganda, kidnapping, sabotage, and street tactics. For each of these subjects, the author explicitly delineates characteristics for their successful implementation through simple, straightforward language and the frequent use of lists. When discussing wounded comrades, he suggests, "One of the precautions we must take is to set up first-aid courses ... in which guerrillas can learn the rudiments of emergency medicine." As an instructional document, the *Minimanual* achieves its rhetorical force through adherence to conventions, making complex and unfamiliar military strategies accessible and easy to follow.

## CRITICAL DISCUSSION

Upon its publication, the *Minimanual of the Urban Guerrilla* immediately instigated international controversy. Simultaneously banned by noncommunist governments and the recipient of much media attention throughout the world, the book was soon translated into numerous languages, including Spanish, English, and German. According to scholar William Ratliff, the *Minimanual of the Urban Guerrilla* was the "first widely read book on urban guerrilla warfare" circulated by revolutionary

Because of the widespread adoption of the *Minimanual of the Urban Guerrilla,* scholarship of the work has fallen into two camps: study of the text's practical applications and that of its historical role. Marxist and communist revolutionaries have pored over the manual as an influential text for antigovernment resistance, whereas counterrevolutionary experts and governmental bodies such as the FBI and CIA have studied the text to anticipate and prevent guerrilla activities in combat, as well as by analyzing the applied tactics and their efficacy. In the article "Terrorist Targeting of Police," William F. Jasper invokes Marighella's emphasis on police attacks as an example of the work's legacy, which he asserts is a "standard handbook" for Islamic extremists. The text is also often included in historical accounts of Cold War-era political turmoil in Latin America and is looked to as an important illustration of the wider guerrilla warfare movement of the time.

## BIBLIOGRAPHY

### Sources

Deakin, Thomas J. "The Legacy of Carlos Marighella." *FBI Law Enforcement Bulletin* 23.10 (1974): 19–25. Print.

Huffman, Richard. Notes to "Book: *Minimanual of the Urban Guerrilla." Baader-Meinhof.com.* Baader-Meinhof.com, 20 Oct. 2011. Web. 21 Jan. 2013.

Jasper, William F. "Terrorist Targeting of Police: The Global Terror Network Launched by the Soviet KGB in the 1960s, Now Dressed in Jihadist Garb, Continues a Decades-long War against Law Enforcement in the Non-communist World." *New American* 17 Aug. 2009: 17+. *Academic OneFile.* Web. 21 Sept. 2012.

Ratliff, William. "Revolutionary Warfare." *Violence and the Latin American Revolutionaries.* Ed. Michael Radu. New Brunswick: Transaction Books, 1988. 28. Print.

"The Urban Threat: Guerilla and Terrorist Organizations: Introduction." *Small Wars Journal.* N.d. Web. 13 Sept. 2012.

### Further Reading

Castro, Daniel. *Revolution and Revolutionaries: Guerilla Movement in Latin America.* Wilmington: SR Books, 1999. Print.

Chilcote, Richard H. *The Brazilian Communist Party: Conflict and Integration 1922–1972.* New York: Oxford UP, 1974. Print.

Cronin, Isaac. *Confronting Fear: A History of Terrorism.* New York: Thunder Mouth, 2002. Print.

Dobson, Christopher. *The Carlos Complex: A Study in Terror.* New York: Putnam, 1977. Print.

Kushner, Harvey. *Encyclopedia of Terrorism.* Thousand Oaks: Sage, 2003. Print.

Post, Jerrod M. *The Mind of the Terrorist: The Psychology of Terrorism from the IRA to alQueda.* New York: Palgrave, 2007. Print.

*Elizabeth Boeheim*

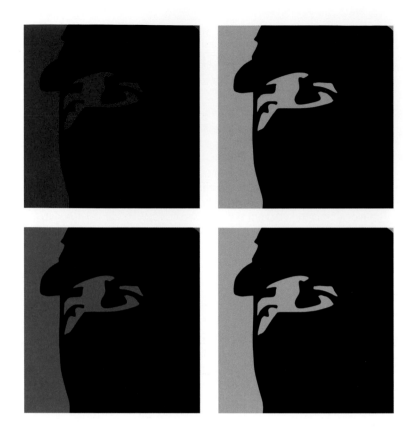

*Minimanual of the Urban Guerrilla* serves as a framework and outlines strategies adopted by many guerrilla movements around the world.
© PHILIPP KAMMERER/ ALAMY.

groups throughout Latin America and reported to have been distributed by Fidel Castro's Cuban government. Guerrilla groups, including Marighella's own Ação Libertadora Nacional (ALN; National Liberating Action), soon began implementing their tactics. Meanwhile, popular outlets such as the *New York Times* and *Time* magazine reported on the text and its dangerous influence on the changing nature of combat in Latin America.

Marighella was assassinated less than a year following the publication of his seminal work, and even though the guerrilla resistance in Brazil soon collapsed thereafter, the influence of the *Minimanual of the Urban Guerrilla* continued to grow throughout the twentieth century. The text served as a framework for later revolutionary movements and a guidebook of maneuvers. Several Latin American guerrilla groups at the end of the 1960s and early 1970s—including Uruguay's *Tupamaro,* Chile's MIR, and Argentina's *Montoneros*—were known to have adopted the *Minimanual's* tenets. Although each of these groups failed to overthrow their repressive regimes, and despite some outdated technology, the *Minimanual* has been used by terrorist organizations that continue to take advantage of the masses of people and maze of structures found in modern cities. As Richard Huffman points out, Marighella's tactics "didn't work in the early seventies and [are] less likely to work now." Nevertheless, even in the twenty-first century, counterterrorist experts have observed the use of Marighella's tactics in armed resistance, notably among Iraqi insurgencies against U.S. occupation.

# THE MONKEY WRENCH GANG

*Edward Abbey*

## OVERVIEW

*The Monkey Wrench Gang,* Edward Abbey's 1975 novel about ecological saboteurs, is a protest of the destruction of the American Southwest by corporate interests and by the U.S. government. The novel concerns a plot by the Monkey Wrench Gang—activists George Hayduke, an ex-Green Beret; "Seldom Seen" Smith, a river guide; Doc Sarvis, an eccentric surgeon; and Bonnie Abbzug, the surgeon's assistant—to blow up the Glen Canyon Dam in Arizona. The novel was so influential among radical environmentalists that the term *monkeywrenching* came into use to describe the practices of ecological sabotage, from spiking trees (a method of booby trapping) to prevent lumber sales to disabling construction equipment and more. Abbey denied that the novel was written as a playbook; rather, it was meant to call attention to the need to preserve the wilderness of the American Southwest as an irreplaceable part of the national character and heritage.

The twentieth century was a time of rapid expansion in the western United States. Several major highway projects made the area more accessible, and populations grew. Oil booms in Texas and Oklahoma contributed to the West's shifting landscape, as did the population boom in California, the seat of the U.S. entertainment industry. The resulting increase in the need for power and water began to significantly affect natural landscapes, causing an outcry from environmental and preservationist groups like the Sierra Club. *The Monkey Wrench Gang,* which was generally treated by critics as an entertaining caper, if not great literature, brought Abbey's concerns, along with his satirical approach to addressing them, to an enthusiastic generation of activists.

## HISTORICAL AND LITERARY CONTEXT

In the 1950s, the U.S. Bureau of Reclamation embarked on a project to manage the water of the Colorado River. Initial plans called for the construction of a dam in Dinosaur National Monument in Utah. However, extensive protests by the Sierra Club eventually forced the government to relocate the project—which became the Glen Canyon Dam—to Arizona. The dam, which was undertaken in 1956 and finished ten years later, caused major physical and ecological changes along the Colorado River, angering many environmentalists.

Abbey, who traveled extensively in the Southwest during the 1940s and 1950s, counted himself among them; indeed, he dubbed the dam's reservoir, Lake Powell, "the blue death."

Abbey began working on *The Monkey Wrench Gang* in the early 1970s, pouring all of his anger over the dam into the novel, which was dedicated to Ned Ludd. Ludd—an early nineteenth-century weaver whose name gave rise to the term *Luddite* to describe one who is averse to technology—was famous for sabotaging machinery in an effort to call attention to the evils of the industrial revolution. By invoking Ludd and making him the hero of the titular characters, Abbey frames *The Monkey Wrench Gang* as something of a wake-up call to his fellow citizens and, as some critics would argue, a commentary on possible routes for addressing the problem, especially for those who found the Sierra Club's agitations too sedate.

Abbey has sometimes been called the Thoreau of the West, and like Henry David Thoreau, he engaged with nature and lamented the diminishing effects of population growth on the American wilderness. Moreover, commentators have noted that, like Thoreau and Ralph Waldo Emerson, Abbey's nature writing is grounded in his moral philosophy and notions of the responsibilities of citizens in a free society. Thoreau and Abbey are often cited as influences on some militant eco-activists, including those who see civil disobedience as an almost compulsory activity and nature-centered writing as a means to educate people before the wilderness is lost. Quoting Abbey in his 2000 introduction to *The Monkey Wrench Gang,* David Brinkley writes, "We can have wilderness without freedom, we can have wilderness without human life at all" but "we cannot have freedom without wilderness."

*The Monkey Wrench Gang* is widely regarded as Abbey's magnum opus; the novel cemented his reputation as an iconoclastic defender of the earth. As of 2012, the book has sold more than a million copies since publication, and was followed by a sequel, Abbey's last novel, *Hayduke Lives!* Abbey remains one of the most influential writers of the twentieth century American Southwest, and *The Monkey Wrench Gang* continues to be required reading for environmental activists.

❖ *Key Facts*

**Time Period:**
Late 20th Century

**Genre:**
Novel

**Events:**
Population growth; damming of the Colorado River

**Nationality:**
American

# ECODEFENSE: A FIELD GUIDE TO MONKEYWRENCHING

David Foreman's 1985 primer *Ecodefense: A Field Guide to Monkeywrenching* reads a bit like a tract written by George Hayduke and is introduced by Edward Abbey himself. Foreman, a member of the radical activist group Earth First!, wrote *Ecodefense* as a practical guide for activists working to stop land surveying, logging, construction, and related practices. After Abbey's introduction, the guide develops a working definition of *monkeywrenching,* which Foreman describes as "nonviolent resistance to the destruction of natural diversity and wilderness." Foreman emphasizes the importance of targeting nonliving things only, as well the importance of being both strategic and ethical. Having laid the ground rules, Foreman goes on to detail various methods of sabotage, from immobilizing equipment to prevent road building and other construction to interfering with timber sales. Tips on general methods for conducting operations follow, and evasive actions to avoid arrest are also presented.

In his forward, Abbey likens monkeywrenching to defending one's home against assault, opining that "the wilderness is our true home … we have the right to defend that home … by any means necessary." Commentators have long argued over how seriously to take Abbey's vision of eco-sabotage, and some are critical of *The Monkey Wrench Gang* for being a blueprint for eco-terrorism. The question remains open, and Abbey's endorsement of Foreman's guide adds an interesting layer to the debate.

## THEMES AND STYLE

*The Monkey Wrench Gang* is a picaresque novel that decries the pillaging of the American Southwest and challenges citizens to take notice that the wilderness—and with it, the American spirit—is vanishing. As the novel opens, a bridge, "bedecked with bunting and streamers and Day-Glo banners," is being opened. Abbey describes the flags, the lines of hot cars idling, and the "electronically amplified techno-industrial rhetoric" pumping out to the crowds. What is supposed to be a proud moment celebrating progress amounts to "five thousand people yawning in their cars, intimidated by the cops and bored to acedia by the chant of the politicians." In contrast to the masses, the members of the Monkey Wrench Gang do not sit sedately in their cars.

The explosion of the bridge in the novel's opening reflects Abbey's desire to overturn popular notions about use of the land in the United States. The spectators gathered for the bridge's unveiling initially think that the fireworks display set off by the Monkey Wrench Gang is the highlight of the show rather than a prelude to soul-driven protest activity. This opening act is merely the first stop in Abbey's road narrative. Back from Vietnam and joyriding through the desert, George Hayduke "felt and shared in the exhilaration

of the sun" as he and his motley band head for "the red cliffs of the canyon country, the purple mesas, the cliff-rose and the blue birds." Critic Ann Ronald argues in *The New West of Edward Abbey* (1982) that the free-ranging heroes of *The Monkey Wrench Gang* deliberately reference the classic Western, but the fact that they traverse a changing landscape serves to underline Abbey's notion that losing wilderness is losing more than land—it is losing the nation's stories.

*The Monkey Wrench Gang*'s humorous tone is often noted as one of the novel's key features. Abbey's satirical novel is populated with over-the-top characters whose bounding exuberance and colorful language, according to some critics, serve to make them more accessible to a readership that otherwise would be put off by the book's grim message. Others have pointed out that Abbey's use of language feels quintessentially American and speaks to deep-seated frustrations with capitalist politics. When "Seldom Seen" Smith complains about the destruction caused by "them bastards from Washington," for example, many readers can relate. Writing for the *CEA Critic* in 1993, Scott Slovic takes a different approach, seeing a deliberate disconnect between the novel's tone and its message. Slovic points to Abbey's use of morally neutral language to describe a destructive act like exploding a newly built bridge as part of a larger message in the novel that the disconnect between moral convictions and human perceptions of events can keep people from engaging meaningfully with their environment.

## CRITICAL DISCUSSION

Following the Vietnam War and Watergate, many American readers were looking for zany entertainment with a bit of social commentary, and *The Monkey Wrench Gang* was published to generally good reviews. The *National Observer* called the novel "sad, hilarious, exuberant, vulgar," while *Newsweek* praised Abbey for developing a new genre, the ecological caper. Beyond literary critiques, some readers expressed concerns about the more anarchist elements of the novel, and especially about Abbey's inclusion of vaguely described but potentially usable plans for eco-sabotage.

One of *The Monkey Wrench Gang*'s more significant legacies is that it played a key role in the development of the eco-activist group Earth First!, which was formed in the late 1970s as an alternative to the more mild-mannered approach of groups like the Sierra Club. Earth First! adopted George Hayduke's motto—"always pull up survey stakes where you find them"—and for its public debut in 1981, the group unfurled a 300-foot banner designed to look like a giant crack down the front of the Glen Canyon Dam. The novel remains a cult classic even though Abbey's gas-guzzling, beer-swilling, sometimes piggish protagonists might seem unlikely environmentalists by today's standards.

*The Monkey Wrench Gang* is the culmination of a number of themes at play in Abbey's oeuvre. Chief among them is, of course, the environmental impact of twentieth-century development. Edward Twining notes that in Abbey's writing, changes to the landscape wrought by humans often result not only in physical modification but in "the profound alteration in the mental landscape all Americans perforce survey." Further, Twining traces Abbey's vision to "his affinity with the long, classic American search for a morality based in our intuitive sense of the grandness of American nature." Rereading Abbey in 2009, Robert Macfarlane considers not how the landscape informs Abbey's writing but how Abbey's writing has informed the cultural landscape. Recounting Abbey's observation of the 1981 stunt by Earth First!, Macfarlane notes that Abbey was able to "witness his imagined scenario of the actual destruction of the Dam, converted into an actual scenario of the imagined destruction of the Dam," adding that Abbey's "provocative" forward to his novel, in which he claims that the book is based on facts, "had proved complicatedly self-fulfilling." Macfarlane goes on to suggest that *The Monkey Wrench Gang* provides contemporary observers with a way to see how literature can create environmental politics in a very real way.

*The Monkey Wrench Gang* author Edward Abbey sitting above Lake Powell in Utah in the 1970s. © JONATHAN BLAIR/ CORBIS.

## BIBLIOGRAPHY

*Sources*

Abbey, Edward. *The Monkey Wrench Gang.* 1975. New York: Harper Perennial Classics, 2006. Print.

Macfarlane, Robert. "Rereading: Robert Macfarlane on *The Monkey Wrench Gang.*" *The Guardian,* 25 Sept. 2009. Web. 30 June 2012.

Ronald, Ann. *The New West of Edward Abbey.* Reno: U of Nevada P, 1982. Print.

Slovic, Scott. "Aestheticism and Awareness: The Psychology of Edward Abbey's *The Monkey Wrench Gang.*" *CEA Critic* 55.3 (1993): 54–68. Rpt. in *Twentieth-Century Literary Criticism.* Vol. 160. Ed. Thomas J. Schoenberg. Detroit: Gale, 2005. *Literature Resource Center.* Web. 30 June 2012.

Twining, Edward S. "The Roots of Abbey's Social Critique." *Coyote in the Maze: Tracking Edward Abbey in a World of Words.* Ed. Peter Quigley. Salt Lake City: U of Utah P, 1998. 19–32. Vol. 160. Rpt. in *Twentieth-Century Literary Criticism.* Ed. Thomas J. Schoenberg. Detroit: Gale, 2005. *Literature Resource Center.* Web. 30 June 2012.

*Further Reading*

Abbey, Edward. *Desert Solitaire.* New York: Touchstone, 1968. Print.

Cahalan, James M., *Edward Abbey: A Life.* Tucson: U of Arizona P, 2001. Print.

Hart, George, and Scott Slovic. *Literature and the Environment.* Westport: Greenwood, 2004. Print.

Hunt, Alex. "The New Atomic Wilderness: Ed Abbey's Post-Apocalyptic Southwest." *Southwestern American Literature* 34.1 (2008): 41+. *Literature Resource Center.* Web. 1 July 2012.

Norwick, Steve. "Nietzschean Themes in the Works of Edward Abbey." *Coyote in the Maze: Tracking Edward Abbey in a World of Words.* Ed. Peter Quigley. Salt Lake City: U of Utah P, 1998. 184–205. Rpt. in *Twentieth-Century Literary Criticism.* Vol. 160. Ed. Thomas J. Schoenberg. Detroit: Gale, 2005. *Literature Resource Center.* Web. 1 July 2012.

*Daisy Gard*

# THE PORT HURON STATEMENT

*Tom Hayden*

## OVERVIEW

*The Port Huron Statement,* published by the Students for a Democratic Society (SDS) in 1962, is the first manifesto of the 1960s New Left movement. Drafted principally by Tom Hayden, a twenty-two-year-old graduate of the University of Michigan, the lengthy polemic was revised and approved by a group of about sixty participants at an SDS convention in Port Huron, Michigan, in June 1962. The document represents a self-conscious attempt by the youth organization to create an "agenda for a generation" that would serve as a platform for a national student movement. The statement combines declarations of philosophical principles and ethical values with analyses of specific policy issues and proposals for engineering fundamental social, political, and economic change in American life.

The statement brought articulate expression to the rumblings of discontent among middle-class youth during the Cold War years. Many of these young people had been inspired by the nonviolent movement against racial discrimination in the South. Embracing the spirit and tactical ingenuity of the civil rights protesters, the Port Huron authors sought to inspire a radical political movement—the New Left—that was not aligned with the Socialist or Communist parties or other sectarian groups whose politics they considered outmoded. Grassroots activism, they argue in their document, "has the function of bringing people out of isolation and into community." Although the statement's detailed political program was not widely embraced, its publication helped to bring the emerging radical perspective of the left into focus. The SDS and other youth-led groups would soon take center stage in the opposition to the Vietnam War and other political issues of that tumultuous decade.

## HISTORICAL AND LITERARY CONTEXT

The statement's opening sentence places its authors within a social context: "We are people of this generation, bred in at least modest comfort, housed now in universities, looking uncomfortably to the world we inherit." When these young Americans were weaned during the 1950s, the United States dominated the world economy but was locked in the tense Cold War with the Soviet Union. The nation's ideological battle against communism had major repercussions on domestic life. Thousands of Americans lost jobs or faced prosecution because they were suspected of being sympathetic to communism or past members of the Communist Party. The air of anticommunism had a chilling effect on activists on the political left, but the first sign of a radical resurgence came with the African American freedom movement. Young people led a number of successful civil rights initiatives, such as the lunch counter sit-ins in North Carolina in 1960 and the Freedom Rides of 1961, which were intended to compel the federal government to enforce a 1956 U.S. Supreme Court decision that integrated interstate transport.

Originated in 1960 by Alan Haber of Ann Arbor, the SDS grew out of an organization he had been leading called the Student League for Industrial Democracy. Haber recruited Hayden, who had been editor of the University of Michigan's newspaper, to become the SDS field secretary after he graduated in 1961. After Hayden was jailed in Georgia in December of that year, along with seven other Freedom Riders, Haber asked him to draft a mission statement for the SDS. The document grew to nearly fifty pages, far beyond its intended length. At the five-day Port Huron conference in a labor union camp, the young activists debated the details of the manifesto, made suggestions for fine-tuning it, and ratified the amended version. Conscious of their ambition to revitalize the American left, the SDS members circulated their statement as a tool to spark the formation of a broad coalition of progressive movements.

*The Port Huron Statement* is indebted to literary traditions of the manifesto genre harking back to the writings of American revolutionaries such as Thomas Jefferson and Thomas Paine. It also owes much to the abolitionists, early feminists, socialists, and political dissidents who had presented broad critiques of American society. A more direct influence on Hayden's viewpoint was the sociologist C. Wright Mills, who had challenged bureaucratic thinking, public apathy, and the "power elite" in the 1950s. One such concentration of power—the military-industrial complex—had been identified by President Dwight D. Eisenhower in his 1961 farewell address.

The statement is now widely viewed as a prescient expression of the progressive political viewpoint that crystallized in the 1960s. When the document was published, the SDS was a small, little-known group, but the manifesto was increasingly embraced as the most ambitious theoretical exposition of the New Left. *The Port Huron Statement* popularized the notion of "participatory democracy," a phrase coined by University of Michigan professor Arnold Kaufman, which has continued to resonate through movements such as Occupy Wall Street in the early 2010s.

## THEMES AND STYLE

As stated in the introduction to *The Port Huron Statement,* the central purpose of the document is to "search for truly democratic alternatives to the present." The statement envisions a revived American democracy driven by a much greater level of civic activity across the population—a participatory, rather than merely representative, democracy. By replacing apathy with activism in the public sphere, individuals win a greater share of influence over the collective decisions that determine their conditions and quality of life. In foreign affairs, the authors call for a retreat from what they characterize as the aggressive militarism of the Cold War. Domestically, they aspire to construct a powerful progressive force in electoral politics by inspiring a fusion of the student, labor, peace, civil rights, and liberal movements. Such a coalition, they imagine, could displace the conservative southern Dixiecrats from their entrenched positions of power within the Democratic party and make the party more responsive to progressive demands.

Rhetorically, the statement aims to persuade young readers to align with its "agenda for a generation." The introduction expresses the authors' collective experience of growing to political awareness: "When we were kids, the United States was the wealthiest and strongest country in the world." The authors state that they contentedly absorbed the American ideals of freedom and democracy as children, but as they matured, their "comfort was penetrated by events too troubling to dismiss." Specifically, blatant racial bigotry and the unsettling shadow of the atomic bomb spurred the authors toward taking responsibility for their citizenship through activism. In the concluding section, they argue that universities represent a potentially powerful base from which to initiate reform: "The bridge to political power … will be built through genuine cooperation, locally, nationally, and internationally, between a new left of young people, and an awakening community of allies."

The bulk of the statement consists of a detailed analysis of the U.S. political and economic systems, which fail, in the authors' view, to live up to the nation's democratic principles. The language is scholarly and often incisive in its social criticism. Although passages on nuclear deterrence and disarmament, the Berlin Wall, and anticolonial revolutions are dry and jargon laden, a palpable passion imbues the sections charging national leaders with placing far too much emphasis on anticommunism. According to the authors, military policy predicated on the assumption of Soviet

## TOM HAYDEN: LIFELONG ACTIVIST

Thomas Emmet Hayden, the principal author of *The Port Huron Statement,* has had a celebrated career in the political arena. Born in Detroit, Michigan, in 1939, he was editor in chief of the *Michigan Daily* during his senior year at the University of Michigan. After graduating, he moved to Atlanta, Georgia, with his first wife, Casey, to organize for Students for a Democratic Society. After the appearance of *The Port Huron Statement,* he became a national figure in the youth movement and played a central role in the demonstrations at the 1968 Democratic National Convention in Chicago and in the Chicago Eight conspiracy trials that followed. (His conviction for crossing state lines to incite a riot was overturned on appeal.)

He made his first of several well-publicized visits to North Vietnam in 1965. He returned in 1972 with actress Jane Fonda and married her a year later. In 1976 he unsuccessfully challenged California senator John V. Tunney for the Democratic nomination before being elected to California's state legislature in 1982 and serving for eighteen years. He made a memorable speech to the street demonstrators outside the 1999 World Trade Organization conference in Seattle, Washington, and has written and edited many books, including *Reunion: A Memoir* (1988), *The Long Sixties: From 1960 to Barack Obama* (2009), and *Writings for a Democratic Society: The Tom Hayden Reader* (2008).

aggressiveness "has been more effective in deterring the growth of democracy than communism." The introduction is particularly powerful, with its generational appeal and a values discussion that centers on defining participatory democracy. In keeping with the participatory ethos, an introductory note calls the statement "a living document open to change with our times and experiences. It is a beginning: in our own debate and education, in our dialogue with society."

## CRITICAL DISCUSSION

Initially, twenty thousand mimeographed copies of the statement were distributed, mostly to other campuses across North America. Many of the Port Huron participants believed their communiqué would be influential, but the document resonated with only a small number of readers. However, two subsequent events fueled a national explosion of student protest: the December 1964 campus conflict at the University of California at Berkeley over free speech rights and the escalation of the Vietnam War in early 1965 under president Lyndon Johnson. The SDS became the most prominent student antiwar group in the late 1960s, and by decade's end, *The Port Huron Statement* was recognized by some as a seminal document.

The development of the SDS has figured largely in the historiography of the 1960s. Several lengthy studies of the movement have been published, starting with *A Prophetic Minority* (1966) by journalist Jack Newfield. Books such as *SDS* (1973) by Kirkpatrick

Activists protest the detention of Tom Hayden during ongoing demonstrations at the Democratic National Convention in Chicago, Illinois, on August 1, 1968. PHOTO BY ART SHAY/TIME & LIFE PICTURES/GETTY IMAGES.

*Student Movements from Port Huron to Today* (2012), he claims that the participatory democracy model still animates political movements, from Mexico's Zapatistas to world trade protesters, Occupy Wall Street, the Arab Spring, and Barack Obama's 2008 presidential campaign. On the other hand, scholar Allen Smith takes issue with standard historical narratives of the 1960s, which he asserts in a 2000 essay in *Peace & Change,* have placed *The Port Huron Statement* on a pedestal and have overestimated its importance. Many other scholars, however, agree that the statement has had a powerful impact. In a 2012 essay for *Dissent,* coeditor and onetime Weathermen member Michael Kazin calls it "the most ambitious, the most specific, and the most eloquent manifesto in the history of the American Left."

## BIBLIOGRAPHY

*Sources*

Hayden, Tom. *Inspiring Participatory Democracy: Student Movements from Port Huron to Today.* Boulder: Paradigm, 2012. Print.

———. *The Port Huron Statement: The Visionary Call of the 1960s Revolution.* Berkeley: Thunder's Mouth, 2005. Print.

Kazin, Michael. "The Port Huron Statement at Fifty." *Dissent* 59.2 (2012): 83–89. *Elsevier.* Web. 10 Sept. 2012.

Miller, James. *Democracy Is in the Streets: From Port Huron to the Siege of Chicago.* New York: Simon & Schuster, 1987. Print.

Smith, Allen. "Present at the Creation … and Other Myths: *The Port Huron Statement* and the Origins of the New Left." *Peace & Change* 25.3 (2000): 339–63. *ArticleFirst.* Web. 10 Sept. 2012.

*Further Reading*

Adelson, Alan. *SDS: A Profile.* New York: Scribner's, 1972. Print.

Gitlin, Todd. *The Sixties: Years of Hope, Days of Rage.* New York: Bantam, 1987. Print.

Hayden, Tom. *The Long Sixties: From 1960 to Barack Obama.* Boulder: Paradigm, 2009. Print.

Hazlett, John Downtown. *My Generation: Collective Autobiography and Identity Politics.* Madison: U of Wisconsin P, 1998. Print.

Horowitz, David. "Port Huron and the War on Terror." *FrontPage Magazine.* FrontPageMag.com, 23 July 2002. Web. 11 Sept. 2012.

Newfield, Jack. *A Prophetic Minority: The American New Left.* New York: Signet, 1966. Print.

Pekar, Harvey. *Students for a Democratic Society: A Graphic History.* New York: Hill and Wang, 2008. Print.

Sale, Kirkpatrick. *SDS.* New York: Random House, 1973. Print.

Sale, *Democracy Is in the Streets* (1987) by James Miller, and *The Sixties: Years of Hope, Days of Rage* (1987) by former SDS president Todd Gitlin, cover the dramatic rise of the student group and its later disintegration into rival factions, including the notorious Weather Underground, a band of revolutionaries that became domestic terrorists. Thanks to this type of scholarship, *The Port Huron Statement* is now recognized as the major founding document of the 1960s white left. The statement has been excerpted in several anthologies featuring the decade's primary documents.

Hayden has been a dominant voice in critical debate over the legacy of Port Huron. In 2005 he republished *The Port Huron Statement,* adding a new introduction. In *Inspiring Participatory Democracy:*

*Roger Smith*

# PRISON POEMS

*Bobby Sands*

## OVERVIEW

*Prison Poems* (1981) is a collection of radical Irish nationalist poems written by Provisional Irish Republican Army (IRA) member Bobby Sands from inside the Long Kesh prison. The poems—written on prison-issue toilet paper with a pen cartridge Sands kept hidden inside his body—rail against the tyranny of the British empire and decry the treatment of incarcerated IRA members (Republicans) as criminals rather than political prisoners. Most of the poems included in the collection were smuggled out of the prison during the last four years of Sands's life and span the duration of both the "Dirty Protest" (wherein Republican prisoners refused to bathe or flush) and the hunger strikes of 1981. The protests, and the poems inspired by them, demand that Republicans be granted the rights guaranteed to political prisoners of war under the Geneva Conventions.

Except for some poems and prose pieces that appeared in Republican publications while he was incarcerated, little of Sands's writing was published during his lifetime. *Prison Poems* was printed in a very small run and received little to no attention until the poems were collected alongside his prose in *Skylark Sing Your Lonely Song* (1985). However, Sands himself became an icon of the Irish nationalist movement. His death triggered a media firestorm, fueling public debates and protests in Europe, Asia, and the Americas. His story remains a point of contention in debates over both Irish nationalism and the rights of political prisoners.

## HISTORICAL AND LITERARY CONTEXT

The IRA picked up where the Irish Republican Brotherhood (IRB) had left off. Though the IRB had secured Irish independence in 1922, Northern Ireland was cordoned off as a separate nation still under British control. In 1969 the IRA split over differences of opinion on how to respond to violence against nationalists. The decidedly militant Provisional IRA (known as the Provos) was formed in the wake of this rift, and the group furthered Northern Ireland independence efforts in a period of violence commonly referred to as "The Troubles." British authorities responded to the escalating violence with increased arrest rates, often interning agitators without trial, claiming authority to do so under the Special Powers Act of 1922. Three hundred

forty-two men were detained in this manner during Operation Demetrius, a concentrated raid carried out on August 9 and 10, 1971. The majority of those imprisoned ended up in Long Kesh, where they were treated even more poorly than standard criminals. In 1972 negotiators from the IRA secured Special Category Status (SCS) for the group's captive members. This meant they were granted the rights provided to prisoners of war under the Geneva Conventions: exemption from prison uniform and work requirements, confinement in dedicated cell blocks housing only IRA detainees, and extra food parcels. However, the British government revoked SCS in 1975, claiming that its provisions "undermined the role of the prison authorities in maintaining discipline."

Sands wrote *Prison Poems* during a series of protests aimed at reinstating SCS provisions. The first uprisings, in 1976, were called "blanket" protests, wherein some three hundred Republican prisoners refused to wear government-issued uniforms, covering themselves instead with the blankets from their bunks. These were followed by the "Dirty Protest," and the period culminated in the hunger strikes of 1981. One hunger strike was called off rather quickly; a second was led by Sands until he and nine other IRA members died of starvation. Sands wrote on toilet paper rolls—even as he became weak and began losing his teeth and hair—stopping only when he was physically unable to hold a pen.

Sands placed himself in auspicious company with his collection of poetry. Though he never commented on his political or literary influences, he would no doubt have had knowledge of Dr. Martin Luther King's "Letter from Birmingham Jail" (1963)—a long letter that responds to fellow activists who had begun to label King as a rabble-rouser and radical—which he wrote in the margins of newspapers, on scraps of paper smuggled into him, and on a legal pad his lawyers were eventually allowed to leave with him. Sands would likely have been less aware of Etheridge Knight's widely acclaimed debut volume of poetry, *Poems from Prison* (1968). The poems document his eight-year incarceration for robbery and examine the social inequities that he felt were at the heart of both his heroin addiction and the petty crimes by which he fueled it.

Sands's collection was not published until shortly after his death, which occurred sixty-six days into the

❖ *Key Facts*

**Time Period:**
Late 20th Century

**Genre:**
Poetry

**Events:**
Irish struggle for Home Rule; persecution of the IRA; IRA Dirty Protest and hunger strikes

**Nationality:**
Irish

# POWER OF THE PEOPLE

On March 5, 1981, just five days into the Irish Republican hunger strikes, Member of Parliament (MP) Frank McGuire of Fermanagh and South Tyrone suffered cardiac arrest and passed away. In the by-election to fill his vacant seat, Irish nationalists saw an opportunity to secure a seat in Parliament, as media attention paid to the hunger strikes had led to a surge in support. To ensure high nationalist turnout in the election, they decided to nominate the hunger strike's orchestrator, Bobby Sands, who was a nationalist icon.

Sands won by a narrow margin on April 9,1981, becoming, at once, the first incarcerated man elected MP and the youngest sitting MP at just twenty-seven years old. When he passed away on May 5 of that year, he had served the fourth-shortest term in Parliament history, at just twenty-five days. His election drew the majority of the media attention over the hunger strikes, as the British government—particularly Prime Minister Margaret Thatcher—was brutally criticized for allowing a sitting MP to starve himself to death.

hunger strike on May 5, 1981. His passing—more specifically, his martyrdom—is seen as having brought more attention to his writing than his writing brought to the nationalist movement. Still, the story of his tenacity, of his refusal to stop expressing himself even as he was dying, made him a legend. He has been immortalized in at least four feature films, a mural depicting him was added to a series of Republican murals along Falls Road in Belfast, and songs written in his honor have been adopted by nationalist movements worldwide.

## THEMES AND STYLE

Crucial to *Prison Poems* are the transgressions of the British government in responding to "The Troubles" and the refusal of fair treatment for those imprisoned as a result. The collection depicts British law enforcement and loyalists as monsters, with poems such as "Modern Times" describing the frequency with which "little children die, / They starve to death … And little girls without attire, / Run screaming, napalmed, through the night." In the face of such tyranny, though, Sands insists in "The Rhythm of Time" that there is a strength inside each Irish nationalist, an inherent yearning for liberty that "has withstood the blows of a million years, / And will do so to the end." Through his own tenacity, Sands exemplified the fortitude he felt was necessary in the struggle for the reunification of the island of Ireland under the Republic.

It is this sense of righteousness that provides most of the collection's rhetorical power. Sands establishes nationalists in a power position by contrasting the "fat dictators … bureaucrats, speculators and presidents" of Britain against Irishman in "rusty chains, / That beset them by their birth." He brings those power

dynamics to bear on his own conditions in "A Place to Rest," resigning himself to the likelihood that he will be allowed to starve to death by "the black devils of H-Block hell" before he and his fellow prisoners are granted SCS provisions. Sands's persistence in the face of certain death, and the sympathetic light in which he was seen thereafter, ensured that the nationalist movement would, at the very least, finally receive the attention he felt it deserved.

As would be expected in the writings of a dying man, the emotional tenor of the work is sweeping and, at times, melodramatic. In "Tom Barry," Sands evokes the efforts of previous generations of nationalists, how "in dusky light, by mist, o'er hills they tread, / A column on the run, / The ghosts of fighters long since dead." In "Weeping Winds," he extends the scope and depth of the resignation from "A Place to Rest," pleading out loud, "Oh! cold March winds your cruel laments / Are hard on prisoners' hearts, / For you bring my mother's pleading cries / From whom I have to part." These are not merely the sentiments of a dying man, however—they are also carefully devised constructs meant to convince as many sympathetic hearts as possible to "join freedom's fight."

## CRITICAL DISCUSSION

*Prison Poems* went largely unnoticed upon its initial release, and even the reprinting of the poems in *Skylark Sing Your Lonely Song* was reviewed in only a handful of outlets. Joe McMinn wrote the most substantive treatment of the latter in *Fortnight* in 1985, calling the conditions under which Sands wrote the poems "simply incredible for anyone who associates learning with leisure." He notes that some of Sands's images "are quite unimaginable" in their horror, and they land so effectively because "the writing is precise, lively and humane. No sign of a monster anywhere." The shock is supplemented, McMinn observes, by the fact that every word of the collection was written "on loo-roll," showing "another grotesque effect of the system behind 'The Troubles.'"

This humanity, and the brutal conditions under which he maintained it, propelled the legacy of Sands. On the thirtieth anniversary of his death in 2011, the *Irish Examiner* printed an article titled "Turning Point in History," which suggests that Sands's death was "one of the most iconic moments of the Troubles" and that he was "the closest Ireland [had] come to a Che Guevara … his hirsute image adorning everything from gable ends to t shirts and posters." And like Guevara, an Argentine revolutionary who was executed in 1967, Sands had gone down as a hero of republicanism and a bulwark of liberty, despite the British government's efforts to defame and obscure his name.

Scholars have begun to discuss Sands not only in the context of civil rights but also within the body politics. Stefan Simanowitz, in a 2010 article for *Contemporary Review,* uses Sands's hunger strikes as contextual background for a discussion of contemporary

Mural of Bobby Sands on Sinn Fein headquarters, Belfast, Northern Ireland, in 2012. © JOE FOX/ALAMY.

hunger strikes, such as that of Nobel Peace Prize-winning human rights activist Aminatou Haidar after she was denied reentry to her native Morocco. In all cases, Simanowitz argues, accounts of hunger strikes move people to support and action, rendering "powerful government[s] so accustomed to using violence and repression to suppress dissent" nearly helpless in the face of just, determined individuals who are content to sit as their bodies waste away. However, the primary inadequacy of hunger strikes staged in prisons, she contests, is that "they are difficult to get publicity for," often relegating the causes motivating them to obscurity.

## BIBLIOGRAPHY

*Sources*

McMinn, Joe. "Blood of a Belfast Supergrass." *Fortnight* 13–26 May 1985: 23. *JSTOR*. Web. 16 Aug. 2012.

Sands, Bobby. *Prison Poems*. Dublin: Sinn Fein Publicity Dept., 1981. Print.

Simanowitz, Stefan. "The Body Politic: The Enduring Power of the Hunger Strike." *Contemporary Review* 292.1698 (2010): 324+. *Academic OneFile*. Web. 16 Aug. 2012.

"Turning Point in History." *Irish Examiner*. Examiner Publications, 5 May 2011. Web. 16 Aug. 2012.

*Further Reading*

"After Bobby Sands." *New Republic* 184.21 (1981): 5–6. *Academic Search Complete*. Web. 16 Aug. 2012.

Golway, Terry. *For the Cause of Liberty: A Thousand Years of Ireland's Heroes*. New York: Simon & Schuster, 2000. Print.

Grant, Patrick. *Breaking Enmities: Religion, Literature, and Culture in Northern Ireland, 1967–97*. Basingstoke: Macmillan, 1999. Print.

Feehan, John M. *Bobby Sands and the Tragedy of Northern Ireland*. Sag Harbor: Permanent Press, 1985. Print.

O'Brien, Conor C. *Passion and Cunning: Essays on Nationalism, Terrorism and Revolution*. New York: Simon & Schuster, 1988. Print.

*Clint Garner*

# SCIENCE OF REVOLUTIONARY WARFARE

*A Handbook of Instruction Regarding the Use and Manufacture of Nitroglycerine, Dynamite, Gun-Cotton, Fulminating Mercury, Bombs, Arsons, Poisons, etc. as Military Science for Revolutionaries*

*Johann Most*

✣ *Key Facts*

**Time Period:**
Late 19th Century

**Genre:**
Manifesto

**Events:**
Rise of anarchist movements; Second Industrial Revolution; economic problems and social unrest in Europe and the United States

**Nationality:**
German

## OVERVIEW

Johann Most published *Science of Revolutionary Warfare: A Handbook of Instruction Regarding the Use and Manufacture of Nitroglycerine, Dynamite, Gun-Cotton, Fulminating Mercury, Bombs, Arsons, Poisons, etc. as Military Science for Revolutionaries* (1885) as an instructional manifesto for anarchists who use violence for revolutionary means, culturally instilling the idea of *attentat*, or "propaganda by deed." This motto, coined and popularized in Europe a few decades earlier, led to the nearly synonymous pairing of "anarchism" with "violence" in the public eye. The majority of the pamphlet details the manufacture of explosives, with the rest offering letter-writing tricks to maintain anonymity and secrecy, tips to enhance economic viability in the movement, advice on how to best serve one's cause if caught, and vitriol against the rich.

Most, a German national, had ties to German Americans who sought to establish violent anarchism in working-class immigrant groups. After being spurned by Friedrich Engels for his interpretation of Karl Marx's *Das Capital* and being exiled from both Germany and the German Social Democrat movement for his incendiary writings, Most found a welcoming audience in the American *lumpenproletariat,* a group of disillusioned immigrants whose dreams of advancement were crushed by industrial exploitation and social oppression. They hungrily devoured his German-language newspaper and pamphlets. *Science of Revolutionary Warfare,* which was sold at picnics, mass meetings, and anywhere sympathetic comrades gathered, provides arguments bolstering the anarchist cause and proposing to end economic strife and social injustice—factors that made the work immediately popular. Commanding, instructive, and incendiary, *Science of Revolutionary Warfare* is now considered crucial to the late-nineteenth-century American anarchist movement and is still widely influential to terrorists and revolutionaries. Among scholars and political scientists, the work is frequently referenced as a model for the idea of "propaganda by deed" espoused by most modern terrorist groups.

## HISTORICAL AND LITERARY CONTEXT

The French Revolution of 1848 and Marx and Engels's *Communist Manifesto* (1848) laid the groundwork for a European proletariat uprising similar to the one Most later encouraged in the United States. Around the same time, anarchism, an ancient political philosophy that opposes hierarchical organization, reemerged, adding another level of revolutionary thought. Jean-Jacques Rousseau's works influenced early nineteenth-century manifestos on anarchism, including manifestos by Pierre-Joseph Proudhon and William Godwin and *The Anarchist's Manifesto* (1850) by Anselme Bellegarrigue. In the second half of the nineteenth century, the second Industrial Revolution sparked global disputes over working hours and conditions, child labor, and fair pay. The world was aflame in calls to action in every sphere, from politics to literature and the arts.

By the time *Science of Revolutionary War* was published, increased economic problems had exacerbated unrest in Europe and the United States. As speculative investments burst, banks failed, and wages fell, workers organized and protested. In the United States, the 1880s saw the beginning of coherent radical movements and organized protests, inspired by the revolutions of Europe and aided by improved literacy, print technology, and mobility. Just before writing *Science of Revolutionary War,* Most joined a group of militants in drafting the "Pittsburgh Proclamation," a declaration that drew rhetorically and stylistically from the 1776 *Declaration of Independence* and the *Communist Manifesto.* Addressed to "fellow workmen," it was the organizational proclamation of the International Working People's Association (IWPA), a movement central to class struggle and aligned with Most's philosophies.

A charismatic hybrid of theoretical writers such as Marx and Peter Kropotkin and unpredictable, impulsive activists such as Mikhail Bakunin, Most quickly gained a following in Europe and the United States. Most was repeatedly jailed in Germany and Austria for his incendiary speeches and an anticzarist attack in his newspaper *Freiheit* (*Freedom*), and again when he republished an article that seemingly spurred

President McKinley's assassination in 1902. In the United States, *Freiheit* joined various anarchist periodicals such as *Alarm* and *Liberty* in establishing a formal anarchist movement. A prolific writer, Most published the rallying "Hymn of the Proletariat" in 1883; it was sung by radicals in Germany and America for decades after Most's death, inspiring solidarity and action.

With *Science of Revolutionary Warfare*, bomb-making rose to the fore of anarchist ideologies and literature. Hungry for change, workers flocked to Most's radicalism, quickly incorporating "propaganda by deed" into otherwise peaceful demonstrations. In 1886 a labor protest in Haymarket Square in Chicago turned violent when a deadly bomb was thrown. Many believed that the unidentified perpetrator had been strongly influenced by Most's polemics and created the bomb using Most's instructions. "It would be no exaggeration to say," writes Paul Avrich, that Most was "the most vilified social militant of his time." A majority of scholars agree that Most's promotion of action (and his explanatory guide to bomb-making) cohered and closed ranks in revolutionary parties, greatly influencing later anarchist and terrorist organizations, the "agitprop" of Soviet Russia, and the negative connotations of "propaganda" as its used today.

## THEMES AND STYLE

Although in other works Most calls violence a last resort, he presses for it in *Science of Revolutionary War*, arguing that "the existing system will be quickest and most radically overthrown by the annihilation of its exponents. Therefore, massacres of the enemies of the people must be set in motion." He positions anarchists as morally above the villainized rich, and he repeatedly underscores the labor of his followers. In one passage, he gleefully suggests, "Just imagine this bomb had been planted under the table at a high society banquet, or had been thrown through a window onto their table—it would have achieved wonderful results!" The word *their* depersonalizes those at the hypothetical banquet—itself a term that evokes decadence and sinful gluttony to a starving people. Most's use of "wonderful" here emotionally guides his readers' responses to the hypothetical situation.

The pamphlet shifts from technical instruction to manifesto and back frequently, merging methods and reasons together in one seamless text. In doing so, scientific instructions become political propaganda and vice versa. Thus, *Science of Revolutionary Warfare* promotes Most's pet notion, "propaganda by deed," in its style, form, and content. Often, fervor for his ideals surfaces momentarily in words and phrases but is quickly squelched as the calm, informative tone resurfaces. Mixing strong invectives such as "NOW LET'S GET ON WITH IT!!" with coldly imparted instructions describing the chemical properties of nitroglycerine and other ingredients for bombs, Most uses the connotations of "science" to impart a tone of rationality to his politics. He also uses his expertise in one field to bolster his authority in the other. By juxtaposing scientific and

## *FREIHEIT* AND FRICTION: MOST'S INCENDIARY NEWSPAPER

Johann Most was widely known in anarchist circles even before he wrote *Science of Revolutionary Warfare*. His speeches and pamphlets were roundly heard and read but his newspaper, *Freiheit*, gave him the most consistent interactions with the protean world of politics. For at least a decade before publishing *Science of Revolutionary Warfare*, Most had been putting his experience as a printer and bookbinder to use, circulating what Martin Miller deems some of "the most extreme pro-terrorist articles … that have been published anywhere." Running for nearly thirty years, *Freiheit* began in Germany, moving with Most when he immigrated to the United States in 1882. His loyal followers kept it running during his imprisonments and for five years after his death in 1905.

*Freiheit* was also a hotbed for Most's public disputes with other anarchists, such as Benjamin Tucker of *Liberty* and his former protégée Emma Goldman. After Goldman and Alexander Berkman attempted to assassinate industrialist Henry Clay Frick during the Homestead Strike, Most denounced them, calling their plot a ploy to raise sympathy for Frick and damaging to their shared cause. Berkman and Goldman attested they had been upholding Most's philosophy of "propaganda by deed," and Goldman demanded a retraction of his accusation. When he failed to deliver one, she took a whip to him—literally—during a public lecture.

political instructions, Most insinuates that if his methods are correct, so are his arguments, suggesting to his readers that he is a logical expert to be followed.

For many of Most's immigrant readers, the German-language pamphlet takes on an empowering tone, reminding them that though they may stumble with the language of the land, the universal language of violence will right the scales of society. He calls his tactics those of "modern warfare," dismissing his targets as "enemies" and "riff-raff of the upper-class variety" while ennobling his readers as "revolutionaries." He also aligns his readers with historically renowned figures, such as Napoleon, who gained fame in the French Revolution a century earlier, and with American Revolutionary figures who supported the "right to bear arms," stretching the idea of "arms" to include dynamite. By using the polarizing language of warfare and by invoking war heroes, Most attempts to persuade his readers that to act as he suggests will be not only effective in their battle for social justice but also right and good.

## CRITICAL DISCUSSION

Early tributes to *Science of Revolutionary Warfare* appeared in similarly sympathetic periodicals such as *Alarm*. As rapidly as it was circulated, the work was tied to violence. Wherever there was social unrest and oppression in the United States in the late nineteenth

*Tsar Alexander II of Russia.* Johann Most was imprisoned by the British after he expressed his delight over the assassination of Alexander II and urged emulation. *ALEXANDER II OF RUSSIA.* (ENGRAVING) (LATER COLOURATION)/ PRIVATE COLLECTION/ PHOTO © TARKER/THE BRIDGEMAN ART LIBRARY.

century, it seems *Science of Revolutionary Warfare* was there. Just after the Haymarket Affair, an article in the *New York Times* named *Science of Revolutionary Warfare* "Anarchy's Red Hand," and the widely read *Anarchy and Anarchists* (1889) by police captain Michael Schaack quickly and indelibly linked Most and his pamphlet to the Haymarket violence. Schaack accused Most of "driving" men to "lawlessness" and of teaching "the public how to commit murder" in his pamphlet. These works and others also tie *Science of Revolutionary Warfare* to future bombings and terrorist acts.

With its promotion of the practice of "propaganda by deed," *Science of Revolutionary Warfare* exacerbated the negative connotations of both "propaganda" and "anarchist." "Propaganda by deed" became a media-magnetizing spectacle that fused violence to language, described by Café Terminus bomber Émile Henry as the "voice of dynamite." Problematically presupposing that the message could be widely interpreted as intended, the act became the message. According to Sarah Cole, the idea of "allowable violence" associated with Most's "propaganda by deed" spread and "partially underwrote the movement." Outside of social and political movements, today the manifesto's legacy can be seen most directly in William Powell's *Anarchist's Cookbook,* a 1971 manual written to protest U.S.

involvement in the Vietnam War, filled with "recipes" of questionable validity for explosives and drugs.

*Science of Revolutionary Warfare* rarely garners critical attention as more than an influential historical document. However, it has recently been utilized to elucidate contemporary literary productions. Scholars such as Alex Houen have turned to Most's pamphlet as a catalyzing point that intertwines science, violence, and anarchism. Hoeun finds that dystopian novels centered upon a Victorian fear of science, a kind of proto-cyberbunk mode, were inspired by Most's rhetoric. The work's literary impact can also be felt in sympathetic novels such as *A Hazard of New Fortunes* (1890) by William Dean Howells and Henry James's *The Princess Casamassima* (1886). Joseph Conrad modeled his unsympathetic and bombastic protagonist in *The Secret Agent* (1907) on Most and drew from anarchist politics in other works. Such literary productions, Sarah Cole argues, interrogate the exuberantly spectacle-driven performance that "propaganda by deed" suggests.

## BIBLIOGRAPHY

### Sources

Avrich, Paul. *The Haymarket Tragedy.* Princeton: Princeton UP, 1986. Print.

Cole, Sarah. "Dynamite Violence and Literary Culture." *Modernism/modernity* 16.2 (2009): 301–28. *Project Muse.* Web. 16 Sept. 2012.

Houen, Alex. *Terrorism and Modern Literature: From Joseph Conrad to Ciaran Carson.* Oxford: Oxford UP, 2002. Print.

"Rioting and Bloodshed in the Streets of Chicago." *New York Times.* 5 May 1886: 1. *ProQuest.* Web. 20 Sept. 2012.

Schaack, Michael. *Anarchy and Anarchists. A History of the Red Terror and the Social Revolution in American and Europe. Communism, Socialism, and Nihilism in Doctrine and in Deed. The Chicago Haymarket Conspiracy, and the Detection and Trial of the Conspirators.* Chicago: Shulte, 1889. *Google Book Search.* Web. 16 Sept. 2012.

### Further Reading

Butterworth, Alex. *The World That Never Was: A True Story of Dreamers, Schemers, Anarchists, and Secret Agents.* New York: Vintage, 2011. Print.

Grob-Fitzgibbon, Benjamin. "From the Dagger to the Bomb: Karl Heizen and the Evolution of Political Terror." *Terrorism and Political Violence* 16.1, (2004): 97–115. *University of North-Texas Department of Political Science.* Web. 16 Sept. 2012.

Merriman, John. *The Dynamite Club: How a Bombing in Fin-de-Siècle Paris Ignited the Age of Modern Terror.* New York: Houghton, 2009. Print.

Miller, Martin. "The Intellectual Origins of Modern Terrorism in Europe." *Terrorism in Context.* Ed. Martha Crenshaw. University Park: Pennsylvania State UP, 1995. 27–62. Print.

Trautmann, Frédéric. *The Voice of Terror: A Biography of Johann Most.* Westport, CT: Greenwood, 1980. Print.

*Katherine Bishop*

# THE SECRET AGENT

*Joseph Conrad*

## OVERVIEW

*The Secret Agent,* a 1907 novel written by Joseph Conrad, tells the story of Mr. Verloc, a businessman and secret agent for a foreign embassy who finds himself enmeshed in a plan to detonate a bomb in London. The story's plot alternates between Verloc's home life, focusing largely on his relationship with his wife, Winnie, and her brother, Stevie, and his political life with his friends, a group of communist anarchists. As Verloc gets more deeply entrenched in plotting the bombing, he finds it more difficult to keep his family life separate. Both his worlds collide when Stevie is killed in the bomb attack. The novel is based on a true event, the bombing of the Royal Observatory in 1894. Conrad's book examines how a public act of terrorism can be propaganda in itself and influence not only individuals but the politics of a country.

Though *The Secret Agent* did not garner large book sales upon its first publication, it found a lasting legacy in the century that followed. The novel eventually gained a cult following and has been described as a classic of terrorism literature. *The Secret Agent's* significance lies in its ability to show not only how a person might find himself committing a terrorist act but also the scope of consequences that follows in the wake of such an act. Conrad's novel is notable in that it examines both the reasoning behind and reactions to a historical act of terrorism.

## HISTORICAL AND LITERARY CONTEXT

On February 15, 1894, Martial Bourdin, a French anarchist in London, was carrying a bomb that accidentally detonated outside the Royal Observatory. Bourdin died shortly after the incident, leaving his terrorist act shrouded in mystery. London had seen a trend of bomb detonations, including an 1885 attack against the London Bridge and the House of Commons, among other major landmarks, and another attack against the London Underground the same year. Prior to Bourdin's attack, the bombings in London had been carried out primarily by the Fenians, a group of Irish nationalists. Bourdin's bombing marked one of the first attacks with international ties.

Conrad began writing this novel at the same time the Western world was seeing a rash of similar terrorist acts. In general, their goal was to create mass confusion and panic, thus disrupting social order as embodied by a government or policing body. The overall aim was to tear down the existing social structure so that a better one could be built in its place. In Chicago in 1886, in what became known as the Haymarket Affair, someone threw a homemade bomb following what had been a peaceful labor demonstration, killing at least eleven people. Although it was not determined who the perpetuator was, many believed that the bombing, like the Bourdin attack, was the work of anarchists using violent methods to incite chaos and prompt political change.

Following the Greenwich bombing, authors such as David Nicoll and the Rossetti sisters published pamphlets that tried to make sense of the terrorist act, with the Rossettis (under the name Isabel Meredith) later turning their writings into the novel *A Girl Among the Anarchists* (1903). Conrad's novel *The Secret Agent* is among a number of early-twentieth-century novels that might be considered "terrorist literature." Jack London's "The Enemy of All the World" appeared the same year as *The Secret Agent* and features a young university student who becomes a murderer and then a terrorist.

Conrad's novel did not enjoy as much literary success as his other works, such as *Heart of Darkness* (1902), but it did receive more attention as the twentieth century progressed. As a work examining terrorist activity and its influence on the world, *The Secret Agent* influenced literature that followed it. In 1911 Conrad wrote *Under Western Eyes,* which examined another act of terrorism, in this case a political assassination. Both novels gained popularity during times of high terrorist activity, and following the September 11, 2001, attacks in New York City, *The Secret Agent,* in particular, was being cited as a classic in the genre.

## THEMES AND STYLE

At the heart of *The Secret Agent* is the theme of political life versus familial life. Central to the plot is Verloc's home life with his wife and brother-in-law, giving readers not only a way to humanize the criminal minds behind the violence but also a model for the public's feelings in the face of terrorist actions. The novel opens with a description of Verloc's daily activities, describing his surroundings as quite ordinary. His shop is "one of those grimy brick houses which existed in large quantities," and his shop windows are

### ⁜ *Key Facts*

**Time Period:**
Early 20th Century

**Genre:**
Novel

**Events:**
Rise of anarchism; growth of terrorism; Haymarket Affair

**Nationality:**
English

# UNDER WESTERN EYES

Four years following the publication of *The Secret Agent*, Joseph Conrad revisited the theme of terrorist activity with his novel *Under Western Eyes*. This novel focuses on the story of Russian student Razumov, who comes into contact with an old friend, Victor Hadlin, who confesses he has assassinated a political leader. Razumov agrees to help his friend to escape, only to end up a secret agent himself when Hadlin falls into a trap that leads to his execution.

Like *The Secret Agent*, *Under Western Eyes* centers on ordinary people involved in extraordinary political events. Whereas *The Secret Agent* highlighted the effect of the anarchist's actions upon the outside world, however, *Under Western Eyes* attempts to understand a similar event from the inside perspective of the terrorist. The depictions of the revolutionaries are not caricatures but are realistic representations, making *Under Western Eyes* a unique twist on terrorist literature. In this novel, Conrad revisits familiar themes, particularly that of familial relationships and political duty. Like Winnie and Verloc in *The Secret Agent*, Razumov and his love, Hadlin's sister, find that their love cannot withstand the aftershocks of Razumov's own ties to anarchism and his guilt over Hadlin's death.

filled with "nondescript packages." His shop, like his life, may be easily overlooked by the passerby. In presenting Verloc as an everyman, Conrad characterizes the terrorist not as a monster but the man next door. Beneath this commonplace façade, however, Verloc's door is described as "suspiciously ajar" at night, drawing attention to the fact that not all is right with the man.

Rhetorically, Conrad highlights the everyman aspect of his characters by creating a band of anarchists who—with the exception of the bombing at the novel's end—are largely unsuccessful in their attempts at terrorism. He describes Verloc's political allies, the so-called anarchists of the novel, as almost cartoonish. The Professor, for example, one of Verloc's political associates, is presented as the stereotype of the reader's perception of a terrorist: a man of mystery, nameless except for his nickname, and a mad genius who uses his chemical knowledge to make a bomb that he carries with him, strapped to his chest, at all times. He is a failed scientist, angry with what he perceives to be immoral and unfair in the world around him. What readers do not expect is the final violent act of the book, rendered not by one of the story's stereotypical villains but by Verloc's young wife, the innocent with the "full, rounded form," the "clear complexion," and the "tidy" hair.

The Secret Agent reads in the style of a typical thriller. The plot moves quickly as it follows the cat-and-mouse game between Mr. Verloc and his opponent, Chief Inspector Heat, leaving little room for

emotional language. The most emotionally charged moment comes at the novel's climax when Winnie discovers her husband's role in the Greenwich bombing and her brother's death. The language, which has maintained the neutral tone of an omniscient narrator, turns colorful, with Verloc "huskily" growling his words to his wife, who is "trembling all over" as she realizes Verloc is responsible for the murders. Her recollection of the bombing is given in agonizing detail as the carnage is described as "mangled limbs" and "decapitated" heads and bodies that had to be picked up with a shovel. The language returns to its detached tone as Winnie stabs her husband to death, placing Winnie on the same level as the anarchists who commit murderous acts.

## CRITICAL DISCUSSION

*The Secret Agent* received good reviews in the year of its debut, but it was not widely read among the general public. The *Times Literary Supplement* highly praised the book, noting "how narrow a gulf is fixed" between the anarchist/terrorists and the everyman. A review in *Nation* complemented Conrad for his ability to look into "the dim recesses of human motive." In the years that followed, readers were so convinced by Conrad's story that rumors persisted that he had studied the Greenwich bombing in detail, though he put those speculations to rest by stating that he had not read any of the newspapers at the time nor was he even in London during the bombing.

In the century following the book's initial publication, *The Secret Agent* continued to be read, resonating in particular during times of terrorist activity. Tom Reiss reevaluated Conrad's work for the *New York Times* in 2005, noting that *The Secret Agent* "has acquired a kind of cult status as the classic novel for the post-9/11 age." Following the attacks on the United States on September 11, 2001, readers could relate to Conrad's treatment of a terrorist act, particularly in the reaction of Winnie Verloc as she discovers her husband's role. This for many readers, including Reiss, is the reason the novel is considered relevant even today: *The Secret Agent* is "the most brilliant novelistic study of terrorism as viewed from the blood-spattered outside."

Often compared to other so-called "terrorist literature," *The Secret Agent* has also provoked discussion on its own terms. Much of the criticism written about the novel surrounds the politics in the novel's world as they relate to the anarchy at the heart of the story. Alex Houen and Christian Haines both examine the novel's "entropolitics," or, as Haines describes it, "the political implications of social/political chaos." This theory examines the fin-de-siècle Victorian culture as it unravels under the pressure of acts of terrorism. Other criticism, such as that by Merritt Abrash and Paula Marantz Cohen, seeks to compare Conrad's novel to the 1936 Alfred Hitchcock film *Sabatoge*, which was based on *The Secret Agent*.

## BIBLIOGRAPHY

### Sources

Abrash, Merritt. "Hitchcock's Terrorists: Sources and Significance." *Literature Film Quarterly* 39.3 (2011): 165–73. *MLA International Bibliography.* Web. 22 July 2012.

Cohen, Paula Marantz. "The Ideological Transformation of Conrad's *The Secret Agent* into Hitchcock's *Sabotage.*" *Literature Film Quarterly* 22.3 (1994): 199–209. *MLA International Bibliography.* Web. 22 July 2012.

Haines, Christian. "Life in Crisis: The Biopolitical Ambivalence of Joseph Conrad's *The Secret Agent.*" *Criticism* 54.1 (2012): 85–115. *Literary Reference Center.* Web. 16 July 2012.

Houen, Alex. "*The Secret Agent*: Anarchism and the Thermodynamics of Law." *English Literary History* 65.4 (1998): 995–1016. Print.

Reiss, Tom. "The True Classic of Terrorism." *New York Times.* 11 Sept. 2005. Web. 16 July 2012.

Rev. of *The Secret Agent,* by Joseph Conrad. *Nation.* 28 Sept. 1907. Rpt. in *Conrad: The Critical Heritage.* Ed. Norman Sherry. Cambridge: Cambridge UP, 1983. 191–93. Print.

Rev. of *The Secret Agent,* by Joseph Conrad. *Times Literary Supplement.* 20 Sept. 1907. Rpt. in *Conrad: The Critical Heritage.* Ed. Norman Sherry. Cambridge: Cambridge UP, 1983. 185. Print.

### Further Reading

Buffington, Robert. "Conrad's Bourgeois Tragedy." *Sewanee Review* 117.3 (2009): 495–98. *Literary Reference Center.* Web. 24 July 2012.

Casten, C. "An Episode from Anglo-Irish History in Conrad's *The Secret Agent.*" *English Language Notes* 10.4 (1973): 286–89. *Humanities International Complete.* Web. 24 July 2012.

Houen, Alex. *Terrorism and Modern Literature, from Joseph Conrad to Ciaran Carson.* Oxford: Oxford UP, 2002. Print.

McLeod, Deborah. "Disturbing the Silence: Sound Imagery in Conrad's *The Secret Agent.*" *Journal of Modern Literature* 33.1 (2009): 117–31. *MLA International Bibliography.* Web. 24 July 2012.

Meredith, Isabel. *A Girl Among the Anarchists.* Lincoln: U of Nebraska P, 1992. Print.

Nicoll, David. *The Greenwich Mystery.* London: Sheffield, 1897. Print.

Oliver, Matthew. "Conrad's Grotesque Public: Pornography and the Politics of Reading in *The Secret Agent.*" *Twentieth Century Literature* 55.2 (2009): 209–31. *Literary Reference Center.* Web. 24 July 2012.

Rice, Tom. "Condomization in *The Secret Agent* and *Under Western Eyes.*" *Conradiana* 40.2 (2008): 129–45. *Literary Reference Center.* Web. 24 July 2012.

Sherry, Norman, ed. *Conrad: The Critical Heritage.* London: Routledge, 1973. Print.

Stînğă, Valentina. "From 19th Century Propaganda by the Deed to 20th Century (Im)Mediation: Joseph Conrad's *The Secret Agent* and Don DeLillo's *Mao II.*" *Language and Literature: European Landmarks of Identity* (2010): 385. *Directory of Open Access Journals.* Web. 24 July 2012.

Watt, Ian. *Essays on Conrad.* Cambridge: Cambridge UP, 2000.

### Media Adaptations

*Sabotage.* Dir. Alfred Hitchcock. Ed. Charles Frend. Perf. Sylvia Sidney, Oscar Homolka, John Loder. Gaumont British, © 1936. Film.

*Joseph Conrad's The Secret Agent.* Writ. and adapted by David Thomas and Gillian Greenwood. Dir. and prod. David Thomas. Ed. Melvyn Bragg. Host by V. S. Pritchett and Keith Carabine. Cast Brian Glover, Frances Barber, Hywel Bennett et al. Home Vision, 1988. VHS.

*The Secret Agent.* Dir. Christopher Hampton. Perf. Bob Hoskins, Patricia Arquette, and Gérard Depardieu. Twentieth Century Fox Film Corporation, 1996. Film.

*Lisa Kroger*

Joseph Conrad's novel *The Secret Agent* is the fictional story of a man who becomes involved with anarchism, espionage, and terrorism. PETER HINCE/ STONE/GETTY IMAGES.

# THEORIES

# "ART OR PROPAGANDA?"

*Alain Locke*

## OVERVIEW

Alain Locke's short essay "Art or Propaganda?" appeared in 1928 at the height of the Harlem Renaissance. With this piece, Locke made a firm statement about the purpose of art created by African Americans (or any subjugated group of people): art created for its own sake is vastly preferable to propaganda. "Art or Propaganda?" fits in with a potent rhetorical tradition in African American letters that uses forceful, elegant language to assert the rights and abilities of African Americans. It also engaged in an important twentieth-century conversation about the purpose of art—by African Americans and more generally. The piece values the politics inherent in artistic creation rather than overtly propagandistic arguments and themes.

"Art or Propaganda?" appeared as an opening editorial in the short-lived arts magazine *Harlem: A Forum of Negro Life*. "Art or Propaganda?" established the tenor and goals for the journal, most notably its aim to be a publication for the African American community featuring a wide array of opinions, perspectives, and artistic styles. Locke declares: "Should we not then have a journal of free discussion, open to all sides of the problem and to all camps of belief? Difficult, that—but intriguing." With this statement, Locke responds to other thinkers on the issue of race in the United States and on the purpose of art. His most notable interlocutor was W. E. B. Du Bois, founder of the National Association for the Advancement of Colored People (NAACP), but Locke also responds to the international cultural and artistic movements of modernism, which had a profound impact on art and thinking about art. By engaging in dialogue with both prominent African American thinkers and broader cultural movements, Locke's essay participated in the prominent trends of the time.

## HISTORICAL AND LITERARY CONTEXT

From approximately 1919 through the 1930s, the African American community experienced a flowering of art that invigorated their fight for equality. During the period a large number of African Americans abandoned near slave-like conditions in the South to work in factories and shipyards and as domestics in Northern and Midwestern cities. This period also included a sharp uptick in racial violence, including riots and lynchings. African Americans struggled to survive under institutional oppression, and elite African Americans sought to wage this battle with the tools of art, education, and intellect. The unofficial capital of this movement was the Harlem neighborhood of New York City, which is why this period is now referred to as the "Harlem Renaissance," though people at the time were more likely to speak of a "New Negro" Renaissance or Movement. At this time in particular, African American artists found a market for their work among wealthy whites who, disenchanted with modern life, created a "vogue" for things they deemed "primitive" or more "pure." There were also greater opportunities for publication owing to an increase in magazines and journals edited by and publishing houses owned by African Americans. This complicated history created a tangled, vibrant milieu for African American artists.

"Art or Propaganda?" weighed in on the contentious issue of politics in art. At the time, thinkers were divided on whether art should be overtly political or whether it should be open to represent anything. This debate led some, such as Du Bois, poet Countee Cullen, and novelist Jessie Fauset, to create idealistic works depicting the lives of elites. Yet it led others to depict working-class black life, as in the jazz-based poems of Langston Hughes, the novels of Claude McKay, and the novels, plays, and folklore of Zora Neale Hurston. These authors argued that they were realistically representing black experience, but such works offended many black elites who thought these texts catered to white readers' racist beliefs.

If anyone was suited to argue against propaganda, it was Locke. Like Du Bois, Locke was highly educated—the country's first African American Rhodes Scholar and a PhD in philosophy, educated at Harvard and Oxford. Locke is best known as editor and contributor to the volume *The New Negro* (1925), which showcased the important work being done during the Renaissance. For his part, Du Bois was a very public intellectual, writing and speaking extensively about black experience and political issues. Despite their shared belief that the black elite—what Du Bois dubbed the "Talented Tenth"—should lead the charge toward equality, Du Bois and Locke disagreed on the role of art in political endeavors.

The perspectives of Locke and Du Bois represent the most prominent sides in an ongoing debate.

**✛ Key Facts**

**Time Period:**
Mid-20th Century

**Genre:**
Essay

**Events:**
Harlem Renaissance; rise of modernism; fight for African American rights

**Nationality:**
American

# AFRICAN AMERICAN MODERNISM

Art of all kinds flourished during the first half of the twentieth century. In visual art, post-Impressionism segued into Cubism and featured influences from so-called "primitive" cultures such as Native American or African cultures. In literature, poets broke with established forms and topics whereas fiction writers experimented with perspective, narration, and the traditional structures of novels. This flourishing was accompanied by other cultural changes including new technologies, sciences, political philosophies and movements, and the horrors of World War I (1914–1918). Artists responded to this changing world in their work, often reacting with exuberance and excitement or, more frequently, dismay and despair. A common attribute of these various movements was either essays describing the tenor of "modern" art or manifestos expounding on the goals and merits of a specific movement. Thus, Locke's "Art or Propaganda?" participates not only in debates among African American intellectuals about the purpose and goals for art by African Americans but also in the broad cluster of artistic movements and new styles that characterized the period. As Houston Baker Jr. argues, the Harlem Renaissance was an important example of one such movement, and some scholars suggest that "African American modernism" would be a fruitful, even preferable, term.

Du Bois believed that African American art should directly engage in the politics of racial uplift, that it should always function as propaganda. Locke disagreed. In "Art or Propaganda?" he refutes Du Bois's perspective (while never naming Du Bois directly) by claiming that propagandistic art is never as good as art developed from the individual for the community. However, Locke still makes a political argument. He claims that art created without political goals will have a greater effect on the politics of equality than biased propagandistic art. "Art or Propaganda?" thus becomes a manifesto in the contentious debate over race, politics, and art taking place at the time, a debate that continues among African American scholars and artists today.

## THEMES AND STYLE

In "Art or Propaganda?" Locke makes an argument for "art for art's sake" but then deepens it by declaring that such art better serves the battle for equality. Locke declares that his "chief objection to propaganda" lies in how it exacerbates inferiority because it "speaks under the shadow of a dominant majority whom it harangues, cajoles, threatens or supplicates." He adds as an aside that propaganda also suffers from the "besetting sin of monotony and disproportion." With his primary claim, Locke contends that by howling against the oppressor, propaganda uses and, therefore, reinscribes, the terms of oppression. He uses his secondary claim to suggest that propaganda's "monotony and disproportion" make it ineffective at engaging audiences. Together, these two issues undermine propaganda's effectiveness, which leads to his point that art as "group expression, or even at times … [as] free individualistic expression" better counters inequality by functioning on its own terms rather than within the bounds of oppression.

Because "Art or Propaganda?" is an opinion piece, Locke can write it as a manifesto of art while arguing for the importance of art itself. He notably uses metaphors drawn from Christianity, a tradition in African American letters, to make his points. He states that propaganda equates to "too many Jeremiahs … and too much of the drab wilderness." He argues that, in contrast to these old-fashioned naysayers, the movement of the "younger generation" of African American artists should draw on David as its "patron saint," creating art that "should confront the Phillistines [sic] with its five smooth pebbles fearlessly." Locke thus holds up hero-artists (the Davids) over hand-wringing propagandists (the Jeremiahs). He continues this theme, asserting that for true artists, art is their religion: "Beauty, however is its best priest." He rounds out the comparison between art and propaganda, stating, "psalms will be more effective than sermons." Here, "psalms" evoke art whereas "sermons" suggest the doom-and-gloom prophesies of Jeremiah. Locke also employs other rhetorical strategies, including using leading questions to set up his response, which displays his academic training and experience. He also draws readers in by repeatedly using the communal pronouns "we" and "our," signaling that his audience, other African Americans, has a shared goal to address these issues. Strategies such as shared knowledge of Biblical metaphors, rhetorical questions, and communal pronouns serve to "bring the reader" along, so to speak, with his thinking.

Locke's use of religious themes as rhetoric and his logical yet impassioned argumentative style situate "Art or Propaganda?" in a long tradition of African American writing that includes the nineteenth-century slave narratives of Frederick Douglass and Harriet Jacobs, the folklore and essays of Du Bois, and the speeches and essays of Martin Luther King Jr. Such writing uses language and allusions appropriate for an educated audience, a rhetorical strategy designed to refute the belief in the intellectual and emotional inferiority of African Americans. Locke makes calculated concessions, acknowledging the current generation's "debt" to propaganda-based publications and organizations, and admits that "propaganda itself is preferable to shallow, truckling imitation." Yet he maintains the need for a venue more focused on artistic expression and dedicated to the diversity of opinion and styles in the African American community. Here he reflects his training as a philosopher while engaging in the prominent debates of the time. He likewise maintains his importance as a mentor to the second generation of Renaissance artists.

## CRITICAL DISCUSSION

The inaugural edition of *Harlem* featured essays, stories, poems, and illustrations by several prominent Renaissance writers and artists. Despite its solid intellectual and artistic grounding, *Harlem* lacked the vigor of other publications—such as its predecessor, *Fire!!*—and was impaired by having Wallace Thurman as its primary editor, because Thurman rubbed many people the wrong way. In short, the whole volume—"Art or Propaganda?" included—met with mixed reviews that reflected the contentious and ongoing debates within various factions in African American arts and letters.

Scholars rarely discuss "Art or Propaganda?" at length, although it is often anthologized. Those who do analyze the piece usually consider it within Locke's larger body of work rather than in its original organ of publication. Pulled out of the context of *Harlem,* scholars generally view "Art or Propaganda?" within Locke's developing philosophies, which include his evolving perspective on the issue as seen in his 1936 follow-up, "Propaganda—or Poetry?" Critics also often contrast his perspective with that of Du Bois, which points to both the ongoing importance of Du Bois in discussions of the Harlem Renaissance and to Locke's being such a worthy opponent for him. Indeed, the frequent appearance of "Art or Propaganda?" in anthologies signals its importance to an ongoing historical debate.

Contemporary scholars often seek to understand Locke within larger cultural contexts. Everett Akam defends Locke as an important philosopher who was a proponent of self-identity, which Locke thought the New Negro was uniquely able to understand. Tommy Lott sees in Locke's arguments against propaganda his belief that neither a dominant nor minority culture's representation of the minority can be accurate because their "respective representations will be only propaganda and counterpropaganda." Taking "Art or Propaganda?" apart from *Harlem* also allows critics to view Locke as participating in larger cultural trends, as Lott does in examining Locke's interest in sciences or as George Hutchinson does in his study of intersections between the Harlem Renaissance and other modernisms. Hutchinson claims that Locke rejected the notion of separate cultures between races but, "nonetheless, he believed in the continuing importance of race to the understanding of culture and affirmed the 'cultural racialism,' as he called it, of the Harlem Renaissance." These scholars all seek to recover Locke from relative obscurity (particularly as compared to Du Bois) and to understand his work in broad contexts.

## BIBLIOGRAPHY

*Sources*

Akam, Everett H. "Community and Cultural Crisis: The 'Transfiguring Imagination' of Alain Locke." *American Literary History* 3.2 (1991): 255–76. Print.

Hutchinson, George. *The Harlem Renaissance in Black and White.* Cambridge: Belknap P of Harvard U, 1995. Print.

Locke, Alain. "Art or Propaganda?" *The Making of African American Identity: Vol. III, 1917–1968.* National Humanities Center, 2007. Web. 29 July 2012.

Lott, Tommy. "Du Bois and Locke on the Scientific Study of the Negro." *Boundary* 27.3 (2000): 135–52. Print.

*Further Reading*

Baker Jr., Houston. *Modernism and the Harlem Renaissance.* Chicago: U of Chicago P, 1989. Print.

Calo, Mary Ann. "Alain Locke and American Art Criticism." *American Art* 18.1 (2004): 88–97. Print.

Du Bois, W. E. B. "Criteria of Negro Art." *The Crisis* 32 (1926): 290–97.

Glick, Elisa. "Harlem's Queer Black Dandy and the Artifice of Blackness." *Materializing Queer Desire: Oscar Wilde to Andy Warhol.* New York: SUNY P, 2006. 83–106. Print.

Portrait of Alain Locke, circa 1925, by Winold Reiss. NATIONAL PORTRAIT GALLERY, SMITHSONIAN INSTITUTION/ART RESOURCE, NY.

Harris, Leonard, ed. *The Philosophy of Alain Locke: Harlem Renaissance and Beyond.* Philadelphia: Temple UP, 1989. Print.

Harris, Leonard, and Charles Molesworth. *Alain L. Locke: Biography of a Philosopher.* Chicago: U of Chicago P, 2008. Print.

Locke, Alain. *The Works of Alain Locke.* Ed. Charles Molesworth. Oxford: Oxford UP, 2012. Print.

————, ed. *The New Negro: Voices of the Harlem Renaissance.* 1925. New York: Touchstone, 1997. Print.

Miller, Monica L. "The Black Dandy as Bad Modernist." *Bad Modernisms.* Eds. Douglas Mao and Rebecca L. Walkowitz. Durham: Duke UP, 2006. 179–205. Print.

*Sarah Stoeckl*

# "CRITERIA OF NEGRO ART"

*W. E. B. Du Bois*

## OVERVIEW

W. E. B. Du Bois originally delivered "Criteria of Negro Art" at the Chicago NAACP conference in June 1926. It was later published in *The Crisis,* the NAACP's magazine, in October 1926 as one of the ongoing Negro in Art symposiums. The text outlines Du Bois's view that the works of black artists should be propaganda for furthering the cause of racial equality for African Americans. Prominent members of the Harlem Renaissance, including Alain Locke, Langston Hughes, and James Weldon Johnson, acknowledged Du Bois's work as propaganda, although not everyone agreed with his message. "Criteria of Negro Art" has as its main theme that black writers should use their art to precipitate change in their racial status. Du Bois emphatically states: "Thus all art is propaganda and ever must be, despite the wailing of the purists. I stand in utter shamelessness and say that whatever art I have for writing has been used always for propaganda for gaining the right of black folk to love and enjoy. I do not care a damn for any art that is not used for propaganda."

When Du Bois spoke these words in June 1926, he was highly critical of events occurring in the Harlem Renaissance, a movement he had helped pioneer. He was suspicious that the movement was being controlled by white publishing houses and agents who only sanctioned works they deemed as depicting black people in comical, bawdy, and other stereotypical ways. Du Bois believed black artists should strive to produce art that depicted their race more realistically rather than in ways that pandered to white audiences. His work received mixed reviews, but it resonated throughout the movement for decades, creating a rift among black writers.

## HISTORICAL AND LITERARY CONTEXT

Du Bois wrote "Criteria of Negro Art" at a turning point in the Harlem Renaissance when a younger generation of writers was beginning to branch out in new directions and much of the political motivation of the movement had faded. Du Bois believed white publishers and editors strove to limit the image of blacks to caricatures; thus, publishers wanted only writers with literature palatable for white audiences. Du Bois believed African American writers should respond by using their art as propaganda to further the progress of racial equality.

In Du Bois's opinion, young black writers focused on the aesthetics of their craft more than its message. Harold Cruse suggests why Du Bois's argument may have produced division in African American literary circles.

> Ironically the view of the Negro intellectuals involved in the Harlem Renaissance was also limited. Only one man saw deeply into the social implications of the movement: W. E. B. Du Bois. He outlined his insights in "The Criteria of Negro Art," … but he did not carry his analysis far enough. One reason was that Du Bois was not functioning as a creative artist but as a voice in the politics and economics of civil rights organizations. … The three writers who wrote specifically about the Harlem Renaissance and were also representatives of it—Langston Hughes, James Weldon Johnson, and Claude McKay—all failed the kind of analysis the movement demanded.

Du Bois touched on this concept five years earlier in his essay "Negro Art," stating: "We want everything that is said about us to tell the best and highest and noblest in us. We insist that our Art and Propaganda be one. We fear that evil in us will be called racial, while in others it is viewed as individual. We fear that our shortcomings are not merely human." In contrast, George Schuyler's "The Negro Art Hokum" (June 1926) questions whether there is such a thing as "Black Art." Langston Hughes's "The Negro Artist and the Racial Mountain" (June 1926) acknowledges separatism but hopes for the day when a black artist might be free of the restrictions of race. Du Bois's essay served as a stern warning for African American writers who attempted to avoid politics in their art. Cruse explains:

> In this speech, W. E. B. Du Bois went on to describe Negro art in its functional relationship to the civil rights movement and its aims as Negro cultural expression within the context of the American nationality. It was a brief exposition, but it was, undoubtedly, the very first time the theme was ever voiced by a ranking Negro leader, and the decade of the Harlem Renaissance was the proper historical moment for it to be expressed.

✣ *Key Facts*

**Time Period:**
Mid-20th Century

**Genre:**
Essay

**Events:**
Popularization of Harlem Renaissance literature; racial discrimination

**Nationality:**
American

## SOME BACKGROUND ON DU BOIS

William Edward Burghardt Du Bois was born February 23, 1868, to Alfred and Mary Du Bois. His mother's family were free blacks from Massachusetts and Du Bois experienced little racism during his childhood. He went on to become the first African American to earn a doctorate degree from Harvard. His case study "The Philadelphia Negro" gained him notoriety as a sociologist, and he later taught at Atlanta University.

By the early 1900s, Du Bois was among the nation's most prominent civil rights leaders, but his ideas often clashed with Booker T. Washington's "accommodationist" views, known collectively as the Atlanta Compromise. Du Bois cofounded both the Niagara Movement (1905) and the NAACP (1910) with other civil rights leaders. He served as director of publicity for the organization and editor of its periodical, *The Crisis,* from 1910 to 1933.

In Du Bois's most famous work, *The Souls of Black Folk* (1903), he said, "... the problem of the 20th century is the problem of the color line." He continued to pursue this idea throughout his career, urging black writers and artists to focus on the advancement of their race over aesthetics in their craft. Du Bois died in Ghana, Africa, on August 27, 1963, just one day before Martin Luther King gave his "I Have a Dream" speech.

Du Bois's essay led African American writers to question the purpose of their work, with some asserting that creating propaganda rather than art further diminished the black writer. Alain Locke responded to Du Bois in his essay "Art or Propaganda?" (1928): "My chief objection to propaganda ... is that it perpetuates the position of group inferiority even in crying out against it." As the Harlem Renaissance drew to a close, focus shifted from art as propaganda for racial equality to art as an aesthetic born of but not limited to the black experience.

### THEMES AND STYLE

The main theme of Du Bois's "Criteria of Negro Art" is that African American art should be rooted in propaganda. All black writers should dedicate their craft to the betterment of their race, he asserted, rather than pandering to white audiences for the purpose of publication. He believed the new generation of black writers should focus their works on the truth of the African place in American culture. He plays on Keats's poetic adage "Beauty is truth, truth beauty," in stating:

> How is it that ... a fighting organization ... struggling for the right of Black men to be ordinary human beings ... can turn aside to talk about art? ... What has Beauty to do with Truth and Goodness—with the facts of the world and the right actions of men?—Beauty sits above

Truth and Right I can conceive, but here and now and in the world in which I work they are for me unseparated and inseparable.

Du Bois urges his audience not to lose sight of the initial goals of the Harlem Renaissance movement. He cautions black writers not to fall prey to the complacency of success, arguing that the growing stature of black writers appears to offer for both black and white artists a convenient release from the issue of race. He states:

> They are whispering, "Here is a way out. Here is the real solution of the color problem. The recognition accorded Cullen, Hughes, Fauset, White and others shows there is no real color line. Keep quiet! Don't complain! Work! All will be well!"
>
> I will not say that already this chorus amounts to a conspiracy. But ... there are today a surprising number of white people who are getting great satisfaction out of these younger Negro writers because they think it is going to stop agitation of the Negro question.

Throughout "Criteria of Negro Art" Du Bois employs an impassioned if not emphatic tone. His language is direct—"I do not care a damn for any art that is not used for propaganda"—and he maintains this ideal with "the white public today demands from its artists ... racial pre-judgment that distorts the Truth and Justice, as far as colored races are concerned, and it will pay for no other. ... In all sorts of ways we are hemmed in and our new young artists have got to fight their way to freedom." W. E. B. Du Bois believed the only way for African American writers to keep their hard-won freedom was to keep their art rooted in the propaganda of equal rights and racial equality.

### CRITICAL DISCUSSION

Du Bois's "Criteria of Negro Art" stirred debate in the community of African American writers. While many civil rights leaders agreed with Du Bois, a majority of young black writers, especially those whose work already had received critical acclaim, disagreed that art's sole purpose should be rooted in the betterment of their race. Anne E. Carroll describes Du Bois's work in relation to that of James Weldon Johnson:

> Johnson insisted that literature might serve the purpose of undermining racism, both by presenting positive images of African Americans and by demonstrating the achievements of African Americans in the arts. This argument, of course, would be much more explicitly made in the following years by Du Bois ... in his essay, "Criteria of Negro Art". ... But younger artists like Langston Hughes and Wallace Thurman, who insisted the artist needed freedom to create as he or she saw fit, also would famously rebuke the argument. Johnson's statement, then, was an important early volley in this debate.

Du Bois was a champion of civil rights, and his legacy as a writer lies more in essays and sociological studies than the creative arts like poetry or fiction. Henry Louis Gates explains:

> The confusion of realms, of art and propaganda, plagued the Harlem Renaissance in the 1920s. A critical determination … meant that only certain literary treatments of Black people could escape community censure. The race against Social Darwinism and the psychological remnants of slavery meant that each piece of creative writing became a political statement. … Black literature became to be seen as a cultural artifact or as a document and witness to the political and emotional tendencies of the Negro victim of white racism. Literary theory became the application of a social attitude.

"Criteria of Negro Art" influenced writers of Du Bois's time as well as future African American authors in their views on art, propaganda, and segregation. Pulitzer Prize winner David Levering Lewis, in describing former NAACP Chairman of the Board Joel Spingarn's "Segregation—A Symposium," remarks that, "like the watershed 'Criteria of Negro Art' eight years earlier, [it] was designed to motivate informed controversy … Joel Spingarn, still prompted by philosophical integrity, expressed appreciation for Du Bois's broaching of implications of segregation, then went on to underscore that the NAACP had 'always regarded segregation as an evil.'" Du Bois's watershed essay forced African American writers to choose whether their work would be political or merely aesthetic, or, in essence, whether they would be considered artists or black artists.

Historian Carter Godwin Woodson. W. E. B. Du Bois initially delivered the "Criteria of Negro Art" in a speech given as part of a 1926 NAACP conference celebrating Woodson's accomplishments.
© BETTMANN/CORBIS.

## BIBLIOGRAPHY

*Sources*

Carroll, Anne E. "James Weldon Johnson." *Harlem Speaks: A Living History of the Harlem Renaissance.* Ed. Cary D. Wintz. Illinois: Sourcebooks, Inc., 2007. 343–360. Print.

Cruse, Harold. *The Crisis of the Negro Intellectual.* New York: Morrow, 1967.

Du Bois, W. E. B. "Criteria of Negro Art." *The Crisis* Oct. 1926: 290–97. The Portable Harlem Renaissance Reader. Ed. David L. Lewis. New York: Viking Penguin, 1994. 100–05. Print.

———. "Negro Art." *The Crisis* June 1921: 55–56. Du Bois on Reform: Periodical-based Leadership for African Americans. Maryland: AltaMira Press, 2005. 227–229. Print.

Gates Jr., Henry Louis. "Preface to Blackness." *African American Literary Theory: A Reader.* Ed. Winston Napier. New York: New York UP, 2000. 147–64. Print.

Lewis, David Levering. *W. E. B. Du Bois: The Fight for Equality and the American Century 1919–1963.* New York: Henry Holt and Company, 1993. Print.

Locke, Alain. "Art or Propaganda?" *Harlem* Nov. 1928: 12. The New Negro: Readings on Race, Representations, and African American Culture 1892–1938. Eds. Gates, Henry Louis and Jarrett, Gene Andrew. New Jersey: Princeton University Press, 2007. 260. Print.

*Further Reading*

Du Bois, W. E. B. The Correspondence of W. E. B. Du Bois. *1, Selections, 1877–1934.* Ed. Herbert Aptheker. Amherst: U of Massachusetts P, 1973. Print.

———. *A W. E. B. Du Bois Reader.* Ed. Andrew G. Paschal. New York: MacMillan, 1971. Print.

Lewis, David Levering. *W. E. B. Du Bois: A Biography.* New York: Henry Holt and Company, 1993. Print.

Lewis, David Levering, and Deborah Willis. *A Small Nation of People: W. E. B. Du Bois and African American Portraits of Progress.* New York: Amistad, 2003. Print.

*Ron Horton*

# "FREUDIAN THEORY AND THE PATTERN OF FASCIST PROPAGANDA"

*Theodor W. Adorno*

✥ **Key Facts**

**Time Period:**
Mid-20th Century

**Genre:**
Essay

**Events:**
Rise of fascism in
Europe; World War II;
holocaust

**Nationality:**
German

## OVERVIEW

"Freudian Theory and the Pattern of Fascist Propaganda," an essay written by German sociologist, musicologist, and philosopher Theodor W. Adorno in 1951, uses psychology to explain the effectiveness of fascist propaganda. Writing in a dense and academic style, he connects propaganda to Freud's theories of group psychology. Adorno quotes heavily from Freudian theory to frame his analysis and focuses on propaganda's power to influence otherwise liberal-minded citizens to work against their own rational interests. He identifies a psychological basis for propaganda's successful appeal to the mob mentality, and he works toward a complex understanding of the power of group identification in an age when borders and identities had become very fluid.

Throughout the 1940s, Adorno focused on understanding fascism's success in Europe. "Freudian Theory and the Pattern of Fascist Propaganda" organizes this analysis into a working psychoanalytic system, although it was initially overlooked in favor of Adorno's larger-scale works. By distilling his observations into a single essay, Adorno sets the stage for a systematic understanding of how fascists were able to influence people on such a massive scale, the key being their exploitation of mass psychology through propaganda. Beneath successful forms of propaganda, he suggests, is a sort of psychoanalysis in reverse: they exploit an unconscious understanding of human psychology to override the individual ego in favor of a more primal group identity. Adorno focuses on fascism, but he notes that any movement could potentially make use of mass psychology. Thus, while this essay is principally a discourse on fascism, it is especially valuable today as a cipher to unlock the secrets of all forms of propaganda and the many forms of mass culture.

## HISTORICAL AND LITERARY CONTEXT

In the decades following World War I, Germany was required to pay steep reparations as a condition of their surrender. In an attempt to speed up the payment of reparations, the German government rapidly inflated its currency; this action, along with the privations of the worldwide Great Depression, led to a decade of extreme impoverishment. Many radical groups formed in these desperate times, including the Nazi Party. Aided in part by a powerful propaganda department and exploiting a strong current of nationalism, the Nazis eventually rose to prominence and consolidated their power soon thereafter. As part of their agenda, the Nazis began aggressively expanding their territory while imposing ever harsher restrictions on minority groups within it.

For German Marxists like Adorno, who was himself the son of an assimilated Jewish father, the rise of fascism was a matter of grave concern, even after the triumph of the Allies in World War II. The prototypical fascist success story may be the German Nazi Party, but even after the Nazis lost the war, fascism remained politically relevant in the early Cold War era as a form of opposition to communism. Adorno was concerned both with countering the potential of fascist propaganda and discrediting the ideology that drives fascism in the first place. In this essay, Adorno makes the case that fascism is a fundamentally irrational ideology. He lucidly describes the "irrational" appeal of fascist propaganda, and in doing so, he charts a way for antifascist forces to counter this appeal.

Adorno was a member of a group of social theorists collectively known as the Frankfurt school, so called because of its association with the Institute for Social Research at the University of Frankfurt. Although Marxist in orientation, members of the Frankfurt school were critical of Soviet-style communism and aware of the failures of strict Marxism when applied to developments of twentieth-century capitalism. The group's many famous theorists worked to expand Marxism by incorporating a variety of critical theories in their analyses: Walter Benjamin, author of "The Work of Art in the Age of Mechanical Reproduction," incorporated aesthetic theories in his work; Max Horkheimer, a notable collaborator of Adorno's, often borrowed from philosophy; and Leo Lowenthal integrated elements of Freudian psychology. Adorno incorporated elements from all of these theories and more in his wide-ranging criticisms.

Perhaps the most lasting contribution of "Freudian Theory and the Pattern of Fascist Propaganda" is the connection it forges between mass culture and propaganda. While Adorno begins this essay by commenting on the resemblance between American fascist groups and the vanquished Nazis, he soon hypothesizes that what propelled the Nazis to power was not unique to Nazis nor, for that matter, unique to fascism, but rather grounded in a mass culture driven by group psychology. Both Adorno and subsequent critics have expanded his methodology to help understand the forms and effects of mass culture. His influence can be seen today in the works of such scholars as philosopher and literary critic Umberto Eco, literary theorist Fredric Jameson, and cultural critic Slavoj Žižek, who in many cases share Adorno's insistence on the psychological power of mass culture.

## THEMES AND STYLE

Central to "Freudian Theory and the Pattern of Fascist Propaganda" is the tension between an individual's rational self-interest and propaganda's ability to circumvent that rational interest. Adorno seeks to understand "why modern men revert to patterns of behavior which flagrantly contradict their own rational level and the present stage of enlightened technological civilization" through an application of Freud's theories. The submission of the individual ego to the will of a fascist leader follows the contours of group psychology. In particular, "fascist agitation is centered in the idea of a leader" and "the mechanism which transforms libido into the bond between leader and followers, and between the followers themselves, is that of *identification*" between the leader and the follower. The leader need not be real; rather, the purpose of successful propaganda is to elicit psychological identification with an "enlargement of the subject's own personality, a collective projection of himself" onto any convenient figure.

Propaganda accomplishes this task by rhetorically placing audiences into artificial categories. Adorno notes that most masses begin as "the accidental crowds of the big city," whose lack of group identification makes "it imperative that discipline and coherence be stressed," effectively "making the crowds behave like the Army or Church," even when such hierarchies are unnecessary. Propaganda stresses hierarchy for its own sake and uses the "fetish" for "over-organization" to obscure any lack of natural identification between members of the crowd. Similarly, fascist propaganda creates and reifies "a division between believers and nonbelievers," which "acts as a negatively integrating force," tying a group together through a shared opposition to some arbitrary enemy. Through use of endless repetition, propaganda is able to drown out the normal meaning of certain words and phrases; when this happens, "language itself, devoid of rational signification, functions in a magical way and furthers those archaic regressions which reduce individuals to members of a crowd."

Stylistically, Adorno positions himself and his readers as key figures in the attempt to defeat fascist propaganda. The essay's observations are important

## COLLABORATIVE SCHOLARSHIP: ADORNO, HORKHEIMER, AND THE FRANKFURT SCHOOL

"Freudian Theory and the Pattern of Fascist Propaganda" opens with a footnote stating that "this article forms part of the author's continuing collaboration with Max Horkheimer." Like many of his Frankfurt school colleagues, Theodor Adorno constantly collaborated on his work; indeed, many of his most famous books and essays were actually collaborations with Horkheimer. Often operating on the cutting edge of psychology, philosophy, and social science, the members of the Frankfurt school would bring their specialty to bear on a larger topic and publish the results collectively.

Even when they were publishing separately, Frankfurt school academics shared their ideas and credits freely. Adorno's theories on mass culture are often described as "psychoanalysis in reverse," a phrase which captures how mass culture, like the practicing psychoanalyst, seeks to understand an individual's psychology and then, unlike a psychoanalyst, uses this knowledge to covertly exploit the individual. The phrase describes Adorno's theory so well that it is regularly attributed to him, but in reality the phrase was coined by another Frankfurt scholar, Leo Lowenthal. Adorno, ever the ethical scholar, uses the phrase in his own writings, but is always careful to credit Lowenthal for the "felicitous" expression.

because deployment of manipulative group psychology can be easily undermined simply by recognizing what is happening. Freud "defines the realm of psychology by the supremacy of the unconscious," meaning that by exposing the psychology—making the unconscious conscious—Adorno's essay will thus neutralize the power of fascist propaganda. Fascism presents its worldview as reality, burying its inherent irrationality under a psychological appeal. The historical effectiveness of this appeal means that similar methods can be used by any group to influence mass culture through advertising or Hollywood films; "even the most progressive political movement can deteriorate to the level of the 'psychology of the crowd' and its manipulation, if its own rational content is shattered through the reversion to blind power." Adorno's essay serves as a potent counterpoint to the forces of fascism and propaganda, ending with an idealistic assertion that his work will "in the end awaken those who keep their eyes shut though they are no longer asleep."

## CRITICAL DISCUSSION

Adorno's work on authoritarianism has proved to be among his most enduring contributions, although many in the English-speaking world have found his reliance on theory to be problematic. Writing in 1951, University of Chicago sociologist David Riesman noted that Adorno's work was the "highest and

Known for its use of propaganda, the German Nazi Party issued items such as this cigarette picture book depicting Hitler Youth Day in Potsdam, Germany, 1932. In "Freudian Theory and the Pattern of Fascist Propaganda" (1951), Theodor Adorno discusses the effect of propaganda on groups. HITLER YOUTH DAY, POTSDAM, 1932, FROM 'GERMANY AWAKENED,' 1931 (COLOUR LITHO), GERMAN SCHOOL, (20TH CENTURY)/ PRIVATE COLLECTION/THE STAPLETON COLLECTION/ THE BRIDGEMAN ART LIBRARY.

Reichsjugendtag Potsdam, 1932

most sophisticated level of research" and represented an "impressive attempt" to connect "large-scale and important theory to data which would support and demonstrate it." However, even in his larger-scale work, Adorno's reliance on abstract theories often conflicted with the fact that "society does not stand still," meaning that his theories should not be followed too strictly. Riesman also criticizes the equivalence Adorno draws between the Nazis and fascism in America, noting that fascism is but one of the possible forms of authoritarianism, and "the Puritan character, which qualifies in many ways as 'authoritarian,' actually helped foster a democratic social structure."

As part of Adorno's larger critical project, "Freudian Theory and the Pattern of Fascist Propaganda" is often cited less because of its insights into fascism than because of its insights into propaganda generally. Through the early twenty-first century, Adorno's work has been a touchstone for those seeking to understand how authority circulates and how to subvert this power. To that end, his work contributes to what Oskar Negt calls the "first groping efforts to establish a literary counter public sphere independent of the official publishing industry." As certain cultural forms become ever more pervasive and dominant, scholarly interest in Adorno's essay has only increased. Adorno's observations, written in the wake of the fascist triumph in Europe and the later defeat in World War II, have remained relevant because they help explain the nature of the dueling ideologies of the Cold War and the mass cultures of post-Cold War globalization.

"Freudian Theory and the Pattern of Fascist Propaganda" has become especially important in recent years as critical studies of mass cultural outlets like radio, television, and film have become more popular. For instance, several modern scholars have remarked upon the connection between political propaganda and the putatively apolitical mass culture industry. Robert Babe, for example, notes that "much of what Adorno has to say about fascist strategies of persuasion applies to contemporary commercial advertising." Likewise, Adorno's essay has been read by scholars such as scholar Gulshan Khan as the first instance in which the manipulation of mass psychology is shown to be "directly related to the declining autonomy and spontaneity of the individual in standardized mass culture."

## BIBLIOGRAPHY

*Sources*

Adorno, Theodore W. "Freudian Theory and the Pattern of Fascist Propaganda." *The Essential Frankfurt School Reader.* Ed. Andrew Arato and Eike Gebhardt. New York: Urizen, 1977. Print.

Babe, Robert. "Theodor Adorno and Dallas Smythe: Culture Industry/Consciousness Industry and the Political Economy of Media and Communication." *Revisiting the Frankfurt School: Essays on Culture, Media and Theory.* Ed. David Berry. Burlington: Ashgate, 2011. 91–116. Print.

Benjamin, Walter. *The Work of Art in the Age of Its Technological Reproducibility, and Other Writings on Media*. Cambridge: Harvard UP, 2008. Print.

Khan, Gulshan Ara. "Pluralisation: An Alternative to Hegemony." *British Journal of Politics & International Relations* 10.2 (2008): 194–209. *Academic Search Premier*. Web. 11 Aug. 2012.

Negt, Oskar. "Mass Media: Tools of Domination or Instruments of Liberation? Aspects of the Frankfurt School's Communications Analysis." *New German Critique* 14 (1978): 61–80. *Academic Search Premier*. Web. 2 Aug. 2012.

Riesman, David. "Some Observations on Social Science Research."*Antioch Review* 11(1951): 259–78. *Humanities & Social Sciences Index Retrospective: 1907–1984 (H. W. Wilson)*. Web. 1 Aug. 2012.

*Further Reading*

Adorno, Theodore W. "How to Look at Television." *Quarterly of Film Radio and Television* 8.3 (1954). 213–35. Print.

Comroff, Jean. "Populism and Late Liberalism: A Special Affinity?" *The ANNALS of the American Academy of Political and Social Science* 637.1 (2011). 99–111. *PsycINFO*. Web. 12 Sept. 2012.

Cook, Deborah. "The Rhetoric of Protest: Adorno on the Liberal Democratic Tradition." *Rethinking Marxism* 9.1 (1996). 58–78. Print.

Gagnier, Regenia. "Individualism, Civilization, and National Character in Market Democracies." *Sublime Economy*. Eds. Jack Amariglio, Joseph W. Childers, and Stephen E. Cullenberg. New York: Routledge, 2009. 153–71. Print.

Jacob, Preminda. *Celluloid Deities: The Visual Culture of Cinema and Politics in South India*. Lanham: Lexington, 2009. Print.

Pick, Daniel. "'In Pursuit of the Nazi Mind?' The Deployment of Psychoanalysis in the Allied Struggle against Germany." *Psychoanalysis and History* 11.2 (2009): 137–57. *PsycINFO*. Web. 1 Aug. 2012.

Sumpter, Caroline. "The Cheap Press and the 'Reading Crowd.'" *Media History* 12.3(2006): 233–52. *Communication & Mass Media Complete*. Web. 13 Aug. 2012.

Wheeler, Brett. "Antisemitism as Distorted Politics: Adorno on the Public Sphere." *Jewish Social Studies* 7.2 (2001). 114–48. *JSTOR*. Web. 15 Aug. 2012.

*Taylor Evans*

# GENERAL PLAN OF THE CONSTITUTION OF A PROTESTANT CONGREGATION OR SOCIETY FOR PROPAGATING CHRISTIAN KNOWLEDGE

*Thomas Bray*

✢ **Key Facts**

**Time Period:**
Late 17th Century

**Genre:**
Tract

**Events:**
Foundation of Anglican religious societies for the purpose of education and social reform

**Nationality:**
English

## OVERVIEW

The *General Plan of the Constitution of a Protestant Congregation or Society for Propagating Christian Knowledge* (1698), by Thomas Bray, lays out the organizational charter for the Society for Promoting Christian Knowledge (SPCK). Composed after the society's first meeting in 1698, the *General Plan* outlines the society's purpose under two simple headings. First, the society is to spread the knowledge of Anglican Christianity in the British colonies. Second, it is to educate British citizens about Anglican theology. The *General Plan* calls for the society to be composed of high-ranking clergymen and lay volunteers, and requires that the organization use its funds to support Christian missionaries and to establish Christian schools and libraries.

Although Bray was not the only founding member of the SPCK, the *General Plan* bears the hallmark of his guiding philosophy, which held that knowledge of Christian doctrine would result in godly living. An Anglican clergyman deeply concerned with the spread of orthodox Christianity, Bray was already popular in England for his *Catechetical Lectures* (1696), and in 1696 the bishop of London made him the first commissioner to Maryland. Worried for the religious well-being of Anglicans in England and in the colonies, Bray used his position as commissioner to bring together four other important men as the first members of the SPCK. As the formal statement of the SPCK's purpose, the *General Plan* combines the power of organized Anglicanism with Bray's desire to use education to promote moral living at home and abroad. The document provides the structure for one of the largest outpourings of Christian publishing and missionary work in modern history and marks the impetus for the creation of the oldest Anglican mission organization and the third-oldest publishing house in England.

## HISTORICAL AND LITERARY CONTEXT

In the mid-seventeenth century, religion in Europe was in turmoil. To counteract the loss of practical, everyday morality, German Christians created a series of biblical lectures at Frankfurt in 1670. The movement quickly attracted adherents, such as Anthony Horneck, who moved to England and in 1671 began to preach highly influential sermons in London. These sermons were the catalyst for the foundation of religious societies in London and Westminster in 1678. Early groups such as the Societies for Reformation of Manners were among the ancestors of the SPCK. In addition, Philipp Spener and Augustus Francke, the leaders of the original German coalition, were early correspondents with the SPCK.

Bray's *General Plan* encapsulates the philosophy at the heart of these societies: believers could live a moral life only if they were properly educated in the theological underpinnings of their faith. As a result of this philosophy, the SPCK sought to provide a unified theology that would guide believers to live upright lives. In particular, it responded to the Quakers, who rejected organized Christian doctrine for an "inner light." Thus Bray and his followers would have seen their educational work as the antidote to unorthodox Christianity and theological ignorance. Teaching the poor to read, providing libraries for clergy, and sending missionaries to Native Americans and Quakers were—in Bray's view—the best ways to promote order and moral living among laypeople.

Anglican religious societies in the late 1600s were deeply concerned by people's ignorance about the tenets of the faith. Preachers from these societies—such as Robert South, who decried British morals in his sermon at Westminster Abbey in 1692—painted vivid images of the evil state of the British people. To ameliorate the lack of theological knowledge and the resulting moral downslide, members of religious societies published books and pamphlets to educate clergy and laypeople. These texts zealously promoted the Book of Common Prayer and the Anglican catechism. Bray's own *Catechetical Lectures* was one such book, although he also carried his concerns about morality to the American colonies. His sermon *Apostolick Charity* (1697) was preached in London for missionaries who were sent to the colonies, and he composed a circular letter in 1699 to clergy in Maryland, which expounds upon these issues.

The *General Plan* gave this furor over moral laxity an organized application. On March 8, 1698, the

SPCK met for the first time. Before the society met, Bray had already composed the *General Plan* as the guidelines for the group. Two months after this meeting, Bray added the *Memorial*, which lists the specific actions that would be taken to implement the *General Plan* in the American colonies. With the *General Plan* as their directive, members of the society approached the archbishop of Canterbury and secured financial means to organize schools, establish libraries, and purchase and publish books. These actions occurred in rapid succession in the spring of 1698. Today the SPCK, which was formed by the *General Plan*, still functions as a branch of the Anglican Church.

## THEMES AND STYLE

At the heart of the *General Plan* is the goal of spreading education about Anglican Christianity in England and the American colonies. The *General Plan* calls for the organizational power of the Anglican Church to be mobilized to support these efforts. It states that the SPCK will consist of "clergy of the chiefest note" and of laypeople who are "eminent for their worth" and eager to uphold moral standards, thus making the SPCK a combination of official and lay efforts. Bray calls for the society to support missionaries to America and to create parochial libraries "in order to render both these Missionaries and all the other Clergy … useful and serviceable, in the propagation of the Christian Faith and Manners." Similarly, the *General Plan* declares that in Britain the SPCK will create libraries and that it will also establish schools so that children from impoverished families can learn to read, to write, and to understand Christian doctrine. As a result, the *General Plan* provides the framework for the SPCK's outreach. Its goal is to spread Christian education so that people will, on the basis of believing and understanding the faith, live upstanding moral lives.

After a two-part preamble, the *General Plan* begins with the section "As to the Plantations Abroad," which lists the four goals of the SPCK in the colonies. The plan's second half consists of the section "Propagating of Christian Knowledge at Home." Here, under three headings, Bray lays out the SPCK's plan in Britain. In both realms the SPCK's purpose, as stated by the plan, is to use "the best means and methods of promoting Religion and Learning." Importantly, it does not stop at establishing libraries but specifies that laypeople be given the tools they need—literacy and guidance from the clergy—to be able to use these libraries themselves. The plan, then, is not so much a specimen of propaganda by itself as a directive for spreading Christian ideas.

Stylistically the *General Plan* reads like a charter for a new corporation, elucidating its purpose in crisp, businesslike language. At the same time, several of its headings make clear that the author is motivated by charitable care for the well-being of laypeople. The third point of the section on spreading Christianity in the colonies is concerned with the support of

## THE SPCK: THOMAS BRAY'S LEGACY

After Thomas Bray died in 1730, the SPCK continued its work in the colonies and in England. Eventually the organization was split into several divisions, among them branches focused on the Americas, Scotland, and Wales. Each of these divisions continued to pursue the goals of the *General Plan* in its separate sphere. Today the SPCK works under three arms: publishing, worldwide, and diffusion. The SPCK's publishing house makes hundreds of titles available—not only those that fit with Anglican doctrine but also titles from other Protestant traditions as well as Catholicism. The society's worldwide branch provides teaching aids for educators in Latin America, Africa, and Asia, in a variety of translations. A more recent addition to the SPCK's mission, the diffusion branch, demonstrates the society's attempt to use emerging technologies to continue to promote Christianity. Literacy efforts in prisons are one of the newer avenues the SPCK currently pursues.

In each of these branches, the *General Plan*'s mandate to spread Christian theology through education and literacy continues to be the guiding philosophy. Like Bray, who was renowned during his lifetime for his theological and moral consistency, the SPCK has continued to pursue its original goals with little deviation from its original plan.

missionaries, who "shall most hazard their persons in attempting the conversion of the Negroes or native Indians." This goal of bringing Christianity and literacy to all people was radical for its time. The fourth point of this same section provides for "widows and orphans" of these mission workers, showing Bray's knowledge of the dangers present in the American colonies. Similarly, under the second section, the *General Plan* specifically states that libraries be given to "poor Clergy" and that "poor children" be the focus of the SPCK's schools. Although the plan at first glance seems to be impersonal, its major concern is to reach those who are poor or outcast.

## CRITICAL DISCUSSION

Created at the culmination of popular concern about public morality, the *General Plan* effectively mobilized the Anglican Church to carry out a project of religious education with the goal of reforming laypeople's morals and manners. The minutes from subsequent SPCK meetings describe in detail the steps that Bray and other founding members took to implement the plan. Almost immediately, as Bernard C. Steiner writes in an 1896 essay for the *American Historical Review*, Bray's "success in getting contributions for his libraries [was] marked," particularly in the colonies. Steiner lists thirty libraries that Bray established in America.

Because the *General Plan* is the original charter for the SPCK, it has far-reaching historical significance. In his essay Steiner mentions that the SPCK, still functioning under the goals enumerated by the plan, is "now … venerable and well known" as the

The seal of the Society for the Propagation of the Gospel in Foreign Parts on a stained glass church window in Hampton, Virginia. Anglican priest Thomas Bray helped found this missionary society and promoted missionary activities in his *General Plan of the Constitution of a Protestant Congregation or Society for Propagating Christian Knowledge* (1698). IPS LERNER/UIG VIA GETTY IMAGES.

founder of important public libraries in America. These libraries contained not only religious material but also books on science, ethics, politics, and law, among other "humane" subjects, as Steiner calls them. In a 1939 essay for *Pennsylvania Magazine of History and Biography* on Benjamin Franklin's work with the SPCK, Richard I. Shelling points out that Bray's goal included both poor whites in England and "the Negroes who lived in the British plantations." The *General Plan* thus provided for some of the first American public libraries and for the education of neglected social classes.

Although it is the backbone of an influential organization, the *General Plan* is seldom discussed as a document by itself. In fact, though it was originally published as a tract, printed editions of the *Plan* are difficult to find except as primary sources embedded in histories of the SPCK. Even these histories are outdated; as Isabel Rivers writes in her a 2007 essay for *Historical Journal,* "There is no full recent history of the largest and most important distributor of religious books in the eighteenth century, the Society for

Promoting Christian Knowledge." Aside from histories of the organization published in 1898 and 1959 and a study of eighteenth-century piety written in 1944, the plan's impact on popular publishing and religious education has been infrequently discussed. A few later articles mention the impact of Bray's libraries in British colonies and English parishes, but otherwise the SPCK and its founding document, the *General Plan,* remain untouched by modern scholars.

## BIBLIOGRAPHY

*Sources*

Allen, William Osborne Bird, and Edmund McClure. *Two Hundred Years: The History of the Society for Promoting Christian Knowledge, 1698–1898.* New York: Benjamin Franklin, 1970. Web. 21 Sept. 2012.

Lofaro, Michael A. "Thomas Bray." *American Colonial Writers, 1606–1734.* Ed. Emory Elliott. Dictionary of Literary Biography. Detroit: Gale Research, 1984. *Literature Resource Center.* Web. 21 Sept. 2012.

Rivers, Isabel. "The First Evangelical Tract Society." *Historical Journal* 50.1 (2007): 1–22. *JSTOR.* Web. 21 Sept. 2012.

Shelling, Richard I. "Benjamin Franklin and the Dr. Bray Associates." *Pennsylvania Magazine of History and Biography* 63.3 (1939): 282–93. *JSTOR.* Web. 21 Sept. 2012.

Steiner, Bernard C. "Rev. Thomas Bray and His American Libraries." *American Historical Review* 2.1 (1896): 59–75. *JSTOR.* Web. 21 Sept. 2012.

*Further Reading*

Clarke, W. K. Lowther. *Eighteenth Century Piety.* London: Society for Promoting Christian Knowledge, 1944. Print.

———. *A History of the S.P.C.K.* London: Society for Promoting Christian Knowledge, 1959. Print.

Frohnsdorff, Gregory. "'Before the Public': Some Early Libraries of Antigua." *Libraries and Culture* 38.1 (2003): 1–23. *JSTOR.* Web. 21 Sept. 2012.

Gray, Sarah, and Chris Baggs. "The English Parish Library: A Celebration of Diversity." *Libraries and Culture* 35.3 (2000): 414–33. *JSTOR.* Web. 21 Sept. 2012.

Mandelbrote, Scott. "The English Bible and Its Readers in the Eighteenth Century." *Books and Their Readers in Eighteenth-Century England: New Essays.* Ed. Isabel Rivers. London: Leicester UP, 2001. 47–50. *JSTOR.* Web. 21 Sept. 2012.

*Evelyn Reynolds*

# THE GULF WAR DID NOT TAKE PLACE

*Jean Baudrillard*

## OVERVIEW

*The Gulf War Did Not Take Place*, a trio of essays composed by Jean Baudrillard in 1991, argues that the American military assault on Iraq in February 1991 constituted not an actual war but a simulation of war. Pointing to the live but tightly sanitized television coverage, Baudrillard argues that the Gulf War was a simulacrum, an artificial spectacle in which reality has been confused and replaced by its representation. Pointing to the massive disparity between the United States and Iraq, in terms of military power, he argues that the "war was won in advance" and therefore took place only as a performance. Written in Baudrillard's simultaneously casual and erudite style, *The Gulf War Did Not Take Place* embraces logical contradiction in order to undermine the propagandistic nature of media's seemingly coherent but demonstrably false version of war.

*The Gulf War Did Not Take Place* first appeared as a series of articles in the French newspaper *Libération*. The first of these, "The Gulf War Will Not Take Place," appeared in January 1991 as British and American forces prepared to bomb Iraqi troops, which had invaded the neighboring country of Kuwait, a Western ally. The second article, "The Gulf War: Is It Really Taking Place?" appeared in February in the midst of the American campaign. A brief excerpt from the final article, "The Gulf War Did Not Take Place," was published in March after the Gulf War had ended. Later in 1991 the articles were expanded and collected in book form. At the time, Baudrillard was one of the West's foremost left-wing cultural critics and public intellectuals. As a result, his seemingly irrational denial of the war's existence drew a strong response. Many critics accused him of amorality and failing to engage with reality; others defended the text as an apt critique of postmodern culture.

## HISTORICAL AND LITERARY CONTEXT

Between 1980 and 1988, Iraq was engaged in a long war with Iran. According to Saddam Hussein, Iraq's longtime dictatorial president, the conflict with Iran was part of an effort to curb the threat of Islamic fundamentalism in the region. As a result of a perceived common strategic interest, the United States provided Hussein with military, technological, and economic support. Then, on July 21, 1990, after the end of the Iran-Iraq war, Hussein moved 30,000 troops to Iraq's border with the small, oil-rich state of Kuwait. The military aggression was an outcome of Kuwait allegedly driving down the price of oil, among other issues. Weeks later, Iraqi troops seized control of Kuwait. This alarmed many Western powers, which feared instability in the Middle East and the likelihood of increased oil prices, as Iraq and Kuwait controlled twenty percent of the world's known oil reserves.

By the time Baudrillard began writing the *The Gulf War Did Not Take Place,* the United Nations Security Council had authorized military action against Iraq if Hussein did not remove his troops from Kuwait by January 15, 1991. The collection's first article, "The Gulf War Will Not Take Place," appeared in print January 4. Within two weeks, American forces along with their British allies had begun bombing Iraqi troops in Kuwait, as well as installations in Baghdad. Over the next month and a half, the war was covered, for the first time, in live televised footage. The imagery, though, was tightly controlled and offered a sanitized, one-sided version of the conflict. As Paul Patton writes in his introduction to *The Gulf War Did Not Take Place,* "[W]hat we saw was for the most part a 'clean' war, with lots of pictures of weaponry, including the amazing footage from the nose cameras of 'smart bombs,' and relatively few images of human casualties, none from the Allied forces." Before, during, and after the war, Baudrillard's text offered a counternarrative to that of the American media and government.

*The Gulf War Did Not Take Place* emerged from a larger school of French poststructuralist philosophy and criticism that originated in the late 1960s. Led by such theorists as Jacques Derrida, Jacques Lacan, and Michel Foucault, poststructuralism was a wide-ranging movement that sought to interrogate the underlying structure of language, as well as other culturally determined systems of conveying meaning. Baudrillard first came to prominence in the 1970s for his analysis of capitalist consumerism in such books as *The Mirror of Production* (1975). In the 1980s, he began to focus on the nature of mass communication. In his book *Simulacra and Simulation* (1994), Baudrillard argues that the profusion of mass media in the contemporary, late-capitalist world has undermined the possibility of a stable, underlying reality; rather, all is a simulation of "a real without origin or reality:

### ✣ *Key Facts*

**Time Period:**
Late 20th Century

**Genre:**
Essay

**Events:**
Gulf War

**Nationality:**
French

# JEAN BAUDRILLARD: POSTMODERN PHILOSOPHER

Jean Baudrillard was born in 1929 in Reims, a city in the northwest of France. The son of working-class parents, he was the first in his family to attend university. At the Sorbonne in Paris, he studied German and began to write. After graduating, he worked as a writer and translator and then returned to school to earn his doctorate in sociology. He became a professor at the University of Paris at Nanterre. Massive student riots broke out in May 1968 at Nanterre and other French universities, and he became a member of the Situationist International, a radical left-wing group that sought the end of the capitalist status quo. That same year, his first book, *The System of Objects,* appeared.

Over the next two decades, he remained at Nanterre and wrote widely on politics, economics, semiotics, and culture. Profoundly influenced by Roland Barthes, Ferdinand de Saussure, Jacques Derrida, and other poststructuralists, Baudrillard examined throughout his long career the fraught relationship between signs and signifiers. While he began his career with an affinity to Marxist thought, he became increasingly critical of communist ideology over the course of his career, eventually arguing that Marxist economic theory ignored the significance of consumption. Although he left the university at Nanterre in 1987, Baudrillard retained his links to academia throughout his life, teaching at various other institutions and schools until his death in 2007.

a hyperreal." This allows, he argues, for the manipulation of reality by capitalist forces. These ideas proved central to the argument he made a decade later about the "un-reality" of the Gulf War.

Following the publication of *The Gulf War Did Not Take Place,* Baudrillard continued to write prolifically, publishing numerous texts on various subjects before his death in 2007. He also continued to explore the relationship between reality and militaristic violence. In November 2001 he wrote an article for the French newspaper *Le Monde* about the September 11 attacks on the World Trade Center, arguing that terrorists' actions "might be perceived (maybe with a certain relief) [as] a resurgence of the real, and of the violence of the real, in a supposedly virtual universe." However, he writes, the "violence is not 'real.' It is worse in a way: it is symbolic."

## THEMES AND STYLE

The central theme of *The Gulf War Did Not Take Place* is that the military conflict between the United States and Iraq in 1991 was essentially an artificial simulation. This simulation, Baudrillard argues, is a form of propaganda created through the complicity of governmental and media authorities. According to *The Gulf War Did Not Take Place,* the American air strikes on Iraq and Kuwait were not enacted to make military

or political gains but to manufacture a conception of reality that reinforces the necessity of the capitalist status quo. As Baudrillard writes in the text's second essay, "The media promotes the war, the war promotes the media, and advertising competes with war." This promotion, he argues, "devours our substance, but it also allows us to metabolize what we absorb, like a parasitic plant or intestinal flora, it allows us to turn the world and the violence of the world into a consumable substance."

In making his case for the necessity of exposing the constructed and artificial nature of reality, Baudrillard embraces irrationality and paradox as an antidote to the rationale of those in power. For example, the text's final essay, which appeared after the end of military operations, begins, "Since this war was won in advance, we will never know what it would have been like had it existed." In this sentence's first clause, Baudrillard seems to acknowledge the Gulf War's reality and the American victory in it; in the second clause, however, he declares that it never existed. This form of self-contradiction, which proliferates throughout the book, is indicative of Baudrillard's strategy of undermining the kind of logic upon which the government's and media's simulation of reality is founded.

Stylistically, *The Gulf War Did Not Take Place* is distinguished by an alternately casual and poetic tone that offers readers an alternative to the dominant mode of rational, authoritative discourse. The text's first essay begins in the first-person plural and establishes an affinity between Baudrillard and his reader: "From the beginning, we knew that this war would never happen." As the text proceeds, he employs poetic strategies that turn his often erudite argument into an accessible and engaging polemic. Of the UN's role in approving the American military campaign, he writes, "It is the bellicose equivalent of safe sex: make war like love with a condom!" Elsewhere, he declares that the war is a "virtualisation which is like a surgical operation, the aim of which is to present a face-lifted war, the cosmetically treated spectre of its death, and its even more deceptive televisual subterfuge." These metaphorical leaps allow Baudrillard to puncture the appearance of objectivity and inevitability manufactured by military and media officials in order to justify the war.

## CRITICAL DISCUSSION

When *The Gulf War Did Not Take Place* first appeared, it proved controversial. Among many, the idea of denying the reality of a very real war that caused massive casualties and destruction seemed callous. In the book *Uncritical Theory: Postmodernism, Intellectuals, and the Gulf War* (1992), scholar Christopher Norris offers a blunt, book-length critique of Baudrillard's argument, stating that Baudrillard's argument is not only "absurd" but it represents "the depth of ideological *complicity* that exists between such forms of extreme anti-realist or irrationalist doctrine and the crisis of moral and political nerve" among many left-wing intellectuals. Not all critics were so damning. Stephen Pfohl, in a review of the book's English translation, deemed it "provocative and politically challenging."

As part of Baudrillard's larger body of work, *The Gulf War Did Not Take Place* has been regarded as an important critique of the ways in which the mass media shapes not only public perception but also public policy. Other authors have taken up, in particular, Baudrillard's examination of the media's complicity in U.S. government propaganda about the Gulf War. Douglas Kellner, in his book *The Persian Gulf TV War* (1992), argues, "During the Gulf War, the mainstream media were cheerleaders and boosters for the Bush administration and Pentagon war policy, invariably putting the government 'spin' on information and events concerning the war." In the two decades since its appearance, Baudrillard's argument has continued to inform the way scholars and critics decipher late-capitalist constructions of political and cultural reality.

*The Gulf War Did Not Take Place* has attracted significant scholarly attention, much of which has considered the implications of Baudrillard's denial of the reality of the war. While Christopher Norris argues that Baudrillard's argument represents "degraded and debilitating aspects" of the present culture, others have defended his work. William Merrin in a 1994 article for *Economy and Society* argues, "Baudrillard has been vindicated, that the Gulf War did not take place and that it is continuing not to do so." Other commentators have considered Baudrillard's rhetorical strategy of rejecting the seemingly factual. As Kevin Robins writes in a 1993 article for *Media, Culture, and Society,* Baudrillard's book is "important because it directly confronts our rational pretensions. The scandal of Baudrillard is to distance himself from the cause of Reason."

## BIBLIOGRAPHY

*Sources*

Baudrillard, Jean. *The Gulf War Did Not Take Place.* Trans. Paul Patton. Bloomington: Indiana UP, 1995. Print.

———. *Simulacra and Simulation.* Trans. Sheila Faria Glaser. Ann Arbor: U of Michigan P, 1994. Print.

———. "The Spirit of Terrorism." Trans. Rachel Boul. *European Graduate School.* European Graduate School, n.d. Web. 31 Oct. 2012.

Dixon, Wheeler Winston. Rev. of *The Gulf War Did Not Take Place,* by Jean Baudrillard, and *The Phantom Empire,* by Geoffrey O'Brien. *Film Quarterly* 50.4 (1997): 54–55. *JSTOR.* Web. 31 Oct. 2012.

Gane, Mike, ed. *Jean Baudrillard.* Vol. 2. London: Sage, 2000. Print.

Merrin, William. "Uncritical Criticism: Norris, Baudrillard and the Gulf War." *Economy and Society* 23.4 (1994): 433–58. Print.

Norris, Christopher. *Uncritical Theory: Postmodernism, Intellectuals, and the Gulf War.* Amherst: U of Massachusetts P, 1992. Print.

Pfohl, Stephen. Rev. of *The Gulf War Did Not Take Place,* by Jean Baudrillard. *Contemporary Sociology* 26.2 (1997): 138–41. *JSTOR.* Web. 31 Oct. 2012.

Robins, Kevin. "The War, the Screen, the Crazy Dog and Poor Mankind." *Media, Culture, and Society* 15.2 (1993): 321–27. Print.

*Further Reading*

Baudrillard, Jean. *The Spirit of Terrorism: And Requiem for the Twin Towers.* London: Verso, 2002. Print.

Chesterman, Simon. "Ordering the New World: Violence and Its Re/Presentation in the Gulf War and Beyond." *Postmodern Culture* 8.3 (1998). *Project MUSE.* Web. 31 Oct. 2012.

Gane, Mike, ed. *Baudrillard Live: Selected Interviews.* London: Routledge, 1993. Print.

———. *Jean Baudrillard: A Critical Reader.* Oxford: Basil Blackwell, 1994. Print.

Kellner, Douglas. *The Persian Gulf TV War.* Boulder: Westview, 1992. Print.

Mowlana, H., G. Gerbner, and H. I. Schiller, eds. *Triumph of the Image: The Media's War in the Persian Gulf—A Global Perspective.* Boulder: Westview, 1992. Print.

Redfield, Marc. "Virtual Trauma: The Idiom of 9/11." *Diacritics* 37.1 (2007): 55–80. *Project MUSE.* Web. 31 Oct. 2012.

Rowe, John Carlos. "Culture, US Imperialism, and Globalization." *American Literary History* 16.4 (2004): 575–95. *Project MUSE.* Web. 31 Oct. 2012.

Sifry, Micah L., and Christopher Cerf. *The Gulf War Reader: History, Documents, Opinions.* New York: Times Books, 1991. Print.

*Theodore McDermott*

A group of young antiwar activists in 1991 protesting the media coverage of the Persian Gulf War. They are wearing sweatshirts decorated with the acronyms of major television broadcasting stations. Jean Baudrillard was also critical of the media's coverage of the war. © MARK PETERSON/ CORBIS.

# INSCRUTABILI DIVINAE PROVIDENTIAE ARCANO

*Pope Gregory XV*

## OVERVIEW

Written by Pope Gregory XV and issued on June 22, 1622, *Inscrutabili Divinae Providentiae Arcano,* a papal proclamation called a "bull," created a new group of officials to oversee the Catholic Church's missionary efforts around the world. Called the Congregation for the Propagation of the Faith, this group provided unifying guidance to the previously disparate collection of priests and monks who sought to convert the inhabitants of Europe, Asia, Africa, and the newly discovered Americas. By delineating the powers, funding, meeting protocols, and goals of the new group, Gregory's bull equipped the congregation to become an efficacious force within the church. Crucially, it also brought the Latin word *propaganda* into common parlance, linking it with the church's efforts to proselytize on a global scale.

With *Inscrutabili Divinae Providentiae Arcano* Gregory sought to reestablish church authority by creating a bureaucracy that would arrange for Catholic teaching to be promulgated around the world. The initial reaction to this mission was mixed. While most Catholics agreed that converting people in newly discovered lands (and reconverting newly Protestant countries) was a priority, specific groups of missionaries worried that their own authority would be curtailed and that the new supervisory group would hamper the arrangements they had already made. These fears were partly realized. With its unlimited powers of jurisdiction over the church in non-Catholic countries, the congregation quickly became one of the most powerful organizations within the Curia, the official governing body at the Vatican. Still functioning in the early twenty-first century, it has many responsibilities, including overseeing marriage law and annulments, religious education, and the translation of written materials. Its leader is nicknamed "the red pope," because he is the most powerful cardinal.

## HISTORICAL AND LITERARY CONTEXT

Starting in 1517, Martin Luther, a German priest, challenged the Catholic positions on salvation, church hierarchy, and the sacraments in a document that came to be known as Luther's Ninety-Five Theses, and northern Europe began to openly reject the Vatican's teachings. From 1545 to 1563, Catholics and their challengers met repeatedly in Trent, Italy, to negotiate

terms, but these meetings, collectively known as the Council of Trent, were fruitless and solidified the schism between the two parties. Galvanized by the council's work, popes in the late sixteenth century opened colleges and seminaries, reorganized the Curia, and created new editions of holy texts in order to reaffirm the dogma of Catholic teaching in the face of the reformers' movement.

Gregory wrote *Inscrutabili Divinae Providentiae Arcano* as part of the Counter-Reformation, or Catholic response to Luther's Ninety-Five Theses and other reformers' criticism, and it carries on the Catholic intellectual tradition that began at the Council of Trent. Another influence on Gregory in writing *Inscrutabili Divinae Providentiae Arcano* was the exploration of the New World. Predominantly Catholic countries, such as Spain, Portugal, and France, were sending expeditions to colonize North and South America, and missionaries accompanied the sailors and planters. In this context, Gregory's bull hints at the serious moral duty of the church to convert not only the natives of newly discovered lands but also the settlers who came from Protestant countries, bringing all souls into the fold of the universal church. As a piece of propaganda, the bull underscores that only the Catholic Church (under the leadership of Gregory XV) can safeguard these souls from the devilish ideas promulgated by other, rival institutions.

Although Gregory was pope only from 1621 to 1623, his bull is the culmination of a literary trend stretching back into the previous century. He drew the idea of a congregation from many sources, including a three-cardinal commission that operated under Gregory XIII and a 1613 book by Thomas à Jesu that presents a plan for a similar group. (This plan, in turn, is based on Antonio Possevino's reworking of a text by Jean Vendeville in 1577.) During the papacy of Gregory XV, the work of the congregation was also enabled and contextualized by a series of other bulls, including *Cum inter multiplices, Cum nuper,* and *Romanum decet,* which gives more details about the congregation's funding sources.

With a stunning level of power, the Congregation for the Propagation of the Faith became one of the most effective groups within the church. It weathered four centuries of reform movements, including the Second Vatican Council (1962–1965), and its notable alumni include Domenico di Gesù e Maria (general of the Discalced Carmelites), Cardinal Domenico Passionei, and Pope Benedict XVI. In 1982 it was renamed the Congregation for the Evangelization of Peoples, a title that minimizes its association with the concept of propaganda and clarifies its goal. In the early twenty-first century, it remains an organization that disseminates religious information and provides Catholic educational opportunities.

## THEMES AND STYLE

Written in Latin in an official Vatican style, with standard opening and closing formulae, *Inscrutabili Divinae Providentiae Arcano* develops the themes of pastoral care and the reunification of the global church. Seeking to bolster and consolidate the Vatican's position as the legitimate head of all Christian worship, the text makes pointed references to scripture and specifically invokes a vision sent to the disciple Peter (who is traditionally viewed as the first leader of the Catholic Church). Gregory presents the vision allegorically, as a command to convert "foolish, impious men from the four parts of the world," leading them to become observant Christians in the Roman style. While explaining this mission to "propagate" the faith worldwide, Gregory also highlights the pitfalls of the reformers' alternative tradition, using a Latin pun: Outside the Roman Church, helpless souls are being "perpetuated [propagari] for the eternal fires prepared by the Devil."

Throughout the brief text of the bull—which features a general introduction, a description of the new congregation's meeting procedures, and an inaugural list of members—Gregory uses the pronoun "we" to make two important points. First, he hints, the office of the pope remains powerful and important enough to use the royal "we," no matter what Protestant reformers may imply. Second, the idea of "we" underscores that the Catholic Church and its leadership function as one united community, with one mission-driven goal. The bull emphasizes this approach from its first sentence, which is addressed to the bishops of the church: "We who have been called to govern the office over which we have watched so attentively … recognize … that our duty is to lead the wretched and errant sheep back to the folds of Christ." This passage also initiates the use of the metaphor of sheep, deploying the biblical language of Jesus's parables to reaffirm the "pastoral" (or "shepherd-like") role of church officials in guiding the laity to embrace and to "propagate" Catholic teachings.

Stylistically, *Inscrutabili Divinae Providentiae Arcano* combines earnest zeal about theological matters with down-to-earth statements about meeting times and places. For example, Gregory recalls being "shaken by pity" as he considered the fate of the souls deluded by the Protestant reform movement. To the pope these souls have been "transformed into beasts," a propaganda-like statement that implies a strong bias against non-Catholic ways of life. This bias is underscored by other instances of severe language: Northern Europe,

## DISSEMINATING PROPAGANDA: THE POLYGLOT PRINTING PRESS

In order to create educational materials and religious texts for use in global missionary work, the Congregation for the Propagation of the Faith acquired a printing press in 1626. Capable of producing liturgies and catechisms in many different languages, the press was an uneasy reminder of bygone tensions. In the previous century, German priest Martin Luther and other reformers had stressed the need for bibles and devotional texts to be produced in the vernacular tongues instead of Latin. The papacy, however, resisted this idea, implying that lay people were incapable of correctly interpreting scripture on their own. With the purchase of the polyglot press, the congregation needed to readdress this issue and decide how best to reach and inform its global target audience. Its decision was a compromise of sorts. In 1631 a decree mandated that foreign-language editions of a text could be printed only alongside a Latin or Italian version of the same document.

In the meantime, the press helped the congregation to promote accessibility in a different way. Starting in 1629, it disseminated free religious materials that had been printed on the press. Although a few publications were sold in later years, the printing that supported missionary work remained free for many years.

for example, has been plagued by "weeds" and "infection" and is gradually becoming lost to "tyranny." In order to save all of the endangered souls in the world, Gregory reports, an organized bureaucracy is needed. By explaining the quotidian details of this bureaucracy, including its funding sources and a schedule for at least three meetings a month, Gregory underscores the link between larger theological concepts and seemingly minor everyday details, implying that the Catholic Church must mobilize on a bureaucratic level to support, defend, and embody its ideas.

## CRITICAL DISCUSSION

Pope Urban VIII, Gregory's papal successor, did much to codify and strengthen the dictates of *Inscrutabili Divinae Providentiae Arcano*. He decreed that the congregation's official rulings are as effective as the pope's, and in 1627 he established the Collegium Urbanum, a congregation-linked seminary. At this institution, scholars trained together, forming social bonds that provided support during years of missionary work. This college became a place where residents of non-Catholic or minimally Catholic countries could receive a religious education in Rome, furthering the mission of the congregation. Later popes, including Innocent X and Pius IX, seconded Urban's decisions, verifying the wide-ranging powers of the congregation to hear cases and issue binding official statements.

More broadly, Gregory's bull received mixed reviews. During the early twentieth century, scholars,

Portrait of Pope
Gregory XV by Guido
Reni. *PORTRAIT OF
POPE GREGORY XV*
(1554–1623) (OIL ON
CANVAS), RENI, GUIDO
(1575–1642)/CORSHAM
COURT, WILTSHIRE/THE
BRIDGEMAN ART LIBRARY.

Although the congregation was a trendy topic to study in the early twentieth century, with essays published on its history in German, Italian, and English, interest substantially declined in more recent years. In the late twentieth and early twenty-first centuries, many books and articles appeared that address aspects of missionary work in the early modern period, but these tend to focus on the interactions between missionaries and would-be converts. Nevertheless, a few works seek to clarify information about the founding and functioning of the congregation. For example, "Antonio Possevino's Plan for World Evangelization," an article written by John Patrick Donnelly in a 1988 issue of *Catholic Historical Review,* points out that Possevino played a vital role in transcribing and altering a text that contributed to the congregation's development.

## BIBLIOGRAPHY

### Sources

Benigni, Umberto. "Sacred Congregation of Propaganda." *The Catholic Encyclopedia.* Vol. 12. New York: Appleton, 1911. *New Advent.* Web. 20 Sept. 2012.

"The Congregation for the Evangelization of Peoples." *The Roman Curia.* The Vatican. Web. 20 Sept. 2012.

Donnelly, John Patrick. "Antonio Possevino's Plan for World Evangelization." *Catholic Historical Review* 74.2 (1988): 179–98. Print.

Egan, Bartholomew. "Notes on Propaganda Fide Printing-Press and Correspondence Concerning Francis Molloy, O.F.M." *Collectanea Hibernica* 2 (1959): 115–24. Print.

Griffin, Joseph A. "The Sacred Congregation de Propaganda Fide: Its Foundation and Historical Antecedents." *Christianity and Missions, 1450–1800.* Ed. J. S. Cummins. Aldershot: Ashgate, 1997. 57–95. Print.

### Further Reading

Borelli, John. "The Origins and Early Development of Interreligious Relations During the Century of the Church (1910–2010)." *U.S. Catholic Historian* 28.2 (2010): 81–105. Print.

McKevitt, Gerald. "Northwest Indian Evangelization by European Jesuits, 1841–1909." *Catholic Historical Review* 91.4 (2005): 688–713. Print.

Pasquier, Michael. "'Though Their Skin Remains Brown, I Hope Their Souls Will Soon Be White': Slavery, French Missionaries, and the Roman Catholic Priesthood in the American South, 1789–1865." *Church History* 77.2 (2008): 337–70. Print.

Stanley, Brian, ed. *Missions, Nationalism, and the End of Empire.* Grand Rapids: Eerdmans, 2003. Print.

*Nancy Simpson Younger*

such as Umberto Benigni and Joseph Griffin, praised the decisive nature of the congregation's creation, citing it as a turning point in church history. Griffin goes even further in an essay in the book, *Christianity and Missions, 1450–1800* (1997), calling the congregation "one of the greatest civilizing forces on earth." During the later years of the century, however, historians and church officials alike ceased using such descriptions. Instead, Catholics began to emphasize the congregation's desire to respect local traditions. To this end, the modern Vatican points out that *Instruction* of 1659, a document created by the Congregation for the Propagation of the Faith, demands that "indigenous clergy" should be promoted whenever possible, and that the congregation is committed to "inculturation," meaning that local customs must be preserved and respected, "except when they stood in opposition to faith or morals."

# MANUFACTURING CONSENT
## The Political Economy of the Mass Media
### Edward S. Herman, Noam Chomsky

## OVERVIEW

Published in 1988, Edward S. Herman and Noam Chomsky's *Manufacturing Consent: The Political Economy of the Mass Media* argues that American media coverage tends to reflect and cater to the dominant political and economic interests in the country—that it is, in effect, a system of propaganda. The book contains a theoretical chapter describing the "propaganda model" by which Herman and Chomsky argue the press functions, while subsequent chapters trace U.S. media coverage of events in several spheres—Central and South America, the Soviet bloc, Vietnam, and Laos and Cambodia—to present case studies in support of the validity of the model. The text provides insight into how "propaganda" might work systemically, less a production of intentional conspiracy and more an effect of social, political, and economic factors that impose filters and frames on the information disseminated.

Published near the end of the Ronald Reagan administration, Herman and Chomsky's theory was likely shaped by their own leftist politics—they famously denounced the Vietnam War and questioned the U.S. media's coverage of the Khmer Rouge in Cambodia. *Manufacturing Consent* equally reflects the authors' critical observation of press coverage of the Cold War arms race, the Iran-Contra scandal, and abuses in communist countries, especially in comparison to the relative lack of attention to human-rights abuses in U.S. client countries such as Israel, El Salvador, and Guatemala. Although often easily dismissed as conspiracy theory, the work's republication in 2002 and 2008 and its adaptation to documentary film in 1992 suggest its continued relevance; notably, the 2002 edition includes a forty-page introduction updating the propaganda model and *Manufacturing Consent*'s original case studies and applying the model to contemporary events. The theory continues to be both heavily critiqued and hotly defended.

## HISTORICAL AND LITERARY CONTEXT

*Manufacturing Consent* contains five chapters of historical case study, events whose media coverage shaped the development of the propaganda model. These chapters primarily examine media coverage of U.S.

foreign policy, which tends to support the current administration's course of action and present events in ways that foreclose avenues of dissent. For example, Herman and Chomsky's first case study compares negative media coverage of the Sandinista government in Nicaragua to more benign coverage of the oppressive, violent regimes contemporaneously operating in El Salvador and Guatemala; though Nicaraguans had more democratic freedoms, Herman and Chomsky argue that the Reagan government's disfavor colored media coverage of events in the country to portray the Sandinistas in an antidemocratic light. Similarly biased coverage of earlier conflicts including Vietnam equally informs the text.

Immediately prior to *Manufacturing Consent*'s publication, the Iran-Contra scandal of 1986 raised questions about U.S. foreign policy and government secrecy. In light of Iran-Contra, U.S. interventionist policies seemed too often motivated by self-interest, albeit veiled in rhetoric about global security, the protection of human rights, and the promotion and spread of democracy. In this atmosphere of mistrust, Herman and Chomsky's accusations of government influence on media coverage found audiences already suspicious of government secrecy. Moreover, in the academy, theories suggesting the malleability of individual identity and consciousness by social and systemic forces philosophically paved the way for *Manufacturing Consent*.

The 1920s "debate" between journalist Walter Lippmann and philosopher John Dewey over the role of journalism and expertise in participatory democracy supplies the title of Herman and Chomsky's text. The "manufacture of consent," the manipulation of the populace by leaders and the press, serves as a shared premise in the debate, just as passive, "mass society" media audiences form a core assumption of 1920s and '30s journalism theory. Herman and Chomsky reference these premises in exploring how the media is structured to manipulate audiences' views. While the Lippmann-Dewey debate is the most obvious antecedent of *Manufacturing Consent*, the work is also, according to Andrew Mullen in his 2010 article in *Media, Culture & Society*, philosophically indebted to the 1960s Marxist-radical theories of the role of media in the production of ideology, as well as to Foucauldian

### ❖ *Key Facts*

**Time Period:**
Late 20th Century

**Genre:**
Theory

**Events:**
Cold War arms race;
Nicaraguan Revolution;
Guatemalan Civil War;
Israeli invasions of
Lebanon; Iran-Contra
scandal; U.S. presidency
of Ronald Reagan

**Nationality:**
American

## THE EXPERTS ON EXPERTISE

The title *Manufacturing Consent* deliberately references Walter Lippmann's side of the Lippmann-Dewey debate, outlined in his *Public Opinion* (1922). Lippmann notes the threats to participatory democracy posed by the interaction of a self-interested, ill-informed public and a commercialized press. Public opinion, according to Lippmann, is not the result of rational processes but an imposition by leaders, a manufactured consent. Lippmann scorns idealistic conceptions of the press as informing the public to help them better participate in their own governance, positing instead that democracy would be better served by the creation of a class of scientific experts to mediate between government and populace. It is here that Dewey's opposition begins.

Herman and Chomsky—both PhDs, prominent intellectuals, prolific writers, and active participants in (and critics of) U.S. democratic processes—take the manufacture of consent as premise. They share Lippmann's skepticism about the press as the best avenue toward an informed public. Although perhaps not the kind of scientific experts Lippmann had in mind, it is possible they cast themselves in the role of the experts Lippmann prescribes to act on the public's behalf. And if so, this would open them to Dewey's attacks on the culture of expertise and the consecration of science as an ideology.

analyses of the interrelationships among power, knowledge, and discourse. Foucault's contention that power dichotomies are strengthened and naturalized through "knowledge," which is itself discursively constructed, informs much of the critical theory of the 1970s and '80s, an academic tradition to which Herman and Chomsky are heir.

Chomsky's *Necessary Illusions* (1989) predicted the legacy of the propaganda model: "One prediction of the model is that it will be effectively excluded from discussion…. Plainly, it is either valid or invalid. If invalid, it may be dismissed; if valid, it *will* be dismissed." Writers, including Mullen, who mourn a lack of attention to *Manufacturing Consent,* maintain that this prediction has come true. Yet though Mullen may argue that attention to the propaganda model has been insufficient and critiques unsubstantiated, his own article is proof of the work's continuing contentiousness. Although widely criticized, *Manufacturing Consent* has been equally passionately defended. It remains a polarizing text in media studies.

### THEMES AND STYLE

As their preface promises, Herman and Chomsky "sketch out a 'propaganda model' and apply it to the performance of the mass media of the United States." Their central claim is that media reports align with dominant market and government forces in the country. The press is essentially a self-censoring body that has internalized the desires and biases of powerful groups, and their reports reflect these biases. Journalism in this

light becomes propaganda. Still, media coverage is not a deliberate campaign of misinformation perpetrated by conspirators; rather, the way in which the media system is structured reinforces bias in favor of those in power and against dissenting views. The structure comprises five "filters" that effectively circumscribe media reports: (1) large, conglomerated mass-media owners who are necessarily oriented toward profit; (2) reliance on advertising revenue; (3) dependence on information from government and "experts" who reflect dominant power interests; (4) the need to avoid flak or negative responses to media coverage; and (5) anticommunism as the national ideology. Arguably the anticommunism filter has since been replaced by the "war on terror" as a defining patriotic discourse that, like the other filters, effectively frames media coverage of U.S. foreign policy and, in Herman and Chomsky's words, "filter[s] out the news fit to print, marginalize[s] dissent, and allow[s] the government and dominant private interests to get their messages across to the public." These filters are so naturalized as structural imperatives of the media system that they may not even be visible to the journalists themselves.

Stylistically *Manufacturing Consent* is thoroughly academic. It lays out the features of the authors' propaganda model, with a subsection describing each of the five filters, and then uses subsequent chapters to test this hypothetical model on several case studies, the results of which confirm the model's relevance and aptitude. The work contains numerous charts quantifying news reporting on issues ranging from elections in Nicaragua, Guatemala, and El Salvador to U.S. involvement in Vietnam. It also frequently calls attention to media silence or relative silence on issues and perspectives that might work against dominant interests. Herman and Chomsky make heavy use of research and example to support their assertions of media bias.

Still Herman and Chomsky have been taken to task for what Nina Eliasoph, writing for the *Journal of Broadcasting & Electronic Media,* calls their "self righteous writing style" and for writing "in the leaden prose of a sectarian tract." Nicholas Lemann concurs, noting in his review of the work for *New Republic* that the authors use "tabular lingo that is supposed to give their views the aura of scientific fact." Attacks on *Manufacturing Consent* get personal, as exemplified by a reviewer Jeffery Klaehn cites in his essay in *Journalism Studies* who suggests that Chomsky's "self interest … warp[ed his] … brilliant mind." The excessive virulence of such critiques might be seen as a fair indictment of poorly executed prose; then again, the persistence of interest in the work may suggest that such critiques are more an indication of how threatening the propaganda model is to the status quo. Insofar as Herman and Chomsky clearly and objectively trace the policing of dissenting voices in the media, their model predicts that their own work will be roundly criticized and even outright dismissed.

## CRITICAL DISCUSSION

Initial critical reaction to *Manufacturing Consent* runs the gamut: opponents (for example, Lemann) generally dismiss it as conspiracy theory, while celebrators consider it, as described by James R. Bennett in his review for *Contemporary Sociology,* a "book [that] will become required reading in journalism, communications, sociology, and political science departments." Middle-of-the-road reviews, such as Walter Laferber's, praise "the book's raw-data comparisons ... [as] compelling indictments of the news media's role in covering up errors and deceptions in American foreign policy of the past quarter-century" while lamenting its tendency to overstate Herman and Chomsky's case. In short, it is impossible to claim mostly praise or condemnation of the work; its most notable critical trend is divisiveness.

The film version of *Manufacturing Consent* testifies to the endurance of the propaganda model; similarly, the model's twentieth anniversary saw a republication of the text with a new afterword and a 2007 conference at the University of Windsor titled "20 Years of Propaganda? Critical Discussions and Evidence on the Ongoing Relevance of the Herman & Chomsky Propaganda Model." Moreover, works such as Klaehn's 2003 article "Behind the Invisible Curtain of Scholarly Criticism: Revisiting the Propaganda Model" reveal continued scholarly interest. Klaehn "considers several of the most prominent criticisms that have been leveled against the propaganda model and responds to each in turn." These criticisms include conspiracy theorizing, failure to theorize audience effects, taking for granted dominant-class interests and media audiences, and determinism. Klaehn attempts to reveal each critique as unfounded and thereby defend the relevance of the propaganda model.

The most prominent trend in criticism of *Manufacturing Consent* is the accusation by Lemann and others that it presents conspiracy theory. Klaehn counters that "the conspiracy theory label is a convenient means by which to dismiss the propaganda model and its explanatory logic out of hand." By Klaehn's account, to view media coverage as conspiracy, as subject to "secret controls that are divorced from normal institutional channels," is to miss the point entirely. It is precisely the "normal institutional channels" that filter and normalize news coverage in support of elite interests. Moreover, the model is systemic, meaning that it attributes responsibility to large, free-market forces rather than to scheming conspirators. Herman and Chomsky go to some trouble in their preface to present the same defense against conspiracy theorizing. Clearly their argument failed to persuade many critics, but readers might be well served by at least questioning the origins of their consent.

Noam Chomsky, author of *Manufacturing Consent,* photographed in 2011. © BERNAL REVERT/ALAMY

## BIBLIOGRAPHY

*Sources*

Bennett, James R. Rev. of *Manufacturing Consent: The Political Economy of the Mass Media,* by Edward S.

Herman and Noam Chomsky. *Contemporary Sociology* 18.6 (1989): 937–38. *JSTOR.* Web. 14 Oct. 2012.

Chomsky, Noam. *Necessary Illusions: Thought Control in Democratic Societies.* Cambridge: South End, 1989. Print.

Eliasoph, Nina. Rev. of *Manufacturing Consent: The Political Economy of the Mass Media,* by Edward S. Herman and Noam Chomsky. *Journal of Broadcasting & Electronic Media* 33.4 (1989): 468.

Herman, Edward S., and Noam Chomsky. *Manufacturing Consent: The Political Economy of the Mass Media.* New York: Pantheon, 1988. Print.

Klaehn, Jeffery. "Behind the Invisible Curtain of Scholarly Criticism: Revisiting the Propaganda Model." *Journalism Studies* 4.3 (2003): 359–69.

Laferber, Walter. Rev. of *Manufacturing Consent: The Political Economy of the Mass Media,* by Edward S. Herman and Noam Chomsky. *New York Times Book Review* 6 Nov. 1988: 27.

Lemann, Nicholas. "White House Watch." Rev. of *Manufacturing Consent: The Political Economy of the Mass Media,* by Edward S. Herman and Noam Chomsky. *New Republic* 9 Jan. 1989: 34–35.

Mullen, Andrew. "Twenty Years On: The Second-Order Prediction of the Herman-Chomsky Propaganda Model." *Media, Culture & Society* 32.4 (2010): 673–90. *Sage.* Web. 14 Oct. 2012.

*Further Reading*

Brahm, Noah Gabriel. "Understanding Noam Chomsky: A Reconsideration." *Critical Studies in Media Communication* 23.5 (2006): 453–61. Print.

Chomsky, Noam. *Letters from Lexington: Reflections on Propaganda*. Boulder: Paradigm, 2004. Print.

Klaehn, Jeffery. "A Critical Review and Assessment of Herman and Chomsky's 'Propaganda Model.'" *European Journal of Communication* 17.2 (2002): 147–82. Print.

Lang, Kurt, and Gladys Engel Lang. "Noam Chomsky and the Manufacture of Consent for American Foreign Policy." *Political Communication* 21.1 (2004): 93–101. Print.

*Media Adaptation*

*Manufacturing Consent: Noam Chomsky and the Media*. Dir. Mark Achbar and Peter Wintonick. Perf. Noam Chomsky, Mark Achbar, and Edward S. Herman. Zeitgeist Films, 1992. Film.

*Laura Johnson*

# MYTHOLOGIES

*Roland Barthes*

## OVERVIEW

*Mythologies* (1957) by Roland Barthes is a seminal, foundational work for the fields of semiotics (the study of signs) and cultural theory. It contains a collection of short essays analyzing various elements of popular French culture, followed by a longer, more theoretical essay explaining Barthes's semiotic approach to demythologizing contemporary "myths." The short essays are highly intelligent but not overly theoretical. They represent one of the earliest attempts to apply literary criticism to ostensibly nonliterary phenomena such as advertisements, news articles, and popular pastimes. In the book's final essay, "Myth Today," Barthes defines *myth* as the means through which the ideology of the dominant class is made to seem normal and natural. Barthes's semiotic approach to demythologizing has been widely employed to analyze not only the mechanics of blatant propaganda but also the inherent propagandistic elements in all popular media, particularly advertising.

The short essays in the first section of *Mythologies* were originally written between 1954 and 1956 as a series of articles for the literary magazine *Les LettresNouvelles*. The articles were popular, well received, and less academic in tone than Barthes's previous book on literary criticism, *Writing Degree Zero* (1953). *Mythologies* critiques the dominant influence of bourgeois, or upper middle-class, culture in France at the time. According to Barthes, contemporary advertisements and news journalism perpetuated an ideology that status quo values were simply the natural way of the world. *Mythologies* was widely read only after 1965, when Barthes came to national prominence as the result of his well-publicized conflict with the conservative literary critic Raymond Picard. To literary critics and semiologists, *Mythologies* is an important early example of structuralism and semiology. More broadly, the text became a touchstone for those who sought to analyze an increasing barrage of mass-mediated messages and advertisements.

## HISTORICAL AND LITERARY CONTEXT

After World War II, France's colonial empire gradually fell apart politically; however, the French ruling class sought to sustain France's influence abroad and to present its colonial presence as ethical, desirable, and natural. Economically, French consumer goods were being manufactured at increasingly affordable prices, leading to a proliferation of corporate advertising, marketing, and branding. These developments enticed Barthes to turn his critical semiotic attention away from literature and toward magazine advertisements and news stories about domestic and foreign politics.

In 1954 France lost its colonies in Indochina, and in 1956 it had to fight to maintain its control of the Suez Canal in Egypt. Both events occurred during the period when Barthes was writing the monthly essays that would constitute the first part of *Mythologies*. Barthes was further developing his own structuralist, semiotic form of literary criticism at the time. These monthly essays, in dialogue with immediately relevant popular media—including staged wrestling, laundry detergent advertisements, and news coverage of domestic affairs—provided Barthes with a series of case studies that allowed him to test and refine his demythologizing approach to media.

Several prior approaches to literary and cultural criticism inform *Mythologies,* including Karl Marx and Friedrich Engels's critique of ideology (*The German Ideology*; 1845), Ferdinand de Saussure's semiology, Freudian psychoanalysis, American New Criticism, and Jean Paul Sartre's existentialism (*What Is Literature*; 1949). Barthes synthesized and expanded these critical approaches into his own unique method of demythologizing—a kind of structuralist semiotics that could be applied to text or images. Much literary criticism prior to structuralism emphasized the author's intention and his own biographical circumstances. Structuralism challenged this emphasis and sought for an explanation of the work in the structure of the text. This approach led to an increased interest in the functioning of language itself. *Mythologies* became a key text in the development and popularization of structuralism.

*Mythologies* has subsequently influenced the fields of semiotics, literary criticism, media theory, and cultural studies. It established a novel connection among literary criticism, the study of signs, and popular culture. Academics and journalists have applied Barthes's method of demythologizing to a dizzying array of topics, such as cowboy hats, political press conferences, names of lipsticks, special effects in Asian movies, Word War II propaganda posters, the use of archive footage in television news bulletins, and

✣ *Key Facts*

**Time Period:**
Mid-20th Century

**Genre:**
Essays

**Events:**
Disintegration of French colonial empire; rise of advertising industry

**Nationality:**
French

# BARTHES'S "THE DEATH OF THE AUTHOR" (1967)

Ten years after *Mythologies,* Barthes wrote "The Death of the Author," arguably his most influential essay. The essay concludes with his famous statement that "the birth of the reader must be ransomed by the death of the Author." Barthes argues that the intention of the biographical author of a text is not as important as the reader's past experience with language and his or her current reading of the text itself. In this sense, the text is written by the reader, in conjunction with all the other texts the reader has ever read (because these previous texts influence the reader's understanding of what each word means in the current text). Because there are multiple readers and multiple readings and rereadings of any single text, a text may have multiple layers of meaning and multiple legitimate interpretations.

It is particularly ironic that much of the subsequent scholarly debate over the interpretation of Barthes's own corpus hinges on trying to discern Barthes's own "true" biographical opinion of his earlier work. Jacques Derrida honored the spirit of "The Death of the Author" by titling an essay he wrote upon Barthes's death "The Deaths of Roland Barthes." The implication is that there always were (and always will be) multiple ways of reading the texts of Barthes.

depictions of eating in silent films. *Mythologies* was also subsequently coopted by corporations as a tool to help them make more persuasive advertisements. Barthes himself later questioned the value of demythologizing when his insights were used only to construct more robust mythologies that were increasingly resistant to demythologizing.

## THEMES AND STYLE

In *Mythologies,* Barthes expands Saussure's basic explanation of the *sign* to encompass a new, "second-order" explanation of the *myth.* According to Saussure's system, a *signifier* (for example, the word *wine*) plus a *signified* (the idea of wine itself) equals a *sign* (a unified relationship between the sign and what it signifies—a meaning). Barthes then takes Saussure's unified *sign* to a second, even more abstract level of signification, the level of *myth* or *metalanguage.* According to Barthes's system, Saussure's first-order *sign* (the holistic meaning of wine) itself becomes a new second-order signifier, which then combines with a new second-order signified (the concept of French robustness) to equal a *myth* (the cultural signification of wine). Understanding Barthes's second-order, semiotic system is crucial to demythologizing advertisements, literature, and even objects themselves. In Barthes's system, the initial first-order signifier need not be a word. It may be an image or even a human behavior.

Although *Mythologies* is not explicitly a myth, Barthes later feared that the work may have become its

own myth. Barthes's goal is not to mythologize but to demythologize. He pays close attention to previously marginalized cultural details, frequently treating them with a detached playfulness but always and ultimately foregrounding the social implications of the myths he exposes. For example, regarding theatrical (staged) wrestling, Barthes acutely observes, "What the public wants is the image of passion, not passion itself." Structurally, the first section of *Mythologies* applies Barthes's semiotic method to several specific examples of cultural myths, while the final section explains the theory behind his method. In a sense, the acute insights of the initial, individual analyses prove the validity or at least the pragmatic usefulness of the theory.

In *Mythologies,* Barthes employs semiotic analysis not for its own sake but as a way of critiquing bourgeois ideology. Ultimately, Barthes's goal is to expose the ways in which semiotic myths function to perpetuate the ideology of the ruling class's status quo. He explains, "Bourgeois norms are experienced as the evident laws of a natural order—the further the bourgeois class propagates its representations, the more naturalized they become." Technically, myths use the self-evidence of the first-order sign (a photograph of a bottle of wine is obviously real) to naturalize the ideology of the second-order myth (there is nothing inherently "robust," "healthy," or even "French" about wine). Because both sign systems are in play at the same time, the consumer of the myth is unaware of these slippages and distortions. Barthes says, "*Myth hides nothing*: its function is to distort; not to make disappear…. Myth is neither a lie nor a confession: it is an inflexion." His focus on the semiotic function rather than the content of myth is the key to his ability to demythologize.

## CRITICAL DISCUSSION

As Barthes continued to alter his own position toward semiotics and structuralism between 1957 and his death in 1980, critical reaction to *Mythologies* and its role in Barthes's corpus shifted as well. In the mid-1960s Barthes's structuralism was mischaracterized and harshly attacked by Picard. However, by 1972 the literary critic Paul de Man was impressed with Barthes less as a structuralist emiotician than as a demythologist: "Barthes is primarily a critic of literary ideology and, as such, his work is more essayistic and reflective than it is technical." Barthes himself was constantly revising and undermining his own previous positions. Toward the end of *Mythologies,* he begins demythologizing his own practice, noting that demythology speaks its own kind of slippery, third-order metalanguage.

*Mythologies* has become more influential for its insightful critique of ideology than for its novel semiotic theory. Even so, in "Barthes's Relevance Today" (2008), the semiotician Harri Veivo states that "in teaching semiotics, Barthes's early *Mythologies,* despite the 51 years that separate the present from its publication, is hardly superseded as an introduction to critical social semiotic analysis." *Mythologies* establishes a precedence for critical, suspicious reading of both literature and media. Such critical reading is a precursor for cultural studies, media theory, and poststructuralist forms of literary criticism such as deconstruction.

Most Barthes scholars acknowledge two distinct periods in his writing: an earlier period marked by a focus on semiotics and structuralism—to which *Mythologies* belongs—and a later "literary" period, in which Barthes celebrates the difficulty, if not impossibility, of rigorous demythologizing. Nevertheless, there is disagreement on the relationship between these two periods. In his book *The Future of the Image* (2007), the philosopher Jacques Rancière suggests that Barthes had a reversal of heart and repented of semiology, "his sin of … having wished to strip the visible world of its glories, of having transformed its spectacles and pleasures into a great web of symptoms and a seedy exchange of signs." The literary theorist Jonathan Culler takes a different view, arguing in "Barthes, Theorist" (2001) that Barthes's semiotic phase is the more significant: "It is the early and middle Barthes and not the late, nostalgic or sentimental Barthes, to whom we should return." Finally, some critics see not a break but a continuation between the two periods: a transition from structuralism (an interrogation of language) to poststructuralism (an interrogation of structuralism itself). In *The Work of Mourning* (2001), Jacques Derrida finds the seeds of Barthes's abandonment of structuralism as early as *Writing Degree Zero*: "In this book of 1953 … the taking leave or the exit is underway." Elena Oxman, in her essay "Sensing the Image: Roland Barthes and the Affect of the Visual" (2010), suggests that "Barthes's later writings must be viewed … as a critique of the scientific assumptions that had driven his early work … as an 'attempt at self-criticism.'"

**BIBLIOGRAPHY**

*Sources*

Barthes, Roland. *Mythologies*. New York: Hill, 2012. Print.

Culler, Jonathan. "Barthes, Theorist." *Yale Journal of Criticism: Interpretation in the Humanities* 14.2 (2001): 439–46. *MLA International Bibliography.* Web. 11 Oct. 2012.

A girl playing with a doll. In his 1957 book *Mythologies,* Roland Barthes argues that children's toys precondition them to the gender roles that they will one day assume. © BEAU LARK/CORBIS.

De Man, Paul. "Roland Barthes and the Limits of Structuralism." *Yale French Studies* 77(1990): 177–90. *MLA International Bibliography.* Web. 11 Oct. 2012.

Derrida, Jacques. *The Work of Mourning.* Chicago: U of Chicago P, 2001. Print.

Oxman, Elena. "Sensing the Image: Roland Barthes and the Affect of the Visual." *Substance: A Review of Theory and Literary Criticism* 39.2 (2010): 71–90. *MLA International Bibliography.* Web. 11 Oct. 2012.

Rancière, Jacques. *The Future of the Image.* London: Verso, 2007. Print.

Veivo, Harri. "Barthes's Relevance Today." *Sign Systems Studies: An International Journal of Semiotics and Sign Processes in Culture and Nature* 36.1 (2008): 7–10. *MLA International Bibliography.* Web. 11 Oct. 2012.

*Further Reading*

Barthes, Roland. "The Death of the Author." *Aspen* 5–6 (1967). *UbuWeb.* UbuWeb. Web. 11 Oct. 2012.

———. *Writing Degree Zero.* New York: Hill, 1968. Print.

Culler, Jonathan D. *Barthes: A Very Short Introduction.* Oxford: Oxford UP, 2002. Print.

Sontag, Susan, ed. *A Barthes Reader.* New York: Hill, 1982. Print.

*Curt Cloninger*

# A New Look at the Language Question

*Tom Paulin*

✤ *Key Facts*

**Time Period:**
Late 20th Century

**Genre:**
Pamphlet

**Events:**
Hunger strikes at Maze Prison resulting in the deaths of Bobby Sands and nine other Republican political prisoners; violent conflict escalating between Loyalist and Republican paramilitary groups

**Nationality:**
Irish

## OVERVIEW

Tom Paulin's *A New Look at the Language Question* (1983), a pamphlet published by the Field Day Theatre Company in Derry, Northern Ireland, examines and promotes the precept that retention of distinctly Irish languages is crucial to the maintenance of Irish national identity. The document was the first in a series of fifteen pamphlets released by the company in an effort to articulate the theories put into practice by its plays. By citing Noah Webster's *Dictionary of American English,* as well as the emergence of Scottish and Canadian English dictionaries, Paulin eschews old antagonisms between Irish Gaelic and English to focus instead on separatist arguments for the recognition of what he calls "Hiberno English," or Irish English. In so doing he relates to British and unionist readers that the Field Day company supports efforts toward the formation of an independent, unified Ireland.

Although Paulin's pamphlet received little attention outside the theater's small but growing fan base, Field Day's body of work as a whole prompted an unprecedented level of peaceful public discourse surrounding issues of Irish identity. With the support and participation of such prominent nationalist figures as Seamus Deane and Seamus Heaney—both renowned authors and critics who would eventually serve on the theater company's board of directors with Paulin— Field Day's various projects cultivated a new understanding of the links between language, culture, and political power. Acting as a counterbalance to IRA violence throughout the 1980s, the Field Day enterprise spearheaded by Paulin's pamphlet signaled a shift in the tenor of the nationalist movement from militancy to cultural awareness.

## HISTORICAL AND LITERARY CONTEXT

The "language question" had been raised in Ireland since the Acts of Union in 1800, though the subject moved to the foreground of Irish nationalist concerns during the English ordnance surveys of Ireland in the 1830s and 1840s. The seemingly innocuous surveys of land recently incorporated under the English Parliament's control succeeded in replacing traditional Irish place names with anglicized versions and provided precise ordnance (artillery and explosives) coordinates to the English army. Many of the proponents of Irish language retention passed away in the Great Famine of the 1840s and 1850s, relegating the question to relative obscurity until the Gaelic revival at the end of the nineteenth century.

In 1980 Brian Friel produced the play *Translations,* the debut performance of the Field Day Theatre Company. The play reexamined the ordnance surveys, arguing in the process that neither a full transition to English nor a full reversion to Irish Gaelic would serve the interests of Ireland. Released three years later, Paulin's *A New Look at the Language Question* (1983) served as a companion piece to the play. It expanded on Friel's postulation that in order to remain relevant in an increasingly globalized world, the business of which was conducted predominantly in English, Ireland would have to find a place for both languages in defining its national identity. In Paulin's estimation, the standardization and recognition of a distinctly Irish dialect of English was a crucial step toward reconciling opposing camps within Ireland and toward emancipating Northern Ireland from British control.

The pamphleteering enacted by Paulin and Field Day drew on a rich tradition traceable most clearly to the Levellers and Diggers of 1640s England. The two groups, circulating pamphlets and declarations in support of an egalitarian English republic following the deposing of the monarchy in 1648, are often cited as the forebears of modern socialism, the manifesto as a form, and modern understandings of republicanism. Their ideas and methods found iteration in Ireland nearly a century and a half later through the United Irishmen, which in the 1790s lobbied against the proposed Acts of Union and for equal representation in Parliament. The Irishmen, and nearly every generation of nationalists who succeeded them, relied on the circulation of pamphlets as the primary means of dispatching their dictums and demands.

Paulin and his cohort at Field Day in their own pamphleteering attempted to reconcile a centuries-old tradition with a desire to advance more progressive nationalist tactics. Rather than setting down aims and goals in constitutional language as their forebears had, Field Day members used the pamphlet as a means to supplement their stage productions with elaborations of the linguistic and cultural theory examined therein. While the group's efforts have produced few tangible political results, the media attention the group received helped foster a renewed international interest in Irish culture.

## THEMES AND STYLE

Central to *A New Look at the Language Question* is the argument that both unionist and nationalist views of "the language question" are problematic. Paulin argues that "traditionally, a majority of Unionist Protestants have regarded the Irish language as belonging exclusively to Irish catholic culture," which he sees as emblematic of an "essentially racist ethic" at the heart of some unionist attitudes. Equally problematic, Paulin argues, is the rather "old-fashioned Nationalist concept of the 'pure Gael'" rooted in agrarian idealism, which he feels will render Ireland culturally obscure, if not obsolete, in an increasingly modern world. In Paulin's estimation the reconciliation of these two extremes lies in the recognition of a distinctly Irish dialect of English, which he claims "lives freely and spontaneously as speech" but "lacks any institutional existence and so is impoverished as a literary medium" for the expression of Irish identity.

Paulin's primary rhetorical strategy is to present a brief history of the English language to illustrate the roles it played in the establishment of an English national identity. He cites the Elizabethan and Jacobean periods as representing the "peak of creative power" for the English language, noting that writers of the period "formed sentences by instinct or guesswork rather than by stated rule." It is this creative power, he argues, that unified the English public into something resembling a nation of people rather than just a nation by law. The incorporation of this imaginative written language—previously encountered only in speech and regarded as base and barbarous—into standardized English dictionaries transformed them from book to "sacred natural object, one of the guardians of the nation's soul." Paulin holds the same to be true of American, Canadian, and Jamaican English dictionaries and insists that the establishment of such a volume for Irish dialects would galvanize the Irish public in a united front for national sovereignty.

Driving Paulin's arguments is a sense that language, government, and consent to be governed are inextricably linked. He surmises at one point that the main question the compiler of a dictionary should keep in mind is, "for what nation am I compiling this lexicon?" If the question is answered earnestly and from a place of great national pride, Paulin offers that the resultant work can become "the scholarly equivalent of an epic poem or of a prose epic like *Ulysses*." Somewhat anticlimactically, Paulin concludes in the closing passages that "the publication of *A Dictionary of Irish English* or the rewriting of the Irish Constitution" in a language other than standard British English "appear to be impossible in the present climate." The result, he submits almost in resignation, "is a living, but fragmented speech, untold numbers of homeless words, and an uncertain or a derelict prose" with which to articulate Irish identity.

# THE FIELD DAY PAMPHLETS

When the Field Day Theatre Company's board of directors (at the time composed of Tom Paulin, Seamus Deane, and Seamus Heaney) decided to publish a series of pamphlets expanding on the theoretical frameworks of their stage productions, critics were skeptical. Many theatergoers had been less than impressed with the brief theoretical materials included as program notes in the productions' playbills, and they surmised the pamphlets would contain more of the same. While some critics maintained their earlier skepticism, the series gained the favor of those who had been eager to support the company's messages and were hesitant only in supporting its methods.

The pamphlets were released in groups of three, with each series focusing on a single theme or issue of nationalist political theory. Published in 1983, the first three—Paulin's *A New Look at the Language Question,* Heaney's *An Open Letter,* and Deane's *Civilians and Barbarians*—looked at the language question, each adopting a different theoretical approach and tone. For instance, while Paulin's was more discursive and was presented in somber, academic prose, Heaney's was an ironic, self-deprecating epistolary poem written to the editors of a British poetry anthology, objecting that he was in fact Irish not British. Field Day has since embarked on other publishing projects, including a controversial anthology of Irish literature.

## CRITICAL DISCUSSION

Paulin's pamphlet received little to no critical attention upon its release, as they addressed much of what they had to say about the language question in their critiques of Brian Friel's *Translations*. Indeed, critical attention to Field Day's activities was predominantly reserved for the group's stage productions. Perhaps because of the political tension surrounding Field Day's work, particularly during the 1980s, which still saw significant violence from the IRA in Northern Ireland, substantive critical treatments of the theater's pamphlets did not begin surfacing until well after the last of the series had been published in 1988.

After Field Day's final stage production in 1989, critics and scholars began to examine the contributions of the project as a whole. By 2000 comprehensive treatments had emerged, with Marilynn Richtarik's *Acting Between the Lines: The Field Day Theatre Company and Irish Cultural Politics 1980–1984* being one of the most substantive. Richtarik suggests that—much as Field Day had likely planned—"the title of Paulin's pamphlet set the keynote for the entire series," with the phrase "the language question" implying "either a new vision of the Irish nation and its language, a critique of traditional Irish nationalism, or both." She further suggests that Paulin's "fascination with dialect" lends his arguments a decidedly separatist (or nationalist) bent. Indeed nationalism was at the foreground of Field Day's agenda. The group's efforts, as Richtarik

Photograph of Northern Irish writer Tom Paulin in 2008. DAVID LEVENSON/ GETTY IMAGES.

seems to agree, have helped foster a political environment in Northern Ireland more conducive to open dialogue than guerrilla violence.

Although scholars still afford relatively little attention to *A New Look at the Language Question* itself, treatments of the various Field Day projects have largely maintained Richtarik's stance. Tim Gauthier, writing for the *Companion to Brian Friel* (2002), asserts, "[T]he publication of the pamphlets had a profound effect on the ways in which the Field Day Theatre Company were perceived, its actions were construed, and its plays read." Without the pamphlets, spearheaded by Paulin's socio-linguistic treatise, the company's plays might have been found lacking in theoretical legitimacy. Gauthier notes, however, that many of Field

Day's critics have dismissed claims that the company was "opening up new channels for dialogue," insisting instead that across its various projects Field Day was merely "propounding old political views in new packages." Gauthier counters this view by offering that the rhetorical strength of the projects is located not in the novelty of Field Day's stances but in its willingness not only to hear but also to consider in earnest viewpoints other than its own—a quality most evident in the decision to finish the pamphlet series with three volumes written by non-Irish authors.

## BIBLIOGRAPHY

*Sources*

Gauthier, Tim. "Friel and Field Day: Field Day Pamphlets (1983–1988)." *Companion to Brian Friel* 32 (2002): 387–416. *Literary Reference Center.* Web. 10 Sept. 2012.

Paulin, Tom. *A New Look at the Language Question.* Derry: Field Day Theatre, 1983. Print.

Richtarik, Marilynn J. *Acting Between the Lines: The Field Day Theatre Company and Irish Cultural Politics 1980–1984.* Washington: Catholic U of America P, 2001. *Questia.* Web. 10 Sept. 2012.

Simon, Sherry, and Paul St-Pierre. *Changing the Terms: Translating in the Postcolonial Era.* Ottawa: U of Ottawa P, 2000. Web. 10 Sept. 2012.

*Further Reading*

Eagleton, Terry, Fredric Jameson, Edward W. Said, and Seamus Deane. *Nationalism, Colonialism, and Literature.* Minneapolis: U of Minnesota P, 1990. Print.

Friel, Brian. *Translations.* London: Faber & Faber, 1981. Print.

O'Malley, Aidan. *Field Day and the Translation of Irish Identities: Performing Contradictions.* Hampshire: Palgrave Macmillan, 2011. Print.

Paulin, Tom, and Sophocles. *The Riot Act: A Version of Sophocles'* Antigone. London: Faber and Faber, 1985. Print.

Richards, Shaun. *The Cambridge Companion to Twentieth-Century Irish Drama.* Cambridge: Cambridge UP, 2004. Print.

*Clint Garner*

# "THE PARANOID STYLE IN AMERICAN POLITICS"

*Richard Hofstadter*

## OVERVIEW

Richard Hofstadter's 1964 essay "The Paranoid Style in American Politics" is a seminal work of cultural and rhetorical analysis. The essay defines "the paranoid style"—a recurrent mode of American thought and discourse—through historical case studies. Hofstadter's examples range from eighteenth- and nineteenth-century conspiracy movements to the conservatism of his time in the mid-twentieth century. "The Paranoid Style in American Politics" soberly diagnoses the type of "overheated, oversuspicious, overaggressive, grandiose, and apocalyptic" discourse that Hofstadter claims has episodically animated American politics, especially in periods of "ethnic and religious conflicts." In so doing, it has served as an important resource for rhetoricians and historians studying the effects and effectiveness of such dialogue.

"The Paranoid Style in American Politics" was adapted from a lecture that Hofstadter, already a two-time Pulitzer Prize recipient, delivered at Oxford in 1963. It appeared in *Harper's* in 1964, and Hofstadter included it as the title essay of a book he published in 1965. Although the essay was controversial—particularly among liberals who resented Hofstadter's contention that the paranoid style is not limited to the right wing—it was generally well received. It is still cited as a potent critique of American conservatism and a foundational text in conspiracy theory rhetoric. In 2010 *Newsweek* placed *The Paranoid Style in American Politics and Other Essays* on a must-read list that the magazine described as "a sort of literary road map to the most important stories of the moment, as explained by some of the best minds in their diverse fields." Similarly, a 2008 piece in *The Wall Street Journal* listed Hofstadter's collection as one of the five best books on conspiracy thinking.

## HISTORICAL AND LITERARY CONTEXT

Events in the decades before the essay's publication had predisposed Americans to anticommunist paranoia and prompted an outpouring of conspiracy rhetoric. From the socialist leanings of Franklin Delano Roosevelt's New Deal to the Korean War to China's adoption of communism to the rise of the Soviet Union, circumstances both at home and abroad seemed to substantiate anticommunist anxieties, culminating with one of the most infamous conspiracy theories:

Joseph McCarthy's allegations in the early 1950s of communist infiltration of the U.S. State Department. Indeed, Hofstadter was afforded numerous contemporary examples of the ability of conspiracy theories to gain adherents, and he sought to expose these theories as an important trend in American thought.

The most immediate example was the rise of Barry Goldwater, who easily won the 1964 Republican presidential nomination on a surge of conservative popularity. Hofstadter argues in his essay that Goldwaterism was the latest manifestation of a paranoid tendency in the American political landscape. Although he traces this mindset back to eighteenth-century American mistrust of the Bavarian Illuminati and nineteenth-century anti-Masonism and anti-Catholicism, he sees twentieth-century right-wing political rhetoric as a unique instance of the paranoid style. The rhetoric of his contemporaries was, Hofstadter writes, "more vivid," their writings more "personal," and their proponents more "mainstream" than was the case with previous conspiracy theorists. Whereas past movements had often concerned themselves with conspiracies that had begun abroad, American anticommunists focused on enemies who were local, a twist that added an element of betrayal to the paranoid style. What's more, their rhetoric was more apocalyptic than previous instances of the paranoid style in that it positioned the United States and its values as already undermined and weakened by enemy forces, to the point that reclaiming these virtues would necessitate an epic battle of good versus evil.

"The Paranoid Style in American Politics" fits solidly in Hofstadter's oeuvre. His Pulitzer-winning *The Age of Reform* (1956) and *Anti-Intellectualism in American Life* (1963) both exhibit a similar desire to examine the American social and cultural landscape. Although Hofstadter has been criticized for using the psychological term "paranoia" without concern for its clinical definition, his forays into psychology provide insights into the social history of the United States that might not otherwise be gleaned. Hofstadter generally offers big-picture cultural analyses—he is less concerned with the archival minutiae of historical research than with drawing overarching conclusions that can be broadly applied.

Due in part to "The Paranoid Style in American Politics," Hofstadter is widely viewed as an innovator

### Key Facts

**Time Period:**
Mid-20th Century

**Genre:**
Essay

**Events:**
Korean War; McCarthyism; rise to prominence of Barry Goldwater

**Nationality:**
American

# PARANOIA IN CONTEXT: RICHARD HOFSTADTER'S OTHER WORKS

To understand "The Paranoid Style in American Politics," it is useful to consider the overarching scope of Richard Hofstadter's other writings, which include *Social Darwinism in American Thought, 1860–1915* (1944), *The Age of Reform* (1955), and *Anti-Intellectualism in American Life* (1963). In all of these works, Hofstadter borrows concepts from other fields to shed light on historical events. For example, he delves into ideas from literary studies such as irony and paradox, cultural forces from anthropology such as myth and tradition, and notions from psychology such as anxiety and the unconscious.

Whereas prior historians had placed much emphasis on economic circumstances and class conflict as influences, Hofstadter concerns himself with making broad claims about the American zeitgeist as it has shifted, transformed, and reiterated itself over time. Similarly, whereas historians have traditionally engaged in detailed archival study to draw conclusions, Hofstadter develops big-picture perspectives on political events and movements, and is known for a writing style that is engaging without being consumed with scholarly detail, an approach that has been widely critiqued.

in historiography. As A. E. Campbell writes in a revised edition of *The Paranoid Style in American Politics and Other Essays,* his "emphasis on symbolism and myth-making, on the emotional forces in political life" became "almost the orthodoxy of the most gifted American historians." His books are still widely read, often serving as broad-based cultural studies that are cited to buttress analyses of conspiracy theories or anti-intellectual movements both contemporary and past. Furthermore, they are held up as examples of engaging scholarly writing.

## THEMES AND STYLE

The main thrust of "The Paranoid Style in American Politics" is the prevalence of conspiracy theorizing in American political discourse. The paranoid style, which Hofstadter describes as "a way of seeing the world and of expressing oneself," is a fundamental, "ineradicable" aspect of American identity, a mode of discourse through which "movements of suspicious discontent" call attention to "the existence of vast, insidious, preternaturally effective international conspiratorial network[s] designed to perpetrate acts of the most fiendish character." Examining multiple episodes throughout American history, he distills the essential characteristics of conspiracy propaganda.

The major case study Hofstadter uses to achieve the essay's rhetorical effect involves the mid-twentieth-century preoccupation with communism and intellectualism as threats to "[t]he old American virtues"—"competitive capitalism" and "national security and

independence." Whereas past conspiracy movements had been seen as originating in Europe, this one, according to Hofstadter, "also embraces betrayal at home." He lays out three central elements cited by theorists to support the presence of a conspiracy: (1) a widespread plot to install federal controls of the economy and make the United States socialist or communist, (2) powerful American political leaders who are in on the plot, and (3) "a network of Communist agents" in the United States controlling "education, religion, the press, and the mass media" in a way that has brainwashed American citizens.

Using examples such as the hysteria over communism, Hofstadter systematically identifies characteristics of "the paranoid style," a multilayered definition that is the most widely cited part of his essay. He observes that the rhetoric of various conspiracy theories has some common themes. The first involves the depth of the conspiracy, which is presented by a paranoid spokesperson as so deeply entrenched that it necessitates "an all-out crusade." Like millenarian rhetoric, paranoid rhetoric pinpoints the present moment as critical in the fight against the enemy forces. Another theme is the power of the conspirators, who are portrayed as brainwashing the populace by hijacking systems such as education, religion, and the media. Defeating these enemies will require brute force, and no compromise is permissible. A third theme is the paranoid spokesperson's collection of evidence regarding the particular conspiracy. The spokesperson "carefully and all but obsessively accumulates 'evidence'" of the conspiracy. Ironically, Hofstadter notes, the paranoid style presents the world as cleaner and more controlled than it actually is, since all events can be traced to the deliberate, premeditated actions of the conspirators.

## CRITICAL DISCUSSION

As Monika Bauerlein and Clara Jeffery write in a 2010 essay for *Mother Jones,* Hofstadter's work became "an instant classic—not because it was so elegantly written, but because in just a few pages it described with deadly accuracy one of the major strains of our national dialogue." Nevertheless, many conservatives were put off by Hofstadter's leftist position. Other critics questioned his credibility in diagnosing paranoia, given his lack of training in psychology. However, a majority of reviewers felt that the essay, in keeping with Hofstadter's reputation, provided keen insights into America's ideological history and served as a conceptual tool that would inform future analyses.

Although Hofstadter was well known before the publication of "The Paranoid Style in American Politics," the essay increased his fame, and it remains one of the works for which he is best remembered. In the essay, he codifies a definition of conspiracy discourse that has subsequently been broadly applied. This resonance can be seen in references to his work in publications ranging from *The Wall Street Journal* to *Newsweek.* Moreover, Hofstadter's definition of conspiracy rhetoric

Senator Barry Goldwater speaks to a crowd in Raleigh, North Carolina, during his presidential campaign on September 17, 1964. Richard Hofstadter wrote "The Paranoid Style in American Politics" as Goldwater and other conservatives were taking control of the Republican Party. AP PHOTO.

has been applied to a wide variety of people and topics—from slavery and Watergate to Al Gore and Rush Limbaugh. The 9/11 attacks also spawned a large outpouring of conspiracy theories, which led to more Hofstadter citations from cultural critics, a testament to the continued relevance of his work.

Hofstadter's application of social psychology to history has been frequently adopted by historians, though his legacy has spread beyond the field of history. He is also viewed as an early exemplar of a now prolific subfield that examines conspiracy rhetoric. On a political level, his work is often seen as providing a negative view of American conservatism and creating a legacy of diagnosing, or pathologizing, conservatism that continues today. According to Gerald Russello in a 2012 review for *Academic Questions,* this legacy "is largely devoted to figuring out where conservatives 'come from' and treats the conservatives' concern about liberty versus order, or the claims of tradition, as the result of something else: displacement by modernity, for example, or a 'situationist' ideology" that often traces conservatism back to "some form of extremism." In short, "The Paranoid Style in American Politics" has widened the gap between left and right in the United States and encouraged the alignment of intellectualism and leftist politics.

**BIBLIOGRAPHY**

*Sources*

Bauerlein, Monika, and Clara Jeffery. "Patriot Games: From Blowhardery to Nihilism to … Treason?" *Mother Jones* Mar. 2010: 4. *General OneFile.* Web. 14 Sept. 2012.

Campbell, A. E. Rev. of *The Paranoid Style in American Politics and Other Essays,* by Richard Hofstadter. *International Affairs* July 1967: 615–16. *JSTOR.* Web. 14 Sept. 2012.

Hofstadter, Richard. *The Paranoid Style in American Politics and Other Essays.* Cambridge: Harvard UP, 1965. Print.

Holland, Max. "Five Best." *Wall Street Journal* 2 Feb. 2008: W8. Web. 14 Sept. 2012.

Russello, Gerald. "Conservatism under Academic Scrutiny." Rev. of *The Paranoid Style in American Politics and Other Essays,* by Richard Hofstadter. *Academic Questions* 25.1 (2012): 174–81.

"What You Need to Read." *Newsweek* 9 Aug. 2010: 52–55.

*Further Reading*

Barkun, Michael. *A Culture of Conspiracy: Apocalyptic Visions in Contemporary America.* Berkeley: U of California P, 2003. Print.

Brown, David S. *Richard Hofstadter: An Intellectual Biography.* Chicago: U of Chicago P, 2006. Print.

Eysenck, H. J. Rev. of *The Paranoid Style in American Politics and Other Essays,* by Richard Hofstadter. *Political Science Quarterly* 81.4 (1966): 645–46. *JSTOR.* Web. 14 Sept. 2012.

Fenster, Mark. *Conspiracy Theories: Secrecy and Power in American Culture.* Minneapolis: U of Minnesota P, 1999. Print.

Frank, Thomas. "From John Birchers to Birthers." *Wall Street Journal* 21 Oct. 2009: A21.

Hayes, Christopher. "9/11: The Roots of Paranoia." *Nation* 25 Dec. 2006: 11–14.

Hofstadter, Richard. *Anti-Intellectualism in American Life.* New York: Vintage, 1963. Print.

*Laura Johnson*

# "POLITICS AND THE ENGLISH LANGUAGE"

*George Orwell*

## OVERVIEW

The essay "Politics and the English Language," by English author and journalist George Orwell (the pen name of Eric Arthur Blair), was published in 1946. In it, Orwell correlates what he sees as the corruption of modern English with the corruption of critical thinking skills, which ultimately leads to corrupt governments like the fictional totalitarian state he wrote about in *Nineteen Eighty-Four* (1949) or the very real Fascists he fought against in the Spanish Civil War of the 1930s. The essay champions plain language and original imagery over florid prose and stale metaphors, identifying offenses common to each of the latter and offering six concrete rules for eliminating such faults from one's own writing. Because Orwell ties imprecise language to political barbarisms, the essay is often seen as an attack on propagandists and apologists—liberal and conservative alike—who may use abstract terms like *liberate* or *pacify* as political cover for committing atrocities around the world.

Published in the literary journal *Horizon* in April 1946, "Politics and the English Language" appeared just eight months after the end of World War II, when much of the world was wondering how the political crisis in Europe had been allowed to escalate to such dire proportions. Orwell placed the blame on lazy thinking caused by an inadequate understanding of language and its impact, writing, "One ought to recognize that the present political chaos is connected with the decay of language, and that one can probably bring about some improvement by starting at the verbal end." Unsurprisingly, "Politics and the English Language" was enthusiastically received by English teachers, who likewise believed in the power of language studies to foster creativity, individualism, and critical thought. It became a staple in college composition courses almost overnight. The essay has been at the center of numerous academic debates about the nature of language over the years and remains a powerful statement on the power of words. Orville Schell, in his introduction to *What Orwell Didn't Know: Propaganda and the New Face of American Politics,* calls it "one of our most durable literary monuments on language and propaganda."

## HISTORICAL AND LITERARY CONTEXT

Orwell served in the Indian Imperial Police in the British colony of Burma (now Myanmar) in the 1920s, when the British Empire still controlled numerous Asian states. His experiences led him to reevaluate the meaning of government aims to "civilize" or "modernize" a people through force. He left the Imperial Police in 1927 and began his career as a writer, penning a number of articles on social issues like free speech, workers' rights, and poverty. He became an ardent socialist and outspoken critic of fascism in the 1930s, traveling to Spain in 1936 in support of the socialist Republicans and their fight against Francisco Franco's fascist regime.

During World War II, Orwell worked for the British Broadcasting Company (BBC), writing and broadcasting wartime propaganda, euphemistically referred to as "news commentaries," from 1941 to 1943. The experience gave him extensive insight into the process of manipulating language to gain political influence, and upon his resignation he set to work on a series of essays that explored how propaganda could be so influential while in fact saying so little. In "Propaganda and Demotic Speech" (1944) he decries political language's "remoteness from the average man," a problem he seeks to rectify in "Politics and the English Language." Orwell's other essays of the period, including "The Prevention of Literature" (1946) and "Writers and Leviathan" (1948), advance similar arguments, the former attacking "the organized lying practiced by totalitarian states" and the latter, the dangers of "yielding oneself over to orthodoxies and 'party lines.'"

Orwell went on to expound upon his ideas about the relationship between muddy language and the abuse of political power in his celebrated novel *Nineteen Eighty-Four* (1949), which features a totalitarian government that forces its citizens to use a modified form of English called Newspeak. As Orwell explains in an appendix to the novel, "Newspeak was designed not to extend but to diminish the range of thought, and this purpose was indirectly assisted by cutting the choice of words down to a minimum." While "Politics and the English Language" advocates the use of simplified language, it does so in order to promote the expression of ideas in a clear and straightforward manner, to "let the meaning choose the word and not the other way around." Newspeak, on the other hand, imposes "ready-made phrases" that "think your thoughts for you."

"Politics and the English Language" is Orwell's most widely read nonfiction work. Its interrelated

### ✦ Key Facts

**Time Period:**
Mid-19th Century

**Genre:**
Essay

**Events:**
Spanish Civil War; World War II; growth of propaganda

**Nationality:**
English

# ORWELL THE PROPAGANDIST

Operating under his given name of Eric Blair and under the designated staff number 9889, George Orwell worked with the BBC's Eastern Service to provide morale-boosting entertainment and education to British soldiers stationed in India during World War II. From August 1941 to November 1943, he served first as talks assistant and then talks producer, writing, coordinating, and appearing in news programs and literary discussions known as "cultural broadcasts" that were intended to counter German propaganda efforts in the area. Though he was opposed to British rule in India—a conclusion he reached after serving as a colonial policeman in Burma—Orwell took the job partly in response to his dismay at having been rejected for military service due to a lung condition and partly in the hope that he might contribute to the ultimate downfall of fascism in Europe.

As documents released by the BBC show, Orwell was highly praised by his superiors, and he appeared to find great satisfaction in his work, often inviting fellow writers, including T. S. Eliot, E. M. Forster, and William Empson, to contribute to his programs. When he left the BBC in 1943, his resignation letter noted that he had never once been forced to say anything over the air that he would not say privately, but his journals and letters of the time paint a different picture, often acknowledging that he was contradicting his socialist beliefs by serving under an imperialist government. In later years he would denounce his work for the BBC entirely as "bilge," but the fact remains that one of the world's great literary opponents of propaganda was at one time himself a propagandist.

concerns of establishing rules for good writing and beginning the process of "political regeneration" in a period marked by international conflict and social unrest have made the essay influential in the fields of both politics and literature. Though it was initially perceived as common-sense writing advice, academic debates in the 1970s and 1980s over whether words could be said to have objectively "true" meanings brought the essay under increased scrutiny. Those who argued that words held inherent meanings found solace in Orwell's insistence that one must first conceive of a "concrete object" and then "find the exact word that seems to fit it." American poet Wendell Berry's 1980 essay "Standing by Words" is often seen as an extension of Orwell's argument in "Politics and the English Language," adapted to respond to the language debates of the time.

## THEMES AND STYLE

Orwell's aim in "Politics and the English Language" is a simple one, but its ramifications are far-reaching. He is primarily concerned with bad writing habits, but as he explains in the introductory paragraph, "If one gets rid of these habits one can think more clearly, and to think clearly is a necessary first step toward political regeneration: so that the fight against bad English

is not frivolous and is not the exclusive concern of professional writers." The essay deftly connects its practical writing tips to the fight against what Orwell views as a dangerous trend toward an unthinking, robotic society that would be susceptible to the will of despots. "This reduced state of consciousness," he warned, "if not indispensable, is at any rate favourable to political conformity."

Orwell reinforces his assertion that abstruse writing is a sign of unclear thinking by grounding his essay in concrete examples rather than generalizations and broad claims. In order to buffer himself from charges that his essay was motivated by ideology or political dogmatism, the examples he chooses to represent the most egregious faults committed by contemporary writers do not come from right-wing politicians and speechmakers, but from figures on the left, such as Professor Harold Laski, who was chairman of the socialist-leaning Labour Party at the time the essay was written, and Professor Lancelot Hogben, who was also active in the Labour Party. Another example is taken from an anonymous Communist pamphlet. The one example of good writing that he does provide is a passage from the biblical book of Ecclesiastes, a source considered unassailable by some, and which likewise presents itself as offering objective truths for those who care to listen.

Orwell aligns himself in the essay with common, everyday people and makes the mealy-mouthed intellectual and the soulless politician his primary targets, portraying the former as "some comfortable English professor defending Russian totalitarianism" and the latter as "some tired hack on the platform mechanically repeating the familiar phrases." Although Orwell was himself closer to being "some comfortable English professor" than the ordinary people with whom he identified himself, much of the essay is written in conversational vernacular, which at first appears to be the logical result of a writer following his own advice. But the apparent effortlessness of his language, as is the case with the works of many argumentative writers and speakers dating back to Socrates, is in fact a conscious strategy to gain the assent of his readers. As John Rodden writes in *The Unexamined Orwell*, "The plain style of 'Politics and the English Language' masks an intricate art of argumentation. ... It is a writing strategy that demands consummate mastery of the language."

## CRITICAL DISCUSSION

"Politics and the English Language" was published in a relatively obscure literary journal during the period between the publication of Orwell's most famous and well-received works of fiction. After *Animal Farm* and *Nineteen Eighty-Four* were established as major literary works, and particularly after the author's death in 1950, critics began to take a closer look at some of his lesser-known essays, articles, and stories. When the essay was included in the posthumous anthology *A Collection of Essays* (1954), it was mostly cited as an apt teaching tool, with reviewer Mary Hazard singling it out as "a model of prose analysis."

As Orwell's stature continued to grow throughout the twentieth century, based largely on the seemingly endless relevance of his dystopian view of society, critical esteem of "Politics and the English Language" grew with it. Events like the Vietnam War underscored the essay's political dimensions, as phrases like "defenseless villages are bombarded from the air, the inhabitants driven out into the countryside, the cattle machine-gunned, the huts set on fire with incendiary bullets: this is called *pacification*" eerily conveyed both the carnage taking place in Southeast Asia and the rhetoric used to justify it. As literary theory emerged as an important academic discipline, however, some scholars began to dismiss the work as overly simplistic and dismissive of nuanced thought. Carl Freedman, in particular, sparked controversy by attacking the essay as "false and dangerous" and complaining of its "dogmatic evasion of complexity." Such critiques gained momentum throughout the 1980s, and by the time of the fiftieth anniversary of the essay's publication, critics who still found Orwell's insight to be of value to the budding writer were on the defensive. As Sanford Pinsker lamented in 1997, "Orwell has a hard time passing muster among the composition theory crowd."

Nevertheless, Orwell remains one of the most influential and widely read authors of the twentieth century, and "Politics and the English Language" is counted among his most significant works of nonfiction. Lynn Z. Bloom placed the essay on a list of "extremely popular canonical essays" in 1999, noting that the work had been reprinted in major essay anthologies no less than 118 times in a forty-four-year period. It should come as no surprise that the essay has retained its relevance in the twenty-first century, for as long as individuals and nations are willing to go to war on behalf of abstract notions of duty and patriotism, there will always be those who seek to gain political influence and control behind a mask of what Orwell calls "euphemism, question-begging and sheer cloudy vagueness."

## BIBLIOGRAPHY

### Sources

Bloom, Lynn Z. "The Essay Canon." *College English* 61.4 (1999): 401–30. Print.

Freedman, Carl. "Writing, Ideology, and Politics: Orwell's 'Politics and the English Language' and English Composition." *College English* 43.4 (1981): 327–40. Print.

Hazard, Mary E. "Bargain Books." Rev. of *A Collection of Essays*, by George Orwell. *Clearing House* 34.7 (1960): 445. Print.

George Orwell in about 1949. © EVERETT COLLECTION INC./ALAMY.

Pinsker, Sanford. "Musing about Orwell's 'Politics and the English Language'—50 Years Later." *Virginia Quarterly Review* 73.1 (1997): 57–71. Print.

Rodden, John. "Literacy and the English Language." *The Unexamined Orwell*. Austin: U of Texas P, 2011. 245–52. Print.

Schell, Orville. "Follies of Orthodoxy." Introduction. *What Orwell Didn't Know: Propaganda and the New Face of American Politics*. Ed. András Szántó. New York: Public Affairs, 2007. xvii–xxxi. Print.

### Further Reading

Berry, Wendell. "Standing by Words." *Hudson Review* 33.4 (1980–81): 489–521. Print.

Carr, Craig L. *Orwell, Politics, and Power*. New York: Continuum, 2010. Print.

Gallant, James. "War within War: The Weapon of Language in the Sixties." *Worcester Review* 5 (1982): 16–21. Print.

Goodheart, Eugene. "Orwell and the Bad Writing Controversy." *CLIO* 28.4 (1999): 439–43. Print.

Kingsbury, Melinda Spencer. "Orwell's Ideology of Style: From 'Politics and the English Language' to *1984*." *Journal of Kentucky Studies* 19 (2002): 108–13. Print.

Rai, Alok. "The Roads to Airstrip One." *Orwell and the Politics of Despair: A Critical Study of the Writings of George Orwell*. Cambridge: Cambridge UP, 1990. 113–49. Print.

Reznikov, Andrei. *George Orwell's Theory of Language*. San Jose: Writers Club, 2001. Print.

*Jacob Schmitt*

# THE PRINCE

*Niccolò Machiavelli*

## OVERVIEW

Since its first printing during the early part of the sixteenth century, Niccolò Machiavelli's *The Prince,* or *Il Principe* in its original Italian, has been one of the world's best-known and most fervently debated political treatises. From correspondence, historians believe an original version of the work was distributed in 1513, though its initial formal publication was not until 1532, five years after the author's death. Sometimes called the first work of "modern" sociopolitical philosophy, it is written in the form of direct, pragmatic instruction on strategy and conduct to the political rulers of its time. The book's endorsement of immoral and often ruthless means to achieve political goals has in modern times made the author's name synonymous with greed, cynicism, and a hunger for power. *The Prince*'s focus on despotism has also prompted some philosophers and historians to theorize that it is actually a work of satire, or at least a cautionary tale meant to instruct people on how to avoid the perils of authoritarian rule. Today, politicians and policies that are seen as particularly cruel, dishonest, or cunning are sometimes labeled "Machiavellian."

Written in the first person and originally published in vernacular Italian rather than formal Latin, *The Prince*'s concentration on realism and "effective truth" over ethics and idealism quickly set it apart from previous prominent social doctrines. Machiavelli writes that in order to establish and hold on to power, a "new prince" must maintain a virtuous public image while doing whatever it takes behind the scenes to bend his peers and subjects to his will. Today the book is commonly associated with the often-quoted political quandary of whether "the end justifies the means." Though Machiavelli was often openly disdainful of "philosophical inquiry"—preferring to focus instead on real-world experiences and examples—he nonetheless is considered an innovative and important sociopolitical philosopher and is credited with contributing to a number of areas of modern Western thought.

## HISTORICAL AND LITERARY CONTEXT

Machiavelli served as an envoy for the Republic of Florence during the early 1500s, traveling extensively throughout Italy and France while earning a reputation as a keen judge of both people and political organizations. After the fall of the republic in 1512, he was imprisoned and tortured for a short time before being exiled to a farm outside the city. Once there, he turned his attention more seriously toward writing, and references to *The Prince* began to appear in his correspondence within a year.

Perhaps desperate to regain his standing in government, Machiavelli personally dedicated *The Prince* to Florence's incoming ruling family, presenting it as a book of advice for the "new princes" on the most effective ways to establish and maintain power over the long term. The book appeared at a time of considerable political upheaval in Europe, so Machiavelli's ideas about personal preservation, as well as his endorsement of a strong, durable state, may have been particularly attractive to Italy's new regime and to leaders around the continent.

Before publication of *The Prince,* political theorists—many of whom were funded by the Catholic Church—largely urged leaders to value virtue above all else. It was commonly held that kings who desired long, prosperous reigns and the ability to pass their offices on to their children should strive to be benevolent, thereby earning the trust of their subjects and the right to rule through moral decency. Machiavelli proved to be inventive as one of the first who dared to criticize this notion, shunning the concept of a connection between morality and the ability to rule. Instead, he argues in *The Prince* that the only way to differentiate between legitimate and illegitimate uses of power is through real-world results (in other words, success or failure) and that the only true concerns of a new prince should be "maintaining the state" and protecting his personal influence.

Though debate still rages over how to interpret many of Machiavelli's theories, he is often viewed as an important link between "ancient" and "modern" political thought. As one of the first philosophers to address what he saw as the role of true human nature in politics and to argue that the legitimacy of a government's laws rests entirely upon its ability to enforce them, he brought new and controversial areas of inquiry to the field of political theory. His apparent support of brutal and dishonest practices in *The Prince* has tantalized, frustrated, and angered scholars, sparking debate and discussion that continues to this day. In many ways, the theories presented in the book have come to symbolize everything detractors view as wrong with modern politics. Nonetheless, Machiavelli's provocative stance on leadership and power continues to make him one of the most discussed political theorists in both academia and popular culture.

## THEMES AND STYLE

Textbook-style royal advice manuals (or "mirror of princes" books, as they were known) were a popular form of political writing during the Middle Ages and the Renaissance. But *The Prince* may have been the first to comment so frankly on the human condition and the nature of power. Throughout the work, Machiavelli argues that authority stems only from a leader's ability to maintain it, by force if necessary. Fear, he writes, is preferable to admiration or approval in order for a prince to keep his subjects in line, and violence and dishonesty are more effective than legality and transparency in the interest of maintaining the state.

> "One can say this in general of men," he writes, "they are ungrateful, disloyal, insincere and deceitful, timid of danger and avid of profit … Love is a bond of obligation which these miserable creatures break whenever it suits them to do so; but fear holds them fast by a dread of punishment that never passes."

Throughout *The Prince*, Machiavelli employs a direct rhetorical strategy, offering clear and bold instructions to the rulers of his day. In discussions of the work as propaganda, it should be noted that *The Prince* differs in several basic ways from what we have come to view as "propaganda" today. Machiavelli lived at a time when only select members of the ruling class were expected to be literate, and though advances in printing technology began to speed the dissemination of news and ideas during the Renaissance, it is unlikely he ever expected his work to reach the general population. Because his writing was intended solely for a small audience of powerful men, he does not attempt to engage the lower classes at all. He also does not mince words or employ more modern literary techniques such as symbolism or narrative. Instead, he delivers his message as succinctly as possible.

Because he is writing only for people in power, Machiavelli makes no attempt to soften or camouflage the message of *The Prince*. In fact, it is exactly his insistence on realism and his seemingly callous endorsement of tyranny that have made him such a notable figure in political theory. His language reflects the direct and somewhat removed tone of a teacher lecturing a student. Centuries later, Machiavelli's writing was described by *New York Times Review of Books* writer Isaiah Berlin as "singularly lucid, succinct, and pungent—a model of clear Renaissance prose."

## CRITICAL DISCUSSION

Machiavelli initially dedicated *The Prince* to two specific members of Florence's new ruling family, but there is some doubt among modern scholars about whether either would have actually read it. Since the book was

# HOW DID MACHIAVELLI'S IMPRISONMENT INFLUENCE *THE PRINCE?*

Niccolò Machiavelli was forty-three years old when he wrote *The Prince*, considerably late in life for a Renaissance man and career public servant to begin extolling the virtues of iron-fisted autocratic rule. Given the circumstances of his own imprisonment, torture, and eventual banishment by Florence's ruling Medici family less than a year before the completion of the book, historians naturally assume a correlation between the two.

Machiavelli's family had been prominent in Florence since the thirteenth century. But after he was jailed and interrogated under suspicion of plotting against the Medicis in early 1513, he was reduced to poverty, living on a small farm outside Florence and working in a tavern. Since Machiavelli had dedicated his life to serving the republic, it is easy to assume that he was drawing on personal experience (albeit perhaps bitterly) when he advised in *The Prince* that high moral character and righteousness matter little in determining a politician's success.

Amid his personal ruin, historians believe Machiavelli purposefully crafted *The Prince* to be provocative in order to curry favor with the Medici family. Those who consider the work to be either simple pandering or deft satire bolster their arguments by pointing out the obvious gulf between Machiavelli's career in republican politics and the tyrannical theories expressed in the book. Whether Machiavelli had truly lost faith in the idea of the republic or wrote *The Prince* as a sly parody of Italian politics remains up for debate, though his later writings in *Discourses on the First Ten Books of Livy* have a far more republican slant.

not widely distributed until after the author's death in 1527, nearly all the immense critical discussion of his work has taken place posthumously. According to the *Cambridge Companion to Machiavelli*, he was largely denounced during the latter part of the sixteenth century as an "atheist and defender of tyranny." The first criticism of the book, written by Cardinal Reginald Pole in 1539, even charges that *The Prince* was written "by Satan's own hand," and by 1559, Machiavelli's name had been added to the list of authors banned by the Catholic Church. By the seventeenth century, however, scholarly questions about the book's true intent, coupled with further analysis of the more republican focus of his later works, began to foster significant disagreement about Machiavelli himself and what he truly had hoped to accomplish with *The Prince*.

Critical response to the book has been divided throughout history. As early as the late 1500s, well-known scholars of philosophy and international law such as Alberico Gentili had begun to believe Machiavelli meant *The Prince* as a scathing satire aimed at Italian politics. This argument has been echoed by numerous subsequent critics, among

Portrait of Cesare Borgia and Niccolò Machiavelli talking to Cardinal Pedro Loys Borgia and his secretary. MONDADORI PORTFOLIO/ELECTA/ART RESOURCE, NY.

them twentieth-century historian and Pulitzer Prize-winning author Garrett Mattingly, who contends that Machiavelli could not have actually meant what he wrote in *The Prince*. Philosophers such as Baruch Spinoza (1632–1677) and Jean-Jacques Rousseau (1712–1778), meanwhile, portray the book as a warning about the actions of tyrants and an aid in resisting authoritarian regimes. Still others have been content to merely take the work at face value and continue to indict it as a cynical and cold-blooded endorsement of oppression.

The passage of time has done little to quell debates about *The Prince*. In popular discussion, Machiavelli is seldom given credit as a satirist or even as a particularly nuanced political thinker. His name is typically evoked pejoratively in order to criticize modern Western politicians who seem to lack empathy for the people they govern. In a 2005 essay titled "Machiavelli and U.S. Politics," Lawrence M. Ludlow even argues that *The Prince* "neatly characterize[s] the behavior of most U.S. politicians for the past century." Regardless of—or perhaps because of—the scholarly disagreement surrounding *The Prince*, Machiavelli's theories continue to be discussed and viewed as relevant centuries after his death. As Berlin writes: "There is something surprising about the sheer number of interpretations of

Machiavelli's political opinions. There exist, even now, over a score of leading theories of how to interpret *The Prince*. ... There is evidently something peculiarly disturbing about what Machiavelli said or implied, something that has caused profound and lasting uneasiness."

## BIBLIOGRAPHY

*Sources*

Berlin, Isaiah. "The Question of Machiavelli." *New York Times Review of Books* 4 Nov. 1971: 20–32. Web. 12 July 2012.

Ludlow, Lawrence M. "Machiavelli and U.S. Politics. Part 1: Pattern and Perception." *The Future of Freedom Foundation*. 15 Aug. 2005. Web. 12 July 2012.

Najemy, John M., ed. *The Cambridge Companion to Machiavelli*. New York: Cambridge UP of New York, 2010. Print.

Nederman, Cary. "Nicolò Machiavelli." *The Stanford Encyclopedia of Philosophy*, 2009. Web. 12 July 2012.

*Further Reading*

Anglo, Sydney. *Machiavelli: The First Century*. Oxford: Oxford UP, 2005. Print.

Cassirer, Ernst. *The Myth of the State*. New Haven: Yale UP, 1946. Print.

DeGrazia, Sebastian. *Machiavelli in Hell,* Princeton: Princeton UP, 1989. Print.

Deitz, Mary. "Trapping the Prince: Machiavelli and the Politics of Deception." *American Political Science Review* 80 (1986): 777–799. Print.

Femia, J. V. *Machiavelli Revisited.* Cardiff: U of Wales P, 2004. Print.

Machiavelli, Niccolo. *Discourses on the First Decade of Titus Livius.* Project Gutenberg, 2004. Web. 15 July 2012.

Mattingly, Garrett. "Machiavelli's Prince: Political Science or Political Satire?" *The American Scholar* 28 (1958): 482–491. Print.

Patapan, Haig. *Machiavelli in Love: The Modern Politics of Love and Fear.* Lanham: Lexington Books, 2006. Print

Ridolfi, Roberto. *The Life of Nicolo Machiavelli.* U of Chicago P, 1963. Print.

Von Vacano, D. A. *The Art of Power: Machiavelli, Nietzsche, and the Making of Aesthetic Political Theory.* Lanham: Lexington Books, 2007. Print.

*Chad Dundas*

# PROPAGANDA

*Edward Bernays*

✤ **Key Facts**

**Time Period:**
Mid-20th Century

**Genre:**
Treatise

**Events:**
World War I; founding of
the Committee on Public
Information

**Nationality:**
American

## OVERVIEW

Published in 1928, *Propaganda* is a hugely influential work by Edward Bernays, who argued that overcoming chaos and conflict within society required the scientific manipulation of public opinion. Although the term "propaganda" has come to be closely associated with despotic governments and carries negative connotations, Bernays took a positive view of the tactic. In *Propaganda* he argues that the sheer size of the human population creates a need for control: a small group of people who understand human psychology and behavior must foster cooperation and ensure a functioning society. This "invisible government," the true ruling power of the nation, molds the minds of the people, shapes their tastes, and suggests their ideas. Bernays's work pioneered and furthered techniques in both propaganda and public relations. So large was his influence that he has been called the "father of public relations," as well as the "father of spin."

In the aftermath of World War I, in which propaganda had been used extensively, the study of propaganda together with its methods and ethics took on a new importance. Having worked on American propaganda projects during the war, Bernays came to view propaganda as a tool that, harnessed, could redirect the negative impulses of humanity for economic and public benefit to create a flourishing society—a kind of utopia. *Propaganda,* however, received largely negative reviews upon its release, mainly because of the public's sensitivity to the devastation of the war. The adverse reaction to his ideas only grew when the German Nazi Party's propaganda mastermind, Joseph Goebbels (who had a copy of *Propaganda* on his bookshelf), used mass manipulation to justify the extermination of the "inferior" non-Aryan races. Ultimately, however, Bernays's ideas would become most influential in the fields of public relations and advertising, softening critical reactions to the work.

## HISTORICAL AND LITERARY CONTEXT

During World War I, American and European governments took control of the media and propaganda became a sophisticated strategic enterprise, promoting national pride and vilifying people of other nationalities and races. In 1917, as part of the American propaganda agenda, President Woodrow Wilson founded the Committee on Public Information, an organization charged with increasing public support for American participation in the war. Bernays contributed the idea that the United States could help achieve democracy in Europe. Wilson was so impressed with Bernays's work that he invited him to the 1919 Paris Peace Conference, where the Allies met to determine the fate of the Central Powers.

In the United States, a recession following the war caused high unemployment rates, cuts in wages, business bankruptcies, and farm failures. Bernays became increasingly interested in determining how the slogans and campaigns he and his colleagues had developed during the war could be utilized during peacetime. By shaping public opinion, he believed, propaganda could accomplish economic and political goals.

Bernays's work combined several philosophies: the crowd control ideas of French social psychologist Gustave Le Bon (author of *The Crowd: A Study of the Popular Mind,* 1896), who believed that so-called subordinate groups could be manipulated by the media; British neurosurgeon Wilfred Trotter's pioneering work on the herd mentality (including *Instincts of the Herd in Peace and War,* 1919); and many concepts from the psychoanalytical work of his uncle, Sigmund Freud, most notably his belief that people behaved differently when they were in groups than when they were isolated. A former coworker on the Committee on Public Information and one of the most notable political journalists of the time, Walter Lippmann (who wrote *Public Opinion* in 1922), became a major influence on Bernays's thinking and the development of his ideas. Lippmann, more critical of propaganda than Bernays, believed that traditional notions of democracy had been rendered obsolete by information overload. As a result, he concluded that the well-informed should "manufacture the consent" of the masses by providing them with simplified concepts of the world and its problems. Bernays quotes heavily from Lippmann in *Propaganda* and further explores his colleague's ideas on the manipulation of large populations in his future work in public relations.

*Propaganda* played a large role in popularizing Freud's ideas, and it initiated the public relations industry's extensive use of psychology. One of Bernays's most lasting and significant contributions was his belief that the news, more trusted by the public, is a better medium than advertising for carrying a message. He also pioneered the practice of integrating third-party authorities, such as doctors and lawyers, into public relations campaigns, believing that recruiting experts or leading figures in the targeted field would automatically increase the influence on any group associated with the third party (for example, the pervasive "three out of four dentists recommend" is still an advertiser's boon). In 1990 *Life* magazine listed Bernays among the one hundred most influential Americans of the twentieth century.

## THEMES AND STYLE

The central theme of *Propaganda* is that the success of a democratic society depends on the purposeful direction of the thoughts and actions of its people by the largely anonymous corporate elite. Bernays writes, "We are governed, our minds are molded, our tastes formed, our ideas suggested, largely by men we have never heard of … vast numbers of human beings must cooperate in this manner if they are to live together as a smoothly functioning society." In addition, he maintained that the public was being inundated more than ever before with complex information requiring increasingly specialized knowledge and that Americans needed guidance in thought and action in order to forward their own best interests. He described this as the "new propaganda." It is important to note that Bernays drew a firm line in the sand between advertising and public relations. He viewed public relations as a more important and higher calling because it focused not simply on the sale of commercial goods but instead on the larger problems facing the country. For Bernays, public relations represented an essential part of governance.

*Propaganda*'s rhetorical strategy is based on an appeal to logic, or logos. Bernays begins with a straightforward outline of his reasoning: "If we understand the mechanism and motives of the group mind, it is now possible to control and regiment the masses according to our will without them knowing it." He then applies the argument in a methodical, step-by-step process to areas relevant to the growth of a healthy society, including business, politics, women's activities, education, social service, art, science, and, especially, the development of a strong economy. The world exists in a state of increasing chaos, he warns, now playing on emotion, or pathos—specifically on fear—and this chaos must be systematized.

Bernays's confident tone is reflected in his stylistic and syntactical choices. Typically, his prose is accessible and straightforward, and a current of urgency runs through the work as a whole. Any business, Bernays writes, "cannot afford to wait until the public asks for its product; it must maintain constant touch, through advertising and propaganda" in order to stay afloat. Emphasizing the importance of what he perceives as universal truths, Bernays renders dissent illogical: his methods provide the only path to success in modern society.

## THE SPIN DOCTOR AT WORK

Throughout his lifetime Edward Bernays worked on countless public relations campaigns. Many are remembered as examples of effective, even brilliant marketing. He played an important role in the first National Association for the Advancement of Colored People (NAACP) convention held in 1920 in Atlanta, Georgia, promoting the vital contributions of African Americans to the whites living in the South. The campaign earned Bernays an award from the NAACP. Perhaps his most famous effort was on behalf of the American Tobacco Company, during which he arranged for a group of young models to march in the 1929 Easter parade in New York City smoking Lucky Strike cigarettes and posing as women's rights marchers carrying "torches of freedom."

History reviews other displays of the power of Bernays's beliefs and techniques less favorably. One of his campaigns was conducted on behalf of the United Fruit Company, known today as Chiquita Brands International. In 1954 Bernays helped the corporation and the U.S. government overthrow democratically elected Guatemalan president Jacobo Árbenz Guzmán. Bernays's propaganda, branding Árbenz as a communist, was disseminated extensively in the United States. The event promoted the use of the term "banana republic," which originally referred to the Central and South American banana-producing countries.

## CRITICAL DISCUSSION

*Propaganda* was immediately met with claims that it promoted deception. In March 1929 *Forum* magazine printed a debate between Bernays and social psychologist Everett Dean Martin (author of *The Meaning of a Liberal Education*, 1926) titled "Are We Victims of Propaganda?" The two disputed the proper role of propaganda in contemporary society and the ethics of manipulating the public's actions and thoughts. Martin argued that the aim of Bernays's brand of propaganda was "to 'put something over' on people, with or without their knowledge and consent"; he said of Bernays's projected leaders, "Their rule is pure impertinence." Bernays maintained that truth and propaganda did not need to be mutually exclusive and that minorities could similarly fight tyranny among leaders using the same methods he had described. Bernays and many of his contemporaries were also criticized for representing lobbying groups.

Because of the subsequent use of its theories and techniques to serve destructive ends, *Propaganda* has a complicated and highly contested legacy. In a review of Larry Tye's 2002 biography of Bernays, *The Father of Spin*, for *PR Watch*, public relations scholars John Stauber and Sheldon Rampton argue for the historical importance of the author's work: "It is impossible to fundamentally grasp the social, political, economic and cultural developments of the past

DISTRIBUTED BY
WORLD FILM
CORPORATION

"UNIS POUR LA PAIX
AVEC LA VICTOIRE"

THIRD
UNITED STATES OFFICIAL WAR PICTURE

UNDER
FOUR FLAGS

PRESENTED BY DIVISION OF FILMS
COMMITTEE ON PUBLIC INFORMATION
GEORGE CREEL, CHAIRMAN.

TAKEN BY THE OFFICIAL PHOTOGRAPHERS
OF THE ALLIED ARMIES

A poster for the 1917 World War I film *Under Four Flags* that depicts four soldiers, one from each of the Allied nations. George Creel's Committee on Public Information presented the film. A member of this committee, Edward Bernays, used this experience to shape the field of public relations and write *Propaganda* (1928). © EVERETT COLLECTION INC./ALAMY.

one hundred years without some understanding of Bernays and his professional heirs in the public relations industry." Scholarship on Bernays and *Propaganda* has focused on the author's role in establishing public relations as a staple of modern advertising and politics as well as the ethics and legacy of his ideas.

Bernays remains most widely discussed in the world of public relations, where study centers on the various applications of his ideas and the reasons he was so influential. In a 1984 essay in *Public Relations Review,*

Marvin N. Olasky noted, "Journalists compared statements ... by Bernays to the thoughts of Goebbels or, alternately, Stalin. But Bernays was able always to escape criticism of that kind. He escaped much less scathed than one might expect ... partly because there was, for many, little arguing with success." Writing for the *Boston Globe* in 1990, Diane E. Lewis summarized the substantial and wide-ranging impact of Bernays's work: "High-tech marketing techniques and the electronic media have turned Bernays' theory of mass psychology and the power of suggestion into a multimillion-dollar industry, transforming politics, business and the American psyche."

### BIBLIOGRAPHY

*Sources*

Bernays, Edward L. *Propaganda.* Brooklyn, NY: Ig, 2004. Print.

Bernays, Edward L., and Everett Dean Martin. "Are We Victims of Propaganda?" *Forum* March 1929. Print.

Colf, Richard T. "Who's the Father of Public Relations?" *Public Relations Strategist* 13.4 (2007): 24–27. Print.

Lewis, Diane E. "PR's Founder Also Its Conscience." *Boston Globe,* New York Times Co., 4 Oct. 1990. *Highbeam Research.* Web. 17 July 2012.

Olasky, Marvin N. "Retrospective: Bernays' Doctrine of Public Opinion." *Public Relations Review* 10.3 (1984): 3–12. *SciVerse.* Web. 1 Aug. 2012.

Stauber, John, and Sheldon Rampton. Rev. of *The Father of Spin: Edward L. Bernays and the Birth of PR,* by Larry Tye. *PR Watch* 6.2 (1999). Web. 5 Feb. 2012.

*Further Reading*

Bernays, Edward. *Biography of an Idea: Memoirs of Public Relations Counsel.* New York: Simon, 1965. Print.

———. *Crystallizing Public Opinion.* Brooklyn, NY: Ig, 2011. Print.

Collins, Ross F. "This Is Your Propaganda Kids: Building a War Myth for World War I Children." *Journalism History* 31 (2012): 13–22. *Highbeam Research.* Web. 17 July 2012.

Cutlip, Scott M. *The Unseen Power: Public Relations, A History.* New York: Routledge, 1994. Print.

Ewen, Stuart. *PR! A Social History of Spin.* New York: Basic, 1996. Print.

Tye, Larry. *The Father of Spin: Edward L. Bernays and the Birth of Public Relations.* New York: Picador, 2002. Print.

*Colby Cuppernull*

# PROPAGANDA

*The Formation of Men's Attitudes*

*Jacques Ellul*

## OVERVIEW

French historian and sociologist Jacques Ellul's *Propaganda: The Formation of Men's Attitudes,* published in English in 1965, defines the deep roots and toxic effects of propaganda and its interactions with technology in the modern age. Organized into five chapters with titles progressing from "The Characteristics of Propaganda" to "The Necessity of Propaganda" and "The Socio-Political Effects," Ellul's work analyzes propaganda as an intrinsic part of a hypertechnological society. His innovative examination delineates and explores various perspectives for classifying propaganda, not merely as a tool for immediate persuasion but also as a pernicious replacement for spiritual connection and community. In Ellul's view, it matters little whether propaganda issues from a "good" or "bad" regime. Ultimately, the constant bombardment of governmental and commercial messaging is a prevailing and predictable trend in modern culture and is antithetical to individual thought and identity.

*Propaganda: The Formation of Men's Attitudes* resonated in a society that was quickly becoming overwhelmed by the rapidity of technological changes and the rise of propaganda messages that accompanied them. Originally published in French in 1962 under the name *Propagandes,* Ellul's work appeared as governments around the world were combining developments in technology and behavioral science with manipulation of the private media to refine methods for affecting public opinion. The author's analysis of the consequences of expanding societal dependence on technology and the individual citizen's increasing vulnerability to the persuasive power of propaganda calls upon readers to examine and challenge the growth of these powerful forces.

## HISTORICAL AND LITERARY CONTEXT

During the first half of the twentieth century, advances in communications technology greatly expanded the reach and role of propaganda. In 1917 the U.S. government, under the leadership of president Woodrow Wilson, formed the Committee for Public Information, which successfully "sold" the idea of entering World War I to a reluctant population using techniques of journalism and advertising. This marriage of media and government continued during the 1920s and 1930s as a campaign of anticommunist propaganda was employed to discredit labor organizers and other social activists. The use of propaganda intensified again during World War II as the Office of War Information employed a number of professional print and broadcast journalists (including its director, Elmer Davis, who had worked for both *The New York Times* and Columbia Broadcasting) to produce persuasive materials that roused and maintained support for the war effort.

By the 1950s television had overtaken radio as the most popular public source of information and entertainment, providing a more vibrant platform for propaganda than ever before. Although the French lagged somewhat behind such nations as the United States and United Kingdom in public acceptance of the new medium, there were one million TV sets in France by 1958, and virtually all broadcasting was under the control of the government. President Charles de Gaulle (1959–69) made effective use of television for propaganda during the colonial war in Algeria (1954–62), and in the United States president Dwight D. Eisenhower (1953–61) established the President's Committee on International Information to forge connections with private media organizations in order to spread government messaging. After World War II, the Cold War developed between the Soviet Union and the United States and its Western allies, fostered by deep mistrust and ideological incompatibility. In 1954 tensions within American society heightened as Eisenhower initiated Operation Candor, a government project that employed media figures to impress upon the public the gravity of the Soviet threat. The president reinforced this ongoing state of alarm by referring to the period as "an age of peril." Ellul's *Propaganda* emerged from the author's alarm at his perception of a different peril, deriving from the immersion of the public consciousness in an atmosphere of constant propaganda.

Although the postwar period of the 1950s and early 1960s is often popularly perceived as an age of conformity, there did arise a literature of rebellious inquiry that challenged socially enforced norms and assumptions. Some writers not only supported but

### ✣ Key Facts

**Time Period:**
Mid-20th Century

**Genre:**
Theory

**Events:**
Cold War; increased popularity of television; presidency of Dwight D. Eisenhower

**Nationality:**
French

# BRANDING: A NEW FRONTIER OF PROPAGANDA

The turn of the twenty-first century saw an upsurge in the philosophy and practice of branding, a practice Jacques Ellul would surely recognize as a model of sociological propaganda. Brand names began appearing on products as makers of manufactured goods needed to distinguish their products from others on the market. Unique names and labels evolved into distinctive qualities of strength, goodness, or freshness associated with different brand names. The next step of branding involved imparting distinctive qualities of discernment or glamour to the purchaser of a particular product, and many products implicitly promised happiness and success to those who used them.

By the 1990s branding had become so sophisticated that in many cases the product itself was secondary to the lifestyle or identity associated with it. Indeed, the practice of branding, or the establishment of a deep emotional association in order to gain popular acceptance and inspire loyalty, became widespread among such noncommercial concerns as the U.S. Army, religious groups, and even nations. This type of branding represents both vertical and horizontal propaganda as conceived by Ellul. The vertical messaging is accomplished by groups of highly skilled propagandists who mount intricately planned advertising campaigns to sway the emotions of consumers, while the consumers themselves participate in horizontal propaganda to spread the message to other consumers.

also helped create the status quo, such as journalist Walter Lippmann, who participated in Wilson's Committee for Public Information and expounded an elitist theory of democracy in his 1955 *The Public Philosophy.* Others, such as George Orwell in *Animal Farm* (1945) and *1984* (1948), used allegory and science fiction to expose societal ills. Philosophers such as Michel Foucault in *Folie et Déraison* (*Madness and Civilization*; 1961) cast a light on power dynamics in modern society, while other French writers such as Albert Camus in *L'Étranger* (*The Stranger*; 1942) explored the alienation of the individual. Ellul preceded his study of propaganda with his 1954 analysis of modern ideas of progress, *La Technique, ou, L'Enjeu du Siècle* (*The Technological Society*).

Frequently quoted in any study of the meaning and effects of propaganda, Ellul's *Propaganda* remains one of the most thorough analyses of the subject. His seminal perspective on the unremitting campaign of social propaganda that glorifies technological progress is particularly relevant in postmodern twenty-first-century culture, as technology takes an expanding role in everyday life. Later works exploring the phenomenon of propaganda, such as Garth S. Jowett and Victoria O'Donnell's *Propaganda and Persuasion* (1999), are often viewed in comparison with Ellul's original vision.

## THEMES AND STYLE

Ellul clearly states the focus of his work in the preface of *Propaganda*: "Having suffered, felt, and analyzed the impact of the power of propaganda on myself, having been time and again, and still being, the object of propaganda, I want to speak of it as a menace which threatens the total personality." He quickly makes the connection between propaganda and technology, stating, "The study of propaganda must be conducted within the context of the technological society." He then delineates the distinction between political and sociological propaganda, claiming that the technological society uses the latter "to prevent [mechanization and technology] from being felt as too oppressive and to persuade man to submit with good grace." Most of Ellul's study is devoted to the origins and effects of sociological propaganda, which he ties to political and economic interests: "Mass production requires mass consumption, but there cannot be mass consumption without widespread identical views as to what the necessities of life are." This homogenization of needs and desires leads to the degradation of the spiritual life of the individual: "Propaganda strips the individual, robs him of part of himself, and makes him live an alien and artificial life."

Ellul employs a wealth of examples to illustrate his thesis. Stating that "propaganda as a phenomenon is essentially the same in China or the Soviet Union or the United States or Algeria, engendering certain identical results in Communism or Hitlerism or Western democracy," he uses cases from each in making his various points, ensuring that readers of differing political ideologies will find points of reference. He uses categories and classification to make his complex subject more easily comprehensible, distinguishing not only the political and the sociological, but also making a number of other distinctions, such as that between agitation and integration propaganda, and vertical and horizontal propaganda. With persistent and convincing logic, the author outlines his case for a new definition and perception of propaganda, and the societal conditions necessary for its existence: "Modern man ... is in the position of needing outside help to be able to face his condition. And that aid is propaganda."

Ellul's narrative is dense and detailed but written in accessible, even engaging, language that pulls the reader from point to point: "The time is past when propaganda was a matter of individual inspiration, personal subtlety, or the use of unsophisticated tricks. Now science has entered propaganda, as we shall reveal." His tone is scholarly, and somewhat ironically he avoids questions of morality and uses scientific argument and language to persuade his mid-century audience. For example, he discusses "the objective situation of man which generates this need for propaganda."

## CRITICAL DISCUSSION

*Propaganda: The Formation of Men's Attitudes* was published in English in 1965 to general critical interest. *New York Times* reviewer Seymour Lipset (1966)

Government propaganda posters on a wall in Pyongyang, North Korea, 2007. © MARKA/ALAMY.

commended the book for "bringing together important recent findings about the effects of propaganda." Editor Saul Padover, in a review of Ellul's *The Political Illusion* (1967) published in the *Saturday Review,* recognizes Ellul's innovative insights: "His analysis of modern society reminds one of the child who blurted out that the emperor was naked." In his 1965 introduction to *Propaganda,* Konrad Kellen comments on Ellul's methodical approach and his refusal to offer pat solutions: "Ellul reaches neither a pessimistic nor an optimistic conclusion. … His super-analysis ends with a warning, not a prophecy."

A half century after its publication, Ellul's study of propaganda remains dynamic and relevant as society continues to struggle with concepts of modernity and the far-reaching consequences of technological development. The author's exhaustive examination of the characteristics of societal persuasion is still considered authoritative, and his conclusions are frequently called up to assist modern writers in assessing a wide range of contexts of propaganda, from the former German Democratic Republic to the U.S. war with Iraq. Ellul was a prolific writer who followed *Propaganda* with numerous works of philosophical analysis of society, technology, ethics, and spirituality. In 1988 the journal *Ellul Forum* was founded to elucidate and expand the author's ideas. One of its writers, Randal Marlin, described Ellul's legacy: "That Jacques Ellul is one of the world's leading thinkers in the area of propaganda becomes clearer with each passing decade."

Propaganda and technology remain major topics of contemporary thought, and scholars continue to examine Ellul's ideas. Although he points out inconsistencies in the author's arguments, Marlin says "Ellul was right about the direction in which propaganda was headed." Shawn Parry-Giles challenges *Propaganda*'s assertion of the universality of societal messaging: "Ellul's foundation propaganda principle … denies the cultural influences that determine how a text is 'read' in its historical-cultural context." Samuel Hope in a 1996 essay for *Arts Education Policy Review* eulogizes the author after his death: "Like those of all great thinkers, his works disturb and enlighten. As we in the late twentieth century begin to face the opportunities and challenges of a world that is increasingly technical, Ellul's logic, clarity, and faith in the grandeur of the human spirit can make a positive contribution."

## BIBLIOGRAPHY

*Sources*

Ellul, Jacques. *Propaganda: The Formation of Men's Attitudes.* New York: Vintage, 1973. Print.

Hope, Samuel. "Homage to Jacques Ellul." *Arts Education Policy Review* 97.5 (1996): 38–39. Print.

Lipset, Seymour Martin. "Forcing a Free Choice." Rev. of *Propaganda: The Formation of Men's Attitudes,* by Jacques Ellul. *New York Times* 6 Mar. 1966: BR24. Print.

Marlin, Randal. "Problems in Ellul's Treatment of Propaganda." *Ellul Forum* 37 (2006): 9–12. Print.

Olsen, Curt. "Bernays vs. Ellul: Two Views of Propaganda." *Public Relations Tactics* 12.7 (2005): 28. Print.

Padover, Saul. Rev. of *The Political Illusion,* by Jacques Ellul. *Saturday Review* 29 Apr. 2012: 27. Web. 4 Oct. 2012.

Parry-Giles, Shawn J. "'Camouflaged' Propaganda: The Truman and Eisenhower Administrations' Covert Manipulation of News." *Western Journal of Communication* 60.2 (1996): 146–53. Print.

*Further Reading*

Chomsky, Noam. "Early History of Propaganda. Spectator Democracy. Engineering Opinion. Public Relations." *Alternative Press Review* Fall 1993: n. pag. Web. 17 Sept. 2012.

Cone, Stacey. "Pulling the Plug on America's Propaganda." *Journalism History* 30.4 (2005): 166–76. Print.

Cunningham, Stanley B. *The Idea of Propaganda: A Reconstruction.* Westport: Praeger, 2002. Print.

Ellul, Jacques. "The Ethics of Propaganda: Propaganda, Innocence, and Amorality." *Communication* 6 (1981): 159–75. Print.

———. *The Technological Society.* New York: Knopf, 1964. Print.

Moore, Rick Clifton. "Hegemony, Agency, and Dialectical Tension in Ellul's *Technological Society.*" *Journal of Communication* 43.3 (1998): 129–44. Print.

St. John III, Burton. "A View That's Fit to Print: The National Association of Manufacturers' Free Enterprise Rhetoric as Integration Propaganda, 1937–1939." *Journalism Studies* 11.3 (2010): 377–92. Print.

*Tina Gianoulis*

# THE PUBLIC AND ITS PROBLEMS

*John Dewey*

## OVERVIEW

*The Public and Its Problems* (1927) is a work of political philosophy by American John Dewey. Partially written in response to Walter Lippmann's *Public Opinion* (1922) and *The Phantom Public* (1925), it refutes Lippmann's notion that the average citizen is too overwhelmed by the complexity of modern life to make informed decisions without the intervention of experts who can discern facts from politically motivated falsehoods and propaganda. Instead, Dewey suggests, "only when the facts are allowed free play for the suggestion of new points of view is any conversion of conviction as to meaning possible." In other words, democratic societies can only thrive and become meaningful when the entire population is engaged in the free exchange of ideas and perspectives. At its core, *The Public and Its Problems* celebrates participatory democracy and the collaboration of ordinary individuals within society as a safeguard against the concentration of power in the hands of an elite few.

Dewey wrote *The Public and Its Problems* in the wake of World War I, as an increasingly industrialized U.S. economy began to rely on specialized knowledge and more concentrated work roles to meet the demands of a new age. Such fragmentation exposed major incompatibilities between the traditional idea of the United States as a loose affiliation between self-sustaining individuals and the reality of its deep interdependence. "The social situation has been so changed by the factors of an industrial age," writes Dewey, "that traditional general principals have little practical meaning.... There is too much public, a public too diffused and scattered and too intricate in composition." Both Lippmann and Dewey agree that such splintering of the public is a hindrance to social unity. But whereas Lippmann suggests that those with the highest level of expertise be employed to cut through jargon and propaganda and discern the facts of a matter prior to bringing it before the public, Dewey argues for an increase in public education and dialogue that will empower the public as a whole and protect against an unfair centralization of knowledge and power. His theories were well received and continue to exert an influence on progressive politics, policy, and philosophy to this day.

## HISTORICAL AND LITERARY CONTEXT

Great shifts took place in the global political situation in the aftermath of World War I. The Ottoman, Austro-Hungarian, and Russian empires crumbled, and several new nations were formed in their place. Such upheaval gave rise to debate among political theorists as to what features constitute a nation and which form of government was least likely to promote oppression, exploitation, and ultimately totalitarianism. In the United States, politicians and business leaders were alarmed by the rise of communism in Europe (particularly the Bolshevik Revolution in Russia) and began to view political activists with suspicion in what came to be known as the first "Red Scare." Increased specialization and a growing inequality between the rich and the middle class had ushered in new social divisions and laid the foundation for the Great Depression, and philosophers like Dewey and Lippmann sought solutions to the tensions that threatened the future of the nation by defining the modern democratic state and the bonds that hold it together.

*The Public and Its Problems* emerged from a series of lectures that Dewey delivered at Kenyon College in 1926. While his critiques were aimed at the specific policies advocated by Lippmann, they were borne of a general dissatisfaction in the direction of the U.S. government after the war. As Laura M. Westhoff points out in her 1995 piece in *History of Education Quarterly*, Dewey was disappointed that the war had failed to foster an era of world peace and was "appalled by the manipulation of public opinion, by paranoia, and by the subsequent suspension of civil liberties resulting from the government's mobilization programs and the Red Scare of 1919.... A war ostensibly about 'democracy' had made American government less responsive to the people." The only remedy to this trend, argued Dewey, was a voting public—a "Great Community" as he describes it—unified by its concern for the common good and galvanized by the confidence that results from a thorough education. The alternative, a society governed by a handful of experts, was doomed to failure because "a class of experts is inevitably so removed from common interests as to become a class with private interests and private knowledge, which in social matters is not knowledge at all."

Dewey and Lippmann were not the only theorists to engage in debate over the proper methods of fostering and maintaining a democratic society in the early twentieth century. American thinkers including Harold Lasswell, Jane Addams, James Harvey Robinson, George Herbert Mead, and W. E. B. Du Bois

❖ *Key Facts*

**Time Period:**
Mid-20th Century

**Genre:**
Treatise

**Events:**
World War I; Great Depression; conflict between capitalism and socialism

**Nationality:**
American

# JOHN DEWEY AND SOCIALISM: THE CASE OF THE DEWEY COMMISSION

Although John Dewey is best remembered for his defense of democracy, his ideas were heavily influenced by the tenets of socialism, which prizes cooperation and public ownership of goods and the means of their production over the accumulation of private property and wealth as championed by capitalism. Many of Dewey's ideas borrow from European democratic socialism (though he was critical of Karl Marx, a leading architect of socialist thought), and he was an early supporter of the Soviet Union, the first country to put socialist ideas into widespread practice.

Initially, Dewey's writings were touted by the Soviets as evidence of the spread of socialist thought. Then, after serious infighting led to a split in Soviet leadership between the totalitarian and bureaucratic Joseph Stalin with the more democratic-leaning Leon Trotsky (who was expelled from the Soviet Union in 1929 during the Stalin-led Moscow show trials), Dewey became an outspoken critic of Stalin and his brand of socialism. In 1937, at the age of seventy-eight, Dewey served as the head of the Commission of Inquiry into the Charges Made against Leon Trotsky in the Moscow Trials—what later came to be known as the Dewey Commission. The commission refuted the charges made against Trotsky and issued a 400-page report, titled *Not Guilty*, which stands as one of the first liberal critiques of Stalinism as a corruption of true socialist ideals.

each contributed specific visions of the role of the individual in society and the role of society in shaping government during this period. Literary authors also sought to portray the disintegration of the public in postwar society, most notably F. Scott Fitzgerald in *The Great Gatsby* (1925). Even journalist and satirist H. L. Mencken offered his take on modern democracy in his *Notes on Democracy* (1926). Dewey himself had already published a number of works exploring the way in which the public shapes and is shaped by democracy, including 1916's *Democracy and Education,* and he went on to pursue similar themes in future works, including *Individualism: Old and New* (1930) and *Liberalism and Social Action* (1935).

Dewey remains a vital and canonical philosopher of progressive liberalism. His books are taught in education, sociology, psychology, and political science classes across the country. Although his reputation in philosophy and political science circles has wavered over the years, historical events such as World War II, the boom-and-bust cycles of the U.S. economy, and the rise of globalism have confirmed the relevance of *The Public and Its Problems*. As the United States again faces growing disparity between the wealthy and the middle and lower classes, and as education and social reform continue to be important political issues, Dewey's work remains influential among leading progressive thinkers.

## THEMES AND STYLE

The central theme of *The Public and Its Problems* is that democracy is only possible in the modern world of mass communication, pluralism, and propaganda insofar as the public sphere is characterized by mutual concern for the consequences of our actions rather than a constant clash of partisan special interests. If U.S. society continues to view itself in the light of classical liberalism—the notion that every person is a unique and self-contained individual who serves the world best by tending to his or her own self-interests—it will inevitably embody the misguided conclusions that Dewey attributes to Lippmann, namely that "the state, the public, is a fiction, a mask for private desires for power and position." Such convictions ignore the fact that every individual is the product of a community and that the shared concern for the well-being of others in these communities makes the notion of a public sphere, and democracy itself, possible. However, Dewey argues that the will of the individual does not always need to bend toward the will of the collective. Rather, the individual must view himself in relation to the larger community from which he springs and must participate in that community through the sharing of knowledge and ideas. Simply put, "Communication can alone create a great community."

Opposed as he is to the kind of top-down, expert-guided approach to democracy advocated by Lippmann, Dewey does not present his argument in *The Public and Its Problems* as a kind of polemic against Lippmann's entire system of thought. On the contrary, he acknowledges that they both seek solutions to the same problem. "In spite of attained integration, or rather perhaps because of its nature," he writes, "the Public seems to be lost; it is certainly bewildered." To this he attaches a footnote acknowledging his "indebtedness" to Lippmann, "not only as to this particular point, but for ideas involved in my entire discussion even when it reaches conclusions diverging from his." By engaging with Lippmann and others in philosophical dialogue, Dewey underscores the importance of his project, giving it a sense of urgency and universality by confirming that other respected thinkers had attempted similar analyses. Furthermore, by framing his argument as an exchange of ideas and a modification rather than an outright refutation of Lippmann's approach, Dewey makes *The Public and Its Problems* a literal embodiment of the kind of democratic communication he prescribes.

Dewey's style is somewhat elliptical and vague; indeed, he is often criticized for a lack of concrete policy proposals. However, underneath its occasional rhetorical obscurity, *The Public and Its Problems* contains a clear progression of ideas, focusing first on the individual, then the local community, then the Public, and finally on democracy as a form of government that can only exist when all of these preceding factors are aligned. Dewey's rational and logical development of ideas contributes to his ability to influence his readers.

His strategy is to work up from the foundational ideas to the broader suggestions. In this way, the reader is able to easily follow him as he develops his thoughts, and the writer is able to address counterarguments and opposing viewpoints as he guides the reader through his own thinking.

## CRITICAL DISCUSSION

Initial reaction to *The Public and Its Problems* was positive and reflected the elevated reputation Dewey had already achieved as well as the intelligence of his new work. Writing in the *International Journal of Ethics,* Stephen C. Pepper equates Dewey with another innovative proponent of American democracy, revered poet Walt Whitman, and calls the book "calmly eloquent, moving, penetrating, compelling." In his evaluation of *The Public and Its Problems* in *Philosophical Review,* T. V. Smith praises Dewey's conclusions as important guidelines for future generations, writing, "Not merely as a plea but as a program this book is magnificent."

Over time, *The Public and Its Problems* has remained relevant for two significant reasons. First, Dewey's reputation as one of the leading liberal philosophers and writers has stood the test of time. Although his theories were somewhat buried under the renewed celebration of individualism in the 1960s and 1970s, a resurgent effort to bridge the gap between various social groups in the 1980s and 1990s made what was termed the "Dewey-Lippmann Debate" a central feature of sociopolitical scholarship. Second, *The Public and Its Problems* contains ideas and theories that are applicable to almost any time period. As a result, scholars, critics, readers, and philosophers have held a continued dialogue with the text and its ideas.

The dominant trend in contemporary criticism reflects this unique strength of the book. Most critics spend their time analyzing Dewey's work as it relates to their own time and applying his ideas to the particular historical moment in which they live. In *Argumentation and Advocacy,* scholar Robert Asen suggests that the problem of a diffused public that Dewey describes remains a problem of contemporary America. He notes, however, that Dewey "did not object to multiplicity but to uncoordinated multiplicity." As a solution to such uncoordinated multiplicity, journalism scholar Carl Bybee suggests in his essay in *Journalism and Communication Monographs* that "the path for Dewey was a turn to what might be called public journalism," something that several critics see taking shape in our era of Internet reporting and social media. There exists an ongoing trend to view the public as fractured, and as a result Dewey's ideas for solving this problem have remained relevant. In an article in *Philosophy & Rhetoric,* Paul Stob, a philosopher and scholar, writes that "'the public' may not be as fractured as some believe, or, better, it will not be as fractured as some believe if the public continues to forge a fruitful discourse and manifest better versions of itself." The ideas Dewey put forth in *The Public and*

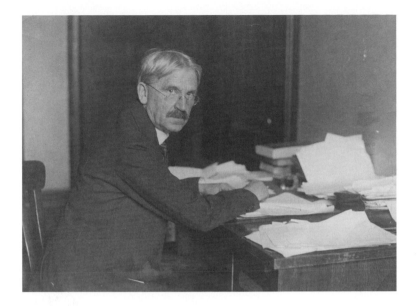

*Its Problems* remain relevant today because many of the same problems exist. In this way, the text has been tremendously influential and continues to inform the work of countless scholars, philosophers, and writers.

John Dewey, author of *The Public and Its Problems.* THE NEW YORK PUBLIC LIBRARY/ART RESOURCE, NY.

## BIBLIOGRAPHY

*Sources*

Asen, Robert. "The Multiple Mr. Dewey: Multiple Publics and Permeable Borders in John Dewey's Theory of the Public Sphere." *Argumentation and Advocacy* 39 (2003): 174–88. Print.

Bybee, Carl. "Can Democracy Survive in the Post-Factual Age?" *Journalism and Communication Monographs* 1:1 (1999): 29–62. Print.

Smith, T. V. Rev. of *The Public and Its Problems,* by John Dewey. *Philosophical Review* 38.2 (1929): 177–80. Print.

Stob, Paul. "Kenneth Burke, John Dewey, and the Pursuit of the Public." *Philosophy & Rhetoric* 38.3 (2005): 226–47. Print.

Pepper, Stephen C. Rev. of *The Public and Its Problems,* by John Dewey. *International Journal of Ethics* 38.4 (1928): 478–80. Print.

Westhoff, Laura M. "The Popularization of Knowledge: John Dewey on Experts and American Democracy." *History of Education Quarterly* 35.1 (1995): 27–47. Print.

*Further Reading*

Boisvert, Raymond. *John Dewey: Rethinking Our Time.* Albany: SUNY P, 1997. Print.

Caspary, William R. *Dewey on Democracy.* Ithaca: Cornell UP, 2000. Print.

Crick, Nathan. *Democracy & Rhetoric: John Dewey on the Arts of Becoming.* Charleston: U of South Carolina P, 2010. Print.

Fishman, Stephen M., and Lucille McCarthy. *John Dewey and the Philosophy and Practice of Hope.* Champaign: U of Illinois P, 2007. Print.

Kloppenberg, James T. *Uncertain Victory: Social Democracy and Progressivism in European and American Thought, 1870–1920.* New York: Oxford UP, 1986. Print.

Rogers, Melvin. *The Undiscovered Dewey: Religion, Morality, and the Ethos of Democracy.* New York: Columbia UP, 2007. Print.

Ryan, Alan. *John Dewey and the High Tide of American Liberalism.* New York: W. W. Norton, 1995. Print.

Talisse, Robert B. *A Pragmatist Philosophy of Democracy.* Oxford: Routledge, 2007. Print.

*Colby Cuppernull*

# PUBLIC OPINION
*Walter Lippmann*

## OVERVIEW

*Public Opinion* is a philosophical work published in 1922 by journalist and social and political philosopher Walter Lippmann. In the book, Lippmann analyzes the problem of maintaining a well-informed electorate in democratic societies as the world becomes increasingly complex, fragmentary, and filled with ideological bias and "stereotypes," a term he coined to describe the prevalence of preconceived notions in the general public. "The pictures inside the heads of these human beings, the pictures of themselves, of others, of their needs, purposes, and relationship, are their public opinions," he writes, adding, "democracy in its original form never seriously faced the problem which arises because the pictures inside people's heads do not automatically correspond with the world outside." Ultimately, Lippmann advocates for the formation of a kind of impartial public truth commission— "an independent, expert organization for making the unseen facts intelligible to those who have to make the decisions"—to alleviate the distorted worldviews and political gridlock that are the result of partisanship, propaganda, and the "unworkable fiction that each of us must acquire a competent opinion about all public affairs."

Following World War I, propaganda and its use became the subject of heated debate among intellectuals, philosophers, and politicians. As the United States became more influential in the global community and as socialism and communism gained a foothold in Europe, leading thinkers of the time began to analyze democracy and the role of the public within it. *Public Opinion* served as an important catalyst for debate, particularly Lippmann's assertion that an impartial group of intellectuals could disentangle itself from emotion and political allegiances to identify a core group of facts on which political leaders and the public in general would base its opinions. It has since contributed to the use of Lippmann's name among political theorists as shorthand for the view that modern democratic societies function best under the careful guidance of nonpartisan experts.

## HISTORICAL AND LITERARY CONTEXT

When World War I began in 1914, the United States faced tremendous opposition from the public to becoming involved. As a result, propaganda campaigns were designed and implemented in order to increase support for military intervention. Once the United States joined the war, these campaigns became even more important to the cause, emphasizing the dangers of spies and depicting the Germans as blood-thirsty villains. The end of the war saw the Bolshevik Revolution install a communist, socialist government in Russia. From this cultural milieu emerged a number of thinkers and scholars who began to focus on the workings of a democratic society and debate the role of propaganda and other forms of control or influence on the larger population.

In 1917 Lippmann served as special assistant to Secretary of War Newton D. Baker, and during the war he represented the United States on the Inter-Allied Propaganda Board, a collective effort by Allied nations to secure and maintain support for the war effort around the world. In 1918 he helped draft President Woodrow Wilson's famous "Fourteen Points" speech, which largely defined the terms of surrender ratified at the Paris Peace Conference of 1919. Lippmann also became a major player in an organization referred to as the "Inquiry" that was charged with coming up with a plan for postwar peace. Lippmann then left government service, and in 1920 he published *Liberty and the News,* a study of the influence of biased journalism on democracies. This work is considered a forerunner to the more expansive exploration of the distillation of information in *Public Opinion.*

Lippmann was not the first intellectual to tackle the problem of public opinion in a world of diverse political, social, religious, economic, and educational backgrounds. In *Public Opinion,* he cites a range of theorists who have taken into account the fact that most citizens are "self-centered" and "see the whole world by means of a few pictures in [their] head." This insightful group of philosophers, deemed by Lippmann "political thinkers who have counted," includes such giants as the ancient Greek thinkers Plato and Aristotle, fifteenth-century historian and political theorist Niccolò Machiavelli, and seventeenth-century philosopher Thomas Hobbes. An important contemporary influence on Lippmann's work was the psychological discoveries of Sigmund Freud, who argued that humans are as much controlled by the irrational aspects of the mind—the dark and mysterious subconscious—as they are by the rational, conscious

*Key Facts*

**Time Period:**
Early 20th Century

**Genre:**
Philosophy

**Events:**
World War I; rise of socialism and communism

**Nationality:**
American

# MR. LIPPMANN GOES (BACK) TO WASHINGTON

In 1964 President Lyndon Baines Johnson awarded Walter Lippmann the Medal of Freedom, the highest honor the U.S. government can bestow upon a civilian. During the ceremony, Johnson referred to Lippmann as a "profound interpreter of his country and the affairs of the world." The president added that "he has enlarged the horizons of public thinking for more than five decades through the power of measured reason and detached perspective." Unfortunately, the relationship between Johnson and Lippmann would later sour.

In the years following this recognition, Lippmann became increasingly critical of the war in Vietnam. As the famous thinker, writer, and journalist became more vocal in his critiques of the war and Johnson's handling of it, the relationship between Lippmann and the White House turned. In the end, history would reach many of the same conclusions as Lippmann regarding the war in Vietnam. Ten years after his Medal of Freedom award, Lippmann died in New York at the age of eighty-five. His death was commemorated by then-President Gerald Ford, who noted that "as a newsman, political analyst, and author, Walter Lippmann played a major role for more than half a century in the development of public dialogue and in shaping a new standard of journalism."

mind. Such theories provided an important foundation for Lippmann's critique of a society that forms opinions based on ill-formed and nebulous "pictures in [their] head." Lippmann acknowledges this in his introduction, noting that "the study of dreams, fantasy and rationalization has thrown light on how the pseudo-environment is put together."

Since its initial publication, *Public Opinion* has divided readers. Critics such as the philosopher John Dewey and political theorist Noam Chomsky, for example, attack Lippmann for advocating what they see as an elitist view of democracy in which the general public is subject to the whims of a few intellectuals. Others vigorously defend his legacy, noting that Lippmann does not decry the voting public as incompetent; rather, as Michael Schudson observes in *International Journal of Communication,* "what he insists on in *Public Opinion* is that we must reject a view of democracy that is premised on the 'omnicompetence' of citizens." Despite such conflicting readings, Lippmann's ideas, particularly those on the ways in which the public forms its opinions, have been extremely influential. Political scientists still employ much of his research, theory, and philosophy designing campaigns and legislature. His stance on the necessity of maintaining an objective and critical disposition in the face of government propaganda and the misrepresentation of reality by special interests has been particularly influential—if not always adhered to—in the field of journalism.

## THEMES AND STYLE

The central theme of *Public Opinion* is that the original concept of American democracy, in which a relatively small and centralized electorate was expected to hold informed opinions on public policy and events based on a shared group of established facts, is untenable in modern, industrialized, and increasingly diverse societies. Because of a variety of factors—preexisting cultural or religious beliefs, differing educational backgrounds, a lack of access to facts about world events and little time to devote to studying them, government censorship and propaganda—citizens cultivate an insular and incomplete understanding of the world, a "pseudo-environment" that leaves them highly susceptible to manipulation. "Man is no Aristotelian god contemplating all existence at one glance," Lippmann writes. In order for democracy to function as it was initially conceived, he suggests that there must exist a filtering body to gather, verify, and disseminate facts to legislators and voters on which they can form educated opinions.

Lippmann makes his argument in a linear fashion, building from one conclusion to the next. After a brief introduction in which he establishes the foundation of his inquiry and summarizes his conclusions, he then moves through the book's seven other sections, describing how objective facts are rendered unattainable to the general public; how this phenomenon leads to the formation of stereotypes and "pseudo-environments"; how such incomplete "pictures" leave most of the population open to manipulation by "the skillful propagandist" who can tap into broadly held stereotypes and gin up fear, outrage, and the will to act; how such widespread susceptibility threatens democracies; how "interposing some form of expertness between the private citizen and the vast environment in which he is entangled" is necessary; and, finally, how an appeal to the public's capacity for reason over its preference for generalization and stereotypes can lead to better democracies and a better world. Lippmann moves his theories from the abstract and philosophical to the realm of concrete public policy by citing examples from contemporary and historical world events and applying his conclusions to them. The most notable example he uses is the recently concluded Great War, arguing that "it was only Berlin, Moscow, Versailles in 1914 to 1919, not Armageddon, as we rhetorically said. The more realistically men have faced out the brutality and the hysteria, the more they have earned the right to say that it is not foolish for men to believe, because another great war took place, that intelligence, courage and effort cannot ever contrive a good life for all men."

Lippmann's style is spare and direct. He moves fluidly from one idea to the next, guiding the reader through his thought process in a way that leaves little room for disagreement. While his assessment of the political situation of his day is noticeably dour ("The world is vast, the situations that concern us are intricate, the messages are few, the biggest part of opinion must be constructed in the imagination"), he sees such pronouncements as the starting point for a social project of real consequence ("the perplexities of government and industry are conspiring to give political science this enormous opportunity to enrich itself and to serve the public").

## CRITICAL DISCUSSION

Initial reaction to *Public Opinion* was mixed. Theorists and philosophers such as Edward Bernays, the so-called "father of public relations," were greatly affected by the work, and they found in it the foundations for their own thoughts on democracy and the art of persuading the public. Other theorists, including Dewey, were critical of the work and its seeming lack of faith in the American public. One early reviewer, Clyde L. King, writing in *The Annals of the American Academy of Political and Social Science,* identified the book's potential impact not only in the field of political science but also across a number of areas of thought. He wrote, "A critique of this kind is needed in political science and is just as useful to economics or to sociology, and for that matter to business, for the limitations to attention and the inaccuracies of the pictures in our minds and the clutch of the stereotypes which we judge are just as applicable to business and to making a living as to government."

Lippmann's legacy is undoubtedly formidable. What seems most remarkable about it is just how widely his ideas have spread and the number of fields they have influenced. Gretchen Soderlund, a communications scholar, neatly summarizes Lippmann's impact, noting that in many studies "Lippmann becomes historical shorthand for connoting (1) broad historical and cultural shifts, (2) emerging media practices, and (3) institutional transformations occurring in the wake of World War I. Lippmann thereby becomes in these works the embodiment of decisive changes rather than a subjective expression of them, an emphasis that contributes to the aura of realism shrouding the author's work." Soderlund goes on to point out that "the title of Ronald Steel's impressive biography, *Walter Lippmann and the American Century,* suggests that to chronicle Lippmann's life is tantamount to detailing the collective experience of a major twentieth century nation." In short, while Lippmann's lasting impact has been in the field of media studies, the appeal and influence of his ideas touch almost every aspect of twentieth-century thought.

The most prevalent trend in current studies of Lippmann and his work is to evaluate the writer's thoughts on the media, the responsibilities of the producers of said media, and its role in forming public opinion. Given the proliferation of opinions in the "new media" of online journalism and informal social networks, Lippmann's concerns in *Public Opinion* have proven more perceptive than first imagined, and

Walter Lippmann in 1941.
© BETTMANN/CORBIS.

scholars continue to apply his ideas to contemporary issues. For example, media scholar Susan Herbst writes that "Lippmann—if he were alive today—would applaud self-reflection and self-critique among journalists. We could use a bit more of it, in fact." Herbst also notes that "practicing journalists—the men and women who struggle with stereotyping and the burdens of objectivity on a daily basis—might find new motivation for studying their own craft if they took a few days off to read and reflect on the ideas in *Public Opinion.*" Lippmann's theories on the proper role and potential impact of the media remain important to this day.

## BIBLIOGRAPHY

*Sources*

Herbst, Susan. "Walter Lippmann's Public Opinion, Revisited." *International Journal of Press/Politics* 4.2 (1999): 288–93. Print.

Lippmann, Walter. *Public Opinion.* New York: Harcourt, Brace, 1922. Print.

King, Clyde L. Rev. of *Public Opinion,* by Walter Lippmann. *Annals of the American Academy of Political and Social Science* 103 (1922): 153–54. Print.

Schudson, Michael. "The 'Lippmann-Dewey Debate' and the Invention of Walter Lippmann as an Anti-Democrat 1986–1996." *International Journal of Communication* 2 (2008): 1031–42. Print.

Soderlund, Gretchen. "Rethinking a Curricular Icon: The Institutional and Ideological Foundations of Walter Lippmann." *Communication Review* 8.3 (2005): 307–27. Print.

*Further Reading*

Blum, D. Steven. *Walter Lippmann, Cosmopolitanism in the Century of Total War.* Ithaca: Cornell UP, 1984. Print.

Childs, Marquis, and James Reston, eds. *Walter Lippmann and His Times.* New York: Harcourt, 1959. Print.

Goodwin, Craufurd D. "The Promise of Expertise: Walter Lippmann and the Policy Sciences." *Policy Sciences* 28.4 (1995): 317–45. Print.

Riccio, Barry D. *Walter Lippmann: Odyssey of a Liberal.* New Brunswick: Transaction, 1993. Print.

Splichal, Slavko. *Public Opinion: Developments and Controversies in the Twentieth Century.* Lanham: Rowman & Littlefield, 1999. Print.

Steel, Ronald. *Walter Lippmann and the American Century.* Boston: Little, Brown, 1980. Print.

Whipple, Mark. "The Dewey-Lippmann Debate Today: Communication Distortions, Reflective Agency, and Participatory Democracy." *Sociological Theory* 23.2 (2005): 156–78. Print.

*Colby Cuppernull*

# RHETORIC

*Aristotle*

## OVERVIEW

Around 335 BCE, ancient Greek philosopher Aristotle composed his treatise *Rhetoric* to explore the argumentative element in oratory and place the subject within a philosophical framework. He defined and analyzed the many components of rhetoric, dividing the treatise into three parts: The first book explores the speaker's persuasive function, the second discusses the role of the audience, and the third examines the stylistic devices of oratory. Aristotle's *Rhetoric* made numerous contributions to the theory of rhetoric and it influenced many later rhetoricians. The ultimate aim of rhetoric is to persuade an audience effectively; consequently, Aristotle's treatise has been studied by propagandists for centuries.

The rise of democracy in ancient Athens made public speaking increasingly important for the average citizen. In both the bustling law courts and the political arena, the faculty of persuasion became a necessity in daily life. These cultural conditions created a demand for individuals who could speak and reason well, and so people consulted traveling teachers called Sophists in order to learn the art of persuasion. Plato, Aristotle's mentor, condemned the Sophists' style of rhetoric as immoral, but Aristotle attempted to reconcile the intense rivalry between rhetoric and philosophy in his treatise. Aristotle's *Rhetoric* was highly praised by numerous Peripatetics, as the adherents to Aristotle's philosophy were known, and it attained an enormous authority, influencing not only classical writers such as the ancient Roman orator Cicero but also later philosophers such as Averroës, Thomas Aquinas, and Thomas Hobbes. Contemporary rhetoricians consider Aristotle's *Rhetoric* the most important work on persuasion ever written.

## HISTORICAL AND LITERARY CONTEXT

The most dramatic turning point in Greek history, the Battle of Chaeronea, took place in 338 BCE—just a few years before Aristotle composed the *Rhetoric*. King Philip II of Macedon defeated the Thebans and Athenians, thus marking the triumph of both an outsider and absolute monarchy over democracy and the old powers of Hellenic city-state politics. Philip was murdered two years later, and his son Alexander, Aristotle's pupil, succeeded him. These events marked the dawning of the Hellenistic period. As a result of the political crises, oratory and the art of persuasion reached their pinnacle of influence within Athens under the guidance of two great rhetoricians, Isocrates and Demosthenes.

Aristotle had left Athens in 343 to tutor Alexander in the Macedonian capital of Pella. When he returned to Athens in 335, Aristotle founded his school, the Lyceum, which met in an area dedicated to the god Apollo Lykeios, and he began to compose his most important works, including the treatise *Rhetoric*. During these years of political upheaval and uncertainty, the need to acquire power to control not only one's personal fate but also the direction of Athenian political policy by means of persuasion grew increasingly urgent. In his monumental work *A History of Greece*, J. B. Bury concludes that "Rhetoric had been carried to such perfection, that the best years of a man's youth were absorbed in learning it." The Athenians enthusiastically endorsed rhetoric by taking great pleasure in hearing and criticizing elaborate speeches, relishing oratory as high entertainment. With such value placed on formal persuasion in Athens, it was only fitting that the philosophic and scientific mind of Aristotle undertook to dissect and define the components of rhetoric.

In Athens, the fifth and fourth centuries BCE were marked by an intense rivalry between philosophy and rhetoric. The Sophist Gorgias, for example, popularized new persuasive methods in his work *Encomium of Helen*, in which he attempted to reveal the relativity of truth. Plato condemned the Sophists in multiple dialogues, pointing out the deceptive nature of rhetoric and its consequent moral dangers. Isocrates, in turn, claimed that Platonism went against common sense with its exaggerated intellectualism. The youthful Aristotle entered the debate with the now lost treatise *Gryllus*, a polemic against Isocrates that mimics the ideas of Plato. At this time, Aristotle did not consider rhetoric to be an art (*techne*). We know of *Gryllus* because it is mentioned in other ancient sources, which indicate that the work offers a glimpse into Aristotle's formative thoughts on rhetorical theory and provides some insight into the development of ideas that led to the creation of his masterwork, the *Rhetoric*.

Aristotle's *Rhetoric* is considered by many to be the most important and influential work on formal persuasion ever written. The Peripatetics of the Hellenistic age admired and expressed in fuller form Aristotle's

✣ *Key Facts*

**Time Period:**
4th Century BCE

**Genre:**
Treatise

**Events:**
Rise of democracy; Battle of Chaeronea; founding of the Lyceum

**Nationality:**
Greek

# ARISTOTLE: A BIOGRAPHICAL NOTE

Aristotle was born in 384 BCE in the small town of Stagira on the northeast coast of the Chalcidice peninsula. Aristotle's father, Nicomachus, was the physician to Amyntas II, king of Macedon. Aristotle's interest in physical science and biology had its roots in his upbringing. He intended to follow his father's profession, but this plan changed when both of his parents died. At the age of seventeen, Aristotle moved to Athens and enrolled at Plato's Academy, where he remained for nineteen years—until Plato's death. Aristotle then traveled to Assos and married Pythias, who bore him a daughter. After three years in Assos, he moved to Mitylene. While living in Assos and Mitylene, Aristotle devoted a great deal of time to the study of natural history, especially in his explorations of the island lagoon of Pyrrha. He traveled to Pella in 343 to educate Prince Alexander, the future conqueror. In 335, he moved back to Athens and founded his school of philosophy, the Lyceum. He taught here for nearly thirteen years and composed his greatest works during this time. After his wife's death, he became involved with Herpyllis, who bore him a son named Nicomachus. Aristotle died not long after Alexander the Great. The works of Aristotle have significantly influenced higher education in the Western world. His ethical, political, rhetorical, and epistemological treatises are still considered the finest introductions to these subjects.

rhetorical system. Theophrastus, for example, developed Aristotle's rhetorical delivery with emphasis on facial expressions, and Hermagoras expanded Aristotle's forensic and deliberative branches of rhetoric. In ancient Rome, Aristotle's *Rhetoric* profoundly influenced the divisional structures of Quintilian's *Institutio* and Cicero's *De invention* and *De oratore*. The text of the *Rhetoric* was lost for centuries; it was the last of Aristotle's works to be recovered in the Middle Ages. It was translated into Arabic and then translated into Latin (from the Arabic) in 1256. From the sixteenth century to the present, numerous translations and commentaries have been published. Contemporary academicians have frequently scrutinized the construction of the work and have analyzed the psychological concepts in the treatise.

**THEMES AND STYLE**

Central to Aristotle's *Rhetoric* is the opening declaration that "Rhetoric is the counterpart of dialectic" and the moral implications of this statement. In direct contrast to the views Aristotle expressed in the earlier treatise *Gryllus*, he now asserts that rhetoric is not a form of immoral deception. He now believes that rhetoric involves logical reasoning, and he concludes that it is an art (*techne*). Furthermore, he identifies rhetoric as a key element of philosophy. Aristotle acknowledges that rhetoric is potentially dangerous unless used by those of good moral character. In *The Idea of Propaganda*, Stanley Cunningham points out that rhetoric

is not by necessity propaganda, despite the fact that the terms are often used interchangeably. As Cunningham notes, propaganda "exploits information, skews perceptions, disregards values such as truth, poses as knowledge, and supplies ersatz certainties." Rhetoric, in contrast, is often truthful. On the one hand, Aristotle stresses the importance of arguing both sides of a question; on the other hand, he concludes that the best rhetoric is truthful and that "We must not make people believe what is wrong." Rhetoric, according to Aristotle, is intended to help counteract false arguments; therefore, it provides a defense against propaganda.

Aristotle defines rhetoric as "the faculty of observing in any given case the available means of persuasion." He differentiates his theory of rhetoric from the theories of his predecessors by making the focus of the rhetorician's argument a logical proof, the enthymeme, which he posits as the most important form of persuasion. (Earlier theories relied on the use of emotional appeals and distracting lines of argument.) In Aristotle's view, persuasiveness and truth were closely linked; therefore, a rhetorician's success depends upon the degree to which he is able to prove the truth of his argument using reason. The technical means of persuasion lie in establishing the speaker's character (*ethos*); guiding the emotional response (*pathos*) of the audience; and the argument of the speech itself (*logos*). A speaker who is able to convince an audience that he is of good character is more likely to gain his hearers' belief and trust; likewise, a speaker who is able to arouse the emotions of the audience so that it is warmly disposed toward him is more likely to be heard. Finally, a speaker who is able to prove that something is the case successfully employs the most important means of persuasion, the enthymeme, which, according to Aristotle, should optimally have the form of a deductive argument. Aristotle holds that rhetoric is most important in the following contexts: a deliberative setting, such as a political debate; a forensic argument made in court; or an epideictic, or ceremonial, speech, such as a funeral oration. The *Rhetoric* discusses the techniques appropriate to each of these contexts. In addition, the work provides lists of *topoi*, or patterns upon which certain kinds of arguments can be based. Some of the topoi are quite specific, providing examples of language that can be used to arouse an audience's emotions, for example, while others provide only general instruction on how to construct an argument, suggesting, for example, that a speaker reflect back upon an opponent a criticism made by that opponent.

Stylistically, the language of Aristotle's *Rhetoric* is philosophical and unemotional. The philosopher maintains a detached and authoritative voice throughout the work; for example, he claims "The subject can plainly be handled systematically, for it is possible to inquire the reason why some speakers succeed through practice and others spontaneously." He coins and defines numerous rhetorical terms and logically proves their persuasive function. Although many of Aristotle's statements are original and even controversial, they often seem commonsensical because of his advanced ability in logical proofs. By providing clear and concise examples throughout the work, Aristotle effectively makes the means of persuasion available for propagandists. Aristotle wrote the *Rhetoric* in the same philosophical and authoritative manner as he did his other works on a variety of topics such as *Poetics, Nicomachean Ethics,* and *Metaphysics.*

## CRITICAL DISCUSSION

The initial reaction to Aristotle's *Rhetoric* is relatively unknown. The preserved text was neither published nor was it readily available outside Aristotle's personal library for many years. In his monograph "The Audience for Aristotle's *Rhetoric*," Edward Clayton argues that Aristotle's students were his primary targeted audience and, therefore, widespread publication of this esoteric treatise was not deemed necessary. Aristotle's *Rhetoric* influenced many Peripatetics, such as his successor at the Lyceum, Theophrastus. Theophrastus provides an extension of Aristotelian thought in his work *Lexis,* placing greater value on bodily gestures and further developing such strategies as the rhetorical deduction. In 83 BCE, the Roman general Sulla seized Aristotle's works and sent them to Rome, where they were published and admired. In his *De inventione,* Cicero adheres to Aristotle's conclusion that the rhetorician's work takes the form of speeches that are laudatory, political, or forensic in nature (the *tria genera causarum,* or three kinds of cases), and in *De oratore* he repeatedly refers to Aristotle's *Rhetoric* as the authoritative text on the subject.

The legacy of Aristotle's *Rhetoric* cannot be overstated. In their preface to *Rereading Aristotle's Rhetoric,* Alan Gross and Arthur Walzer recognize the tremendous influence of the work and make the following claim: "[Alfred North] Whitehead's observation that the history of philosophy is one long footnote to Plato can for us be transferred to the *Rhetoric.* All subsequent rhetorical theory is but a series of responses to issues raised by that central work." Numerous translations of the *Rhetoric,* as well as commentaries and critical works about it, have been published since ancient times; for example, the twelfth-century philosopher Averroës wrote a brief but highly influential commentary, Thomas Hobbes provided a fine translation of the *Rhetoric* in the seventeenth century, and Amelie Oksenberg Rorty has more recently re-examined the text in her insightful critical essays.

Although the *Rhetoric* has been appreciated for centuries, the understanding of its significance is a phenomenon of twentieth- and twenty-first century interest in speech communication and critical theory. Among contemporary audiences who have taken a particularly keen interest in Aristotle's *Rhetoric* are

Aristotle and Plato: detail from *The School of Athens,* a fresco in the Palace of the Vatican painted by Raphael in 1510–11. ARISTOTLE AND PLATO: DETAIL FROM *THE SCHOOL OF ATHENS IN THE STANZA DELLA SEGNATURA,* 1510–11 (FRESCO) (DETAIL OF 472), RAPHAEL (RAFFAELLO SANZIO OF URBINO) (1483–1520)/VATICAN MUSEUMS AND GALLERIES, VATICAN CITY/THE BRIDGEMAN ART LIBRARY.

classical philologists, students of ancient philosophy, teachers of composition, communications scholars, and literary critics. Contemporary scholarship has focused on such issues as the structure of the text and psychological elements in the work. In her essay "Structuring Rhetoric," for example, Amelie Oksenberg Rorty tackles both of these scholarly trends, exploring the role played by different types of psychological knowledge in the structure of Aristotle's theory of rhetoric. Rorty argues that the "intractable problems" that Aristotle's theory leaves unresolved continue to be "mirrored in our own deliberations about public and political discourse." She observes that, like Aristotle, audiences today continue to view oratory "pragmatically, as directed to finding the most efficacious argument to produce the most satisfactory results," and, like Aristotle, they continue to "construe the 'satisfactory result' morally."

## BIBLIOGRAPHY

*Sources*

Aristotle. *The Complete Works of Aristotle.* Ed. Jonathan Barnes. Trans. W. Rhys Roberts. Princeton: Princeton UP, 1995. Print.

Bury, John B. *A History of Greece.* New York: Random, 1900. Print.

Clayton, Edward. "The Audience for Aristotle's *Rhetoric.*" *Rhetorica* 22 (2004): 183–203. Print.

Cunningham, Stanley. *The Idea of Propaganda.* Westport: Praeger, 2002. Print.

Gross, Alan, and Arthur Walzer. *Rereading Aristotle's Rhetoric.* Carbondale: Southern Illinois UP, 2000. Print.

Rorty, Amélie Oksenberg. "Structuring Rhetoric." *Essays on Aristotle's Rhetoric.* Ed. Rorty. Berkeley: U of California P, 1996. 1–33. Print.

*Further Reading*

Allen, Barry. *Truth in Philosophy.* Cambridge: Harvard UP, 1993.

Crowley, Sharon, and Debra Hawhee. *Ancient Rhetorics for Contemporary Students.* Boston: Allyn, 1999. Print.

Engberg-Pedersen, Troels. "Is There an Ethical Dimension to Aristotelian Rhetoric?" *Essays on Aristotle's Rhetoric.* Ed. Amélie Oksenberg Rorty. Berkeley: U of California P, 1996. 116–141. Print.

Garver, Eugene. *Aristotle's Rhetoric: An Art of Character.* Chicago: U of Chicago P, 1994. Print.

Jaeger, Werner. *Paideia: The Ideals of Greek Culture.* Trans. Gilbert Highet. Vol. III. Oxford: Oxford UP, 1944. Print.

Kennedy, George A. "The Composition and Influence of Aristotle's *Rhetoric.*" *Essays on Aristotle's Rhetoric.* Ed. Amélie Oksenberg Rorty. Berkeley: U of California P, 1996. 416–25. Print.

Thorp, John. "Aristotle's Rehabilitation of Rhetoric." *Canadian Journal of Rhetorical Studies* 3 (1993): 13–30. Print.

*Greg Bach*

# "TALKS AT THE YAN'AN FORUM ON LITERATURE AND ART"

*Mao Zedong*

## OVERVIEW

Mao Zedong's "Talks at the Yan'an Forum on Literature and Art," delivered on May 2 and 23, 1942, and published a year later, underscores the importance of literature and art in the Chinese Communist Revolution. Presenting a series of problems that compromise the revolutionary value of art, the "Talks" offer correctives for artists who, according to Mao, do not fully understand their role in supporting the masses. Mao's basic position is that art should be created for the people and by the people, that the political import of creative work takes precedence over its aesthetic quality, and that revolutionary art should be evaluated by its effects rather than by its intentions. His "Talks" constitute perhaps the single most influential document in the history of art in modern China. In the seventy years since they were first given, the "Talks" have inspired and guided the production of thousands of pieces of communist propaganda.

Mao's "Talks" were given at Yan'an, a small, remote city in north-central China located near the endpoint of the Long March—a retreat made by the Chinese communist army that ended in 1936. Yan'an served as a headquarters for the revolution from 1936 to 1948 and, as such, attracted revolutionary thinkers and artists from Shanghai and many other places. These new arrivals joined the veteran communists in living in caves while they set up schools and other institutions to facilitate the development and spread of communist ideas. Many intellectuals associated with the so-called May Fourth Movement also influenced the culture of Yan'an, and they offered their suggestions and criticisms to the Communist Party. By 1942, however, tension had arisen between the May Fourth group and the communists. The party called the Yan'an Forum to address the attitude and mission of revolutionary intellectuals, many of whom were May Fourth writers who, Mao believed, were out of step

÷ *Key Facts*

**Time Period:**
Mid-20th Century

**Genre:**
Speech

**Events:**
May Fourth Movement;
Chinese Civil War

**Nationality:**
Chinese

Dancers in traditional Chinese folk dress performing in front of a portrait of Mao Zedong with soldiers looking on (1952). Ten years earlier Mao had delivered his "Talks at the Yan'an Forum on Literature and Art," which outlined the approved style of art and literature. © MICHAEL NICHOLSON/CORBIS.

## PRIMARY SOURCE

### EXCERPT FROM "TALKS AT THE YAN'AN FORUM ON LITERATURE AND ART"

[...] Our meeting today is to ensure that literature and art become a component part of the whole revolutionary machinery, so they can act as a powerful weapon in uniting and educating the people while attacking and annihilating the enemy, and help the people achieve solidarity in their struggle against the enemy. What are the problems which must be solved in order to achieve this purpose? They are questions relating to our position, attitude, audience, work, and study.

The question of our position. We identify ourselves with the proletariat and the broad popular masses. Communist Party members must also identify themselves with the Party and with its basic character and policy. Is it true that some of our workers in literature and art still lack a clear and correct understanding of this question? I think so: many comrades have frequently strayed from their correct position. ...

What does the existence of these questions among our writers and artists in Yan'an tell us? It tells

us that three incorrect working styles still exit to a serious degree among our writers and artists, and that many shortcomings such as idealism, foreign dogmatism, idle speculation, contempt for practice, and isolation from the masses still exist among our comrades, a situation that requires a realistic and serious movement to correct our work styles.

Many of our comrades are still not very clear about the difference between the proletariat and the petty bourgeoisie. Many party members have joined the party on an organizational level, but haven't made a full commitment on the ideological level, or any commitment at all; these people still carry around a lot of exploiter's filth in their heads and are fundamentally ignorant of what proletarian ideology, communism, and the party are. They think that proletarian ideology is just the same old story. Little do they realize that it is by no means easy to acquire: some people spend a lifetime without ever getting close to being a true party member and invariably end up leaving the party. Of course, some people are even worse: on the organizational level, they join the Japanese party,

with communism's populist mission. Mao's "Talks" soon traveled far beyond their immediate context; they became almost instantly foundational to communist theory and art, and they have shaped the artistic production of China ever since.

### HISTORICAL AND LITERARY CONTEXT

As Mao points out, literature and art had played a significant role in the revolutionary struggle since May 4, 1919. On that day, the gathering of students to protest the transfer of Shandong province to Japan (a provision of the World War I peace treaty) sparked a cultural movement. The subsequent May Fourth Movement called for a cultural shift away from Western-style intellectualism and Chinese traditionalism and toward a more politicized and modern understanding of culture. The movement, in turn, facilitated the birth of the Chinese Communist Party in 1921. The production of revolutionary art grew in the 1930s, during the war between Chinese communists and the Nationalist government. The government's violent persecution of left-wing activity radicalized many writers and students, who increasingly turned to communism. Over time, many intellectuals associated with communism or the older May Fourth Movement traveled to Yan'an to observe the social experimentation going on there.

By the early 1940s conflict had developed in Yan'an between the newly arrived intellectuals and the peasants, soldiers, and veterans of the Long March. The tension was due in part to the intellectuals' distaste for physical labor. In China at the time, young educated people rarely performed working-class jobs to finance their early intellectual or artistic endeavors. Mao recognized that this gap in experience had separated the priorities of writers and artists from the needs of the newly literate mass of Chinese people. He chose to address this pervasive divide in the Yan'an "Talks."

Much of the theory presented in Mao's "Talks" did not originate with him; earlier versions of the ideas he presents had begun to appear in China in the 1920s. May Fourth intellectual Qu Qiubai preceded Mao in his opposition to the Westernization of Chinese literature, and much of Mao's theory of revolutionary art derives from Leninist literary theory and policy. Mao's ideas also overlap considerably with those of Lu Xun, a writer lionized by Mao and quoted multiple times in the "Talks." However, as scholar Bonnie S. McDougall argues in her 1980 commentary and translation of the "Talks," Mao's thinking is deeper and more comprehensive than that of most left-wing writers of his day. McDougall points out that the leader excels at emphasizing the importance

Wang Jingwei's party, or the Special Branch of the big bourgeoisie and big landlords party, but afterwards they also bore their way into the Communist party or Communist-led organizations, advertising themselves as "partymembers" and "revolutionaries." As a result, although the vast majority of people in our party and in our ranks are true, nevertheless, if we are to lead the revolutionary movement to develop in a better way and be the sooner completed, then we must conscientiously put in order our internal affairs on both ideological and organizational levels. We have to put things in order ideologically before we can tackle the organizational level and begin an ideological struggle between the proletariat and non-proletarian classes. An ideological struggle has already begun among writers and artists in Yan'an, which is very necessary. People of petty bourgeois origins always persist in expressing themselves through a variety of ways and means, including literature and art, propagating their own proposals and urging people to remake the party and the rest of the world in the image of the petty bourgeois intelligentsia. Under these conditions our job is to raise our voices and say, "Comrades, this game of yours won't work, the proletariat and the popular masses can't accept your terms; following your course would be in fact following the big landlords and big bourgeoisie; that way we'd run the risk of losing our party, our country, and our own heads." Who are the only people we can rely on? We must rely on the proletariat and its vanguard to remake the party and the rest of the world in their image. We hope that the comrades who are writers and artists recognize the seriousness of this great debate and participate actively in the struggle directed toward the enemy, friends, comrades, and ourselves, so that every comrade is strengthened and our entire ranks are genuinely united and consolidated on both the ideological and organizational level.

SOURCE: "'Talks at the Yan'an Conference on Literature and Art': A Translation of the 1943 Text with Commentary," pp. 58, 83–84, translated by Bonnie S. McDougall. Copyright © 1980 by Center for Chinese Studies, The University of Michigan. All rights reserved. Reproduced by permission.

of his audience, the politics of form, and the process of literary creation.

The Yan'an "Talks" had two primary immediate effects: the first was the suppression of the critical strain of May Fourth-style writing that prevailed in the months leading up to the "Talks"; the second was an increased focus on popular cultural forms derived from peasant traditions. An example of the latter was the *yangge* peasant dance, which had been developed into a revolutionary play called *The White-Haired Girl*. The play was performed at the Yan'an Forum as a model of revolutionary art that reflected Maoist principles and guidelines. Today Mao's "Talks" not only provide a useful example of left-wing literary criticism and theory, but they also offer insight into the historical period from which they emerged. Moreover, the "Talks" enable contemporary readers to see how Mao—through his practical approach, persuasive tone, and charismatic turns of phrase—was able to inspire and carry out a communist revolution on a grand scale.

## THEMES AND STYLE

Throughout his Yan'an "Talks," Mao reiterates that in a class society, all aesthetic values are class based and therefore political, which is the reason that the goals of art and the criteria for evaluating it cannot be separated from politics. Encouraging artists to reflect on this knowledge as they create a classless society through revolution, Mao stresses the importance of a "cultural army" to unify and galvanize the revolutionary efforts of the common people, who constitute more than 90 percent of the population. He emphasizes the need for a "living Marxism which plays an effective role in the life and struggle of the masses, not Marxism in words." Thus, as art must serve politics, popularization and accessibility must take precedence over the raising of aesthetic standards.

The perspective and structure of Mao's "Talks" reflect his powerful insight and his direct, pragmatic approach. He establishes himself as a voice of practical logic: "in discussing a problem, we should start from reality and not from definitions." Setting up his speech in a problem-solution format, he systematically disabuses his audience of artists and writers of the middle-class biases and prejudices that they still carry. Moving through a series of mistaken beliefs about art, he redefines the terms of the argument by making it less abstract. He evaluates these beliefs by considering their actual revolutionary potential: "Many comrades like to talk about 'a mass style.' But what does it really mean? It means that the thoughts and feelings of our writers and artists should be fused with those of the masses of workers, peasants, and soldiers." Rhetorical questions like this help Mao to carry his point home.

# CENSORSHIP OF CHINESE LITERATURE AND ART: A LEGACY OF THE "TALKS"

Perhaps the most general and lasting effect of the "Talks at the Yan'an Forum on Literature and Art" has been the censorship of Chinese artistic production since the 1940s. Recent Chinese literature, art, and entertainment tend to focus on the bright side of life, to provide moral uplift, and to avoid superstition and grim subject matter. Furthermore, Chinese cultural productions eschew satire and humor to avoid treading on any political toes, and they are expected to depict Chinese history and historical figures heroically.

Yet while censorship often suppresses creativity, it may spur it as well. A great example is the work of Ai Weiwei, a controversial photographer, sculptor, architect, and performance artist whose studio was demolished by the Chinese government. Ai also has been detained as punishment for his violation of the government's tastes and preferences. Government censorship inspired Ai to create a self-surveillance performance project (Weiweicam.com), which endeavors to depict what life in a fully censored China would be like. The project was shut down by the government in April 2012, but the existing feed still appears online and receives inspiring commentary from loyal fans.

He anticipates the question "Then does not Marxism destroy the creative mood?" by answering with a twist: "Yes, it does. It definitely destroys creative moods that are feudal, bourgeois, liberalistic, individualist, nihilist, art-for-art's sake, aristocratic, decadent, or pessimistic." Speaking in the first person at times, he also uses personal anecdote as a rhetorical device to establish common ground with his audience. Citing his own original distaste for manual labor and the peasant lifestyle, he explains that, after having considered the corruption of bourgeois life, what he once thought was a "dirty" way of life now seems the "clean" one.

In their simple, direct vocabulary and phrasing, Mao's "Talks" model the popular accessibility and practicality that he asks artists and writers to adopt. He sets up familiar, easily graspable binaries such as "political" and "artistic," "good" and "bad," "content" and "form," "motive" and "effect," and "unity" and "struggle." His tone toward his audience is firm, as he is ultimately inflexible in his views—"writers who cling to an individualist, petty-bourgeois stand cannot truly serve the masses"—yet he endeavors to seem moderate and compromising as he carefully and patiently articulates the appropriate approach to the aesthetic binaries he summons. He uses metaphor sparingly but effectively; for instance, he explains that the people's "prime need" is not "more flowers on the brocade" but "fuel in snowy weather." In line with his advocacy of a "bright" outlook, he speaks with hope, tempered by a realistic understanding of the size of the task at hand: "There will be genuine

love of humanity—after classes are eliminated all over the world." Indeed, the "Talks" remain a justification for the severe censorship of artistic and intellectual freedom under communism.

## CRITICAL DISCUSSION

In the months following the Yan'an Forum, voices critical of the Communist Party's methods were quickly quieted, as artists and writers tried to follow the guidelines provided by Mao. In the following years, more than eighty editions of the "Talks" were published, and Mao's ideas spread rapidly. Early treatments of the "Talks" by those sympathetic to Mao's politics, such as Jaroslav Prusek's *Die Literature des Befreiten China* ("The Literature of the Liberated in China"; 1955) and Wang Yao's *Zhongguo xin wenxue shi gao* ("Draft History of China's New Literature"; 1954), focus on clarifying and propagating the political import of the talks. Western discussions of the "Talks," such as those found in C. T. Hsia's *History of Modern Chinese Fiction* (1961), Douwe Fokkema's *Literary Doctrine in China and Soviet Influence* (1965), and Merle Goldman's *Literary Dissent in Communist China* (1967), tend to be dismissive of Mao's artistic theory. They perceive it as simplistic propaganda shaped entirely by a political and moral agenda rather than by aesthetic concerns.

The popularity of the "Talks" has waxed and waned over time; more attention was paid to them in the 1940s and the late 1960s than in the 1950s and more recent years. During the periods of praise for the "Talks," they have been cited to rally support for a variety of artistic and intellectual revivals and suppressions. Before 1950, as mentioned above, the "Talks" inspired the turn toward popular forms and the silencing of critical voices in Yan'an; after 1950 a revival of both China's classical tradition and May Fourth literature ensued. Chinese literary policy became more permissive during the 1950s, when Zhou Yang, vice-minister of culture and vice director of the Department of Propaganda, invited writers to explore topics less political in nature. However, that period of liberality ended when control of artistic production tightened during the Cultural Revolution (1966–76) and Zhou was persecuted and dismissed by Mao's wife, Jiang Qing, as a counterrevolutionary force.

Western scholarship of the past thirty years has revised its earlier reductive understandings of Mao's thinking and explored the complexities of the "Talks" more carefully. Scholars of the 1970s and 1980s in particular sought to reconsider Mao's ideas at a time when communist studies were relevant and still interesting to global intellectuals. John Bryan Starr's *Continuing the Revolution: The Political Thought of Mao* (1982) distinguishes between "historically universal, general, and specific ideas" in his discussion of the validity of the "Talks." McDougall's significant 1980 translation of and commentary on the 1943 edition of the "Talks" redeem their value as literary theory—an approach that had been neglected in Eastern and Western scholarship.

## BIBLIOGRAPHY

*Sources*

McDougall, Bonnie S. *Mao Zedong's "Talks at the Yan'an Conference on Literature and Art": A Translation of the 1943 Text with Commentary.* Ann Arbor: Center for Chinese Studies, U of Michigan P, 1980. Print.

Womack, Brantly. Rev. of *Continuing the Revolution: The Political Thought of Mao,* by John Bryan Starr; *The Emergence of Maoism: Mao Tse-tung, Ch'en Po-ta, and the Search for Chinese Theory 1935–1945,* by Raymond F. Wylie; *Mao Zedong's 'Talks at the Yan'an Conference on Literature and Art': A Translation of the 1943 Text with Commentary,* by Bonnie S. McDougall. *Journal of Asian Studies* 41.4 (1982): 825–28. Print.

Wylie, Raymond F. *The Emergence of Maoism: Mao Tse-tung, Ch'en Po-ta, and the Search for Chinese Theory 1935–1945.* Stanford: Stanford UP, 1980. Print.

Zedong, Mao. *Selected Readings from the Works of Mao Tse-tung.* Peking: Foreign Languages Press, 1971. Print.

*Further Reading*

Denton, Kirk, ed. *Modern Chinese Literary Thought: Writings on Literature, 1893–1945.* Stanford: Stanford UP, 1996. Print.

Fei, Faye Chunfang, ed. and trans. *Chinese Theories of Theater and Performance from Confucius to the Present.* Ann Arbor: U of Michigan P, 1999. Print.

Guo, Sujian. *Post-Mao China: From Totalitarianism to Authoritarianism?* Westport: Praeger, 2000. Print.

Lenin, Vladimir Il'ich. "Party Organisation and Party Literature." *Collected Works.* Vol. X. Moscow: FLPH, 1962. 48–49. Print.

Peng, Lu. *A History of Art in 20th Century China.* Trans. Bruce Gordon Doar. Milano: Charta, 2010. Print.

*Sarah Gardam*

# THE WRETCHED OF THE EARTH

*Frantz Fanon*

## OVERVIEW

*The Wretched of the Earth* (1961), an analysis of decolonization by Frantz Fanon, explores the psychological effects of colonialism and proposes a theory of revolution and anticolonial struggle. In fiery prose, Fanon draws from his own encounters with racism and colonialism not only in his native Martinique but also in France and in his adopted home of Algeria. *The Wretched of the Earth* comprises several essays, a number of psychiatric case studies, and a concluding manifesto that calls for a new "history of man." Fanon exposes the atrocities of colonialism obscured by European humanist discourse and denies the possibility that decolonization can ever be peaceful. He also addresses the challenges posed by nation building, condemning the role of the corrupt, native, intellectual elite during the postindependence of former colonies and rejecting notions of continental and racial identity that were popular at the time.

Following its publication, *The Wretched of the Earth* received mixed reviews, particularly in relation to Fanon's controversial views on violence. The text has been called both the bible and *Mein Kampf* of decolonization. Despite this paradox, *The Wretched of the Earth* has had a major impact in the years since its publication. Although aspects of the text have little applicability outside of the anticolonial context, many of Fanon's ideas have been reappropriated by later scholars, revolutionaries, and equal-rights activists.

## HISTORICAL AND LITERARY CONTEXT

Many former European colonies gained independence in the aftermath of World War II. The process of decolonization was often nonviolent, although some nations were forced to engage in extended struggles for self-determination. From 1954 until 1962 Algeria fought a particularly bloody war of independence. After its colonization in 1830, Algeria had rapidly become home to a sizable European settler community known as *pieds-noirs*. The entrenchment of this population and the country's proximity to France contributed to the belief that French Algeria was not a colony but an integral part of France. This perception led to a protracted conflict that continued even after most of Africa and the majority of France's other colonies had already gained independence.

Seven years had passed since the outbreak of the Algerian War of Independence when *The Wretched of the Earth* was published. The French army had reinstituted the use of torture, a move that horrified many French intellectuals, especially in the wake of World War II. However, the official French political discourse of the time suppressed this dissent. In addition to the atrocities committed by the army, acts of terrorism were carried out by both the right-wing *Organisation armée secrète* (OAS), which supported the preservation of French Algeria, and the *Front de libération nationale* (FLN), a group dedicated to Algerian independence. Although Fanon was born in Martinique and educated in France, he became a member of the FLN and worked as one of their publicists. *The Wretched of the Earth* promotes the perspective of the colonized and was written to engineer support for the nationalist cause, especially among the French left.

*The Wretched of the Earth* emerged as part of a larger literature focused on decolonization. In 1960 the *Declaration of the Right to Insubordination in the Algerian War*, known as *The Manifesto of the 121* (after the number of its original signatories), condemned the use of torture by the French army and supported the Algerian cause. However, this document was concerned with the right of French soldiers to refuse to fight in the war in Algeria and was not addressed to the Algerian people. Fanon had previously written on the psychological effects of racism in *Black Skin, White Masks* (1952), and he focused on the colonial struggle in Algeria in *A Dying Colonialism* (1959). Fanon's fourth essay in *The Wretched of the Earth*, "On National Culture," was a reaction in part to philosophies such as Pan-Africanism and *Négritude* that he believed promoted a reified and static postcolonial identity that was rooted in the past rather than the present.

Although some critics condemned Fanon's endorsement of violence in *The Wretched of the Earth*, the text has been influential in a variety of contexts and has generated an extensive body of scholarship. When Fanon died just months after completing *The Wretched of the Earth*, the Paris police seized copies found in bookstores. The text affected the ideas of later leaders, revolutionaries, and artists, including Bobby Seale and Huey Newton, founders of the American Black Panther Party; Steve Biko, founder of the South African Black Consciousness movement; Ali Shariati, one of the intellectual leaders of the Iranian Revolution; and Ngugi Wa Thiong'o and Ayi Kwei Armah, writers from Kenya and Ghana respectively. *The Wretched of the Earth* remains the focus of scholarly debate and criticism even today.

## THEMES AND STYLE

In *The Wretched of the Earth*, Fanon is primarily concerned with the process of decolonization, which must include both physical and psychological revolution if the colonized are to prevail over the systematic oppression and dehumanization of colonialism and become a functioning member of the new nation. Fanon recognizes the vital role of class struggle, but he emphasizes the importance of race in the division of power within the colonial context: "In the colonies the economic infrastructure is also a superstructure. The cause is effect: You are rich because you are white, you are white because you are rich." Since colonialism represents "the organization of a Manichaean world, of a compartmentalized world," Fanon asserts that there is no easy path to liberation: "decolonization is always a violent event." When Fanon turns to nation building, he is critical of the African bourgeoisie and the intellectual elite who look to history and tradition for an understanding of national identity that is static and reified. Fanon argues that "[c]ulture eminently eludes any form of simplification." He further rejects notions of continental or racial identity. Culture must be national; it is "the collective thought process of a people to describe, justify, and extol the actions whereby they have joined forces and remained strong." Fanon questions the legitimacy of the colonial narrative that claimed to rest on European humanist values and also destabilizes predominant Pan-African ideologies that were shaping the newly independent nations of Africa.

The argument for decolonization is presented in *The Wretched of the Earth* through the use of essays, case studies of the mental disorders caused by colonialism and war, and a closing manifesto. In his four essays, Fanon addresses different aspects of decolonization, beginning with the actual struggle for independence and ending with the formation of the nation. The case studies draw from Fanon's encounters as a psychiatrist with both French and Algerian patients at the psychiatric hospital in Blida, Algeria, as well as his private treatment of FLN revolutionaries. By approaching the conflict through a psychiatric lens, Fanon is able to expand these encounters into universal theories on the psychological effects of colonialism and decolonization. The final chapter of *The Wretched of the Earth* constitutes a manifesto addressed to the people of the Third World. Embracing Marxist and universalist rhetoric, Fanon makes an idealistic call: "For Europe, for ourselves and for humanity, comrades, we must make a new start, develop a new way of thinking and endeavor to create a new man." Through the combination of three different formal approaches, Fanon undermines European humanism and situates the future, of both the Third World and Europe, in the hands of the formerly colonized.

Stylistically, Fanon employs a universalist tone as he lays out his theory, while his use of French colonial terminology and Arabic words locates him within the Algerian context. Fanon makes repeated reference to the Third World and its people, a designation that encompasses every colonized, newly independent, and underdeveloped nation. At the same time, however, he uses the Arabic word *fellah*, which roughly means peasant, in general discussions of the colonized subject. For example, he makes reference to "the fellah, the unemployed and the starving," indicating his familiarity with French and, specifically, Algerian colonialism. Fanon's claim that he is speaking for and to the Third World signals a rebellion against the colony's dependence on the *metropole* and undermines the belief that new nations must rely on colonial structures and language for their foundation.

## CRITICAL DISCUSSION

Following its publication, as Algeria moved closer to independence and other revolutionary movements began to take shape around the world, *The Wretched of the Earth* provoked a range of reactions in France, Africa, and the United States. Marxists condemned

## THE PSYCHOLOGICAL IMPACT OF COLONIALISM: A TUNISIAN PERSPECTIVE

In 1957, the year after Tunisia gained independence from France, Albert Memmi published *The Colonizer and the Colonized*, in which he provides a description of the colonial dynamic through a series of "portraits." As a Tunisian Jew, Memmi occupied a liminal position between the colonizing population and his Muslim compatriots, which he believed allowed him to identify with both sides. Memmi observes that the colonizer relies on the continued presence of the colonized for his existence and the perpetuation of the colonial system that privileges him. Memmi refutes the existence of the benign colonial, arguing that every European occupies a position of economic and racial superiority in the system even if he or she is not as privileged as other Europeans. By exploring the psychological effects of colonialism on both sides of the colonial project, Memmi demonstrates that the systematic dehumanization and exploitation of colonialism damages the colonized psyche as it simultaneously destroys the colonizer's soul and that the colonial situation is ultimately untenable and revolt is inevitable. Memmi's goal was to portray the particularities of his encounter with colonialism in Tunisia, but *The Colonizer and the Colonized*—much like *The Wretched of the Earth*—has been adopted by oppressed peoples around the world. He dedicates the American edition to "the American Negro," illustrating the argument that colonialism takes many forms.

Celebrations in Algiers, Algeria, in 1962, marking Algeria's independence from France. Frantz Fanon supported African independence in works such his 1961 book *The Wretched of the Earth.* © THE PRINT COLLECTOR/ALAMY.

Fanon's emphasis on race and the psycho-affective realm rather than class and questioned his focus on the rural masses instead of the proletariat. Fanon was also criticized for developing a generalized theory of revolution and decolonization based predominantly on the case of Algeria. However, the debate around *The Wretched of the Earth* mostly concerned the book's first chapter, "On Violence." In "Frantz Fanon: A Gospel for the Damned," Aristide R. Zolberg denounced the text's "murderous humanism," while Jean Paul Sartre, in his 1961 preface to *The Wretched of the Earth,* affirmed the necessity of violence in decolonization. Sartre stresses that the nation, and with it a new humanism, can only be born of violence: "[K]illing a European is killing two birds with one stone, eliminating in one go oppressor and oppressed: leaving one man dead and the other man free."

As part of Fanon's larger body of work, *The Wretched of the Earth* has been regarded as a broader call for ideological transformation and revolution rather than a historically specific theory of decolonization. In "Race and Nation: Ideology in the Thought of Frantz Fanon" (1980), Paul Nursey-Bray argues that "for Fanon, the end product of revolutionary struggle is nothing less than the creation of a new set of human possibilities, not just for the colonized, but for all mankind." In his 1993 article, "Frantz Fanon as a Democratic Theorist," Hussein M. Adams similarly settles on Fanon in his search for "indigenous [African] political theories favouring democratization," asserting that he "outlines a theory of democratized development through an emphasis on decentralization and participation." More recently, Homi Bhabha, in his 2004 forward to the new English translation of *The*

*Wretched of the Earth,* makes the case for "a critique of the configurations of contemporary globalization," drawing a comparison between its victims and the oppressed subjects of colonialism. He turns to Fanon to emphasize "the need for something like a 'right' to equitable development."

Much of the scholarship on *The Wretched of the Earth,* like early criticism of the book, focuses on Fanon's theory of violence. In *Holy Violence* (1982) B. Marie Perinbam differentiates between violence, which she defines as "coercion and physical force," and the "holy violence" endorsed by Fanon, which she describes as "a distinctive force creative beyond belief, and frightening beyond comprehension, compelling and dangerously powerful." Hannah Arendt however, in her 1970 work *On Violence,* advances her widely cited critique of Fanon's belief (which was further radicalized by Sartre in his preface) that the violence of revolutionary struggle leads to a new humanism: "no body politic I know of was ever founded on equality before death and its actualization in violence."

## BIBLIOGRAPHY

*Sources*

Adam, Hussein M. "Frantz Fanon as a Democratic Theorist." *African Affairs* 92.369 (1993): 499–518. Print.

Arendt, Hannah. *On Violence.* New York: Harcourt, 1970. Print.

Bhabha, Homi K. Foreword. *The Wretched of the Earth.* By Frantz Fanon. New York: Grove, 2004. vii–xli. Print.

Nursey-Bray, Paul. "Race and Nation: Ideology in the Thought of Frantz Fanon." *The Journal of Modern African Studies* 18.1 (1980): 135–42. Print.

Perinbam, B. Marie. *Holy Violence: The Revolutionary Thought of Frantz Fanon.* Washington: Three Continents, 1982. Print.

Sartre, Jean-Paul. Preface. *The Wretched of the Earth.* By Frantz Fanon. New York: Grove, 2004. xliii–lxii. Print.

Zolberg, Aristide R. "Frantz Fanon: A Gospel for the Damned." *Encounter* 27.5 (1966): 56–62. Print.

*Further Reading*

Bhabha, Homi. "Interrogating Identity: Frantz Fanon and the Postcolonial Prerogative." *The Location of Culture.* New York: Routledge, 1994. 40–65. Print.

Blanchot, Maurice. "Declaration of the Right to Insubordination in the Algerian War [Manifesto of the 121]." *Political Writings, 1953–1993.* Trans. Zakir Paul. New York: Fordham UP, 2010. 15–17. Print.

Fanon, Frantz. *A Dying Colonialism.* Trans. Haakon Chevalier. New York: Grove, 1965. Print.

Horne, Alistair. *A Savage War of Peace: Algeria, 1954–1962.* London: Papermac, 1987. Print.

Macey, David. *Frantz Fanon: A Life.* London: Granta, 2000. Print.

*Media Adaptation*

*Franz Fanon's Blues: The Wretched of the Earth.* Dir. Rasuma. Ital Film, 2008. Film.

*Allison Blecker*

# SUBJECT INDEX

Bold volume and page numbers (e.g., **3:269–272**) refer to the main entry on the subject. Page numbers in italics refer to photographs and illustrations.

# C

# K

# N

"Talks at the Yan'an Forum on
Literature and Art" (Mao Zedong),
**1:** *363, 363–367*

*Talks for Girls* series, **1:**64

*Tallow Waa Telee Ma* (Farah), **2:**292

Taner Akçam, **1:**246

*Taohua shan (The Peach Blossom Fan)*
(Kong), **3:**241–244, *243*

Tappan, Mary Jennie, **2:**125

Tarnac 9, **1:**265–267, *267*

Tarrant, R. J., **2:**136, 209

*The Task* (Cowper), **1:**37, 38, 189, 190

Tate, Claudia, **2:**56, 354, 355

Tatlock, J. S. P., **1:**231

Tatsumi, Takayuki, **2:**232

Tawil, Raymonda, **2:**25, 26

Tax, Meredith, **2:**318

Taxes, **1:**131

*Taxi* (al-Khamissi), **2:66–68,** *68*

Taylor, Aline Mackenzie, **2:**298

Taylor, Apriana, **2:**14

Taylor, Charles, **1:**236

Taylor, Frederick Winslow, **3:**136

Taylor, John, **2:**76

Taylor, Lois, **2:**29

*Tazmamart Cell 10 (Tazmamart Cellule 10)*
(Marzouki), **1:**141–142

Tazmamart Prison, **1:**141–143, *143*

*Te Kooti* (Taylor), **2:**14

Te Ture Whenua Maori Act (1939),
**2:**15

Tea Act (England, 1764), **2:**159

Teachout, Terry, **2:**48

*Teahouse* (She), **2:**288

*The Tears of the Indians* (Phillips), **1:**35

*La Technique, ou, L'Enjeu du Siècle (The
Technological Society)* (Ellul), **1:**348

*The Technological Society (La Technique,
ou, L'Enjeu du Siècle)* (Ellul), **1:**348

Technology
  *Brave New World* (Huxley), **3:**7–10, *9*
  *A Canticle for Leibowitz* (Miller),
  **3:**67–69, *69*
  *Do Androids Dream of Electric
  Sheep?* (Dick), **3:**73–75, *75*
  *Dyke Manifesto* (Lesbian Avengers),
  **2:**96–97
  *Ecotopia* (Callenbach), **3:**77

  *Erewhon* (Butler), **3:**83–85, *85*
  *Fahrenheit 451* (Bradbury),
  **3:**329–332, *331*
  *I, Robot* (Asimov), **3:**105–108, *107*
  Luddites, **1:**285
  *News from Nowhere* (Morris),
  **3:**120–122, *122*
  *Propaganda* (Ellul), **1:**347–350,
  *349*
  *Silent Spring* (Carson), **1:**137–140,
  *139*
  *Tono-Bungay* (Wells), **3:**53–56, *55*
  *We* (Zamyatin), **3:**136–139, *138*
  *WikiLeaks Manifesto* (Assange),
  **1:**144–148, *145*
  *Woman on the Edge of Time*
  (Piercy), **3:**142

*Technology Review* (journal), **1:**147

Tel-Troth, Thomas. *See* Swetnam,
Joseph

*Telefon* (Wagner), **3:**28

Televangelism, **3:**93

Television, **3:**3, 101, 128
  *See also* Mass media

Temara Detention Facility, **1:**142

Temperance movement, **1:**64–66, *66,*
84–87, *86*

*The Tempest* (Shakespeare), **1:**174,
**3:**208

Temple, John, **1:**239–241, *241*

Temple, William, **3:**90

*The Temple of Boredom: Science Fiction,
No Future* (Sante), **2:**218

Temple-Thurston, Barbara, **2:**226

*Ten Best Bad Novels* ( *Time* magazine),
**3:**29

Ten Hours Act (England, 1847), **3:**156

*Ten Nights in a Barroom and What I
Saw There* (Arthur), **1:**87

Ten-Point Plan. *See Black Panther Party
Platform and Program* (Newton and
Seale)

*Ten Thousand Lives (Maninbo)* (Ko Un),
**1:242–244,** *244*

Ten Years' War (Cuba, 1868–1878),
**3:**294, 295

Tenant farmers, **1:**166, *171*

Tenements, **1:**105–108, *107*

Tennyson, Alfred Lord, **3:**200–202,
*202*

*Terminator* (film), **3:**84

Terrill, Ross, **1:**81, 83

Terrorism
  *Anil's Ghost* (Ondaatje), **3:**313–315,
  *315*
  *Green Book* (Irish Republican
  Army), **1:**268–270, *270*
  *Manifesto for Armed Action*
  (Meinhof), **1:**279–281, *281*
  *Mao II* (DeLillo), **2:**257–259, *259*
  *Minimanual of the Urban Guerrilla*
  (Marighella), **1:**282–284, *284*
  9/11 terrorist attacks, **1:**134, 317,
  335, **2:**258, 259
  *Science of Revolutionary Warfare*
  (Most), **1:**294–296, *296*
  *The Secret Agent* (Conrad),
  **1:**297–299, *299*
  *The Turner Diaries* (Pierce), **3:**360
  war on, **1:**144–148, **3:**101, 304
  *WikiLeaks Manifesto* (Assange),
  **1:**144–148

*Terrorist Targeting of Police* (Jasper),
**1:**284

Testimonials, **1:**232–234, *234*

Testimonio, **1:**112–115, *114,*
**2:**98–101, *100*

*Tetsuwan Atomu (Astro Boy)* (film), **1:**72

*Texas Studies in Literature and Language*
(journal), **2:**252

Thackery, William Makepeace, **3:**55, 91

*Thanatopsis* (Bryant), **2:**148

Thanhouser, Edwin, **3:**157

*Thank You for Smoking* (Buckley),
**3:49–52,** *51*

*Thank You for Smoking* (film), **3:**50

Thatcher, Margaret, **1:**27, 28, 292,
**3:**273

*Theatre Arts* (journal), **3:**326

*The Theatre in America During the
Revolution* (Brown), **3:**286

*Theatre Journal,* **2:**48, **3:**287

*Their Eyes Were Watching God*
(Hurston), **2:**56

*Them!* (film), **3:**265

*The Theme of Totalitarianism in English
Fiction* (Klawitter), **3:**36–37

*Theological Discourse of the Lamb of God*
(Harvey), **1:**8

Theology, liberation, **3:**254

# W

# AUTHOR INDEX

The author index includes author names represented in *The Literature of Propaganda*.
Numbers in **Bold** indicate volume, with page numbers following after colons.

# TITLE INDEX

The title index includes works that are represented in *The Literature of Propaganda*. Numbers in **Bold** indicate volume, with page numbers following after colons.